Introduction to Sociology:
A Collaborative Approach

Ashbury Publishing LLC

Ashbury Publishing LLC

Introduction to Sociology:
A Collaborative Approach

Rene L. O'Dell • XueMei Hu • Barbara Miller • Beverly Farb

Sally Stablein • Kwaku Obosu-Mensah • Alyce B. Bunting

Saadi N. Hassan • Cheryl Boudreaux • Mita Dhariwal • Martyn Kingston

Bruce D. LeBlanc • Mark Shelley • Chris Biga • Brenton Roncace

Editor: Brenton Roncace
Book design by Jade McCoy
Cover photography by Margarit Ralev

Introduction to Sociology: A Collaborative Approach / Rene L. O'Dell, XueMei Hu, Barbara Miller, Beverly Farb, Sally Stablein, Kwaku Obosu-Mensah, Alyce B. Bunting, Saadi N. Hassan, Cheryl Boudreaux, Mita Dhariwal, Martyn Kingston, Bruce D. LeBlanc, Mark Shelley, Chris Biga, Brenton Roncace

ISBN 978-0-9791538-3-9

Ashbury Publishing LLC, Boise, Idaho, 83712
www.ashburypublishing.com

Contents ─────────

Chapter 6 Deviance And Social Control 159

Chapter 7 Social Stratification In The United States And Globally 183

Introduction to Sociology:
A Collaborative Approach

Meet the Authors _____

Rene L. O'Dell
Chapter 1 An Introduction To Sociology

A student once told me, "Sociology is like opening the back of a clock and learning how it ticks." I took my first sociology course in high school as an elective; it soon became my very favorite class that I actually looked forward to attending. When I graduated, I attended Irvine Valley College as a sociology major. At the time, I didn't realize that it was going to become my profession.

My first passion was social work dealing with abused and neglected children. I decided to attend Cal State Fullerton, obtaining both a bachelor's and a master's degree in sociology. My goal was to be a social worker by day and a professor by night. When presented with the opportunity to teach, I decided to pursue that avenue exclusively. I was right back at the place that I started, Irvine Valley College—very ironic.

Without the people that you love, your dreams are just your own. I have been very blessed to be supported by my loving husband Patrick and my family—especially my mother and my friends. In case you are wondering, the picture was taken in front of Disney's California Adventure in Anaheim, California. I am standing next to the letter "a" in the word "California." This picture is very appropriate because every student of mine has the ability to achieve this letter grade and that is what I hope for everyone taking this course.

Dr. XueMei Hu
Chapter 2 Society And Culture and Chapter 4 Social Structure And Social Interaction

I am Dr. Xuemei Hu. I obtained my bachelor's degree in English and American literature in 1986. I earned my master's degree in sociology in 1991 and my doctorate in sociology in 1996 at the University of Hawaii at Manoa. I have twelve years of teaching experience at the college/university level. My sociological interests of study include social stratification, marriage and family, social problems, racial and ethnic relations, distance learning education, and student learning outcome assessment. I currently hold the position of senior professor in sociology at Union County College in New Jersey.

I was born and raised in Hangzhou, China. Being both bilingual and bicultural, I was employed by College of Education at University of Hawaii (UH) to implement Project CLASS (Chinese Language Achievement through Sequential Study), a federally-funded program by Department of Education in Washington, D.C. I served as Project Coordinator and held the rank of UH Specialist to introduce the study of Chinese language. In this capacity, I served as liaison, trained and supervised teachers, taught workshops to disseminate the curriculum, and wrote annual reports to Department of Education which was published by the Education Resources Information Center (ERIC) as a curriculum entitled Mandarin Chinese for Elementary Students that includes textbooks, teacher's manuals, and workbooks.

Dr. Barbara Miller
Chapter 3 Socialization

I was born in Tulsa, Oklahoma. I studied piano at a young age, and, at the age of eleven, played as a soloist with the Minneapolis Symphony Orchestra. I trained in Lake Placid, New York as a figure skater, winning three national titles and pair skating with Dick Button. I was the alternate member of the 1948 Olympic team. I met my husband of fifty years while skating on a float in the Rose Parade. Teaching ice skating paid for my education. I have also run five marathons, some with my Pasadena City College students.

Educators love learning and I am no exception. I have gone to law school and nursing school, and I have kept my Emergency Medical Technician (EMT) license active for 14 years. I love studying and teaching abroad; in 2009, I spent the spring in Oxford, England teaching two psychology and two sociology courses. I live near the Pacific Ocean and enjoy chasing dolphins in a kayak with my grandsons. I have taught at Pasadena City College for 41 years and wear two hats—psychology and sociology; however, my doctorate is in education. I say I shall retire every year, but I love my job too much to stop.

Dr. Beverly Farb
Chapter 5 Groups And Organizations

Beverly Farb has taught at Everett Community College for 12 years. She teaches a broad variety of courses including: Introduction to Sociology, Introduction to Psychology, Social Psychology, Criminology, Family, Cross-Cultural Medicine, and Global Studies. Beverly has served as adjunct faculty at Simon Fraser University in British Columbia, Canada. She has also worked as a mental health counselor with the homeless. Beverly Farb earned

both her doctorate in sociology and her master of marriage and family therapy degrees at the University of Southern California.

Sally Stablein
Chapter 6 Deviance And Social Control

I grew up in the City of Orange in Southern California. I moved from Orange County to San Marcos, California, where I attended Palomar Community College, receiving an associate of arts degree in general studies in 1995.

From there I attended California State University San Marcos and fell in love with sociology. I had a passion for the topics of deviant behavior, violence and culture, race and ethnicity, social stratification, and gender issues.

During my time at Cal State San Marcos, I figured out what I would do with my education: I wanted to teach sociology! I graduated in 1998 with a bachelor of arts degree in sociology.

From there I attended Humboldt State University in Northern California. My focus was teaching, and in addition to continuing the same passions, I adopted a new one—environmental sociology. Humboldt County is a beautiful place and you can't help but become aware of environmental issues.

I received a master of arts degree in sociology from Humboldt State University in 2001 and moved from Humboldt to Broomfield, Colorado. Humboldt was a great place, but it can be very hard to make a living there.

My first teaching job was at Red Rocks Community College in 2002. From there I started teaching at several schools in the Denver Metro area. In 2007, I received a full time position at Red Rocks Community

College, where I plan to stay for quite a while.

At Red Rocks, I teach several classes that include: Introduction to Sociology, Deviant Behavior, Death and Dying, Contemporary Social Problems, Sociology of Gender, Violence and Culture, and Sexuality. With the Psychology Department, I am currently co teaching a Deviant Behavior and Sexuality class that ends with a trip to Amsterdam. I am also working on an Environmental Sociology class that will, hopefully, be offered soon, as Red Rocks has gone green!

I have been in Colorado for a little over seven years. I miss the ocean, but the mountains have taken its place; Colorado is home to me now!

Dr. Kwaku Obosu-Mensah
Chapter 7 Social Stratification In The United States And Globally

I was born and raised at Oyoko, a small town in the Eastern Region of Ghana. My secondary (high school) and higher education landed me in the Ghanaian towns of Nkonya Ahenkro, Hohoe, and Accra. After a stint as a teacher at Osu Presby Secondary School in Accra, I left for Nigeria for my first major employment as a high school teacher at St. John's Anglican Grammar School (Ode Lemo, Ogun State) and later at Asabari Grammar School (Saki, Oyo State).

In 1985, I enrolled at the University of Bergen, Norway, and obtained my master's degree in sociology in 1990. My minors were in administration and organization science, methodology of social sciences, and pedagogy.

After a couple of years as a lecturer at Høgskolen i Bodø (Bodø University College) in Bodø (Norway), in 1992 I enrolled at the University of Toronto for my Ph.D. degree in sociology. Upon completion of my doctorate in 1998, I worked as a career counselor and a teaching assistant at the University of Toronto before moving to Jackson, Tennessee, to take an assistant professor position at Lane College in 2000. In 2001, I accepted a visiting assistant position at Western Kentucky University, Bowling Green. In 2002, I accepted an assistant professor position at Lorain County Community College in Elyria, Ohio. In total, I have ten years of teaching experience and I have presented papers at over 50 conferences in Norway, Canada, Germany, and the United States. In addition to courses in sociology, I teach international studies. At the moment, I am an associate professor.

I have lived in, studied in, or visited 12 countries around the world. My hobbies are soccer, traveling, listening to music, organizing functions, fishing, reading, and discussing international affairs.

Dr. Alyce B. Bunting
Chapter 8 Race And Ethnicity

Dr. Alyce B. Bunting has been a professor of sociology, criminal justice, and psychology at Texarkana College in Texarkana, Texas, since 1993, where she regularly teaches sections of Introductory Sociology, as well as Marriage and Family, and Juvenile Delinquency classes. She has also created and offered internet courses in introductory sociology and general psychology at Texarkana College. As an adjunct professor at Texas A&M – Texarkana, Dr. Bunting has taught courses in race and ethnicity and criminology.

Dr. Bunting was born in Hope, Arkansas. After completing her high school education at Liberty-Eylau High School in Texarkana, Texas, she entered Stephen F. Austin State University in Nacogdoches, Texas, from which she received a bachelor of arts degree in sociology and criminal justice in December, 1976. She entered the Graduate School of Stephen F. Austin University in August, 1978, and was awarded a master of arts degree in sociology in December of 1980. In the fall of 1999, she entered the Graduate School of Texas A&M University-Commerce and was awarded a doctor of education degree with a major in supervision, curriculum, and instruction-higher education in December 2004. In 1977, she married Joe Bunting, and they are the parents of three adult sons.

A perpetual student herself, Dr. Bunting enjoys the challenge of creating new courses and preparing new lectures. But as much as she enjoys teaching a variety of courses on various topics in both sociology and

criminal justice, she most enjoys teaching introductory sociology classes where she can watch her students' interest grow as they come to see the relevance of the discipline to their own lives.

Dr. Saadi N. Hassan
Chapter 9 Inequality And Stratification By Gender And Age

I was born in Baghdad where I received two bachelor's degrees from the University of Baghdad, one in English language and the other in business administration. I taught English as a second language in Baghdad High School for two years. I joined the British Iraq Petroleum Company where I served for about twenty years, holding administrative positions in the Human Resources Department as Training and Career Development Coordinator and Senior Government Relations Coordinator. After the nationalization of the foreign oil companies in 1972, I was appointed as Director General of Human Resources and Administration Affairs of the nationalized oil company in Kirkuk which was named the North Oil Company.

In 1980, I migrated to the United States and joined the Sociology Department at the University of Kentucky. I obtained my master's degree in sociology in 1982 and started working towards a Ph.D. in the same field. In 1984, I went to Sudan with my advisor/professor, Milton James Cougherour, to do field research on the role of social networks in the diffusion of new technology for agricultural development.

I obtained my Ph.D. in sociology in 1986 from the University of Kentucky. During the period from 1983 to 1987, I was an adjunct professor of sociology at the University of Kentucky. I joined Somerset Community College in 1988 where I continue to teach sociology.

Dr. Cheryl Boudreaux
Chapter 10 Families

Professor Cheryl Boudreaux, Ph.D., teaches in the Sociology Department (Death and Dying, Families in Society, and Love, Sex and Gender) at Grand Valley State University, Allendale, Michigan. Dr. Boudreaux has served two terms as the elected president of the Michigan Sociological Association (MSA) and is an active member of the Society for the Study of Social Problems (SSSP), currently serving as vice president of the organization and the chair of the Family Division. Dr. Boudreaux is a photographer/sociologist that sees images as a significant part of the social construction of reality.

Specializing in the study of transformations of

consciousness or worldviews, Dr. Boudreaux's research includes race consciousness, spiritual transformations of consciousness, and changing images of death and dying. Professor Boudreaux earned a Ph.D. in sociology at Brandeis University, Waltham, Massachusetts, an M.A. at Boston College, Chestnut Hill, Massachusetts, and a B.A. at University of California San Diego, La Jolla, California.

Professor Boudreaux's research and theories of transformation inform her teaching in sociology as well as her advocacy and interest in working toward social justice. She has written and presented papers on Marriage and Family, Images of Death, Dying and Terrorism, and Race Consciousness in Health and Illness.

Mita Dhariwal
Chapter 11 Education And Religion

I was born and educated in India. I have a bachelor's in sociology from California State University, Fresno, and a master's in sociology from Utah State University. I have also done post-graduate work at the University of California, Riverside. I have worked with the Peace Corps, teaching language and culture seminars at University of California, Berkeley. I have also taught women's studies and sociology courses at Bakersfield College for the last 35 years, specializing in population studies.

Dr. Martyn Kingston
Chapter 12 States, Markets And Politics

Dr. Kingston is a professor of sociology at Southern Utah University and is currently a visiting professor of marketing at the Eccles School of Business, University of Utah. Dr. Kingston has a B.A. (Honors) and M.A. in urban planning from Manchester University, England, a M.A. and Ph.D. in sociology from Harvard University, and an M.B.A. from the University of Utah. He has held teaching positions at several universities and colleges including Olympic College, Williams College, the University of Puget Sound, and the University of Washington, Tacoma. Martyn's sociological interests include political and economic sociology, stratification, urban studies, race and ethnicity, and comparative historical sociology. Martyn was born and raised in Europe and still enjoys travelling and seeing the world. An avid skier and rugby enthusiast, Martyn now lives in Park City, Utah, with his wife and four young children.

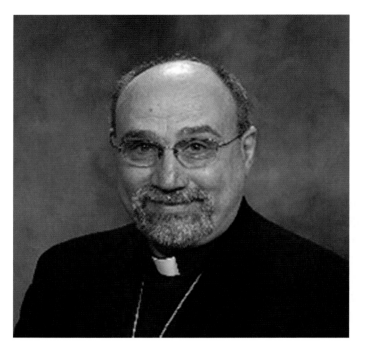

Dr. Bruce D. LeBlanc
Chapter 13 Health And Population

Bruce D. LeBlanc is a professor of sociology and psychology at Black Hawk College, Moline, Illinois. He holds an Ed.D. in post-secondary social sciences from the University of Sarasota, an M.A. in sociology from Idaho State University, an M.A. in transpersonal studies from Atlantic University, and an M.P.A. from the Consortium of the California State University. He is a board-certified sexologist with the American College of Sexologists and a certified sexological instructor/advisor for HIV/AIDS prevention. His research interests focus on marginalized or under-studied social phenomena, including sexuality and the aged, female homosexuality, and the social psychological dimensions of spirituality. Additionally, he is an autocephalous Catholic bishop holding dual affiliations with the Transformational Catholic Church, and the Ecumenical Catholic Church.

Dr. Mark Shelley
Chapter 14 Urban And Environmental Sociology— Urban Portion

Mark Shelley is Dean of the Liberal Arts Division and teaches sociology and psychology at Yavapai College in Prescott, Arizona. After having lived and worked in Southeast Asia for several years, he began his teaching career in 1985. In addition to his study of the Vietnamese community in Milwaukee, he has written on Southeast Asian groups in the Encyclopedia of American Immigration. Other published work includes "The Dark Engine of Illinois Education: A Sociological Critique of a 'Well-Crafted (Testing) Machine,'" (Educational Policy, with Drs. William Rau and Frank Beck, Illinois State University), and "Building Community from 'Scratch': Social Forces at Work among Urban Vietnamese Refugees in Milwaukee" (Sociological Inquiry). Mark co-wrote a chapter on Latinos and Asians in the book entitled "Perspectives on Milwaukee's Past," which was edited by Margo Anderson and Victor Greene and published by the University of Illinois Press. He currently serves on the Editorial Review Board for a new introduction to psychology text by John Cacioppo and Laura Freberg (Cengage Learning). His research interests focus around urban issues—race, ethnicity, education, inequality, homelessness, and inner city communities—and the psychology of men. Mark received a B.A. in history from York University in Toronto, an M.A. in educational psychology from California State University-Northridge, an M.A. in cross-cultural studies from Fuller Theological Seminary, and his Ph.D. in urban studies from the University of Wisconsin-Milwaukee.

Dr. Chris Biga
Chapter 14 Urban And Environmental Sociology — Environment Portion

Chris Biga is an Assistant Professor in the Department of Sociology, Anthropology, and Emergency Management at North Dakota State University. Chris earned a Ph.D. in sociology from Washington State University. His primary research focuses on the intersection of environmental sociology and sociological social psychology. Specifically, explaining environmentally significant individual behaviors through self meanings of identities. Currently, Chris is investigating how shared values across identities (environmental, gender, and consumer) influence the occurrence of environmentally significant individual behaviors. Outside the office, Chris enjoys mountain biking, skiing, and backpacking, but spends most of his free time playing with his son.

Brenton Roncace
Chapter 15 Collective Behavior, Social Movements And Social Change

I was born in Baltimore, Maryland, later moving to South Carolina and then to Idaho. I earned my bachelor's and master's degrees in criminal justice administration from Boise State University. For the last six years, I have taught criminal justice classes at Boise State University under the titles of adjunct instructor, special lecturer, and visiting assistant professor. Collective behavior, occurring both in free-world and correctional settings, is a concept thoroughly covered in the academic field of criminal justice. While attending graduate school, I worked at a shelter serving homeless and at-risk youth and later worked with youth at a community corrections treatment facility.

CHAPTER ONE

An Introduction To Sociology

Rene L. O'Dell

Once you have read this book, you will never look at people the same way again. Sociology is guaranteed to change how you view yourself and other people. If you have enjoyed *people watching*, this book will teach you methods of understanding people almost to the point of being able to predict human behavior. This first chapter will lay a foundation for the entire book and include such topics as the origin of sociology, sociological theory, and sociological research.

Sociology Defined

Let's start by providing the simple definition. **Sociology** is *the scientific study of human society and social interaction*. Auguste Comte coined the term in 1838 to describe a new way of thinking about and understanding our social world. If we looked at the word origin, sociology comes from a combination of the Latin word *socius*, which means "associate," and a Greek-derived suffix of "ology" which has come to mean "study." We loosely translate "associate" to mean people in general. Putting the pieces together, we end up with our earlier definition—the study of people.

The definition has been expanded because sociology also includes the study of how people interact with one another, the groups that comprise society, the institutions of society, how institutions and people affect one another, and much, much more. The goal of sociology is to study and understand the modern society in which we live.

When we study sociology, we should use the "sociological imagination." According to C. Wright Mills, the **sociological imagination** is the equivalent of using a pair of lenses to look at a situation in a different light. Another way to say it would be walking in someone else's shoes in hopes of understanding his or her point of view. We find that our own personal struggles and tribulations can actually be viewed in a larger social context that others in society may be experiencing as well. We also come to realize that society influences the way we think, feel, and act.

Sociological Perspective

To understand phenomena occurring in our social world, we must have tools and techniques that help guide the way in which we approach a topic. Sociology questions what most people consider "common sense" or "personal choice."

Take, for example, the fact that you are in college getting a higher education. Why is it that you are enrolled in college? Most people will say it is because they want to get a good job that will yield them a large paycheck. Enrollment in college actually has little to do with the personal choice of being there. Would a person have the ability to obtain the job he desires without having an education? For the most part, people need to have a degree in their field to get a better job. Society has thus influenced the decision to enroll in college. Therefore, it is very important to keep in mind the first maxim of sociology, that things are not always as they seem.

Sociology uses the **sociological perspective** developed by Peter Berger in 1963. First we are able to see *the general in the particular*. This allows individuals to categorize people based on characteristics they have in common. Categories could include men or women, old or young, rich or poor, majority

or minority, and so on. Once people are grouped into these categories by society, they are treated a particular way according to that category. Personal life experiences are also shaped by the various categories in which we are placed.

The sociological perspective also allows us to see the *strange in the familiar*. By understanding what falls into certain categories based on what is the same, we are also able to see what is different.

The sociological imagination and perspective provide us with general knowledge for the larger picture of the **sociological paradigm**. This framework allows us to study society using sociological tools, methods, and assumptions in analyzing data and research.

Global Perspective

It would be naïve to think that your personal actions do not influence other people. No one person can go through life without affecting others around him or her. For that reason, we must consider others within our own society.

Would it be going too far to say that your actions or beliefs could also reach across the world? Especially with technology and the creation of the World Wide Web, people are more interconnected now than ever. The Internet allows for communication and contact with individuals with whom we might never have interacted. At the touch of a button, the Internet takes people to destinations around the world.

With that in mind, we should consider not only the people that comprise our own society, but other nations as well. This concept of **global perspective** studies the impact of our society on other nations, and also their impact on us. This does not only include the impact of our westernized culture on other nations, but also how other cultures change our society. Using a global view allows us to answer questions like, "How do we as Americans view other nations?" and "How do other nations view Americans?"

Where we live greatly shapes our lives. Have you ever thought about how your life would be different if you were born or raised in another country? What opportunities might you gain or lose? What language would you speak? What type of viewpoint or beliefs would you have? The type of nation that you live in molds the person you become.

There are three different types of nations determined by standards of living and wealth. At the top of the list are high-income nations like the United States, Japan, and Germany, where the wealth is high and so are the standards of living. The countries that fall into this category have been referred to as first-world countries and are now considered developed countries.

Application: Global Perspective

<u>The impact of our society on other nations, and their impact on us.</u>
When studying sociology, we must remember the "big picture." We must keep in mind that our culture influences other societies and vice versa.

Certainly our Western society has affected other cultures around the world.

McDonald's is located in more than 100 countries around the world and you can find a Burger King restaurant in more than 65 countries and U.S. territories. In Ireland, one noticeable difference is that these two fast-food chains offer fountain drinks, while many restaurants and pubs only serve canned or bottled soda, which they term "single-serve."

On the other hand, we are also able to see the impact of other cultures on our society. For example, if you were to walk into a food court at a mall, you would have many ethnic cuisines to choose from and enjoy.

Pictures (top left and right): McDonald's, China; McDonald's Mexico

There are middle-income countries, like Russia and most of Latin America. These countries tend to have midrange scores on indicators such as life expectancy and poverty rates. Although this classification of countries has been used in the past, the category has all but disappeared, and most countries are now classified as either first-world (developed) or third-world (developing).

At the bottom are low-income countries struggling to develop, where most of the citizens are poor. Most of Africa and parts of Asia fall into this category previously known as third-world countries, and now as developing countries. The standard of living in these countries does not even meet the most basic needs of food, clothing, and shelter for large portions of the citizens. Other social problems encountered include unsafe drinking water, low education, and diseases like AIDS. People who reside in low-income nations are very disadvantaged, and the nations themselves have little ability to solve their own problems.

These three categories of nations do not necessarily convey an accurate description of the many societies that comprise the world. They do, however, illustrate that the standards of living are not equal amongst all nations. Keeping a global perspective in mind allows sociologists to study commonalities and differences among the many nations of the world. Societies are more alike than what was previously thought. For example, every society has social problems, but the variation lies in the types of problems and the extent to which they are suffered.

Origins Of Sociology

The field of sociology developed as a response to changes that were drastically transforming society. There were three major social revolutions that occurred, including technological advancements, the formation of cities, and political changes. Established in Germany, France, and England, these social changes fostered sociology as a new academic discipline.

Technological Advancements

During the late 18th and early 19th centuries, the Industrial Revolution led to many changes in the structure of societies.

Technology, without a doubt, has an impact on the ways in which people live. It was never truer than during this period. Many people during the Middle Ages worked at home or in small groups where employment was dictated by the individual. For the vast majority who were farmers, going to work meant opening their back door and tilling their own land. This all changed when technology advanced, producing new methods of producing energy, first by water power and later by steam.

With new advancements in the methods of production, people flocked to factories, mills, and mines in search of employment. Labor shifted from being about personal employment to being community-based. Instead of being their own bosses, people now worked for others in large anonymous groups.

Formation Of Cities

Changes in technology gave rise to cities as people were forced to live close to where they worked. Factories became a central focal point in the concentration of where people lived, and cities were formed around factories. Life in the city was drastically different than rural living. People now interacted with large groups of people at work and in the community, and there was more crime and less available living space.

Political Changes

As people were making more money by working in the factories, they started challenging the Divine Right of Kings for political rule. The focus moved from doing God's will to seeking more individualism.

Results Of Change

Together these three major revolutions changed the ways in which people interacted with one another, the types of communities in which people lived, and the rules by which they were governed.

Sociology was formed by the cumulative efforts of Auguste Comte, Karl Marx, Emile Durkheim, and Max Weber as they attempted to understand society's changes. These key players, along with some marginal voices, will be discussed later in this chapter.

Sociology As A Science

Auguste Comte is considered the father, or founder, of sociology. He was the first to attempt to understand society in its modern context, versus imagining an idealistic society.

Comte's thinking centered on the notion that society moved and developed through three stages. The first, known as the *theological stage*, included the time period through 1350. During this period, people's lives revolved around the notion of God's will. Theories and the belief in the divine structured and shaped society. The *metaphysical stage* was a transition from theory to natural order.

The last stage Comte called the *scientific stage*. Many great thinkers arose from this era, such as Isaac Newton, Galileo Galilei, and Nicolaus Copernicus. Science was the medium utilized to understand the physical world. Comte believed that the only way to understand social phenomena was to use the methodological approach of *positivism*.

Compared with other sciences like philosophy, physics, and astronomy, society is governed by the collection of data. As a positivist, Comte believed that without empirical data, we would not have concrete knowledge. Research must use the scientific method in order to gain knowledge of society. Comte believed that if we were able to understand society based on science, we would be able to prescribe remedies for change.

In earlier times, during the theological stage, our understanding of society was at a low point. Entering into the last stage of positivism, our understanding of society is much greater. As time moves forward, so should our knowledge of society. It begs the question: Does time equal knowledge? Thinking about it in a modern context, do we as a society know more today than we did fifty years prior? Based on this theory, Comte proposed that as we study sociology, we should seek to ask two basic questions: "Why does a society change?" and "Why does a society not change?"

Like other sciences, sociology uses the scientific method, conducting research and analyzing results to systematically study society. For this very reason, sociology is thus considered to be in the field of science. To be considered a science, however, a discipline must also be founded on well-defined laws. For example, the law of gravity states that if you drop something, it will fall to the ground no matter where you are located on planet Earth. Sociology, on the other hand, does not have any laws, contrary to Comte's notion. What is true in our society may or may not be true elsewhere, and what applies to one person certainly does not apply to all people. Critics use this fact to point out that sociology (along with other social sciences) should not be considered a science. This is why sociology is deemed a "soft science." In the absence of laws, the data is collected and interpreted, and then conclusions are drawn. Although some might downplay the importance of science, it is still considered a crucial part in understanding society, as human behavior is complex and multifaceted.

Applications In Sociology

Forming in the mid-1800s, sociology is one of the youngest of all academic disciplines. Sociology as an academic discipline came to America in the early 20th century. It was first introduced as a department at the University of Chicago in 1892. Since that time, it has rapidly spread and expanded into an exciting field of study.

Topics In Sociology

Wherever you can find human life, you can find a topic in sociology. Because sociology deals with human behavior, the topics are vast and broad. Some of the more popular topics include: marriage and family, sex roles and gender, delinquent behavior and crime, race and ethnicity, and economics and politics.

Careers In Sociology

Sociology attracts a variety of people who are interested in a wide array of topics. To be recognized in the field of sociology, a person must have an advanced degree like a master's or a doctorate. Once that degree is obtained, a person is considered a sociologist.

Why would someone want to become a sociologist? What can you do with a degree in sociology? Some degrees and majors have a direct link to a person's job. For example, if a person receives a degree in psychology, chances are that person will be a psychologist. For sociology, there isn't necessarily a specific job called a "sociologist."

Sociologists work in many different fields, often pursuing diverse specialties. Because sociology deals with human behavior of all sorts, it offers a broad base of knowledge for any type of job. So what can you do with a sociology degree? The answer is that the possibilities are limitless.

If an individual were to receive a bachelor's degree with sociology as either a major or minor, possible jobs might be in public relations, human resources, sales, advertising, or market research. Knowledge of human behavior in these fields is imperative. If a person wishes to sell products, or attempt to reach people through advertising, knowledge of humans and their behavior is a key component. Without this understanding, they might not be able to connect with their target groups.

Sociology is also important for anyone interested in a career involving interaction with large groups of diverse people. This would include individuals who want to work in politics or in a nonprofit organization performing community outreach.

A sociology degree is often used as a foundation for higher degrees outside the field of sociology, like law and medicine. Many universities actually make sociology courses a requirement to obtain a degree in the medical field. One of the more obvious reasons is that doctors and other medical professionals interact with people when they are at their weakest points. How can a medical staff member treat patients without some understanding of basic human behaviors?

Although a degree in sociology does not apply to one specific job, sociologists tend to gravitate toward the fields previously mentioned. When an advanced degree in sociology is obtained, the predominate jobs are teaching at the college level and conducting research. Many times, sociologists divide their time between these two occupations.

Application: What can I do with a sociology degree?

Here is a list of some famous sociology majors:

Politics:	Actors:
President Ronald Reagan	Robin Williams
Rev. Martin Luther King	Dan Akroyd
Rev. Jesse Jackson	Regis Philbin

* Partial list adapted from the website of the American Sociological Association.

Other Social Sciences

Sociology is only one field of study in a grouping of social sciences. Other fields include anthropology, psychology, political science, economics, and social work. Anthropology is the science most closely related to sociology. Whereas sociology studies society in its modern context as a whole, anthropology studies various cultures worldwide and some societies that might no longer exist.

Although similar in their methods, each social science analyzes data according to its own theories. Hence, if each were to examine the same situation, each would have its own point-of-view and analysis.

Part Two: Sociological Theories

The main goal in studying sociology is to analyze and comprehend the meaning of our social world. To do this, theories must be applied. A **theory** is an *integrated set of propositions that connects facts in order to gain an understanding of a specific phenomenon and to illustrate relationships.* The purpose of sociological theory, then, is to make generalizations in an attempt to understand human behavior in the modern world. Although there are many sociological theories, this book seeks to highlight the three major paradigms: structural functionalism, social conflict, and symbolic interactionism. These theories help guide research and explain social phenomena, and may be applied to any research topic.

Structural Functionalism

One of the major schools of sociological thought is the **structural functionalism** approach that views society as an intricate *structure with many different levels or parts all working in collaboration for stability.* Structural functionalists base their thinking on three major concepts.

First, each part provides a function that keeps society working like a well-oiled machine. These different parts include social groups, institutions, and individual interactions, to name just a few. Sociologist Herbert Spencer (1820-1903) stated it another way, comparing society to a human body. Within the body are various organs and other parts that are required to keep the body running in a healthy way. Just like your body needs the brain, heart, and stomach internally, and the arms, legs, and skin externally, society needs many building blocks to function properly, maximizing ability and potential. Even though some people may be of the opinion that certain parts are not needed, structural functionalists would contend that all parts are necessary for the complex system to maintain stability.

Second, structural functionalism is a macro-oriented approach, and, as such, seeks to look at the big picture. Society as a whole is composed of many building blocks like family, peers, government, religion, and the media. Sociologists seek to identify the social structures that exist and the roles they play in shaping our lives. Together, these building blocks comprise one functioning entity.

Lastly, as the name suggests, the structural functionalism paradigm seeks to look at functions. Robert Merton (1910-2003) expanded on the notion of functions, dividing them into two different categories: intended (manifest) and unintended (latent). **Manifest functions** are *consequences of a social situation that are intended and expected.* In other words, they are the result of the functions that were projected and served their purpose. **Latent functions** are *unintended or unexpected consequences of a social situation.*

Applying Merton's functional principles to schooling, the manifest function is to get an education. A latent function might be that children interact with other peers their age and make friends. So the goal or purpose of schooling is to acquire an education, but, as a side benefit, friends are also earned.

Merton believed that negative consequences, whether intended or unintended, could also be produced. We call the negative functions *dysfunctions* because they disrupt equilibrium. A dysfunction occurs when an object is not serving its purpose and stability is threatened.

Application Of Theory

Emile Durkheim (1858-1917) was one of the pioneers of the structural-functionalist paradigm. Growing up in France, his research focused on anthropology and sociology. He covered a wide variety of topics over his lifetime—religion, suicide, crime—and provided many insights into the development of sociology as an academic field.

Durkheim, along with other functionalists, believed society was held together by a shared **social consensus** in which almost all members wanted the same outcomes and worked cooperatively to achieve them. Durkheim categorized this consensus into two different forms of social cohesion: mechanical solidarity and organic solidarity.

Mechanical solidarity involves people doing similar work and sharing the same values and beliefs. This type of solidarity is often found in traditional societies that are moderately small and non-complex. An example of this would be a farming community in which everyone knows everyone, incomes are tied in some way to farming, and people share the same values and beliefs.

Conversely, in **organic solidarity**, people work in a wide variety of specialized occupations and, thus, gain social consensus from their need to rely on one another for goods and services. In a large city, for example, people depend on others to provide them with food, clothes, safety, health care, and entertainment, as no one can provide all of that for themselves in an urban environment.

Students can increase their involvement by joining campus clubs.   Source: Rene L. O'Dell

Application: Durkheim's Social Integration

Example : Completing College

Durkheim explored the concept of social integration in relationship to committing suicide. Those people who were less tied to society were more likely to commit suicide.

Expanding on the notion of social integration, let's apply it to college students.

Hypothesis: Individuals who are more involved at their college institutions are less likely to drop out of college.

What this means: Get involved at your college—join clubs, get a part-time job at the college, spend time getting to know staff members and fellow classmates, and attend sporting events, theater productions, and musical performances.

The more people who are counting on you to be there, the less likely you will be to disappoint them. The more ties and connections you make, the harder it is to pull away.

Throughout Durkheim's research, a theme of society and integration emerges. Durkheim viewed society as a separate entity apart from people, playing a vital part in our lives. Durkheim wanted to investigate why some people committed suicide, while others did not.

In his book *Suicide*, he found that people had higher rates of suicide based on three variables. Individuals were more likely to commit suicide if they were single or widowed or divorced versus being married. People also had higher rates of suicide if they were without children. Lastly, individuals had higher rates if they practiced Protestant religions versus Catholicism.

Durkheim analyzed these results to show that individuals who were less integrated into society had higher rates of suicide. By integration, Durkheim was referring to connections to social structures. Those people who were more connected were less likely to kill themselves because other individuals, like their spouses or children, needed them.

Additionally, Durkheim concluded that those people who had abnormally high amounts of social integration would also be more likely to commit suicide. This could be due to the stress of having too many people making demands on the individual.

Social Conflict Perspective

The second major school of thought is the **social conflict perspective**, which *views society as a compound filled with inequalities with regards to allocation of resources*. The social conflict perspective is macro-oriented and, as such, focuses on the big picture or large-scale phenomena. While the structural functionalist approach states that grouping people into categories is beneficial and functional, the social conflict approach highlights those categories as a method used to put certain groups of people at a disadvantage. In our society, for example, race, social class, and gender are all areas where you can see inequalities in terms of education, wealth, and power.

Every society has a limited amount of resources that must be divided, in some manner, among its members. While some societies attempt to distribute the resources so that people have similar social standings, that is not the case in the United States. Under the assumption that all people cannot have all the resources or society would crumble, there is a vast difference between those individuals at the top with many privileges versus those at the bottom without any privileges at all.

The social conflict approach is guided by the assumption that there is a constant struggle to gain or keep power. The standard of living for those privileged individuals is threatened by those people who are not privileged. Dominant groups in society—like Caucasians, men, the rich, and heterosexuals—must protect their privileges, while minorities, women, homosexuals, and the poor struggle to gain more for themselves. Going a step further, social conflict theorists state that not only will the dominant group protect its interests, it will also exploit the weak for the benefit of the strong.

Each of the variables of gender, race, and social class are important in understanding the conflict approach. They are sometimes categorized into sub-groupings called *gender conflict or race conflict* approaches.

Social conflict theorists believe that the structure of a society and the institutions found within it perpetuate disparity between its members. It is fully the fault of the social system that certain individuals are left disadvantaged. In other words, the structures of society reinforce and generate an imbalance in the arena of social equality. You are able to see inequalities in politics, the workplace, and in universities and other educational settings.

Although this viewpoint of society may appear to be negative, social conflict theorists are actually seeking social change. By gaining an understanding of the inequalities that are inherent in society, the goal is to reduce inequality by disbursing resources more equitably. This change may only occur as a result of a revolution where the disadvantaged overthrow the system.

Application Of Theory

Karl Marx (1818-1863), a German who lived in Great Britain, is considered one of the key founders of the social conflict theory. He was a philosopher, political activist, and sociologist who is probably best known for his work *The Communist Manifesto*.

Karl Marx's entire philosophy was centered on the roles of social class and economics. According to Marx, conflict arose in society due to the structuring of people into social classes. As the opening line of his manifesto states, *"The history of all hitherto existing society is the history of class struggles."*

When viewing society, Marx believed that people were divided into two social classes or categories; they were either part of the Bourgeoisie or part of the Proletariat. The Bourgeoisie included the owners of the factories and was considered the ruling class or the "haves" (versus the "have-nots"). The people who were in this group had the ability to determine how the factories were run and what the labor wage would be. Because they had control, they were said to own the "means of production."

The Proletariat included the workers in the factories and was also described as the subordinate class, or the "have-nots" of society. The individuals in this category were subjected to the terms set by the Bourgeoisie. These included their working conditions and also their pay. Marx even went so far as to say that the Proletariat was enslaved by the Bourgeoisie.

According to Marx, society imposed these two

social classes on people. In other words, either a person owned the means of production or a person worked for the means of production. There were no other choices. This created a divide between the two classes of society and contributed to **class conflict** between the owners and the workers. All conflict theorists believe that people battle over scarce resources, and in this case money became the scarce resource and the basis for all class struggle.

During the time that Marx was living, capitalism was the thriving economic force. Marx saw the capitalist system as corrupt because it was his view that factory owners were the only ones who benefited economically from a good purchasing market.

One way for factory owners to receive more money was to pay workers less. Getting more labor out of the workers, while paying them the least amount of money possible, increased the power of the Bourgeoisie. From this, they were able to benefit from increased "labor power," which contributed to their status as part of the ruling class. In the end, workers were powerless against the factory owners who exploited them.

In this situation, the capitalist system created an environment that was hostile and competitive as individuals strived for the same privileges. Marx predicted that the workers would eventually get tired of the poor treatment that they received. He believed that they would overthrow the capitalistic system, and a new system would emerge.

The global revolution movement that Marx was so positive would occur has, as yet, failed to materialize. Even today, it is evident that some of these conditions of class struggle still exist in society.

Symbolic Interactionism

The third major theory in sociology is the **symbolic interaction** approach, which states that *society exists due to the everyday interactions of people*. This framework is considered a micro-oriented theory. Whereas structural functionalists and conflict theorists seek to explore society as a whole, symbolic interactionists stake their claim in sociology by focusing on small-scale phenomena. They are interested in individuals and the small groups that comprise a society.

Symbolic interactionism revolves around two basic concepts or themes. First, each society contains symbols or labels from which meanings are derived. Second, the meanings that are attached to items require social interaction. To explain further, the material and non-material components of every culture are defined by the interactions of individuals in that society. Attaching labels to objects in society creates cohesion among individuals.

Objects themselves do not have inherently embedded meanings and, therefore, the definitions will vary by person and by culture. The definitions will also change over time, just as the people in society change. In short, objects only have the meanings that people attach to them. Without the interactions of people, objects themselves do not carry any meanings or significance. Symbolic interactionists are interested in the labels that we attach to our world, their meanings, and how they change over time.

Herbert Blumer coined the term "symbolic interacionism" in 1969, and he is largely responsible for the development of the theory and its methodologies. Previous theorists, like Max Weber, George Herbert Mead, and Charles Horton Cooley, are credited with creating the foundation and basic concepts of interaction.

Although not originally associated with this school of thought, Max Weber (1864-1920) is probably the best known symbolic interactionist. Weber, a German, was a political economist and sociologist who studied the sociology of religion and of government. One of his most famous writings is "The Protestant Ethic and the Spirit of Capitalism."

Whereas Comte was a positivist and believed that science was necessary to evaluate society, Weber was an anti-positivist. Weber believed that to understand society, the focus must be on individuals and their cultural values. To do this, researchers must evaluate the meanings of symbols, their values, and their norms as per the culture.

Application Of Theory

Hand gestures can be found in every society. These symbols have various definitions depending

Overview: Early Women of Sociology

Harriet Martineau (1802-1876), an English writer and philosopher, is generally considered the first woman of sociology. One of her contributions to sociology included translating Auguste Comte's writing into English, which brought sociology to more people. Martineau focused her studies on women's rights, slavery, the workplace, and factory laws. She also wrote the first text on sociological research in 1838.

Jane Addams (1860-1935) was a social worker in Chicago, Illinois. She co-founded Hull House, a community-based center offering classes for adults and children, an art gallery, and many other facilities. Throughout her life she indirectly provided many insights to the discipline of sociology. She was a friend and colleague to George Herbert Mead and other members of the Chicago School of Sociology.

on the culture. In our westernized society, extending the middle finger while all other fingers form a fist sends a very powerful message. In the United States, this gesture is labeled "flipping the bird," "giving someone the finger," or "flipping someone off." In another culture, this gesture could be assigned a different meaning or no meaning at all. To have the equivalent effect in another culture, a different gesture might be used. For example, several Middle Eastern countries use our "thumbs-up" gesture, while in the United Kingdom they use our "v-sign," to convey a meaning similar to that of the obscene gesture. For a symbol to carry any meaning or significance, it must be recognized by the people in a culture. Some symbols have multiple meanings depending upon the individual and the context in which they are being used.

Other Sociological Theories

Although sociology is governed by the aforementioned three major theories, there are many others that will be discussed in later chapters as they are applicable to specific topics within sociology.

Marginal Voices In Sociology

While the discipline of sociology is largely shaped by Comte, Durkheim, Marx, and Weber, other theorists should be recognized for their contributions as well. These marginal voices include Jane Adams, Harriet Martineau, and W.E.B. Du Bois, to name just a few (see above).

Also, because sociology studies society in its modern context, the discipline is continuously developing and expanding. Since the formation of the discipline, many other theories and theorists have had an impact on the way that we look at our social world.

Part Three: Sociological Research

As previously stated, sociology is a science; therefore, the conclusions that are drawn are the results of conducting research. As a result, it is very important to understand the methods and terminology of research studies in order to understand society.

Research Perspectives

There are three different perspectives on collecting sociological data: scientific, interpretive, and critical. Each of these three perspectives focuses on different methods and techniques when gathering and analyzing data. Sociologists use a variety of research methods to learn about society.

Scientific Sociological Research

Scientific sociological research is probably the most popular and widely used method of conducting research. This method employs the use of science and empirical data. Sociologists who use this method like to focus on debunking commonly held beliefs. By collecting research, sociologists are able to "prove" or "disprove" what most people would believe is common sense.

For example, most people in the United States would say that they married their spouses because they loved them. In fact, people would query a person if he or she gave any other answer to that question. Sociologists who have studied this topic actually find that the reason you date and ultimately marry a person has little or nothing to do with love. Shocked or insulted? Don't be. There are many factors that go into deciding who people date and later marry. Family, peers, religion, social class, race, and government are just a few of the things that influence who we choose as marital partners.

One might ask a question like, "What role could the government possibly play in who I choose to marry?" Well, if a woman loved her biological brother, could she marry him? Not in America, where we have laws against that happening. As a matter of fact, all societies have laws regarding who a person can marry, based on factors like age, gender, and blood relationship. The government certainly has a say in who a person can marry. Even though people might give love as their reason to marry, it simply isn't true. There are many social structures that ultimately make our decisions.

Interpretive Sociological Research

The second method for conducting sociological research is known as interpretive sociology. This study of society focuses on meanings that people attach to their world. An interpretive sociologist would suggest that although science is crucial when collecting data, it is missing the vital ingredient of interpretation. Interpretive sociologists wish to find out not only what people are doing, but the meanings that people attach to their actions.

Interpretive sociologists use different methods of data collection than scientific sociologists. Because they are searching for the meanings that people attach to their behavior, oftentimes researchers will ask about a respondent's feelings or thoughts. These two things are dismissed in scientific research because they are difficult to measure.

Critical Sociological Research

Critical sociology focuses on the notion that society is not a natural system with fixed order. In this case, the goal in conducting research would be to change society. Critical sociologists collect data and research with the goal of changing society. They often look for issues within a society and then consider methods for solving those problems. An interpretative sociologist would review the data and consider why the problems exist, while a critical sociologist wouldn't necessarily care about the how or why. This method for collecting "research" is often used by conflict theorists who would like a restructuring of society.

How To Collect Sociological Data

Sociologists collect data and analyze the results just as any other scientist would. They formulate a **hypothesis**—a tentative statement about how various variables are related to each other—collect data, run statistical tests, and analyze results.

Sample Population

When conducting research, the first item that sociologists need to decide is which group of people should be studied and to whom the findings can be applied. A **population** is *the entire group of people to be studied*. It can be all the people in the United States, males in California, or expectant mothers located in the South, just to name a few examples.

Of course, gathering information from each member of a population would be time-consuming, costly, and virtually impossible, especially if the number of members is in the millions. Because of these factors, sociologists gather data from only a select number of people as a *sub-grouping*, or *sample* population.

Size Of Sub-Grouping

Because researchers are only collecting data from a select number of people, the size of the group becomes very important. Let's say a researcher posed the question, "Who do you believe is the best sociology professor ever?" The results showed that 100 percent of the people asked believed that Professor X was the best. That would be pretty impressive, right? Then, if we looked at the size of the population sampled and found it to be only one person, the results of 100 percent would not be very significant after all. A good sample size can be determined statistically by the number of people who fall into the population being researched.

Samples And Application Of Data

A **sample** is simply a smaller group of individuals selected from a larger population. The results of a research study can only be applied to the entire population if each person who falls into the population has had an equal opportunity to participate in the study as part of the sample. This would be known as a **random sample**. If a sample is not truly random, the results may only be applied to the people who actually provided the data.

Let's use the previous example. What if the sample was not random, and only the family members and friends of Professor X were surveyed? The results could then only be applied to the people who provided the data: 100 percent of family members and friends of Professor X believe that he is the best sociology professor. Would it be accurate to state that the results reflect the opinion of every student at the university where Professor X teaches, or all college students in the nation? It would not, which illustrates why collecting data from a random sample is very important.

Sometimes researchers use **stratified sampling**, which goes beyond a random sample by making sure that the people randomly selected to be in the sample match the proportions of the population being studied. If a population were 60 percent female, for example, researchers using this method would want to make sure that their sample contained 60 percent females.

Type Of Data

There are two different types of data that can be collected. Scientific sociologists like to focus on collecting **quantitative data**, or *data that can be measured in numbers.*

When collecting data, they use questions in which a respondent is limited to answering on a scale. An example of a quantitative question might be, "On a scale of one to five, where five means that you are very happy to be enrolled in college and one means that you are very unhappy, please choose the number that applies to you." Being an optimist and a fan of higher education, I will assume that an individual gives an answer of five. The researcher would then take that answer, along with all the other response numbers, and compute how happy students are to be enrolled in college, on average. This result is very objective because the respondents had to choose from a limited number of responses.

The second type of data that can be collected is **qualitative data**, or *data that can be qualified.* This method is widely used among interpretive sociologists who like to understand meanings. Researchers who use this method often use open-ended questions to which respondents are free to give any answer.

Let's change the previous research question into a qualitative format. The revised question might be, "Please describe how you feel about being enrolled in college and why." By using an open-ended question, respondents have the opportunity to explain their answers instead of simply choosing a number. Results of this kind of research are subjective.

If a respondent gives an answer of three on the scale of happiness, it is left to the researcher to describe the person's level of happiness. Using the qualitative method, on the other hand, allows the respondent to explain that she is somewhat happy because she is getting her college education, but is somewhat unhappy because she is tired from the demands of working and going to school. Overall, she feels somewhat happy.

Researchers may not be interested in the "why" of an answer; they might only be looking for the "what." It is up to researchers to decide which type of data should be collected. Both types of data are

Overview: Reliability & Validity

Reliability: Consistency in measurement.

Validity: Accurately measuring what is intended to be measured.

Review the three targets below. Are the results reliable, valid, neither, or both?

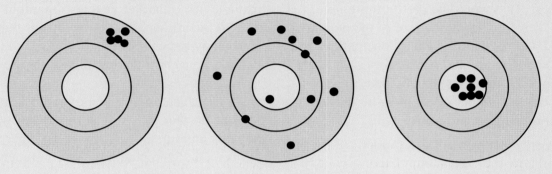

useful in different situations, and researchers often use a combination of the two.

Variables

Once sociologists know whom they wish to gather information from and what type of data to collect, they need to determine the variables. A **variable** is a *concept whose values change from case-to-case*. Variables assign numerical scores or category labels; in research, common variables include race, gender, age, social class, marital status, education, and religion. The education of people will vary; some may have less than a high school education and others will have advanced college degrees. The same goes for gender, where the categories will be male, female, and, possibly, intersex individuals.

Variables can be either dependent or independent. In research, there is only one dependent variable—the variable that changes—while the independent variables are those causing the changes.

As an example, let's use a research question related to drinking among college-age students. We might ask their age, race, gender, and how frequently they consume alcoholic beverages. The dependent variable is alcohol usage, because it is expected to change in relation to other variables. Age, race, and gender would be independent variables. The results might show the amount of drinking will vary

depending on the gender of the respondent. Perhaps the researcher learns that males drink more than females. The frequency of alcohol consumption might also change in relation to the age or race of a respondent; thus, how often alcohol is consumed may depend upon age, race, or gender.

A research study may have many variables depending on the topic being studied. For elementary purposes, there will only be one dependent variable and one or more independent variables in the examples included in this chapter.

Measurement Of Variables

Once the variables for a research study have been determined, researchers must assign them a value. **Measurement** is the *process of systematically assigning values to concepts for the purpose of research*. In other words, the variables must be defined.

Depending on how important a variable is to a study, it can be defined broadly or narrowly. Let's use the same three variables as before: race, gender, and age. Race might be defined as Caucasian, African-American, Hispanic, Asian, Middle-Eastern, or other. A researcher would list as many, or as few, race categories as needed to represent the population he wished to sample. If the researcher was only interested in comparing African-Americans and

Caucasians, those might be the only two categories listed for the study.

Definitions of variables must be generally accepted, and not far-fetched. As an example, consider a researcher who wants to study children in African-American families. Could the researcher define the variable "child's age" as 0-32 years? This definition would not be accepted because they aren't many 32-year-olds that would be considered children in our society. If, instead, the researcher defined "child's age" as 0-18 years, most people would accept that definition.

Importance Of Defining Variables

The definition of a variable is very important. The results of a research study are determined by the variables and how they are manipulated. If a variable isn't given an acceptable definition, the results will be skewed and, therefore, useless.

Some variables are more difficult than others to define. For example, the variable of gender is fairly standard and there are not many choices for the definition. The variable of singlehood, on the other hand, could be quite difficult to define. To determine the status of singlehood, a researcher might have to ask questions like, "Are you currently dating?" or "When was the last time that you went out on a date?"

Reliability And Validity

The entire process of collecting data and manipulating variables can become valueless if the method of measurement is not reliable. **Reliability** refers to *consistency*, or receiving the same results every time. For example, if a researcher conducted the same study again using the same methods, he should receive the same results. To explain it a different way, if a person were to step onto a scale ten different times, and each time the results read the same amount, then that scale would be said to be reliable.

The measurement indicator used for the research study must also be valid or accurate. **Validity** means that *the indicator accurately measures what it is intended to measure*. If a person who weighed two-hundred pounds stepped onto a scale and it said that person only weighed one-hundred pounds, then the

scale would not be valid; it would not be producing accurate results. To be considered valid, the scale would have to give the measurement of two-hundred pounds.

Sometimes an exam, a form of measurement, is not a true assessment of a person's knowledge. Researchers have discovered that if a test is administered to the same people multiple times in a short time-frame, the test loses its validity. For example, if a person were handed the same word search puzzle ten different times on a given day, what would be the chances that he would eventually master that puzzle? Would that prove he is great at conquering word search puzzles, or would it prove that he had mastered that one particular word search? As a matter of fact, by the tenth time, the person might not even look for the words, but just circle them immediately.

Researchers must be careful in the selection of their measurement so that it will be both reliable and valid. Without meeting these two demands, the results of the research will be inadequate for application to the target population.

Relationships Between Variables

The purpose of conducting sociological research is to determine how variables are related. For example, how much does race influence a person's level of education, or what is the role of social class in the amount of alcohol consumed?

A **correlation** exists when two or more variables change together. This can be either a positive or a negative change. Although variables might change together, this does not necessarily mean that one variable actually causes a change in the another. Correlation, instead, refers to *establishing that there is a relationship between variables*. For example, the number of cell phone users has increased steadily over the past years. The number of automobile accidents has also increased. This shows a correlation between the number of cell phone users and the number of automobile accidents. Many people might, therefore, conclude that cell phone users cause more automobile accidents. This conclusion might be true in specific cases, but it cannot be said that cell phone users cause more accidents without further study and analysis. Neither could it be said that a decline in cell phone use would result in a decrease in the number of accidents.

A **spurious correlation** occurs when two variables change together, but the change is being caused by a third variable. For instance, as shoe size goes up so does the frequency of sexual activity for a person. Does this mean that the size of a person's shoe dictates how often he or she will have sex? If researchers were to come across these results, they would have to test other variables to see what is actually causing the change. In this case, the third variable is age. A child's foot is very small and children do not participate in sexual activity. As they reach adulthood, though, their feet have grown much larger, and sexual activity has also begun.

When manipulating variables, researchers are looking for cause and effect, where a change in one variable causes a change in another. To prove a cause-and-effect relationship, a timeline must be established to demonstrate that the cause occurred before the effect. As previously mentioned, when Durkheim studied who was most likely to commit suicide, he found that a lack of social integration was the cause, and people ending their own lives was the effect.

Methods Of Collecting Data

Once a research question has been established and the variables have been decided upon, the next step is to figure out how the data will be collected. There are many methods that can be utilized to collect data. Each of the following methods has advantages and disadvantages. It is up to researchers to select a process based on factors like time, money, topic and data.

Experiment

One research method is to conduct an **experiment**; this would occur in a controlled environment where the variables could be closely managed. In this type of research there are generally two groups of respondents randomly classified into either an experimental group or a control group. The **experimental group** is the one exposed to independent variables like treatments or services. **Control group** participants are not exposed to the variables. The results from the two groups are then compared. This form of research is generally used for clinical research studies.

Advantages: Certainly, if the experiment were conducted in a laboratory, unknown conditions would have less chance of interfering with the outcome. A researcher is able to predict obstacles.

Disadvantages: Oftentimes, experiments conducted in a laboratory lack real-life application because it is difficult to account for all unforeseen variables.

Survey Research

This method is the most popular and widely used form of data collection. One reason for its popularity is that there are many variations of surveys that can be used. Survey research can be conducted over the phone, in person, or over the Internet. In this case, researchers would create a questionnaire and then administer it in the chosen method. Researchers might also choose to use multiple forms of survey research by starting with one method and following up with a second or third.

Advantages: Administering a survey is useful when attempting to reach large numbers of people. It is fairly cost-effective, and people in general are usually willing to answer a few questions. Also, answering a survey over the phone or through the mail allows a participant to remain relatively anonymous. If the subject matter is sensitive, a researcher might get more truthful responses with a phone survey versus an in-person interview.

Disadvantages: One of the major drawbacks to this method is that it might take more time to collect the data. Mailed surveys, for example, often do not get returned in a timely manner, if at all. It usually takes hundreds of mailed surveys to receive even one completed questionnaire back. Individuals might throw out the survey as junk mail, or they might intend to complete it but forget or return it too late.

Also, when interviewing individuals, researchers might not get truthful answers because respondents may tend to provide the answers they believe the researchers want, or one that the respondent decides is more suitable. As an illustration, if a researcher asked a 25-year-old female the number of sexual partners she has had, she might give a lower number (so as not to be viewed as promiscuous) or a higher number (to prove she has had experience).

Observation

Another method of collecting data is by observing a particular population. This observation takes place in the population's natural setting. For example, if a researcher wanted to see how mothers interact with their children during playtime, perhaps he would go to the park and watch mothers and their children. This technique has two components. First, the researcher must write down the group's actions, being both objective and factual. Second, the observations must be analyzed by applying theory. This type of observation is known as **detached observation**, because the researcher observes from a distance without actually getting involved.

A variation of observation involves the researcher joining the group and participating in the activity. **Participant observation** allows a researcher to observe a group's behavior from within the group itself. The people who are being studied may or may not know that they are being observed. Depending on the topic in question, a group might reject an outsider, making research difficult. This method of participant observation is widely used among anthropologists who wish to study various cultures.

Advantages: Many things can be learned by studying people in their natural environments. Often, a researcher will receive the most realistic responses by seeing how people interact in real-life situations.

Disadvantages: One disadvantage to using this method is that people might behave differently if they know that they are being watched, a phenomenon known as the **Hawthorne effect**. This first came to light in a series of studies on factory workers between 1924 and 1932. Although the change in behavior is generally positive, the results of a research study using this method would not be valid if the changes noted were found to be temporary and unrealistic.

Secondary Data Analysis

One method of collecting data is to get the data from another rather than actually gathering it yourself. In this case, researchers are able to tap into databases hosted by other researchers who collected the data. The best example of this is the U.S. Census Bureau. In its database, census data has been compiled and made available in one place, allowing researchers to select variables and run statistical analyses.

A variation of this method is *content analysis* in which a researcher looks at a variety of content, such as marriage, divorce, birth, and death certificates, and police or other public records. This method helps researchers look at patterns of behavior that occur over time. They might also review media like movies, television shows, advertisements, and magazines. In this case, no respondents would be physically involved in the study, only their information.

Advantages: Conducting research can be costly and time-consuming, and this method is the cheapest and, most likely, the easiest. Because the data is collected from another source, it saves the researcher time, allowing him or her to move to the second step, which is analyzing the data.

Disadvantages: One major disadvantage of this method is the lack of variables. If researchers did not collect the data for themselves, then certain variables in which they are interested in might be missing. When conducting their own research, sociologists are able to use any variables and are also able to follow up with respondents if they need more information. When pulling variables out of a database, if a certain variable does not exist, researchers are not able to get the information. In other words, they must choose only from the available variables. Additionally, a researcher might enjoy collecting data and interacting with respondents. Generally, sociologists are interested in the topics they research and might miss the process if they do not collect the data themselves.

Overview Of All Methods

Deciding on the method of collecting data is up to the researcher. The best methods to use will depend on the topics and the populations being studied.

ASA Guidelines

Whenever research is collected, scientists are bound by certain ethics and rules that govern their work. This is true for sociology as well. The American Sociological Association (ASA) provides guidelines and specific rules to which sociologists must adhere.

Probably the most important ethic is that researchers are to protect the physical and psychological well-being of the respondents. This means that the researcher must not purposefully harm the respondent and should also attempt to foresee any potential problems that may arise and take appropriate actions. Researchers should also protect the privacy of the people participating in the study and maintain confidentiality.

Participants will generally sign a consent form that explains the study and the terms and conditions of participation. The consent form will also state that a respondent's personal information will be protected.

Once a study has been conducted, the findings should be published without excluding any aspect of the results. Once in a while, a researcher might uncover results that are disturbing; it would be unethical for him to just "sweep it under the rug" by deciding not to disclose that portion of the findings. This extends to sharing techniques and methods with other professionals in the field, should they ask for the information. Conducting research allows for the creation of a body of knowledge. Therefore, professionals should impart their expertise to others to facilitate better understanding of the results and reproduction of the studies.

Other Areas Of Concern

Researchers should also be culturally sensitive to the population they are studying. In seeking

---

Overview: How To Conduct A Research Study

Choose a Topic/Select your Population: What question would you like to ask, and who would you like to answer it?

Choose and Define Variables: Consider the group that you are studying when selecting the variables and make sure that the definition is acceptable.

Select a Method of Collecting Data: There are many types of methods to choose from, such as experiments, surveys, observations, or secondary analyses.

Measurement: Make sure that the measurement for analyzing the data is both reliable and valid.

Remember the ASA Guidelines: While conducting the research keep in mind the rules that govern research, especially those protecting respondents.

Analyze the Results: You are looking to see how the variables are related and to analyze the results by applying theory.

---

information from a certain ethnic group, researchers should be aware of the group's dynamics and lifestyles. This is especially true in America, where there are many people of diverse backgrounds. Although this isn't an ethical standard provided by the ASA, it is common courtesy to afford such consideration to all respondents.

When conducting research, it is very easy for a person's biases to interfere with the results. Weber suggested that anyone who conducted research should be objective, and assumptions should not be included in the research process. In other words, researchers must suspend all beliefs, assumptions, biases, and prejudices. If a sociologist were to conduct research and relate it to preconceived notions, the results would be tainted and, therefore, invalid. Some common biases relate to gender, race, age, or social class.

Most of the time, conducting objective research is a virtually impossible task. Researchers choose the topics and the methods of collecting data, and they are also the ones analyzing the results, so the studies are already subject to bias. Therefore, instead of trying to be completely objective themselves, researchers should strive for value-free research, untainted by their own views.

Summary

This chapter provides a foundation for the study of sociology, helping you to see the general in the particular and the strange in the familiar. The field of sociology is continually growing and expanding through three categories of sociological research: scientific, focusing on empirical data; interpretive, striving to understand the meanings people attach to their world; and critical, working towards the goal of changing society. The origins of sociology lie in the formation of cities, political changes, technological advancements, and the results of change. The viewpoints of the three main schools of thought in sociology introduced in this chapter—structural functionalism, social conflict, and symbolic interactionism—will be discussed throughout this book as they pertain to topics ranging from religion to the environment.

Review/Discussion Questions

1. What is a theory?
2. What is the difference between organic and mechanical solidarity?
3. Who was Karl Marx?
4. What are some of the methods used by sociologists to collect data?
5. If you were going to conduct sociological research, what would you study?
6. Do you think your behavior would change if you were under constant observation?

Key Terms

Class conflict occurs between the owner class and the worker class as they struggle for control over scarce resources.

Control groups are those in which participants are not exposed to the variables.

Correlation exists when two (or more) variables change together.

Detached observation involves a researcher observing behavior from a distance without actually getting involved with the participants.

Experiments are controlled environments in which variables can be closely managed.

Experimental groups are those exposed to the independent variables, such as participation in a program or receiving a medication.

Global perspective studies the impact our society has on other nations, and also the impact of other nations upon our society.

Hawthorne effect describes a phenomenon in which people modify their behavior because they know they are being monitored.

Hypotheses are tentative statements about how different variables are expected to relate to each other.

Latent functions are consequences of a social situation that are neither intended nor expected, and are often unrecognized.

Manifest functions are the intended and expected consequences of a social situation.

Measurement is the systematic process of assigning values or labels to concepts for research purposes.

Mechanical solidarity is a form of social cohesion in which people do similar work and share the same values and beliefs.

Organic solidarity is a form of social cohesion in which people work in a wide variety of specialized occupations, and thus gain their social consensus from their need to rely on one another for goods and services.

Participant observation allows a researcher to observe a group's behavior from within the group itself.

Populations are entire groups of people to be studied.

Qualitative data measures intangibles like people's feelings and can include focus group results, interviews, and observations.

Quantitative data is data that can be measured in numbers.

Random samples are those in which each person who is part of the population has an equal opportunity to be selected for participation in a study.

Reliability refers to consistency, or receiving the same results every time the same study is conducted.

Samples are smaller groups of individuals selected from larger populations.

Social conflict perspective views society as a compound filled with inequalities in regard to the allocation of resources.

Social consensus occurs when nearly all members of a society want to achieve the same goals and work cooperatively to achieve them.

Sociological imagination is the process of achieving a better understanding of our own experiences. We do this by discovering our place within society, including our experiences with social institutions and the historical period in which we live.

Sociological paradigms provide frameworks that allow us to study society and analyze data and research using sociological tools, methods, and theories.

Sociological perspective involves being able to see the general in the particular.

Sociology is the scientific study of human society and social interaction.

Spurious correlation occurs when two variables change together, not because of a causal relationship between the two, but because of a third variable. This result reminds us that "correlation does not imply causation."

Stratified sampling makes sure that the people randomly selected to be in the sample match the proportions of the population being studied.

Structural-functionalism views society as an intricate structure, with many different levels or parts all working together in collaboration for stability.

Symbolic interactionism contends that society exists due to the everyday interactions of people.

Theories are integrated sets of propositions that are intended to explain specific phenomena and to show relationships between variables in order to gain understanding.

Validity means that indicators used in research, like rating scales, accurately measure the concepts they are intended to measure.

Variables are attributes that may change their values under observation. Variables can be assigned numerical scores or category labels.

Bibliography

American Sociological Association (2008). <http://www.asanet.org/> (2008).

Buchmann, C., & DiPiete, T. (2006, August). The Growing Female Advantage in College Completion: The Role of Family Background and Academic Achievement. American Sociological Review, 71 (4).

Blumer, H. (1969). Symbolic Interaction: Perspective and Method. Englewood Cliffs, NJ: Prentice-Hall.

Comte, A. (1975). Auguste Comte and Positivism: The Essential Writings. New York: Harper & Row.

Durkheim, E. (1957). Suicide. (J. A. Spaulding & G. Simpson, Trans.). Glencoe, IL: Free Press of Glencoe.

Marx, K. (1964). Selected Writings in Sociology and Social Philosophy. (T. B. Bottomore, Trans.). New York: McGraw-Hill.

Merton, R. (1938, October). Social Structure and Anomie. American Sociological Review, 3 (5).

Mill, J. S. (1961). August Comte and Positivism. Ann Arbor: University of Michigan Press.

Venkatesh, S. (2008). Gang Leader for a Day. New York: Penguin Press.

CHAPTER TWO

Society And Culture

XueMei Hu

In Chapter One, you learned that sociology is the scientific study of human society and social interaction. Components of the definition include humans, societies, social interactions, and science. The lenses through which sociologists analyze the world in which we live are broad concepts like society and culture, structural concepts like social institutions, and cultural concepts like beliefs and values. Sociologists ask the following questions. What is society? How did societies change over time? What is culture? What role does culture play in society?

Sociologists use both macro and micro levels of analysis to study human society and social life. *Macrosociology* focuses on broad aspects of society. Conflict theories and functionalist theories use the this approach—focusing on large-scale groups and events—to analyze social classes and examine how groups with different social economic status are related to one another. For example, in a macro-level analysis, you as a sociologist would examine how social institutions like family and school have functioned to increase or decrease teenage pregnancies. *Microsociology*, by contrast, focuses on social interaction—how people interrelate. For example, microsociology can be used to explain why students might feel comfortable when interacting with their professors in classrooms, but awkward when meeting them in supermarkets. Both macrosociological and microsociological approaches help us understand social life in society. Chapter 2 explores society and culture. Social interaction is the central focus of Chapter 4.

Society changes over time. Culture and society are different components, but they are closely connected simply because a society has knowledge, beliefs, norms, and values that constitute a culture. Without culture, society cannot exist. Our culture moves at such a fast pace that we are constantly changing and adapting to new trends and new technologies. Society exists within a culture as a subgroup of a larger populace, and, similarly, culture changes with society. For example, without culture, we would not be humans, simply because we would not use language to express ourselves. In what follows, we begin with the concept of society and describe and explore the different types of societies in which human beings have lived, past and present. Then we turn to studying components of culture and cultural diversity.

Society

People live together in society as a group made up of all kinds of people from different backgrounds. Our differences make up the society and the world that we live in today. In most cultures, people have a desire to build a better life and want to live in a safe, secure environment. Some people hope for peace and try to respect each other, while others 'stir the pot' and cause trouble. What everybody experiences in society and how society works is the focus of this section.

What is society? **Society** refers to a diverse group of people who share a distinctive culture in a defined geographic location. A society can be a city, a township, a tribe, or an association. There are two components of the term *society*. First, we think of a society as a group of people bound by such factors as race, ethnicity, gender, social class, or age. Second, a group of people shares a mainstream culture, and sub-groups inherit their sub-cultures from the mainstream. Whatever the criteria may be, the constant factor is the presence of human beings.

Societies change constantly. In order to fully appreciate and understand what life was like at any point in history, one must understand what the society at that time perceived as normal. *How did societies change over time?* Gerhard Lenski (1995) described how societies have changed over the past 10,000 years, emphasizing the role of technology in shaping any society. Lenski applied the term *sociocultural evolution* to the social changes that occur as a society invents and adopts a new technology. Societies with simple technology can support a small number of people and remain traditional or industrial. By contrast, societies with advanced technology can support not only a large population, but also increased standards of living.

Society shapes technology as much as technology shapes society. Technology influences changes in society and has done so throughout history. In fact, many historical eras are identified by their dominant technology: Stone Age, Iron Age, Bronze Age, Industrial Age, and Information Age. Where people live and what modes of production they use to provide food are related to subsistence technology.

Subsistence technology refers to the methods and tools used to acquire basic daily necessities. Based on Lenski's perspective that social change occurs through technological innovation and different levels of subsistence technology, social scientists have identified five types of societies influenced by their technology: hunting and gathering societies, horticultural and pastoral societies, agrarian societies, industrial societies, and post-industrial societies.

The earliest fossil remains of modern humans date to more than 100,000 years ago. Early societies evolved from small bands of hunters and gatherers that relied primarily on their biological skills to large industrial societies based on sophisticated technologies. In the following, we will discuss Lenski's societal stages, followed by a list of large-scale social changes that have occurred in the last 100,000 years of human history.

Evolution Of Societies

Hunting And Gathering Societies

All early hominids, from 2 million to 30,000 years ago, and modern Homo sapiens, until 15,000 years ago, lived as hunters and gatherers. They took their food directly from the environment, rather than maintaining gardens, fields, or domesticated animals. It would be nearly impossible to live as a hunter-gatherer today; in fact, it is generally illegal to hunt on public lands except during special hunting periods. People in **hunting and gathering societies** used simple subsistence technology to hunt animals and gather vegetation. Today we still can find a few hunting and gathering societies like the Aka and Pygmies of Central Africa, the Bushmen of southwestern Africa, the Aborigines of Australia, the Kaska Indians of northwestern Canada, and the Batek and Semai of Malaysia.

Technology And Simple Tools

In early hunting and gathering societies, technology consisted of simple tools made of natural materials like spears, nets, bows and arrows, and traps for hunting. The forces of nature were their enemy because storms and droughts could destroy their food supply. For survival purpose, hunters and gatherers worked together and shared. As technologically simple societies, hunters and gatherers spent most of their time hunting for game and gathering plants to eat. There was no stable food supply and there was no surplus food.

Size And Density

Hunting and gathering societies were small by today's standards, usually consisting of fewer than 40 people. There were thousands of these societies scattered about the planet. Population densities were about 0.6 persons per square mile. A hunting and gathering society needed several hundred square miles of territory, as they were constantly on the move looking for new food supplies. As a result, they had no permanent settlements.

Social Institutions

Social institutions were primitive and informal by today's standards. In hunting and gathering societies, kinship—family—was the major institution and also the basic social and economic unit. Food was acquired and distributed through kinship ties. Hunters and gathers were nomadic, constantly moving to find new sources of plants or to follow migrating animals. Therefore, they did not have private residences or households. The family protected their children and taught basic survival skills. Young children and older people were involved in supplying food, but healthy adults were expected to acquire most of it.

Most of these societies allowed divorce, and it appears to have been very common in some. Infanticide (15-50% of all live births) and abortion also appears to have been common. The economy was primitive; males were hunters, while females were gatherers. Except in the Arctic, gathering provided 60 to 80 percent of the food supply. Hunters and gatherers were thought to have worked about 15 hours per week in locations where the climate was not extreme. Religion was based on *animism*, the belief that spirits inhabit virtually everything in the world. Politics were somewhat democratic, with decisions reached through discussion and consensus. Some societies did have a chief or headman, but their power was limited. Education was informal. There were initiations into various stages of life (e.g., adulthood). Art and leisure consisted of music, dancing, and storytelling. Games were based on physical skill and chance. There are no records of these societies having games of strategy (Sloss, 2008). Warfare existed but was rare and ritualistic.

Social Equality

Hunting and gathering societies were relatively egalitarian. People or groups experienced difficulties in building power bases because they could not accumulate a surplus of food and there were few resources. Women and men were relatively equal because they were all involved in the supply of food, though, in some societies, there was a division of labor where men were hunters and women were gatherers. Private ownership of land was virtually absent. Constant moving made it difficult for anyone to accumulate much wealth. Outstanding people such as religious leaders could not receive material rewards since there was no surplus of food.

Horticultural And Pastoral Societies

Many societies gave up hunting and gathering for horticultural and pastoral pursuits for three reasons. First, the supply of large game animals as a source of food was depleted because growing human populations with better tools had overhunted them. Second, there was an increase in the number of humans without enough food available to feed them. Third, there were weather and environmental changes.

About 10,000 years ago, a number of groups discovered that they could cultivate plants. Others found that they could tame and breed some of the animals they hunted, primarily goats, sheep, cattle, and camels. As a result, between 13,000 and 7,000 BCE (Before the Common Era), hunting and gathering societies branched into two directions—horticultural and pastoral. Which direction they chose was based on water supply, terrain, and soil quality.

Horticultural Societies

Horticultural societies used hand-powered tools

in raising crops to acquire food. These societies existed in more fertile regions better suited for raising crops. People used hoes to work the soil and digging sticks to punch holes in the ground to plant seeds. The use of tools made planting more efficient and productive. Horticulturalists were able to cultivate the soil more deeply so that they could raise crops in the same areas for longer periods of time. People were able to settle for a longer time in the same area. These inventions also allowed horticultural societies to grow food for more people. The first horticultural societies began in fertile areas of the Middle East (Lenski, Nolan, & Lenski, 1995).

Size And Density

Horticulture had the effect of producing larger food supplies which produced larger populations. While hunting and gathering societies rarely had more than 40 people, simple horticultural societies averaged 1,500 people, with an average density of 13.8 per square mile, while more advanced groups had more than 5,000 people with an average density of 42.7 per square mile. Horticultural societies were characterized as multi-community because they were linked politically and economically.

Technology And The Domestication Revolution

The Domestication Revolution occurred over thousands of years. It represented a fundamental break with the past and changed human history. Horticultural societies were based on the cultivation of plants by the use of hand tools like hoes and digging sticks. Because these groups no longer had to abandon an area as the food supply ran out, they developed permanent settlements. These more dependable food supplies ushered in changes that touched almost every aspect of human life. With more food than was essential for survival, no longer was it necessary for everyone to produce food. This allowed groups to develop a division of labor, and some people began to specialize in making jewelry, tools, weapons, and so on. This led to a surplus of objects, which, in turn, stimulated trade. With trading, groups began to accumulate objects they prized, such as gold, jewelry, and utensils. These changes set the stage for social inequality. Private ownership of land remained virtually absent.

Mobility

People in horticultural societies moved less than those in hunting and gathering societies. A few advanced horticultural societies may have had truly permanent settlements, but most moved every few years. Gardens were usually made by clearing forested areas using slash-and-burn techniques and then planting the crops. As the forest reclaimed the garden and the soil lost nutrients, people would move on to make new gardens. Thus, horticulturalists formed permanent settlements and moved only when the soil gave out and the water source was

The Domestication Revolution

Food Supply	Food supply became more dependable and available.
Large Societies	A dependable food supply made it possible to support large societies.
Surplus Food	For the first time in human history, food surpluses became common.
Division of Labor	Food surpluses freed workers to do crafts and specialize.
Trade and Barter	Surplus food and crafts were traded with others.
Accumulation of Goods	Some people accumulated more valued goods than others.
Wars	People had possessions worth fighting over.
Slavery	Captives from battles were forced to do less appealing work.
Social Inequality	Some people accumulated much over time, while others accumulated less.
Hereditary Wealth	The wealthy passed their benefits on to their children.
Concentrated Power	Wealth and power became concentrated in the hands of a few. Chiefs, kings, and feudal societies emerged.

depleted.

Social Institutions

The family, or kinship, was still the primary social institution. Matriarchies, with the mother's side of the family wielding the power, were more common but not the most common form of household. Some societies had very complex and intricate systems of marriage rules, and marriage itself became an economic activity as 83 percent of advanced horticulture societies required the purchase of brides. Female infanticide was also common, especially in warring societies. Horticulturalists created complex systems for tracing family lineage. Education was informal and not a social institution. In horticultural societies, religion was often based on ancestor worship. Lenski believed this was a result of living close to the graves of their dead. The economy revolved around the cultivation of plants. Primary responsibility for this activity differed from one society to another. Females were responsible for cultivation in about 39 percent of the societies and males were responsible in 28 percent, with men and women sharing responsibility in the remaining 33 percent of societies. Since there was some food surplus, other full-time occupations like priests, artisans, and soldiers arose. Politics was more complex than in hunting and gathering societies, and legal codes were developed. There was often a headman or shaman. Recreation included art, music, and dancing. Games of physical skill were still common (90%), games of chance declined (34%), and strategy games were introduced (10% of simple societies and 57% of advanced). Compared with hunting and gathering societies, there were increases in head-hunting, cannibalism, and human sacrifice (Sloss, 2008). Murder and intergroup violence appeared to be rather common, as was slavery. Warfare increased in frequency.

Social Inequality

Horticultural societies were less egalitarian than hunter-gatherer societies. With the surplus of food, people began to weave cloth and carpets, make crafts, or serve as priests. Some people produced more, received more material rewards, and became richer. The idea of property rights came into be-

ing as people formed more permanent settlements. People with the greatest material surpluses not only enjoyed economic advantages, but also gained higher statuses and more power than others. They had the ability to control others. Slavery was fairly common. Social inequality emerged in horticultural societies, with elites using government power backed by military force. Warfare increased in frequency. Private ownership of land was still virtually absent.

Pastoral Societies

Hunter/gatherer societies living in areas not suitable for growing plants, such as mountainous areas with low annual rainfall, adopted pastoral societies. **Pastoral societies** used technology that supported the domestication and herding of animals to acquire food. These societies first appeared about 12,000 to 15,000 years ago. Most pastoral societies had secondary means of subsistence, usually small scale horticulture or agriculture. True pastoral societies are rare today (Lenski, Nolan, & Lenski, 1995).

Size And Density

Pastoral communities were usually small, averaging 72 people, with several dozen communities forming a society with a total population of approximately 6,000. Domesticating animals and growing plants increased food production and became a more reliable source of food than hunting and gathering. With more food came an increase in population from dozens of people to hundreds or thousands.

Mobility

Most of these groups remained nomadic (90%), following their animals to fresh grazing lands and water sources. In desert areas they traveled from water hole to water hole. In mountain areas they moved up and down the terrain as the weather changed. We can still find societies today that mix horticulture and pastoralism throughout South America, Africa, and Asia.

Social Institutions

The family remained the primary social institution. These societies were very male-dominated because men controlled the food supply. Religion, education, and politics remained relatively informal in pastoral societies. Pastoralists believed that God was directly involved in the well-being of the world, with an active role in human affairs. The religions of Christianity, Islam, and Judaism developed in pastoral societies, with God often likened to a shepherd and humans to domesticated animals such as sheep. Politics was based on a simple form of government that was backed up by military force. The economy was primarily men's work. Warfare was more frequent than in hunting and gathering societies, and most fights were over grazing areas. Slavery was more common in pastoral societies than in others; in some areas, being a slave was a hereditary status. Education was informal and not a social institution.

Social Inequality

Pastoral societies were less egalitarian than those of hunter-gatherers. Social status was based on the size of one's herd. These societies were very patriarchal (male-dominated) in customs, and newly married couples were likely to live with the husband's family. Women had very few rights. Gender inequality was greater in pastoral societies than in those of hunters and gatherers because men raised the animals and were engaged in food production, while women contributed little in this area. Social inequality emerged in pastoral societies with elites using government power supported the military.

In summary, some families acquired more goods than others in horticultural and pastoral societies. This led to feuds and wars because groups now possessed animals, pastures, croplands, jewelry, and other material goods to fight over. War, in turn, opened the door to slavery; people found it convenient to let their captives do their drudgework. Social inequality remained limited, however, as the surplus itself was limited. As individuals passed on their possessions to their descendants, wealth grew more concentrated and social inequality became more common. As people learned to domesticate plants and animals, they were able to produce and accumulate a food surplus. This food surplus resulted in a more complex division of labor allowing for

trade among groups and the accumulation of material goods. This surplus also resulted in the subordination of females by males, the development of the state, and rule by the elite.

Agrarian Societies

Another technological revolution occurred in the Middle East about 5,000 years ago, which led to the emergence of agrarian, or agricultural, societies in Mesopotamia and Egypt, and later in China. This period of history is called the *dawn of civilization*. **Agrarian societies** are based on the technology of animal-drawn plows that supported large-scale cultivation to acquire food. Along with these plows, other breakthroughs of this period included irrigation, writing, numbers, the wheel, and the use of various metals. Agrarian societies are classified as pre-industrial economic structures, as are those of the hunter-gatherers, horticulturalists, and pastoralists. Agricultural workers in these societies engaged in primary sector production, meaning that they attempted to extract raw materials and natural resources from the environment to be consumed or used without much processing.

Technology

Unlike the hoes and digging sticks used in horticultural societies, the animal-drawn plow made it possible for people to produce large surpluses of food. With these plows, farmers could cultivate bigger fields than the garden plots planted by horticulturalists. Plows not only could turn and aerate the soil to make it more fertile, but also control the weeds that might kill crops. In this way, farmers were able to reap several harvests every year from the same plot of land. Due to the resultant increase in surplus food and the transportation of goods using animal-powered wagons, the population of agrarian societies expanded. According to Nolan and Lenski (1995), about 100 BCE, the agrarian Roman Empire contained some seven million people spread over two million square miles. Greater production led to a relatively high level of division of labor and specialization. Dozens of distinct occupations arose including farmers, builders, and metalworkers. Money was invented as the standard of exchange; the old barter system—trading one thing for another—was abandoned.

Size And Density

Agrarian societies were larger and denser than previous societies. They could support over 100,000 people with densities of more than 100 people per square mile. Modern agrarian societies often had rapidly expanding populations. For the first time, farming allowed people to be born, live to be an adult, and die in the same place. Agrarian societies were the first societies to develop cities.

Social Institutions

Agrarian societies developed more elaborate and complex institutions, though the family was still primary. The economy was principally composed of family-based businesses. For farmers, the farm was the family business. For urban craftsmen and shopkeepers, their shop was family-owned and operated. The economy established monetary systems of exchange, increasing available markets because products could be sold to people who did not produce things. The value of individualism was amplified. Religion was very powerful, providing a rationale for giving surplus items to leaders. In agrarian societies, religion defined loyalty and hard work as moral obligations and reinforced the power of elites. The "creator" and "involved" gods that originated in horticultural and pastoral societies were still part of the ideology. In simple agrarian societies, the gods were seen as being concerned about the individual's moral conduct. As societies advanced and began to include various sub-cultures, monotheism replaced multiple gods. Politics was primarily a feudal system based on heredity. Emperors and pharaohs were given absolute power to control political systems, and people were ordered to obey and work for them. Education was expanded as an institution, although only a small number of people were actually educated. Elites had time for cultured activities like the study of philosophy, art, and literature. This was not yet mass education. Leisure activities included art, music, and dancing. Much of the entertainment was raucous and crude; cock fights, gladiatorial combat, and public hangings were common. Warfare was constant in agrarian societies. Standing armies became common and fought each other, wiping out earlier types of societies (Lenski, Nolan, & Lenski, 1995).

Social Inequality

Social inequality was very extreme, with landlords and peasants serving as the two main classes. Landlords owned the land and passed it along through generations of their families. A large number of people were peasants or slaves, and they produced the harvests. Peasants signed agreements with landowners to cultivate a parcel of land in exchange for part of the harvest. The landlords became richer and more powerful as they exploited labor, rent, and taxation from the peasants.

Gender inequality also increased in agrarian societies. Since large-scale farming required intensive labor and greater physical strength than horticultural societies, men were more involved in food production and, thus, were given a position of social dominance. Women might not be included in agrarian tasks and were, instead, left with support tasks such as cooking, caring for children, and weeding. As more men owned land, women's lives grew more restricted and they became a kind of property. Marriage meant the transfer of that 'property' from a father's side to a husband's residence. According to Nielsen (1998), men demanded that women practice premarital virginity and marital fidelity so that "legitimate" heirs could be produced to inherit their land and other possessions. Gender inequality continued to exist as the division of labor between women and men was very obvious in areas of the Middle East. Women were engaged in unpaid work in the private sphere inside the home, while men were involved in paid work outside of the home which provided men with higher status and social dominance.

Industrial Societies

The Industrial Revolution first began in Britain and then spread to other nations through the process of diffusion, including the United States. **Industrial societies** are based on technology that mechanizes production to provide goods and services. Industrial technology changed the nature of subsistence production and the distribution of goods. In agrarian societies, men and women worked in the home or in the fields. In industrial societies, large-scale agri-businesses replaced family-based farms and ranches. Industrialization brought about changes to the modes of production. New sources of energy—steam, internal combustion, and electricity—allowed factories to emerge as the primary means of producing goods. Industrialization attracted agricultural workers seeking employment in factories where they were paid an income. Workers engaged in secondary-sector production, processing raw materials into finished products. Industrial technology gave people the power to transform rural and agrarian societies into urban and industrial societies.

Technology And The Industrial Revolution

Industrial societies are characterized by their use of machines rather than animals (including humans) for power. The planet's first industrial society was England, about 280 years ago. Technology-driven changes have been particularly evident in the past century. The invention of the steam engine brought about other inventions and discoveries. In terms of transportation, trains, steamships, and automobiles came into being. By 1900, railroads crossed the country, steamships traveled the seas, and steel-framed skyscrapers reached far higher than any of the old cathedrals that symbolized the agrarian age (Macionis, 2008). These changes were followed by automobiles, which created greater mobility and spread-out societies. Inventions such as electric lights allowed people to work around the clock. Electricity powered houses full of modern appliances like washing machines, air conditioners, refrigerators, and stereos. Electric communication began with the telegraph and telephone, to be followed by radio, television, and computers. Aircraft shortened traveling times, leading to a "smaller" world and, eventually, globalization.

Size And Density

Sizes and densities of industrial societies were far higher than those of previous societies, with populations numbering in the millions and densities of hundreds of people per square mile. Population size began to stabilize as birth rates dropped.

Mobility and settlements

For the first time, the majority of people lived in urban rather than rural settings. In industrial societies, most people live and work in urban areas because of job opportunities. Industrialization is characterized by a high level of division of labor and occupational specialization. Over time, government agencies grew in size and scope. More occupations and jobs were created as new corporations and companies were established. Workers were required to have stronger educational backgrounds and possess mechanical or technical skills. A person's occupation became very important because paid work not only brought income and social networks, but also individual status.

Social Institutions

Industrialization transformed social institutions and changed family structures. In pre-industrial societies, the family played a multifunctional role by providing food, shelter, jobs, care, socialization, and religious worship. Industrialization reduced the traditional importance of the family and took over many of these roles as the social institutions of economy, education, and politics grew. The economic system tends to be capitalistic, with dominant monopolies. As more and more people pursued education and careers, they postponed marriage or remained single. Along with other technological changes, contraception revolutionized sexual mores. Another effect of industrialization was the entry of women into the labor market. Women earned wages and became financially independent. A vast array of living arrangements came into being, including single-by-choice people, divorced people, single-parent families, childless families, and blended families.

Religion remained a powerful institution. While science took over the primary function of "explaining" how the natural world works, church membership in the United States increased steadily from 17 percent in the 1700s to more than 63 percent in the 1990s. Education became a major institution. Children were required to receive formal education and both parents and children could be imprisoned for non-attendance. Warfare remained constant as people around the globe competed for limited resources. Politics was based on democratic forms of government. In industrial societies, democracy increased the demand for a greater political voice and also influenced other nations. As the "Four Little Dragons" (Taiwan, Singapore, South Korea, and Hong Kong) and NICs (newly industrialized countries), such as Mexico and Brazil, became industrialized, many people in these nations enhanced their demands for political participation.

Social Inequality

Industrialization had the greatest effect on raising the standards of living. Due to mass production and industrial technology, people could afford durable goods and enjoy comfortable lives as their incomes rose over time. Improved sanitation and advanced medicine extended life expectancy. Elites benefitted from industrial technology first, and though the standards of living rose in industrial societies, social inequality remained a compelling issue. As men entered the labor market and became breadwinners, women were seen as homemakers and financially dependent. Even with the entry of women into the labor market, there was an income gap between women and men. This division of labor increased the economic and political dominance of men. Likewise, minorities and people of color were discriminated against in the labor market.

Post-Industrial Societies

Societies, especially post-industrial societies, are the playing fields of sociologists, whereas pre-industrial societies are usually the domain of anthropologists. Like the United States, many industrialized countries have become post-industrial societies with the advent of computers and new information technology. Sociologist Daniel Bell (1973) coined the term post-industrialism. A **post-industrial society**, or postmodern society, is based on computer technology that produces information and supports a service industry.

Information Technology Society

What is characteristic of these advanced industrial societies is their heavy reliance on information technologies. Major job categories are involved in creating, organizing, or transferring information.

The media has a huge influence on the world today. The information disclosed could be local, national, or international. News about disasters is shown and reported within seconds of occurring—flooding in Washington, tornadoes in the Midwest, fires in California, earthquakes in Japan, a tsunami in Thailand, a war in Iraq, and genocide in Darfur, to name just a few. We live in a world where technology enables us to see what is happening globally.

In this new information technology society, people produce knowledge that generates material

Paying on credit card.   Source: Lotus Head

goods, services, or more knowledge. In post-industrial societies, formal education becomes a very important social institution. It is crucial to upward social mobility because people need to learn information-based skills and obtain degrees for their jobs. Workers also need to learn technical skills and complete their work using computers and other forms of high technology.

Service Sector Economy

Post-industrial societies are associated with service economies based on tertiary-sector production. Tertiary-sector production is the provision of services instead of goods. In a service economy, this means of production is the primary source of income for workers and profit for owners and corporate shareholders. People provide services for others and are employed in jobs such as fast-food, transportation, banking, letter and package delivery, travel, education, health care, real estate, advertising, sports, and entertainment. In 1957, the United States became the first society on the globe to have more than half of its working population employed in the service sector. Today, about 75 percent of the work force is in the service sector. Education is the largest employer in the United States, with health care being second largest. Both fields employ more people than the industrial sector.

Consumer Society

Post-industrial societies are also associated with consumer societies. With the invention of the credit card, post-industrial societies became cashless, which encouraged people to consume more material goods and services. As consumers, people are bombarded with commercials that imply status if they buy brand-name products like Porsches, Rolex watches, Louis Vuitton bags, Chanel clothes and accessories, and other high-end merchandise. Celebrities endorse new trends every season that people are then expected to wear to be part of the "in-crowd". As a result of media exposure, consumers can become very fashion-conscious.

Post-industrial societies are at the heart of globalization. The emergence of a *global village*, where people around the globe interact and communicate with each other via electronic technologies like cell phones, television, faxes, iPods, e-mail and instant messenger services, and the Internet. Although the

Societies	Control of the Food
Hunting and Gathering	First and only type of society until 15,000 years ago. Small (40 people) and nomadic, with little specialization. Religion: animism. Technology: spears.
Horticultural / Pastoral	Domestication of plants (gardening) and animals (herding) about 15,000 years ago. Increased population (200-5,000 people). Lacked permanent settlements. Increased specialization and stratification. Slavery common. Increased warfare. Religion: horticultural societies - ancestor worship; pastoral societies - active god(s). Technology: hoes and digging sticks.
Agrarian	6,000 years ago. Invention of plow controls weeds and maintains fertility of soil. Population increased (100,000+ people). First permanent settlements (cities). Increased specialization and stratification. Gender and class stratification most extreme. Constant warfare. Monetary economies and hereditary political systems. First educational institutions evolve. Religion very powerful and concerned with moral conduct. Technology: animal-drawn plow (natural power or physical labor).
Industrial	Machine power replaces animal and human power. Population in the millions, with hundreds of people per square mile. Urban living for the majority. Corporate/state capitalism replaced family businesses. Education and science have expanded roles. Increased inter-society trading. Democratic governments emerged. Technology: steam engine and fuel-powered machinery.
Post-Industrial	Service sector became largest employer. Production and control of information became a major activity. Specialization continued to increase. Increased control of environment. Technology: creation, organization, or transfer of information using computers and other forms of high technology.

information revolution originated in wealthy countries, new information technologies spread through the worldwide flow of material goods, information, and population. In this way, societies have become more connected, and a global culture has been advanced. With globalization, companies have become diverse and transnational. Companies with large global presences include Google, Yahoo, Disney, Coca-Cola, and Wal-Mart. Since Wal-Mart opened their first international store in 1991, it has grown tremendously and currently has more than 3,000 stores outside the United States.

In sum, societies progress based on their level of technology and their food supply (as shown in Table 2.2). A technologically literate person recognizes the rate of change and accepts the reality that the future will be different from the present, largely because of technologies now coming into existence ranging from Internet-based activities to genetic engineering and cloning.

Culture

The word culture comes from the Latin root *colere*, meaning to inhabit, to cultivate, or to honor. **Culture** refers to a particular society's or social group's way of life, encompassing a set of distinctive spiritual, material, intellectual, and emotional features of a society or social group. A way of life also includes norms, values, traditions, customs, beliefs, art, literature, lifestyles, and sanctions. Culture includes how we live and shapes not only what we think, but also how we behave. Additionally, it suggests that people living together grow and change over their lifetimes.

Importance Of Culture

Culture provides a way of living, thinking, behaving, and interpreting the world. It is essential for our individual survival and for our interaction with others. Cultures include the languages used to communicate and the types of foods consumed. The foods may differ in texture, taste, and color, but they all relate to the resources that are, or were, available to a society. All cultures have their own customs and celebrations based on past experiences, like bull-

fighting in Spain and the Festival of the Giants in Puerto Rico.

Globally, there are almost 7,000 languages, which suggests the existence of just as many cultures. People tend to view their own cultures as normal, but often feel uncomfortable and experience culture shock when they enter an unfamiliar culture. **Culture shock** refers to the personal disorientation that people feel when they experience a culture different from their own. The term was introduced for the first time in 1958 to describe the anxiety produced when a person moves to a completely new environment. Culture shock expresses a lack of direction, a feeling of being lost and not knowing what is appropriate or inappropriate. People may experience culture shock in the United States if they venture into the Amish countryside in Ohio or into Chinatown in New York. In the military, new recruits experience culture shock when they step off the bus and enter basic training or "boot camp," where the goal is to turn them into soldiers, sailors, airmen, or marines.

Different practices might sound quite surprising to members of other cultures. In the Old West, an Apache warrior would eat the heart of an enemy that had truly tested him so that he could keep some of his foe's spirit and ferocious strength. People in some cultures eat human flesh, such as a son eating a piece of his dead father to increase his own manhood. These people believe that the practice allows them to absorb some of the characteristics of the dead person or to regenerate life after death. In most cultures, cannibalism remains one of the ultimate taboos. If a person grew up eating the dead, though, he would probably learn and accept this cultural practice as normal (Arens, 1979).

Culture Is Learned

We are not born with culture. Children learn how to survive and how to express themselves through agents of socialization like family members and peers, schools and mass media. People learn their traditions by growing up in a society and living together in a community. As they get older and learn more, they have a sense of social order and social justice. Culture provides the rules of behavior within a society. These learned rules of social behavior make us alike. While some of these rules can be very surprising to a member of another culture, others are more or less the same across cultures. Respect for elders, hierarchy of authority, and gender roles are examples of shared rules. Some rules of behavior may also be constant, passed down from one generation to the next. The best way to instill values in a child is to set up a role model because children learn by example. If they see tolerance, understanding, and respect for other people in their role models, those are the qualities they will learn.

What behaviors are not learned? An *instinct* is an unlearned, biologically determined behavior pattern common to all members of a species that occurs predictably whenever certain environmental conditions exist (Kendall, 2008). For example, spiders are born able to build webs, they do not learn how. Their instinct to build webs is triggered by basic biological needs such as protection and reproduction. The instinctive behavior of humans is attributed to reflexes and drives. A *reflex* is unlearned because it is a biologically determined response to a physical stimulus. Examples include sneezing after breathing pepper in through the nose, or blinking an eye when a speck of dust gets in it. *Drives* are unlearned, biological impulses common to all members of a society that satisfy needs like sleep, food, water, and sexual gratification. However, expressions of these biological characteristics are learned according to culture. For example, we learn to eat with our hands or with a pair of chopsticks, or to chew our food with our mouths closed. It is also a learned response to use a tissue or turn our head away when we are sneezing.

Culture is shared. People share customs, traditions, and beliefs that they have learned in their communities. Almost all cultures have similar cultural components that people participate in to survive each and every day. Sharing a culture with others makes it possible to interact with people around us. With technological advances and migration, people share different lifestyles as they cross the lines between cultures.

Culture is inherited. Culture is inherited through your parents and your upbringing. It is human nature to be grounded in the culture in which one has

been immersed in since birth. Culture is developed and passed down from one generation to the next. For example, parents of different cultures are taught to love and care for their children, while children are instructed to respect their parents and love their families. No matter what the culture, the traditions of family are usually upheld. In some cultures, parents put their children through rites of passage. Even though those rites may differ from one culture to the next, the tradition of passing culture from parent to child is the same. In some countries, parents may have their children go on their first hunt or get tattooed. We teach our children norms and values. We teach them to cook, clean, and raise families of their own. Family traditions are demonstrated all across the globe. Unlike other species, we, as humans, cannot rely on instinct for our survival. We learn culture after we are born—how to express ourselves and how to treat people as we want to be treated—and we survive because of everything we learn. The culture that we have learned is shared and inherited by people around us. People embrace different cultures, which can bring in personal learning experiences and different skills to strengthen teamwork and productivity in the workplace.

Material And Nonmaterial Culture

Material Culture

Culture can be divided into two categories, material and nonmaterial. Every culture has a variety of physical creations and artifacts. **Material culture** refers to these tangible creations that are made and used by members of a society. Material culture includes raw materials and resources like cotton and potatoes. Through technology, these raw materials are turned into finished products like clothing and potato chips. Technology is one important element of culture, and, as discussed previously, a culture's level of technology has an impact on the way of life of a society.

The material culture of a society may reflect its cultural values. For example, because Americans value science and technology, they invent new ma-

An Amish horse and buggy crossing the intersection in Strasburg, PA.   Source: Nancy Brammer

terial culture items which lead to cultural changes. The material culture of one population may sound strange to another. For example, the Amish culture values tradition, but one concession to modern civilization has been the Amish horse-drawn buggy (Nolt, 1992).

Material culture involves our basic needs, which are important because we must have our daily necessities in order to survive. Food, shelter, and clothing are universal items of material culture. We all need a place to live, clothes for our bodies, and food to consume that will sustain life, provide energy, and promote growth. However, what, how, and when we eat is a major difference between different cultures.

Nonmaterial Culture

Nonmaterial culture refers to abstract or intangible things that influence our behavior. The way people dress and the way they eat is determined by nonmaterial culture. Food is a universal item of material culture, but the way people eat—a nonmaterial item—varies widely from one culture to the next. For example, people in Japan and China eat food with chopsticks, while people in Western countries eat food with spoons and forks. Some people chew food with their mouths open; Americans chew food with their mouths closed. When Americans finish the food on their plates, it usually means that the food was good. In other countries, when a plate of food is completely finished it is taken to mean that not enough food was given, which is an insult. We may also notice cultural differences in the selection of foods. A pork chop served for dinner might insult the majority of people in Saudi Arabia, while it is likely to please many people in the United States. Nonmaterial culture expresses our beliefs and values, our way of thinking. For example, some people believe in Christianity while others believe in Buddhism, and those beliefs affect their behavior.

Customs And Rituals

Nonmaterial culture expresses our customs and rituals. Customs and rituals associated with weddings are examples of nonmaterial culture. In the Middle East, a woman is set up in an arranged marriage with a man she hardly knows. Looking at arranged marriages helps one to appreciate the dating rituals in America. Here we meet and date one person after another until we find the person we want to marry, then we take final plunge, hoping and praying that he or she is the right one. In Sudan, there is an egg-breaking ceremony, called *nincak endog*. In this ceremony, the man has an egg broken over his head to pronounce him the master of his home. This concept may be foreign to another society. In many countries, the groom is required to give gifts to the bride's family, but this practice would make other people feel like a possession. In an African village, women iron their daughters' breasts when they hit puberty to flatten them. According to their customs, it protects their daughters from being raped or forced into marriage at a young age. It is not a ritual to harm their children, but to protect them and allow Them To Enjoy Being Children.

Components Of Nonmaterial Culture

Nonmaterial culture varies from culture to culture. However, all cultures include beliefs, values, norms, and language, because these four components influence our behavior and shape our society.

Beliefs

Beliefs are a central component of nonmaterial culture. **Beliefs** refer to specific ideas that people think to be true or untrue; they represent a mental acceptance that certain ideas are real and others are not. Human beings have a free thought process and are able to explore their beliefs. Since achievement is an American core value, each of us believes that we are able to reach our goals. Beliefs may be based on cultural influences, trust, faith, scientific research, experience, or any combination of these.

Values

Values direct our lives because they help people who share a culture to make decisions about how to live. The difference between beliefs and values is that beliefs are specific, while values are abstract standards. **Values** refer to collective ideas about what is right or wrong, good or bad, desirable or undesirable in a particular culture (Williams, 1970). Values come in pairs of positive and negative values, such as respect or disrespect, success or failure, beautiful or ugly, and happy or unhappy.

We use values to justify our behavior. Values provide us with the standards by which we evaluate people and judge behavior or objects. For instance, people in the United States and Japan value achievement and hard work, but people in the United States value individualism whereas Japanese people value collectivism. Cultures in higher-income countries value self-expression, while cultures of lower-income countries are more concerned with survival and tradition.

A consistent value across cultures is success. Survival is a natural instinct that is shared even with animals, though as humans we innately seek more than survival. We can each relate to survival and success. People with different cultural backgrounds have different definitions of success. For some, success is being a millionaire. For others, success is giving everything to the less fortunate. Success can be having a strong family or enough money to pay the bills each month. Which category we fall into is primarily determined by our culture. One similarity shared by all societies is the deep desire to have a sense of belonging, whether it comes from a family, social group, or religion. As human beings, we all have the need to love and be loved, to accept and be accepted.

In summary, values determine our preferences, guide our way of thinking, and shape our behavior. We create and view cultural values as standards by which we define what is right or wrong. In this way, we are judged on how well we follow and live these values each day. All cultures wish to reproduce their own values through procreation, education or familial ties. We observe different core values across cultures. For example, in Australia, tolerance, fairness, and personal enjoyment are considered core values. Can you identify core American values?

Core American Values

It is important to share values because they provide us with the standards by which we evaluate people's behaviors. Functionalists tend to believe that shared values are essential for the maintenance of a society, and scholars have researched core values from a functionalist perspective. Because there are so many subcultures, the impacts of acculturation, assimilation, and pluralism make it difficult to identify core American values. Nonetheless, sociologist Robin Williams (1970) identified 10 core values shared by the American people. Many scholars maintain that the following values are still important to people in the United States in 2009.

1. *Achievement and success.* Americans value personal achievement. Individuals are encouraged to compete, to do better than others in school and at work, in order to gain wealth, power, and prestige.
2. *Individualism.* Americans advocate individual ability and independent actions. Americans expect people to work hard and "move up the ladder."
3. *Efficiency and practicality.* Americans place great value on efficiency and want to get things done faster. In workplaces, Americans seek out ways to increase efficiency and focus on accomplishing realistic goals.
4. *Science and technology.* Americans develop new technologies and use them, along with science, to control nature and human society. Americans appreciate advances in every area and, because of technology and science, America became the superpower in the world.
5. *Progress and material comfort.* Americans aim to make continuous improvements and expect rapid social change. Material possessions are considered to be a sign of comfort, and a high level of material comfort includes basic necessities as well as new items of material culture like Land Rovers and iPhones.
6. *Morality and humanitarianism.* Americans em-

phasize volunteer work and the notion of helping others both domestically and globally. Helping others is associated with the idea of morality.

7. *Freedom and liberty.* Americans value individual freedom. People have freedom of speech, freedom of the press, and other freedoms which are considered to be basic human rights.
8. *Activity and work.* Americans are engaged in all kinds of activities that bring them satisfaction. People who are diligent and hard-working are praised for their successes. Americans view their work as their life and value it because it brings them an income and social status, which result in material comforts and a social network.
9. *Equality.* Americans emphasize having an equal chance to achieve success. Equality of opportunity has significantly pervaded American society. However, there is still a discrepancy between legal equality and social inequality. Equality is viewed as equality of opportunity instead of equality of outcome.
10. *Racism and group superiority.* Americans follow mainstream culture and value their racial and ethnic groups as well. There is a value of reinforcing ethnocentrism since Americans who value basic human rights and freedoms feel superior to those societies that deprive their citizens of these rights. Americans also feel obligated to exert their culture and values on those nations that repress fundamental, natural rights that are inherent to all people. The key is to strike a balance with the cultural focus of ethnocentrism. It is not of value if a certain culture is judging the values, traditions, and beliefs of another just because they are different. We can consider it discrimination if one culture feels superior to another strictly because of differences in religion, dress, customs, or color. These are differences that do not harm anyone or threaten any culture. If these differences are viewed equally, positive cultural diversity and gaining knowledge from one another become possibilities.

We have called attention to work as a core American value. We value work because it brings us income and status. Workers in the United States put in more hours than anywhere else in the industrialized world. In addition, European workers take an average of four to six weeks of vacation each year, while workers in the United States average two weeks.

Americans value morality and humanitarianism. As one example of this, Dr. Carl Lum and his fellow Aloha Medical Mission volunteers have provided free medical care to people in the Philippines, Vietnam, Cambodia, Laos, China, Burma, Africa, and Bangladesh. Dr. Lum and 30 other Aloha Medical Mission volunteers participated in a five-month humanitarian and goodwill mission to Southeast Asia aboard the Navy hospital ship USNS Mercy. "The area we were working in was potentially dangerous, so we were closely associated with the military people protecting us," said Dr. Lum. He added that, "An amazing 1,500 surgical patients were screened" at Zamboanga, but it was possible to accept only about 125, "so there were many very disappointed people" in the Philippines.

Dr. Lum and his Aloha Medical Mission volunteers have performed more than 75 missions in 15 nations aboard the U.S. Navy ships USNS Mercy and USS Peleliu. Volunteers pay their own airfare and expenses and take their own supplies.

As culture in the United States grows and changes, it becomes more diverse and pluralistic, making the job of specifying core values more difficult. Five years after Williams created his list, James Henslin (1975) added six more core values: education, religiosity, environmentalism, leisure, self-fulfillment, physical fitness, romantic love, and monogamy.

Value Contradictions

In many ways, cultural values are in harmony, but that is not always the case. **Value contradictions** refer to values that conflict with each other either within, or across, cultures. For example, the values of racism and group superiority contradict the values of freedom, democracy, and equality. Societies regard some groups more highly than others and have done so throughout history. In the United States, the slaughter of Native Americans and the enslaving of Africans are the most notorious examples. We pursue equality of opportunity, but there is still a discrepancy between legal equality and social inequality in terms of sex and race. For example, we have laws and amendments for equal rights, while men in the same or similar positions are still paid more than women. These same issues come into play in regard to minority groups.

Value contradictions can also involve two different cultures. For example, the Japanese value collectivism while Americans value individualism. Different values might bring about different measures of performance. For example, students from some Asian countries value respect for authority. When they come to the United States, they might agree with everything that the professor says in the classroom. They sit quietly and are reserved about speaking up even though they may have differing opinions. A professor who is not familiar with Asian culture might think that the student does not participate in class discussions. By contrast, in American universities, a good student is expected to ask questions, share personal opinions, and even challenge the professor at times.

Value contradictions produce strain, and that can lead to confusion about our beliefs. Although the government of the United States claims to value equal opportunity, it does not allow women to join infantry divisions in the army. Some people learn to accept reality, adhering to the law and living with the value contradictions, but others try to fight against social inequality and change the law.

Ideal Culture And Real Culture

People are expected to act according to stated values and norms, but they sometimes deviate. This means that people's self-reporting of their values sometimes differs from their actual behavior. Sociologists refer to this discrepancy as a gap between ideal culture and real culture. **Ideal culture** refers to the rules of expected behavior that a society has accepted in principle—what people "should" do. **Real culture** refers to the values that are actually practiced by people in a society. Ideal culture specifies law-abiding behavior while real culture specifies illegal behavior. For example, a person may claim to be a law-abiding citizen (ideal cultural value), but then keep a person's wallet found on the ground (real cultural value). A woman may believe that a child is a gift from God (ideal cultural value), yet have an abortion (real culture value).

Norms

The first building block of culture consists of norms. **Norms** refer to established rules of expected behavior that develop from a society's or a group's values. Every society establishes norms, or ways of reflecting the values of a culture. While values provide standards for behavior, they do not state specifically how we should behave. Norms specify expected behaviors and clarify what is considered normal or acceptable. It is important to be aware that norms considered acceptable by one culture may be rude or inappropriate in another. For instance, in some cultures it is customary to kiss people upon meeting them, whereas that behavior might be considered offensive and pushy to another culture. Some norms are proscriptive. *Proscriptive norms* state what behavior is unacceptable. By contrast, *prescriptive norms* state what behavior is acceptable. Both prescriptive and proscriptive norms apply to all aspects of society, though informal norms are not enforced. Formal norms are considered more important and are typically based on laws and enforced by sanctions.

Sanctions And Social Control

We live in a controlled setting where we follow norms which are the basic rules of everyday life. Developed by the people in a society or group, norms promote conformity and are essential to the stability of society. Norms make our everyday lives orderly.

Following or breaking the rules of expected behavior prompts a response from society in the form of a reward or a punishment. These rewards for normal behaviors and penalties for abnormal behaviors are referred to as **sanctions**, and they function as a system of social control mechanisms. *Social control mechanisms* are the means used by society to maintain social order and regulate people's behavior. Sanctions can be either positive or negative. We apply positive sanctions to encourage people to continue an appropriate or acceptable behavior. Ex-

amples of formal positive sanctions include money, awards, career advancement, and scholarships. An approving smile, a happy face sticker, and a thumbs-up gesture are all examples of informal positive sanctions. Negative sanctions are used to discourage people from continuing unacceptable behaviors. Formal negative sanctions include fines and time in jail or prison. Examples of informal negative sanctions include dirty looks, raised eyebrows, sad face stickers, negative gestures, and gossip.

Human beings are creatures of adaptation and, when they are exposed to rules of expected behavior and sanctions, they are more likely to follow these shared norms. People who have been to Singapore, for example, find it amazing to see how clean the city is as a result of their culture of severely punishing individuals for littering and defacing property. Tour briefings stress the importance of not littering, because something as small as spitting gum onto a sidewalk can result in an enormous fine or jail time.

Formal And Informal Norms

All norms are not of equal importance; they are categorized based on their relationship to social order and the stability of society. Norms that are less essential to the stability of society are considered informal norms. *Informal norms* are unwritten rules of behavior that are understood and shared by people. Folkways and mores are types of informal norms. People in a group are expected to follow informal norms in order to conform. When an individual follows informal norms, other people may respond with informal positive sanctions like smiling or making positive gestures. However, if an individual violates informal norms, others might apply negative informal sanctions like frowning or scowling. The norms that are most essential to the stability of society are formalized. *Formal norms* are written down and enforced by formal sanctions. Laws are the most common type of formal norms, and violations of laws are punished through formal sanctions ranging from fines to the death penalty.

Folkways refer to everyday customs within a society that may be violated without formal sanctions. Folkways provide unwritten rules of expected behavior shared by a group and fall under the category of informal norms. They are not considered to be crucial to social stability. In the United States, examples of folkways include brushing our teeth every day, quietly chewing our food, and saying thanks when someone does us a favor.

Mores refer to strongly held, informally enforced norms with moral overtones. These norms are considered to be more important to a society than folkways, but not as important as actual laws. William Graham Sumner (1969) coined the term mores (pronounced "more-ays"). Mores reflect the core values of society and are considered to be crucial to the social order of a society. We insist on conformity, and we punish violators with negative sanctions like gossip, loss of employment, and jail because mores are essential to the well-being of a group. As an example, we are supposed to send our kids to school, where they receive a compulsory education. **Taboos** refer to the most strongly held mores. Their violation is considered to be extremely offensive. Having sex with one's mother or sister is an example of a violation of the incest taboo which prohibits sexual or marital relations between certain groups of kin. Genocide—the act of destroying racial, religious or ethnic groups—would be considered a multicultural taboo, and the United Nations has even deemed it to be a criminal act. Some mores may be considered normal in one culture but abnormal in another. For example, some cultures embrace dog, chicken, and bull fighting, while American culture considers it animal cruelty and unethical.

In summary, mores and folkways are types of informal norms. Mores distinguish between right and wrong and involve serious moral issues, while folkways draw a line between appropriate and inappropriate behaviors. A female student who comes to her classes barefoot might raise eyebrows for breaking the unwritten rules or folkways. However, if she arrives in the classroom wearing only a bra and underwear, she would be violating mores.

Laws

The second building block of a culture is its laws. **Laws** refer to formal norms enacted by legislatures and enforced by formal sanctions. Laws are designed to protect innocent people and punish viola-

tors. Laws are divided into two main categories, civil and criminal. *Civil law* covers private disputes between individuals or groups. Individuals who lose lawsuits may experience negative sanctions like having to provide monetary compensation to the winning party. *Criminal law* involves crimes against the public. It is possible for an event to encompass both types of law. For example, if an individual broke into a car and stole a stereo, that event could trigger both a private and a public wrong. The person whose stereo was stolen would have suffered a private injury and could, therefore, file a civil lawsuit against the wrongdoer for the replacement cost of the stereo. A government prosecutor could file a criminal case against the perpetrator for the crime of burglary.

Symbols

Symbols comprise the third building block of culture. Human beings use their senses to experience the world around them, and they translate their observations and thoughts into symbols. A **symbol** refers to anything that carries a meaning and represents something else. Symbols include written, verbal, and nonverbal language like signs and body language. The world of symbols changes, with new symbols being created all the time. The invention of new technologies like the Blackberry, which has three pages of abbreviations such as "h/o" (homeowner), "tt" (talked to), and "cc" (credit card), makes it easier for us to quickly transfer information. Symbols help us communicate with each other in at least two ways.

First, symbols convey the meanings shared by people in a society. In the United States, red roses represent love, while yellow roses symbolize friendship. A yellow ribbon can show support for troops overseas, and people may tie them around trees in front of their homes in support of a family member or friend fighting in a war. Some symbols may be recognized in many countries, like the peace symbol and the golden arches that symbolize McDonald's. Religious symbols are often recognized in many countries, like the crucifix or cross symbolizing the death of Jesus Christ which has been around for over 2,000 years. The Red Cross and Red Crescent symbols represent medical facilities and aid. Other symbolic meanings can vary from culture to culture. The color red symbolizes revolution in some communist countries, good luck in China, passion and aggression in the United States, and purity in India. The color white signifies purity in the West but mourning and death in the East.

Second, symbols can reflect a person's socioeconomic status. We may judge people by their job, the way they dress, the kind of car they drive, the area in which they live, and the items of material culture they consume. All cultures make judgments based on such indicators. Americans, for instance, can sometimes appear to be obsessed with dress, which is used as a sign of status.

Language

Language refers to an organized system of symbols that people use to think and communicate with each other. It attaches meanings to actions, as well as to sounds and writing. Not only does it allow people to communicate with one another, but it is also the key to transmitting culture to the next generation. Language is the heart of culture; it allows human beings to express themselves. All languages fuse symbols with distinctive emotions. Globally, there are almost 7,000 languages, suggesting the existence of at least as many different cultures (U.S. News & World Report, 2001). The world's three most widely spoken languages are Mandarin Chinese, English, and Spanish.

Functions Of Language

Language is powerful and the words we choose make a difference. Johnson O'Connor is credited with saying, "If you want to succeed, your vocabulary must equal the average level of your colleagues, but if you want to excel, your vocabulary must surpass that of your colleagues." O'Connor was the founder of the Human Engineering Laboratory, now called the Johnson O'Connor Research Foundation. Language is the greatest cultural item on which human activities depend. Without language, cooperation and communication would be very difficult. The significance of language is what draws people to study origins, differences, and interconnections of languages.

First, people can use both verbal (spoken) and nonverbal (written or gestured) language to express themselves. One of the basic characteristics of human beings is their ability to share experiences, feelings, and knowledge. Language is how we express our thoughts and ideas to those around us. We can use our language to persuade others to our way of thinking. Critical thinking skills enable us to use language to the fullest in our thought processes and problem-solving by bringing clarity and an understanding of all sides of a situation. Language is the chief vehicle though which we can tell others what we have in mind, what we are, and what we want to do so as to constitute a sense of self and become a part of a group.

Second, language enables us to interact with other people to survive. If we travel to a foreign country and there are no signs in English, we may be lost. Research findings by Frederick II, Emperor of the Holy Roman Empire in the 13th century, supported this. Some newborn babies were selected to be nurtured as usual, but the use of language (speech, songs, and lullabies) was prohibited. It turned out that all these babies died. These findings tell us that language helps us to interact and survive in a society. Language is not only a human characteristic, but also a trait of other animals. It has been found that other animals use sounds, gestures, touch, and smells to communicate with each other. Human use

Table 2.1 Mostly Widely Spoken Languages in the World

Language	Approx. Number of Speakers
1. Chinese (Mandarin)	1,075,000,000
2. English	514,000,000
3. Hindustani[1]	496,000,000
4. Spanish	425,000,000
5. Russian	275,000,000
6. Arabic	256,000,000
7. Bengali	215,000,000
8. Portuguese	194,000,000
9. Malay-Indonesian	176,000,000
10. French	129,000,000

Source: Ethnologue, 13th Edition, and other sources.
1. Encompasses multiple dialects, including Hindi and Urdu.

of language differs from that of other animals in that animals use expressions limited to immediate and present situations. Nonhuman animals are not able to conceive of past or future situations. For example, nonhuman animals—even the most linguistically capable chimps—cannot pass along aspects of culture to their offspring.

Cultural transmission refers to the process through which one generation passes culture, including language, to the next. As human beings, we possess a native language that separates us from other animals. It is a fact that language is developed within the first few years of a person's life. Children worldwide exhibit similar patterns of language acquisition even though they may be learning different languages.

Language And Reality

Does language determine reality? In 1929, anthropologist and linguist Edward Sapir, and his student Benjamin Whorf, observed that the Hopi Indians of the Southwest could not state a word in the past, present, or future tense because there were no verb tenses in their language. From their observations, Sapir and Whorf concluded that people in a particular society perceive the world and create reality through the cultural lens of language. Therefore, it is our culture that determines our language, which in turn determines the way that we categorize our thoughts about the world and our experiences in it. *The Sapir-Whorf hypothesis* suggests that language expresses our thoughts and does more than describe reality. It holds that language is culturally determined and helps us interpret reality. The hypothesis states that people's thoughts are determined by the categories made available by their language. Since people can conceptualize the world only through language, language precedes thought. Therefore, the word symbols and grammar of a language organize the world for us.

Most sociologists do not agree that language determines reality simply because we can shape our view of reality through experiences and other venues. Language may affect our interpretation of reality, but language does not determine reality. For example, children have learned how to eat food with a spoon or chopsticks long before they learn the words for these items.

Gender And Control Function Of Language

Scholars suggest that language and gender are intertwined. This means that language reflects cultural assumptions about men and women in a particular society. This is the control function of language. The English language almost seems to ignore what is feminine. The control function of language is illustrated by the custom of women taking the last name of the man they marry. This function is also reflected in our pronoun usage, such as when men attach female pronouns to valued objects—consistent with the concept of possession. The gender games begin at birth when an "it" becomes a "he" or "she." Naming the baby perpetuates the *he/she* persona. It is highly unlikely that a baby boy will be named Rachel or Anna or a girl named Tom or Jack. A small girl cries and *she* is pampered, a small boy cries and he is told to dust himself off and be strong. The English language uses the masculine form to refer to human beings in general, and uses the word *man* to include both women and men. For example, words like chairman and policeman indicate examples of gender bias, using the word man to ignore women. Another way to show gender bias in the English language is through the use of the pronouns *he* and *she*. Since paid work may be segregated between women and men, we expect nurses, secretaries, and elementary school teachers to be referred to as *she*, but presidents, CEO, lawyers, and engineers referred to as *he*.

Culture Diversity

Diversity is a very powerful word, with a meaning that encompasses much more than most people might realize, or even believe. Diversity involves acknowledging the fact that everyone is unique and accepting each person for that very reason. The world is made up of people from all walks of life. For instance, on any given day you may come in contact with people of all different races, religions, ethnicities, political viewpoints, and sexual orientations. The television show *The Real World*, featured on MTV, illustrates diversity in action. The show actually takes seven strangers from all parts of the United States, regardless of their differences. It is the casts' responsibility to live and work together for six months, working through any disagreements they might have with one another. Not only does the show depict what it is like for people from all walks of life to live together, but it also shows how they grow together. In some ways, this show has helped us rethink how we perceive differences.

Cultural Diversity: Mosaic Culture

Culture diversity refers to a variety of cultural differences both within a society and across societies. According to the Merriam-Webster Online Dictionary (2009) diversity is defined as the inclusion of diverse people (like people of different races or cultures) in a group or organization. According to Kottak & Kozaitis (2003), sociocultural diversity means diversity "based on such variables as ethnicity, race, religion, gender, age, class, occupation, region, sexual orientation, and differential 'abledness'," indicating the importance of considering the needs and wants of a variety of cultures and ethnic backgrounds, rather than just race and culture.

It is important to be aware that our culture is not the only culture in the world. It is equally important to learn how to interact with people who are different from us. If we are not aware of the differences between cultures, there may be times when we offend others unintentionally. Understanding cultural diversity helps us to be more conscientious of our surroundings and more inclusive of other people.

Diversity As An Asset

People learn many things from each other. According to research findings, children learn from each other thanks to a diverse way of thinking. Diversity is an important aspect of the business world, and a diverse staff is an asset to a company. No matter what type of business, there will be some representation of diversity. Within the business world, diversity can encompass employees, customers, and vendors. In the past, a business could afford to be exclusive and focus on any one culture or group; this is not the case anymore. A business of any sort must embrace the essence of what it means to be diverse.

Subcultures

Subculture refers to distinctive lifestyles and values shared by a category of people within a society. A subculture is a group of people who share a distinctive set of cultural beliefs and behaviors that differ in some significant way from that of the larger society. Thus, subcultures are subgroups of a society's population. This concept has been applied to cultural differences based on gender, age, ethnicity, religion, geography, occupation, and social class, and even those subgroups thought to be deviated or marginalized from the larger society. Different groups of people residing in a society may also live or work in one or more subcultures. For example, if you are a 20-year-old, wealthy male singer with an Italian cultural background, you fall within the subcultures of upper class, Generation Y, Italian-American, and entertainer. Video game enthusiasts, traditional Chinese-Americans, Ohio State football fans, the Southern California "beach crowd," and the Old Order Amish all display subculture patterns and lifestyles.

Ethnic Subculture

People who share different lifestyles related to an ethnicity, language, or cultural activity may consider themselves to be members of a specific subculture. Though almost everyone participates in subcultures, they may not have much commitment to them. The United States is a pluralistic society, made up of many ethnic groups. Examples of ethnic subcultures include British or Anglo Americans (Caucasians), Native Americans, African-Americans, Latinos/Latinas (Hispanic-Americans), Asian-Americans, and Middle Eastern-Americans. "White ethnics" are people from European countries other than England, like Irish-Americans, Italian-Americans, Polish-Americans, and Jewish-Americans.

Some subcultures are concentrated in large communities; people with the same ethnic backgrounds often stick together. In New York City, Korean Americans, Italian-Americans, and Puerto Rican-

Generation Timeline

1922-1945	1946-1964	1965-1980	1981-2000
Veterans, Silent, Traditionalists	Baby Boomers	Generation X, Gen X, Xers	Generation Y, Gen Y, Milennial Echo Boomers

Americans display distinctive subcultures with different food, music, and lifestyles. People who experience these subcultures enjoy different material cultures and are exposed to different customs and traditions. People in different ethnic subcultures are distributed throughout the United States. Chinese Americans are the largest segment of the Asian American population, and the majority live in San Francisco, Los Angeles, and New York. Chinatowns located in these cities represent visible ethnic subcultures, where people speak Mandarin Chinese or Cantonese and follow core values such as respect and loyalty. Chinese language is taught in schools in Chinese communities. *Huaxia Chinese School* is a nonprofit organization dedicated to teaching Chinese language (Mandarin) and culture classes. Being the largest of its kind in the United States, the school consists of 18 branches, serving more than 6,000 students in New Jersey, New York, Pennsylvania, and Connecticut.

Age And Subculture

Subcultures can also be examined in terms of age and generations. There are four generations: traditionalists, baby boomers, Generation X, and Generation Y. Traditionalists value privacy, hard work, formality, and respect for authority. Baby boomers value peer competition, challenge, change, success, body language, and inclusion. Generation X values entrepreneurial spirit, independence, creativity, access to information, feedback, and quality of work life. Generation Y values positive reinforcement, autonomy, diversity, money, and technology as a tool for multitasking.

Generation Y, including people born between 1980 and 2000, has developed work characteristics and tendencies from doting parents, structured lives, and contact with diverse people. They need to understand why they are performing tasks and how they tie into company goals. People in this group tend to be independent thinkers who speak up without regard to power structure, and they don't thrive well in strict hierarchical work structures. They are quite adept at using technology and are able to quickly learn new technologies. Their informal communication styles include many slang words derived from texting, reality television, and popular music.

Social Class And Subculture

Different social classes have different lingoes or phrases that they tend to use, which can create different groups within a society. Family background and culture also play a role in creating divisions. People who grow up in the same country or location will be raised by different families with different communication styles. One family might teach their children manners and how to speak clearly and use proper English. Another family might teach their children to use slang and disregard authority figures.

Negative Results Of Subcultures

Cultural differences can set people apart from each other and result in negative consequences. In the 1990s, for example, a civil war in the area formerly known as Yugoslavia in southeastern Europe was triggered by extreme cultural differences. The population of this country used two alphabets, had three main religions, and spoke four languages. It was home to five major nationalities and divided into six republics influenced by seven surrounding countries. As a result, cultural conflict led to the 1990s civil war. These different subcultures helped produce confusion, conflict, and violence.

Subcultures involve not only cultural differences, but also domination by one culture. When sociologists study how subculture participants interact with the dominant culture, they limit the scope of inquiry to more visible groups like ethnic enclaves in large urban areas. Many people view the United States as a *melting pot* where many nationalities blend into a single "American" culture (Gardyn, 2002). Oftentimes we view the dominant or mainstream culture as maintained and favored by the majority, while subcultures are seen as the domain of minority or subordinate groups. With the United States becoming a more multicultural and diverse society, sociologists now prefer to emphasize multiculturalism.

Countercultures

Subcultures exist within the mainstream culture of a society, but have distinguishing practices or norms that identify them as a distinct group. They are not opposed to the basic principles of the culture that surrounds them but maintain their own distinct identities within the overall cultural norms. **Counterculture** describes a cultural group whose values and norms are opposed to those of the mainstream and dominant culture. A counterculture is a group that strongly rejects and rallies against the dominant culture, opposing accepted lifestyles and seeking alternatives. During the 1960s, some young people rebelled against some of their parents' values like material comfort and competition. Other examples of rebellion include skinheads, Black Panthers, the Ku Klux Klan, and hippies who favored a culture of "free love" and a cooperative lifestyle.

Ethnocentrism And Cultural Relativism

Ethnocentrism refers to the tendency to judge other cultures using the standards of one's own culture. The world has a long history of ethnocentrism. The word ethnocentrism derives from the Greek word *ethnos*, meaning "nation" or "people," and the English word *center*. A common idiom for ethnocentrism is "tunnel vision." Ethnocentrism is a basic attitude expressing the belief that one's own ethnic group or culture is superior to others, and that its norms and standards can be applied in a universal manner to all cultures. The term was first used by the American sociologist William Graham Sumner (1840–1910) to describe the view that a person's

own culture can be considered central, while other cultures or religious traditions are reduced to less prominent roles (1969). The flip side of ethnocentrism is xenocentrism. *Xenocentrism* refers to a preference for the cultural beliefs of other societies and groups and the belief that they are superior to their own. For example, when items of Japanese material culture dominated the world, some people were on the verge of obsession, preferring everything from the language to the cultural practices of Japan.

Functions Of Ethnocentrism

According to the functionalist perspective, ethnocentrism performs functions that can be either positive or negative. The first function of ethnocentrism is to promote unity, which can help people to pursue and achieve group goals. Ethnocentrism may also lead to in-group favoritism like the "promote from within" policies of many organizations, including the government. The second function of ethnocentrism is to encourage conformity, which promotes order and stability. The third function of ethnocentrism is to reinforce nationalism. Patriotism is a love of, and loyalty to, one's country, which is crucial during times when solidarity is needed, such as wars and economic crises.

Ethnocentrism serves to maintain a sense of solidarity and allegiance to one's culture by promoting group pride and commitment. Many groups are proud of their heritage and may voice their beliefs to ensure that others are aware of their culture. Reinforcing an ethnocentric view of one's own culture as a means of instilling pride and respect is acceptable when coupled with tolerance and respect for other cultures.

Dysfunctions Of Ethnocentrism

When a belief is "too" strong, there is a risk of negative effects, and people are often admonished to avoid having "too much" pride. The first dysfunction of ethnocentrism is that it can lead to making judgments based on false assumptions about cultural differences. Some people may be so entrenched in their own cultures that they refuse to understand and learn about the beliefs of others. They may be intolerant and refuse to accept the ways of others.

When people's cultural differences are discounted, generalizations, stereotypes, and biases may surface. We see these biases in groups like the Ku Klux Klan. If we use our culture as a universal yardstick, we can misjudge other people and cultures. Sometimes people make small judgments that they don't even notice. For example, when we see people in Britain drive on the left side, do we say that they are driving on the *wrong side* of the road? When we see Japanese read from right to left, do we think that Japanese books are *backward*? These judgments can affect how we look at other people and their cultures.

Second, ethnocentrism discourages integration. Promoting the view that one's own race or ethnicity is superior to others based on bias or prejudice is simply an ignorant and deplorable act. In the past, ethnocentrism was practiced by people and groups, and also nations, that tried to divide and conquer the world for the sole purpose of making other nations assimilate into their culture and way of life. In this way, other cultures could be eradicated completely.

Third, ethnocentrism accompanies outsider-group hostility which can lead to intergroup conflict, violence, or support for discriminatory behavior. Ethnocentrism is closely related to racism, xenophobia, prejudice, mental closure, and an authoritarian personality structure. Social scientists have speculated that limited contact with members of outsider-groups can lead to stereotyping. Research surveys reveal a high level of education can effectively reduce ethnocentrism, and that, typically, men express ethnocentrism more than women.

The fourth dysfunction of ethnocentrism is preventing beneficial social change. Social scientists in the 19th century operated from an ethnocentric point of view. Anthropologists studied primitive tribes, for example, to illustrate how human civilization had progressed from "savage" customs toward the accomplishments of Western industrial society. In order for societies to progress, they need to adopt items from other cultures through the process of diffusion, rather than refusing to accept them outright. Ethnocentrism gives people a solid place to stand, but it should not be the final word. In this multicultural society, we should encourage cultural diversity and tolerance.

Cultural Relativism

Cultural relativism is the opposite of ethnocentrism. Cultural **relativism** refers to a tendency to judge another culture by its own standards. For example, when we see Japanese eating raw fish, we would put our feet in their shoes and respect their way of life, and maybe even try the food, instead of calling it "disgusting." *Reciprocal inclusivity* suggests that if we are strong enough to reach out and communicate with other people, they will be inclined to reach out to us. Cultural relativism goes hand in hand with cultural diversity and multiculturalism; the term *salad bowl* is the metaphor of cultural relativism. In a multicultural society, different cultures are described as equal, and a mutual respect for each other's cultures is promoted.

In a multicultural society, we can see that one culture is not superior to any other culture—each is unique and has its own merit. Each culture has something of value to offer that can potentially enhance another. Therefore, it is important to increase cultural diversity awareness, striking a balance with the cultural focus of ethnocentrism. It is not of value if cultures judge the values and beliefs of another just because they have different religions, dress, customs, or skin colors. These differences do not harm anyone or threaten any culture and, if they are viewed as equal, we make it possible for positive cultural diversity and the sharing of knowledge to take place.

When cultures falsely assume something about another culture, a level of hate can start to build. We should remember that we were created equal, but different. In thinking back to slavery, African-Americans were treated as inferior to whites, causing a lot of pain and segregation among blacks and whites today. No culture should have the right to treat other cultures as if they are inferior.

Multiculturalism

Multiculturalism not only embraces the uniqueness of disparate groups, but also the idea of many different groups being part of the same whole. **Mul-**

ticulturalism refers to the coexistence of diverse cultures with equal standing in a society. Multiculturalism holds that various groups with different cultures in a society should have equal rights and statuses, rather than living in a hierarchy. It encompasses many cultures without practicing ethnocentrism.

Multiculturalism brings greater value to the United States. Immigrants from different cultural backgrounds enter the country, integrate into the mainstream culture, and still maintain their heritage. Since the United States has more diverse groups than any other nation, it needs to embrace the concept of multiculturalism because its people value freedom and equal opportunity. Multiculturalism favors cultural diversity and represents a sharp change from the past, when a person or group had to adopt the dominant traits of the majority culture. Multiculturalism promotes equality for all cultures.

High Culture And Popular Culture

In everyday life, we usually use the concept of culture to indicate different forms of art. If you go to the opera and ballet regularly, people think that you are "cultured." Sociologists use the terms "high culture" and "popular culture" to help people understand different forms of culture. **High culture** refers to cultural patterns that appeal to the upper class or elite of a society. High culture may include opera, classical music, ballet, live theater, and other activities typically enjoyed by members of the elite. In pre-industrial societies, elites did not produce harvests and, therefore, had time for cultured activities like the study of philosophy, art, and literature. High culture usually appeals to the upper classes because they have the resources such as leisure time, money, and cultural capital, like the knowledge and education that helps them enjoy the activities. Many types of high culture originated outside the United States and were introduced here through the process of diffusion. By contrast, much of popular culture was created and developed in the United States. **Popular culture** refers to cultural patterns that appeal primarily to the middle and working classes and are widespread within a population of a society.

Russian ballet.

Source: Andrews Kovas

Examples of popular culture include movies, television soap operas and reality shows, rock concerts, spectator sports, and the new music culture of Hip Hop, R&B, BET, and MTV.

A Global Culture

Some scholars argue that all cultures are becoming Westernized or Americanized. The so-called Americanization phenomenon seems to be a consequence of the recent globalization in our world. The process of Westernization is called **cultural imperialism**, referring to the widespread infusion of one culture into the cultures of other societies. Nowadays, we see many American icons in any country in the world, such as McDonald's and Coca-Cola. Another example of cultural imperialism is the infusion of the English language into nations where other languages are dominant.

Critics argue that cultural imperialism neglects various cross-culture influences. They argue that the spread of popular culture is likely to produce a global culture, and we have witnessed the birth of such a culture due to the diffusion of material culture, information, and population.

International trade has exported a variety of material cultural items from one country to another throughout the world. Global cultures include items from various societies and cultures. Some people would like to curb the globalization process because they fear losing their own cultures, but it is very difficult to stop. For example, music, movies, food, and clothing in the United States reflect African, Asian, and Caribbean cultural influences. It is also common to see tattoos with Japanese Kanji or Chinese characters on Americans. Cultural diffusion has taken place on a global basis.

Modern communication systems and diffusion of information make it possible for the existence of a global culture. Telecommunication, electronic devices, satellite communication, and the Internet spread news and information to every corner of the world. Many of the communication devices we buy in the United States are made in foreign countries like China, Japan, Taiwan, and Mexico.

Global migration brings diverse cultures together to form a global culture. Push and pull factors encourage people to migrate to another country for job and education opportunities. Transportation technology such as air travel shortens the distance from one country to another and makes sightseeing, and even relocating, much easier. People witness the impact of Westernization or Americanization on other countries, and many are also aware of a new phenomenon, the so-called Asianization of America. Asianization is the term used to describe the influence of Asian culture on America (Berg, 2008). Living in the United States, we are discovering many Asian products ranging from food and movies to nonmaterial culture items such as Buddhism, meditation, Taiji, karate, and feung shui.

Cultural Change

Culture constantly changes and grows. Our pioneer culture was much different from the culture we have now. American culture will continue to change and grow because of immigrants who bring their ideas and cultural items with them to the United States. This process has enriched our culture and knowledge. We depend on television, newspapers, radio, the Internet, and magazines to stay informed and to learn. These same sources can bring about social change and diversity. Without the ability to adapt, people would suffer culture shock and, perhaps, choose ethnocentrism.

Cultural Lag

When a change takes place in the material culture of a society, nonmaterial culture must adapt. However, not all cultural components adapt at the same pace. According to William Ogburn (1964), technology generated new items of material culture faster than nonmaterial cultures could accept or catch up with them. Ogburn referred to this inconsistency as cultural lag. **Cultural lag** is a discrepancy between material culture and nonmaterial culture that disrupts a way of life for an individual. Technology plays an important role in adding new cultural items to material culture. Those who fail to adapt to new technologies and the changes they cause can experience culture shock or culture lag. An instance of culture lag that comes to mind is that it now seems odd to see someone actually writing a check at the register in a store, with debit cards being so accessible.

Sources Of Culture Change

Social changes are set in motion by discovery, invention, and diffusion. Discovery and invention are internal sources that bring about cultural change. Diffusion can be considered an external source of cultural change.

Invention is the process of reshaping existing cultural traits into a new form. Technology plays an important role in shaping and adding to the material culture of society. Culture changes because people invent new items. Because Americans value technology and science, they keep inventing new items which, in turn, make culture change possible. In industrial societies, the invention of the steam engine and fuel-powered machinery stimulated many other changes. Other inventions that have had an impact on cultural change include electricity, household appliances, computers, the telephone, cars, automatic weapons, atomic bombs, iPods, and Blackberry devices.

The invention of the computer was just an invention, not a change in culture. Culture change occurred when computers were accepted and adopted by society. The computer has now become part of our lives and changed our lifestyles. First, the computer is more of a means of socialization than the telephone. In today's information technology society, people who use computers have created a whole new culture. They have e-mail, instant messaging, Facebook, and other ways to communicate. With web cams, they can even watch each other over the Internet. People post their entire profiles on sites such as Facebook, often with pictures of all kinds. These are just some of the new ways to communicate that computers have brought about. The computer is widely accepted, and some people use them to communicate because it is cheaper than using a telephone. Teenagers, especially, use instant messaging and Facebook to communicate. Finally, the computer has changed language patterns and social circles, and has provided instant access to information, allowing people to self-educate and self-help. The use of technology has formed our younger generations into different social patterns that might widen the generation gap if the aging generations refuse to catch up.

Discovery is the process of knowing and recognizing something previously in existence, and it is the second source of social change. There are different types of discoveries. Archaeological discoveries include dinosaur bones in Alberta, Canada, and the Gobi Desert. Penicillin and vaccines are examples of medical discoveries. Galaxies and extraterrestrial moons are examples of astronomical discoveries. New chemical compounds and a glue for self-adhesive notepaper are examples of chemical discoveries. In terms of mathematical discoveries, the concept of zero was discovered separately by the Babylonians, Mayans, and Hindus. Modern algebra was based on the theories of Évariste Galois. Some discoveries are accidental. In 1946, Percy Spencer was walking by a magnetron and realized that a candy bar in his pocket had melted. He got the idea to place popcorn in front of the magnetron to see what would happen, and it all popped. This was the beginning of the microwave oven.

Diffusion, the third cause of cultural change, is the spread of cultural traits from one group or society to another. Factors such as migration, communication, and trade account for diffusion. Generally, cultural traits originate in a particular area and spread outward to a larger expanse of territory. For example, multinational corporations and businesses establish facilities or outlets in foreign countries; thus, the appearance of a Starbucks coffee shop or a Wal-Mart store in another country is a form of diffusion.

Sociological Perspectives On Culture: Functionalist, Conflict, And Interactionist

Sociological perspectives help us appreciate how culture aids us in understanding ourselves and the surrounding world. In the following sections, we will examine culture at the macro level of analysis.

A micro-level approach to the personal experience of culture is the focus of Chapter 4.

Functionalist Theory

The functionalist theory argues that society needs every aspect of culture for survival, emphasizing cultural patterns and functions in a society. The key question posed by this approach is whether every part in society performs its functions and contributes to its smooth operation. The function of culture is to meet human needs. Functionalists tend to believe that shared values are essential for the maintenance of a society, and culture is considered a complex strategy for meeting human needs.

Different cultural traits provide a variety of functions that help maintain society. Cultural values direct our lives, give meaning to what we do, and bind people together. In a multicultural society, we are exposed to different cultures and may experience difficulty crossing cultural boundaries and barriers. However, we can find many common patterns across such barriers. George Murdock (1945) compared hundreds of cultures and identified dozens of cultural universals. **Cultural universals** refer to traits that people share across cultures. If cultural traits and patterns are found everywhere, they must be functional and useful in society. Families are a cultural universal, functioning everywhere to socialize children and control sexual reproduction. The modern Olympic Games have been bringing cultures together for more than 100 years, illustrating that the drive to compete is something else that all cultures share. Music is something that easily crosses cultures, and rock bands like the Rolling Stones have had sold-out concerts on all continents. Movies are another example. Movies are premiered all over the world in different languages. Great literature and famous authors also have works that sell out all over the world. JK Rowling's *Harry Potter* books and movies, for example, crossed cultural divisions and are enjoyed by millions of people around the globe.

Conflict Theory

Conflict theory links culture to social inequality. The key question of this theory is who benefits from societal arrangements and why. From the conflict perspective, cultural traits are not equally distributed. Any cultural pattern benefits some people at the expense of others in society. Karl Marx argued that culture is molded by the political and economic systems of a society. For example, the political system in the United States is democracy, and the economic system is capitalism. Democracy and material comfort have become American core values. We have developed our culture through our political and economic structures. Based on our capitalistic culture, much of our lives revolve around earning materialistic rewards and profit. When we adopt the multicultural doctrine, we learn that we can prosper from what diversity has to offer, but we still do it from a business point of view.

At the macro-level of analysis, our political and economic systems have shaped our cultural values of democracy and material comfort. In turn, those values allow some people to become wealthier and dominate others, leading to social inequality. For example, rich oil executives can benefit from high gas prices while others have to struggle to pay higher prices. This may not seem fair because one dominant group gets to live in luxury and the rest of the masses pay for it.

Proponents of the conflict approach argue that a "culture of poverty" arises among people who experience extended periods of economic deprivation. Conventional society imposes its norms on people who are adapted to a poor environment and used to that lifestyle. Eventually, when people become educated and aware of the strains of inequality, they will initiate social change. The civil rights movement and the women's movement are the two examples in the United States.

Symbolic Interactionist Theory

Both functionalists and conflict theorists focus on macro-level analysis. Symbolic interactionists examine culture on a micro-level and view society as a sum of social interactions. From this perspective, people create and interpret cultural traits, further changing them as they interact with each other in everyday life situations. Symbols and language allow people to communicate and interact with each other because they provide shared meanings.

According to symbolic interactionalists, our behavior is not determined by values and norms. We negotiate and reinterpret our values and norms in every social situation we experience, because each person defines the situation from his or her point of view and responds accordingly. In this way, we shape reality and modify culture based on our different definitions of reality. Reality is an arena of interwoven potentialities. We may be more controlled by culture than we maintain. For example, with the invention of new material cultural items like laptops and cell phones, we may want to slow down, but find it difficult because society is conditioned to be able to get information anytime, anywhere. Symbolic interactionists also explore how people preserve and change culture through their interactions with people around them. They highlight how we shape culture and in turn shape ourselves through our interactions with others.

Summary

Societies were able to progress based on their food supplies and levels of technology. Society and culture are closely connected. Society exists within a distinctive culture, and culture is the way of life of a particular society or group. There are different cultures, both nationally and globally, and they change constantly. Cultures provide people with different ways of seeing, hearing, and interpreting the world, and different ways of thinking. Cultures can be either material or nonmaterial. Material culture refers to the tangible things made by a society, while nonmaterial culture includes intangibles like beliefs, symbols, language, values, and norms. Beliefs are the ideas that people think to be true, and symbols refer to anything that represents something else. Language serves as the primary means of communication among members of a group or society. Every society establishes norms which reflect the values of a culture. Values provide standards for behavior, while norms specify ways of reflecting the values of a culture. The United States is a multicultural society, and as we experience cultural change, our culture becomes more diverse.

The functionalist theory emphasizes the functions of culture and shows that cultural systems operate to meet human needs. Conflict theory contends that these systems fail to address human needs equally, allowing some elites to dominate society at the expense of others. According to symbolic interactionists, people create, maintain, and change culture through their interactions with others. Functionalist and conflict theorists are interested in a macro-level analysis of culture, while symbolic interactionists focus on the micro-level analysis of social interactions.

Review/Discussion Questions

1. Can you share any customs or practices from another culture that might shock people in the United States?

2. Can anyone think of any other examples of value conflicts? What do you think we can do to learn how to live with the contradictions or reduce the discrepancies between legal equality and social inequality or equality of outcome?

3. How can we deal with these kinds of value contradictions across cultures in the workplace?

4. Can anybody provide additional examples of discrepancies between people's stated values and their actual behaviors?

5. People are sometimes on the verge of anger as a result of culture differences. What would you think if you heard these questions: "Why do they eat with stupid sticks in Japan!" and "Why do I have to take off my shoes to eat!"?

6. Give three examples of violating school folkways. What are the possible consequences for each type of violation? Give three examples of mores.

7. The Olympics are coming soon. Don't they ban certain hand gestures? Do you think that certain hand gestures mean different things in other places? What happens if some gestures are not welcome in other countries?

8. List three cultural items that were passed on to you from earlier generations. List three new cultural items that have emerged in your own generation.

9. Give three examples of culture shock that you have experienced in the United States or other countries.

10. What is *Tex-Mex*? Do you think that Ebonics and Tex-Mex should be taught because many people use them?

11. Do you think that a company should hire an employee who speaks Ebonics or Tex-Mex in an interview? Why or why not?

12. When we see people in Britain drive on the left side of the road, do we say that people in Britain drive on the "wrong side" or the "opposite side"? When we see Japanese read from right to left, do we think that Japanese books are backward?

13. Do you think that we have to be careful in how ethnocentrism is reinforced in a multicultural society?

14. What causes people to dislike an entire group of people? Is it possible to change attitudes? Are there any theories to explain the existence of prejudice?

15. Is it arrogant when Americans believe that people in the United States should all speak English and adapt to their way of life?

16. Make a list of six subcultures that are part of your life. Which ones are the most important to you?

17. Do you think that multiculturalism is a good way to strengthen the achievement of diversity, or do you think that it draws its share of criticism?

18. Western and Southern businesses and people are more liberal in their organizations and casual in their business relationships. In Midwestern and Eastern states there is a bigger push for precision and efficiency in business and more formal business relationships. Are these statements true? What is your observation?

19. Do you think that we should promote pluralism or multiculturalism? Where do you draw the line to allow a culture to thrive without threatening the dominant values and norms?

20. Can anyone list fads that represent popular culture in the United States and across cultures?

21. Do you think Ebonics would be suitable for children to learn? Is it another fad that will go out of style?

Key Terms

Agrarian societies are based on the technology of animal-drawn plows that support large-scale cultivation to acquire food supplies.

Beliefs are specific ideas that people think to be true.

Counterculture describes a cultural group whose values and norms are opposed to those of the mainstream and dominant culture.

Cultural imperialism refers to the widespread infusion of a society's culture into the cultures of other societies.

Cultural lag is a discrepancy between material culture and nonmaterial culture that disrupts an individual's way of life.

Cultural relativism refers to people judging another culture by its own standards.

Cultural transmission refers to a process through which one generation passes culture to the next.

Cultural universals refer to the culture traits that people share across cultures.

Culture refers to a way of life that is carried on by a particular society or social group.

Culture diversity refers to a variety of cultural differences within a society and across societies.

Culture shock refers to the disorientation that people feel when they experience an unfamiliar culture.

Diffusion is the spread of cultural traits from one group or society to another.

Discovery is the process of knowing and recognizing something previously in existence.

Ethnocentrism refers to a tendency to judge another culture based on the standards of one's own culture.

Folkways refer to everyday customs that may be violated without formal sanctions within a society.

High culture refers to cultural patterns that appeal to the upper class or elite of a society.

Horticultural societies use hand tools to raise crops in order to acquire food.

Hunting and gathering societies use simple subsistence technology to hunt animals and gather vegetation.

Ideal culture refers to the rules of expected behavior that people should follow.

Industrial societies are based on technology that mechanizes production to provide goods and services.

Invention is the process of reshaping existing cultural traits into new forms.

Language refers to an organized system of symbols that people use to think and to communicate with each other.

Laws refer to formal norms that are enacted by governments and enforced by formal sanctions.

Material culture refers to physical or tangible creations that members of a society make and use.

Mores refer to strongly held, formally enforced norms with moral overtones.

Multiculturalism refers to the coexistence and equal standing of diverse cultures within a society.

Nonmaterial culture refers to abstract or intangible things that influence our behavior.

Norms refer to established rules of expected behavior that develop out of society or group values.

Pastoral societies use technology that supports the domestication of animals in order to acquire food.

Popular culture refers to widespread cultural patterns that cppeal primarily to the middle and working classes.

Post-industrial (Postmodern) societies are based on computer technology that produces information and supports service industries.

Real culture refers to the values that people actually have.

Sanctions refer to rewards for normal behaviors and penalties for abnormal behaviors.

Societies are diverse groups of people who share distinctive cultures in defined geographic locations.

Subculture refers to distinctive lifestyles and values shared by a category of people within a larger society.

Symbol refers to anything that carries a meaning and represents something else.

Taboos refer to strongly held mores, the violation of which is considered to be extremely offensive.

Values refer to collective ideas about what is right or wrong, good or bad, desirable or undesirable in a particular culture.

Value contradictions refer to values that conflict with each other, either within a culture or across cultures.

Bibliography

Ager, S. (2008). Evolution of Chinese characters. Retrieved on August 05, 2008, from Omniglot Web site: http://www.omniglot.com/writing/chinese_evolution.htm

All About Philosophy (2002). Ethnocentrism. Retrieved on June 27, 2008, from All About Philosophy Web site: http://www.allaboutphilosophy.org/ethnocentrism-faq.htm

Altonn, H. (2006). Team gets OK for Myanmar mission. Retrieved on July 28, 2008, from Honolulu Star Bulletin Web site: http://starbulletin.com/2007/10/04/news/story11.html

Arens, W. (1979). The Man-Eating Myth: Anthropology & Anthropophagy. New York: Oxford University Press.

BBC (2006). The Amish. Retrieved June 17, 2008, from BBC Web site: http://www.bbc.co.uk/religion/religions/christianity/subdivisions/amish_1.shtml

Bell, D. (1973). The Coming of Post-industrial society. New York: Basic Books.

Berg, Y. (2008). Asianization - The Influence of Asia on America. Retrieved on July 18, 2008, from Topics Online Magazine Web site: http://www.topics-mag.com/globalization/asianization.htm

Bernstein, N. (2007, January 20). Correction Appended. Retrieved on July 12, 2008, from New York Times Web site: http://www.nytimes.com/2007/01/20/nyregion/20philanthropy.html?pagewanted=1&fta=y

Brad, I. (1995). Amish Religious Traditions. Retrieved June 17, 2008, from Amish Country News Web site: http://www.amish-news.com/amisharticles/religioustraditions.htm

Burleson, D. (2007). Consulting Tips for Foreign cultures and religions. Retrieved on June 30, 2008, from Burleson Consulting Website: http://www.dba-oracle.com/consultant_religon_culture_guidelines.htm

Chapman, G. (2004). The Five Love Languages: How to Express Heartfelt Commitment to Your Mate, Men's Edition. Chicago, IL: Northfield Pub.

Democracy Central (2008). U.S. workers still lag Europe in vacation stakes. Retrieved on August 25, 2008, Web site: http://democracycentral.blogspot.com/2005/08/us-workers-still-lag-europe-in.html

diversity. (2009). In Merriam-Webster Online Dictionary. Retrieved February 23, 2009, from http://www.merriam-webster.com/dictionary/diversity

Eckert, P., & McConnell-Ginet, S. (2003). Language and Gender. New York: Cambridge University Press.

Erickson, R. (1997). The laws of ignorance designed to keep slaves (blacks) illiterate and powerless. Education, 118 (2), 206 - 210. Retrieved on July 7, 2008, from MasterFILE Premier Database Web site: http://www.aafny.org/proom/pr/pr20041014.asp

Gardyn, R. (2002, July/August). The Mating Game. American Demographics, 24(7), 33-37.

Gerzon, M. (2003). Becoming Global Citizens. Finding Common Ground In a World of Differences. Retrieved on July 20, 2008, from the Mediators Foundation Web site: http://www.mediatorsfoundation.org/relatedreading/becoming_global_citizens.pdf

Heatwole, C. A. (2008) Cultural diffusion. Retrieved on August 05, 2008, from http://www.emsc.nysed.gov/ciai/socst/grade3/geograph.html

Henslin, J. M. (1975). Introducing Sociology: Understanding Life in Society. New York: Free Press.

Hoorman, J. J. (2008). The History of Amish and Mennonite Cultures. Ohio State University Extension Agent. From the Clark County Economic Development Corporation and Tourism Bureau Website: http://www.clark-cty-wi.org/historya&m.htm

Huaxia Chinese school (2008). Huaxia Chinese schools. Retrieved on August 11, 2008, from Huaxia Chinese School Web site: http://www.hxcs.org/

Indiana University Southeast (2008). Horticultural and Pastoral societies. Retrieved on August 05, 2008, from Web site: http://homepages.ius.edu/GSLOSS/ttpastor.HTM

Kendall, D. E. (2008). Sociology in our times. Belmont, CA: Thomson/Wadsworth.

Kim, J. H. (1997). Bridge-makers and Cross Bearers. Atlanta, GA: Scholars Press

Koch, W. (2008). 401 children taken in raid of Texas polygamist compound. Retrieved on July 03, 2008 from USA Today Web site: http://www.usatoday.com/news/nation/2008-04-07-Polygamy_N.htm

Kottak, C. P., & Kozaitis, K. A. (2003). On being different: diversity and multiculturalism in the North American mainstream. Boston: McGraw-Hill.

Lenski, G. E., Nolan, P., & Lenski, J. (1995). Human Societies: An Introduction to Macrosociology (7th ed.). New York: McGraw-Hill.

Macionis, J. (2008). Sociology: A Global Introduction. New York: Pearson Prentice Hall.

Murdock, G. P. (1945). The common denominator of cultures. In R. Linton (Ed.), The Science of Man in World Crisis (pp. 123-142). New York: Columbia University Press.

National Academy of Sciences (2008). Technologically Speaking. Retrieved on July 28, 2008, from The National Academy of Sciences Web site: http://www.nae.edu/nae/techlithome.nsf/weblinks/KGRG-55SQTT?OpenDocument

Nielsen, Donald A., (1998) Three Faces of God: Society, Religion, and the Categories of Totality in the Philosophy of Emile Durkheim. State University of New York Press.

Nolt, S. M. (1992). A History of the Amish. Intercourse, PA: Good Books.

Ogburn, W. F. (1964). Scientific writings of William Fielding Ogburn. In O. D. Duncan (Ed.), On Culture and Social Change (pp. 349-360). Chicago, IL: University of Chicago Press.

Province of Manitoba, Canada (2008). Inventions, Innovations, and Discoveries. Retrieved on August 05, 2008, from Web site: http://www.edu.gov.mb.ca/k12/tech/imym/6/tblm/tmod_1_3a_1.pdf

Robinson, B. A. (2004). The Amish: History in the US and Canada:1700 to now. Retrieved June 17, 2008, from Ontario Consultants on Religious Tolerance Web site: http://www.religioustolerance.org/amish2.htm.

Sailer, S. (2001). Hispanics in America. Retrieved July 26, 2008, from Google Archive Search Web site: http://news.google.com/archivesearch?scoring=t&hl=en&um=1&lnav=ent5&sa=N&q=hispanics+in+america

Sloss, S. (2008). Agrarian societies. Retrieved on August 05, 2008, from Indiana University Southeast Web site: http://homepages.ius.edu/GSLOSS/tth&g.HTM

Sloss, S. (2008). Horticultural and pastoral societies. Retrieved on August 05, 2008, from Indiana University Southeast Web site: http://homepages.ius.edu/GSLOSS/tth&g.HTM

Sloss, S. (2008). Hunting and gathering societies. Retrieved on August 05, 2008, from Indiana University Southeast Web site: http://homepages.ius.edu/GSLOSS/tth&g.HTM

Sloss, S. (2008). Industrial societies. Retrieved on August 10, 2008, from Indiana University Southeast Web site: http://homepages.ius.edu/GSLOSS/tth&g.HTM

Sloss, S. (2008). Post-industrial societies. Retrieved on August 05, 2008, from Indiana University Southeast Web site: http://homepages.ius.edu/GSLOSS/tth&g.HTM

Smitherman, G. (1986). Talkin and Testifyin: The Language of Black America. Detroit, MI: Wayne State University Press.

Sumner, W. G. (1969). The Forgotten Man and Other Essays. Freeport, NY: Books for Libraries Press.

Tarrant County College District (2008). Horticultural and Pastoral societies. Retrieved on August 04, 2008, from Tarrant County College District Website: http://www.tccd.edu/uploadedfiles/employees/2469/courses/SOCI%201301/Handouts/Ch%206%20%20%20Pastoral%20Societies%20%20%20Horticultural%20Society.doc

U.S. News & World Report (2001, June). The Tower of Babel is Tumbling Down – Slowly. U.S. News & World Report.

Williams, R. M., Jr. (1970). American Society: A Sociological Interpretation (3rd ed.). New York: Knopf.

CHAPTER THREE

Socialization

Barbara Miller

This chapter will convince you of the importance of the socialization process by exposing you to a variety of sub-topics, theories, authors, and researchers who have contributed to our understanding of how this process works in our lives and how it affects individuals and society.

Socialization

Socialization is a process whereby we internalize our culture's values, beliefs and norms; through this experience we become functioning members of our society. It is a complex, intricate task, and the process lasts a lifetime. It teaches members the skills necessary to satisfy basic human needs and to defend themselves against danger, thus ensuring that society will continue to exist. Socialization also teaches individuals the expected behaviors associated with their cultures and provides ways to ensure that members adhere to their shared way of life by having and enforcing rules and laws (Ferris, Stein, & Meyer, 2008). The importance of the socialization experience can hardly be overstated. It gives us our humanity. We might still eat with our hands if mothers didn't insist on our using utensils and learning manners. We learn socialization through four major processes:

1. Explicit instruction is an important means for socializing the child. Teachers, religious leaders, and, especially, parents use this repeatedly.
2. Socialization can take place through conditioning. As we age, we start to reward our own behavior. Conditioning can involve positive reinforcement, negative reinforcement, or punishment. Positive reinforcement feels pleasant. Negative reinforcement, such as being told not to touch a hot stove, can prevent something bad from happening to us. Punishment is something negative being done to us. Through all three avenues, we hope to change behavior (Dodgen & Rapp, 2008).
3. Socialization results from role modeling. A child watches another person's behavior and begins to act the same way.
4. Socialization can occur through innovation. If, through experimentation or change, we come across a behavior pattern that solves a problem, we repeat the pattern.

It is important to note that although natural limits exist on what we *possibly* can accomplish, socialization plays a very large role in determining what we *actually* do achieve. Inherited attributes can either grow or wither in the socialization process. Suppose certain infants are born with high levels of **intelligence**, the capacity for mental or intellectual achievement, and of **aptitude**, the capacity to develop physical or social skills, but their parents are physically and mentally abusive. Those inherited traits are likely to fail to reach their full potential. On the other hand, if those same infants were born with parents who were loving and nurturing, those traits would have a better chance to flourish (Thio, 2005).

Three Functions Of Socialization

1. We learn the language of a culture, including body language and other nonverbal forms of language. We enter a network of social relationships while living in the respective culture, learning how to get along with others.
2. We learn the norms of the culture such as not laughing loudly at a funeral.

3. We determine what we want from life—what is valuable and worth achieving—such as getting a good job, getting married, and having children (Dodgen & Rapp, 2008).

Sociologists ask, "Are people more programmed by their genes or by their upbringing?" What if we fail to be socialized?

Failure To Socialize

Today there are real-life cases of children who have lived in extreme social isolation. Some were kept in an attic and fed by shoving a pie plate through a crack beneath the door. When found, these children never smiled, talked, or laughed, and most of them died before reaching maturity. Kingsley Davis studied several similar cases to better understand the relationship between human development and socialization, since there was an opportunity to control one variable—that of nurture (Ferris et al., 2008). The three cases below are classic examples.

The first case, Anna, was born to an unwed mother, a fact that outraged the mother's father. The mother hid Anna in her attic and barely kept her alive. Anna was never touched nor talked to, and never washed; she just lay in her own filth. At age six she was found, unable to walk or talk, lying on the floor with her eyes vacant and face expressionless (Thio, 2005).

Isabella was also born to an unwed mother, one who was a deaf mute; both were kept in a secluded dark room by the mother's father. When discovered, Isabella showed great fear and hostility toward people, and the only sound she could make was a strange croaking (Thio, 2005).

Genie was deprived of normal socialization for many years, kept tied to her potty seat, barely able to move her hands and feet. Her father tied and caged her in a crib, covering her head with a rag. She was beaten if she made any noise, could not stand straight, and had the intelligence of a one-year-old when she was found at the age of thirteen (Thio, 2005).

At each stage of life, we acquire new knowledge

and learn social skills appropriate for that stage. The socialization process is not a perfect process, nor does it always occur. On any given day, newspapers and radio and television broadcasts offer us numerous indications that there are individuals who exist in our society that have not completely learned our norms. Unfortunately, in the United States and other cultures, there are adults who physically, sexually, and psychologically abuse their children and spouses (Curry, Jiobu, & Schwirian, 2008). We might say that these people failed to be socialized. What, precisely, is gained by socialization and how does our prolonged adolescent period affect the formation of cultural values and norms?

The Nature/Nurture Debate

In the 1920s, early sociologists at the University of Chicago spoke of the "tabula rasa" (Durkheim, 1956) which means "empty slate," and implied that every experience in life makes a mark on our slate. By the time we reach adulthood, we are the sum total of the marks on the slate. This narrow view discounted the impact of genes, or heredity. Today, *sociobiology* stresses the *nature* side of the longstanding nature versus nurture debate. Edward Wilson, a Harvard professor, coined the term sociobiology, in the 1970s, and claimed that social behavior was influenced strongly by evolution; today, sociobiology and evidence from brain studies have given more credence to the importance of nature. According to one sociobiological theory, humans have four basic needs:

1. To acquire objects and experiences;
2. To bond with other humans in long-term relationships involving mutual care and commitment;
3. To learn and to make sense of the world and ourselves; and
4. To defend ourselves and our loved ones, our beliefs, and our resources from harm (Tischler, 2007).

Opponents of sociobiological theories claim that these conjectures are a product of animal studies, and people's behavior does not always fit conveniently into animal study results (Dodgen & Rapp, 2008). Studies of identical twins, reared apart, have given us insight into the nature/nurture debate since we are able to control one major variable—that of nature. A question often asked is "are racial differences in IQ genetic?" Because there are no black-white pairs of identical twins, we cannot use twin studies to determine the answer to this question. Anthropologists claim that differences in IQ are due to societal advantages, and whites are more likely to be better educated, privileged, and advantaged. How the brain develops is of interest here. The brain of a fetus is altered by its genes and by its own and its mother's hormones. All brains are feminine unless acted upon by male hormones during two periods—one occurring in *utero* and the other at *puberty*. The hormone is nature, in the sense that it can be altered by drugs taken by the mother. It is also nature in the sense that it is a product of the body's biology (Duffy, 1996). This discovery has gradually altered the views of many psychologists regarding the relationship between *gender* and *education*. An increasing number realize that the competiveness, mathematical ability, and spatial skills of boys are the product of their biology (genes and hormones), not their family, and that the characteristic reading, verbal, linguistic, and emotional interests of girls are also biological. Many homosexuals have thought all along that their sexual preference was biologically predetermined. Studies of identical twins show that if one twin is homosexual, there is a high likelihood that the other will be also, but a non-identical twin has only a one-in-five chance of being homosexual (Duffy, 1996). Men are thirty times more likely to commit murder than women of all ages, and no doubt testosterone (nature) makes males more innately aggressive. Yet, young men in Chicago are thirty times as likely to murder as men in England and Wales, which has nothing to do with nature and a lot to do with nurture (Dodgen & Rapp, 2008).

Theories Of Personal Development

As infants develop, they grow not only biologically and emotionally, but socially as well. As infants get older, their personalities begin to show more and more. **Personality** refers to those patterns of thoughts, feelings, and self-concepts that make us distinctive from each another. Along with the development of personality, infants begin to develop their own sense of *self*, meaning they become aware of their existence, feelings, and personal and social identities. When infants are born, they do not understand that there is a difference between them and their parents. Later they learn that they are one person and their parents are separate persons. Eventually, they understand that they are small and that their parents are large, and that they are referred to as sons and daughters, while parents are referred to as mothers and fathers (Popenoe, 2000).

Harry Harlow: Contact Comfort

Few researchers were more significant than Harry Harlow in helping us to understand the importance of nurturing a baby. He initially thought that the baby-to-mother attachment occurred chiefly because the mother fed the child, but there were other components at work. His startling findings created a new appreciation of "contact comfort," and today we realize that the nurturing provided by a caregiver is absolutely essential to the life of a neonate. After World War I, hundreds of babies in orphanages died mysteriously, puzzling those caring for them. When autopsies were performed, no cause of death could be determined; the description of these babies' deaths was that they just "wasted away." The disease was named *marasmus* from the Greek word for "wasting away." Nurses were apparently so understaffed that they only had time to prop up a bottle in each baby's crib and change diapers, infrequently. There was no time to hold a baby or nurture it in any way. Harlow's studies, forty years later, solved the mystery when he discerned that cuddling and holding a baby was essential to the baby's very existence. He also discovered that maternalism *per se* is not instinctual but is a result of learned behavior—another earth-shaking finding (Belsky, 2004). In his studies of rhesus monkeys, Harlow offered them two "dolls," one made of wire that had a feeding tube attached and another made of soft cloth with no feeding tube. When frightened, monkeys ran to the soft, cuddly doll rather than to the tube-feeding doll. Before these studies, behaviorists insisted that infants were "attached to the reinforcing stimulus that feeds them" (Belsky, 2004, p. 109). In another study, Harlow took newly born monkeys away from their mothers and raised them in isolation to study the effects. The monkeys who received no nurturing or mothering were abnormal in their behavior. They bit and scratched and were highly aggressive; they would not socialize with other monkeys introduced into their cages. They rocked obsessively and were terrified of trainers and peers. They refused to mate, so were inseminated, and when they gave birth they refused to *mother* their offspring—sometimes even killing them. Because these monkeys had never been nurtured, they knew nothing about the experience (Belsky, 2004). Prior to Harlow's studies, maternalism was considered innate, automatic. The fact that it is not helps explain why many abused children grow up to abuse their children, a fact supported by research. Now let us explore which experiences socialize us.

Charles Cooley: Looking-Glass Self

Charles Horton Cooley's **looking-glass self** theory claimed "we are influenced by our perception of what we think others think of us." Cooley felt that the sense of self developed through our imagining the reaction others have to us. There are three steps:

1. We imagine how we look to others (e.g. Are we friendly?);
2. We imagine other people's judgments of us (e.g. Do they find us boring?); and then
3. We experience some kind of feeling about ourselves based on our perceptions of other people's judgments (Ferris et al., 2008).

In effect, other people become a mirror or looking glass for us. In Cooley's view, we are not born with a *self* nor does the *self* emerge merely because of biological maturation. Instead, the *self* is a social product that develops only through interactions with other people (Sullivan, 2007). To Cooley, even

Mother kissing her baby.

Source: Benjamin Earwicker

though our perceptions are not always correct, what we believe is more important in determining our behavior than what is real. W.I. Thomas echoed the same idea when he noted, "If men define situations as real, they are real in their consequences. If we can understand the ways in which people perceive reality, then we can begin to understand their behavior" (Tischler, 2007). Normally we strive to behave in ways that are consistent with our perceptions of ourselves. If, for instance, we view ourselves as kind, we behave toward others in a fashion consistent with that self-concept; that is, we will be kind. Thus, the looking glass can be self-reinforcing (Sullivan, 2007).

The *self-concept* provides the foundation for all later socialization. One distinctive feature of human beings, compared with other animals, is that humans are self-aware. As early as two, we realize that we are unique or different from others. With development comes awareness that other people have needs, views and perceptions different from our own, and that is the beginning of the *self*. Cooley and Mead

did much to help us understand how social experience develops personality. Human beings are unique among animals in part because we are able to put ourselves in another's shoes. We can imagine, for instance, what it would be like to be somebody else, or how another person might view us. We are not born with this ability; infants have no sense of themselves as something separate from their surroundings. As Sullivan puts it "one develops this awareness of *self*, this sense of our own identity, through interaction with other people; the *self-concept,* which is the perception that we all have about who we are—our unique characteristics and attributes—is vital to understanding our nature and worth as human beings" (Sullivan, 2007, p. 77).

George Herbert Mead: Role Taking

George Herbert Mead developed a theory in which the central figure is the *self*, postulating that the self is that part of an individual's personality composed of self-awareness and self-image. Mead rejected the idea that personality was guided by biological drives, as Freud would assert, or even biological maturation, as Piaget would claim. (More about Freud and Piaget will be covered in later sections.) For Mead, the self developed only as the individual interacted with others (Mead, 1934). Without interaction, as in the cases of isolated children, the body grew, but no *self* emerged (Giddens, 2008). Secondly, Mead continued, understanding intention required imagining a situation from another person's point of view. Using symbols, we imagine being in another person's shoes and see ourselves as that person does. This capacity lets us anticipate how others will respond to us even before we act. Mead felt that a child learned about the self through *play* and later through *role-taking*. In other words, when children play they may pretend to be a nurse, or firefighter. In doing so, the child assumes the role of that person and judges or imagines life from that point of view, thus *role-plays* life. Mead claimed that there were two parts to the self: the "I" and the "me." The self is both a subject and an object. When we refer to "I" it is as the subject component, the creative part of ourselves, whereas the "me" is the object component or the conforming part of ourselves. Realistically, children are not merely given a self by their parents, they find and construct a self. By age two, they even recognize themselves in the mirror (Giddens, 2008; Rathus, 2000).

Mead used a term—**significant others**—that has endured and is now even used in social circles. We pay more attention to the judgments of some people than we do others; those people whose approval and affection we desire the most are labeled significant others. Parents are a child's first significant others. By age twelve, most children have developed an awareness of other people and have gone through three stages as they mature and expand their social world (Mead, 1934). The first is called the *preparatory stage* in which the child interacts chiefly through imitation, seeking parental approval. In the second, called the *play stage*, the child moves beyond imitating others to act out imagined roles. In the third stage, the *game stage*, children take on the roles of several people at once and readily transfer the games to real-life situations (Mead, 1934; Rathus, 2000). Aside from their parents, children are also influenced by **generalized others**. These

people are not necessarily close to the child but still help influence the child's internalization of societal values. The next contribution to be examined is that of Freud.

Sigmund Freud: The Unconscious

Sigmund Freud, in 1917, felt that to understand human development, we must analyze the symbolic meanings of behavior and the deep inner workings of the mind. Psychoanalysis and the interpretation of dreams were his legacy. Freud felt there were three structural elements within the mind:

1. The **id**, which is totally unconscious and consists of biological drives.
2. The **ego**, which is the part that deals with the real world. It operates on the basis of reason and helps to integrate the demands of both the *id* and the *superego* (Ferris et al., 2008).
3. The **superego**, which is the "executive branch" of personality because it uses reason to determine whether something is right or wrong

The **superego** is likened to our conscience, which keeps us from engaging in socially undesirable behavior. It develops as a result of parental guidance, particularly in the form of rewards and punishments, when we are children. It inhibits the urges of the *id* and encourages the *ego* to find morally acceptable forms of behavior (Freud, 1953). Freud emphasized early experiences and thought that as children grew up, their focus on pleasure and sexual impulses shifted from the mouth, to the anus, and eventually to the genitals. His five stages of psychosexual development are:

1. Oral
2. Anal
3. Phallic
4. Latent
5. Genital (Santrock, 2007; Ferris et al., 2008).

In the *oral stage* (ages 0-1) infants gain pleasure through the mouth, and feeding and sucking are key activities. Dependency and trust begin in this stage. During the *anal stage* (ages 2-3) the child's focus is on the anus, and toilet training occurs. In the *phallic stage* (ages 3-6) a child's focus is on the genitals. The superego develops and masturbation is common. It was the *phallic stage* that probably received the most attention, especially as it related to gender socialization. At this stage, children recognize the anatomical distinction between the sexes. This is also the time when sexual curiosity is at its peak. Children focus gratification on the clitoris for a girl and the penis for a boy. According to Freud, girls come to believe that the penis, unlike the barely noticeable clitoris, is a symbol of power denied to them. The result is *penis envy*, which culminates in a girl's wish to be a boy (Freud, 1953). She views her mother as inferior because she, too, does not have a penis. The girl's *libido* or sexual energy is transferred to the father, who becomes the girl's love object. This experience was called the *Electra complex*. Resolution occurs when the girl's wish for a penis is replaced by the wish for a child. A male child is more desirable than a female because he brings a penis with him. In the *latency stage* (ages 6-11) gender identity develops; boys and girls ignore each other, but sexual needs lurk in the background. In the *genital stage* (adolescent years) puberty kicks, in and the focus is once again on the genitals as boys and girls search for love and a partner (Santrock, 2007; Ferris et al., 2008).

According to Freud, our adult personality is determined by the way we resolve conflicts between the sources of pleasure at each stage and the demands of reality. In understanding the *self*, Freud believed sexual development had an indelible influence on the individual's identity (Ferris et al., 2008). Freud's greatest contribution to the understanding of our *self* is his belief that just below the surface of the mind exist powerful areas called the subconscious and the *unconscious*. He proposed that *unconscious* energy is the source of conscious thoughts and behavior. For example, one might dislike a coworker at the office and unconsciously express it by working hard to make the coworker look lazy.

Sigmund Freud once said, "Civilization tends to breed discontent in the individual." No normal person wants their drives for self-expression, free-

dom, creativity, or personal eccentricity to be totally suppressed." In other words, if we were completely socialized, we would become extremely unhappy and probably neurotic or psychotic (Thio, 2005).

Critics of Freud point out that his theories were dominated by sex, that his work focused only on males, and that his studies devalued women (Macionis, 2007). During the span of Freud's career, he became an internationally known figure, even though his research threatened the existing political, social, and moral climate of his times. At that time, sex was not a subject for public discussion. Freud lived and worked under totalitarian and fascist regimes where independent thinking was discouraged. In 1938, during the Nazi invasion, he was forced to leave Austria, and his sisters were put to death in German concentration camps. Although Freud's ideas generated much controversy, especially in light of the fact they surfaced during the Victorian Era, they had a profound impact on the social sciences, and students will ponder his theories for years to come (Ferris et al., 2008).

Erik Erikson: Identity Crisis

Erik Erikson helped us understand the factors that influence our human development. Erikson studied with Freud in Vienna and postulated eight stages of human development. He built these on Freud's work but added two important elements. First, he stressed that development is sequential and that a person continues to pass through stages even during adulthood. Secondly, Erikson paid greater attention to the social and cultural forces at each step of development. Erikson's theory has been called the "single most important theory of adult personality development" (Belsky, 2004, p. 22). His model assumes that:

1. A fixed set of stages for the life course exists.
2. These stages unfold over time just as physiology develops over time.
3. At each stage, the person faces a challenge with a positive and negative pole.
4. A healthy personality will achieve the goal of the positive pole and then have the resources to tackle the challenge of the next stage (Novak,

2008).

Each of the eight life stages, called "psychosocial" (instead of Freud's term "psychosexual"), amounts to a crisis of sorts brought on by two factors: biological changes and social expectations. At each stage, the person is pulled in opposite directions in order to accommodate, or hopefully resolve, the crisis. In normal development, the individual resolves the conflict somewhere toward the middle of the opposing options. For example, few people are entirely trusting, while very few trust nobody at all. Most of us are able to trust at least some people, thereby forming enduring relationships, while at the same time staying alert to being cheated or misled by those who are unscrupulous (Tischler, 2007). Erikson's eight stages appear below:

1. Trust vs. mistrust
2. Autonomy vs. shame and doubt
3. Initiative vs. guilt
4. Industry vs. inferiority
5. Identity vs. role confusion
6. Intimacy vs. isolation
7. Generativity vs. self-absorption
8. Integrity vs. despair (Belsky, 2004).

In the first years of life, stage one occurs, involving the crisis of *trust vs. mistrust*. During this period, infancy sets the stage for a lifelong expectation that the world is a good place. The second stage (ages 1-4) is labeled *autonomy vs. shame* and doubt, in which a crisis develops if the child is punished too harshly. The third stage (ages 4-5) is *initiative vs. guilt,* during which time preschool children are asked to assume responsibility for their bodies, behavior, toys and pets; if they are irresponsible, they may develop feelings of guilt and anxiety, creating the crisis. Stage four (ages 6-12) is called *industry vs. inferiority*, wherein children are mastering knowledge and intellectual skills; the danger is the child can feel incompetent and inadequate, creating a crisis. Stage five, *identity vs. role confusion*, occurs during adolescence at a time when young people are exploring new roles and career paths, thus producing identity confusion. Stage six (ages 20-30), *intimacy vs. isolation*, occurs as adults form intimate relationships. Intimacy was described by Erikson as "finding oneself yet losing oneself in another" (Santrock, 2007, p. 23). If this effort is unsuccessful, isolation may result. Stage seven (middle age), *generativity vs. self-absorption*, a person becomes more concerned with others beyond their family and focuses their attention on how future generations will live. The last stage is labeled *integrity vs. despair* and occurs in old age when we reflect on the past. If we feel remorse and regret, doubt and gloom may produce a crisis of despair (Belsky, 2004). Each of Erikson's stages has a "positive" pole, such as trust, and a "negative" pole, such as mistrust. In the healthy solution to the crisis of each stage (of primary importance to Erikson), the positive pole dominated, but Erikson emphasized that some exposure or commitment to the negative side is inevitable. Gail Sheehy (1976) in her book *Passages* spoke of six predictable stages that occur in our lives, and these are reminiscent of Erikson's stages. Sheehy's stages are presented in the section on *socialization in the later years*. Following Erikson was an equally important cognitive developmentalist, Jean Piaget.

Jean Piaget: Cognitive Development

Jean Piaget, born in 1894 in Switzerland, published volumes about how children develop.

Early in his career he worked with Alfred Binet, a French psychologist who was devising the original intelligence test. It was as though Piaget could get into the mind of a child and see precisely how the child viewed the world. He had three children late in life—Laurent, Lucienne, and Jacqueline—and as is true with people who bear children late in life, Piaget was fascinated with every minuscule detail of his children's developmental changes. He spent sixty years writing extensively in a remote cottage in the French countryside. It is rumored that even his wife did not know where he wrote his books and articles, so he could be certain of privacy (Miller, 1980). Piaget observed four distinct stages that children experience:

1. Sensorimotor stage
2. Preoperational stage

3. Concrete operational stage
4. Formal operational stage (Rathus, 2000; Santrock, 2007; Belsky, 2004).

In the first stage, *sensorimotor* (ages 0-2) children assimilate, or test the outer world through their senses, and especially with their mouth. They taste, touch, smell, look, and listen; it's all about the senses (Santrock, 2007). Reality for the infant corresponds to whatever his senses tell him. He learns that objects come in different sizes and colors; some are soft and others prickly. Some taste terrible, others taste wonderful. During this stage, one particularly delightful development occurs— *object permanence*. This is the understanding that objects continue to exist even when they cannot be seen, heard, or touched. If a puppy goes behind a couch he is gone, to an infant. Later on, when we see the infant looking everywhere for the puppy, we know the child has developed object permanence.

The *preoperational stage* (ages 2 to 7) is characterized by the use of language and the ability of the child to use his imagination. Children can attach meanings only to specific experiences and objects, but, lacking abstract concepts, they cannot judge size, weight, or volume. In one of Piaget's best-known experiments, he placed drinking glasses containing equal amounts of water on a table. One glass was tall and skinny, the other short and wide; he then asked children ages five and six if the glasses contained the same amount of water, and they all insisted that the taller glass held more. He then poured the water into a measuring cup, showed them the amount, then poured it back into the original container and asked them the same question. Their answer was still the same, showing that they could not process this abstract concept. However, by the age of seven, they realized that the amount of water is the same—only the container is of a different shape.

The *concrete operational stage* (ages 7 to 11) shows us that children have a realistic understanding of their world. Their thinking is on the same wavelength as adults. Children can manage logic and understand why things happen. While they can reason about concrete objects, they cannot yet think

abstractly in a scientific way.

In the last stage (ages 12 and over) children manage the *formal operational stage* where they can think critically as well as abstractly. They understand cause and effect, and, when faced with a problem, children at this stage are able to review all of the possible ways of solving it and go through them theoretically in order to reach a solution (Santrock, 2007; Belsky, 2004; Rathus, 2000).

According to Piaget, the first three stages of development are universal, but not everyone reaches the *formal operational stage*; it depends largely on a person's education. Adults of limited educational attainment tend to continue to think in more concrete terms and, of interest, they retain a tendency toward egocentrism.

As an educator, Piaget called all teachers *facilitators* and claimed there are no teachers, only learners. He urged parents and educators to allow children to discover the world on their own; he abhorred pushy parents (Giddens, 2008). Piaget is probably the best known developmental psychologist to date; his theories appear in virtually every textbook on child development.

Abraham Maslow: Hierarchy Of Needs

Maslow published his *hierarchy of needs theory* more than fifty years ago, and it is probably the most popular and oft-cited theory about precisely what motivates people to behave the way they do (Maslow, 2008). Maslow was born in New York in 1908 and died in 1970, although various publications appeared in Maslow's name in later years. Maslow's original hierarchy of needs model was developed between 1943 and 1954 and was first widely published in *Motivation and Personality*. He believed each of us is motivated by needs. Our most basic needs are inborn, having evolved over tens of thousands of years. Maslow said that needs must be satisfied in a given order; once the needs of one level are met, aims and drives shift to the next higher level of the hierarchy. If needs are thwarted it causes stress. Physiological needs must come first. If needs like air, water, food, and sleep are not satisfied, a person's energy must be spent in pursuit of them. Higher needs such as esteem and love will have to wait. The second most important needs to be satisfied concern safety, so that we can be free from the threat of physical and emotional harm. Such needs might include "living in a safe area, medical insurance, job security and financial reserves" (Maslow, 1987). In other words, if a person feels endangered, higher needs will not receive much attention. Next are social needs. Social needs are those related to interactions with others and may include the need for belonging and the need for giving and receiving love. Social needs are followed by esteem needs. After feeling a sense of "belonging," the need to feel important arises; esteem needs bring self-respect, a sense of accomplishment and recognition. At the top of Maslow's pyramid-shaped hierarchy is self-actualization, which means finding self-fulfillment and realizing one's potential. Self-actualized people are characterized by being problem-focused, possessing an ongoing freshness and appreciation of life, wanting to achieve maximal personal growth and having the ability to have "peak experiences" (Maslow, 1987).

Self-actualization is the level that most fascinates students, so we shall let Maslow describe this level as persons who have:

1. A keen sense of reality and objective judgment, rather than subjective.
2. The ability to see problems in terms of challenges and situations requiring solutions, rather than as personal complaints or excuses.
3. A need for privacy and are comfortable being alone.
4. Reliance on their own experiences and judgments. They are independent and don't rely on culture and environment to form opinions and views.
5. Autonomy, and are not susceptible to social pressures. They are nonconformists.
6. A democratic, fair, and non-discriminating sense. They embrace all cultures, races, and individual styles.
7. Social compassion and humanity.
8. An acceptance of others as they are rather than trying to change them.
9. A sense of comfort with themselves, despite any

unconventional tendencies.
10. A few close intimate friends, rather than many surface relationships.
11. A sense of humor directed at oneself or the human condition, rather than at the expense of others.
12. Spontaneity. They are natural and remain true to themselves, despite the wants of others.
13. An excitement and interest in all things, even the most ordinary.
14. Creativity; they are inventive and original.
15. The ability to have peak experiences that leave a lasting impression (Maslow, 1987).

Norwood proposed that Maslow's hierarchy can be used to describe the kinds of information that individuals seek at different levels. For example, those at the lowest level seek *coping information* in order to meet basic needs. Persons at the safety level need *helping information* in order to be safe and secure. Belongingness creates a need for *enlightening information*. Persons at the esteem level need *empowering* information so their ego can be developed. Persons in self-actualization need *edifying* information which probably includes seeking a "higher power, some power beyond themselves" (Norwood, 2002). In addition to the five-level theory, there are later adaptations of the hierarchy based on Maslow's work; these later models add levels that include "*cognitive, aesthetic,* and *transcendence* levels of need. For many people, self-actualizing commonly involves each and every one of the newer levels. Thus, the original five-level *hierarchy of needs* model remains a definitive classical representation of human motivation; and the later adaptations perhaps serve best to illustrate aspects of self-actualization (Maslow, 1987).

Lawrence Kohlberg: Theory Of Moral Development

Kohlberg was the principal academician to ask where we get the concept of moral development. How do we come to judge situations as right or wrong? Sunday school and church might teach children about right and wrong, but not all children go to church. Parents might teach about right and wrong by modeling it, but not all children get their values from their parents. Early researchers were leery of studying moral development because they didn't want to offend religious groups or step on the toes of what parents clearly defined as "their job." This is analogous to sex education being taught in schools today, meaning that many parents say, "I'll teach my children about sex, thank you" and then don't do it. Kohlberg believed that it is only during adolescence that we become capable of developing a moral code that guides our lives (Curry et al., 2007). To measure the presence of this moral code, Kohlberg wrote scenarios and asked people to respond to the moral dilemmas presented. Kohlberg discovered that three levels (or six stages of morality) were discernable. Additionally, stage development always moved upward, and the three levels of moral thought—*pre-conventional, conventional* and *post-conventional* were found in all cultures tested (Miller, 1980). Each level actually has two stages, but this discussion will be confined to the general term levels, to avoid confusion.

In the earliest stage, **pre-conventional morality**, people are thought to obey laws chiefly to avoid punishment or to gain some benefit. It is considered good to do something nice for another person, but only if that person would do something nice in return. Even though pre-conventional morality refers chiefly to children's behavior, adults participate in it, too. For example, we might look both ways to see if a policeman is watching and then turn illegally in our car, or we find a $10 bill on the sidewalk, look around to make sure no one is watching, and put it in our pocket. This is pre-conventional thinking. In the second level, **conventional morality**, people incorporate society's rules and laws into their own value system and behave accordingly. Most adults and adolescents operate in this level (Curry et al., 2007; Miller, 1980). They obey rules not only to win approval or gain rewards, but also because they feel they are doing the right thing. Loyalty becomes an important concept, and some people feel it takes precedence over all other commitments. **Post-conventional morality** is the highest level attainable. At this level, people use broad ethical principles to guide their behavior, such as showing respect for human dignity, equality, and, of late, respect for one's environment—even for the rights of animals and other living creatures. People operating at this level are often instigators of social change and are in the forefront of social movements. One famous post-conventional act was that of Martin Luther King, Jr., in his peaceful protest march in 1963. Followers ignored a court order, and some were arrested and jailed. Dr. King concluded that racial inequality was a higher principle than obeying a court order (Curry et al., 2007).

One criticism of Kohlberg's theory is that he used only boys as subjects for his investigation; another is that very few people ever reach the highest (stage six) post-conventional level. The following story is one of Kohlberg's most widely known dilemmas, and he used it to determine in which level a person was operating:

In Europe, a woman was near death from a special kind of cancer. There was one medicine that a druggist in the same town had recently thought might save her. It was a form of radium that the druggist had recently discovered. The druggist was charging ten times what the drug cost him to make. He paid $200 for the radium and charged $2,000 for a small dose of the drug. The sick woman's husband, Heinz, went to everyone he knew to borrow the money, but he could only get together about $1,000. He told the druggist that his wife was dying and asked him to sell it to him cheaper or let him pay later, but the druggist said, "No, I discovered the drug and I'm going to make money from it." Heinz got desperate and broke into the man's store and stole the drug for his wife (Miller, 1980, p. 35).

If, after reading this, you thought in terms of whether Heinz would be punished for his actions, (i.e., "If Heinz stole the drug he would go to jail") you would be classified as operating at the *pre-conventional level*. Your concern would focus on the external consequences for Heinz rather than any internalized moral sense. If you're thinking, "Heinz shouldn't steal the drug because that is not law-abiding, and laws must be obeyed," your response would be classified at the *conventional level*. If your concern was, "No matter what society says, Heinz had to steal the drug for his wife because nothing outweighs the universal principle of saving a life," you were at the *post-conventional level* of moral thinking.

When Kohlberg conducted studies with children of different ages, he discovered that at age thirteen, pre-conventional answers were universal in every culture. By the age of fifteen, most children around the world were reasoning at the conventional level (Miller, 1980). When Kohlberg described the advances in moral thinking that take place during adolescence, he made an important point: Teenagers are famous for questioning society's rules, for seeing the injustice of the world, and for getting involved in idealistic causes; however, these factors can add to the already emotional storm characteristic of the teen years (Belsky, 2004). Gilligan criticized Kohlberg's use of male children in his sample because, according to Gilligan's research, males approach morality from a different perspective than females. "Whereas males define morality in terms of justice, females define morality in terms of responsibility" (Gilligan, 1982, p. 326). Another criticism focused on whether we can depend on an actual link between moral thought and moral behavior.

All societies have value systems that specify what is right or wrong. Today, most people have strong opinions not only about moral and immoral behavior, but also about how moral behavior should be taught and whether it should be taught in school or left up to parents.

Gender And Socialization

Gender refers to learned behavior as to how we are expected to act as males or females in society. This learning occurs in good part through the socialization process (Sullivan, 2007). Our **gender role** refers to how we should act as males or females, whereas **gender typing** refers to acquiring behavior considered appropriate for one's particular gender. Research has shown that much of our behavior as males and females is not a function of biology, but rather of learning (Ferris et al., 2008). This finding leads to the distinction that sociologists make between *sex and gender*. **Sex** refers to the biological

and physiological characteristics of sexual identity. Masculine and feminine, by contrast, are used as gender-specific terms. The way parents treat children reinforces gender. Parents might be rough-and-tumble with a boy. With a girl, they might smile more and hold them closer, for longer periods of time (Dodgen & Rapp, 2008). We will put a female child in long pants, but we would never put a male child in a pink dress. Even height and low birth weight help socialize us by the way our parents react to us. Biologists claim that we are born with tendencies to be introverted or extroverted, hormones give males a push toward greater aggression, and even intelligence is thought to be as much as 70 percent inherited (Dodgen & Rapp, 2008; Sullivan, 2007).

The Social Learning Theory

Precisely how do children learn their gender roles? According to *social learning theory, conditioning* and *imitation* have significant influence: "people learn by watching others and imitating the ones we emulate" (Belsky, 2004, p. 14). Children are rewarded for behaving in ways that parents consider appropriate for their gender, and punished for not doing so; therefore, they eventually conform to society's expectation of gender roles. A boy learns to hide his fears and pain because he has been praised for being brave and scolded for crying. Children also learn by imitation. They tend to imitate their same-sex parent and certain adults because they are powerful role models and people who are able to reward or punish them (Thio, 2005, p. 247). Androgyny, the presence of masculine and feminine characteristics in the same person, is being encouraged today because it helps avoid the limiting quality and rigidity of old, stereotypical ways. Young marriages are seen as a healthy blending of roles—dads change diapers and moms service the car, and neither feels abused.

Occupations often show gender discrimination, and some professions are still male-dominated. The U.S. Census Bureau (2004) showed that even though more females go to college, more males graduate and finish graduate degrees, especially in certain fields. For instance, only one out of five

Girls playing with dolls.   Source: Morgue File

bachelor's degrees in engineering is awarded to women (Sullivan, 2007). *Sexism*, the belief that one sex is innately superior to the other, has had a negative impact on women and produces inequality in two ways, especially in the work world. At each level of occupational skill, men receive higher pay than women and many women believe they get passed over for promotions in favor of men. However, our society has made great strides with respect to gender equity, in part because of the influence of the feminist movement (Gilligan, 1982).

Children are given verbal cues from parents about their gender behavior. By age two, children have a pretty good idea of what gender is. They know if they are a boy or a girl, but not until age six do children understand that a person's sex does not change, and that sex differences between girls and boys are anatomically based. Many toy stores and catalogs still classify products according to gender (Dodgen & Rapp, 2008). Adults feel the push toward acting in accordance with gender roles, too. Society claims that women are supposed to be shy, easily intimi-

dated, and passive. Men are to be bold, ambitious, and aggressive. Women should pay attention to their appearance and it's acceptable to be emotional, even to cry easily, but men should hold back emotions and not cry (Thio, 2005). Women need male protection and are expected to be intuitive and unpredictable; men are leaders and expected to be logical, rational and objective. Even though our culture has modified some of these values, certain *gender stereotypes* persist and will continue to affect our opportunities and life events (Thio, 2005).

Socialization Is Reciprocal

Is there a "downside" to socialization, or is it perfect? We wonder if we are just prisoners of socialization, shaped and influenced to such a great extent by others and by society. Are our ideas as individuals unique and independent, or just a sorry illusion? Ferris (2008) suggests that it is true that the process of socialization is rather homogenizing, that people are pushed toward conformity to help the culture run smoothly. He asks, "Does this press us toward some sort of lowest common denominator, toward the mainstream?" Or is it true that no two people are ever really alike or ever entirely "finished." The process by which we become socialized is ongoing; we are not merely passive players, receiving all the influences around us. We are spontaneous, intelligent, and creative, and we exercise free will. We are interpreting, defining, making sense of, and responding to, our social world. That gives us a great deal of personal power in all situations. The socialization process is reciprocal in that we are shaping society at the same time society is shaping us (pp. 137-138).

Agents Of Socialization

Every society has individuals, groups, and institutions that provide varying amounts of socialization during the life course, and some, like *family*, have a greater impact than others. *Schools, peers,* the *media* and, eventually as an adult, the *work world* are also powerful socializing agents, as are the police and even religious leaders. These agents limit our choices by rewarding compliance to rules and punishing noncompliance. Socializing agents also act as role models, serving as especially important reference points for our thoughts and actions (Curry et al., 2007). Humans, however, are not simply passive subjects waiting to be programmed or instructed; individuals come to understand and assume social roles through an ongoing process of social interaction. The impact of any certain agent is not the same for all people, and no two people experience the same type of socialization because of the influence of other factors like social class and educational level. **Primary socialization** begins in infancy and childhood and is the most intense period of cultural learning (Giddens, 2008). It is the time when children learn language and the basic behavioral patterns that form the foundation for later learning. **Secondary socialization** takes place later in childhood and into maturity. In this phase, other agents of socialization take over some of the responsibility from family (Tischler, 2007). **Anticipatory socialization** involves learning the skills and values

needed for future roles. This type of socialization begins during adolescence. We prepare for future roles by working part-time jobs, taking certain self-help courses in college, reading books and articles, talking with mentors, and trying out anticipated roles (Giddens, 2008). Three key factors influence the effectiveness of anticipatory socialization:

1. The visibility of the future role.
2. The accuracy with which the future role is presented.
3. The agreement society has about the role.

To the sociologist, **roles** are cultural norms that define the behaviors expected of an individual occupying a particular status (Ferris et al., 2008). Sometimes we get mixed messages from the culture about what is really expected when we play a given role.

Day Care

Today, children are brought up in single families; some are cared for by two mothers and two fathers (divorced parents and stepparents). Most American mothers work outside the home or return to work relatively soon after the birth of children. For that reason, we can almost include day care and nursery schools as *agents of socialization*. Critics of the *day care movement* in our culture believe that only parents can give children the love, attention, and intimate involvement that they need to develop into emotionally healthy and socially competent adults (Belsky, 2004). Proponents claim that day care helps children learn to be independent of "s-mothering" (of which some mothers are guilty) and that research indicates that children exposed to day care do as well, or better than, children raised exclusively in the home (Sullivan, 2007).

Family

In the family network, we first learn about intimacy, emotions, and power; we also learn the components of culture and social structure, including language, norms, and values. The family usually protects us and provides us with nourishment and affection. Family also determines such ascribed statuses as racial and ethnic background and influences other statuses including socio-economics and religion. These statuses have an impact on how we are raised. For instance, parents from different backgrounds raise their children in different ways and expect different things from them. Working-class parents tend to encourage obedience, conformity, respect, cleanliness, and neatness. Middle-class parents are more likely to encourage curiosity, self-direction, and expressiveness (Sullivan, 2007). Later in life, a strong social support network makes aging experiences easier because within the family, elders can feel useful, loved and accepted. All things considered, the family remains the major agent of socialization in a sequence of development connecting the generations (Giddens, 2008).

Schools

A significant part of the socialization process occurs in schools. Our schools tend to have female teachers and male principals. So, from the beginning of their education, children see males in positions of authority and dominant over females. By giving misbehaving male students extra attention, female teachers encourage qualities such as independence—even aggression. Female students are expected to be quiet and conforming. Without realizing it, teachers reward students for behaving in a way consistent with their own gender-role stereotypes (Sullivan, 2007).

Schools, especially because attendance is mandatory, have a powerful effect in America, not only because they teach intellectual pursuits and job preparedness, but because of something sociologists label the *hidden curriculum*. The hidden curriculum refers to teachings in school that prepare children to accept the requirements of adult life and to fit into the social world society provides. Children learn to be quiet and punctual in class, accept and respond to a teacher's authority, and show respect to the principal; these rules are later linked to their job experience. Riding the school bus, eating lunch in the cafeteria, bringing a note from home when absent, all add to the experiential base that children receive from going to school. School provides children with a rich source of new ideas to shape their sense of self. When children progress in school, parents

tend to accept and respect their children, regardless of how successful they are with the "four R's," but teachers, who replace parents as authority figures in school, are more demanding. Poor performance and low grades bring rebukes and cause a sense of failure, especially with middle-class youth.

Conflicts in schools complicate our lives; issues like school prayer, free lunches for the poor, sex education, and other controversies give grief to educators and to parent-teacher organizations. With so many children coming home to an empty house after school, another issue arises. Researchers are finding that more young people get into trouble with the law because of the lack of supervision. These so-called "latchkey kids" are deprived of proper socialization by absentee parents and exposed to improper socialization by street friends who are up to no good. Juvenile crime rates triple after the school-day ends at 3 p.m., and more than 75 percent of first-time sexual encounters take place in the homes of someone whose parents are still at work. Research reveals that, compared to children who have some adult supervision, young people who are home alone are more likely to smoke, drink, and use marijuana, as well as get poor grades and have encounters with the police. After-school programs, community education centers, YMCAs, and playground supervisors are some of the measures being used to combat the increase in after-school delinquency (Thio, 2005). Despite the many problems inherent in trying to socialize our youth in schools, all of the trouble in the world is worth the price when we see our children fulfill their potential and grow up to be responsible, productive, well-adjusted citizens.

Peer Groups

Peer groups may have the next most powerful impact to that of family. Peers are those people who are our social equals, our pals, those friends whom we cherish and emulate. The **peer group** is defined as same-aged friends with similar interests and social positions (Sullivan, 2007). Parents may play the most significant role in teaching basic values, but peers have the greatest influence on lifestyle choices, such as length of hair, social activities, and the use of bad language (Tischler, 2007). Negative

Friends.

Source: Patti Gray

effects are felt on college campuses as well as in the ghetto, and, for some youth, peer-group experience can lead to wasted lives and violence. Teenagers band together for identity, status, and shared drugs and other criminal acts if parental guidance is missing. Davis Elkind's research indicated that "the power of the peer group is in direct proportion to the extent that the adolescent feels ignored by the parents" (Tischler, 2007, p. 123).

The family is eventually supplanted by the peer group as young people spend more and more time in school and with social activities. Because of the fact that children have so much freedom early in life, parents have probably lost control by age ten (Miller, 1980).

The Media

One problem with today's media is that it's a one-way form of communication, creating an audience that tends to receive passively whatever news and program content is brought to it. By the time our young people reach eighteen, they will have viewed more hours of television than they have spent in school classrooms. Because young children are so impressionable, and because many parents use the television as a babysitter, social scientists have become increasingly concerned about its role in socialization. The impact of television is greater on males than on females, and it is more substantial on children who are more aggressive to begin with and on children between the ages of eight and twelve. Music, such as rap and hip-hop, may contain lyrics that are inconsistent with mainstream cultural values and have a negative effect on the young, as may playing certain video games. These can cause children to become more aggressive, at least in the short term (Thio, 2005). Currently, iPods, cell phones, Xboxes, and MySpace raise new concerns about the power of the media to influence our youth. Some believe that adolescence, or the teen years, bring turbulence not only from biological and hormonal changes, but also from cultural inconsistencies. Consider these examples: schools recommend sexual abstinence and then hand out condoms in high school; an adult at eighteen may face going to war, but he cannot order a beer. Adolescence is indeed a time of social contradictions, when people are no longer children but are also not yet adults (Macionis, 2007). Researchers are concerned that the public may get socialized by the media into a world that does not exist. However, we do not make decisions in isolation, nor do we simply absorb everything we see or hear. Instead, we usually choose those mediums and messages that suit our own purposes and pay attention to programs that are consistent with our own experiences (Curry et al., 2007; Sullivan, 2007). Sullivan believes that the media is a powerful agent of socialization for the young and can, and does, erode cultural and family values.

Adult Socialization

Adult socialization is the process by which adults learn new statuses and roles. It differs from primary socialization in two ways. First, adults are much more aware than young people of the processes through which they are being socialized. Some people deliberately invite socialization processes into their lives, pursuing advanced education or changing careers. Others may reject choices that were forced upon them within a **total institution**, such as a prison or psychiatric hospital, where people are cut off from the larger society and forced to follow a strict set of rules. In addition, an adult has more control over how he wants to be socialized and so can generate more enthusiasm for his own growth. Acquiring a new hobby, traveling to a foreign country, or taking up jogging can provide a way to channel energy and introduce change. Adults, like children, continue their **developmental socialization** process, learning to be more competent in their assumed roles (Tischler, 2007).

Work

Work gives purpose and direction to our lives and helps provide for our families' needs; *work* exists in every culture, but only in industrial societies do we go each day to places of work separate from our homes. In agrarian societies, people farm land close to where they live; therefore, work in these communities is not as clearly distinct from other activities

as it is in the Western world. Wilbert Moore studied *occupational socialization* and identified four stages in the process, which follow:

1. We must make a career choice and, based on that choice, we have to decide where and how much training we shall need to enter that career.
2. We experience anticipatory socialization which may last a few weeks or a few years and involves trying out different aspects of the future role.
3. We experience conditioning and commitment when we actually take our job of choice and when we start out very excited about our new duties.
4. The fourth stage is labeled continuous commitment. At this stage, the job becomes an integrated part of our self-concept (Sullivan, 2007).

The work world requires many adjustments, such as being friendly, but not too friendly, and learning to dress appropriately for a given job. In one example, a young management trainee was rebuked for wearing his keys snapped to his belt. "Janitors wear keys there; executives keep them in their pockets," said his boss. Today, because we live such long lives, we may have a dozen or more jobs and five or six careers during our lifetimes.

Quitting work permanently also necessitates many adjustments. When we're young, maturing means taking on new roles and responsibilities (Tischler, 2007). When we age, the opposite happens, as people leave behind roles, like work, that have given them identity, pleasure, and prestige. Retirement for some people means restful recreation and leisure time, but for others it can mean lowered self-worth and downright boredom (Giddens, 2008). Some occupations require **resocialization**, which is the process of leaving behind old selves and developing new ones; for example, the armed forces use basic training to socialize recruits to accept killing as a necessary part of their work. The financial crisis and high unemployment rates we are experiencing today are factors that have had a great impact on the necessity of resocialization (Tischler, 2007). Many citizens are being laid off or encouraged to take early retirement. Our current flat economy has demanded more change than we have experienced in decades.

Socialization In The Later Years

Old age begins around age 65. With people living longer, the elderly population is growing nearly as fast as the U.S. population. About one person in every eight is over 65 years old and the elderly now outnumber teenagers. By 2030, the number of seniors will double to 71 million, and almost half of the country's population will be over forty (Macionis, 2007). The elderly population grew more than ten times in size from 1900 to 2003, going from 3.1 million to 36 million people. Now that baby boomers are retiring, the next two decades will provide a large population whose collective energy, good health, and productivity will likely redefine what it means to be old (Giddens, 2008). Elders who have a healthy sense of self, of who they are, age well. They are less likely to identify themselves as old because they see themselves as being "who they always have been" (Hillier & Barrow, 2007, p. 35). Moen believes that we are on the cusp of what she calls "retirement scripts," the set of social expectations that guide perceptions of what is possible during the decades following middle age (1995). Aging poses a number of challenges to every person. These challenges come from at least three sources: social attitudes toward elders, physical decline, and the loss of social roles (Novak, 2008).

Ageism

Ageism (the process of stereotyping people based on their age) is a source of frustration to elders because of the self's sensitivity to the perceptions of others. Robert Butler said that ageism "reflects a deep-seated uneasiness on the part of the young and middle-aged—a personal revulsion to and distaste for growing old, disease, and disability. It also is associated with fear of powerlessness, uselessness and death" (Novak, 2008, p. 3). Older people even try, unsuccessfully, to distance themselves from being old by attempting to stay middle-aged forever. Some refuse to take advantage of reduced fares on buses and discounts in restaurants; they would rather pay

more than admit advanced age. Most people feel that "old" is five years older than they are (Novak, 2008). Physical decline is especially challenging for those people who get their self-esteem from playing sports. Limitations like having to give up driving, or contracting diseases such as Alzheimer's and Parkinson's, can prevent successful aging. Shakespeare offered one view of physical aging as "sans teeth, sans eyes, sans taste, sans everything" (Novak, 2008, p. 139). The loss of social roles shrinks our world; studies recommend playing bridge, joining organizations for seniors, going to church, and seeking friends who have similar values and levels of aging. It's all in one's attitude, this successful aging concept.

Three Theories On Aging

Three ways for people to adapt to changes as they age are: the *disengagement theory*, the *activity theory*, and the *continuity theory*. Disengagement is a withdrawal from society, consciously or unconsciously, due to the decline of one's strength and energy; it occurs socially as well as physically. The activity theory is almost the opposite of the disengagement theory. This theory suggests that activity leads to the highest satisfaction possible in later life, especially if we find the activities meaningful (Novak, 2008). The continuity theory suggests that our personality does not undergo radical change during the life course. A person who applies successful strategies from the past to current and future challenges helps maintain continuity. Each of these three theories helps us understand how people adapt to change as they age. For instance, perhaps the disengagement theory applies best to people in late old age who have less energy to keep active; they may welcome disengagement and find satisfaction in a less active lifestyle (Novak, 2008).

Gail Sheehy became renowned after her book *Passages* identified six predictable stages in one's life. Those stages are:

1. *Pulling up stakes*, ages 22-28, when we distance ourselves from parents and become our own person. We try to establish intimate relationships.
2. The *trying twenties*, ages 28-33, when we are

still trying to separate from our parents, but we reappraise our choices and take another look at our goals in life.

3. *Passages to the thirties*, ages 33-40, when we feel we are established in an adult world and have set out on our true course in life.

4. But *I'm unique*, ages 40-45, when we start to question our true course in life and we have nothing more to prove to our parents. We start to ask if this is the only way to be. It is a period of disillusionment.

5. *Deadline decade*, ages 45-60, when we question our lives, values, and ourselves and wonder if there is time to do everything that we want to accomplish in life. We try to develop other aspects of ourselves and may begin mentoring or caretaking (Sheehy, 1976).

6. *Renewal*, ages 60 and up, when we mellow toward the world and ourselves and become more people-oriented. We begin to look inward rather than focusing on our jobs and other outside stimulations (Dodgen & Rapp, 2008; Sheehy, 1976).

Perhaps we should add a seventh stage now that we are living well past 60, and in it we might refer to changes that take place from 70 to 90 years of age that are similar to those discussed above in the disengagement, activity, and continuity theories.

Gerontology

College courses containing gerontological studies have added greatly to our understanding of the entire process of aging. (*Geron* in Greek means old person.) These courses contain a sub-section called *geriatrics* which focuses mainly on diseases of the elderly, like arthritis, Alzheimer's, and Parkinson's. Macionis states, "For most of the population, gray hair, wrinkles, and declining energy begin in middle age. After about fifty, bones become more brittle, injuries take longer to heal, and the risk of chronic illnesses like diabetes becomes greater. Life-threatening conditions such as heart disease and cancer rise steadily. Sensory abilities such as taste, sight, touch, smell, and especially hearing, become diminished as we age (Macionis, 2007). In low-income countries,

being old lends status and influence because elders control most of the wealth and, subsequently, are shown great respect. At the dinner table, no family member takes a bite of food until the elder member starts. Their intelligence is undisputed and they are thought to have great wisdom from having lived so long. In contrast, an elder's status is low in this country. Many families feel burdened by elder care, and today families are providing care for as many as four generations at a time—not always gracefully. Females are often overburdened with a job and caring for children, spouses, parents, and grandparents. In the future, wealthy nations will need to use resources wisely to serve a growing elderly population; and elders, in turn, will need to "give back" because their self-esteem improves when they are contributing to their society (Macionis, 2007). Keeping busy and playing useful roles enhances our health late in life. Our culture can create policies and social opportunities for older people with this in mind.

Elizabeth Kubler-Ross: Five Stages Of Dying

Elizabeth Kubler-Ross described five stages that she observed in virtually all terminally ill patients. These stages are taught to nurses and doctors all over the world because it provides them with a glimpse of what it's like to be dying and helps them be more compassionate. The first stage is *denial*, the second *anger*, then *bargaining*, *depression* and, finally, *acceptance*. In the denial stage, the patient is certain there is a mistake in the diagnosis. "You have the wrong x-rays" is a typical reaction. In the anger stage, nurses realize that complaints and constant criticism of things like wrinkled sheets and bad food are to be expected. Bargaining surfaces when we feel that we are losing all control over our lives. Patients try to make "deals" with their nurse, their doctor, or God: "I will consent to that last surgery only if you will let me go to my grandson's graduation" or, "God, if you will let me have one more summer at the cottage, I'll leave the church $50,000." The next stage, depression, is difficult to witness, especially for family members who see "the fight" go out of their loved one. In the accep-

Elderly women resting.

Source: Janet Burgess

tance stage, the patient is peaceful and logical. In making family members sensitive to this stage, they are advised to stop pushing for miraculous treatments and more surgery. Instead, it is recommended that they encourage the writing of a will and ask about special wishes regarding the dispensation of personal items. Burial preferences should also be discussed. At this point, no longer paralyzed by fear and anxiety, patients whose lives are ending set out to make the most of the time they have left, and they say their good-byes (Giddens, 2008).

It is useful to distinguish among different age categories of the elderly, such as the *young old* (ages 65-74) the *old old* (ages 75-84), and the *oldest old* (age 85 and older). The *young old* are the people most likely to be economically independent, healthy, active, and engaged. The *oldest-old*, the fastest-growing segment of the elderly population, are the most likely to encounter poor health, finan-

cial insecurity, isolation, and loneliness; however, these differences are not solely due to aging. The *young old* group came of age during the post-World War II period of strong economic growth. They are more likely to be educated, to have had stable employment, and to have acquired wealth in the form of a home, savings, and investments (Novak, 2008). These advantages are much less likely to be enjoyed by the *oldest old*, partly because their education and careers began at an earlier time, when economic conditions were not so favorable (Treas, 1995).

Science and technology have extended our lives, pushing death and dying later in our old age. A recent study of 1,227 deaths of older people showed an average age of 80 at the time of death; 45 percent of these died in a hospital, 25 percent died in a nursing home, and 30 percent died at home. Hospice care has become a viable alternative to the usual health care methods. The emphasis is on dying with dignity, and we can either go to a hospice or have hospice personnel come to our homes. In 1970, when this nation adopted hospice care, the American Medical Association (AMA) was opposed to it; philosophically, the values of the two groups were at odds. When doctors take the Hippocratic Oath, they declare that everything will be done to keep a patient alive. The goal of hospice care is to keep patients comfortable; if in severe pain, the patient can request an injection of pain medication, and family members can be present day and night. Medicare covers most hospice expenses because they are lower than those incurred during a stay in a hospital.

Death challenges our moral and ethical codes. Oregon has physician-assisted suicide, but most states do not. Long-term care insurance is heavily advertised and prohibitive in cost. Do we want a funeral service or a wake, cremation or a coffin and plot? Have we made adequate financial arrangements for a durable power of attorney or a family limited liability partnership (LLP)? Should we discuss a do-not-resuscitate (DNR) order with our doctor? These and other matters occupy our late-in-life thoughts. At least people in our society plan ahead better now than in previous years, and planning ahead is vital to those who are left behind. Most family members will carry out the wishes of the deceased if they know what they are.

Recent research has focused on hundreds of centenarians, and these studies are showing some surprises about the elderly (Cutter, 2008). Centenarians were found to share the same characteristics of healthy aging, with the most important factors being maintaining close relationships with family and friends and possessing a healthy mental and physical lifestyle. One centenarian, Maurice Eisman, offered his advice for long life: "Never stop learning." To demonstrate that these centenarians were in tune with today's culture: nearly half of all respondents could identify the most recent *American Idol* winner, 19 percent used cell phones and automatic teller machines, and 3 percent had dated someone they met on the Internet (Hitti, 2008). It is projected that by the year 2025, this country will have at least 275,000 centenarians. These and other studies offer optimism for those in their elder years (Hitti, 2008).

Summary

This chapter has presented many aspects of the socialization process and shown it to be a central force in affecting who we are and how we behave. We are indebted to authors and researchers who spent years studying all of the ramifications of socialization so that we could gain a better understanding of how it affects us and our society. After looking at many facets of the socialization process, we can take with us a greater awareness and appreciation of it.

Review/Discussion Questions

1. What are some agents of socialization?
2. According to Elizabeth Kubler-Ross, what are the five stages of dying?
3. What is pre-conventional morality?
4. Where do you stand on the nature versus nurture debate? Which do you think has the strongest influence on who we are?
5. When you were a child, which occupation did you envision yourself performing when you grew up? How does it match with what you do now?
6. According to Cooley's looking-glass theory we are all influenced by our perception of what we think others think of us. Do you think this is true? In what ways have you let others people's judgment of you alter your behavior?

Key Terms

Adult socialization is the process by which adults learn new statuses and roles.

Ageism is the process of stereotyping people based on their age.

Anticipatory socialization involves learning the skills and values needed for future roles.

Aptitude is the capacity to develop physical or social skills.

Conventional morality is Kohlberg's term for people incorporating society's rules and laws into their own value systems and behaving accordingly.

Developmental socialization is the process by which people learn to be more competent in their currently assumed roles.

Ego is Freud's term for the part of the personality that deals with the real world on the basis of reason and helps to integrate the demands of both the id and the superego.

Gender refers to learned behavior involving how we are expected to act as males and females in society.

Gender role refers to how we should act as males or females.

Gender typing refers to acquiring behavior that is considered appropriate for one's particular gender.

Generalized others are people that are not necessarily close to a child but still help influence the child's internalization of societal values.

Id is Freud's term for the part of the personality that is totally unconscious and consists of biological drives.

Intelligence is the capacity for mental or intellectual achievement.

Looking-glass self is Cooley's theory that we are influenced by our perception of what others think of us and develop our self-image on that basis.

Peer group includes a person's same-aged friends with similar interests and social positions.

Personality refers to a person's patterns of thoughts, feelings, and self-concepts that make him or her distinctive from others.

Post-conventional morality is the highest level of morality available, according to Kohlberg. At this level, people use broad ethical principles to guide their behavior, such as showing respect for human dignity, equality, and, of late, respect for one's environment—even for the rights of animals and other living creatures.

Pre-conventional morality is Kohlberg's term for abiding by the law chiefly to avoid punishment or to gain some benefit.

Primary socialization is the period during which children learn language and basic behavioral patterns that form the foundation for later learning.

Resocialization is the process by which people must leave behind their old selves and develop new ones.

Secondary socialization takes place later in childhood and into maturity. In this phase, other agents of socialization take over some of the responsibility from family.

Sex refers to the biological feature of sexual identity that each of us plays, such as in reproduction.

Significant others are those people who are the closest to, and have the strongest influence on, a child, and whose approval and affection they desire most.

Socialization is the process whereby we internalize our culture's values, beliefs, and norms. Through this experience, we become functioning members of our society.

Superego is Freud's term for the part of the personality that acts as the "executive branch" because it uses reason and it deals with whether something is right or wrong.

Total institutions are places where people are cut off from the larger society and forced to follow a strict set of rules.

Bibliography

Belsky, J. (2004). Experiencing the Life Span: Class Test Version. Boston: W. H. Freeman & Company.

Berk, L. E. (2006). Development Through the Lifespan. Danbury: Allyn & Bacon.

Butler, R. N. (1969). Age-ism: Another form of bigotry. The Gerontologist, 9, 243-246.

Corey, G., & Schneider Corey, M. (2005). I Never Knew I Had a Choice: Explorations in Personal Growth. Belmont, CA: Wadsworth.

Curry, T., Jiobu, R., & Schwirian, K. (2007). Sociology for the Twenty-First Century. Upper Saddle River: Prentice Hall.

Cutter, J. (2008). Living Well to 100. MedicineNet. <http://www.medicinenet.com/script/main/art.asp?articlekey=51451> (2008).

Dodgen, L. I. & Rapp, A. M. (2008). Sociology: Looking through the Window of the World. Dubuque, IA: Kendall/Hunt Publisher Co.

Duffy, K. G. (Ed.). (1996). Annual Reports: Psychology (95/96). New York: McGraw-Hill/Dushkin.

Durkheim, E. (1956). Education and Sociology. New York: Free Press.

Ensher, G. L., & Clark, D. A. (2009). Families, Infants, and Young Children at Risk. New York: Paul H. Brookes Co.

Feldman, R. S. (2006). Understanding Psychology. Boston: McGraw-Hill.

Ferris, K., Stein, J., & Meyer, A. E. (2008). The Real World : An Introduction to Sociology. Boston: W. W. Norton & Company.

Freud, S. (1927). A General Introduction to Psychoanalysis. New York: Boni and Liveright.

Freud, S. (1953). A Religious Experience. In J. Strachey (Ed.), Standard edition of the complete psychological works of Sigmund Freud. London, UK: Hogarth Press. , 1064.

Giddens, A. (2008). Essentials of Sociology (2nd ed.). New York: Norton and Company.

Gilligan, C. (1982). In a Different Voice : Psychological Theory and Women's Development. New York: Harvard University Press.

Hillier, S. M., & Barrow, G. M. (2007). Aging, the Individual, and Society. Belmont, CA: Brooks/Cole.

Hitti, M. (2008). Healthy Tips for Centenarians. WebMD. <http://www.webmd.com/healthy-aging/news/20080729/10-healthy-aging-tips-from-centenarians> (2008).

Kendall, D. E. (2007). Sociology in Our Times : The Essentials. Belmont, CA: Thomson/Wadsworth.

Kubler-Ross, E. (1969). On Death and Dying. New York: MacMillan.

Lawrence, P., & Nohria, N. (2002). Driven : How Human Nature Shapes Our Choices. San Francisco: Jossey-Bass.

Lemert, C. C. (2008). Social Things : An Introduction to the Sociological Life. New York: Rowman & Littlefield, Inc.

Lightfoot, C. (2008). The Development of Children (6th ed.). New York: Worth Publishers.

Lindsey, L. L. & Beach, S. (2000). Sociology: Social Life and Social Issues. Upper Saddle River, NJ: Pearson.

Macionis, J. J. (2007). Society: The Basics. Upper Saddle River, NJ: Pearson Prentice Hall.

Maslow, A. (1987). Motivation and Personality (3rd ed.). New York: Harper and Row.

Maslow, A. (2008). Maslow's Hierarchy of Needs. <http://Chiron.valdosta.edu/whuitt/col/regsys/Maslow.html> (2008).

Mead, George H. (1934). Mind, self & society from the standpoint of a social behaviorist. Chicago, IL: University of Chicago Press.

Miller, B. (1980). The Contribution of Lawrence Kohlberg to the Study of Moral Development. Unpublished dissertation.

Norwood, G. (2002). Maslow's Hierarchy of Needs. <http://www.deepermind.com/20maslow.htm> (2002, May).

Novak, M. (2008). Issues in Aging. Boston: Pearson/Allyn & Bacon.

Popenoe, D. (2000). Sociology. Upper Saddle River, NJ: Prentice Hall.

Rathus, S. A. (2000). Essentials of Psychology. Fort Worth: Harcourt Brace College Publishers.

Rymer, R. (1993). Genie: An Abused Child's Flight from Silence. New York: HarperCollins.

Santrock, J. W. (2007). Child Development (11th ed.). Boston: McGraw-Hill.

Schaefer, R. (2009). Sociology: a brief introduction (8th ed.). New York: McGraw-Hill.

Schaie, K. W., & Abeles, R. P. (Eds.). (2008). Social Structures and Aging Individuals: Continuing Challenges. New York: Springer Publishing.

Sheehy, G. (1976). Passages: predictable crises of life. New York: Dutton.

Sullivan, T. J. (2007). Sociology: concepts and applications in a diverse world (7th ed.). Danbury, CT: Allyn & Bacon.

Thio, A. (2005). Sociology: A Brief Introduction (6th ed.). Boston: Pearson/Allyn & Bacon.

Tischler, H. L. (2007). Introduction to Sociology (9th ed.). Belmont, CA: Wadsworth/Thomson Learning.

Treas J. (1995). Older Americans in the 1990s and beyond. Population Bulletin, 50 (2).

U. S. Census Bureau (2004). Educational Attainment. <http://www.census.gov> (2008).

CHAPTER FOUR

Social Structure And Social Interaction

XueMei Hu

In society, we structure our behavior through the statuses that we occupy and the roles that we play. As human beings, we have considerable ability to shape the patterns of social interaction and creatively build reality through such interactions. In this chapter, we will first examine social structure with a macro-level perspective. We will explore how the structure determines the statuses we hold, the roles we play, and the groups and social institutions to which we belong. Then we will move on to the study of social interaction, through which we build reality.

Building Blocks Of Social Structure

In order to understand human behavior in society, we need to understand **social structure**, which refers to the social relationships that exist within society. Social relationships in a society guide our behavior and provide us with the framework for interacting with others. Our behavior is patterned by social influences and guided by social structure. Human beings rely on this structure to make sense of situations in everyday life. As an example of social structure, imagine that you are now listening to a lecture by a professor in a classroom. You hold the status of a student and play the role of a student, while your professor occupies the status of an instructor and plays the role of an instructor. There is a relationship between the students in the social group (classmates) and the instructor. Both you and your instructor behave according to learned behaviors and attitudes based on your respective statuses in the social structure.

Society uses social structure to set the rules of everyday life. Society is cooperation; it is community in action, with females and males of all ages, and all races and ethnicities, interacting within groups and social institutions of a particular society. If there are clear-cut rules to follow, human beings know how to act and react in relation to others. Society is the outcome of conscious and purposeful behavior; it is the complex sum of mutual relations.

The building blocks of society include statuses and roles, groups, and social institutions, as illustrated in Chart 4.1. In every society, people rely on social structure to make sense of their life experiences. The following section provides a macro-level analysis of statuses and roles, examining the ways in which society sets the rules of everyday life.

Statuses And Roles

How an individual behaves in society is determined by two factors: status and role. In every society, people build lives that are based on the statuses they occupy. Statuses and roles are part of the basic framework for living in society.

Status

Status refers to a social position—characterized by rights and duties—that is held by a person. Our status guides our behavior in different social situations and is an important part of how we define ourselves. Before we can deal with anyone, we need to know who the person is (Simmel, 1955). A social position that someone occupies may carry a great deal of prestige, as in the case of a CEO or a lawyer, or little prestige, as in the case of a factory worker. The status of an ex-convict may be looked down upon. Therefore, status is an indicator of social identity, which helps define our relationships to others.

Ascribed Status And Achieved Status

People may attain statuses through events over which they have no control (ascribed status), or through personal effort and choice (achieved status). An **ascribed status** is a social position that a person receives at birth or assumes involuntarily later in life. We inherit ascribed statuses at birth based on biological factors such as race, ethnicity, gender, age, and the social class of our parents. Examples of ascribed status include being a son, a Hispanic American, a poor person, a teenager, or a woman. Some people inherit ascribed statuses based on the social class of their parents. Popular culture in the United States has created a list of babies who are born into the status of celebrity, such as Brad Pitt and Angelina Jolie's twins, who are likely to be in the spotlight their entire lives because of their famous parents.

An **achieved status** is a social position that a person earns through personal effort and choice, like education, occupation, and income. These statuses can be earned or accomplished, and thus they are voluntary. They can also be positive or negative. If you are an honors student, CEO, computer engineer, or professor, you have earned positive achieved statuses through direct effort. In modern American society, when individuals have been successful in their education and careers, their level of financial se-

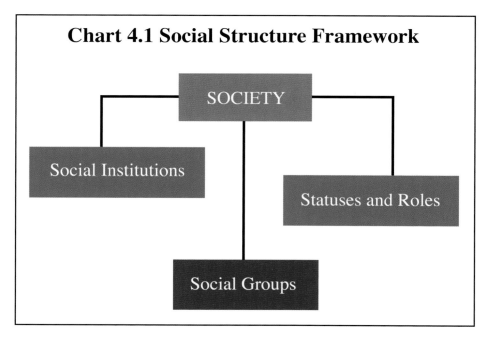

Chart 4.1 Social Structure Framework

SOCIETY

Social Institutions

Statuses and Roles

Social Groups

curity typically changes their status. If a person does not make an effort, perhaps dropping out of high school, he or she earns a negative achieved status. Achieved statuses can reveal a great deal about a person's background and values.

Each status provides guidelines for behavior. Like other parts of the social structure, a status sets limits on what we can and cannot do. How we behave in groups is determined by statuses. Everybody occupies multiple statuses in society, some ascribed, some achieved. If asked who you are, you may make a list of your statuses. You might answer, "I am a daughter, a mother, a wife, a student, a woman, an African-American, and a store manager." Our statuses are often a combination of ascribed and achieved factors.

Can An Ascribed Status Influence Achieved Status?

Equality is considered an American value, but there is still a discrepancy between legal equality and social equality. Theoretically, it is possible for any person to experience upward social mobility. Anyone can become highly educated, successful in their occupation, and earn a high income through their efforts. However, those born into certain conditions and circumstances may be at an advantage or disadvantage to gain certain achieved statuses. People born into wealthy and prominent families often have better opportunities to achieve high levels of education and obtain prime jobs because of their social connections. On the other hand, those born into poor families have to set themselves apart from the competition to get those same opportunities. Though there are many laws like affirmative action to protect minority groups, ascribed statuses can hinder the attainment of certain achieved statuses.

Male and female cultures differ, with each having a direct impact on achieved statuses in the workplace. Male culture deters the advancement of women into management positions, and contributes to communication gaps. Andrew Agapiou refers to men in the workplace as gatekeepers and believes that men and women are trying to find ways in which they might work together and "comfortably reconcile issues of gender" (Agapiou, 2002, p.

697). Michael Peterson points out that "success for women emphasized values, the corporate culture, and work/family balance" (RTO Online, 2005, p. 1). Peterson continues by drawing a comparison, stating that, "In contrast, male-oriented culture is based on the assumptions that work is for the purpose of achievement and fortune, and that for a business to be successful it must recognize the importance of achieving results" (RTO Online, 2005, p. 2).

Women's roles have changed significantly since the early 1960s, when they were generally depicted in the media solely as wives and mothers (Schaefer, 2006). The Civil Rights Act of 1964 created the Equal Employment Opportunity Commission (EEOC) to enforce laws designed to prevent employment discrimination, extending the act beyond the original grounds of Title VII—race, color, sex, national origin, and religion—to include pregnancy, age (40 and over), and disability. It also extended coverage to governmental entities (U.S. Equal Employment Opportunity Commission, 2002). The EEOC protects the rights of all individuals to be considered for jobs based solely on their abilities, and to have a work environment free from abusive practices.

Other factors can affect a person's achieved statuses. Youth can be an advantage, because many employers believe that younger people will stay with their organizations longer, but it can also be a disadvantage if youth is equated with inexperience. Along the same lines, age can be an advantage if it is considered to be a sign of experience and maturity, but a disadvantage if it is thought to indicate that a person is nearing retirement and may not be as focused on his or her career. Height, weight, personality, race, ethnicity, and many other factors can also come into play when a person wants to achieve a certain status.

Master Status

Each of us occupies many statuses in life. Among these, one status may matter more than the others. A status that determines a person's overall social position and identity is called a **master status**. A master status overshadows our other statuses, and can be either ascribed or achieved. For example, a high-paying occupation may be a master status for some people since it reflects education, income, and social status.

A master status can have positive and negative consequences. If you are very wealthy, your wealth is likely to become a master status because it cuts across other statuses. When a person suffers from cancer, close friends might avoid him or her because of the illness. Illness or disability can be seen as a master status because others may see people only in those terms. For example, Stephen Hawking is severely disabled by Lou Gehrig's disease and, for some, his master status is that of a person with disabilities. Because Hawking is one of the greatest physicists who has ever lived, however, his outstanding achievements have given him another master status, that of world-class physicist in the ranking of Einstein (Henslin, 2008).

In society, we tend to socialize with people who are similar to us and, thus, our statuses usually match and fit together. However, some people also want to socialize with people who are different. **Status inconsistency** occurs when people have a mismatch between their statuses, such as an 18-year-old girl marrying a 60-year-old man. People may feel conflicted about such situations because statuses are characterized by built-in expectations or norms that guide behaviors. Status inconsistency deviates from expected behaviors and can create uncertainty or discomfort.

Status Set

A **status set** includes all of the statuses that a person occupies at a given time. Our status set defines who we are in society, and multiple roles attached to each status define what we do. You may simultaneously be a father, computer engineer, and husband, or a daughter, student, part-time store clerk, and grandchild. Over each stage of our life cycle, we gain and lose statuses and our status set changes. When you are a 2-year-old male toddler, you may be a son to your parents and a younger brother to a sister. As you grow up, you may also become a student, or even a filmmaker in a television production class. You may graduate from law school and become a lawyer, in addition to being a son and a brother. If you marry, you also become a husband, and, possibly, a father. You might even become a single person again because of divorce. Therefore, status sets can and do change over the course of our lives.

Role

Sociologists see roles as essential to our social behaviors. How we behave in society is determined not only by the statuses we occupy, but also by the roles we play. **Roles** refer to socially defined expectations associated with a given status. When we occupy a status, we play a corresponding role. Roles are characterized by behaviors, privileges, rights, and obligations. For example, as you occupy the status of a student, you are expected to play the role of student. This means that you have the right to ask questions and voice your opinions in class, but you are also obligated to attend class, read the material, do the homework, take the tests, and complete any other assignments.

Role Expectation And Role Performance

Sociologists differentiate between role expectation and role performance. **Role expectation** relates to the expectations required of a role, while **role performance** covers the actual delivery of those expectations. If a woman is a mother, the role expectation attached to that status is that she care and provide for her child. The role performance would be her actual day-to-day mothering activities.

Role Set

Each person holds many statuses at any given time; thus, everyday life is a mixture of multiple roles. Robert Merton introduced the term role set. **Role set** refers to a number of roles that can be attached to a single status. If you occupy the statuses of mother, daughter, and manager, each of those statuses is linked to a different role set. First, you occupy the status of a mother. You play a *maternal role* when engaging in child-rearing responsibilities like teaching basic skills and providing economic and emotional support. You also play a *civic role* when driving your children to school and extracurricular activities. In addition, you play a *model role* when you control your behavior to set a good example. In your second status, as a wife, you play a *marital role*, such as being a sexual partner to your husband, and a *domestic role*, such as doing chores. Finally, in the status of manager, you play an *administrator role* when you meet with supervisors and complete the payroll on time. You also play a *leadership role* when you make plans, set deadlines, resolve problems, and implement projects.

Role Conflict And Role Strain

People in modern societies pursue their educational goals and careers in order to make a living. As a result, they must to learn how to juggle the responsibilities of their multiple statuses and roles. It is not always easy to maneuver between family, work, and school, and people holding multiples statuses, playing multiple roles, are more likely to be physically and emotionally overburdened. **Work spillover** is the effect that paid and volunteer work can have on individuals and families, absorbing their time and energy and impinging on their psychological states. On the positive side, family and friends can help alleviate workplace stress. On the negative side, the demands of our home lives may impinge on our concentration, energy, and availability at work.

Role conflict refers to conflicting demands that are connected to two or more coexisting statuses. If you are a working mother and part-time student, you may often experience the conflicting demands of work, child care, and school assignments. Because of role conflict, people sometimes postpone marriage or put off having children in order to pursue career success. For example, let's consider an extroverted manager who desires interpersonal closeness appropriate to a workplace. In addition to this role as more of a friend, he or she also needs to act as a boss and manage the staff effectively to achieve organizational goals. Role conflict might occur when this type of manager needs to reprimand an employee that is under-performing, especially if the manager is aware of the personal difficulties of the employee, such as him or her going through a divorce.

Role strain refers to conflicting demands connected to one single status. A college student may

hold only that status, but tasks ranging from school work for each course to extracurricular activities may be physically and emotionally draining. Similarly, many single mothers raising children on their own are overburdened financially, physically, and emotionally.

Role Strain And Role Conflict

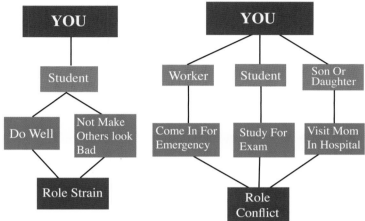

Role Exit

People often move from one role to another—student to employee, single male to husband, married mom to divorced mom. **Role exit** refers to the process by which people disengage from a role. Ex-husbands, ex-alcoholics, ex-nuns, and ex-doctors are examples of people who have experienced a role exit. Each "ex" role has common elements. According to Helen Ebaugh, the exit process begins when people come to doubt their ability to continue in a certain role. When they want to disengage from a role that they have been playing, they picture alternative roles and may eventually decide to pursue a new life. Exes move on and build a new image that is still influenced by the past role. An ex-nun may be fearful of wearing makeup and oversized sunglasses, learning new social skills, and interacting in different social networks. According to Ebaugh's observations, ex-nuns who enter the dating scene after decades in the church are often surprised to learn that sexual norms are very different from those they knew when they were teenagers (1988).

Groups

Groups are the second major building block of society. In sociology, a **group** refers to a collection of people characterized by more than two people who share frequent interaction, a sense of belongingness, and interdependence. Like statuses and roles, the groups to which we belong can become social forces and thus influence our behaviors. When we belong to a group, we are obligated to behave according to the expectations of other group members. In addition, each member of a group occupies a status and is expected to play a corresponding role. In this way, people within a group are interdependent and cooperate in order to build consensus and survive together. The topic of groups will be covered more thoroughly in Chapter 5.

Social Institutions

Social institutions are the third building block of society. **Social institutions** are organized beliefs, rules, and practices established by society to meet its basic needs. Social institutions include family, education, religion, economics, politics, and health care. These social institutions—each with its own groups, statuses, and roles—weave the fabric of society and shape our behaviors. Social institutions will be covered in depth in Chapters 11 through 14.

Social Interaction

Social interaction is of major importance in sociology because it is the foundation of meaningful relationships in society. We are all social creatures and enjoy interacting. **Social interaction** refers to reciprocal communication between two or more people through symbols, words, and body language. Our daily lives are organized around the repetition of similar patterns of social interaction. Studying these social interactions shows us how people can act together to shape reality and enables us to better understand social institutions and entire societies.

Sociological Perspectives

Functionalist theory emphasizes supportive interactions, with people treating others as supporters or friends. Conflict theory on social interaction emphasizes oppositional interactions, contending that people treat others as competitors or enemies. Symbolic interactionists interpret others' behaviors

Social Institution	Basic Needs	Groups or Organization	Statuses	Roles
Family	Regulate sexual activity, reproduce, socialize child	Kinship	Son, daughter, father, mother grandparent	Provide food and shelter, respect parents
Religion	Explain why we exist and suffer	Church, cult, denomination	Priest, minister, worshipper	Read and adhere to texts
Education	Transmit skills and knowledge across generations	School, college PTA, AAUP, sports team	Teacher, dean student, football player	Get good grades, follow teaching ethics
Economy	Produce, distribute goods and services	Banks, buying clubs, stores	Employee, boss buyer, seller	Earn income, pay bills on time
Politics	Exercise power, regulate relationships	Political party, congress, government	President, senator, voter, lobbyist	Distribute power equally, vote
Healthcare	Initiate activity to heal the sick and prevent illness	HMOs, hospital pharmacies, health insurance	Doctor, nurse, patient, insurer, pharmacist	Follow work ethics, follow doctor's order

and act accordingly. Each of these three approaches strives to answer the question of why people do what they do.

Functionalist Perspective: Supportive Interactions

The functionalist perspective on social interaction examines societies, social structures, and social systems primarily on a macro-level. The functionalist perspective emphasizes the way that parts of a society are structured to maintain its stability. It looks at a society in a positive manner; all of its parts work together, supporting each other and contributing to the survival of the society. People are viewed as being socially molded, not forced, to perform societal functions. Order in a society, as viewed by a functionalist, is maintained when its members cooperate with one another. Functionalists emphasize social stability.

Emile Durkheim and Talcott Parsons were responsible for the development of the functionalist perspective, and the contemporary functionalist perspective on supportive interactions derives its foundation from Durkheim. Supportive interactions are positive ways in which we communicate with others, reinforcing solidarity and unity in groups. Two examples of positive supports are making each transition positive and attempting to understand things from the other's point of view. Transitions like greetings and goodbyes can be made more positive through rituals that offer a sense of support, such as handshakes, hugs, and enthusiastic words. When you listen to people speak, remain calm and respectful, and allow them to express their emotions. This will minimize the chances of offending someone.

One of the most important characteristics of a great communicator is the ability to really listen to other people. Learning to actively listen can help us move past our assumptions and overlook distractions. If a speaker feels he or she is not being heard, it has a negative impact on that speaker's ability to communicate effectively in a specific situation, and both the speaker and the listener lose. It is essential to interact in a caring and encouraging manner in order to develop positive social skills. If other people experience trouble in a situation, we should provide support and help them work through the difficulties. Even routine interactions can incorporate supportive factors. For instance, non-English speakers may have a hard time keeping up with the pace of our speech, or maybe our mouths are speaking faster than we can think and our words become jumbled. We need to think about how others process what we are saying in order to make our interactions more supportive.

Exchange And Cooperation

Supportive interactions are based on exchange and cooperation. Exchange means that two individuals offer each other something to obtain a reward, such as a symbol of approval or prestige, in return. Cooperation means that two or more individuals work together to achieve a common goal. Spontaneous cooperation occurs in an emergency. On May 12, 2008, a powerful earthquake measuring 7.9 on the Richter scale struck Sichuan province in southwestern China, killing thousands of people. The American Red Cross worked with the International Red Cross, the Red Cross Society of China, the Red Crescent Movement and other partners to provide aid for those people affected by the disaster.

Reciprocity

Supportive interactions are often reciprocal. Speakers want to give and receive support in interactions, simultaneously conveying and receiving acceptance and preserving the autonomy of both parties. Previous research on the presence or absence of supportive communication has overlooked how support is conveyed and how some message characteristics accomplish multiple goals. By highlighting these multiple goals, politeness theory integrates previous research on the dilemmas of supportive communication and characteristics of helpful and unhelpful messages. **Politeness theory** is the idea that communicators change and adopt their messages to protect and save the "face" or image of their listeners. The communicator's goal, then, is to get his or her intended message across without insulting, embarrassing, or discomfiting the listener.

Conflict Perspective: Oppositional Interactions

The conflict perspective on social interaction also focuses primarily on macro-level analysis of societies, social structures, and social systems. According to the conflict perspective, social behavior is understood in terms of conflict between different groups or individuals. In contrast to the functionalist view of stability, conflict sociologists see societies as being engaged in constant struggle and change.

According to Karl Marx, conflicts between classes of society are inevitable because workers are exploited as a result of capitalism. Individuals are perceived as being shaped by power and authority, and order in a society is maintained through social forces. This perspective contends that social inequality exists, with different groups competing for scarce resources, and these conflicts lead to social change. Contemporary conflict perspective on social interaction is derived from this foundation, with a focus on oppositional interactions between groups and individuals. An example occurs when a dominant group uses an ethnocentric idea to evaluate another group. Ethnocentrism uses one's own cultural standards or norms as a basis to evaluate another culture. If one group is considered ideal, then all others are judged based on how far they differ from that norm. This can produce some irrelevant comparisons and conclusions, benefitting one culture at the expense of others. This brings up the old insider/outsider debate in which the people on the "inside" make value judgments on practices and procedures that are unique and customary in that society or culture. According to the conflict perspective, there is no value to reinforcing ethnocentrism because there is no group, as a whole, that is superior in intelligence, physical attributes, humanity, religion, social earnings, or the arts to any other.

Oppositional Interactions: Competition, Conflict, And Coercion

According to conflict theory, people treat others as competitors, and sometimes even as enemies. In competition, each person or group tries to gain control over limited resources before the others.

Conflict in social interactions is inevitable when individuals respond to each other with a different pace or attitude. Even simple words like "soon," "urgent," "shared," "polite," and "respectful" have different meanings for different individuals. If we encounter conflict, we should step back and listen before reacting. Listening is the key to any interaction, and to any professional or personal relationship. Coercion occurs when one person or group forces its will upon another. Usually, a dominant group uses threats or physical force to get subordinate groups to accept its will.

Symbolic Interactionist Perspective: Interpreting Interactions

Social interaction is the foundation for all relationships and groups in society. Functionalist and conflict theories provide a macrosociological analysis because they focus on large-scale structures and events. For example, from a macro-level perspective, you as a sociologist would examine how social institutions like families and schools have helped to cause teenage pregnancies. By contrast, the symbolic interactionist perspective provides a microsociological overview. Sociologists studying the problem of teenage pregnancy would ask how teenagers are influenced in their daily interactions and their behaviors within small groups. In other words, symbolic interactionists study the small scale in order to understand the large scale.

The origins of this approach can be traced to the Chicago School. George Herbert Mead and Herbert Blumer (1900-1986) coined the term *symbolic interactionism*, and Mead is credited with founding the interactionist perspective. Mead was a professor at the University of Chicago, and there he focused on the analysis of one-to-one situations and small groups. He paid particular attention to body language, such as a frown or nod, and asked how other group members affected these gestures (Schaefer & Lamm, 1998). Symbolic interactionists study behavior—how people react to their surroundings, including material things, actions, other people, and symbols. The interactionist view of society is that

Talking and listening to one another.

Source: Carlos Paes

we influence each other through everyday social interactions. Interactionists believe that individuals create their own social world through interactions, and social order is maintained when people share their understanding of everyday behaviors. From this perspective, social change is seen to occur when the positions and communications of the individuals and small groups change.

Interpreting Supportive Interactions

The symbolic interactionist perspective focuses on the process of interaction, interpreting people's behaviors and acting accordingly. *Social interaction* refers to reciprocal communication between two or more people through symbols, words, and body language; it is the process by which we respond to others. This definition involves two components. First, interaction involves supportive interchanges, mutual dealings, and reciprocal results. Secondly, the inter-

action takes place between two or more people. Communication demands respect. We expect people to communicate with respect when that is how we communicate with them. If we are being rude to one another, we have a breakdown in communication. Communication should also incorporate honor so that, we can honor people even if they are not honorable.

People interpret social interactions and shape reality. Social interaction occurs when people interact and communicate through the use of symbols. According to the symbolic interactionist perspective, human beings create and use symbols to convey shared meanings. They also know how to interpret the meanings of the symbols to understand social interactions. Symbolic interaction takes place nonverbally in a variety of ways, including facial expression, posture, tone of voice, and gestures like handshakes, bows, and hugs. *Symbols* refer to anything that represents something else. Examples of symbols include language based on words, both written and oral, and nonverbal language like signs and body language. For example, a gift of red roses is a symbol of love, and a gift of chocolate to a new officemate is a symbol of welcome and friendship. People interpret social interactions through the shared meanings of such symbols.

Interpreting Oppositional Interactions

In the business world, you might have noticed a difference in the way people speak to one another depending on their corporate positions. Managers are usually authoritative and direct when speaking to subordinates. Subordinates may exhibit a certain giddiness when speaking to people in a higher position, especially if they are eager to please. People also treat those from other social classes very differently. For example, people of a higher social class sometimes speak very slowly and are condescending towards those of lower classes. Why does this happen, and does it frustrate you? Do you put the blame for this on both parties? Consider a manager and an employee. Is it possible that the manager makes the employee feel uncomfortable, while the employee allows the manager to be intimidating? This might suggest the need for training, one session focusing on how to manage with a focus on empowering employees, and another on building self-esteem.

Symbolic Interaction: Principles And Shared Definitions

Social interaction is the foundation of meaningful relationships in society. Having a good foundation or structure is the backbone of our interactions with others. Symbolic interactionists consider society the sum of social interactions between people and groups. Symbolic interactionists focus on understanding how people make sense of their everyday social interactions and their world.

Shared Definition Of A Situation And Human Behavior

Symbolic interactionists seek to understand human behavior from an individual viewpoint. Ev-

erybody defines a situation differently, and those definitions become the foundation for how everyone behaves.

Let's look at specific scenarios. When you see a woman struggling with a heavy object, you quickly come to her aid because you consider yourself to be a helpful person. You have done this on two occasions. In one instance, the lady was very happy after you lent a hand and offered to buy you a cup of coffee. In another instance, you were shocked when you were told to back off. People define situations differently and thus react differently to situations based on those definitions. Think of yourself as a young man. If a 55-year-old woman offers to help with something you are struggling with, how would you define the situation and how would you react to her and behave? Maybe the woman is offering to help because she has the capabilities to help you, or maybe she always wants to help others from a humanitarian perspective. Do you decline or accept her invitation? If you decline, is it because of pride?

People with different personalities will act toward, and respond to, each other in different ways. It is important to share the meanings of how we behave. For example, some people greet others by saying "Good morning," while others hug. The Chinese and Japanese greatly value respect for authority figures and the elderly. In Japan, it is said that a long time ago when a worker was forced to criticize his boss in front of his colleagues, he killed himself afterward because of his disrespectful behavior. In traditional societies, if you as a student ask questions in class, it is likely to be considered a challenge, assault, or disrespectful behavior. If you try to correct a Japanese professor's pronunciation, it is also considered disrespectful behavior. In the Hispanic community, people enjoy a "touchy-feely" culture because they grow up in an affectionate environment. People give hugs and kisses when saying hello or goodbye. When men say hello to women, touching each other—like patting a shoulder or holding the waist while giving a kiss—is a sign of friendship. However, it might be considered a sign of a sexual harassment in the mainstream culture or in other subcultures. People who share meanings about how to interact with each other also under-

The busy streets of New York City.   Source: Gayle Lindgren

stand that there are lines that should not be crossed. Problems are more likely to occur when meanings are not shared.

Different generations do not always share meanings related to social interaction. Members of Generation X would not behave the way their parents or baby boomers did due to different shared meanings. However, we might notice that the older we get, the more we act like our parents as our shared meanings change.

Consequences Of The Definition Of A Situation

Symbolic interactionists further contend that the definition of a given situation has consequences and affects social interactions now and in the future. According to symbolic interactionists, our behavior and subjective reality are shaped by our social interactions with others. Sociologists Charles H. Cooley

and George Herbert Mead explored how individual personalities are developed by social experience. Every time we engage in a new interaction, we have to define and interpret the situation. In a new encounter, we have to negotiate the situation all over again. We try to make sense of our situations and either derive shared meanings from them or comprehend the outcome.

Global Diversity In Social Interactions

Race, ethnicity, gender, and social class often influence people's perceptions of shared meanings and how they interact with each other. The way we respond to people has a lot to do with the way we live. In New York City, for example, the lifestyle is fast-paced and people are too rushed to have idle conversations. In areas with a slower pace, we find people more prone to converse with strangers. Interactions within a given society have certain shared meanings across cultures. For example, in the United States, working lunches are the norm and it is not uncommon to discuss business with a meal. Other societies close deals with different norms and shared values.

Dramaturgy: Social Interaction As Drama

Dramaturgical analysis is a perspective of social interaction that compares everyday life to a dramatic presentation in a theater, as if everybody in real life were performing on a stage. Social interaction is affected by both verbal and nonverbal communication.

Dramaturgy

Erving Goffman (1922-1982) was a sociologist who studied social interaction. He developed **dramaturgical analysis**, which is a perspective that compares everyday life to a theatrical performance in order to study social interaction. This view asserts that we live our lives just like actors and actresses performing on a stage. Central to this analysis is a process called the *presentation of self*, meaning an individual's effort to create specific impressions in the minds of others. Presentation of self involves representing ourselves in ways that are favorable to our own interests or image. Dramaturgical analysis involves such elements as behaving like actors, the presentation of self, impression management, face work, performing rituals, and front and back stages.

Behaving Like Actors

Individuals depend on social context and act accordingly. Our script is based on the statuses that we occupy and the roles that we play in everyday situations. As we present ourselves in everyday life, we try to create impressions in the minds of others. We follow societal standards and present ourselves to other people. We sometimes change or modify our behavior in accordance with what a particular group of people expects of us. At work, we may be diligent and respectful. When we are out with friends, we might swear and drink alcohol, possibly because of peer pressure. In everyday situations, we try to control how others perceive us by modifying our behavior in response to their reactions and to correspond to an ideal role like best employee, best friend, or best group member.

The Presentation Of Self

From the dramaturgy perspective, performance is the heart of social interaction. It involves presenting the self, which Goffman described as impression management (1959). **Impression management** refers to our efforts to present favorable images to the people around us. Everybody holds status and plays roles, just like actors playing parts in a play with dialogue and actions for their characters. The actors perform their parts in order to create specific impressions in the minds of the audience. Everybody in real life is doing the same thing whether they are trying to impress a boss, a teacher, or a date. Goffman referred to the conscious and unconscious efforts of people in conveying information about themselves as performances. These performances will vary by the setting or physical location in which they occur. Everyone's performance is a presentation of self, making an effort to make the right impressions on people.

The fact that people attempt to play the best possible role is also called **face work**. We make every effort to give the best possible performance in order to avoid "losing face," but, in reality, we are often in danger of losing face because there can be so many differences in the criteria, definitions of situations, and cultural norms and values used to measure performance. **Face-saving behavior** refers to the techniques that people use to salvage their performances when they encounter a potential or actual loss of face. Face is a multi-faceted term. The meaning is linked to culture and terms like honor and humiliation. One of the most familiar meanings of "saving face" is not being disrespectful to others in public. The word face can be interchanged with credibility or reputation.

Different cultures place different levels of importance on face-saving behavior. In American culture, saving face is not so much about honor as it is about ego. In Hispanic culture, face is held in very high regard. People of this culture tend not to say "no" in order to avoid confrontation. People might be considered as lacking respect for others in public if they cut in front of people who have been waiting patiently in a line. In most social interactions, all of the role players have an interest in keeping the play going so that they can maintain their overall definition of the situation.

Controlling a situation can be difficult at times, especially when you cannot predict how people are going to react. Some people do not play their roles well and upset the people around them. Everyone in this world fears looking stupid or feeling embarrassed, though some more strongly than others. If you as a contestant during a show forget your lines while performing, you just keep going and do your best to give a good performance. If you stop, everyone will notice the error. Nonverbal expressions are sometimes used as a way to save face. Some people smirk slightly or lower their heads to control their feelings and save face. Sometimes, people might forgive the role failures of others, knowing that the next time they could be the one failing in a role.

Performing Interaction Rituals

On a stage, presentation of self includes the way we dress (costume), the objects we carry (props), and our tone of voice and gestures (manner). When we interact with each other, we also take the setting into consideration. We may yell and cheer loudly at a football game, but speak softly in a fancy restaurant. In a very casual atmosphere where everyone is laughing and joking, we are able to relax. At a fairly quiet party in a more sophisticated setting, being loud and trying to get noticed by everyone would be a negative breach of interaction rituals. If we are at a meeting that has structure, we do not want to be the person blurting things out or moving around and creating a distraction. In real situations, we judge how to best create a favorable image and impress those around us.

Front Stage And Back Stage

Social interaction involves both a front stage and a back stage, like a theater. The **front stage** is the place where a person plays a specific role in front

of an audience. The front stage is characterized by onstage and outward performance, where we behave in ways that others expect. When we are on the front stage, we are onstage performers. Professors giving lectures in classroom are onstage performers and they keep certain styles of behavior in check. In theater, actors are taught to project with their voices and to embody their characters. Actors also spend time studying the parts they will play. When we play roles in real life situations, we need to learn the right mannerisms, customs, and colloquialisms before attempting to truly impress one or more people.

A student in an online learning environment can also be considered on a front stage, because communicating with classmates and responding to the professor on discussion topics is how a student makes his or her impression and gets a grade. Teamwork is a front stage setting as well. Effective team-building and impressing your teammates require a combination of clear goals, empowerment, trust, authentic participation, innovative approaches, proper leadership, and the ability to manage risks and make constructive changes.

The **back stage** is the place where a person does not play a specific role because there is not an audience. The back stage resembles the backstage of a theater. For example, when you are sitting in a class in session, you are on the front stage because there is an audience consisting of your professor and classmates. When the class is dismissed, you may return to your dorm room, which is a back stage environment if there is no audience. When the professor returns to her office, she is behind the stage and can relax.

The need for impression management is most intense when role players have minority group statuses. For example, women often have to work harder than men to prove that they are capable of performing tasks.

The dramaturgical approach studies social interaction as a theatrical presentation. Although this approach helps us understand the roles we play and the audiences who judge our performances, it has some critics. This approach focuses on appearances, which some people argue ignores the underlying substance and does not place enough emphasis on the ways in which social interactions are influenced by occurrences within the larger society. Supporters say that this approach captures the essence of society because it makes sense of the work in which we participate.

The way we dress shows whether we are front stage or back stage. On the front stage, such as at work, we not only speak professional English but may also dress up and wear jewelry. Our posture is upright. When we come home, we might say that we are on the back stage. The jewelry comes off and we might change into sweats and lounge on the sofa with our feet up.

Nonverbal Interaction: Body Language And Personal Space

Nonverbal Interaction

Social interaction requires a great deal of nonverbal communication. While verbal and written communication is important, nonverbal skills make up a significant percentage of our daily life. **Nonverbal interaction** is the exchange of information among people without the use of speech. This concept refers to communication using body movements, gestures, and facial expressions. People create conventions of nonverbal interaction and pass them on to the next generation. Nonverbal interaction carries special meanings in our interaction with others. In some cultures, it is important to make eye contact when speaking, while in others this behavior may be viewed as inappropriate or threatening. So much of what we convey is not in the words we use, but in the subtle undertones of gestures and body language. Personal experience can cause a listener to have a completely different understanding of the message conveyed, even when the people involved in the dialogue speak the same language. Socialization is a life-long learning process of social interaction through which we acquire physical and social skills. Nonverbal interaction requires a great deal of socialization.

Functions Of Nonverbal Interaction

There are three important functions of nonverbal interaction. First, nonverbal messages convey interpersonal attitudes. Even though you are not talking, your nonverbal actions convey messages or your attitudes toward someone. In certain circumstances, silence can let another person know that you are angry. Rolling your eyes at another's statement conveys a negative attitude. Waving to someone can mean hello or goodbye. Holding hands can suggest intimacy. Eye contact may initiate interaction, and not looking at someone during a conversation may suggest awkwardness or a lack of intimacy.

Second, nonverbal interaction can also function as a way to express emotions. Having your head hung down and walking slowly indicate depression, while a smile and upright posture indicate happiness. Examples of nonverbal expressions of emotion include pats, hugs, smiles, frowns, furrowed brows, tight jaws, tapping fingers, and shoulders that are either squared or slumped. Expressing emotions lets other people know how we are feeling so they can respond appropriately. It allows us to share our feelings with others without having to verbally disclose anything.

Third, nonverbal messages help us handle ongoing interactions. An example of this would be if someone yawned while you were talking to them, it would let you know that he or she was tired so that you could wrap up what you were saying. On the other hand, an intent look would indicate an interest in the conversation and encourage you to continue.

Nonverbal expressions often occur subconsciously, and people do not always realize that these communications are taking place. This definitely opens the door to the possibility of misinterpreting the message, especially when individuals of different cultures are interacting and nonverbal communications have ambiguous meanings. In the following section, we discuss nonverbal interactions in the form of body language (facial expressions, eye contact, gestures, and tone of voice) and personal space.

Hugging.

Source: Anissa Thompson

Body Language

Body language plays a vital part in the interpretation of our words. How we say things is often just as important as what we say. People use parts of their bodies to convey information to others through body language. Body language includes facial expressions, eye contact, touching, head movements, body position, and gestures. This type of nonverbal interaction is symbolic of our relationship with others. People use nonverbal cues to expand on what is said with words, and sometimes body language speaks louder than our mouths. Who sustains eye contact? Who touches whom? Though most nonverbal communication is culture-specific, research shows that humans share the same basic emotions. Three ways in which emotional life differs across cultures are: (1) what triggers an emotion, (2) how people display emotions according to the norms of their culture, and (3) how people cope with emotions.

Facial Expressions

Facial expressions are a major aspect of body language. Facial expressions are a type of nonverbal interaction that crosses cultural lines, sharing our attitudes toward others. According to Ekman and Friesen (1978), New Guinea natives identified facial expressions of six emotions: happiness, sadness, anger, disgust, fear, and surprise. Smiling, for instance, shows pleasure. Laughter expresses happiness and bonds people together. Laughter is not about getting a joke, it is about getting along. Laughter is a powerful bonding tool that is used to signal readiness for friendship and to reinforce group solidarity. The physiological indicators of emotion are similar in people from different cultures. Facial expressions are similar both in people who can see and in people who have been blind since birth. This observation suggests that facial expressions are innate, because blind people could not have learned these expressions through observation.

Most facial expressions are created and interpreted depending on place and time. The meanings that are attached to them may be different even though the facial expressions are identical. For instance, the intensity with which people smile, cry, or show anger, sorrow, or disgust, varies from culture to culture. For example, many Asian cultures suppress facial expressions as much as possible because their culture dictates that people are less animated. Many Mediterranean (Latino and Arabic) cultures exaggerate grief or sadness, while most American men hide these emotions.

Eye Contact

Eye contact is another component of body language and is a means of showing interest in the target object. Dr. Peter Marsh says, "How we look at other people, meet their gaze and look away can make all the difference between an effective encounter and one that leads to embarrassment or even rejection." Whether it is a loving gaze, a hostile stare, a nervous glance, or a refusal to look altogether, the duration of the contact (or lack thereof) reveals our interest in the other party and the situation (Bremer, 2004). Eye contact may cause misunderstandings unless we use it with an "acceptable" level of personal assertion or physical motion in a conversation.

People use eye contact in a variety of ways. It can be used to get someone's attention or initiate a social interaction, such as when a student in your classroom "catches your eye," initiating an interaction between the two of you. Looking at people and meeting their gaze are the first steps toward striking up friendships and making positive impressions. By contrast, looking downward or off into the distance discourages interaction. The best advice is to make short frequent glances in social situations. Making eye contact for too long a duration can be seen as threatening, distorting the subtext of interest.

Eye contact depicts interest and honesty or sincerity. One measure of romantic love is eye contact.

If you like someone, you are more likely to have more eye contact with him or her. In addition, eye contact is often used to control an interpersonal interaction. In normal conversation, eye contact plays an important role as the regulator of turn taking. To start a conversation with someone, you need to first establish eye contact. If that person looks back, "permission" has been granted to begin speaking. If people do not wish to be interrupted, they usually look away and continue talking. When they want interaction, they will pause and make direct eye contact. The eyes might also be a signal of non-listening behaviors, telling us that our message is somehow lacking and we are losing the attentiveness of our audience.

Eye contact is sometimes used in the field of investigations as an indicator of whether or not a person is lying. Detecting lies can be difficult. Ekman (1985) suggests scrutinizing four elements of a performance, including words, voice, body language, and facial expression. When you sit through an interview, more than 50 percent of the message received by interviewers is picked up through nonverbal expressions and body positions. Body positioning is one of the most telling signs. People who are being open and honest will often move toward the interviewer and open their arms and body while speaking, to visually convey the message that they have nothing to hide. People trying to cover up the truth often attempt to put distance between themselves and the interviewer and speak with arms crossed or a closed stance which equates to shutting out other people. People telling the truth are often focused and able to maintain eye contact. Those being less than truthful frequently let their eyes wander and move their head in all directions while trying to draw on ideas to strengthen their story. These are observations, though, and not absolutes.

Global Diversity In Eye Contact

The use of eye contact is molded through the development of a person's cultural background. Different cultures or religions have different views on this topic. Westerners see direct eye-to-eye contact as positive. In Western cultures, people make intermittent eye contact while speaking to demonstrate interest and trustworthiness. In American culture, if eye contact is not returned, it can be taken as a sign of disrespect. It is also disrespectful when they do not look away periodically. People in the Middle East use very intense and prolonged eye contact to gauge someone else's intentions and will move in very close to better see the other person's eyes. They believe it shows interest and helps them determine the truthfulness of the other person. A person who does not reciprocate is seen as untrustworthy.

In some countries, including Bahrain, it is disrespectful for a woman to make eye contact with anyone, especially a male. People are not to look at women out of curiosity because the women would be blamed by their husbands and suffer punishment. In Japan, Africa, Latin America, and the Caribbean, people avoid eye contact to show respect. In Japan, eye contact with a superior is considered offensive; direct eye contact is interpreted as an invasion of a person's privacy and an act of rudeness. When bowing to your sensei, it is a symbol of humility to lower your eyes and keep them on the ground while bowing, but on the tatami mat it is important to maintain eye contact with your opponent. Koreans will not look you in the eye as you pass by because they believe that it is disrespectful. In Latino culture, direct eye contact may also be viewed as a sign of disrespect. Among Hispanics, avoidance of direct eye contact is sometimes seen as a sign of attentiveness and respect, while sustained direct eye contact may be interpreted as a challenge to authority. Native Americans regard direct prolonged eye contact as invasive and it is avoided to protect the personal autonomy of the people interacting.

Gestures

Gestures are another form of body language that has many different shades of meaning. In addition to our face and eyes, our hands also speak on our behalf. Hand gestures can request a ride, express love, convey an insult, or make a demand that someone stop. Gestures are continually used to convey meanings when nothing is actually said and to supplement spoken words. For example, rapidly waving the arms adds urgency to the single word "Hurry!" Shrugging your shoulders adds an air of indiffer-

ence to the phrase "I don't know." Human beings create symbols, including gestures, and know how to interpret the meanings of the symbols according to their cultures.

A gesture created in one culture or subculture can have different meanings from the same gesture created in another culture. What may be a generous gesture in one culture may be offensive in another. If two people are speaking the same language, but are from two different cultures, there may still be communication barriers if they interpret the meanings of the same gesture differently. In Japan, for example, bowing shows rank and status. Hands in pockets are considered disrespectful in Turkey. Sitting with legs crossed is offensive in Ghana and Turkey. Showing the soles of one's feet is offensive in Thailand, Saudi Arabia, and other Muslim nations. Many Asians don't touch the head because it houses the soul and a touch puts it in jeopardy. In Iraq, etiquette requires that Muslims use their left hand to clean and wipe after they use the bathroom.

Tone Of Voice

The tone of a person's voice plays a major role in communication. People express themselves through body language to such an extent that it is sometimes hard to tell if someone is being sarcastic or not. Tone is, therefore, an important factor in communicating with others. Speaking in a normal voice is an effective way to communicate. When people start talking in elevated voices, others may shut them out and not listen to what they are saying. People may view them as being disrespectful and immature. However, it seems that there are no guidelines for a normal voice in real life situations. Let's say that we meet a man who speaks to us in an elevated voice. We may misinterpret his elevated (abnormal) voice and describe him as disrespectful or rude. If we later learn that he has a loss of hearing in one ear, we may realize that his "abnormal" voice was normal for him, and that we have judged him unfairly. Thus, it is not easy to define a normal voice in our daily interactions. "Generic language" or tone may be a better term to use. Inclusive language must take these types of issues into account in order to improve communication.

Personal Space

Personal space is another component of nonverbal interaction. **Personal space** is the private area surrounding a person. Some people like to be really close to others while others tend to give people more space. According to some observations, Type A personalities are less likely to respect personal space than Type B personalities. The use of space involves power. Masculinity has been traditionally associated with greater amounts of personal space, or surrounding area over which a person makes some claim to privacy. Also, men tend to intrude on a woman's space more often than women intrude on a man's space.

Personal space varies from culture to culture. For example, in the United States it is rude to stand too close to someone while speaking. This may show that we, as a culture, are more private and withdrawn than other cultures. Americans generally prefer to stand about five feet apart when participating in a conversation—a distance that can seem unfriendly to people of other cultures. In South America, for instance, personal space and comfort distances tend to be quite small; people stand very close to one another to talk, even when they do not know each other very well, perhaps demonstrating that the culture is more comfortable with intimacy among peers. People raised in the Middle East are also socialized to want a very close speaking distance, as are people from Germany and Japan. Factors that determine the allocation of personal space include age, gender, relationship, power differential, social class, and culture.

Anthropologist Edward Hall (1966) described four distance zones for personal space. Intimate distance, from zero to 18 inches, is reserved for close social contacts like lovers, parents, and children. Personal distance, from 18 inches to 4 feet, is the zone for friends and acquaintances. Social distance, from 4 to 12 feet, is the space reserved for formal settings such as interviews. Finally, public distance, beyond 12 feet, is maintained by those performing to an audience. In social interaction, it is the norm to maintain a greater distance if the relationship does not deserve intimate or personal distance. If these spaces are invaded, people may try to regain their space by backing up or giving a dirty look to the intruder as if to say, "Don't invade my space."

Types Of Social Interaction

Social interactions are complex in their manifestations and interrelationships. They can be overt or covert, active or passive, brief or long-lived. They can be organized or disorganized, direct or indirect, narrow or universal. There is clearly a diversity of patterns and types. How can we make sense out of this complexity? Successful social interactions are governed by cultural conventions that are often shared by the people around us. According to Sociologist Robert Nisbet (1970), there are five types of social interaction—molecular cement—that link individuals in groups from the smallest to the largest: exchange, cooperation, conflict, competition, and coercion.

Exchange

Exchange is the most fundamental form of social interaction, in which people treat others as supporters or friends. Exchange means that two or more individuals each offer something in order to obtain a reward in return. Exchange is characteristic of supportive interactions and it must be fair and equitable. People interact and communicate based on a norm of reciprocity, weighing costs and benefits to decide whether they want to maintain the relationships. Social interactions involve smiling, talking, threatening, fighting, negotiating, and discussing. When people say hello to you, you expect them to return the greeting. The exchange is symbolic. Smiles and appropriate greetings symbolize friendship. Vulgar gestures and harsh words communicate hostility. A calm and reasonable tone represents professionalism. People of different groups respond to each other according to reciprocity. Governments of different countries interact with each other based on humanitarianism or costs and benefits. Fair exchanges solidify social structure and social relationships.

Cooperation

Cooperation involves two or more people work-

Field hockey match.   Source: Wilf Ratzburg

ing together as friends or supporters to achieve a common goal. As the saying goes, "Two heads are better than one." In society, people interact with each other, combining their efforts and assets, in order to accomplish tasks. Cooperation is characteristic of supportive interactions.

Traditional cooperation is based on customs. In hunting and gathering societies, men hunt animals and women gather berries and fruits for survival. On family-based farms, kinship members work together to raise crops. In today's formal organizations, there is a high level of division of labor, requiring the cooperation of thousands of people to achieve goals. Contractual cooperation involves planning and team work. A multinational corporation requires more cooperation to globalize cultural traits in a diverse workplace. If a diverse team is assigned a project, the members need to communicate effectively with each other, set deadlines, hold people accountable,

and have a backup plan in place. If a team member doesn't contribute, the others must also be able to pick up the slack early enough to avoid a stressful situation. In this scenario, team members are supposed to cooperate in favor of team objectives and goals. Learning what motivates each individual within the team is the key to success.

Competition

Competition means that two or more people follow mutually accepted rules to achieve the same goal before each other. Conflict is characteristic of oppositional interactions, with people treating each other as competitors, or sometimes even as enemies. Competition is one of the characteristics of capitalism. Competition sometimes leads to better outcomes than cooperation. In society, people always compete for limited resources. Colleges compete for the best students and professors. Nonprofits compete for donations and grants. Religious organizations compete for members. Politicians compete for votes and government agencies compete against each other for funding. Individuals compete for vacant jobs. In each case, candidates try their best to impress someone through their interactions. Younger generations grow up by playing games and value competition. They become more productive when they are engaged in a competitive project. Businesses compete in the marketplace by increasing the quality of their products while containing costs so that their products can be sold at competitive prices. Thus, competition can be beneficial.

Conflict

Conflict occurs when people who dislike or hate each other interact. Conflict is characteristic of oppositional interactions, with people treating each other as enemies or competitors. Conflict can be caused by individuals or groups competing for a prized goal, each wanting to defeat the other. Conflict can also occur when people from different cultures misunderstand each other. When team members fail to participate and complete their assigned share of work, conflict may emerge. Conflict over assignments, evaluations, raises, and promotions may take place between an employee and his or her supervisor. Conflict may result if two boys are chasing the same girl, leading to violence. Conflict may also result when a student and teacher disagree about grades. Conflict at the international level includes terrorist attacks and wars. In times of war and conflict with other groups or countries, solidarity and cohesion unite people in the face of a common enemy. Conflict is sometimes necessary and beneficial because it can lead to social change.

Coercion

Coercion is characteristic of oppositional interactions. It means that one person or group forces its will upon another. In coercions, the individual or group with power, called the **superordinate**, uses the threat of violence, deprivation, or some other punishment to control the actions of an individual or group with less power, called the **subordinate** (Simmel, 1955). Coercion may be considered an illegitimate power. For example, your supervisors have the right to assign your shift, but they do not have the right to make you clean their personal cars. Peer pressure can also be a form of coercion.

Communication And Interaction Differences

Communication

Good communication is essential and can help us in our personal and professional lives. Effective communication is a two-way street. If the sender is unclear, or the receiver misunderstands, it cannot be defined as true communication. Communication consists of the sender, encoding, the channel, decoding, the receiver, feedback, and context. Problems with communication can pop up at every stage of the communication process; there is always the potential for misunderstanding and confusion. To be an effective communicator, a person needs to get his or her point across without misunderstanding and confusion. The goal should be to lessen the frequency of problems at each stage of this process with clear, concise, accurate, and well-planned communications.

Communication with people of different cultures is especially challenging. The same words can mean different things to people from different cultures, even when they speak the same language. Many languages are difficult to translate, and some words cannot be translated exactly, making communication very difficult. The person speaking might think he or she is saying one thing and the person listening could be thinking the opposite. In a society consisting of so many different cultures and people with diverse backgrounds, it is hard to please everyone. It is important for people to use inclusive communication, understanding and recognizing their audience, in order to avoid claims of a hostile environment. **Inclusive communication** refers to an exchange where all parties are entitled to respect and the opportunity to express themselves; they are fully included. Inclusiveness provides definition and guidelines to the process of communication. If we learn to treat everyone with respect, it makes for a more enjoyable atmosphere in our real lives. The key to preventing any wrongdoing is to stay updated and educated on what is acceptable and what is not. Once that framework exists, there is no excuse for harassing behavior or a hostile environment.

Oftentimes, it is not so much what we say, but how we say it. Keeping this in mind, and not leaving people out of interactions, increases our opportunities for positive and effective interactions with others. Many of us speak without thinking first about how a seemingly innocent statement could be construed in a negative or hostile manner. It is important to simply be aware of what you are saying and how you say it.

Verbal Communication

In face-to-face communication, meaning is conveyed through words, tone, and body language. We may experience great joy when we communicate with someone face to face because we know what we are saying and how we are saying it and can sense that he or she understands. However, when communicating in writing, the person sending the message must be able to convey a positive and encouraging tone, and cannot be sure how the receiver is interpreting what has been written. Some people find it much easier to get their opinions or words out by writing them down rather than speaking; it gives them time to organize their thoughts and go over exactly what they want to express. When people share the same pattern to communicate with each other, it is considered normal; it is apparent that consideration has been given to the subject matter and group norms. But when someone deviates from the pattern, it is likely to be considered abnormal or deviant.

Barriers To Verbal Communication

Communication is affected by all of the same factors that influence a person's culture, including gender, age, economic background, occupation, sexual orientation, disability, education, geographic region, dialect, race, and ethnicity. Communication is an essential part of transmitting guidance and direction from top to bottom, and it is made more difficult when differences exist.

Age Differences

A cultural barrier to communication exists between the younger generation and the older generation. The older population may have a hard time understanding the current language of the culture due to variations over their lifetimes. English-speaking younger generations tend to talk faster and use more slang than previous generations. When young people use the word "phat," (pronounced "fat") they are not referring to the actual size of something, but the quality. Phat means excellent or nice. Young men call each other "dawg" or "dog" as a term of endearment or bonding; for the older generation, "dog" is a man who runs around on a woman or treats her badly. A major characteristic of the younger generation would be a vast knowledge of technology. They are practically born with a computer keyboard and video game controller in their hands.

Sociolinguist Penelope Eckert studied the variation in speech related to social categories within a high school. Her study revealed a correlation between speech and social status, identifying two categories—jocks and burnouts—in the high school population. The jocks traditionally helped to maintain the school's formal social structure. They participate in athletics, organized school activities, and student government. The burnouts had their main social networks in their neighborhoods. This split exists in many high schools throughout the United States. Speech patterns are set during the teen years as we emulate people we admire. Because the jocks and burnouts move in different circles, they talk differently.

Different Accents

Accents compound communication barriers between people. Everybody has an accent, in addition to cultural ways of articulating things. Every country has more than one accent that people exhibit when speaking. In the United States, we have different accents throughout the country, and variations of ways to use words. Just because two people are speaking the same language does not mean that they will understand each other. People that live in upper New York, Wisconsin, and southern Louisiana have completely different accents that may make it hard for them to understand each other in a conversation. Individuals from Massachusetts speak differently than those from California. People from California speak differently than those from Alabama.

Dialect And Regional Colloquialisms

Other pieces of language that can affect communication are dialect and regional colloquialisms. Language is different from state to state in the United States. For example, on the East Coast, people say "soda," and on the West Coast, they say "pop." In the East, they say "bag," and in the Midwest, people say "sack." Unlike people in Manhattan or the Bronx, people in Maine are very laid back, and so is the tempo of their speech. When they respond to someone from New Jersey who is in a hurry to get directions, they politely and carefully tell the anxious visitor the best way to get to where they are going. In the workplace, if you have co-workers from New York, Tennessee, and Texas, you will find language differences.

Regional language differences also exist in other countries. In Italy, there are many dialects spoken in the different cities and towns where people live. If you come from the area around Naples, you may have a hard time understanding other Italians in different parts of the country.

We acquire the regional patterns of language where we live. Even race and class can determine our speech patterns. Within a multicultural society, it is important to understand and acknowledge differences in speech patterns. It is important to realize that in business there is also a set pattern of speech that can affect communication.

Social Class And Education

Social class and education may play a role in determining different dialects. Individuals from lower income levels tend to develop speech that differs from those earning higher incomes. The same applies to educated and uneducated individuals. Vocal tone and how loudly someone speaks may also act as barriers to communication. Economic differ-ences can hinder communication, possibly because of a lack of exposure on both sides. For example, farmers may not have the time to travel the world and delve into the arts. On the flip side, wealthy socialites may be unlikely to find pleasure in a barn dance or hayride. If you put people from these two groups in a room together, the conversation might be minimal.

In summary, verbal communications can take on different meanings from state to state in the United States. There are different cultures, including the ways holidays are celebrated, the ways people cook, the ways people greet one another, and the ways people travel. All of these differences can create cultural barriers to communication. There is no way for an individual to become aware of every cultural norm to avoid these barriers. Instead, everyone simply needs to respect different cultures by maintaining an open mind and being willing to learn as things occur. The more languages you know, and the more ways to communicate that you can use, the better off you are. Understanding people's cultures has become increasingly important due to growing diversity. We need to speak with the intent of understanding diverse ideas, use words that will not offend, trust the intelligence of others, work with them to share ideas, eliminate judgment, and be willing to ask questions to clarify and answer questions for the same reason. We can use these strategies to validate and embrace others.

Differences Between Women And Men

Gender can be a factor in communication breakdowns, whether we examine nonverbal or verbal communication. Men and women tend to communicate differently. When these communication styles collide, it can lead to all kinds of misunderstandings. It is important to take into account how societies link human traits to being female or male when studying personal performances. This begins during the socialization process, when boys are taught to be masculine and girls are taught to be feminine.

Speaking Different Genderlects

As we all know, a dialect is a local or regional feature of a language. Deborah Tannen coined the word **genderlect** to explain linguistic variations based on gender. Women are more likely to ask permission, express feelings, attempt to initiate conversations, and attempt to keep conversations going. In task-oriented, mixed-gender groups, men talk much more than women. However, in friendly conversations amongst friends, women like to talk more than men.

What do men and women usually talk about? Men like to talk about public things like sports, cars, and the news. Women like to talk about personal and private things, like their problems, other women, clothing, and cooking. Both men and women like to discuss work-related issues and romantic relationships.

Women and men are different in speech styles. In their speech, women use more qualifiers, such as *I guess, I think,* and *I suppose.* Women use more disclaimers than do men. Women might say that "This probably is not important." Women use more tag questions than do men. For example, women might ask "Do you want to go to a movie tonight, or not?" Women are more likely to use polite words than men. For example, women may say "Would you please take out the trash?"

Who dominates interactions between men and women? Men like to dominate conversations, control the content, and make jokes. In different gender groups, men disrupt women more than women disrupt men. Men interrupt women eight times more. Women like to ask more questions in conversations, and men like to make comments during conversation. Men often have delayed responses in conversations that shorten interactions. Women have quick responses that lengthen interactions.

Who initiates the topic of conversation? Men like to pick out topics of conversations more than women. Boys and men like to make jokes and tell humorous stories. Girls and women like to laugh more than men.

How do men and women define home? Men think of home as a place where speaking is non-existent. Women think of home as a place where speaking is plentiful. Who discloses the most in public and private settings? Men like to talk more in public. This is because men like to establish authority, which is more appropriate in the workplace, so that is where most of their conversations would occur. Women like to talk more in private. They like to establish intimacy, so most of their conversations would be at home (Williams & Anderson, n.d.).

Nonverbal Communication Between Women And Men

There are also gender differences between men and women in nonverbal social interactions. Whenever two or more people are together and aware of each other, it is impossible for them not to communicate. Even when you are not talking, you communicate by the way you position your body and tilt your head, your facial expressions, your physical distance from others, and so on.

How do men and women use body language? Women maintain more eye contact with people during interactions. Men use nonverbal communication indirectly, standing farther away, making less frequent eye contact, and using fewer hand gestures. However, men are more likely to stare at other people (especially men) in order to challenge them and assert their own status (Pearson, 1985). Researchers have found that women tend to smile more than men, and the meanings associated with smiling seem to vary with gender. Touching patterns also vary, with men tending to touch women more than women touch men. Women express a wider range of emotions through their facial expressions. Some people see animated expressions as a sign of a lack of control, though, which means that women may be viewed as emotional, moody, and unpredictable. Additionally, too much smiling may be seen as a sign of shallowness or insincerity, and women smile more than men.

Tone of voice definitely plays a role in the communication process. You can be saying something that on the surface sounds benign, but your tone can cause it to be perceived as something totally different. If your tone of voice is flat, you will seem to be disinterested. Too sharp a tone, and you can seem angry or overly excited. Communication is a combination of verbal communication, including tone, and nonverbal, like gestures and proxemics. When you put those things together, you have a mixture that can work well, but often doesn't. If one of the items is off, like the right words said with a contradictory tone, the message gets garbled.

Practicing The Gendered Game Of Proxemics

In gender-mixed groups, men's proxemics differ from women's. In the United States, men spread out while women constrict. Men usually sprawl with their legs spread apart and hands stretched away from the body, taking up considerable space around them. Women are more likely to draw themselves in with "ladylike" postures such as closing or crossing the legs and placing the hands near the body to use only a little space. Perhaps women became accustomed to this posture because traditionally they wore dresses, while men wore pants and could position themselves more openly. These patterns can differ from one culture to another. For example, European men take up less space than American men.

Male domination reigns in the gendered game of proxemics. A more direct way for men to dominate women involves invading their personal space. Men touch shoulders and signify their dominant status. Men often let their hands rest on women's shoulders, but women rarely do the same to men. A similar proxemic domination prevails in interactions of mutual affection. When an intimate couple walks down the street, the man may place his arm around the woman's shoulders, but the woman is far less likely to put her arm around the man's shoulders. Doesn't this merely reflect the fact that the man is usually taller, so it would be uncomfortable for the sexes to reverse position? The answer is "no." The same ritual of men playing the powerful protector, and women the helpless protected, is often observed when both are about the same height, or even when the man is slightly shorter. If the man is too short to stretch his arm around the woman's shoulders, they still will not reverse positions, instead settling for holding hands. If a tall female does put her arm around a shorter male's shoulders, chances are that she is the mother and he is her child (Tannen, 1990,

1994a). In the world of gender inequality, a man is likely to cringe if his girlfriend or wife treats him like a child by putting her arms around his shoulders.

According to Tannen, even in the most intimate moments between men and women, the males dominate. When both are lying in bed, the man typically lies on his back, flat and straight, but the woman lies on her side, her body nestled against his. She may place her head upon his shoulder with his arms around her. It is a picture of an unequal relationship, with the man appearing strong and protective and the woman weak and protected.

Social Interaction And Gender Inequality

Sociologists try to relate gender differences in social interaction to power and inequality. It is traditionally thought that men are more outspoken, and women are more nurturing; therefore, they may interpret situations differently.

In many cultures throughout the world, women are patronized and viewed as the weaker sex. Women are commonly perceived as being unfit for any forms of higher education and executive positions. Because of societal pressures and expectations, women may retreat to a life of raising children and cooking meals for their husbands. In the United States, we view the shaking of hands as an acceptable practice for both men and women. In the Somalian culture, however, women and men do not shake hands because they view women as subordinate. In most cultures, men are given more leniency.

In cross-gender interactions, men talk and interrupt women more than women interrupt men. In same-gender conversations, men disclose less personal information and restrict themselves to safer topics like sports, politics, and work. Men's styles of both verbal and nonverbal communication fit more closely with positions of dominance, women's with positions of subordination.

Summary

We live in a society where our behavior is determined by social structure, which guides behavior. The building blocks of society encompass status, role, social groups, and social institutions and provide structure to our lives. Social interaction is the foundation of all relationships and groups in society. The functionalist perspective looks at society in a positive manner and sees it as stable, with all of its parts supporting each other and working together. Under the functionalist view, every aspect of society contributes to its survival. The conflict perspective on social interaction also focuses primarily on macro-level analysis, examining societies, social structures, and social systems. Symbolic interactionists study people's everyday behaviors and how they react to their surroundings. In social interaction, it is important to understand principles and shared definitions in order to avoid or overcome barriers. Interactionists look at society from the micro-level perspective and focus on face-to-face interactions between two or more people. Since society is made up of individuals with different backgrounds, and individuals are engaged in interactions every minute of the day, society can be viewed as the sum of the interactions of individuals and groups. People with different cultural backgrounds define situations differently and then respond and behave according to their definitions. This can cause misunderstandings and affect interactions. Dramaturgical analysis compares everyday life to a theatrical presentation to understand social interaction. Presenting ourselves in ways that are most favorable to our own interests or image is known as presentation of self.

There are five types of social interaction: exchange, cooperation, conflict, competition, and coercion. Nonverbal interaction is the exchange of information using body movements, gestures, and facial expressions rather than speech. Nonverbal interactions can regulate our social interactions; eye contact and body posture signal whether or not we want to talk to someone. Communication is an essential part of transmitting guidance and direction. Communication is difficult even without having the cultural aspect added to the equation. Age, geographic region, social class, education level, race, ethnicity, gender, and dialect can be barriers to good communication.

Review/Discussion Questions

1. Do you think that external factors, such as gender and age, are sometimes barriers to upward social mobility?
2. In what ways do race and ethnicity contribute to the formation and fulfillment of other statuses?
3. Status–Role Matrix: Construct a matrix of your own status and role relationships.
4. List your statuses and roles and then analyze your possible role expectations, role performance, role conflicts, and role strains. Does your analysis help you explain irritating behavior? How helpful are the concepts of social structure in analyzing your individual behavior?
5. Give an example of role conflict and an example of role strain in your real life.
6. Role-play and identify barriers to clear communication.
7. Explore the types of role conflict that working women today might experience and provide some coping strategies.
8. How do people make sense of their everyday social interactions from a symbolic perspective?
9. What kinds of shared meanings are necessary for social interaction in a classroom?
10. Provide an example illustrating that how people define a situation becomes the foundation for how they behave.
11. What consequences does the definition of a situation have? How does the definition of a situation affect future social interaction?
12. A student said, "I find that when I try to impress or pretend to know more than I do, I end up just the opposite. I believe in being the best me I can be. If you like me, it is okay but if you

don't, that is okay too. Life is pretty miserable when we try to please everybody. I decide to be myself." What do you think that we can do to please everybody?

13. What is meant by face work? Give examples of face-saving behavior. Do you think that such actions tend to make us feel better about ourselves? If yes, why?

14. Can you share any strategies for treating everyone with respect and avoiding conflict when we are communicating?

15. Why is it so important for us to learn and use nonverbal communication?

16. What is the relationship between personal space and power? Give an example to illustrate it.

17. When communicating with other genders, races, and ages, how do you try to acknowledge different styles?

18. Explore examples of nonverbal communication that you see on your favorite television shows. Provide examples from other cultures and social classes as well as some that cross gender lines.

19. Compose a list of the different ways men and women communicate their feelings in nonverbal communication.

20. Identify some styles of miscommunication and provide tips for effective communication.

Key Terms

Achieved status refers to a social position that a person earns through personal effort and choice.

Ascribed status refers to a social position that a person receives at birth or assumes involuntarily later in life.

Back stage is the place where there is no audience and the person does not play a specific role.

Dramaturgical analysis is the perspective of social interaction that compares everyday life to a theatrical performance.

Face-saving behavior refers to techniques that people use to salvage their performance when they encounter a potential or actual loss of face.

Face work describes when we make an effort to give our best possible performance to avoid "losing face."

Front stage is the place where a person plays a specific role in front of an audience.

Genderlects are the linguistic styles that reflect the different worlds of women and men.

Groups are collections of people characterized by more than two people, frequent interaction, a sense of belongingness, and interdependence.

Impression management refers to our efforts to present favorable images to the people around us.

Inclusive communication refers to an exchange where all parties are entitled to respect and the opportunity to express themselves.

Master status is a status that determines a person's overall social position and identity.

Nonverbal interaction is the exchange of information among people without the use of speech.

Personal space is the private area surrounding a person.

Politeness theory is the idea that communicators change and adapt their messages to protect and save the "face" of their listeners.

Roles are socially defined expectations associated with a given status.

Role conflict refers to conflicting demands connected to two or more statuses.

Role exit is the process by which people disengage from a role.

Role set refers to a number of roles attached to a single status.

Role strain refers to conflicting demands connected to a single status.

Social institutions are established ways that society organizes to meet basic needs.

Social interaction involves reciprocal communication between two or more people through symbols, words, and body language.

Social structure refers to the social relationships that exist within society.

Status refers to a social position that is held by a person and characterized by rights and duties.

Status inconsistency occurs when people experience mismatch between their statuses.

Status set refers to all the statuses that a person occupies at a given time.

Subordinates are individuals or groups with less or little power in a coercive interaction.

Superordinates are individuals or groups with more social power in a coercive interaction.

Work spillover refers to the effect that work has on individuals and families, absorbing their time and energy and impinging on their psychological states.

Bibliography

Agapiou, A. (2002, November). "Perceptions of gender roles and attitudes toward work among male and female operatives in the Scottish construction industry." <http://www.informaworld.com/smpp/content~content=a713763888~db=all~order=page > (2008, June 16).

Bremer, J. (2004) "The "eyes" have it: the fundamentals of eye contact." <http://www.bremercommunications.com/Eye_Contact. htm> (2008, August 16).

CNN.com. (2008, June 23). "First female four-star U.S. Army general nominated." <http://www.cnn.com/2008/US/06/23/woman. general/index.html> (2008, July 20).

Ebaugh, H. R. F. (1988). Becoming an Ex: The Process of Role Exit. Chicago: University of Chicago Press.

ECG. (n.d.). "Bridge the gap of language styles: a legacy that holds women back." <http://ecglink.com/library/ps/gap.html> (2008, June 17).

Eckert, P. (1989). Jocks & Burnouts: Social Categories and Identity in the High School. New York: Teachers College Press.

Ekman, P. (1985). Telling Lies: Clues to Deceit in the Marketplace, Politics, and Marriage. New York: Norton.

Ekman, P., & Friesen, W. V. (1978). Facial Action Coding System: A Technique for the Measurement of Facial Movement. Palo Alto, CA: Consulting Psychologists Press.

Edgecomb, A. (2008). "Lt. Gen. Ann E. Dunwoody is nominated to receive the 4th star." <http://www.army.mil/-newsreleases/2008/06/23/10287-lt-gen-dunwoody-nominated-to-receive-4th-star/> (2008, July 23).

Goffman, E. (1959). The Presentation of Self in Everyday Life. Garden City, NY: Doubleday.

Goffman, E. (1974). The Presentation of Self in Everyday Life. New York: Overlook.

Goldsmith, D. (2008). "Managing Conflicting Goals in Supportive Interaction and Integrative Theoretical Framework." Communication Resource, 19 (2), 264-286. <http://crx.sagepub.com/cgi/content/abstract/19/2/264> (2008, August 6).

Hall, E. T. (1966). The Hidden Dimension. Garden City, NY: Doubleday.

Henslin, J. M. (2008). Sociology: A Down-to-Earth Approach. New York: Allyn & Bacon.

Hello and Welcome. (2005). "Inclusive communication toward inclusive communication strategy in the city of Edinburgh." (2005). <http://www.inclusivecommunications.co.uk/> (2008, July 14).

Inter Tribal Council of Arizona. (2003). "Fort Yuma-Quechan Tribe." <http://www.itcaonline.com/tribes_quechan.html> (2008, August 6).

Johnson, C., & Kreger, J. (2008). "Muslim Women in the Workplace Reaching Beyond   Stereotypes to understanding." <http://www.diversitycentral.com/learning/cultural_insights.html> (2008, June 30).

Kendall, D. E. (2008). Sociology in our times (7th ed.). Belmont, CA: Thomson/Wadsworth.

Nisbet, R. A. (1970). The Social Bond: An Introduction to the Stud of Sociology. New York: Alfred A. Knopf.

Omi, M., & Winant, H. (1994). Racial Formation in the United States: From the 1960s to the 1990s. New York: Routledge.

Pearson, J. C. (1985). Gender and Communication. Dubuque, IA: W.C. Brown Publishers.

RTO Online. (2005). "Is your workplace culture male or female? Answer may affect worker loyalty, health and productivity." <http://www.rtoonline.com/content/Article/Jan05/LuminariStudy013105.asp> (2008, June 17).

Schaefer, R. T. (2006). Sociology: A Brief Introduction. Boston, MA: McGraw-Hill.

Schaefer, R. T., & Lamm, R. P. (1998). Sociology (6th ed.). New York: McGraw-Hill.

Simmel, G. (1955). Conflict (K. H. Wolff, Trans.). Glencoe, IL: Free Press.

Social interaction. <http://www-dept.usm.edu/~antsoc/socio/davehunt/soc101/social%20interaction.htm> (2008, July 9).

Tannen, D. (1990). You Just Don't Understand: Women and Men in Conversation. New York: Morrow.

Tannen, D. (1994a). Talking from 9 to 5. New York: William Morrow.

Tannen, D. (1994b). Gender and Discourse. New York: Oxford University Press.

U.S. Equal Employment Opportunity Commission. (2002). Federal Laws Prohibiting Job Discrimination Questions and Answers. <http://www.eeoc.gov/facts/qanda.html> (2008, August 2).

Williams, S., & Anderson, B. (n.d.). Defining Genderlects. <http://www.wiu.edu/users/scw105/genderlects.htm> (2008, August 14).

CHAPTER FIVE

Groups And Organizations

Beverly Farb

Using the "sociological imagination," we can see that social forces have extraordinary power over individuals (Mills, 1956). Of all social forces, groups exert their power the most directly. This can be either wonderful or terrifying. Have you ever wondered:

(*On the wonderful side*)
- How marriage increases lifespan?
- How social rituals can reduce crime?
- How acquaintances help reduce poverty?
- How local communities can reduce corporate harm?

(*On the terrifying side*)
- Why every major religion in the world has a history of violence, even though they teach peace and universal love?
- How American soldiers, dedicated to defending our nation, could be guilty of torture and abuse?
- Why race and gender continue to affect our available choices in America, land of equal opportunity?
- Why so many people are willing to give up their creativity, freedom, dignity, close relationships, and personal happiness for a job?

Studying the nature and power of groups helps to answer all of these questions and more.

What Counts As A Group?

A **social group** is more than just a collection of individuals. In a group, there is a sense of shared identity, or "we," that is established through shared interaction. People in a grocery store or at a bus stop are not a true group. Although they share a space and a purpose, they form only a **social aggregate**. But this can change. Imagine this crisis: a bus crashes into a telephone pole as it approaches a stop. Suddenly, the people at the bus stop are transformed into a true group. They interact with energy, perhaps shouting to each other about what to do. They share an identity, too: "we" are now the people who have witnessed this tragedy.

However, a tragedy is not necessary; there is another way that an aggregate can transform into a group. Over time, if the same aggregate continues to assemble, the individuals will begin chatting and getting to know each other. In that case, "we" are the people who wait for this bus at this time of day.

A **social category** is not a true group either. Members of a category share a trait, such as a status (e.g., being a student) or condition (e.g., having cancer). Gender, race, age, and social class are characteristics that form categories, not groups; the people who share such traits do not necessarily interact, nor must they perceive themselves as part of a larger "we."

Others who do not share the same trait often perceive those who do share it as a group, and this is a crucial mistake. This misperception is one of the roots of prejudice. It encourages people to respond to members of a category as if they shared far more than that. Even when a prejudice is positive, like "Asians succeed in school" or "teenagers have lots of energy," such expectations tend to place unnecessary limits on social interaction.

Can categories be transformed into groups? Yes, just as with aggregates, a crisis can cause a transformation. For example, in 2001, the crisis of a devastating terrorist attack turned the category "New Yorkers" into a group. People were suddenly showing affection to strangers and making sacrifices for each other. Even the criminals in the city were drawn into the social embrace—crime rates dropped significantly for a period of several weeks. Likewise, immediately after the Oklahoma City bombing of 1995, crime rates dropped just as sharply (Kuntzman, 2001).

Another way for categories to change into groups is through political action. For example, Karl Marx noticed that "factory workers" were just a category, a mass of lonely individuals each struggling separately to survive. Marx wanted to make this category into a group: a powerful army. If the workers could only realize that "we" all suffer together because of a common enemy (namely, the capitalist system), then "we" could unite in fulfilling our common destiny (namely, to destroy that system).

Other political movements have echoed this idea. Feminist leaders, for example, encourage women to unite, to see themselves as part of a powerful coalition with the strength to overcome the system of male privilege. Such political action has been only partially successful. All workers have not united, and neither have all women. Instead, much smaller groups have formed, such as workers unions and women's rights organizations.

Why Do People Join Groups?

Joining groups is a matter of survival. Individuals are far better able to feed, protect, and shelter themselves when they work together. As discussed above, times of crisis remind people of this need for cooperation.

Yet there are other human needs that drive people toward each other. Emile Durkheim believed that social belonging is necessary for two reasons:

1. Humans need guidance on how to think, act, and feel. Such guidelines for how to live are called **norms**. Durkheim argued that only social groups can provide norms. Individuals trying to exist alone are hopelessly confused.
2. Humans need to share experiences and feel that they are part of something larger than themselves. Without this kind of bonding, said Durkheim, individuals are unbearably isolated.

In fact, Durkheim believed that confused and isolated individuals are more likely to commit suicide. If he was correct, this is yet another way that groups are necessary for survival.

Current studies do seem to confirm, over and over again, that people need strong social connections. Deep involvement in a wide variety of strong social networks is correlated with living longer and healthier. A "longer and healthier life" includes a reduced likelihood of suicide, mental illness, and physical illness. This holds true whether the social network is a religious community, a friendship group, an extended family, or a marriage. (Davis, Morris, & Kraus, 1998; Kana'iaupuni, Donato, Thompson-Colon, & Stainback, 2005; Valliant, 2002; Wills & Fegan, 2001). Even a deep attachment to a pet appears to enhance mental and physical health (Allen, Blasovich, & Mendes, 2002; Pachana, Ford, Andrew, & Dobson, 2005).

Where Do Groups Get So Much Power?

At the beginning of this chapter, I stated that groups have extraordinary power over individuals. We have discussed how much individuals need groups. Since groups tend to punish, sometimes even cast out, members that disappoint them, individuals are highly motivated to meet group expectations. When individuals obey the norms of a group, it is called conformity. How do groups ensure the conformity of their members? Their main tools are: internalized norms, identity control, and the power of division.

Internalized Norms

Most of the norms we conform to every day are invisible to us; we follow them completely unaware. For example, we don't imagine that we are conforming when we smile in greeting other people. When such norms are broken, though, we suddenly notice them. A person who consistently fails to smile in greeting soon discovers that social consequences follow, like disapproval, perhaps resentment or suspicion, and withdrawal (for a thorough discussion of this idea, see Garfinkle, 1967).

We tend to be most unaware of norms that are fully internalized. Such social rules have been so completely accepted that our obedience is automatic. When this is so, there is no need for external control.

Authority is one kind of internalized norm. Authority is power that is socially accepted, often so completely that it is not questioned. For example, in a typical college class, students start the first day by helping to establish the teacher's authority. They obey norms when they sit, listen, and write. As the weeks pass, the teacher's authority may be challenged, but likely by only a few. Often the only challenges are quiet absences or privately missed assignments. The conformity level in a college classroom is high, usually without obvious enforcement. This is because each of the participants has internalized the rules of school, including teacher authority, early in life.

The authority of the teacher is *not* a personal trait belonging to that individual. Instead, this power lies in the status and role of the person. A status is a person's position in a social arrangement (e.g., teacher or student), and a role is a set of expectations attached to a status (e.g., grading, lecturing, writing, answering questions). The individuals involved are entirely replaceable. One day, all of the people in the classroom will be dead and gone, but the class will still continue. New members will occupy the old statuses and play the old roles. In this sense, groups can be immortal.

Identity Control

The fact that most of our conformity is automatic lends groups enormous and effortless power. But equally important, groups have power because they shape individual identity.

A **reference group** is any group that an individual admires enough to use as a standard for his or her own identity. The individual may or may not be a member of the reference group. For example, suppose that I admire the dedication of Mother Theresa and those who worked with her to alleviate poverty. That reference group may inspire me to volunteer at homeless shelters and give to charities. It may even keep me humble to mentally compare my contribu-

Best friends.

Source: Anissa Thompson

tions to theirs. Note that a reference group can have a significant influence over an individual's behavior and self-concept, even at a great distance and after some or all of its members have died. In this case, the conformity is managed entirely through the individual's own imagination.

Of course, reference groups can also be much closer to home. In fact, they could actually be a person's primary or secondary groups. **Primary groups**, such as family or friends, are organized around togetherness and assumed to be long-lasting—perhaps eternal. Meanwhile, **secondary groups**, like classmates and coworkers, are organized around a task and assumed to be short-term.

Primary groups have the earliest and deepest hold on our identities. For this reason, they have greater ability to demand conformity than secondary groups. This helps explain why basic values are more effectively taught at home than at school.

Business men and women who act with integrity are no different than their dishonest peers as far as the number of ethics courses they took in college (Conroy & Emerson, 2004). The difference between them is how pro-social values were taught in their primary groups.

We can see how deeply individual identity is rooted in primary groups by considering "borrowed glory" and "borrowed shame." If a member of my family (primary group) earns an award, my whole family glows in the light of it, shouting "We rock!" But if one of my coworkers (secondary group) earns an award, while I'm happy for him or her, it doesn't have any consequence for my identity. There's no borrowing of the glory. Likewise, imagine that one of my close friends was arrested for a crime. I'd be devastated. In a way, the shame would also rest on me. Meanwhile, if one of my classmates were arrested, maybe I'd simply consider it an interesting story to tell.

Secondary groups can transform into primary groups if they last long enough. For example, when a cohort of students spends several years participating in the same classes, they will begin to experience the dynamics of a primary group. They will imagine their bonds lasting forever and begin to borrow glory and shame. The behavior of each individual will become more dependent on that group. The same can be seen among coworkers who have shared their place of employment for years.

Even though primary groups have superior power, don't underestimate the potential identity control in secondary groups. Individuals are vulnerable to secondary groups because humans are likely to live up (or down) to social expectations. Obviously, there are exceptions to this kind of rule, but recent research continues to confirm this as a general tendency. (For some examples, see McFarland and Pals, 2005; Nath, Borkowski, Whitman, & Schellenbach, 1991; Sanders, 2002.)

In one classic example, Rosenthal and Jacobson (1968) demonstrated the power of teacher expectations through a series of experiments. The researchers began with a pool of equally intelligent children. They then lied to teachers, pretending that some of the children were especially smart and about to "bloom." By the end of eight months, the academic achievement of the expected bloomers was significantly superior to that of the other students. This occurred despite the fact that none of the students knew they had been labeled one way or the other. It was enough that the expectation existed in the teacher's mind. How could a teacher's private thoughts result in a student's real-life academic achievement? Through the way the teacher responded to the student. Although the teachers in this experiment were not aware of doing so, they answered the supposed bloomers more frequently and thoughtfully than they did the others. The "bloomers" were given more challenges and opportunities.

The Power Of Division

Both sources of group power that we have discussed—internalized norms and identity control—seem to operate largely without the conscious awareness of the people involved. There is another powerful group dynamic that works just as inadvertently: the formation of **in-groups** and **out-groups**.

Any formation of a valued "we" can be called an in-group. Unfortunately, this automatically defines anyone who isn't part of it as "they," the out-group. The more valuable the in-group, the sharper the division between "we" and "they." Naturally, "we" are more immediately relevant to the daily living of each "I" than "they" are. We certainly have more contact and mutual understanding with each other than with anyone outside the group. It is a small step, then, to imagine that we are essentially different from them. Now add the human tendency toward self-serving bias (for a summary of studies demonstrating such bias, see Aronson, Wilson, & Akert, 2005). Given this self-serving tendency, the belief that "we are essentially different from them" becomes "we are superior to them." Another small step, and the members of the out-group are viewed with contempt and suspicion.

Even though such enemies are created unintentionally, the automatic animosity between in-groups and out-groups can have severe consequences.

Application: The Connection Between Peace-Loving And Violence

At the beginning of the chapter, I asked, "If every major world religion preaches peace and universal love, why does each have a history of violence?" Examples of violence in the history of Christianity include the Crusades of Medieval Europe and, more recently, the Ku Klux Klan in America. Buddhism is often considered an exception to this rule, but its followers have not always been peaceful—for example, the Samurai warriors of Japan.

The puzzling connection between peace-loving religions and violence can be explained by returning to our discussion of the sources of group power. Religion provides individuals with deeply internalized norms, firm identities for each member, and a highly valued in-group. Remember that the very existence of an in-group defines everyone else as an out-group. That basic fact sets the stage for conflict.

Even the best intentions of religious people, and the most sincere preaching about peace and love, cannot erase it.

Once powerful in-groups and out-groups are established, is it possible to dissolve them? Sherif and his colleagues ran an experiment to find the answer (Sherif, Harvey, White, Hood, & Sherif, 1961). They assembled a collection of unconnected children and divided them randomly into two groups. They then encouraged each of the new groups to form a strong sense of "we" through creating group rituals (e.g., chants and games) and symbols (e.g., a flag and a name). As each in-group developed, animosity toward the other group—the out-group—followed. Although this began automatically, Sherif's research team decided to purposely magnify the effect. They set the groups against each other in competitions and played little tricks, like making sure that half of the available food was spoiled.

They succeeded in maximizing inter-group hatred. But the researchers' final goal was to test how inter-group hatred, once created, might be overcome. At first, they tried getting the groups together in shared activities. That didn't help. For example, none of the children was interested in watching a movie because they were too busy taunting and throwing things at each other. What did finally work was setting up a series of emergencies (e.g., the bus broke down, the pipes burst) so that all of the children in both groups were forced to work collectively. Mutual need broke the divide. By the end of the experiment, Sherif boasted, there were best friend pairs across what used to be enemy lines.

As of this writing, the United States is still at war in Iraq and Afghanistan. Officially, the conflict is not about religious differences. Yet the animosity between the largely Christian West and the largely Muslim Middle East is certainly fueled by the in-

U.S. troops in Iraq.

Source: Master Gunner

group/out-group dynamic. Could we borrow the wisdom of Sherif's experiment? Could we arrange a mutual need that would break the divide between the United States and its enemies? Social scientists call such a need a **superordinate goal**. Negotiators in the Middle East have been trying for many decades to find one that would unite opposing sides.

The trick in finding a superordinate goal is to expand the definition of "we" to include everyone and to join in a common effort. Instead, in the current war against terrorism, definitions of "we" are more solidly exclusive than ever. In order to conduct a successful war, leaders must strengthen, not dissolve, a nation's sense of "we." That's why President Bush called Iraq, Iran, and North Korea the "Axis of Evil" (State of the Union Address, 2002). He was making a purposeful connection to the times of WWII when the United States could feel confident that its fight was righteous against the "Axis" of Italy, Germany, and Japan. His attempt makes perfect sense if our goal is to strengthen a separate "we." But suppose that terrorism is created in the first place by that in-group/out-group dynamic? In that case, we want to solve this problem by going in the opposite direction.

Conformity: Wonderful Or Terrifying?

At the beginning of the chapter, I suggested that the power of groups can be either wonderful or terrifying. Much of that power is achieved through demanding conformity.

On The Wonderful Side

Conformity can be wonderful: getting good grades in school, obeying the law, maintaining healthy habits, and showing kindness to others. All of these types of conformity are associated with significant benefits for the individual. As we discussed earlier, health and long life are among the rewards that groups can offer.

How can groups provide so much? Part of the answer is through **social ritual**. Social rituals are set behaviors that symbolize a relationship. Such rituals can be complex like a wedding ceremony or simple like a daily hug. The simple, daily rituals are the ones that are associated with positive results for individuals. For example, children who grow up in families with a lot of ritual—like eating sit-down meals, preserving holiday traditions, and following a bedtime routine—are less likely than other children to engage in crime, drug abuse, or early sex (Kiser, Bennet, Heston, & Paavola, 2005; Pollard & Hawkins, 1999).

On The Terrifying Side

Unfortunately, history has repeatedly shown how conformity can go wrong. The worst example of this was the Holocaust, the slaughtering of millions of people who failed to fit Adolf Hitler's idea of human perfection. Hitler could not have accomplished such an enormous crime by himself. His plan required the conformity of thousands of followers. The rest of the world now sits in judgment, asking, "How could the German people go along with it? How could their soldiers obey such terrible orders?"

Sociology offers a terrifying answer: they did it for the same reasons that anyone goes along with anything. As we discussed earlier, it is normal for individuals to obey authority without thinking, to play familiar roles without complaint, to conform identity to group expectations, and to divide into in-groups and out-groups. Conformity is essential to all human societies, and the people involved in this atrocity were no different than anyone else in the world. It means that the Holocaust might happen anywhere.

A social psychologist named Stanley Milgram tried to prove that Americans can be just as horribly obedient as the Nazi soldiers were (Milgram, 1963). In the 1960s, Milgram did a series of experiments on American college students and community members. He told the experiment volunteers that they must deliver electric shocks to someone they could hear but not see. Milgram explained that the shocks would help the unseen person learn academic information more effectively, since the person would only receive shocks if he answered questions incorrectly. The unseen person was an actor; he didn't actually receive any shocks. But Milgram made the volunteers believe that they were really shocking someone. He had a convincing "shock machine" with blinking lights, lots of electric switches, and bright red danger signs. The unseen actor answered the experimenter's questions wrong on purpose so that the volunteers would have to shock him. As the experiment went on, the actor shouted out in distress, saying something like, "Please don't shock me anymore. It hurts, and I have a heart condition." The volunteers would turn to the experimenter and ask for permission to stop. But the experimenter, who was wearing the white lab coat that symbolizes scientific authority, would say something like, "No, you can't stop. You'll ruin the experiment. You must continue for the sake of science." Sixty-five percent of the volunteers continued to send shocks until the actor no longer responded, and was possibly dead. Milgram had found what he wanted: ordinary Americans who would kill an innocent victim because they were told to do it.

The volunteers in Milgram's experiments were not mentally ill, nor were they criminals. In fact, Milgram made sure that all of the volunteers were mentally and socially stable by giving them a series of psychological tests before allowing them to participate. The Nazi soldiers were just ordinary people, too.

Of course, a set of controlled laboratory experiments cannot truly match the social conditions surrounding the Holocaust. Admittedly, Milgram's work can only suggest what might have been involved. Furthermore, Milgram's samples were small, not representative of the whole nation. His studies could not truly yield accurate conclusions about "the average American."

Knowing the limits of this kind of research tempts me to breathe a sigh of relief. I might say to myself, "Americans couldn't really be that obedient, especially not now. People are much less impressed by authority these days." Unfortunately, recent research does not support such an optimistic conclusion about resistance to misused authority.

A new study, conducted by psychologist Jerry Burger in 2006, has attempted to replicate Milgram's experiments (as of this writing, it is still in press for publication, but the paper is available on his website). Because of ethical concerns, in Burger's study the volunteers were not pressured to

continue until the actor pretended possible death. Instead, they were pushed to continue only after the first verbal plea for mercy. Burger reasoned that, since most of the participants in Milgram's study who went that far also continued to the end, this would provide a reasonable comparison. While 82 percent of Milgram's participants continued to deliver shocks after the first plea to stop, 70 percent of Burger's did the same. Although the percentage in the replication study is slightly lower than in the original, this still means that most participants obeyed authority despite substantial personal misgivings.

Application: Heroes Who Are Villains

At the beginning of the chapter, I asked how American soldiers, dedicated to defending our nation, could be guilty of torture and abuse. I was referring to the scandal at the Abu Ghraib prison in Iraq. At Abu Ghraib, soldiers in the U.S. Army and agents of the C.I.A. extracted confessions from prisoners who were suspected of violent opposition to the new government. In order to do so, some of them used torture (e.g., starvation, injury). In some cases, the abuse of prisoners went far beyond what was imagined as useful in gaining confessions (e.g., forced sexual acts, humiliation) (Hersh, 2004).

So far, it has not been proven that any of this activity was officially authorized. But even if the torture was not directly ordered, these incidents are still examples of conformity to social expectations. Besides the obvious group dynamics of conformity, there are two more social conditions at Abu Ghraib that help explain this disturbing set of individual behaviors: **deindividuation** and **dehumanization**.

Deindividuation: Lost In A Role

Deindividuation occurs when a person loses his or her individual identity and effectively "disappears" into a group. Social roles and crowds are the likeliest places to lose someone.

Earlier in our discussion, I mentioned that social roles carry their own power and a tendency to endure, regardless of which individuals might be playing the parts. In a sense, individuals can "disappear" into their roles. When individuals accept roles, they are showing a willingness to allow social norms, rather than personal factors, to determine their behavior. Some roles include harmful behavior, such as that required of a soldier in a war. An individual given such a role becomes far more willing to cause that harm than if the behavior was considered a matter of personal choice.

The power of social roles in overwhelming individual conscience was demonstrated in a classic experiment conducted by Philip Zimbardo, a social psychologist like Stanley Milgram (Zimbardo, 1972). Zimbardo and his team created a pretend prison, complete with barred windows and bare cots, in the basement of the psychology building at Stanford University. The volunteers in the experiment were randomly assigned to play one of two prison roles: either guard or inmate. Those assigned to be inmates were arrested on schedule by the real Stanford police, handcuffed in front of uninformed neighbors, stripped and deloused, given uniforms, and given prison numbers to replace their names. Those assigned to become prison guards were also given uniforms and a command to keep control of the prisoners. Then Zimbardo settled in to watch what he thought would be a two-week play.

Within just a few days, the volunteers were no longer acting; they were suffering a true loss of individual identity. Some of the guards became sadistic, humiliating and harassing the prisoners. Some of the prisoners became suicidal. Just as Milgram had done, Zimbardo had tested all of the experiment participants to make sure that they were emotionally and socially stable before beginning. Therefore, he was certain that the disintegration of the volunteers was entirely created by the social situation. Zimbardo was delighted; this was just what he wanted to prove. It was a graduate student who challenged him and asked, "What are you doing?" Only then did Zimbardo admit that he was doing harm in the name of science, that he himself had lost his conscience to his social role.

At Abu Ghraib, the soldiers and agents who tortured prisoners in order to extract confessions saw themselves as fulfilling their roles, "just doing our jobs." Their motive was to meet the goals of their organizations. It is unlikely that they would have committed so much violence on their own.

Deindividuation: Lost In A Crowd

At Abu Ghraib, the abuse of prisoners could not have continued without the silence of many observers who were afraid to intervene. Many did not approve of what was happening, but they did nothing to stop it. Once again, this is a kind of deindividuation, each person refusing to stand out, preferring to remain faceless in a crowd.

Deindividuation explains why so many people will refuse to help an injured stranger on the street. None of the individuals passing by is responsible for doing anything. Even when a group of onlookers is talking to each other about what happened, each person is just "part of the crowd." This is also known as the **bystander effect**. A recent example was caught on a surveillance camera in Connecticut when a 78-year-old male pedestrian was struck by a car. The driver was chasing another driver and didn't even slow down after striking the man. The victim lay paralyzed but still alive while pedestrians and other motorists paused and then left without helping. Finally, a police officer on his way to deal with a different incident came to the man's rescue (Fox News Network, 2008).

If you are ever in trouble in a public place, it is important to break the spell of deindividuation by asking specific individuals for help. Even making eye contact increases the likelihood of getting help. Anything that reminds someone that he or she is an identifiable individual will increase that person's sense of responsibility (Kerr & Bruun, 1983; Latane & Darley, 1968).

Dehumanization

With deindividuation, there are still individuals in hiding who have personal feelings of empathy for the victims of violence. But with dehumanization, personal empathy is absent. The victims of violence are considered less than fully human and, therefore, are not deserving of full human rights. The victims seem to be part of an extreme out-group, no longer even part of the species. **Dehumanization** is when individuals deprive others of their humanity.

As we discussed, some soldiers at Abu Ghraib

were violent toward prisoners because they imagined that their roles required it. Yet, there were some soldiers who went far beyond the demands of the role. They took pleasure in degrading the prisoners and eagerly maximized prisoner suffering.

The U.S. military *does not* purposely teach its soldiers to behave this way. But it *does* train soldiers to dehumanize their opponents. Most soldiers are ordinary people who care. How can caring individuals be trained to kill? By dehumanizing the enemy. Obliterating the enemy must become like winning at a computer game. Violence against those who have been dehumanized becomes not only acceptable, but also desirable.

At Abu Ghraib, conformity, deindividuation, and dehumanization were combined. Given this social context, abuse and torture are not truly surprising.

Standing Up To Groups

Despite the intense nature of group power, it is possible, after all, for individuals to resist. In some cases, there are social factors that help the individual to do so. Individuals are most likely to stand up to groups successfully when they have at least one ally, self-confidence, high social status, and a smaller group to resist.

Having An Ally

As it happens, Milgram was once a teaching assistant for another famous researcher of conformity, Solomon Asch. In Asch's experiments, volunteers were shown a straight line and then asked to choose which of three other lines matched the first in length. The correct answer was obvious. Every one of the seven people in the room answered easily. But after a few successes, as they continued to match up lines, six of the seven people began to answer incorrectly. They did this purposely because they were in on the experiment. The seventh person, the only actual subject, was then left to decide whether to report the obvious truth or to conform to the group and report the same wrong answer as everyone else. About 75 percent of the subjects gave in at least once, although it was more typical to give in about one-third of the time (Asch, 1955).

However, in further experiments, Asch discovered that if even one other person in the room would answer truthfully, the subjects were far more likely to do so themselves. Milgram also discovered that his subjects were far likelier to resist conformity when given a positive model who resisted first. Curiously, in Burger's replication of Milgram's study, the presence of a resistant model made no difference. But other recent research continues to confirm the helpfulness of even one ally in resisting the pressure to conform to group errors (Choi & Levine, 2004; De Dreu & West, 2001; Ng & Dyne, 2001).

Having Self-Confidence

An individual can only successfully resist a group when armed with self-confidence. After Asch's experiments were over, he asked participants why they were sometimes willing to agree with clearly wrong information. Many of them stated that they had begun to doubt their own judgment. Even among the 25 percent of subjects who never gave in, many reported having private doubts about the accuracy of their own perceptions. This is remarkable given the simplicity and clarity of the visual material.

When individuals value a group enough to accept group decisions against their own better judgment, it is called **groupthink**. Social scientists once believed that groupthink was most likely to happen when groups were in crisis and didn't have time to consider alternatives, isolated without outside reality checks, and had high status providing extra faith in the rightness of the group (Janis, 1972). But psychologist Robert Baron (2005) argues that groupthink is far more common, and is an ordinary feature of daily life everywhere. According to his investigation, there are two main causes of groupthink:

1. Group members with low self-efficacy are likely to follow the lead of those who are more confident. Such individuals tend to suppress their own, often valid, reservations. **Self-efficacy** is personal confidence that one can accomplish what is desired and manage what is necessary.
2. Group members are likely to spend most of their time and energy talking about the information

that everyone already agrees on. For this reason, they often miss unique information that each member could otherwise offer.

Having High Status

Besides self-confidence, high status is helpful in standing up to groups. As groups form, members automatically and rapidly fall into a hierarchy, with some members having more power and privilege than others. This holds true even in small, temporary groups, like discussion groups in a class. Relative status within the group emerges as members form impressions of each others' likely contributions. (Berger, Wagner, & Zelditch, 1985; Correll & Ridgeway, 2003).

Members of the group with the lowest status have only their conformity to offer. The highest status members, since their contributions are considered so valuable, earn idiosyncrasy credit (Hollander, 1958). **Idiosyncrasy credit** is group permission for nonconformity. In other words, high status members are allowed to break the rules—at least some rules, sometimes, to some degree. Group members tend to agree on who has such credit and how much (Estrada, Brown, & Lee, 1995).

Someone with high status may choose to spend his or her idiosyncrasy credit on helping someone with lower status stand up to the group. This includes allowing newcomers to introduce changes (Lortie-Lussier, 1987). Spending social credit this way is not motivated so much by kindness as by wisdom. Groups are more likely to make successful decisions when they accept dissent and innovation. In turn, the success of the group secures the continuation of idiosyncrasy credit (Hollander, 2004).

Having A Smaller Group To Face

The smaller the group, the easier it is to stand up against it. However, Milgram didn't believe that. In his experiments, conformity was already maximized by the time the group had grown to four members. For that reason, social scientists often cite four as the magic number, though more recent research shows conformity continuing to increase with group size (Walther et al., 2002).

Larger groups become less flexible (Idson, 1990). This is because they must create a formal set of rules to avoid disintegrating. These rules help coordinate efforts and avoid confusion and conflict. But they also add a rigid layer of group expectations, making conformity that much harder to resist.

As groups grow, it is difficult to stay aware of each member, and attention usually focuses on a smaller subgroup of leaders. Each member who is not a leader is at least one step removed from the decision center. They become dependent on the expertise of the few (Bonner & Baumann, 2008). Once again, the individual who would like to be different has an increasingly difficult task.

Diversity: An Unappreciated Benefit

Although both groups and individuals are significantly benefited by diversity, both strongly prefer homogeneity. **Diversity** refers to the existence of differences, whether within groups or between groups. The opposite of diversity is **homogeneity**, or sameness.

The Benefit Of Diversity For Groups

Diversity within groups can help members come to more accurate conclusions and solve problems more effectively and creatively. As we were just discussing, when individuals stand up to groups, groups tend to benefit. Dissenters can introduce unexpected information, different points of view, and new strategies. Even when a dissenter is completely wrong, just the fact that someone said or did something different tends to make group members more willing to explore alternatives. This usually results in higher quality group decisions (Brodbeck, Kerschreiter, Mojzisch, Frey, & Schulz-Hardt, 2002; Nemeth & Kwan, 1987).

Groups can also take advantage of diversity by assigning different tasks to different members according to ability and desire. When members specialize, the group can accomplish tasks that are greater, both in number and in complexity.

The Benefit Of Diversity For Individuals

Individuals know that they depend on the help of family and friends, but they often underestimate how much they need acquaintances. For example, a diverse **social network** of acquaintances is essential to most successful job searches. Family and friends cannot know of all the best job opportunities, and strangers would not be motivated to share them. Sociologist Mark Granovetter (1983) called the importance of diverse acquaintances "the strength of weak ties." He and later researchers have documented the benefits that such ties provide:

- Valuable information (not only job opportunities, but news and fresh ideas).
- Increased flexibility and creativity in thinking and behavior.
- Strength in resisting unhealthy conformity to local norms.
- Increased acceptance of dissimilar others (including willingness to racially integrate).
- Involvement in political action.
- Success in establishing small businesses (Ruef, 2002).

The Preference For Homogeneity

Despite the benefits of diversity, we know from our previous discussion that groups strive to stay homogenous, using all the tools of conformity. Individuals, too, prefer homogeneity. For example, people tend to marry others who are like themselves. Typically, spouses are similar in social class, race, religion, personality, level of attractiveness, I.Q. score, and life experiences (for a summary, see Baumeister & Bushman, 2008, and Hamon & Ingoldsby, 2003). Marriages that cross social lines, like interfaith and interracial marriages, are often—though not always—at greater risk for divorce (Chan & Smith, 2001; Heaton & Pratt, 1990).

Individuals show the same desire for homogeneity in other kinds of groups, as well. Some examples include work teams, counseling groups, military divisions, and neighborhoods. In all of these, feelings of personal satisfaction and loyalty to the group are enhanced when members are similar to each other (Kemelgor, 2007; Meir, Hadasi, & Noyfeld, 1997; Mouritzen, 2006; Perrone & Sedlacek, 2000).

Application: Sorry, Not A Small World After All

As strong as weak ties may be, they do have limits. You have probably heard about the "small world" phenomenon. This is the idea that everyone in the world is connected to everyone else within six acquaintance links, or six "degrees." Unfortunately, this is not true, even though some textbooks are still reporting it as a fact.

It was Milgram who introduced the "small world" idea in 1967. He performed experiments in which he asked volunteers to deliver a letter to a complete stranger. Although they had the stranger's name and address, the volunteers were not allowed to simply mail it—they could only pass the letter on to an acquaintance they knew by first name. Then that person must do the same, and so on. Milgram reported that after repeated trials, on average, it took six first-name acquaintances to deliver the letter to the target stranger. Milgram's findings were embraced at once, not only by the American public but by social scientists.

Eventually, psychologist Judith Kleinfeld (2002) pointed out that Milgram's "small world" conclusion could not be true for the following reasons:

- Most of Milgram's letters never reached the target stranger.
- Milgram's original samples were white and well-educated. Such limited samples cannot represent all of America, much less the world.
- Follow-up studies demonstrated that familiar social divisions such as class and race interfered with letter delivery.

Kleinfeld suggested that only some of us enjoy a "small world." High status individuals are well-connected with each other, just like members of a small town. Among such populations, strangers are not far removed from each other. Yet these miniature worlds are isolated pockets relative to the rest of the world.

Application: Inequality In A Land Of Opportunity

At the beginning of the chapter I asked, "If America is the land of equal opportunity, why do race and gender continue to make such a difference?" First, I want to establish that they really do, and then I'll offer four possible explanations.

Below is a chart that shows how race and gender shape the incomes associated with different educational degrees. Even though education is the most powerful tool for upward mobility in the United States, educational degrees do not bring the same financial rewards to everyone.

Patterns In The Chart

- Within each category, the higher the educational degree, the higher the yearly income. In other words, education is helpful to everyone, both genders and all races.

- When you compare categories, the inequalities by race and gender are clear. For example, white Americans who have bachelor's degrees make $3,420 more per year than black Americans who also have bachelor's degrees. Males of all races who have bachelor's degrees make $15,733 more per year than females of all races who also have bachelor's degrees.

- Being a woman is a greater financial disadvantage than being a person of color. That disadvantage increases as degrees advance.

- Contrary to stereotype, Asian-Americans *do not* have a consistent advantage over white Americans.

Possible Explanations

How can this disturbing reality be explained?

For 2005, Median Yearly Income by Degree Earned, Race, and Gender

	High School	Associate's Degree	Bachelor's Degree	Master's Degree	Doctoral Degree	Lawyers/ Doctors
Both Sexes, All Races	26,505	35,009	43,143	52,390	70,853	82,473
RACE						
White (alone, not Hispanic)	28,617	36,013	44,992	52,385	71,283	86,853
Black (alone)	22,379	30,590	41,572	48,266	61,849	71,456
Asian (alone)	25,285	31,075	42,466	61,452	69,653	80,939
Hispanic (all races)	22,941	31,437	37,819	50,901	67,274	51,021
GENDER						
Male (all races)	32,085	42,382	52,265	67,123	78,324	100,000
Female (all races)	21,117	29,510	36,532	45,730	54,666	66,055

Source: U.S. Census Bureau. (2006). Current Population Survey: Annual Social and Economic Supplement, Numbers in thousands, People 25 years old and over. Retrieved November 1, 2006 from Current Population Survey website. http://pubdb3.census.gov/macro/032006/perinc/new03_000.htm

Chart was created by Dr. Bev Farb (author of this chapter), using data from seven different U.S. Census tables, November 1, 2006.

I offer four possible explanations: the desire for homogeneity, unequal weak ties, the motherhood penalty, and segregated job markets.

1) Desire For Homogeneity.

Hiring agents are not immune to the pervasive desire for homogeneity. Neither are the managers who control promotions. Just as with marriage, people tend to hire and promote others who are similar to themselves (Essed, 2002; Petersen & Dietz, 2006). Obviously, this reduces opportunities for those who do not resemble the people currently in charge, thus maintaining the pattern of relative privilege.

2) Unequal Weak Ties.

As discussed earlier, weak ties (i.e., acquaintance networks) appear to be the best source of information about job opportunities. This is especially true for college-educated individuals who are searching for higher-end employment. Opportunities for lower-end jobs are usually local and are more likely to be found through the strong ties of friends and family (Granovetter, 1983).

Weak ties between individuals of different racial categories tend to be relatively few and far between. This means that people of color are less likely than whites to hear about the best positions or, if they do, they may find out too late. This reduces the diversity of applicant pools, leaving hiring agents with limited choices even when they are eager to diversify staff.

Women are more likely than people of color to have sufficient weak ties for a job search. But the weak ties of women may be less helpful than those of men. Sociologist Gail McGuire (2002) surveyed more than a thousand employees at a financial services firm. She discovered that the men received a great deal of work-related help from their acquaintances. This included help in getting around bureaucratic hurdles, getting one's work recognized, meeting influential others, and getting promotions. Equal help was offered to both white and black men, but only when their organizational positions were equal, which was rare. Women were offered less help than men regardless of race. This was true even when comparing women and men who had equal positions.

Most workplaces can claim that their official, formal procedures are fair. Discrimination is far likelier to show up in everyday, informal interactions. This is important because such interactions have consequences for promotion outcomes (James, 2000; Powell & Butterfield, 1997). Often, the informal harm is done through exclusion. For example, not being invited to lunch can mean missing out on an informal planning session. Not being included in hallway conversations can mean not even coming to mind for important assignments. When informal exclusion results in missed opportunities, the economic consequences can be serious.

3) The Motherhood Penalty.

Women are still more likely than men to take time off from work, or to work only part-time, in order to care for their young children. This translates into lower incomes despite equivalent education in three ways:

- Direct loss of wages due to fewer hours worked.
- Loss of opportunities for promotions and career-building assignments.
- Automatic responses—unintended but damaging—from employers and managers based on beliefs about mothers.

Such automatic responses were documented through an experiment by Correll and Benard (2005). They gave hiring agents two applicant profiles that were equally strong for the position of marketing director. In an attached memo, one applicant was described as the mother of two children, while the other woman was believed to be childless. The hiring agents were twice as likely to report wanting to hire the childless applicant (84% vs. 47%). They also offered an average of $11,000 more to her. Further, the hiring agents indicated a greater willingness to tolerate absences from the "non-mother." Correll and Benard ran the experiment again, this time with the equally strong applications of a father and a "non-father" and the opposite trend was observed. The father was offered an average of $6,000 more and was granted more tolerance for absences. Employers appear to consider parenthood an asset for men, but a liability for women.

4) Segregated Job Markets.

Women and men still tend to predominate in different kinds of jobs. On the whole, "her" typical jobs pay far less than "his" typical jobs. This is true even when required skills and training are taken into account. For example, in 2004, the median wage for a state-licensed day care provider ("her" job) in the United States was $8.06 per hour. Meanwhile, a refuse collector ("his" job) earned a median wage of $12.38. For both jobs, a completed high school education is preferred, and on-the-job training is available. For the licensed day care provider, additional training hours were required, like first aid and child abuse prevention.

The same pattern is observable in higher-end jobs. In 2004, the median wage for a social worker in a mental hospital ("her" job) was $36,170 per year. Meanwhile, the median wage for a mechanical engineer ("his" job) was $59,880. Both jobs require master's degrees and internships (Bureau of Labor Statistics, 2005).

Neither women nor racial minorities receive an equitable return on their investment in education. Their educations will still benefit them greatly, but not equally.

Bureaucratic Organizations Have A Life Of Their Own

Each social condition that I described above (homogeneity, job markets, etc.) tends to create harmful inequality, but mostly without the conscious intention of anyone involved. Remember that conformity also typically operates without awareness. This is because all social forces have their own power, independent of individual will.

The power of social groups to live above and beyond their members is especially evident in bureaucracies. A **bureaucracy** is defined by the features below (Weber, 1947). Each feature contributes to a bureaucracy's ability to control its members:

1. A set of statuses and roles is arranged in a *fixed hierarchy*.
2. All activity is governed by a strict set of *rules* and tracked by keeping formal *records*.
3. Each status and role is *specialized*, responsible for a small piece of the bureaucracy's overall task. This makes every worker an *expert* in his or her own area.
4. Relationships are intended to be *impersonal* with every individual entirely focused on the demands of his or her bureaucratic role.

This arrangement has both benefits and detriments.

The Benefits Of Bureaucracy

More than any other kind of group, a bureaucracy is designed to provide consistency, efficiency, and neutrality.

Devotion to rules and records maximizes *consistency*. Insisting on rules keeps individual efforts stable and predictable. Maintaining a formal record of what everyone is doing helps bureaucracies enforce those rules. Beyond that, the records provide information useful for tracking progress and analyzing the effectiveness of different strategies.

Specialization maximizes *efficiency*. Remember from our earlier discussion that even small groups benefit from splitting up the work. This is the fastest and easiest way to get a massive or complex task done. Saving time and effort also reduces the need for other resources, such as money, required to keep the bureaucracy running.

The prototypical example of maximized efficiency and consistency is an assembly line. In an assembly line, a product is moved, usually by machine, past a series of workers. Each worker adds a single piece or performs a single operation. Because the product parts are interchangeable, and the process of assembly has been worked out ahead of time, workers do not need to spend any time or effort on creating designs or solving problems.

Henry Ford is often given credit for inventing the assembly line, but the process is much older, used by a variety of militaries to produce weapons, starting with ancient China. It was also used in the

1800s by the U.S. meat industry for butchering (Aeragon, 2006). It would be more accurate to say that in 1913, Ford *perfected* the assembly line, at least enough to achieve a dramatic drop in automobile prices. This placed cars within reach of average consumers.

Efficiency is also served by bureaucracy's expectation that workers will remain impersonal. This minimizes daily distractions. However, staying impersonal offers a deeper benefit: *neutrality*. Transcending the personal keeps the work free from political or emotional concerns. This is especially important when the bureaucracy is one that serves the public. For example, judges in criminal courts used to hand out sentences according to their personal assessments. Unfortunately, that included personal biases. In the mid-1980s, the U.S. government established sentencing guidelines, a bureaucratic list of rules that limited the possibilities. In the years directly following, there was a significant reduction of racial and gender bias in sentencing (Anderson, Kling, & Stith, 1999; Barkan, 2006). As time wore on, however, there began to be complaints that the prosecutor now had too much influence on sentencing and that the biases had simply moved (Bowman, 2005). The federal guidelines were not able to achieve long-term equality, but they are still an example of a worthy attempt at bureaucratic impartiality.

The Detriments Of Bureaucracy

Ironically, each strength of bureaucracy is also a source of difficulty. Each feature seems designed to make human creativity and emotion, and ultimately humans themselves, entirely unnecessary. This arrangement has the power to last far into the future through "bureaucratic inertia" and "routinization."

Weber provided the definition of bureaucracy that we have been using for this discussion. He also hated and feared what he described. He complained that bureaucratic efficiency and consistency are bought at an unacceptable price: the *suffocation of human creativity*. Bureaucratic tasks are purposely spelled out so that creativity will not be necessary. Innovative thought is too slow and effortful. Besides, it might suggest changes in the rest of the

bureaucracy that would cost too much.

When organizations resist beneficial change, this is called **bureaucratic inertia**. The main root of inertia is the complexity that comes with specialization. Rules are carefully designed to ensure that each specialty area makes its proper contribution to the whole. Therefore, making a change in one area usually demands adjustments in several others. A daunting amount of paperwork and meetings is required to shift so many bureaucratic pieces. Workers may resist such extra work if the required change does not make immediate sense for their area, even if it will benefit the overall organization. Their specialized concerns block their view of the "big picture" (Caiden, 1991). Political scientist William West explains one example. When a U.S. president wants to introduce an innovative change in Washington, his main obstacle is not usually Congress. Rather, it is the bureaucratic inertia of his own support staff that tends to frustrate him (West, 2005).

When creativity and change are limited, complained Weber, the human spirit suffers. Bureaucracy squeezes the individual even tighter through the *denial of human emotion*. Weber argued that, although people have always been subject to authority, they used to obey from their hearts. Feelings of devotion once inspired people to obey traditional leaders. Once in a while, a charismatic leader would arise, someone with new ideas who was considered exceptional. Then people would obey with enthusiastic hero worship. But now, lamented Weber, since the Industrial Revolution, authority has become rational, based on a set of logical rules. With rational authority, there is no need for feelings or personal attachments (Weber, 1946).

The main vehicle of rational authority is bureaucracy, and it is specifically designed to inhibit human emotion. Bureaucrats are expected to remain impersonal, concerned only with their own piece of the organizational task. Another way to say this is that everyone must be "professional." For example, when I enter a classroom—whether face-to-face or online—I must leave much of myself behind. The same is true for students. If any of us is especially sad, or angry, or even happy and celebrating, we must put that away and focus on our bureaucratic tasks. If I share a personal story about my life with students, the story had better have an educational purpose. Otherwise, I'm misusing everyone's time. I must not be too capricious about my grading either. I must follow the rules as exactly as possible. Yes, such bureaucratic neutrality is valuable, but also inhuman.

None of us dares to truly be ourselves. We must each play our predetermined roles and eventually be replaced by others who will do the same. In other words, we, personally, are entirely replaceable. This was Weber's final complaint: he was horrified by the *dispensability of human beings.*

Some of us might try to comfort Weber by pointing out that exciting charismatic leaders still show up from time to time. Perhaps they can free us from our bureaucratic non-existence. But Weber would answer that charismatic authority is inherently unstable. It only lasts as long as the leader is both popular and alive. After that, the new ideas and loyal followers may simply vanish. There is only one way for a charismatic leader to leave a lasting legacy: routinization. **Routinization** is the reduction of innovation into bureaucratic routine. Once the leader is gone, followers organize to keep his or her dream alive. In organizing, they are likely to adopt bureaucratic strategies: tasks will be split, rules will be defined, and so on. From Weber's perspective, bureaucracy wins again, trapping us in its "iron cage."

In fact, Weber believed that rational systems like bureaucracies will always triumph. Worse, they will spread everywhere, replacing more human systems all over the world. A present day sociologist, George Ritzer, agrees. He points to McDonald's restaurant as a prime example (Ritzer, 2000).

McDonald's was not the first fast food restaurant chain. That honor goes to White Castle (later White Tower), established in 1921 (Wisconsin Historical Society, 2008). In 1948, the McDonald brothers, Richard and Maurice, were the first to retool their diner for assembly line production. As a result, they no longer needed to pay the wages of skilled chefs. At the same time, they switched to disposable utensils and packaging, which allowed them to fire their wait staff and dishwashers. With maximized speed and minimized prices, they became industry leaders (Costin, 2007). Ray Kroc, a milkshake machine salesman, made a proposal to franchise the restaurant for a percentage of sales, and in 1955 the first franchise opened in Des Plaines, Illinois. In the 1960s, McDonald's began to franchise outside of the United States and it now has restaurants in 119 countries (Parks, 2006).

McDonald's, besides leaping international boundaries, is also being replicated through imitation. Other industries like toy manufacturing and banking are reorganizing to match its strategies and structure. Ritzer describes this process as, "McDonaldization." Given the financial success attached, conforming to this corporate trend is the rational choice. Yet, Ritzer warns that all of Weber's worst fears are coming true. In exchange for "big business" success, humans are giving up what should not be for sale: freedom, dignity, creativity, and close relationships (Ritzer, 2000).

Humanity May Be Underestimated

As for me, I think both Weber and Ritzer have underestimated the power of humanity to shine through rational rule systems. At least four conditions encourage an optimistic view:

1. The difference between informal and formal structure within a bureaucracy.
2. The partial humanization of big business through imitation of the *Japanese model.*
3. The development of alternatives to big business through a variety of "stay local" movements.
4. The ability of local populations across the world to choose their response to global forces.

Informal Vs. Formal Structure

The informal reality of a bureaucracy is not likely to match the formal expectations. The official rulebook is likely to describe only a fraction of the actual behavior in an office. Likewise, the organizational flowchart is supposed to show how authority and information move between positions and in what direction; yet, the actual flow may differ significantly. For example, employees may learn not to make requests of the manager since it is more effective to simply go to her secretary. This **informal organizational structure** of "the way things really work" is not written anywhere. No one has planned it out; it simply emerges as people interact.

According to Weber, people must stay impersonal in order to get their jobs done. But coworkers may easily become friends, especially if work-related frustrations are shared (Sias & Cahill, 1998). Indeed, office friendships influence the use of work-related resources, whether or not work-related information is passed on, and whether or not consensus is reached in group decisions (Lincoln & Miller, 1979; Rawlins, 1992). Boss-to-employee relations are also likely to involve strong feelings, although often hidden, rather than neutrality. Some workers have even reported that being able to trust a boss is more important to them than being able to trust a close friend (Cann, 2004).

The expected bureaucratic neutrality is often saved for customers and clients (Tschanh, Sylvie, & Dieter, 2005). Since neutrality is accomplished through strict obedience, the bureaucrat's contact with the public tends to be rigidly rule-focused, though individual humanity can still break through. This is illustrated by a story from my youth:

> Long ago, I lived in Los Angeles. In those days and in that city, getting your driver's license was an all-day ordeal. At the DMV, every step in the process involved a two hour line (e.g., a two-hour line to take the test, another two-hour line to get the results, etc.). Well, I waited in one of these lines, finally arrived at the front, and discovered to my horror that I had been waiting in the wrong line. Now, if Weber were entirely right, the bureaucrat on the other side of the counter should have said simply, "Next window, please." The regulations would not allow anything else. But, as it happened, there was actually a human on the other side of the counter. Observing the moisture that was beginning in my eyes, she whispered, "I'm not supposed to do this, but I can help you. Here's the form you need…." I burst into full tears and sobbed, "You're my b-best fr-friend!"

Perhaps human emotion and variation is not so easily obliterated after all.

Humanization Of Big Business: The Japanese Model

American business has been humanized through imitating the *Japanese business model*. Despite a disappointing reversal in recent years, many benefits of the original change remain.

In the 1970's, the American business community began to admire the Japanese business model. The Japanese model does not contain any of the bureaucratic features that Weber found so dehumanizing. For example, in a typical American bureaucracy, employees are only welcome as long as they are considered useful by management. Likewise, employees freely abandon companies when they find better opportunities elsewhere. But in Japanese business, there is a personal devotion between managers and employees; both are committed to a life-long relationship (Workman, 2008).

Many American companies have adopted their favorite pieces of the Japanese model. Especially popular has been the Japanese decision-making style. First, the decision-making is *collective*. Decisions are made in teams, so credit or blame is shared. This is in sharp contrast to the typical Western focus on personal performance and incentive plans. Second, decision-making is *bottom-up* instead of *top-down*. Work teams participate in key structural decisions such as how the work will be divided, how it will be completed, and how it will be rewarded. In a typical American bureaucracy, such decisions are designed and enforced by management (Egawa et al., 2007).

As long as the Japanese were envied competitors, the number of American companies eager to imitate them increased. Unfortunately, in the 1990s, Japan suffered an economic downturn. Many companies could no longer honor the life-long commitment between workers and management, so there were record layoffs (Japan Echo, 1998).

Since 2002, the direction of imitation reversed: At least 30 Japanese companies have now adopted some American business practices. Specifically, these companies have introduced performance-based pay. Previously, pay had been seniority-based. They are also now willing to sell off company divisions that are not performing well. Before, they would have protected all employees no matter what. Further, these companies now devote more energy to maintaining shareholders than to sustaining employees. Financially, this strategy has paid off, but humanity-wise, it is disappointing. For example, the distance between rich and poor has noticeably increased since these changes were made (Business in Japan, 2007).

How do I maintain an optimistic view in the face of such events? First, I find it encouraging that business communities, both Japanese and American, have demonstrated the capacity to make substantial changes. It means that Weber's "iron cage" has a door that can be opened. Second, Japanese-inspired changes in American business have survived. Compared with companies before the 1970s, current businesses are more accepting of employee control and innovation. (For examples see Berg, Appelbaum, Bailey, & Kalleberg, 2004; Gallup, 2006.)

Alternatives To Big Business: "Stay Local" Movements

Remember that Weber's nightmare of inescapable bureaucracy has been updated in Ritzer's nightmare of global and eternal corporate control. In direct opposition to such a possibility, *stay local* movements provide alternatives for both workers and consumers. Such movements include:

- The *local business* movement.
- The *local farming* movement.
- The *buy local* movement.
- The *eat local* movement.

Although each of these movements developed independently, they share a common goal. All hope to encourage individuals at the community level to resist corporate harm. For example, when corporations control job markets, workers are at constant

A farmers market in Turkey.

Source: Chris Gander

risk of unemployment because jobs can be auto-mated or sent overseas. Further, when corporations control product markets, they also control prices and quality. While product prices can strike at consumer wallets, product quality can threaten consumer health. Finally, corporate damage can include re-source depletion and pollution, even though many companies only contribute to these by transporting their goods long distances (Pollan, 2006).

One leading developer of local businesses, Judy Wicks (2006), explained the benefits of local control this way:

> Local business owners can provide more fulfilling jobs, healthier communities, and greater economic security in their region. Success can mean more than growing larger or increasing market-share. It can be measured by increasing happiness and well being, deepening relationships, and expanding creativity, knowledge, and con-sciousness.

Unfortunately, Wick was compelled to acknowl-edge the corporate ability to overwhelm such efforts. Many local businesses fail because of big business competition. But it's almost worse to know that if they succeed, eventually, they are likely to be absorbed by the big players. For example, Ben & Jerry's was once a main inspiration for the local movement, but it was recently bought by Unile-ver. Likewise, Odwalla was bought by Coca-Cola (Wicks, 2006).

Despite these defeats, local movements hope to survive through forming alliances with each other. Additional allies have been found in related efforts like the organic farming movement and the "slow food" movement which, of course, is specifically opposed to fast food (Wood, 2008).

Local Choice: Globalization Meets "Glocalization"

Globalization refers to the international spread of cultural items, practices, and ideas that were once local, such as chopsticks, the Olympic Games, and the Internet. Could globalization eventually lead to the development of a single world culture? Some eagerly anticipate such a day, hoping that a unified culture would bring peace and prosperity to all. Per-haps if this occurred we would pool our resources and enjoy the benefits of our collective wisdom.

Others dread the idea of one global culture. A homogenous world, by definition, would have lost its diversity. If the unified culture ends up being a globalized version of corporate America, we would be back to the same Weber/Ritzer scenario we keep discussing.

Many imagine that the West is bulldozing over the rest of a helpless world, but I don't think that gives sufficient credit to local populations. When pieces of a culture are globalized, the receiving pop-ulations do not always simply accept them. Instead, they are likely to take what they want of the global input, mix it with what they want from their local culture, and create something new. When globalized items, practices, and ideas are tailored to meet local needs, this is called **glocalization**.

My favorite example of creative glocalization is offered by the Mam, who are current descendents of the ancient Mayans. The Mam were growing coffee on small plots of land in Mexico when NAFTA (the North American Free Trade Agreement) was signed in 1994. Under NAFTA, participating governments are required to maximize trade across their borders. This was to take place no matter what the costs and meant discarding national laws that protected local businesses from corporate competition. The Mam feared that their little coffee industry would not survive. The Mexican government had been trying to "modernize" Mam coffee production for more than a decade. Despite the government's generous provision of pesticides and chemical fertilizers, the crops were meager (Castillo & Nigh, 1998). Mam coffee growers met to devise a plan. They decided that the chemicals were part of the problem, and they returned to their indigenous farming practices. But the Mam had a new tool this time: direct access to potential buyers through the Internet. They soon discovered that the global community viewed their farming as "organic" and would pay higher-than-av-erage prices for their coffee (Casillo & Nigh, 1998). The success of the new global business, Café Mam, is a triumph of glocalization.

Glocalization tends to be beneficial, even when

it does not result in financial rewards. In Singapore, public housing serves 90 percent of the population and consists of high-rise apartment buildings. The buildings were designed by a Western firm, and each has an open parking garage as the first level. The people in Singapore never use the garage for parking, though. Instead, this space is known as a "void deck" and is used for weddings, funerals, club meetings, after-school parties, and other neighborhood gatherings (Khondker, 2004).

Ironically, when the term glocalization was introduced, it did *not* refer to this kind of local empowerment. The word originally meant that a corporation was tailoring a global product to local tastes in order to increase sales (Robertson, 1994). Actually, corporations still use the word this way. For example, McDonald's glocalizes. In India, Big Macs cannot be sold because beef is prohibited, so the Maharaja Mac is made with lamb or chicken. In Germany, McDonald's offers beer. In Hong Kong, instead of using buns, sandwich ingredients are held between two rice patties, and the list goes on (Adams, 2007).

Perhaps you will not be surprised to hear that George Ritzer is offended by the corporate version of glocalization. Ritzer wants to keep this term for describing local resilience (as I did above). He recommends calling what corporations do **grobalization**. The "gro" is short for "grow" since corporations only want to accommodate local needs in order to fuel their own expansion (Ritzer, 2003).

Application: Whistle While You Work

At the beginning of this chapter, I asked why so many people are willing to give up so much of their humanity for a job. Our discussion of bureaucracies and corporations has provided some partial answers.

Now I would like to turn that question upside down: Which work conditions help individuals to *keep* their humanity? Specifically, what helps to keep people happy and healthy on the job? A list of obvious variables has been confirmed by research as having the expected benefits for job satisfaction and worker health. These include: sufficient pay (Terpstra & Honoree, 2004), sufficient resources to get the job done (Backman, 2000), recognition for achievements (Bialopotocki, 2006), and hope for advancement (Tian & Pu, 2008). There are some others that I will discuss in greater detail: autonomy and leadership, coworker relationships, and the bottom line.

Autonomy And Leadership

Workers appear to thrive best when they have considerable control over their own work through managing their own schedules and choosing between task options, as two examples. This is called **autonomy**. Job autonomy is strongly correlated with both happiness and health (Ala-Mursula, Vahtera, Pentti, & Kivimaki, 2004; Jamal, 2004; Pousette & Johansson, 2002).

Lower-paying jobs, like food service and some factory work, tend to offer less autonomy than higher-paying jobs like college instruction and architectural design. This may be one of the reasons that social class is correlated with life expectancy (along with other variables such as nutrition, access to health care, etc.). Although life expectancy has risen for all social classes over the last three decades, the pattern of inequality remains. Currently, males in the professional class have a life expectancy of 80 years while males in the manual unskilled class have an expectancy of 73 years. Likewise, professional women are likely to live to be 85 while unskilled manual class women are likely to live 78 years (National Statistics, 2007).

Autonomy's direct opposite is **micromanagement**, which is the unrelenting managerial control of the smallest tasks. One study estimated that 80 percent of American workers have been subjected to micromanagement at least once. There appears to be a broad consensus that this strategy results in unhappiness, as well as interfering with job completion (Chambers, 2004).

Workers are most likely to enjoy autonomy when their managers favor a **democratic leadership style**. This means involving workers in most decision-making. In contrast, an **authoritarian leadership style** is characterized by giving commands, and a **laissez-faire leadership style** is typified by leaving workers alone. It comes as no surprise that many studies demonstrate a connection between democratic leadership and high worker satisfaction. Such satisfaction includes feeling competent and valued, having lower stress, and feeling safe from abuse (Abbasi, Hollman, & Hayes, 2008; Hauge, Skogstad, & Einarsen, 2007; Kinjerski & Skrypnek, 2008).

It should be noted that effective leadership is actually more complex than I have suggested so far. Different leadership styles are called for in different situations. For example, in a crisis, authoritarian leadership is necessary to prevent confusion and reduce response time. In a non-crisis situation that is unfamiliar, it is best to proceed cautiously, gather information, and involve all players in democratic brainstorming. Further, when employees are new and inexperienced, an authoritarian style may be necessary. On the other hand, when employees are professional experts, it may make sense for a boss to stay out of the way and adopt a laissez-faire style. Finally, it may be necessary to use each style in sequence: authoritarian at the beginning of a project to get everyone moving, democratic as complexities arise, and laissez-faire once decisions have been made and employees are sent on their way to implement them (Clark, 1997).

Coworker Relationships Matter

Bosses and their leadership styles are important to employee happiness, but perhaps coworkers matter even more. Unfortunately, coworkers can easily reduce job satisfaction. One study found that coworker conflict can create lasting stress, with an individual still reporting painful feelings long after the employment and relationship have ended (Hogh, Henriksson, & Burr, 2005). If coworkers disapprove of an individual's innovation, much of the person's creative joy is diminished, even when management rewards the effort (Janssen, 2003).

The good news is that coworkers are much more likely than not to be a source of happiness (Abualrub, 2006; Ducharme & Martin, 2000). The support of coworkers has even been credited with reducing blood pressure in the face of crisis (Quigley, 2003).

For employees, working in teams can significantly improve individual satisfaction. Studies disagree about whether or not work teams achieve more than individuals working alone. Some researchers claim that they have proven it (Hagman & Hayes, 1986;

Laughlin, Hatch, Silver, & Boh, 2006; Moreland, Argote, & Krishnan, 1996; Valacich, Dennis, & Nunamaker, 1992). Others claim that they have disproven it (Allen & Hecht, 2004; Mullen, Johnson, & Salas, 1991). But that only matters from a management perspective. Employees tend to enjoy group work whether or not the job gets done.

The Bottom Line

Intangible sources of happiness and health, such as relationships with coworkers, matter. Their influence, however, can be overshadowed by the practical bottom line: having a job is a necessary prerequisite to all the rest. For example, having a meaningful and engaging job usually seems important. A survey of more than 107,000 individuals in 49 countries confirmed that job satisfaction is greater when work is intrinsically interesting. But there was an important exception: intrinsic interest did *not* increase happiness in countries where inequality was high and government assistance was low. In other words, under difficult circumstances, nothing but job security would satisfy (Huang & Van de Vliert, 2003).

The Future?

Throughout this chapter we have discussed and documented the incredible power of groups. Yet, along the way, we have identified ways that individuals can be heard and contribute some influence. What does all of this research suggest about the possible future? I predict that groups and individuals will continue to struggle for control.

Post-Marxists believe that any individual, group, or culture that succeeds in grabbing power will eventually lose it. Power is inherently unstable, they argue, because it always contains the seeds of its own destruction. They call this process "the dialectic," as Marx did (Finlayson, 2003). For example, corporate culture seems unstoppable now, but it may self-destruct given enough time. Possibly, corporate degradation of the environment will create a global collapse, and humans will have to start over. Or maybe, corporate monopolies will raise prices and lower wages so much that there will no longer be consumers that can buy their products. Or, if you've got the idea, you can make up your own scenario.

Or maybe Weber was right. Maybe routinization is the eternal force that will keep reasserting itself. One example is a current development in emotional labor. **Emotional labor** (Hochschild, 1983) requires workers to manipulate their feelings in order to serve bureaucratic goals. For example, a waitress is required to give customers a "real" smile. In order to be convincing, the waitress must find a way to actually feel like smiling even when customers are being rude. Long-term emotional labor is likely to result in burnout (Zapf, Seifert, Schmutte, Mertini, & Holz, 2001).

An unusual development in emotional labor is the *FISH!* philosophy. *FISH!* originated in a Seattle fish market as employees found ways of making their job fun. For example, they would throw fish to each other to entertain the customers and speak in rhyme—anything to create surprise and excitement.

Customers loved it, and the company made record sales. What made *FISH!* different from other emotional labor is that it was employee-driven rather than management-driven. However, now that other companies are imitating the idea, this has become a management agenda, no different than any other bureaucratic demand. Using Weber's word, *FISH!* has been *routinized*.

Or maybe, after all, it's Durkheim who understood. No matter what happens, humans will always need groups, and we will always benefit from drawing together. You tell me.

A fish market at Pike Place in Seattle, Washington.

Source: Megan Stevens

Summary

Groups have extraordinary power over individuals. The power of a group is above and beyond the individual wills of those involved. Group dynamics are often acted out without conscious awareness.

Members of a group have shared interaction and identity. Aggregates and categories are collections of individuals that do not count as groups. But these can be transformed into groups through crisis, time or political action.

Groups help individuals survive. This includes increasing their members' mental and physical health as well as their overall lifespan. Groups provide guidance through norms and joy through social bonding.

In return, groups demand *conformity* from their members. Groups achieve conformity by using three main tools:

Internalized norms. When group norms are internalized, members obey automatically without question or complaint. *Authority* is one kind of internalized norm. Its power resides within the structure of *statuses* and *roles* rather than in any individual.

Identity control. From birth, individuals depend on their **primary groups** to help them form a basic sense of self. The individual identity is often merged with the primary group identity. **Secondary groups** also help shape identity through expectation. **Reference groups** can influence identity from a distance through the individual's admiration and imagination.

The Power of Division. Any formation of a valued "we" creates an **ingroup**. By definition, everyone else is part of an **outgroup**. Group identity and loyalty both depend on the clarity of such division. This helps to explain why peace-loving religions across the world have histories of violence. But it is possible to unite conflicting groups through finding a **superordinate goal**.

Conformity can be wonderful when it means healthy habits, academic success, and lawful society. But conformity is terrifying when it means obedience to a destructive agenda. Even stable, compassionate individuals often end up participating in group violence. This can happen because individual identity tends to "disappear" into group identity, a process called **deindividuation**. Examples are blending into a faceless crowd or performing a bureaucratic role. The **bystander effect** is one consequence of deindividuation in a crowd. Even worse, victims of violence are often **dehumanized** (i.e., considered less than human). Their suffering seems deserved and may become a source of delight to those who perpetrate it.

Despite the extreme power of groups, it is possible for individuals to resist. Social factors that help individuals stand up to groups include having:

An ally. Even one other person willing to join the individual can be enough to lend courage for nonconformity.

Self-confidence. A sense of **self-efficacy** strengthens individuals against **groupthink**. In groupthink, individuals accept (even come to believe) group decisions against their better judgment.

High status. Group members with high status enjoy **idiosyncrasy credit** (i.e., permission for nonconformity). They sometimes spend it on helping lower-status individuals stand up to the group.

A smaller group to face. In general, the smaller the group, the easier it is to stand up to it.

Diversity (i.e., the existence of significant differences) benefits both groups and individuals. Diversity helps groups make better decisions through introducing new information and alternative strategies. Individuals also benefit from diversity, especially when it enriches their acquaintance networks. Diverse acquaintance networks are the best source of job opportunities. This is called *the strength of weak ties.*

Despite the benefits of diversity, both groups and individuals strongly prefer **homogeneity** (i.e., similarity between group members). This helps to explain why race and gender still make a difference in the United States, even though we value equal opportunity. For example, the financial rewards of an education differ by race and gender. Besides the pull toward homogeneity, other social dynamics help create this situation. These include unequal weak ties, the motherhood penalty, and segregated job markets. Race and class divisions are part of the reason that it is *not a small world after all*. Unfortunately, members of the Earth are not connected by only six links.

Bureaucracy is a formal organization of statuses and roles. The benefits of bureaucracy include consistency, efficiency, and neutrality. But each of the strengths of bureaucracy is also a source of trouble. The downside includes the suffocation of human creativity, bureaucratic inertia, the denial of human emotion, and finally, the dispensability of humans themselves.

Bureaucracy has a frightening durability. Whatever starts out as new and different will eventually end up as bureaucratic (otherwise, it would disappear all together). This reduction of innovation into bureaucratic routine is called **routinization**. A special case of routinization is **McDonaldization**. This refers to the global spread of bureaucratic efficiency and profitability at the expense of human creativity, dignity, freedom, and relationships.

Yet, just as individuals can stand up to groups (with some help), humanity can also stand up to global routinization (and its incarnation in "big business"). Encouraging social dynamics include:

Informal interaction. Even though the *formal structure* of bureaucracy can be dehumanizing, individuals
    find ways to interact more freely and empathically than the rules might allow.

The Japanese business model. Some Western businesses have been humanized by adopting Japanese
    business practices (such as collective, bottom-up decision-making). Recently, there has been a disap-
    pointing reversal of this trend, but many improvements remain.

"Stay local" movements. Keeping jobs, production, and farming under local control helps to minimize
    corporate damage to workers, consumers, and the environment.

Local power and choice. Around the world, local populations do not simply surrender to **globalization**
    (i.e., the international spread of cultural items, such as McDonalds). Instead, they **glocalize**, taking
    what they want of the global offerings and mixing it with their own cultural items to fulfill their own
    needs. When local needs are met as a part of a corporate strategy to expand profits, this is called
    grobalization.

Workplace happiness. Workplaces are not necessarily as inhuman as many fear. Workers are happiest
    when they enjoy **autonomy, democratic leadership**, supportive coworkers, and job stability.

Predictions about the future of groups depend on your theoretical position. Post-Marxists predict that current global giants will eventually fall as all power systems must. No group or set of groups can rule forever. Weber's followers would not find that comforting. Whatever specific groups may or may not be in power, routinization will eternally dehumanize the world. (One current example is the corporate demand for **emotional labor**). Those who favor Durkheim are the most optimistic. They remind us that groups benefit individuals. They do so in multiple ways, which only groups can and always will provide.

Review/Discussion Questions

1. What are the three main tools groups use to achieve the conformity of their members?
2. How can secondary groups transform into primary groups?
3. If you are ever in trouble, and a crowd of people is nearby, you may not receive help because of the *bystander effect*. What advice is given in the chapter for overcoming this phenomenon?
4. What are four of the features that define bureaucracy?
5. What is the difference between "glocalization" and "grobalization"?
6. Which groups have you been member of, and how did they influence you?
7. Would you rather work for a small independent startup business, or a large well-established bureaucratic one, and why?

Key Terms

Autonomy is when individuals have considerable control over their own work.

Authoritarian leadership styles are characterized by a leader giving commands to subordinates.

Bureaucracies are organizations with statuses and roles arranged in a fixed hierarchy. Activity is governed by strict rules and tracked through the keeping of formal records. Each status and role is specialized so that each person is only responsible for one small aspect of the organization, making each worker an expert in his or her own area. Relationships are impersonal, with everyone's main concern being their own bureaucratic role.

Bureaucratic inertia is an organizational resistance to beneficial change.

Bystander effect is a term used to describe the tendency of individuals not to get involved in emergency situations if they are part of a crowd.

Deindividuation occurs when a person loses his or her individual identity and effectively "disappears" into a group.

Dehumanization involves depriving others of their humanity.

Democratic leadership style is a term for involving workers in the decision-making process.

Diversity is the existence of differences.

Emotional labor requires workers to manipulate their feelings in order to serve bureaucratic goals.

Globalization is the international spread of cultural items, practices, and ideas that were once local.

Glocalization describes when globalized items, practices, and ideas are tailored to meet local needs.

Grobalization is the desire of corporations to accommodate local needs in order to fuel their own expansion.

Groupthink occurs when individuals value a group enough to accept group decisions against their own better judgment.

Homogeneity is the existence of sameness.

Idiosyncrasy credits are permissions granted by a group that allow high-standing members to act in a nonconforming manner, thus allowing them to break group norms.

Informal organizational structure includes any group—not formally planned—that forms within an organization and develops through personal relationships and interactions among its members.

In-groups are those in which an individual is a valued member.

Laissez-faire leadership style involves leaving workers to function on their own.

McDonaldization refers to the global spread of bureaucratic efficiency and profitability at the expense of human creativity, dignity, freedom, and relationships.

Micromanagement is the unrelenting managerial control of even the smallest tasks.

Norms provide guidance on how to think, act, and feel.

Out-groups are those in which an individual is not a member, but is, instead, an outsider.

Primary groups are organized around togetherness and are assumed to be long-lasting.

Reference groups include any group that an individual admires enough to use as a standard for his or her identity.

Routinization is the reduction of innovation into bureaucratic routine.

Secondary groups are organized around a task and assumed to be short-term.

Self-efficacy is a person's confidence that he or she can accomplish what is desired and manage what is necessary.

Social aggregates include people who share a space and purpose but do not interact.

Social categories have members that share similar traits, but do not interact or know one another.

Social groups involve two or more people who have a shared a sense of identity and shared interaction.

Social networks are webs of social ties among individuals and groups.

Social rituals are sets of behaviors that symbolize a relationship.

Superordinate goals involve people or groups working together to achieve a goal that is deemed important to everyone involved. The people tend to become friends and their attitudes, values, and goals will become similar, even if those involved originally disliked one another.

Bibliography

Abbasi, S. M., Hollman, K. W., & Hayes, R. D. (2008). Bad bosses and how not to be one. Information Management Journal, 42 (1), 52-56.

Abualrub, R. F. (2006). Replication and examination of research data on job stress and coworker social support with internet and traditional samples. Journal of Nursing Scholarship, 38 (2), 200-204.

Adams, L. L. (2007). Globalization of Culture and the Arts. Sociology Compass, 1 (1), 127-142.

Aeragon (2006). Industrial politics and economics: The history of the assembly line. <http://www.aeragon.com/02/02-04.html> (2008, August 28).

Ala-Mursula, L., Vahtera, J., Pentti, J., & Kivimaki, M. (2004). Effects of employee worktime control on health: a prospective cohort study. Occupational and Environmental Medicine, 61, 254-261.

Allen, K., Blasovich, J., & Mendes, W. B. (2002). Cardiovascular reactivity in the presence of pets, friends, and spouses: The truth about cats and dogs. Psychosomatic Medicine, 64, 727-739.

Allen, N. J., & Hecht, T. D. (2004). The romance of teams: Toward an understanding of its psychological underpinnings and implications. Journal of Occupational and Organizational Psychology, 77, 439-461.

Anderson, J. M., Kling, J. R., & Stith, K. (1999). Measuring interjudge sentencing disparity: Before and after the federal sentencing guidelines. The Journal of Law and Economics, 42 (S1), 271-301.

Aronson, E., Wilson, T. D., & Akert, R. M. (2005). Social psychology (5th ed.). Upper Saddle River, NJ: Pearson Education.

Asch, S. (1955, July). Opinion and social pressure. Scientific American, 31-35.

Backman, A. (2000). Job satisfaction, retention, recruitment and skill mix for a sustainable health care system. Report to the Deputy Minister of Health for Saskatchewan. <http://209.85.173.104/search?q=cache:XcfAQs6GJ2sJ:www.health.gov. sk.ca/health-worcs+sufficient+resources%2Bjob+satisfaction&hl=en&ct=clnk&cd=30&gl=us> (2008, September 1).

Barkan, S. (2006). Criminology: a sociological understanding (3rd ed.). Upper Saddle River, NJ: Pearson Prentice Hall.

Baron, R. (2005). So right it's wrong: Groupthink and the ubiquitous nature of polarized group decision making. In M. P. Zanna (Ed.) Advances in experimental social psychology, (Vol. 37). San Diego, CA: Elsevier Academic Press.

Baumeister, R. F., & Bushman, B. J. (2008). Social Psychology and Human Nature. Belmont, CA: Thompson Wadsworth.

Berg, P., Appelbaum, E., Bailey, T., & Kalleberg, A. (2004). Contesting time: International comparisons of employee control of working time. Industrial and Labor Relations Review, 57 (3), 331-349.

Berger, J., Wagner, D. G., & Zelditch, M. (1985). Expectation states theory: Review and assessment. In J. Berger & M. Zelditch (Eds.). Status, rewards, and influence. San Francisco, CA: Jossey-Bass.

Bialopotocki, R. N. (2006). Recognition and praise relate to teachers' job satisfaction. Doctoral dissertation. University of Nebraska-Lincoln. <http://digitalcommons.unl.edu/dissertations/AAI3238255/> (2008, September 1).

Bonner, B. L., & Baumann, M. R. (2008). Informational intra-group influence: the effects of time pressure and group size. European Journal of Social Psychology, 38 (1), 46-66.

Bowman, F. O. (2005). The failure of the federal sentencing guidelines: A structural analysis. Columbia Law Review, 105, 1315-1350.

Brodbeck, F., Kerschreiter, R., Mojzisch, A., Frey, D., & Schulz-Hardt, S. (2002). The dissemination of critical, unshared information in decision-making groups: The effects of pre-discussion dissent. European Journal of Social Psychology, 32 (1), 35-56.

Bureau of Labor Statistics (2005). Occupational Outlook Handbook. <http://www.bls.gov/oco/ocos170.htm#earnings> (2005, November 1).

Burger, J. M. (in press). Replicating Milgram: Would people still obey today? American Psychologist. <http://www.scu.edu/cas/ psychology/faculty/upload/Replicating-Milgram.doc> (2008, August 24).

Business in Japan: Special report: Going hybrid. (2007, November 29). The Economist. <http://www.economist.com/specialreports/displayStory.cfm?story_id=10169956> (2008, August 30, 2008).

Caiden, G. E. (1991). What really is public maladministration? Public Administration Review, 51 (6), 486-494.

Cann, A. (2004). Rated importance of personal qualities across four relationships. The Journal of Social Psychology, 144 (3), 322-335.

Castillo, R., & Nigh, R. (1998). Global processes and local identity among Mayan coffee growers in Chiapas, Mexico. American Anthropologist: New Series, 100 (1), 136-147.

Chambers, H. (2004). My Way or the Highway. San Francisco, CA: Berrett Koehler Publishers.

Chan, A., & Smith, K. (2001). Perceived marital quality and stability of intermarried couples. Sociological Imagination, 37, 230-256.

Choi, H. S., & Levine, J. M. (2004). Minority influence in work teams: the impact of newcomers. Journal of Experimental Social Psychology, 40, 273-280.

Costin, R. (2007, April 20). Fast food history. <http://referat.clopotel.ro/Fast_food_history-12767.html> (2008, August 29).

Conroy, S., & Emerson, T. (2004). Business ethics and religion: religiosity as a predictor of ethical awareness among students. Journal of Business Ethics, 50 (4), 383-396.

Correll, S. J., & Benard, S. (2005, August 15). Getting a job: Is there a motherhood penalty? Presented at the American Sociological Association's 100th annual meeting, Philadelphia, PA.

Correll, S. J., & Ridgeway, C. L. (2003). Expectation states theory. In J. Delamater (Ed.), Handbook of social psychology and social research (pp. 29-51). New York, NY: Kluwer Academic/Plenum.

Davis, M. H., Morris, M. M., & Kraus, L.A. (1998). Relationship-specific and global perceptions of social support: Associations with well-being and attachment. Journal of Personality and Social Psychology, 74, 468-481.

De Dreu, C., & West, M. (2001). Minority dissent and team innovation: The importance of participation in decision making. Journal of Applied Psychology, 86 (6), 1191-1201.

Ducharme, L. J., & Martin, J. K. (2000). Unrewarding work, coworker support, and job satisfaction. Work and Occupations, 27 (2), 223-243.

Egawa, S., Ito, A., Kokubo, Y., Ishiguro, D., Boozel, K., Osakada, M., & Ogawa, N. (2007). Who's really running the show? <http://www.winadvisorygroup.com/Who'sReallyRunningShow.html> (2007).

Essed, P. (2002). Cloning cultural homogeneity while talking diversity: Old wine in new bottles in Dutch organizations. Transforming Anthropology, 11 (1), 2-12.

Estrada, M., Brown, J., & Lee, F. (1995). Who gets the credit? Small Group Research, 26 (1), 56-76.

Finlayson, A. (Ed.). (2003). Contemporary political thought: A reader and guide. Edinburgh: Edinburgh University Press.

Fox News Network (2008, June 6). Video of gruesome hit-and-run released by Connecticut police. <http://www.foxnews.com/story/0,2933,363493,00.html> (2008, August 23).

Gallup, Inc. (2006, October 12). Gallup study: Engaged employees inspire company innovation. Gallup Management Journal. <http://gmj.gallup.com/content/24880/Gallup-Study-Engaged-Employees-Inspire-Company.aspx> (2008, August 30).

Garfinkle, H. (1967). Studies in ethnomethodology. Englewood Cliffs, NJ: Prentice-Hall.

Granovetter, M. (1983). The strength of weak ties: A network theory revisited. Sociological Theory, 1, 201-233.

Hagman, J. D., & Hayes, J. F. (1986). Cooperative learning: effects of task, reward, and group size in individual achievement. Report for the Army Research Institute for the Behavioral and Social Sciences, Alexandria, VA. <http://www.storming-media.us/82/8283/A828371.html> (2008, August 26).

Hamon, R. R., & Ingoldsby, B. B. (2003). Mate Selection Across Cultures. Thousand Oaks, CA: Sage.

Hauge, L. J., Skogstad, A., & Einarsen, S. (2007). Relationships between stressful work environments and bullying: Results of a large representative study. Work & Stress, 21 (3), 220-242.

Heaton, T. B., & Pratt, E. L. (1990). The effects of religious homogamy on marital satisfaction and stability. Journal of Family Issues, 11 (2), 191-207.

Hersh, S. M. (2004, May 10). Torture at Abu Ghraib. The New Yorker. <http://www.newyorker.com/archive/2004/05/10/040510fa_fact?currentPage=all> (2008, August 22).

Hochschild, A. (1983). The managed heart: The commercialization of human feeling. Berkeley, CA: The University of California Press.

Hogh, A., Henriksson, M. E., & Burr, H. (2005). A 5-year follow-up study of aggression at work and psychological health. International Journal of Behavioral Medicine, 12 (4), 256-265.

Hollander, E. P. (2004, December 6). Leadership perspectives: influence, inclusion, and idiosyncrasy credit. Speech delivered at the New York Academy of Sciences. <http://www.nyas.org/events/eventDetail.asp?eventID=2256&date=12/6/2004%207:15:00%20PM> (2008, August 25).

Hollander, E. P. (1958). Conformity, status, and idiosyncrasy credit. Psychological Review, 65, 117-127.

Huang, X., & Van de Vliert, E. (2003). Where intrinsic job satisfaction fails to work: National moderators of intrinsic motivation. Journal of Organizational Behavior, 24 (2), 159-179.

Idson, T. L. (1990). Establishment size, job satisfaction and the structure of work. Applied Economics, 22 (8), 1007-1018.

Jamal, M. (2004). Burnout, stress, and health of employees on non-standard work schedules: A study of Canadian workers. Stress & Health: Journal of the International Society for the Investigation of Stress, 20 (3), 113-119.

James, E. H. (2000). Race-related differences in promotions and support: Underlying effects of human and social capital. Organization Science, 11, 5, 493-508.

Janis, I. (1972). Victims of groupthink. Boston, MA: Houghton-Mifflin.

Janssen, O. (2003). Innovative behavior and job involvement at the price of conflict and less satisfactory relations with co-workers. Journal of Occupational and Organizational Psychology, 76 (3), 347-364.

Japan Echo (1998, July 31). Record unemployment: A cloud of anxiety looms over Japan's work force. Trends in Japan. <http://web-japan.org/trends98/honbun/ntj980730.html> (2008, August 30).

Kana'iaupuni, S., Donato, K., Thompson-Colon, T., & Stainback, M. (2005). Counting on kin: social networks, social support, and child health. Social Forces, 83 (3), 1137-1165.

Kemelgor, B. H. (2007). Job satisfaction as mediated by the value congruity of supervisors and their subordinates. Journal of Organizational Behavior, 3 (2), 147-160.

Kerr, N. L. & Bruun, S. E. (1983). Dispensability of member effort and group motivation losses: Free-rider effects. Journal of Personality and Social Psychology, 44, 78-94.

Khondker, H. H. (2004). Glocalization as globalization: Evolution of a sociological concept. Bangladesh e-Journal of Sociology, 1 (2), 1-8.

Kinjerski, V., & Skrypnek, B. J. (2008). Four paths to spirit at work: Journeys of personal meaning, fulfillment, well-being, and transcendence through work. Career Development Quarterly, 56 (4), 319-329.

Kiser, L., Bennet, L., Heston, J., & Paavola, M. (2005). Family ritual and routine: comparison of clinical and non-clinical families. Journal of Child & Family Studies, 14 (3), 357-372.

Kleinfeld, J. (2002). The small world problem. Society, 39 (2), 61-66.

Kuntzman, G. (2001, October 1). Thugs are people, too. Newsweek: American Beat. <http://www.msnbc.com/news/636423.asp> (2001, October 5).

Latane, B. & Darley, J. (1968). Group inhibition of bystander intervention in emergencies. Journal of Personality and Social Psychology, 10, 215-221.

Laughlin, P., Hatch, E., Silver, J., & Boh, L. (2006). Groups perform better than the best individuals on letters-to-numbers problems: Effects of group size. Journal of Personality and Social Psychology, 90 (4), 644-651.

Lincoln, J. R., & Miller, J. (1979). Work and friendship ties in organizations: A comparative analysis of relational networks. Administrative Science Quarterly, 24, 181-199.

Lortie-Lussier, M. (1987). Minority influence and idiosyncrasy credit: a new comparison of the Moscovici and Hollander theories of innovation. European Journal of Social Psychology, 17 (4), 431-446.

McFarland, D., & Pals, H. (2005). Motives and contexts of identity change: A case for network effects. Social Psychology Quarterly, 68 (4), 289-315.

McGuire, G. M. (2002). Gender, race, and the shadow structure. Gender & Society, 16 (3), 303-322.

Meir, E., Hadasi, C., & Noyfeld, M. (1997). Person-environment fit in small army units. Journal of Career Assessment, 5 (1), 21-29.

Milgram, S. (1967). The small-world problem. Psychology Today, 61-67.

Milgram, S. (1963). Behavioral study of obedience. Journal of Abnormal and Social Psychology, 67, 371–378.

Mills, C. W. (1956). The power elite. New York: Oxford University Press.

Moreland, R., Argote, L., & Krishnan, R. (1996). Socially shared cognition at work: Transactive memory and group performance. In J. Nye & A. Brower (Eds.), What's social about social cognition? Research on socially shared cognition in small groups (pp. 57-84). Thousand Oaks, CA: Sage.

Mouritzen, P. E. (2006). City size and citizens' satisfaction: two competing theories revisited. European Journal of Political Research, 17 (6), 661-688.

Mullen, B., Johnson, C., & Salas, E. (1991). Productivity loss in brainstorming groups: A meta-analysis. Basic and Applied Social Psychology, 12, 3-23.

Nath, P., Borkowski, J., Whitman, T., & Schellenbach, C. (1991). Understanding adolescent parenting: The dimensions and functions of social support. Family Relations, 40 (4), 411-420.

National Statistics (2007, October 24). Variations persist in life expectancy by social class. National Statistics: News Release. <http://www.statistics.gov.uk/pdfdir/le1007.pdf> (2008, September 1).

Ng, K. Y., & Dyne, L. V. (2001). Individualism-collectivism as a boundary condition for effectiveness of minority influence in decision making. Organizational Behavior and Human Decision Processes, 84 (2), 198-225.

Nemeth, C. J., & Kwan, J. L. (1987). Minority influence, divergent thinking, and detection of correct solutions. Journal of Applied Social Psychology, 17, 788-799.

Pachana, N. A., Ford, J. H., Andrew, B., & Dobson, A. J. (2005). Relations between companion animals and self-reported health in older women: Cause, effect, or artifact? International Journal of Behavioral Medicine, 12 (2), 103-110.

Parks, B. (2006, December 11). McDonald's and global marketing. <http://www.bizcovering.com/Marketing-and-Advertising/McDonalds-and-Global-Marketing.26899> (2008, August 29).

Perrone, K. M., & Sedlacek, W. E. (2000). A comparison of group cohesiveness and client satisfaction in homogenous and heterogenous groups. The Journal for Specialists in Group Work, 25 (3), 243-251.

Petersen, L., & Dietz, J. (2006). Prejudice and enforcement of workforce homogeneity as explanations for employment discrimination. Journal of Applied Social Psychology, 35 (1), 144-159.

Pollan, M. (2006). The omnivore's dilemma: A natural history of four meals. New York, NY: Penguin Press.

Pollard, J. A., & Hawkins, J. D. (1999). Risk and protection: Are both necessary to understand diverse behavioral outcomes in adolescence? Social Work Research, 23 (3), 145-158.

Pousette, A., & Johansson, H. (2002). Job characteristics as predictors of ill-health and sickness   absenteeism in different occupational types: A multigroup structural equation modeling approach. Work & Stress, 16 (3), 229-250.

Powell, D., & Butterfield, A. (1997). Effect of race on promotions to top management in a federal department. Academy of Management Journal, 40, 1, 112-128.

Quigley, A. (2003, April 9). Social support at work protects the heart. Health Behavior News Service. <http://www.hbns.org/news/support04-09-03.cfm> (2008, September 1).

Rawlins, W. K. (1992). Friendship matters: Communication, dialectics, and the life course. New York, NY: Aldine de Gruyter.

Ritzer, G. (2003). Rethinking globalization: Glocalization/grobalization and something/nothing. Sociological Theory, 21 (3), 193-209.

Ritzer, G. (2000). The McDonaldization of society: An investigation into the changing character of contemporary social life. Thousand Oaks, CA: Pine Forge Press.

Robertson, R. (1994). Globalisation or glocalisation?, The Journal of International Communication 1(1), 33–52.

Rosenthal, R., & Jacobson, L. (1968). Pygmalion in the classroom: Teacher expectation and pupils' intellectual development. New York: Rinehart and Winston.

Ruef, M. (2002). Strong ties, weak ties, and islands: structural and cultural predictors of organizational innovation. Industrial and Corporate Change, 11 (3), 427-449.

Sanders, J. (2002). Ethnic boundaries and identity in plural societies. Annual Review of Sociology, 28, 327-357.

Sherif, M., Harvey, O. J., White, J., Hood, W., & Sherif, C. W. (1961). Intergroup conflict and cooperation: The robber's cave experiment. Norman, OK: Institute of Intergroup Relations, University of Oklahoma.

Sias, P. M., & Cahill, D. J. (1998). From coworkers to friends: The development of peer friendships in the workplace. Western Journal of Communication, 62 (3), 273-300.

State of the Union Address (2002, January 29). President delivers state of the union address. <http://www.whitehouse.gov/news/releases/2002/01/20020129-11.html> (2008, August 22).

Terpstra, D.E., & Honoree, A.L. (2004). Job satisfaction and pay satisfaction levels of university faculty by discipline type and by geographic region. Education. <http://findarticles.com/p/articles/mi_qa3673/is_200404/ai_n9345191> (2008, September 1).

Tian, X., & Pu, Y. (2008). An artificial neural network approach to hotel employee satisfaction: The case of China. Social Behavior & Personality: An International Journal, 36 (4), 467-482.

Tschanh, F., Sylvie, R., & Dieter, Z. (2005). It's not only clients: Studying emotion work with clients and co-workers with an event-sampling approach. Journal of Occupational & Organizational Psychology, 78 (2), 195-220.

Vaillant, G. E. (2002). Adaptive mental mechanisms: Their role in positive psychology. American Psychologist, 55, 89-98.

Valacich, J. S., Dennis, A. R., & Nunamaker, J. F. Jr. (1992). Group size and anonymity effects on computer-mediated idea generation. Small Group Research, 23 (1), 49-73.

Walther, E., Bless, H., Fritz, S., Rackstraw, P., Wagner, D., & Werth, L. (2002). Conformity effects in memory as a function of group size, dissenters and uncertainty. Applied Cognitive Psychology, 16 (7), 793-810.

Weber, M. (1947). The theory of social and economic organization. (A. M. Henderson & T. Parsons, Trans.). Glencoe, IL: Free Press.

Weber, M. (1946). Types of authority. In H. H. Gerth & C. W. Mills (Eds.), Max Weber: Essays in sociology (pp. 224-229). New York, NY: Oxford University Press.

West, W. F. (2005). Neutral competence and political responsiveness: An uneasy relationship. Policy Studies Journal, 33 (2), 147-161.

Charthouse Learning (2008). What is Fish! <http://www.charthouse.com/content.aspx?nodeid=1066> (2008, September 1).

Wicks, J. (2006). Local living economies: The new movement for responsible business. <http://www.vtcommons.org/journal/2006/02/judy-wicks-local-living-economies-new-movement-responsible-business> (2006).

Wills, T. A., & Fegan, M. (2001). Social networks and social support. In A. Baum, T. A. Revenson, & J. E. Singer (Eds.), Handbook of health psychology (pp. 209-234). Mahwah, NJ: Erlbaum.

Wisconsin Historical Society (2008). Roadside Highlight: White Tower Hamburgers. Wisconsin History Explorer. <http://www.wisconsinhistory.org/archstories/restaurants/fast_food.asp> (2008, August 29).

Wood, C. (2008, June 19). Eat for the environment: Take charge, and start to live life in the slow lane. Pharmacy News, 34.

Workman, D. (2008, March 4). Japanese corporate culture: Japan's business model and project management approach. <http://globalization.suite101.com/article.cfm/japanese_corporate_culture> (2008, August 30).

Zapf, D., Seifert, C., Schmutte, B., Mertini, H., & Holz, M. (2001). Emotion work and job stressors and their effects on burnout. Psychology & Health, 16 (5), 527-546.

Zimbardo, P. G. (1972). Pathology of imprisonment. Society, 9 (6), 4-8.

CHAPTER SIX

Deviance And Social Control

Sally Stablein

This chapter provides sociological definitions of deviance and deviant behavior and explores deviance from several theoretical perspectives. In addition, this chapter will cover criminal behavior, crime, and punishment. An important lesson to be gained from this chapter is that individuals convicted of wrongdoing do not always fit the common stereotype of the "street" criminal or deviant person.

What Is Deviance?

Most people think of criminals, "weirdos," or perverts when asked to describe deviant behavior. These definitions are not accurate; in fact, there is a great deal of disagreement about what people consider deviant. In his classic study, sociologist Jerry L. Simmons (1965) asked a sample of the general public who they thought was deviant. Respondents mentioned 252 different kinds of people as deviants, including homosexuals, prostitutes, alcoholics, drug addicts, murderers, the mentally ill, communists, atheists, liars, Democrats, Republicans, reckless drivers, retirees, career women, divorcees, Christians, suburbanites, movie stars, perpetual bridge players, prudes, pacifists, psychiatrists, priests, girls who wear makeup, smart-aleck students, and know-it-all professors. Deviance is not easy to define, and often there is a lack of consensus as to what constitutes deviant behavior.

How Do Sociologists Define Deviance?

From a sociological perspective, **deviance** is anything that violates a cultural norm and elicits a reaction. Deviance is a behavior that violates the standards of conduct or expectations of a group or a society (Wickman, 1991). This simple, but deceptive, definition takes us to the heart of the sociological perspective on deviance, which sociologist Howard S. Becker (1966) described this way: "It's not the act itself, but the reactions to the act, that make something deviant." Deviant behavior is not set in stone; rather, it is subject to social definition within a particular society at a particular time. This means the term is neutral, not simply a judgment about behavior. Deviance is a relative concept, meaning different groups have different norms, and, because of this, deviance varies according to culture, gender, social class, race, ethnicity, and historical context.

Consider tattoos, for example. Tattoos vary greatly from culture to culture. What was once taboo for many has become mainstream. Over the past 20 years or so, tattoos in America have moved from the fringes of society, where they were symbols of membership in certain sub-cultures, to a position of increased acceptance and popularity.

The word tattoo comes from the combination of the Polynesian word *ta*, which means "to strike something," and the Tahitian word *tatau*, which means "to mark something" (Designboom, 2008). Tattoos were widespread among the world's ancient cultures, with the oldest direct evidence coming from the 5,000-year-old frozen body of a man discovered in the Alps, along the Swiss-Italian border, in 1991. Ötzi, as he is called, has 57 tattoos on his body, including a cross on the inside of his left knee, six straight lines above his kidneys, and numerous parallel lines along his ankles.

American society and culture, drawing its influences from Christian Europe, portrayed tattooing as deviant or pagan behavior outside the social norm. It is likely that they based these assumptions on the biblical passage Leviticus 19:28: "Ye shall not make any cuttings in your flesh for the dead, nor print any marks upon you: I *am* the Lord."

The historic voyages of discovery in Polynesia by Captain James Cook began a tradition of tattooing in the British Navy, which likely spread from port to port. The first permanent tattoo shop in the United States was established in New York City in 1846. It began a tradition of tattooing military servicemen from both sides of the Civil War (Designboom, 2008).

The tattoo in American society continued to be associated with enlisted members of the military, criminal elements, and circus performers until the late 20th century, and was representative of a socially deviant or lower-class lifestyle, or exposure to such during the person's lifetime. About this time, tattoos experienced a resurgence in popularity, particularly in North America, Europe, and Japan. The tattoo culture has become a growth industry, seeing an influx of new artists, many of whom have technical and fine art training (Designboom, 2008).

People with tattoos consider them to be artwork that represents something permanent and unique that cannot be taken away, and an art form that is accessible to everyone, regardless of class or station in life (Herman, 1992). Tattooing has always acted as a bulletin board to create an identity for a person. *Collectors*, as they call themselves, talk of becoming tattooed at a point in their lives when they were undergoing personal growth or transformation, and that the tattoos provide a feeling of empowerment. A common theme among tattooed people is the idea of tattoos as *psychic armor* fortifying their mind or spirit, reinforcing their image of themselves, helping to define them, or increasing their sense of power. This is a common historical theme drawn from so-called primitive cultures, as is the adoption of tribal designs as representations of spiritualism, or amulets as protection in warrior cultures (Wiley, 1997).

The image of tattooing as deviance still comes into play, however, even as its popularity increases. Tattooing for women, in particular, can carry social stigmas above and beyond what men may experience. Heavily tattooed women are often viewed as deviants. One of the most popular spots for a woman to have a tattoo is on her lower back, and

Does this woman look like a deviant to you?　　　　Source: Sally Stablein

What is normal? For the most part, societies define what normal is within their culture. For example, in most of the United States, males may walk down the street without shirts on and that's okay, but females, on the other hand, cannot walk around without shirts. That would be breaking the norm. Norms make social life possible by making behavior predictable (Henslin, 2007). Without norms, we would have chaos. Norms lay out the basic guidelines for how we should fulfill our roles and interact with others. Norms bring about **social order**, and social order is necessary in all societies. Our lives of "normal" behavior are dependent on social arrangements, which is why deviance is so threatening. Deviance undermines predictability, the foundation of social life. Human groups develop a system of **social control** as well. There are formal and informal means of enforcing norms by using social control, which will be discussed later in this chapter.

Sanctions

Social norms have within them **sanctions** that promote conformity and discourage nonconformity. A sanction may be defined as any formal or informal reaction to an individual or group behavior that breaks a particular norm. A positive sanction rewards people for positive behavior. A *positive sanction* may be getting an A on your sociology exam or a raise at work. A *negative sanction* could be receiving an F on your sociology test or getting fired from a job.

this is commonly referred to by the slang term *tramp stamp* (National Broadcasting Corp., 2007). Whatever the reason, as the popularity of tattooing increases, its association with deviance may begin to fade as it becomes something of a cultural norm, rather than a violation of what people expect to see in everyday life.

So Who Or What Is Deviant?

Sociologists believe all people are deviants because everyone violates rules from time to time. In sociology, the term deviance refers to all violations of social rules, regardless of the seriousness, from committing a faux pas to exhibiting criminal behavior. Speeding is breaking the law and may result in a speeding ticket—a negative sanction. However, in some locations, speeding is considered the norm, and people may receive negative sanctions from other drivers who are wondering why they are traveling so slowly, even if it is the posted speed limit. As we have discussed, it is very difficult to pinpoint who or what is deviant; deviance is often in the eye of the beholder. Nothing is inherently deviant!

If you truly want to know a person, you need to look beyond the public face, the jobs on the resume, the books on the shelves, and the family pictures on the desk. You may learn more from what is hidden in the drawer—there is always more to us than what we will admit (Schlosser, 2004).

Do your own experiment for fun

Do something harmless that is against the social norms. Violate a folkway such as wearing fingernail polish if you're a man, wearing a shirt inside out, or giving a full-blown reply to the question, "How are you?"

Explanations Of Deviance: Sociobiology, Psychology, And Sociology

Sociobiology

Sociobiology focuses on genetic predispositions. A century ago, most people understood—or more correctly, misunderstood—human behavior to be the result of biological instincts. Early interest in criminality focused on biological causes. In 1876, Cesare Lombroso, an Italian physician who worked in prisons, theorized that criminals stood out physically, having such traits as low foreheads, prominent jaws and cheekbones, big ears, lots of body hair, and un-usually long arms. People with these characteristics were said to commit more crimes (Macionis, 2007).

In the middle of the 20th century, William Sheldon also suggested that body structure might predict criminal behavior (Sheldon, Hartl, & McDermott, 1949). He cross-checked hundreds of young men for body type and criminal history, and concluded that criminal behavior was most likely among boys with squarish, muscular, athletic builds. Sheldon Glueck and Eleanor Glueck (1950) confirmed Sheldon's conclusion but warned that a powerful build does not necessarily cause criminal behavior. Rather, parents tend to be somewhat distant from their powerfully built sons, who in turn grow up and show less sensitivity toward others.

Today, genetic research seeks possible links between biology and crime. In 2003, a scientist at the University of Wisconsin reported the results of a 25-year study of 400 boys. The researchers collected DNA samples from each boy and noted any trouble they had with the law. The researchers concluded that genetic factors, especially defective genes that make too much of an enzyme, together with environmental factors, especially abuse early in life, were strong predictors of adult crime and violence. They noted that these two factors combined were better predictors than either one alone (Lemonick, 2003; Pinker, 2003).

Psychology

Psychological explanations of deviant behavior focus on mental disorders, personality disorders, and individual abnormalities. Some traits are certainly hereditary, but most psychologists think that personality is often shaped by social experience. Classic research by Walter Reckless and Simon Dinitz (1967) illustrates the psychological approach. Reckless and Dinitz began by asking several teachers to categorize twelve-year-old male students as either likely or unlikely to get into trouble with the law. They then interviewed the boys and their mothers to assess how the boys felt about themselves (self-concept) and how they related to others. Analyzing the results, the researchers found that the "good boys" had a strong consciousness, what Freud would refer to as the superego, could handle frustration, and identified with cultural norms and values. The "bad boys" had a weaker consciousness, displayed little tolerance or frustration, and felt out of place with conventional culture. The "good boys" went on to lead successful lives and had fewer run-ins with the law than the "bad boys."

There are no simple answers when it comes to the nature versus nurture debate. What is clear is that every behavior is influenced by multiple forces, from biology to community. Both the biological and psychological views refer to deviance as a trait of the individual, but research currently puts far greater emphasis on social influences than genetics and personality (Kindlon & Thompson, 2000).

Sociology

Sociologists focus on outside factors that contribute to deviant behavior and believe that deviance is a learned behavior. Looking outside the individual answers many questions as to why people behave the way they do. People have reasons for breaking rules or acting out. Outside forces, such as social background, peers, schools and other surroundings, contribute to deviant behavior.

Deviance varies according to cultural norms. For example, in the United States, drug use is considered deviant behavior. This country has spent a great deal of time and money on the war against drugs, and there are serious consequences or negative sanctions for people who use and sell them. The majority of our recent prison population has been incarcerated for drug offenses rather than violent crimes like rape, murder, and armed robbery, as might be expected. As a matter of fact, in some cases people spend more time in jails and prisons for drug offenses than for violent crimes (Schlosser, 2004).

In Amsterdam, drug laws are quite different. There are several *coffeeshops*—cafés selling marijuana and hashish—where people may enter, purchase a cup of coffee and a marijuana cigarette, then sit back and smoke, listen to music, and perhaps play some backgammon or chess, with no worries about getting arrested (Pauker, 2006). Can you imagine?

The United States, on the other hand, has arrested people who use marijuana for medicinal use. The enforcement of state and federal laws regarding marijuana serves to guide its production and set the punishments for its users, suggesting the arbitrary nature of many cultural taboos. Americans not only imprison more people for marijuana, but also smoke more marijuana than any other western industrialized nation (Schlosser, 2004). As you can see, laws are defined differently in different geographical locations. Some may suggest that North America's war against drugs is repressive and hypocritical, while others may suggest that Amsterdam's coffeeshops are absolutely horrible and lack moral character. Deviance is often defined by those who make the laws, and those definitions become part of our cultural norms.

The Functionalist Perspective On Deviance

Durkheim's Functionalist Theory

The key insight of the functional approach is that deviance is a necessary part of the structure of society. This point was made a century ago by the French sociologist Emile Durkheim (1893). Durkheim suggested that there is nothing abnormal about deviant behavior and that it contributes to social order. He believed that deviance performed four essential functions:

1. **Deviance affirms cultural values and norms** – Without deviance, how do we know what is good or evil? There can be no good without evil, and no justice without crime. Deviance is needed to define and support morality.

2. **Deviance promotes social unity** – People typically react to serious deviance with shared outrage. People react to deviant behavior and come together, just as we saw in the aftermath of the destruction of the twin towers on September 11, 2001. In doing so, they reaffirm the moral ties that bind them.

3. **Responding to deviance clarifies moral boundaries** – By defining some individuals as devi-

TABLE 1 B

Mode of Adaptation	Cultural Goals	Institutional Means
Conformity	Accept	Accept
Innovation	Accept	Reject
Ritualism	Reject	Accept
Retreatism	Reject	Reject
Rebellion	Reject/Replace	Reject/Replace

ant, people tend to draw a boundary between right and wrong. To punish deviance affirms the group's norms and clarifies what it means to be a member of the group.

4. **Deviance promotes social change** – Deviant people push a society's moral boundaries, suggesting alternatives and encouraging change. Today's deviance can become tomorrow's morality (Macionis, 2007). For example, rock and roll was said to be immoral in the 1950s, and has since become a multibillion-dollar industry

Robert Merton's Strain Theory

Robert Merton used Durkheim's concept of **anomie**, a social condition in which norms and values are conflicting, weak, or absent, to support his **strain theory**. According to Merton, while some deviance may be necessary for a society to function, too much deviance can result from specific social arrangements or flaws within the social structure. The kind of deviance that will exist depends on whether or not a society provides the means or opportunities, like education and jobs, to achieve **cultural goals** such as financial success. Merton (1968) suggests that some people feel more strain and frustration than others due to their social location and unequal access to the institutional or conventional means to achieve those cultural goals. Everybody in the United States, for example, is socialized with the idea of the American Dream. When people cannot achieve that dream through legitimate ways and mainstream norms, they may attempt to achieve it by means of illegitimate opportunities. However, social class and location within the social structure may determine what kind of illegitimate opportunity structures are available.

Merton (1968) presented five different modes of adaptation to classify where individuals fit into the continuum of adopting cultural values: conformity, innovation, ritualism, retreatism, and rebellion.

The first mode is **conformity**, using socially acceptable means to reach cultural goals. This category probably includes most of us, because, as Merton said, this is the most common mode of adaptation. In industrialized societies, the majority of people try to receive an education and get good jobs. If the economy is poor and people cannot find high-paying jobs, then most are willing to take a less-desirable position. If people are denied access to an Ivy League school, they go to a less reputable school, and if people are unable to take time off work during the day to go to school, they attend classes at night or online, or they may go to a vocational school. Most people take the socially acceptable road to success.

Innovation occurs when a person accepts the cultural goals of society but rejects or lacks the socially legitimate means to achieve those goals. For instance, drug dealers accept the idea of achieving wealth but reject the legitimate processes to achieve that wealth. Innovation is the mode of adaptation most associated with criminal behavior.

Ritualism involves following the rules. *Ritualists* are people who become discouraged and often give up on excelling and advancing in society; instead, they survive by following the rules of their job. People using this mode of adaptation reject cultural goals, but accept **institutional means**. They play by the rules of conventional conduct. For example, a ritualist may be a teacher who becomes disillusioned with teaching and, rather than changing the situation, remains in the classroom where he/she continues to teach without enthusiasm. There are many examples of people who become burned out but stay in their jobs. This is considered deviant behavior because they have abandoned their goals.

Retreatism involves rejecting both cultural goals, such as success, and the institutionally legitimate means to achieve them. Retreatists withdraw from society and include those people who drop out of the pursuit of success by way of alcohol or drugs. Often retreatists stop trying to act like they share the goals of society.

The final response is **rebellion**. Rebels, like retreatists, reject both cultural goals and the socially legitimate means to achieve them. However, unlike retreatists, rebels seek to replace existing goals and means with new ones. As an example, rebels may use political activism as a means to replace the goal of personal wealth with the goal of social justice. Revolutionaries are the most common type of rebels.

Opportunity Theory

Sociologists Richard Cloward and Lloyd Ohlin (1966) theorized that there was a criminal subculture offering illegal opportunities and described it as an **illegitimate opportunity structure**. Crime, therefore, was not simply the result of limited legitimate (legal) opportunities, but also readily accessible illegitimate (illegal) opportunities. Deviance or conformity arises from the relative opportunity structure that frames a person's life.

The 2007 film *American Gangster* is based on the life of Frank Lucas. Lucas grew up facing the barriers of poverty and racial prejudice that lowered his odds of achieving success in conventional terms. Not only was Lucas poor, he also grew up in a time of violence against African-Americans. He witnessed his 12-year-old cousin's murder at the hands of the Ku Klux Klan, apparently for "reckless eyeballing" (looking) at a Caucasian woman. Lucas led a life of petty crime, stealing to help feed his family, and one day got in a fight with a former employer. He left the South for New York City, getting off the bus in Harlem. He started robbing and stealing to survive, eventually meeting one of the most notorious gangsters in Harlem, Bumpy Johnson, who became his mentor. After Johnson's death, Lucas began importing illegal drugs into the United States. Frank Lucas' actions are certainly not justifi-

able or acceptable; however, by applying opportunity theory to his life, we can get a better picture as to why he made the choices he did. People do things for reasons, whether right or wrong, and sociologists are interested in understanding those reasons. Denzel Washington, playing Lucas in the film said, "Do you want to be a somebody or a nobody?" Lucas clearly wanted to be a "somebody," and he achieved that through illegitimate means. The story of Frank Lucas illustrates Cloward and Ohlin's theory that crime is a result of limited legitimate opportunities and readily available illegitimate opportunities (NBC, 2008; Wikipedia, 2009).

Control Theory

Control theory proposes that people's values, norms, and beliefs influence them not to deviate or break the law. People who have not been socialized will not have internalized the values and norms of society and their actions won't be limited to those that are legal or legitimate.

Sociologist Walter Reckless (1973) developed **containment theory** which is based on control theory and focuses on a strong self-image as a means of defending against negative peer pressure. This theory suggests that we have two control systems, inner containment (positive sense of self) and outer containment (supervision and discipline). Each of us is propelled toward deviance, but our inner and outer controls keep us from actually deviating. Our inner controls include morality, conscience, religious beliefs, and ideas of right and wrong. Inner controls also include fear of punishment, integrity, and the desire to be a "good" person (Hirschi, 1969; Rogers, 1977; Baron, 2001). Our outer controls consist of people who influence us not to deviate, such as family, friends, and the police.

Control theory suggests the stronger our bonds to society, the more likely we are to conform to societal norms. Those of us with strong social attachments, commitment to legitimate opportunity, respect for authority, and involvement in legitimate activities like jobs, clubs, sports, and a circle of friends, are people who are most likely to conform to societal norms. On the other hand, people with weak social bonds to society are more likely to deviate from social norms. Bonds are based on attachments and commitments. People may also have a place in society that they don't want to risk, such as a respected place in their families, communities, workplaces, or schools.

Someone with strong ties to society would have much to lose if he or she were to commit a deviant act such as robbing a convenience store. However, a person with weak ties may not be as connected, and therefore may take the risk.

For example, let's apply control theory to "Howard." Howard was recently released from prison and told he could complete his time on parole in a halfway house in the city where he was arrested. Howard was dropped off by the Department of Corrections with 100 dollars to his name. It was his responsibility to find a job and pay for his basic necessities, including his stay at the halfway house, but he was having a difficult time with this process. No one wanted to hire Howard because of his status as a convicted felon. Time was running out for Howard, and feelings of hopelessness were setting in. Howard met up with some old friends and decided to participate in some criminal activity. If he isn't caught, he will be able to pay for his spot at the halfway house and other basic needs. Of course, if he is caught, Howard will go back to prison. At this point, does Howard have a strong bond with society? What are Howard's risks? What are society's risks?

You can see how someone in Howard's circumstances might take the risk and commit the crime versus someone in a college classroom who has much more to lose if caught. Howard's criminal behavior is certainly not okay, but it's clear why Howard makes his decision. Howard doesn't have a strong bond with society, so he is willing to take the risk. Sociologists are interested in the reasons people do the things they do, whether right or wrong.

Conflict Theory

Conflict theory suggests that individuals or groups who have power over others can impose rules to produce social order. From a conflict perspective, all of the major institutions, laws, and traditions of a society serve to support those in power. Laws are an instrument of oppression used to maintain power and privilege, which the ruling class, through the **criminal justice system**, uses to punish the poor.

Conflict theory links deviance to social inequality. Power and social inequality are the chief characteristics of society. The group in power (the elite) makes all the rules and controls the criminal justice system. Laws are passed to protect its power. Breaking those laws is deviant behavior resulting from social inequality.

The group in power may be referred to as the **capital class** because it owns the capital, or means of production. There may also be a working class and a **marginal working class**. Most prison inmates fit into the marginal working class category. Often desperate, these people commit street crimes or have severe drug problems, and, because their crime or behaviors threaten the social order, they are severely punished.

According to conflict theorists, the idea that the law operates impartially, treating people in a fair manner, is a myth promoted by the capital class. Conflict theorists see the law as an instrument of oppression, a tool designed to maintain the powerful in their privileged position.

Conflict theorists suggest that the criminal justice system does not focus on the owners of corporations and the harm they do through pollution, unsafe products, and poor working conditions because its job is to protect those in power. When the working classes rebel, it threatens social order and they are imprisoned.

Feminist Theory

Most theories about deviance assume that they apply to both sexes; what holds true for men typically holds true for women. Feminist theorists disagree. They argue that conventional theories of deviance are about men, and are valid for men, but not applicable to, or valid for, women. They also believe that the status of women as victims and offenders reflects the continuing subordination of women in a patriarchal society. Feminist theorists explain that in a patriarchal society, men and women have been socialized differently and, therefore, have different results as far as deviant behavior. Women are less interested in financial success and more interested in emotional success through close personal relations with others. When women are faced with lack of opportunities to achieve economic success, they are not as likely as men to engage in deviant behavior (Thio, 2006).

The Symbolic Interactionist Perspective

As we examine symbolic interactionism, it will become clearer as to why sociologists are not completely satisfied with biology and personality. Symbolic interactionists emphasize our social environments and how our associations say quite a bit about whether or not we will deviate or conform to societal norms.

Differential Association Theory

Contrary to theories built around genetics, sociologists believe deviance is a learned behavior. Edwin Sutherland (1947) coined the term **differential association** to indicate that we learn to deviate or conform to society's norms based on the groups with whom we associate. This theory contradicts the view that deviance is biological or psychological. Humans are essentially social and need to feel a sense of belonging. Membership in groups, especially peer groups, is a primary way through which people meet this need. Regardless of the group orientations, whether conformity or deviance, the need is the same.

Have your peer groups ever influenced you to engage in deviant behavior?

Eric Harris and Dylan Klebold, the two boys who committed the Columbine High School atrocities in 1999, most likely would not have committed this act without one another. It could be said that differential association is one theory to apply to the boys' violent acts. The two together, through association, planned and acted out the high school shootings at Columbine.

Families have a significant impact on the behavior of children. There are many ways in which family affects the socialization process. Providing a safe and caring environment typically falls on parents and other family members. For several years, at least until children begin school, the family has the important job of teaching children skills, values, and beliefs. Research suggests that nothing is more likely to produce a happy, well-adjusted child than growing up in a loving family (Kindlon & Thompson, 2000).

Friends, neighborhoods, and subcultures also influence and shape individuals. When children start school, they are exposed to many other groups that influence their behavior, whether positively or negatively. Social location will say quite a bit about the different groups with whom the children have contact.

Labeling Theory

Labeling theory is a viewpoint developed by symbolic interactionists which holds that the labels people are given affect their own and others' perceptions of them, and, therefore, cause people to channel their behavior into either deviance or conformity. This theory focuses on how labels help funnel people into or away from deviance. People who commit deviant acts often use **techniques of neutralization** to continue to think of themselves as law-abiding citizens.

Labeling theory does not focus on why some individuals resort to committing deviant acts. Instead, it attempts to explain why certain people are viewed as deviants, delinquents, bad kids, losers, and criminals, while others exhibiting similar behaviors are not. Labeling theory emphasizes how a person labeled as deviant will then accept that label. Sociologist Howard Becker (1966) summed it up with this statement: "Deviant behavior is behavior that people so label."

How do certain behaviors come to be viewed as a problem? Take smoking cigarettes, for example. At one point in time, smoking was considered attractive. On film, actors and actresses were seen smoking all of the time, and those people were

Smoking.

Source: Emre Danisman

considered to be attractive. Today many people view smoking as deviant behavior. What are your thoughts when you see a driver with a lit cigarette and a child in the car? This scene was common just 25 years ago. Some states have banned smoking in restaurants, while some towns have banned smoking in public, including beaches. As illustrated by these examples, views on behavior change over time and implementing specific laws regarding behavior contribute to society's change in perspective.

Primary And Secondary Labels

Edwin Lemert (1951, 1993) observed that some violations of norms, like skipping school or underage drinking, provoke slight reactions from others and have little effect on a person's self-concept. Lemert refers to this as **primary deviance**.

A person's perception may change, however, if someone else notices the deviance and makes something out it. For example, if people begin to describe a young man as an alcohol or drug abuser and

exclude him from their friendship group, he may become bitter, drink or use drugs to an even greater extent, and seek the company of others who approve of his behavior. The response to primary deviance sets in motion **secondary deviance**, by which a person repeatedly violates a norm and begins to take on a deviant identity. The development of secondary deviance states that situations defined as real become real in their consequences (Merton, 1968).

The Saints and the Roughnecks were two groups of high school males who engaged in excessive drinking, reckless driving, petty theft, truancy, and vandalism. None of the Saints were ever arrested, but the Roughnecks were continually in trouble and harassed by the police and the townspeople. Why the difference in treatment? Sociologist William Chambliss (1973) conducted research in the boys' high school based solely on observation and concluded that social class played a significant role in the different treatment the boys received.

The Saints hid behind a façade of respectability

TABLE 1 A Sykes and Matza Techniques of Neutralization

Denial of Responsibility	I am not responsible for what happened because it was either an accident that couldn't be helped or I was the victim.
Denial of Injury	No one got hurt. What's the big deal?
Denial of a Victim	They had it coming! Did you see what she was wearing? They deserved what they got.
Condemnation of Condemners	Who are you to judge? Who are they to judge me?
Appeal to High Loyalties	I had to help my friends. Wouldn't you have done the same thing?

and a higher social status based on their parents' income and the neighborhoods in which they lived. They came from good families, were active in school organizations, received good grades, and planned on attending college. People viewed their acts as a few isolated incidences of "sowing wild oats." The Roughnecks had no respectability. They lived on the other side of town, came from a lower social class, drove around town in beat-up cars, were generally unsuccessful in school, and were always viewed suspiciously regardless of their actions. The Saints and the Roughnecks lived up to the labels the community gave them. The Saints grew up, went to college (all but one), and were successful. Two of the Roughnecks earned athletic scholarships and became coaches, but the rest of the Roughnecks did not do so well. Two of them dropped out of high school, later became involved in separate killings, and were sent to prison. One became a local bookie, and no one knows the whereabouts of the other.

How much of what the Roughnecks became had to do with the fact they were labeled "bad" and received negative treatment from their community? What do you think?

Most people attempt to resist negative labels that others try to pin on them. Some are so successful in this that, even though they participate in deviant acts, they still consider themselves conformists. People who commit deviant acts often use techniques of neutralization to continue to think of themselves as conformists. Sociologists Gresham

Sykes and David Matza (1964) studied boys who behaved deviantly and found that they used five techniques to neutralize society's norms:

Matza and Sykes point out that it is not only delinquents who try to neutralize the norms of mainstream society. Most people tend to justify their actions.

Erving Goffman (1963) says that secondary deviance marks the start of a deviant career. As people develop a stronger commitment to deviant behavior, they typically acquire a **stigma**, which is a powerfully negative label that greatly changes a person's self-concept and social identity. Perhaps this was the case for the Roughnecks. Stigma attributes can also be referred to as physical deformities, or skin color, that discredit one's claim to a "normal" identity. This defines a person's master status, superseding all other statuses the person occupies.

Gays and lesbians face a negative stigma in the United States and other Western societies. The view of same-sex orientation as deviant is very strong in society and is strongly condemned by many religious and cultural beliefs. The gay rights movement began in the late 1940s when many individual gays and lesbians discovered that they were not alone. We have made significant progress with respect to the treatment of gays and lesbians. There are laws, though, that do not favor gay rights, specifically, the Defense of Marriage Act.

The Defense of Marriage Act was passed in 1996. This law states:

1. No state needs to treat a relationship between

A lesbian couple attending a gay rights rally.   Source: Kati Garner

persons of the same sex as a marriage, even if this relationship is considered a marriage by another state.

2. The federal government may not treat same-sex relationships as marriage for any purpose, even if conducted in and recognized by one of the states.

This law clearly denies rights to the gay and lesbian populations, and many believe that social change is needed. However, many people believe society is threatened by the prospect of legal gay marriage because it threatens the natural order.

Social Diversity And Deviance

Social Class And Crime

One of the more interesting sociological findings in the study of deviance is that social classes have distinct styles of crime. Structural functionalists point out that **street crime** is typically committed by lower classes. Street crime includes, but is not limited to, robbery, drug dealing, burglary, prostitution, gambling, and many other crimes commonly referred to as "hustling." Industrialized societies have no trouble socializing the poor into wanting what everyone else has. Television and movies show images of middle-class people enjoying the good life, reinforcing the idea that all Americans can afford society's many goods and services.

The school system, which is the most common route to success, often fails the poor. Facing this barrier, the poor are more likely than their more privileged counterparts to drop out of school. Education failure closes the door to many legitimate ways to achieve financial success.

Cloward and Ohlin (1966) suggested that often a different door opens for the poor. They referred to these different opportunities as an illegitimate opportunity structure. Everybody in the United States is socialized with the idea of the American Dream. When one cannot achieve that dream through legitimate ways and mainstream norms, they may attempt to achieve that dream by means of illegitimate opportunities. Social class and location within the social structure may determine what kind of illegitimate opportunities are available.

White-Collar Crime

The more privileged people in society are not crime-free. They may simply find, or have access to, more sophisticated forms of crime. For example, you certainly have heard about bookkeepers who embezzle from their employers, doctors who cheat Medicare, and people who have knowingly granted bad home loans. In other words, rather than mugging and pandering, the more privileged people in society encounter other opportunities like bribery, embezzlement, and many other types of fraud. Sutherland (1947) coined the term **white-collar crime** to refer to crimes that people of respectable and high social status commit in the course of their occupations.

Corporate crimes are often committed by executives to benefit themselves or the companies that employ them. In December 2001, Enron Corporation declared bankruptcy following the public disclosure of significant debt that had been hidden by fraudulent and labyrinthine accounting practices. Top executives were deeply tied to this scheme and personally received tens of millions of dollars from it. This gigantic fraud was pulled off with the help of Arthur Andersen, formerly one of the top five international accounting firms. While the stock price

Enron.

Source: Sean Graham

of Enron collapsed, senior executives sold hundreds of millions of dollars worth of stock to unwary investors, while employees were prevented from selling their own stock held in their 401(k) retirement plans (Desjardins, 2009).

As we can see, people in higher social classes often lie, cheat, and steal just like people in lower classes. They just have access to different crimes. The cases above happen to be big-name cases where there have actually been arrests and some people have been sent to prison, but this may not always be the case.

What illegitimate opportunity structures can you access?
Have you ever taken office supplies from your place of employment?
Have you ever been late to work, or left early, and not documented your hours correctly on your timesheet?
Have you ever cheated on your taxes?
Have you ever downloaded music and not paid for it?
Have you ever been overpaid and just not mentioned it?

Those of us who are guilty of some of the above practices are probably justifying these actions, just as the juveniles studied by Matza and Sykes did. Most people use techniques of neutralization to continue to think of themselves as conformists and to justify their behaviors.

Functionalists conclude that street crime is the consequence of socializing everyone to equate success with owning material possessions, while denying many of those in the lower classes the means to achieve that success. People from higher social classes encounter different opportunity structures to commit crimes; however, a feminist approach would argue this point.

Gender And Crime

Feminist theory focuses on women offenders. Women are committing a larger proportion of almost all crimes, from car theft to burglary, than they did previously (Henslin, 2007). However, the femi-

nist approach argues that the increase is not great enough to be significant. When women do commit crimes, they tend to commit the types of crimes that reflect their continuing subordinate position in society (Thio, 2006). When women commit fraud, they are most likely to cheat banks through bad credit cards or loans, or they cheat the government by garnering benefits to which they are not entitled. Crimes such as false advertising or insider trading are almost exclusively committed by men because they still have greater access to high-level jobs than women, and those jobs provide more sophisticated opportunities to commit such crimes (Daly, 1989).

Race And Crime

If we were to judge solely by arrest and conviction rates, we might conclude that the gender of crime is male and the race of the criminal is black (Pettit & Western, 2004). African-Americans are arrested at a rate two, three, or even five times greater than statistical probability.

Blacks represent just 12 percent of the U.S. population, yet their percentages in these arrest statistics for 2005 are extremely high. Twenty-three thousand black men earned degrees from colleges and universities in the United States in 1990. In the same year, 2.3 million black men and juveniles passed through the nation's jails and prisons (Kozol, 1995).

TABLE 1 D Percentage of Arrestees who were black, 2005

Offense	Percentage
Gambling	71.1%
Robbery	53.3%
Murder	48.6%
Rape	32.7%
Burglary	28.5%
Drug Offenses	33.9%
Vagrancy	38.4%
Loitering	35.5%
Disorderly Conduct	33.6%

Source: U.S. Department of Justice (2005). Crime in the United States.

Controlling Deviance

Social Control

Every culture, subculture, and group has distinctive norms dictating appropriate behavior. **Social order** is made possible by **social control**, which includes the various ways that a social organization attempts to control the individual. Social control can be defined as all the pressures by which society and its component groups influence the behavior of individuals toward conformity with group norms (Rouck, 1978).

Social control and social order are necessary for society to flourish. Though control and order are often good things, allowing the continuation of the social organization, we should not always assume that they are good. A society that oppresses its people should not be supported simply because control and order are necessary. An organization that is racist or sexist in its orientation, for example, should not be supported if it violates our values. Actually, many changes have taken place because of people who refused to be controlled by social patterns they regarded as unjust. For example, women fought for the right to vote, as did African-Americans. Laborers fought for fair working conditions and protective laws. Many of our rights have come about because people fought for them and took the country in new directions.

People like Martin Luther King, Jr., and Rosa Parks are seen as positive role models that have made significant changes to the structure of our society. However, one might ask about the story of Angela Davis, the communist civil rights activist who was imprisoned for her views during the civil rights movement. Did the U.S. federal government feel she was too much of a threat due to her participation in the Black Panther movement and the struggle for equal rights for African-Americans? She was imprisoned in Marin County, California, when one of her guns was matched to the gun that killed a judge. Some people believe, however, that her real offense was belonging to the Communist Party and participating with the Black Panthers in the civil rights movement. She was trying to get a message across, and, instead, was penalized for it because she was engaging in social action that was perceived to be deviant and she belonged to groups that were actively challenging the existing social order (Giddens, Duneier, & Appelbaum, 2005).

Why are people like Angela Davis, Malcolm X and Louis Farrakhan considered negatively in American history? After all, isn't freedom to express ourselves part of America's core values?

Social control and order are necessary. However, one might question how much control and order? Too little can lead to chaos, and too much can lead to a loss of freedom.

Social Control Methods Used To Control Deviance And Crime

The criminal justice system is a complex set of institutions that includes the police and the courts, a wide range of prosecutors and defense lawyers, and the prison system.

The criminal justice system uses diverse methods to control deviance. For example, crime soared in the 1980s so "3 strikes" laws were implemented in the 1990s with the goal of lowering crime. However, the people in power, as the conflict theorist would suggest, did not limit these laws to violent crimes, and they did not consider that some minor crimes are considered felonies. As the functionalist would say, there were many unintended consequences due to this type of law, such as overpopulated prisons and people doing "hard" time for petty theft. Imprisonment is an increasingly popular reaction to crime, but it fails to teach inmates to stay away from crime. The **recidivism rate** runs as high as 85 to 90 percent (Henslin, 2007).

The table below lists the percentage of 272,000 prisoners released from U.S prisons in 15 states in 1994 and rearrested within three years (Bureau of Justice Statistics, 2002).

Capital punishment, the death penalty, is the most extreme action the state takes to control deviance and crime. There is significant controversy about the death penalty, based on moral and philosophical grounds. DNA testing has given opponents of the death penalty a strong argument: Innocent people have been executed!

What is your position on the death penalty?

Should it be legal, or should it be abolished? Why?

In 1986, Congress enacted mandatory minimum sentencing laws across the United States. These laws apply to 64,000 defendants a year and require specific sentences for specific crimes, allowing

TABLE 1 C Recidivism of U.S. Prisoners

Stealing Cars	79%
Possessing or Selling Stolen Property	77%
Larceny	75%
Burglary	74%
Robbery	70%
Illegal Weapons	70%
Illegal Drugs	67%
Fraud	66%
Arson	58%
Drunk Driving	52%
Rape	46%
Murder	41%

Source: Bureau of Justice Statistics, 2002.

no room for discretion. The laws are designed to be tough on crime and eliminate bias in the courts (Kimmel, 2009). The U.S. Census Bureau and the Department of Justice have both concluded that mandatory sentences have contributed greatly to prison overcrowding. More than 80 percent of the increase in the federal prison population from 1985 to 1995 is due to drug convictions based on mandatory minimums (Alliance Defense Fund, 2008).

The number of police officers in the United States has also increased, doubling over the past 30 years. In 2005, there were nearly 582,000 full-time law enforcement officers in the United States—about 3 for every 1,000 people (Federal Bureau of Investigation, 2005; U.S. Department of Justice, 2005).

The methods used by police to control deviance vary based on the crime. There are informal and formal methods of controlling deviance, with innovative approaches being pursued across the country. New policing strategies were introduced in New York City, with increased enforcement on petty crimes like graffiti and marijuana possession. Boston adopted an innovative multi-agency collaboration unit that focused on gang violence, and numerous other cities have introduced community policing, in which police work with community members to identify potential problems (Thio, 2006).

The larger issues include how to: protect people from deviant behaviors that are harmful to their welfare, tolerate those that are not, and develop systems to ensure fair treatment for those who deviate from societal norms. Deviant behavior can often be dealt with through socialization of the young to help them internalize norms against harmful and illegal behavior. Therefore, informal methods like the influence of families, peer groups, schools, and social pressure are the major crime fighters. They do not do a perfect job, though, and the police have to handle the failures. Responses to crime include formal methods such as hiring more police, building more prisons, and toughening penalties for crimes. One consequence of this approach is that certain people or groups in society suffer tremendously (Donohue, 2005).

The Medicalization Of Deviance

Over the last fifty years, the growing influence of psychiatry and medicine in the United States has led to the **medicalization of deviance**, which is the transformation of moral and legal deviance into medical conditions. Labeling people with disorders that need to be treated by physicians has become quite common. Sociologists believe that confused or tortured minds are not necessarily something internal, and instead may be due to particular life experiences.

Thomas Szasz, a professor of psychiatry, argues that mental illness is simply a term for problem behaviors and not a disease. Some forms of mental illness have organic causes like depression caused by chemical imbalances in the brain, while others are responses to troubles with coping devices or specific circumstances. For example, it is known that many of our homeless population have been labeled or diagnosed as mentally ill. For sociologists, the question that arises is: Were the people mentally ill before they became homeless, or did they become mentally ill after becoming homeless? Could losing your home and your job and being forced to live on the streets make you mentally ill? Professor Szasz suggests that it is our social experiences and not some illness of the mind that underlie bizarre behaviors. What could drive you over the edge?

National Crime Rates

Despite a drop in crime rates, there has been an increase in the number of prison inmates. The number of people in state and federal prisons continues to increase, despite a drop or leveling off in the crime rate in the past few years. This is a direct result of laws passed in the 1990s that led to more imprisonments and longer sentences (FBI, 2005).

The Federal Bureau of Investigation reported a decrease in the number of violent and property crimes reported by law enforcement agencies for the first six months of 2007 compared with the first six months of 2006. Despite the decline, the public views crime as a major social problem.

It remains to be seen whether or not this pattern will continue, and how we will deal with the mandatory minimums and drug offenses that are responsible for overpopulating our prisons.

Hate Crimes

A **hate crime** is a criminal act motivated by bias against a victim's/someone's race, ethnicity, religion, sexual orientation, or disability. The term "hate crime" did not enter the nation's vocabulary until the 1980s, though crimes based on hatred and prejudice are a sad fact both in the past and today.

TABLE 1 F Number of Hate Crimes

Directed Against	Number of Victims
Race-ethnicity	
African-Americans	3,075
Whites	910
Latinos	639
Asian-Americans	280
Native Americans	72
Religion	
Jews	1,084
Muslims	174
Catholics	71
Protestants	58
Sexual Orientation	
Male Homosexual	984
Female Homosexual	221
Homosexual	267
Heterosexual	26
Bisexual	15
Disabilities	
Mental	30
Physical	20

Source: U.S. Department of Justice (2005).

Summary

As we can see after reading this chapter, definitions of deviance and deviant behavior can mean many things depending on culture, social ties, race, ethnicity, gender, social class, and historical context. There are several explanations and theoretical perspectives that help us explain deviance and deviant behavior. Biological, psychological, and sociological theories offer much insight; however, most theories suggest that social environment and one's position within the social structure play important roles in whether or not a person deviates from, or conforms to, societal norms.

The theories of structural functionalism, conflict, and symbolic interactionism allow us to view deviant behaviors from different perspectives. Sociologists are interested in why people do the things they do, right or wrong, and these perspectives can provide some answers.

Social control and social order are necessary, but we should not always assume that all forms of control and order are good. A society that oppresses its people should not be supported simply because control and order are necessary. Organizations that violate our values should not be supported. History should remind us that much change has taken place as a result of people refusing to be controlled by social patterns they regarded as unjust.

The criminal justice system uses several methods to control deviance. Methods vary depending on the crime and may include mandatory sentencing minimums, prison terms, and the death penalty. Despite the fact that national crime rates have decreased, the number of prison inmates has increased.

With hope, this chapter has given you some insight on deviant behavior and an awareness that individuals convicted of wrongdoing do not always fit the common stereotype of the "street" criminal or "deviant" person.

Review/Discussion Questions

1. What are the central ideas of the conflict approach to deviance, and in what ways are economic and cultural conflict involved in the definition and control of deviance?
2. Are all deviants oppressed workers, or is deviance caused by other factors? How so?
3. Define and discuss the definition of deviance. Why is there often disagreement over what constitutes deviant behavior?
4. Discuss the death penalty. Are you for it or against it, and why?
5. It makes sense to apply the theories in this chapter to deviant behavior and street crime. Can we apply these same theories to people who commit white-collar crimes?
6. Do childhood experiences contribute to whether or not a person will deviate or conform? Why or why not?
7. Discuss whether or not the laws of society represent the interests of the public at large (public good) versus the interests of the power elites?
8. Identify and discuss major components of the U.S. criminal justice system.
9. Identify and discuss three different types of crimes.
10. What is Robert Merton's Strain Theory? Do you agree with it?
11. Have others ever labeled you? If yes, did it change or alter your behavior in some way?
12. Give some examples of white-collar crime.

Key Terms

Anomie is a social condition in which norms and values are conflicting, weak, or absent.

Capitalist class includes the people who own the means of production.

Conformity may involve going along with peers and/or following societal norms.

Control theory is the idea that there are two control systems—inner and outer—that work against our tendencies to deviate.

Corporate crimes are the illegal actions of people acting on behalf of the corporation.

Criminal justice systems include police, courts, and prisons making up the system that deals with criminal laws and their enforcement.

Cultural goals are the legitimate objectives of members of society.

Deviance is a violation of rules or norms.

Differential association is a theory of deviance that believes people will deviate or conform depending on their associations.

Hate crimes are criminal acts against a person or a person's property by an offender who is motivated by racial or other biases.

Illegitimate opportunity structures are relative opportunity structures outside laws and social norms that frame a person's life.

Institutional means include approved ways of reaching cultural goals.

Labeling theory is the idea that the labels people are given affect their own and others' perceptions of them, and, therefore, channel behavior either into or away from conformity.

Marginal working class includes the most desperate members of the working class who have few skills and little job security. They are often unemployed.

Medicalization of deviance means to relate deviance to an underlying illness that needs to be treated by physicians.

Primary deviance is the first occurrence of a violation of a norm which the committing actor does not view as deviant. Thus, it would have little to no effect on a person's self-concept.

Recidivism rates represent the number of people rearrested for committing the same types of crimes.

Sanctions are penalties (negative) or rewards (positive) for conduct regarding a social norm.

Secondary deviance is a response to primary deviance by which a person repeatedly violates a norm and begins to take on a deviant identity.

Social control involves techniques and strategies for maintaining order and preventing deviant behavior in a society.

Social order includes social arrangements upon which members depend.

Stigmas discredit a person's claim to a normal identity.

Strain theory is an idea developed by Robert Merton to describe the great strain felt by some members of society when they do not have access to the institutional means to achieve cultural goals.

Street crimes include mugging, rape, and burglary.

Techniques of neutralization are ways of thinking or rationalizing that help people deflect society's norms.

White-collar crimes include illegal acts committed by affluent and/or respectable individuals in the course of business activities.

Bibliography

Alliance Defense Fund (2008). Defense of Marriage Act. <http://www.domawatch.org> (2008).

Baron, S. W. (2001, May). Street Youth: Labour Market Experiences and Crime. Canadian Review of Sociology and Anthropology, 38, (2), 24-31.

Becker, H. S. (1966). Outsiders: Studies in the Sociology of Deviance. New York: Free Press.

Bureau of Justice Statistics (2002). Special Report: Recidivism of Prisoners Released in 1994. <http://www.ojp.usdoj.gov/bjs/pub/pdf/rpr94.pdf> (2009, February 7).

Chambliss, W. J. (1973). The Saints and the Roughnecks. New York: Free Press.

Charon, J. (1996). The Meaning of Sociology (5th ed.). New Jersey: Prentice Hall.

Cloward, R. A. & Ohlin, L. (1966). Delinquency and Opportunity: A Theory of Delinquent Gangs. New York: Free Press.

Daly, K. (1989). Neither Conflict Nor Labeling Nor Paternalism Will Suffice: Intersections of Race, Ethnicity, Gender and Family in Criminal Court Decisions. Crime and Delinquency, 35, 136-168.

Designboom (2008). A brief history of tattoos. <http://www.designboom.com/history/tattoo_history.html> (2008).

Desjardins, J. (2009). An Introduction to Business Ethics (3rd ed.). New York: McGraw Hill.

Donohue, J. (2005). Fighting Crime: An Economists View. The Milken Institute Review, 7 (46) 46-58.

Drug Policy Alliance Network (2008). Mandatory Minimum Sentencing. <http://www.drugpolicy.org/drugwar/mandatorymin> (2008).

Durkheim, E. (1893). The Division of Labor in Society. New York: Free Press.

Federal Bureau of Investigation (2008). <http://www.fbi.gov/homepage.htm> (2008).

Federal Bureau of Investigation (2005). Crime in the United States. <http://www.fbi.gov/ucr/05cius/> (2008).

Giddens, A., Duneier, M., & Appelbaum, R. (2005). Introduction to Sociology. New York: Norton & Company.

Glassner, B. (1999). The Culture of Fear: Why Americans are Afraid of the Wrong Things. New York: Basic Books.

Glueck, S. & Glueck, E. (1950). Unraveling Juvenile Delinquency. New York: Common Wealth Fund.

Goffman, E. (1963). Stigma. Englewood Cliffs, NJ: Prentice Hall.

Henslin, J. M. (2007). Essentials of Sociology: A Down to Earth Approach (7th ed.). Boston: Pearson/Allyn and Bacon.

Herman, J. (1992). [Review of the book Skin and Ink: Artists and Collectors]. The Journal of American Folklore, 105 (415), 83-85.

Hirschi, T. (1969). Causes of Delinquency. Berkeley, CA: University of California Press.

Kimmel, M., & Aronson, A. (2009). Sociology Now. Boston: Pearson/Allyn and Bacon.

Kindlon, D., & Thompson, M. (2000). Raising Cain: Protecting the Emotional Life of Boys. New York: Ballantine Books.

Kozol, J. J. (1995). Amazing Grace: the lives of children and the conscience of a nation. New York: HarperPerennial.

Lemert, C. (1993). Social Theory: The Multicultural & Classic Readings. Boulder, CO: Westview Press.

Lemert, E. M. (1951). Social Pathology: a systematic approach to the theory of sociopathic behavior. New York: McGraw Hill.

Lemert, E. M. (1972). Human Deviance, Social Problems, & Social Control (2nd ed.). Englewood Cliffs, NJ: Prentice Hall.

Lemonick, M. D. (2003, January 20). The Search for a Murder Gene. Time, 100

Wikipedia (2008). Frank Lucas (drug lord). <http://enwikipedia.org/wiki/frank_lucas_drug_lord> (2008).

Macionis, J. (2007). Sociology (11th ed.). Upper Saddle River, NJ: Pearson/Prentice Hall.

McCormack, J. (1999, February 22). The Sorry Side of Sears. Newsweek, a36-39.

Merton, R. K. (1968). Social Theory and Social Structure. New York: Free Press.

Merton, R. K. (2008). The Thomas Theorom and the Matthew Effect. <www.garfield.library.upenn.edu/merton/thomastheorem.pdf> (2008).

National Broadcasting Corp. (2008). Dateline NBC / Crime Reports. <http://www.msnbc.msn.com/id/21654381/page/2/> (2008).

National Broadcasting Corp. (2008, August 3). Hooked: Tattoos Head to Toe. <http://video.msn.com> (2008).

Pauker, J. (2006). Get Lost: the cool guide to Amsterdam (10th ed.). Amsterdam: Get Lost Publishing.

Pettit, B. & Western, B. (2004). Mass Imprisonment and the Life Course: Race and Class Inequality in U.S. Incarceration. American Sociological Review, 69, 151-169.

Pinker, S. (2003, January 20). Are Your Genes to Blame? Time, 98-100.

Pinker, S. (1994). The Language Instinct. New York: Morrow.

Reckless, W. C., & Dinitz, S. (1967). Pioneering with Self Concept as a Vulnerability Factor in Delinquency. Journal of Criminal Law, Criminology, and Police Science, 58 (4).

Reckless, W. C. (1973). The Crime Problem (5th ed.). New York: Appleton-Century-Crofts.

Rogers, J. W. (1977). Why are you not a Criminal? Englewood Cliffs, NJ: Prentice Hall.

Rouck, J. (1978). The Concept of Social Control in American Sociology. Westport, CT: Greenwood Press.

Schaefer, R. T. (2008). Sociology (11th ed.). New York: McGraw Hill.

Schlosser, E. (2004). Reefer Madness: Sex, Drugs, and Cheap Labor in the American Black Market. Boston: Houghton Mifflin Company.

Sheldon, W. H., Hartl, E. M., & McDermott, E. (1949). Varieties of Delinquent Youth. New York: Harper Brothers.

Simmons, J. L. (1965). Public Stereotypes of Deviants. Social Problems, 13, 223-224.

Sutherland, E. H. (1947). Principles of Criminology (4th ed.). Philadelphia: Lippencott.

Sykes, G. M., & Matza, D. (2002). Techniques of Neutralization: A Theory of Delinquency. In E. J. Clarke (Ed.), Deviant Behavior: A Text-Reader in the Sociology of Deviance (pp. 122-127). New York: Worth.

Szasz, T. (2008). Psychiatry <http://www.youtube.com> (2008).

Thio, A. & Calhoun, C. (2006). Readings in Deviant Behavior (4th ed.). Boston: Pearson/Allyn and Bacon.

Thio, A. & Calhoun, C. (2006). Deviant Behavior (8th ed.). Boston: Pearson/Allyn and Bacon.

U.S. Department of Justice (2005). <http://www.justice.gov/> (2008).

USAToday.com (2005, June 17). Timeline of the Tyco International scandal. <http://www.usatoday.com/money/industries/manufacturing/2005-06-17-tyco-timeline_x.htm> (2008).

Wickman, P. M. (1991). Deviance. Pp. 85-87 In Dushkin Publishing (Ed.), Encyclopedia Dictionary of Sociology (4th ed.) (pp.85-87). Guilford, CT: Dushkin Publishing.

Wiley, M. (1997). Filipino Martial Art Culture. Boston: Tuttle Publishing.

CHAPTER SEVEN

Social Stratification In The United States And Globally

Kwaku Obosu-Mensah

Social stratification, meaning the ranking of people within a society, is a very important issue because it determines the living standard of individuals in the society. Stratification also determines how valuable resources are distributed in the society.

Basis Of Stratification

The Ashanti people of Ghana have a proverb that states, "The fingers are not equal." The literal meaning is that our fingers are not of the same length—some are longer than others. Figuratively, this proverb means that human beings are not equal, which implies that in every society some people have more privileges, power, prestige, and burdens than others. The proverb acknowledges that stratification, and consequently, inequality, is endemic to all human societies. It should be remembered that stratification explains differences in lifestyle, attitudes, and social behavior among people.

In human societies, there are various bases of stratification, with a master basis that defines the day-to-day interaction between people in the society. In a typical society, the basis of stratification may be put on a continuum from the most important to the least important factor that determines privileges. Such factors of stratification include class (economic position), status (various forms, like age, profession, gender, and family), caste, and power (for example, party affiliation and noble lineage). The placement of profession is fluid because it can be placed under class as well as under status. Under class, the most important factor is income. Under status, the most important factor is the prestige or respect accorded to individual professions. According to the German sociologist Max Weber (Kimmel & Aronson, 2009), **status** is a recognition given to a person or group. This recognition could be based on an economic factor like income, or on the prestige or respect accorded to a profession.

Income And Wealth

In modern societies, the most important or master basis of stratification is class, followed by the statuses accorded to the different professions. Generally, the factors that determine stratification are achieved through an individual's own efforts. In the United States, a person's profession, which determines income and wealth (*economic determinism*), is the most important factor determining his or her privileges. Thus, access to the necessities of life is determined by a person's income and wealth. People with high income or wealth are highly regarded in modern societies. This explains why people may be drawn toward Bill Gates, one of the richest people in the United States, and might shun a homeless person. If Bill Gates walked into your classroom, your reaction toward him would be different than your reaction toward a homeless person. Thus, you are treating these two individuals differently on the basis of their income or wealth. In modern societies, power gained through political affiliation may not be as important in determining a person's position as income.

A related question is, "Why is income so important in modern societies?" The simple answer is that people in such societies are materialistic. **Materialism** develops after people are able to satisfy their basic needs. Thus, as people are able to meet basic requirements, they tend to spend more money on ostentatious goods and services. This is what sociologist and economist Thorstein Veblen termed **conspicuous consumption**—the public display and consumption of expensive items (Ashley & Orenstein, 2001). When people see the wealthy exhibit their affluence, they want to be like them. It is for this reason that a relatively poor family may be tempted to purchase a larger more expensive home than they can afford, all in an attempt to appear better off then they actually are. It is also true that without an adequate income, one may not be able to meet even the basic needs in a modern society. In modern societies, the accepted ideology is that hard work pays, so those who are poor are not hard-working people. One way of showing that you are a hard-working person is to acquire material goods. Thus, since most people do not want to be stigmatized as not working hard, they acquire material goods. The importance of income in modern societies cannot be overemphasized.

In traditional societies, the master basis of stratification is power and the secondary basis is status. Thus, income and wealth may not be the most important determinant of the stratification system. In such societies, stratification may be based on *ascriptive* factors—factors that individuals do not control. For example, no individual determines the family into which he or she is born.

Tradition may determine the stratification system. For example, by tradition the local or traditional chief may be the most powerful person in a society. Most important decisions may be made by the chief, as tradition has always dictated. Chiefs in Ghanaian towns and villages are typical examples. In every Ghanaian town and village, there is a local leader known as the chief. The chief is selected from the royal family and is accorded the highest position in the stratification system. The chiefs are custodians of *stool*, or common lands, and all development projects in the town should be approved by the chief. In addition, disputes are settled by the chief. It should be mentioned that the power of chiefs in Ghana is waning in the face of modern challenges. Nevertheless, they still wield enormous power over their subordinates.

Prestige

The prestige given to an individual is next in importance in determining a society's stratification system. Prestige differs from wealth and power in that it is entirely subjective. A person may have wealth and power regardless of what others think of him or her, but in order for one to have prestige, one must be perceived by others as having it. In this sense, there exists a **status system** which ranks people based on their social prestige. One area that contributes to this ranking system is a person's profession. In a typical traditional society, a high percentage of the people are illiterate. These illiterates depend on the few literates to read and translate their letters and help them with situations requiring reading or writing. Teachers in such societies, by the singular fact that they are literate, are accorded high status in the society, even though they may not earn high incomes. The same applies to priests who may not be rich but are accorded high status because of their profession. This can result in **status inconsistency**, in which a person is given conflicting statuses; he may have the respect of the people and the prestige that comes with it, but lacks wealth or power.

Power

In human societies, especially in capitalistic societies, **power** is very important—it determines who gets the best of the society's resources. Indeed, the power structure of a society determines every aspect of life in the society. For example, power determines who gives instructions and who obeys instructions. Since power is so important, people in every society try to gain power in order to exert influence and control. To achieve this goal, some people, through interactions and associations, form the power elite. In the United States, the governing elite or **power elite** draws its members from the following areas: (1) the highest political leaders, including the president and a handful of key cabinet members and close advisers; (2) major corporate owners and directors; and (3) high-ranking military officers (Mills Wright, 1958). A combination of these groups of people wields the most power and controls the American society.

Historical Systems Of Stratification

Historically, there are five main systems of stratification. These are egalitarianism, slavery, feudalism, castes, and class systems. In a typical society, two or more of these systems may exist at the same time. For example, during the time of slavery in the United States, the class system was also practiced.

Egalitarianism

This type of structure has the least amount of inequality. Examples of this type of system are the hunting and gathering societies in which everyone works together and then equally shares the proceeds of their combined labor. Some inequalities do exist, particularly in the area of status, with men being viewed more highly than women or children, and with skilled and successful hunters being the most prized. This type of society makes it tremendously difficult to build wealth.

Slavery

Under slavery, some people are owned by others. There are several ways of acquiring slaves. However, the most common methods are capturing and purchasing. That means the people who become slaves have very little, if any, role in their situation. Since nobody works to acquire or achieve the position of slavery, slavery is an *ascribed* status, meaning people are born or forced into slavery.

Slavery is the most extreme form of legalized social inequality because a slave owner always has control over slaves. In slavery, human beings are treated as property. People have the right to do whatever they want to do with their property, so those who own slaves normally do as they wish with their slaves. Slave owners determine the schedule of their slaves' daily routines, as well as when to dispose of or sell their slaves and for how much. In most cases, the children of slaves become the property of the slave owner, just as the puppies your dog gave birth to become your property.

Technically, slavery has been abolished, but the practice still exists in various forms in pockets of countries around the world. On the website of the U.S. Department of State (2007), there is a letter dated June 12, 2007, written by Condoleezza Rice, the former secretary of state. In the letter, she notes that, "Trafficking in persons is a modern-day form of slavery, a new type of global slave trade. Perpetrators prey on the most weak among us, primarily women and children, for profit and gain. They lure victims into involuntary servitude and sexual slavery." The U.S. Central Intelligence Agency estimates that 50,000 people each year are trafficked into, or transited through, the United States as sex slaves, domestics, garment workers, and agricultural slaves. Thus, slavery exists even in America. Most of the slaves in the United States are there for the purpose of labor and sexual exploitation. Though most of these slaves come from East Asia, Mexico, and Central America, quite a number of them are native-born Americans (Central Intelligence Agency, 2008).

In a remote area of Ghana, the people practice a type of slavery called *trokosi*. It is a practice where children, mostly girls, are sent to shrines to atone for the crimes of their relatives. Such supposed crimes might have been committed hundreds of years ago, but the family has to send a replacement when the girl entrusted to the shrine dies. Thus, the punishment for a past crime is perpetual. Let's examine an example. Let's say a hundred years ago, Mr. Kankan borrowed some money from Mr. Kosi but was not able to repay it at the agreed upon time. Mr. Kosi, the loaner, would report Mr. Kankan, the borrower, to a fetish priest in the community. The fetish priest would pay Mr. Kosi, and hence Mr. Kankan would now be indebted to the fetish priest. If Mr. Kosi were not able to pay the loan at the agreed upon time, the fetish priest would require him to send a girl from his family to serve him in his shrine. The fetish priest would threaten that if Mr. Kosi did not comply, he (the priest) would use supernatural powers to kill all of Mr. Kosi's family members. Mr. Kosi's family is made to promise to replace the girl any time the one who was handed over to the shrine dies. The girls handed over to the fetish priest would become his slaves because he would use them any way he wanted, including for sexual exploitation.

Feudalism

Feudalism, also known as the *estate system*, was associated with societies during the Middle Ages. Feudalism was most common in England. By its very nature, feudalism gave rise to a hierarchy of rank. Originally, the ranks were the nobles at the top, and the commoners at the bottom. The commoners were mostly peasants who demographically were the majority of the population. During this period, land was the most important commodity because almost everybody depended on it. The most powerful people in the society, the nobles, apportioned all the land to themselves. Thus, the nobles were a powerful land-holding class.

Under this system, peasants worked on leased land that was owned by the nobles. The peasants swore homage to the nobles and, in return, the nobles promised to protect the peasants and to see that they received justice. There were minor variations of feudalism, but generally peasants were not paid, instead being allotted small plots of land to grow food for themselves and their families. After working long hours for his lord, who was a noble, the peasant could cultivate his allotted plot of land to feed his family, if he still had some energy left. Some people associate the estate system with enclosures. The term **enclosure** was used to describe, among other things, the process by which the most powerful and rich people fenced (enclosed) their land to the exclusion of all others. Before the period of enclosures, there was a sort of communal ownership of land. Consequently, Marxists see enclosures as a ploy used by the rich people who controlled state processes to appropriate public land for their private benefit. Thus, the "enclosure was a plain enough case of class robbery" (Thompson, 1991).

In order to prevent the parceling of land into small pieces, feudalism sanctioned *primogeniture*, by which all property of a deceased landowner was passed on intact to his eldest son. This type of inheritance was one of the factors that contributed to the demise of the feudal system. Younger sons of nobles who could not inherit their fathers' land eventually became priests, merchants, and artisans who eventually challenged the positions of their elder brothers who were the landowning nobles. For example, some of the merchants started cottage industries that attracted peasants from the fields, thus weakening the positions of the nobles. For the first time, some wealthy people—the priests, merchants, and artisans—were not dependent upon land.

Castes

In a **caste system**, people inherit their caste category from their parents. The caste system is maintained through inheritance, and is generally justified and perpetuated through religion. As in slavery, the level of inequality in a caste system is very high. You are born into your caste category and you cannot change it. That means the caste system is based on ascription.

The Caste System In India

Historically, the caste system was most common in India. It is still practiced in some form in present-day India. As noted above, castes are hereditary ranks determined by religion. In India, it is determined by the Hindu religion which believes that the caste you were born into was determined by a previous life. One's caste category determines the type of job one can hold. Thus, there is occupational specialization on the basis of caste. In addition, the caste system determines power relations, residential patterns, and the types of food one can eat. In a sense, one's caste destination determines one's life opportunities.

In India, people are born into four main groups or castes (varnas). The highest caste category, the one considered spiritually and socially superior and the one that enjoys the most privilege, is called the *Brahmin*. Members of this caste category are considered pure. Traditionally, this is the priestly caste, with members of this category performing priestly duties. Since the caste system is based on religion, it is not surprising that the highest caste category is composed of those who supervise religion. In a traditional and highly religious society, people will accord the highest privileges to priests and priestly families. This supports the argument that status is the most important stratification item in traditional societies.

The second highest caste category is the *Kshatriya*. Generally, this caste is composed of the warriors and the political upper crust. During the period when people were consolidating their societies, different groups waged wars against each other. Therefore, soldiering was very important

This Indian sweeper is part of the Shudra caste.   Source: Darrell Rogers

for the survival of every society. This may explain why warrior families are accorded such a high position in the caste system of India.

The third highest caste category is the *Vaishnava*. This category is composed of merchants, traders, and business people. Members of this category ensured that certain important goods were available in the society, hence their relatively average position in the caste category.

At the bottom of the four-category caste system is the *Shudra*. This category is composed of peasants, cleaners, and laborers. They do the menial jobs and their contribution to the society is not as valued as that of the other caste categories already mentioned.

A group called the *Dalit*, or *Untouchables*, is considered so low and unclean that it is not considered part of the caste stratification system. According to Smita Narula, "Dalits are not allowed to drink from the same wells, attend the same temples, wear shoes in the presence of an upper caste, or drink from the same cups in tea stalls" (Mayell, 2003). Traditionally, the Untouchables are tasked with doing dirty jobs like washing blood from accident scenes. Most of them are condemned to begging for their survival. It could be said that they live to beg. In recent times, even though most are still sweepers and mowers, some Untouchables have attained executive posts as mayors, chairmen, and chancellors. In 1992, K.R. Narayanan, an Untouchable, became the vice president of India. He went on to become president in 1997. It should be noted, though, that in India, the position of president is largely ceremonial.

Since people are born into their castes, a person who belongs in one caste cannot move into another. For example, a person born as a Kshatriya can never become a Brahmin. In 1949, the Indian government abolished the caste system. However, as is the case in Third World countries, it is one thing to abolish an established cultural or religious practice, but it is another thing to enforce the abolition. Officially, the caste system has been stopped, but it is still practiced in some parts of the country, especially in rural India.

The caste system is not going away for two main reasons. First, those who are privileged by the system want to maintain their privileges. In many instances, through violence and the threat of violence, members of the upper castes have resisted the upward mobility of the lower castes. National Geographic News (2003) published an article, "India's Untouchables Face Violence, Discrimination" written by Hillary Mayell in which the author noted that:

> Human rights abuses against these people, known as Dalits, are legion. A random sampling of headlines in mainstream Indian newspapers tells their story: "Dalit boy beaten to death for plucking flowers"; "Dalit tortured by cops for three days"; "Dalit 'witch' paraded naked in Bihar"; "Dalit killed in lock-up at Kurnool"; "7 Dalits burnt alive in caste clash"; "5 Dalits lynched in Haryana"; "Dalit woman gang-raped, paraded naked"; "Police egged on mob to lynch Dalits." (p. 1)

The second factor that maintains the caste system is the religious belief of the people, including people of the lower castes and the Untouchables. Hindus believe in reincarnation, and it is believed that an individual's position in the next life is dependent upon the way that person lives today. Thus, if you obey the Hindu God and do what the Hindu doctrine expects of you, you may be rewarded in your next life. If you are a Shudra today and you do what is expected of people of the Shudra category, you may be born into a higher caste in your next life. On the other hand, if you do not obey the Hindu doctrine and you elevate yourself, you may be punished in your next life and relegated to a lower category, or remain in your lower category in the case of the Untouchables. This means that even people in lower castes may resist change because they don't want to be punished through relegation in their next life.

Class Systems

This type of ranking is based on economic factors such as income. People are categorized on the basis of their jobs, income, and wealth. A **social class** is made up of people similarly situated with roughly the same income, power, and prestige. The higher your class, the more privileges you enjoy in society. Under a **class system**, an individual's position is not fixed; instead, it is relatively open as one can move from a lower class to a higher one or descend in the opposite direction. Through education and acquiring additional skills, individuals can make themselves more valuable and thus command more money and move up. In a capitalist society, there are five main types of classes. These are the upper class, the middle class, the working class, the lower class, and the underclass.

The Class Structure In The United States

The Upper Class

The upper class is made up of a group of families who are descendants of successful individuals from generations past. This class is also known as the capitalist class. The fortune of the upper class was made generations ago and handed down from one generation to the next. Their money is *old money*. Members of the upper class are the wealthiest and most influential families in the society. Examples of such families are the Rockefellers, the Carnegies, and the Kennedys.

According to Rossides (1997), the upper class is very exclusive because 2 percent or less of the population belongs to this group. Some researchers, like Kerbo (2009) and Marger (2005), believe that the upper class makes up no more than 1 percent of the population. Members of this class associate in exclusive clubs and tend to marry within their class. Some non-upper-class families eventually move into the upper class category because a capitalist society permits mobility from one stratification group to another; however, more frequently, a person is born into the upper class. Bill Gates is one of the richest men in the United States, but his family is not considered a part of the upper class. This is because the wealth of the family was acquired very recently—and is *new money*.

Whoever has the greatest influence on the government controls the economy. The upper class is politically the most influential class through direct participation in politics, selection of government leaders, the activities of lobby organizations, and organizations established to shape the development of government policy (Kerbo, 2009). At times, its members determine how the people upon whom the president relies, like cabinet secretaries, are chosen. For example, President Jimmy Carter chose his running mate from the Trilateral Commission, which is an upper-class organization. Indeed, many of his cabinet members and special advisers were members of the Trilateral Commission, which was formed in 1973 by private citizens from the European Union, Japan, Canada, and the United States to encourage cooperation among the countries. Of the ninety top appointments made by President Ronald Reagan, 31 were members of the upper-class Council on Foreign Relations, a nonpartisan think tank, and 12 were members of the Trilateral Commission (Domhoff, 2006). An additional 32 were members of the Committee on the Present Danger, an organization of upper-class people (Kerbo, 2009) focused on confronting terrorism. The trend of choosing members of the upper class for important political positions continues today.

The Middle Class

The middle class is also known as the white-collar class because its jobs are not dirty jobs. That is, its members don't engage in strenuous, sweaty work; instead, their jobs are typically non-physical and require many years of educational training. In the occupational structure, members of the middle class receive orders from the elite and give orders to those in the working class. Examples of members of the middle class are physicians, professors, lawyers, office workers, insurance agents, and public school teachers. Since the upper class is virtually off limits to most people, the middle-class level is the one people in lower levels strive to reach. Thus, it is easier for people from lower-class backgrounds to join the middle class than it is for them to join the upper class.

Economic historians have pointed out the importance of a middle class for economic development. David Landes (1998) notes that the "ideal growth and development society" would have "a relatively large middle class" (pp. 217-18). According to Landes, England was the first to industrialize because of "the great English middle class" (p. 221). The notion that the middle class is the driving force behind the economic development of a society is supported

Construction workers.

Source: Herman Brinkman

by Adelman and Morris (1967) when they note that in the economic development of Western Europe, the middle classes were a driving force.

The above is an indication that the general success of every economy is more dependent upon the middle class than it is upon the upper class. Collectively, the middle class earns and spends a lot of money. It is the backbone of the economy; when the size of the middle class increases, the economy booms. In addition, members of the middle class are more likely to demand infrastructure and services from the government—schools, highways, law enforcement, and tax reforms—than any other class. Over the past decade, the middle class in the United States has shrunk in size.

Because the middle class consists of a wide range of professions, it is divided into two categories: upper-middle class and lower-middle class.

The upper-middle class makes up 10 to 15 percent of the population (Rossides, 1997). This class is made up of highly paid professionals like doctors, lawyers, accountants, architects, and professors. Their positions are considered highly prestigious, and they are respected in society. Politically, they are active and very influential.

The lower-middle class is 30 to 35 percent of the population (Rossides, 1997). Compared with the upper-middle class, members of the lower-middle class are paid lower rates and include professionals like public school teachers, nurses, office workers, and technicians.

The Working Class

The working class makes up about 40-45 percent of the population (Rossides, 1997). Members of this class are also known as blue-collar workers.

They perform primarily manual (physical) types of work—in a sense, using their muscles rather than their brains. Examples of working class professions are factory laborers, gas station attendants, construction workers, and farm laborers. Compared with the upper and middle classes, members of the working class earn lower incomes. The children of working-class people often remain at that level; however, many become middle class due to the opportunity of attending college.

The Lower Class

In a capitalist society, the lower class typically makes up 12 to 15 percent of the population (Marger, 2005). Many people in this class are employed part time or intermittently. When employed, they earn very little. Members of the lower class are politically weak. They may be struggling to put food on the table and not have enough time to engage in the political process. Historically, many of them don't even vote. It is very difficult for these people to rise above the lower class because they don't have the money and time to attend college, with many working double shifts to make ends meet. The typical education level is high school or lower. Most of their children remain in the lower class because parents lack the resources to push them up through the stratification system. Members of the lower class bear most of the burdens in society.

The Underclass

The underclass is also known as the poorest of the poor, or the chronically poor. In a capitalist society, the underclass may compose about 3 to 5 percent of the population (Gilbert, 2003). One of the differences between the underclass and the lower class is that while members of the lower class may be unemployed for a short time, underclass members are unemployed for a long time or perpetually. The underclass is outside the mainstream of the American occupational system. Thus, it is not essential to the efficient functioning of a capitalist economy. This class is composed of people who dropped out of elementary school, people who engage in petty crime, as well as some elderly or disabled people. Members of the underclass possess few skills and are not able to secure jobs. Most of these people depend on the welfare system.

Consequences Of Stratification

Income And Wealth Disparity

Position. An individual's position in the stratification system determines that person's wealth and income. Stratification, therefore, denotes income and wealth disparity. In the United States, just like in any other country, some people earn more than others. In the United States, 50 percent of all income goes to the richest 20 percent of people, and only 3 percent of total income is earned by the bottom 20 percent. In 2006, the income of the top

TABLE 1 A Household Wealth in the United States

Percentage of Total Wealth in the U.S.

	1983	1989	1992	1995	1998	2001	2004
Top 1%	33.8	37.4	37.2	38.5	38.1	33.4	34.3
Top 20%	81.3	83.5	83.8	83.9	83.4	84.4	84.7
2nd 20%	12.6	12.3	11.5	11.4	11.9	11.3	11.3
3rd 20%	5.2	4.8	4.4	4.5	4.5	3.9	3.8
Bottom 40%	0.9	-0.7	0.4	0.2	0.2	0.3	0.2

* Includes Top 1%

Source: Wolff, Edward N. (2007). "Recent Trends in Household Wealth in the United States: Rising Debt and the Middle-Class Squeeze," Working Paper # 502. The Levy Economics Institute of Bard College

1 percent increased by 14 percent, while that of the bottom 90 percent dropped by 0.6 percent (Saez & Piketty, 2006).

Education. Income is influenced by education. On average, the higher your educational background, the higher your income. According to statistics provided by the U.S. Census Bureau (2006), people with bachelor's degrees earned an average of $45,211, while those with an associate's degree or some college earned $31,936. On the other hand, high school graduates earned an average of $26,123, and high school dropouts earned $18,641. People with professional degrees make an average of $99,300 per annum.

Government spending. In many ways, the government spends more money on the rich than on the poor. For example, according to Jennifer C. Kerr, an Associated Press writer, two-thirds of U.S. corporations did not pay federal income taxes, even though they made trillions of dollars in sales between 1998 and 2005 (Kerr, 2008). Some of these corporations are owned by the richest people in the country.

Wealth. In 2004, the richest 20 percent of families owned 84.7 percent of America's wealth, while the bottom 40 percent of the population owned less than 1 percent of the wealth. During the same year, the top 1 percent of families owned about 34.3 percent of the nation's wealth.(Table 1 A)

It should be noted that wealth disparity is more pronounced than income disparity. For example, in 2004, the richest 20 percent of the population controlled 84.7 percent of wealth in the country and earned about 50 percent of all income. The bottom 60 percent of households possessed only 4 percent of the nation's wealth, while it earned 26.8 percent of the income (Wolff, 2007).

According to Wolff (2007), between 1983 and 2004, the largest gains in wealth and income in relative terms were made by the wealthiest households. The top 1 percent saw their average wealth rise by over 6 million dollars, or 78 percent; those in the top quintile experienced increases from 78 percent to 92 percent. Wealth increased by 57 percent for the fourth quintile, and 27 percent for the middle quintile. People in the bottom two quintiles lost 59 percent of their wealth. By 2004, the average wealth of the poorest 40 percent of the people had fallen to $2,200.

Debt and stocks. Important measurements of wealth include debt and stocks. All things being equal, the wealthier you are, the less debt you have. Additionally, upper-class people have more financial investments than members of other classes. For example, the richest 1 percent of households own about half of all outstanding stock shares, financial securities, trust equity, and business equity, along with 37 percent of non-home real estate. The top 20 percent of families account for 84 percent of the same assets. The remaining 80 percent of American families own only 16 percent of such marketable assets (Domhoff, 2006).

Hunger. Testifying before the Subcommittee on

TABLE 1 B Poverty Threshold

Size of Family Unit	Weighted Average Thresholds
One Person	$10,294
Two People	$13,167
Three People	$16,079
Four People	$20,614
Five People	$24,382
Six People	$27,560
Seven People	$31,205
Eight People	$34,774
Nine People or More	$41,499

Source: U.S. Census Bureau, Income, Poverty, and Health Insurance Coverage in the United States: 2006

Income Security and Family Support of the House Committee on Ways and Means on February 13, 2007, Robert Rector a senior policy analyst of The Heritage Foundation noted that 13 percent of poor families, and 2.6 percent of poor children, experience hunger at some point during the year. In most cases, their hunger is short-term. Eighty-nine percent (89%) of the poor report their families have "enough" food to eat, while only 2 percent say they "often" do not have enough to eat (Rector, 2007).

Income gap. The income gap between the rich and the poor is increasing. The share of total income going to the top-earning 1 percent of Americans went from 8 percent in 1980, to 16 percent in 2004. In 1978, corporate chief executive officers (CEOs) earned, on the average, 35 times as much as the average worker. In 1989, the gap increased to 71 times, and by 2000 the average CEO typically earned at least 300 times as much as the average worker (Mishel, 2006).

Poverty: What Is It?

In 2006, the U.S. Census Bureau defined a poor person as an individual earning less than $10,294 a year. The poverty level was $13,167 for a family of two and $16,079 for a family of three. (Table 1 B) Though many of the poor work, they don't earn enough money to raise themselves above the poverty level

In 2006, 36.5 million people, or 12.3 percent of the population in the United States, fell below the poverty line. The poverty rate was 8.2 percent for non-Hispanic whites, 10.3 percent for Asians, 20.6 percent for Hispanics, and 24.3 percent for African-Americans. Poverty affects people in various ways. For example, many poor people cannot afford health insurance. Between 2004 and 2006, 47 million (15.5%) Americans did not have health insurance (U.S. Census Bureau, 2007).

Types Of Poverty

There are two main types of poverty: absolute poverty and relative poverty.

Absolute Poverty

Absolute poverty may be termed complete poverty, occurring when people are desperately poor and may not even know where they will get their next meal. Absolute poverty connotes unemployment, homelessness, lack of health insurance, and, at times, going to bed hungry. The man or woman you see scavenging for food in other people's garbage is a typical example of a person who is absolutely poor. Nobody should be absolutely poor, but we find such people in all societies.

Relative Poverty

A college class was once asked, "Is there anybody here who thinks he or she is poor?" The hand of a young lady shot up. She was asked to tell the class why she considered herself a poor person. After struggling for a second, she said she drove an old car. She hesitated again and declared, "I know I am poor." The young lady, who was always neatly dressed, was asked to answer a few simple questions: "Have you ever gone to bed hungry? Do you

TABLE 1 C Poverty Rate by Race

Poverty by Race	Poverty Rate	Number in Poverty
Native Americans	26.6%	0.7 million
African-Americans	25.3%	9.2 million
Hispanics	21.5%	9.2 million
Asian-Americans	10.7%	1.4 million
Whites (non-Hispanic)	9.3%	17.0 million

Source: U.S. Census Bureau. Income, Poverty, and Health Insurance Coverage in the U.S., 2006

TABLE 1 D Median Earnings by Race and Gender

Race	Median Earnings	
	Men	Women
Asian	$50,159	$38,613
White	$47,814	$35,151
Native Hawaiian	$34,641	$31,171
African-American	$34,480	$30,398
Native American	$32,684	$27,370
Hispanic	$27,490	$24,738

own a house? Do you have a job?" Yes, she had never gone to bed hungry, she owned a vehicle, and she had a house and an income, yet she considered herself poor. Obviously, when she compared herself with other people in her milieu, others had more, so she thought she was poor. This type of "poverty" is called **relative poverty**, which is the feeling or thought that you are poor when you compare yourself with other people. People in that category are those who call for changes in society. They are the people who criticize political decision-makers and demand better opportunities for society.

Who Are The Poor?

The overall poverty rate declined slightly from 12.6 percent in 2005 to 12.3 percent in 2006. The number of people living in extreme poverty—that is, those with incomes below half the poverty line—remained the same at 15.6 million people in 2006. For children younger than 18, the poverty rate is 17.4 percent (Census, 2008). This means 2.8 million American children, or nearly one in every six, are poor. In 2006, the number of Americans who lived in extreme poverty was the highest since recorded data first became available in 1975.

Racially, there are differences in poverty. The highest rate of poverty is found among Native Americans (26.6%), followed by African-Americans (25.3%), then Hispanics (21.5%). (Table 1 C)

TABLE 2 A Poverty Rate, Ten Top States

Rank	State	Poverty Rate (%)
1.	Mississippi	21.1
2.	District of Columbia	19.6
3.	Louisiana	19.0
4.	New Mexico	18.5
5.	Arkansas	17.3
6.	West Virginia	17.3
7.	Kentucky	17.0
8.	Oklahoma	17.0
9.	Texas	16.9
10.	Alabama	16.6

Source: U.S. Census Bureau. Income, Poverty, and Health Insurance Coverage in the U.S., 2006

The high poverty rates for Native Americans, African-Americans, and Hispanics are due to a relative lack of education and marketable skills in these groups.

When it comes to earnings, Asian men had the highest median earnings, $50,159, in 2006, followed by white men, with median earnings of $47,814. Native Hawaiian and other Pacific Islander men earned $34,641, while African-American men earned $34,480. Native American and Alaskan Native men had median earnings of $32,684, and Hispanic men had median earnings of $27,490 (Table 1 D). The trends were the same for women, though it should be noted that in each group men earned more than women.

Educational achievement is the most important factor in explaining the high earnings of Asians and whites. Related to high educational achievement are marketable skills. Since Asians and whites tend to have higher levels of education, they have skills that secure them high-paying jobs.

As expected, the rate of poverty is not the same in all states. As noted by Hill (2008), poverty is a major problem confronting the South, particularly Mississippi, where about one out of every five people lives in poverty. Among the top ten states with the highest poverty rates, eight are Southern states. This means, comparatively, that an American is more likely to be poor if he or she lives in the South.

Southern states are poorer than northern states due to less economic development and more limited access to higher education. In 2007, Mississippi ranked at the bottom in academic achievement (LeFevre, 2007). In Mississippi *industrialization*, which is the engine of economic growth, did not come to many areas until the late 20th century. This was because the farmers were less than enthusiastic about bringing in new industry that would compete with them for unskilled black laborers. When mechanized agriculture was introduced to the South, many farm workers lost their jobs. Unfortunately, there were few industrial jobs to absorb these laid-off workers. This contributed enormously to poverty in the region, and, at the same time, many of the young and the educated left the South for the North.

Poverty rates differ by city, as well. Table 2 B shows the top ten cities (250,000 or more in population) with the highest rates of poverty. The poorest cities have the highest concentration of minorities. Incidentally, most of the poorest cities are in the north and have high immigrant populations. Compared with northern states, Southern states are poorer. However there is not as much concentration of poverty in their large cities.

One common characteristic of poor cities is job loss. Detroit, for example, was once considered the

TABLE 2 B Poverty Rate, Top Ten Poorest Cities

Rank	City	Poverty Rate (%)
1.	Detroit, MI	32.5
2.	Buffalo, NY	29.9
3.	Cincinnati, OH	27.8
4.	Cleveland, OH	27.0
5.	Miami, FL	26.9
6.	St. Louis, MO	26.8
7.	El Paso, TX	26.4
8.	Milwaukee, WI	26.2
9.	Philadelphia, PA	25.1
10.	Newark, NJ	24.2

Source: U.S. Census Bureau, 2006 American Community Survey, August 2007

automobile production headquarters of the United States, and is still home to the nation's three biggest automobile companies: General Motors, Ford, and Chrysler. At the height of its industrial boom, Detroit boasted many factories. However, due to competition from foreign companies in the international market, some industries in the Detroit area have closed down. This has created unemployment and, hence, poverty.

Most of the poor are women. Pearce (1978) describes this as the feminization of poverty. Women are more likely to be unemployed and, if employed, a woman is more likely to have a part-time position. Another factor that has contributed to the feminization of poverty is an increase in female-headed households. More women are solely responsible for the financial upkeep of their households because of the higher number of deadbeat fathers. Many women are poor because their wages are lower than the wages of men. In 2006, the median earnings of men were $42,210, and for women they were $32,649, or 77.3 percent of what men earned. Traditional gender roles which socialize women to put family ahead of their education and careers, have also contributed to the feminization of poverty.

Disparity In Life Opportunities

Another consequence of stratification manifests itself in how long an individual lives. Various factors influence longevity, but poverty is certainly the most important factor. More affluent people live longer than those who are less affluent, because the former have easier access to health care, material goods, and better living and working conditions. Income influences what people eat and how they behave. For example, poor people are more likely to be obese, eat fatty foods, abuse alcohol and tobacco, and have high blood pressure and high cholesterol than rich people. A common finding is that life expectancy is higher for high-income people (Brown, 2002). Manchester and Topoleski (2008), note that there is a growing disparity in life expectancy

TABLE 2 C Life Expectancy by Income and Race

Race	Income ($)	Life Expectancy (years)
Asian-Americans	$21,566	84.9
Whites in Appalachia	$16,390	75.0
Blacks	$15,412	72.9
Western American Indians	$10,029	72.7

TABLE 2 D Correlation between Income and Life Expectancy

Retirees	Low Income	High Income
	Age at Death	Age at Death
White Males	78.9	80.8
Black Males	76.8	79.5
White Females	82.1	84.7
Black Females	81.3	85.6

Source: Duggan, James E., Robert Gillingham, and John S. Greenlees (2007)

between individuals with high and low incomes. A study done by Murray (2006) confirmed that rich people live longer than poor people. He found that Asian-American women can expect to live 13 years longer than low-income black women in the rural South. Table 2 C shows that across races, income is an important factor in determining an individual's life expectancy.

The effect of income on longevity can be seen within race as well. For example, wealthy whites live longer than poor whites, and wealthy blacks live longer than poor blacks. (Table 2 D)

The percentage of Americans reporting fair or poor health is considerably higher among people living below the poverty line than it is for those with incomes at least twice the poverty threshold. As noted by the Institute for Research on Poverty (2008), "Poor people are less healthy than those who are better off, whether the benchmark is mortality, the prevalence of acute or chronic diseases, or mental health." In addition, the poor in the United States are exposed to more environmental health hazards. The rich, on the other hand, have access to better health care, encounter fewer financial burdens, and enjoy more services provided by the government like roadways and sewage. These factors add to the longevity of the rich.

Disparity In Worker Satisfaction And Alienation

In general, high-level employees, including professionals, tend to be happier with their work than low-level employees. Workers at lower levels are also more likely to be alienated from their work. One reason they feel alienated and dissatisfied is that these low-level workers always have to take instructions from others. In addition, most of the jobs of low-level employees are repetitive, offering these workers little or no meaning in the work they do. Low-level workers are often not satisfied with their jobs because of their lower rate of pay.

Social Mobility

On Friday, August 15, 2008, the media reported that Donald Trump was buying the Beverly Hills mansion of television personality Ed McMahon. Trump intended to rent the mansion to McMahon after buying the home to prevent it from going into foreclosure, since McMahon could no longer afford to pay his $4.8 million mortgage. It is obvious that Ed McMahon was once financially well-off. However, as of August 2008, he was financially desperate. Technically, he moved from a higher social position to a lower social position. This is an example of social mobility. The term **social mobility** is used to describe the movement of one or more individuals from one social position to another. This move can be the result of **individual mobility** through hard work and perseverance at the individual level. Social mobility can also be the result of **structured mobility**, in which events happening in the society as a whole allow groups of people to move up or down. An example of structured mobility is the reduction of manufacturing jobs in the United States. These jobs had allowed workers with little education and few skills to move upward into the middle class. With many plants shutting down their U.S. factories and moving their production overseas, these once middle-class workers are finding themselves reduced to the working or lower class. Social mobility is more viable in open societies like capitalist societies than in closed societies like communist and traditional societies. This is because the rewards for hard work are higher in open societies than in closed societies.

Types Of Social Mobility

Vertical Mobility

At the University of Ghana in Legon (Accra), there is an amazing story about one of the professors of sociology. This professor started work as a porter at the university. Through private studies, using mostly the university library, he passed the required preliminary courses and was admitted to the University of Ghana for his bachelor's degree. Eventually, he obtained his doctorate from Oxford University in Britain and became a professor at the University of Ghana. Socially, this man moved upward from a menial job to become a professor.

Another man became the branch manager of a

bank in Ghana, West Africa. He misappropriated some funds and was fired, and eventually became a subsistence farmer. Both his income and status diminished substantially. Thus, socially, he moved downward.

Both stories are examples of **vertical mobility**—moving up or down from one social position to another of a different rank and prestige.

Horizontal Mobility

John was a high school teacher but decided to change professions. Consequently, he trained to become a registered nurse, where his income was similar to what he earned as a teacher. Furthermore, in society, nurses and high school teachers attract similar levels of prestige. Thus, movement from being a teacher to being a nurse did not significantly change his income or prestige. This is an example of **horizontal mobility**, which is the movement from one social position to another of the same rank. If both professions attract the same prestige, why would an individual change professions? A person may change professions due to burn-out, which is often the result of exhaustion and decreased interest in one's work, possibly caused by stress.

Intergenerational Mobility

The concept of **intergenerational mobility** is used to describe changes in the social positions of children in comparison to their parents. To have a fair comparison, it may be better for sons to compare their social positions with those of their fathers and daughters to compare themselves with their mothers. This is because the chances of succeeding are different for males and females. On a personal level, it will be helpful to compare yourself with your parent at specific ages. For example, if you are a 20-year-old male, you may compare your position with your father when he was 20 years old. When you turn 40, you may want to compare your position with that of your father when he was 40 years old. Normally, children have access to more resources than their parents had when growing up, so they are expected to do better in their lives.

Intragenerational Mobility

Intragenerational mobility involves changes in social positions within a person's adult life. In this case, you might compare "yourself to yourself" at different stages in your lifetime. Many people reach their peak social position at mid-life and continue to have a high social position, especially as far as income is concerned. They maintain this position until retirement, when the social position diminishes due to lower income at retirement, sickness, or other factors. These are normal or expected factors that explain why a person's social position may change over his/her lifetime. A factor expected to produce intragenerational mobility might be when a person is fired from his/her job. A person occupying a highly respected position in the community may be fired, dramatically lowering his/her status in the community. On the other hand, an individual's status in the society may be enhanced by a job promotion.

Factors That Influence Social Mobility

Social mobility is influenced by, among other factors, the occupational structure (parents' background) of a society, education, gender, race, and ethnicity. It should be noted that these factors work in conjunction with each other. For example, regardless of your gender or racial background, if you acquire a college education, you are likely to secure a higher paying job. Similarly, regardless of your gender or racial background, your parents' background will affect your social mobility in society.

Family Background

Family background is very important in determining an individual's social mobility. Thus, the parents' occupations influence the social mobility of their children. Professionals are more able and willing to spend enough money to ensure that their children acquire higher education and better jobs. Though children typically do better than their parents, they don't tend to move very far from their parents' social positions. Hence, if your parents are lower class, you are more likely to be lower class or, at best, lower-middle class. The higher the social position of a person's parents, the higher that per-

Students celebrate graduating from college.

Source: Kati Garner

son's position will most likely be.

Education

Education level is a predictor of earnings. Irrespective of gender, the higher your educational level, the higher your earnings potential. A study by Webster and Bishaw (2007) showed that in 2006 the median earnings of men who had not graduated from high school were $22,151. This increased to $31,715 for high school graduates and $40,217 for men with some college or an associate's degree. Men who completed college and received a bachelor's degree earned a median of $55,446. The highest median earnings, $73,991, were for men with a graduate or professional degree. The trend was the same for women. Women who did not complete high school earned $13,255 in 2006 on average, while graduating from high school increased

women's earnings to $20,650. Receiving an associate's degree, or attending but not completing college, resulted in median earnings of $26,300, while women who completed a bachelor's degree had median earnings of $36,875. At $49,164, women with graduate or professional degrees earned the most among women.

In various ways, a higher educational background also leads to higher social positions in society. Since higher education levels lead to more employment opportunities and higher incomes, people with higher levels of education attain higher social positions than those with lower educational backgrounds. Higher education may propel an individual into the middle-class, while a high school education might keep an individual in the working-class. The educational background of parents also influences the social positions of their children. Research shows that children whose parents have a higher educational background tend to achieve higher educational levels.

Education is also the strongest single predictor of good health. It is known that individuals with high levels of education are less likely to engage in health-risk behaviors such as smoking and heavy drinking. Women with high levels of education are more likely to seek prenatal care and are less likely to smoke during pregnancy. This explains the low infant mortality rate among children of highly educated mothers.

Gender

Compared with men, women have limited employment opportunities and their salaries are lower. Comparatively, women are more likely to be in lower-prestige occupations and less likely to achieve upward social mobility than men. In some cultures, females are discouraged and, at times, prevented, from pursuing higher education. Thus, gender is a factor in determining an individual's social mobility.

Race And Ethnicity

Overall, minorities have little or no wealth, little savings, and are more likely to lose their jobs. Thus, it is easier for a dominant group member to succeed than for a minority to succeed. Many minorities, compared with dominant group members, are born into poverty. Consequently, they are not able to achieve a higher educational background and, therefore, are not able to move up in the stratification system.

Global Stratification

Comparing countries around the world, it is obvious that there is global stratification. Some countries are more powerful, more privileged, and more developed than others. The differences between countries can be measured using factors like life expectancy, population growth rates, and literacy rates. The infant mortality rate—the number of deaths among children under 1 year of age per 1,000 live births—also illustrates the differences between countries.

When making comparisons, countries are traditionally grouped into three categories: first world, second world, and third world.

First World

First world countries are also known as industrialized nations, core countries, high-income countries, developed countries, and the North. As the term "the North" suggests, most of these countries are located in the Northern Hemisphere. Examples include the United States, Japan, Canada, Britain, Norway, Germany, and other countries in Western Europe. It should be remembered that Australia and New Zealand, which are in the Southern Hemisphere, are also first world countries. First world countries are the richest countries in the world. Most of the people in these countries are employed in the non-agricultural sector of the economy. For example, in the United States, only about 1.4 percent of the population was involved in agriculture, forestry, fishing, or hunting in 2006 (Bureau of Labor Statistics, 2007). It is estimated that by 2016, the percentage of Americans engaged in agriculture will decline to 1.2 percent. On the average, primary products—consumed in their natural state—comprise less than 25 percent of the exports from first world countries (Allen, 2006).

In first world countries, the infant mortality rate is very low. That means that most babies born into these societies survive to at least their first birthdays. The infant mortality rate in the United States is 6.7 deaths per 1,000 live births (Census, 2008). This rate is high compared with other first world countries, but it is very low compared with non-first-world countries. Life expectancy or longevity refers to how long a person is expected to live. People in first world countries typically live longer than those in second and third world countries. For example, a baby born in the United States in 2007 will live an average of 78.2 years (U.S. Centers for Disease Control and Prevention, 2008). Many other first world countries have life expectancy rates higher than the United States.

Second World

Second world countries are known as newly

Street in Busan, South Korea.   Source: Ivan Attilio

industrializing countries, middle-income countries, and semi-periphery countries. Examples include Russia, China, India, South Korea, Malaysia, Brazil, Argentina, and most countries in Eastern Europe and the Middle East. In newly industrializing countries, the agricultural sector of the economy is shrinking in relation to other sectors of the economy. For example, at the start of the economic boom in 1963, the majority of South Koreans were farmers. Sixty-three percent of the population lived in rural areas. In the next twenty-five years, South Korea grew from a predominantly rural, agricultural nation into an urban, newly industrialized country, and the agricultural work force shrunk to only 21 percent in 1989 (Savada & Shaw, 1990). Savada and Shaw also note that South Korean government officials expected urbanization and industrialization to further reduce the number of agricultural workers to well under 20 percent by 2000. Indeed by 2003, the

agricultural sector accounted for only 3.2 percent of South Korea's gross domestic product (Butler, 2006).

The infant mortality rate in second world countries is generally somewhere between the low rate of first world and the high rate of third world nations. In China, a second world country, the infant mortality rate is 22.1 deaths per 1,000 live births, and in India it is 34.6. Life expectancy in second world countries is also between that found in first and third world countries. In India, life expectancy is 68.6 years, in Brazil it is 72.2 years, and in China it is 72.9 years (Infoplease, 2007).

Third World

Third world countries are also known as the South, periphery countries, agricultural countries, low-income countries, and less-developed countries. Third world countries are the poorest countries in the world. They are mostly in Africa, Asia, and Central and Latin America. Though the agricultural sector is declining as a reserve for surplus labor, most of the people in the third world are still employed in that sector of the economy. As noted by Díaz-Bonilla and Gulati (2004), "Although primary agricultural activities are declining over time as a share of the economy, they still represent about one-fourth of total economic activity and 60 percent of total employment in low-income developing countries." Primary products like cocoa, coffee, and bananas make up 75 percent or more of the exports from third world countries.

The infant mortality rate is highest in third world countries. In Angola, the rate is 182.31 deaths per 1,000 live births (CIA, 2008). Life expectancy is also low in many third world countries. In Zambia, for example, life expectancy is 40.5 years (United Nations Development Programme, 2008).

Theoretical Explanation Of Global Stratification

An important question is: "Why are some countries rich and others poor?" To answer this question we need to look at some theories.

Modernization Theory

Advocates of the **modernization theory** argue that societies started as traditional and simple societies and moved, or are moving, toward being modern (developed) societies. Thus, societies go through a number of stages of development. Whether a country is considered developed or not depends upon its position on the traditional-modern society continuum. The more developed and privileged countries moved faster along the stages of development. Such countries provide most of their citizens with access to higher education, faith in science and technology, free press, mass production and consumption of goods and services, political freedom, and other privileges. Conversely, less developed countries fall behind in the stages of development. These countries lack political freedom, are superstitious, and lag behind in science and technology. They also do not provide their citizens with many privileges.

Dependency Theory

Dependency theory advocates argue that some countries are poorer and less developed because they are dependent on more developed countries. According to this school of thought, the more developed countries keep other countries poor through political and economic exploitation. The poor countries are compelled to sell their agricultural and mineral products cheaply, and to buy secondary products at exorbitant prices from the rich countries. The unequal trade relationships siphon wealth out of the poor countries and into the rich ones. As a result, the poor countries are in trade deficit, meaning they buy more than they sell. Since they make less money than what is needed for them to provide basic necessities for their citizens, the poor countries borrow a lot of money from the rich countries. These poor countries are indebted to the rich countries and are dependent upon their good will. In addition, the poor countries are dependent upon the rich ones for exports and investment capital. This unequal relationship resulted from colonialism in which some countries, notably European countries, ruled and exploited other countries.

An important version of the dependency theory is *World-Systems Analysis*, proposed by Wallerstein. According to Wallerstein (1974), world countries can be grouped into core countries, semi-periphery countries, and periphery countries. The world system, according to the proponents of World-Systems Analysis, is dominated by core countries like Japan, the United States, and European countries. The most dominated countries are the periphery, or third world, countries.

Neo-Colonialism

Neo-colonialism is the indirect continuation of colonialism by economic means. Some countries were poor under the rule of foreign European powers. This is because the colonial masters appropriated the products, including the minerals, of the colonized countries. For example, Ghana was colonized by the British for a period of 136 years from 1821 to 1957 (Hatch, 1969). Though Ghana's first encounter with Europeans (the Portuguese) was in 1471, it was not until 1821 that the British colonized

Ghana. During the period that Ghana was a colony of Britain, every important decision was made by the British in their own interests. Britain determined where to export Ghanaian minerals and for how much, and how also to spend the earnings. During that period, Britain decided to use Ghana mainly as a source of raw materials. Thus, British activities in Ghana hindered industrialization because Britain did not encourage industries to locate in Ghana. Consequently, Ghana could not develop as would be expected.

Generally, colonialism around the world ended in the 1970s. An important question is, "If colonialism ended in the 1970s, why are former colonies still poor?" According to one school of thought, the former colonies are still poor because of neo-colonialism. It is argued that through multinational corporations, the former colonial masters are exploiting the former colonies. Most multinational corporations are headquartered in developed countries and have branches in developing countries. This means that multinational corporations repatriate wealth in the form of profits from poor countries to the rich countries of the world. This keeps the former colonies poor.

Sociological Theories On Stratification

Structural Functionalist Perspective On Stratification

In order to clearly understand the position of *structural functionalism* on stratification, we have to examine how structural functionalists would answer the question, "Is social stratification necessary for society?"

The simple answer from structural functionalists would be, "Yes, stratification is necessary and important for a society." According to structural functionalists, inequality is important for the survival of a society because it ensures that its most important needs are met. It also ensures that people who work harder are better rewarded. Every society has some necessary functions that must be performed in order for the society to survive, or to maintain social order. To qualify to perform these functions, people have to invest resources like time and money. Those who invest their time and money to achieve the qualifications and training necessary to perform the society's most important functions should be rewarded more than others. For example, the physician's role is very important in society, and it takes a lot of time and money to train to become one. On the other hand, a person does not have to invest a lot of time and money to train as a garbage collector. Moreover, according to functionalists, a garbage collector's role is not as important as a physician's role. Consequently, a physician should be paid, or rewarded, more than a garbage collector. Stratification motivates people to fill the most important positions in society; it encourages hard work. Thus, stratification is a structural arrangement by society to motivate or induce people to perform the duties that are important for a smoothly running society. These inducements take the form of high rewards for the important jobs in society. According to functionalists like Davis and Moore (1967), stratification is both universal and necessary in the society.

Conflict Perspective On Stratification

Though *conflict theorists* admit that stratification is universal in human societies, they don't believe that it is necessary for a society to run smoothly. Indeed, they believe that stratification is the root cause of tension and conflict in human societies. This is because stratification breeds inequality, and inequality leads to conflict.

Conflict theorists do not accept the functionalists' view that a person's position on the stratification ladder is dependent upon the importance of his or her contribution to a society. They challenge this theory on two main grounds.

First, what criterion is used to determine the importance of professions? For example, who is more important to a society, a farmer or a physician? Many people are quick to say that farmers are more important than physicians because the former produce the food we consume. If farmers are more important or critical to the survival of a society, then, going by the structural functionalist perspective, farmers should earn more than physicians. However, physicians earn more than farmers. Therefore, it is not true that the different professions attract different salaries on the basis of their importance to society.

Second, how do we measure importance regarding different professions? Let's assume that it is true that the physician's role is more important than the role of the garbage collector. The average physician earns about $203,000 per year (Adams, 2006), while a garbage collector may earn about $30,000 per year (Employment Development Department, 2006). Thus, a physician's income is almost seven times as much as that of a garbage collector. Conflict theorists question whether a physician is indeed about seven times more important than a garbage collector. If not, then why are physicians rewarded seven times more than garbage collectors? This shows that it is not the importance of professions that determines how they are valued and rewarded.

Considering the above examples, it is obvious that the factors that determine a person's place on the stratification ladder are not straightforward in society. Conflict theorists assert that the most powerful people determine the stratification system ambiguously, placing some professions above others. Thus according to Mosca (1939), every society stratifies itself along lines of power, which is, thus, the main determinant of stratification.

According to the school of conflict theorists called Marxists, since stratification is not important, and since it is the source of conflict in society, it should be eliminated from society. One way of eliminating stratification in society is to pay people according to their needs, not according to their professions.

According to conflict theorists, one of the reasons that more has not been done to address the above issues in the United States is that Americans tend to have a poor level of **class consciousness**. Class consciousness refers to class members' shared awareness of their rank and status within a society, as well as their interests. Conflict theorists blame this low level of class awareness, in part, on false consciousness. **False consciousness** is used to mean

an attitude held by some employees that does not reflect their objective position. For example, certain employees are not aware that they are exploited by the capitalists. Such employees believe that they are fundamentally different from other workers. For example, a physician who practices at a hospital may think that he/she is different from an assembly line worker because he/she works in a better environment and earns better. However, according to the Marxist perspective since both are employees, they are the same, and they are both exploited.

Symbolic Interactionist Perspective On Stratification

Symbolic interactionists are interested in how stratification affects people's behavior. For example, they are interested in the importance of social class in shaping a person's lifestyle (Schaefer, 2008). After meeting their basic needs, people spend a lot of their resources on ostentatious goods and services. Incidentally, not all people in society are able to meet their necessities. Those at the top of the social hierarchy have met their necessities and consequently spend part of their wealth on luxury yachts, fleets of vehicles, private jets, mansions, and other luxury items. On the other hand, those at the bottom of the social hierarchy have not met their necessities, so they spend a considerable amount of their wealth to meet their day-to-day needs.

Stratification influences people's lifespans. In every society, the rich live longer than the poor because the former have access to better health care and more nutritious food. The definition of crime and the enforcement of criminal law may vary on the basis of the class system. While some actions by the rich may be ignored by police, the same actions, when taken by the poor, may result in arrest and prosecution. The definitions of crime and law enforcement biases tend to stigmatize poor and powerless people. Consequently, interactionists maintain that people are treated differently according to their position in the class system. Thus, stratification influences our lives, how others view us, and how we view ourselves.

Yachts in the harbor at Monte Carlo.   Source: Kursad Keteci

Feminist Perspective On Stratification

Most human societies are patriarchal in the sense that they are male-dominated. Even in developed countries like the United States of America, males dominate females. Even when a man and woman have the same qualifications and experience, men normally earn more than women. Going by the thesis of the functionalists, men are more important than women. In addition, the responsibilities and jobs men hold are more important than the jobs women hold. However, feminists do not agree with the views of functionalists. Since men earn more than women even when they perform the same jobs, it is obvious that rewards like wages are not determined by the importance of the jobs performed; rather, they are determined by a person's sex and gender expectations, according to feminists. Like conflict theorists, feminists assert that power relations determine the structure of stratification in society. The main goal of feminists is the practice of gender equality in society.

Summary

Social stratification and, for that matter, inequality, are universal. The criteria used to stratify people may differ from society to society and may change from time to time. However, the consequences of stratification are the same—some people are more privileged than others. The consequences of stratification include differences in power, income, wealth, health care, and lifespan.

From the perspective of structural functionalists, stratification is positive for the society because it encourages competition and motivates people to work hard. Thus, if you work hard you will secure a high paying job and live comfortably. If you want to be in a higher class, and enjoy the benefits that come with that class, you have to work hard. However, stratification is also the source of conflict in human societies. According to conflict theorists, since stratification breeds inequality, which is the main source of conflict, stratification is not good for a society. For symbolic interactionists, stratification gives some people the power to label others in a society. For example, the richest and most powerful people in a society define crime in a way that favors themselves and stigmatizes the poor and powerless. Interactionists maintain that people are treated differently according to their position in the class system. Feminists state that we live in a male-dominated society in which all important decisions are made by men, at times to the detriment of women. The main goal of feminists is to ensure gender equality in a society.

Review/Discussion Questions

1. What is the basis of stratification?
2. What is conspicuous consumption?
3. In your view, do you think stratification is positive or negative for society? List and explain some advantages and disadvantages of stratification.
4. Do you know anybody who is poor? Why do you consider that person poor?
5. List some families that belong to the American upper class. What are the criteria you used to determine the class of the families you listed?
6. What are the occupations of your father and mother? In which class category do you put your parents? Does your family background give you an edge over other students you know? Explain
7. Who is to be blamed for the plight of the underclass? Is it the government's responsibility to assist the poorest people in the society? Why or why not?
8. Who is more important to the society – a farmer or a physician? Explain your answer. Ask your friends the same question; do they have the same answer as you?
9. Your friend insists that there is too much income and wealth disparity in the society, so there should be, at least, income redistribution to ensure that the gap between the rich and the poor is not too wide. Do you agree? Explain.
10. In a political advertisement, the Republican Party says that Social Security is unfair to African-Americans. The argument is that the retirement age is 66, and the average lifespan of African-Americans is 68 years. That means African-Americans benefit only two years from Social Security while the average white person benefits for about 10 years. The Republicans suggest that Social Security should be privatized so that African-Americans can invest and enjoy their hard-earned money before they die. Do you agree with this argument? Explain.
11. If you have never been to a third-world country, find somebody from such a place and ask him or her to tell you about the conditions of life in that country. Based on the answers from this person, what do you suggest as solutions to third-world poverty?

Key Terms

Absolute poverty is complete poverty, used to describe people who are desperately poor and may not know from whence their next meal will come.

Caste systems are based on stratification, classifying people at birth into social levels in which they remain.

Class consciousness is the shared awareness of class members of their status and rank within a society, as well as their interests.

Class systems are stratification systems in which an individual's position is not fixed but instead is relatively open, allowing the individual opportunities to move between levels.

Conspicuous consumption involves the public display and consumption of expensive items.

Dependency theory advocates argue that some countries are poorer and less developed because they are dependent on more developed countries.

Enclosure is the process by which the powerful and rich people fence (enclose) their land in order to exclude others.

False consciousness is used to mean an attitude held by some employees that does not reflect their objective position.

Horizontal mobility is the movement from one social position to another of the same rank and/or prestige.

Individual mobility is the result of hard work and perseverance by an individual.

Intergenerational mobility describes changes in the social positions of children in comparison to their parents.

Intragenerational mobility relates to changes in social position over the course of person's lifetime.

Materialism occurs when people are able to satisfy their basic needs and have money left over to spend on ostentatious goods and services.

Modernization theory advocates argue that societies started as simple and traditional, then moved, or are moving toward, being modern (developed) societies.

Neo-colonialism is the indirect continuation of colonialism through economic means.

Power determines who gets the best of a society's resources, who gives orders, and who obeys orders.

Power elite is a term used to describe a small group of high-ranking leaders from government, corporations, and the military.

Relative poverty is the feeling or belief that you are poor when you compare yourself with other people.

Social class is made up of people in relatively similar situations with roughly the same power, income, and prestige.

Social mobility is the movement from one social position to another.

Social stratification is the ranking of people within a society.

Status is recognition given to a person or group.

Status inconsistency occurs when a person is given conflicting statuses.

Status systems rank people based on their social prestige.

Structured mobility involves societal events that allow entire groups of people to move up or down the social structure together.

Vertical mobility is the movement from one social position to another of a different rank and/or prestige. This change can be in an upward or downward direction.

Bibliography

Adams, D. (2006). Physician Income not Rising as Fast as Other Professional Pay. American Medical News. <http: www.ama-assn.org/amednews/site/free/prsc0724.htm> (2008).

Adelman, I. & Morris, C. T. (1967). Society, Politics, and Economic Development: a Quantitative Approach. Baltimore, MD: Johns Hopkins Press.

Allen, J. L. (2007). Student Atlas of World Politics. New York: McGraw-Hill.

Ashley, D., & Orenstein, D. M. (2001). Sociological Theory: Classical Statements. Boston: Allyn and Bacon.

Brown, J. (2002). Differential Mortality and the Value of Individual Account Retirement Annuities. In M. Feldstein & J. Liebman (Eds.), The Distributional Aspects of Social Security and Social Security Reform (pp.401-440). Chicago: University of Chicago Press.

Bureau of Labor Statistics (2007). Industry output and employment projections to 2016. November 2007 Monthly Labor Review. Washington, DC: U.S. Government Printing Office.

Butler, R. (2006). South Korea: Economy. <http://www.mongabay.com/reference/new_profiles/289.html> (2008).

Central Intelligence Agency (2008). The World Factbook. <https://www.cia.gov/library/publications/the-world-factbook/> (2008).

Davis, K. & Moore, W. (1966). Some Principles of Stratification. In R. Bendix (Eds.). Class, Status, and Power. New York: Free Press.

Díaz-Bonilla, E. & Gulati, A. (2004). 2002-2003 Annual Report Essay: Developing Countries and the WTO Negotiations. Washington, DC: International Food Policy Research Institute.

Domhoff, W. G. (2006). Who Rules America Now? Boston: McGraw-Hall.

Duggan, J. E., Gillingham, R., & Greenlees, J. S. (2007). Mortality and Lifetime Income Evidence from Social Security Records, Research Paper No. 2007-01. <www.ustreas.gov/official/economic-policy/papers> (2008).

Employment Development Department (2006). California Occupational Guide #460. Sacramento: EDD.

Gilbert, D. (2003). The American Class Structure in an Age of Growing Inequality (6th ed.). Belmont, CA: Wadsworth.

Hatch, J. (1969). The History of Britain in Africa. New York: Frederick A. Preager.

Hill, M. (2008). Solving the Poverty Problem in Mississippi. <http://www.mississippi.edu/urc/downloads/solvingpoverty_problem.pdf> (2008).

Infoplease (2007). Infant Mortality and Life Expectancy for Selected Countries. <http://www.infoplease.com/ipa> (2007).

Institute for Research on Poverty (2008). Health in the United States, Institute for Research on Poverty, University of Wisconsin-Madison. <http://www.irp.wisc.edu/research/health.htm#pubs> (2008).

Kendall, D. (2007). Social Problems in a Diverse Society. Boston: Pearson/Allyn and Bacon.

Kerbo, H. R. (2009). Social Stratification and Inequality. Boston: McGraw-Hill.

Kerr, J. C. (2008). Most Companies in US Avoid Federal Income Taxes. Associated Press. <http://news.yahoo/s/ap/20080812/ap_on_bi_ge/corporations_income_tax> (2008).

Kimmel, M. & Aronson, A. (2009). Sociology Now. Boston: Pearson/Allyn and Bacon.

Landes, D. (1998). The Wealth and Poverty of Nations. New York: Norton.

LeFevre, A. T. (2007). 2007 Report Card on American Education: A State-by-State Analysis. Washington, DC: American Legislative Exchange Council.

Manchester, J. & Topoleski, J. (2008). Growing Disparities in Life Expectancy. Washington, DC: Congressional Budget Office.

Marger, M. N. (2005). Social Inequality: Patterns and Processes. Boston: McGraw-Hill.

Mayell, H. (2003, June 2). India's Untouchables Face Violence, Discrimination. National Geographic News.

Mishel, L. (2006). CEO-to-worker Pay Imbalance Grows, Economic Snapshots: Economic Policy Institute. <http://www.epi.org> (2008).

Mills Wright, C. (1958). The Power Elite. New York: Oxford University Press.

Mosca, G. (1939). The Ruling Class. New York: McGraw-Hill.

Murray, C. J. L., Kulkarni, S., Michaud, C., Tomijima, N., Bulzacchelli, M. T., Iandiorio, T. J., & Ezzati, M. (2006). Eight Americas: investigating mortality disparities across races, counties, and race-counties in the United States. PLoS Medicine 3(9), e260.

Pearce, D. (1978). The feminization of poverty: Women, work and welfare. Urban and Social Change Review, 11, 28-36.

Rector, R. (2007). Statement of Robert Rector, Senior Policy Analyst, The Heritage Foundation. Committee on Ways and Means: Hearing Archives. http://waysandmeans.house.gov/hearings.asp?formmode=view&id=5454 (2008).

Rossides, D. W. (1997). Social Stratification: The Interplay of Class, Race, and Gender. Upper Saddle River, NJ: Prentice Hall.

Saez, E. & Picketty, T. (2008) Striking it Richer: The Evolution of Top Incomes in the United States. <http://elsa.berkeley.edu/~saez/saez-UStopincomes-2006prel.pdf> (2009, Jan. 29).

Savada, A. M., & Shaw, W. (1990). South Korea: A Country Study. Washington: GPO/Library of Congress.

Schaefer, R. T. (2008). Sociology. New York: McGraw-Hill.

Thompson, E. P. (1991). The Making of the English Working Class. Harmondsworth: Penguin, New Edition.

United Nations Development Programme (2008). Human Development Report: 2007/2008 Report. New York: UNDP.

U.S. Census Bureau (2006). American Community Survey. <http://www.factfinder.census.gov/servlet/DTTable?> (2008).

U.S. Census Bureau (2007). People and Families in Poverty by Selected Characteristics: 2006 and 2007. <http://factfinder.census.gov> (2008).

U.S. Census Bureau (2008). Current Population Survey, 2008, Annual Social and Economic Supplement. <http://factfinder.census.gov> (2008).

U.S. Centers for Disease Control and Prevention (2008). Life expectancy at birth, National Center for Health Statistics, CDC. <http://www.cdc.gov> (2008).

U.S. Department of State (2007). Trafficking in Persons Report. <http://www.state.gov/g/tip/rls/tiprpt/2007/82798.htm> (2008).

Wallenstein, I. (1974). The Modern World System. New York: Academic Press.

Webster, B. H. & Bishaw, A. (2007). Income, Earnings, and Poverty. American Community Survey Reports, ACS-08, U.S. Census Bureau. Washington, DC: U.S. Government Printing Office.

Wolff, E. N. (2007). Recent Trends in Household Wealth in the United States: Rising Debt and the Middle-Class Squeeze, Working Paper No. 502. <http://www.levy.org/pubs/wp_502.pdf> (2008).

CHAPTER EIGHT

Race And Ethnicity

Alyce B. Bunting

I am writing this chapter the day after the 2008 presidential election, when, according to the media, history was made. For the first time, an African-American has been elected president of the United States. Senator Barack Obama will become President Barack Obama. For many, the election of a black man shows how far, as a country, we have come in healing our racial divisions. For me, a sociologist, I think it says a lot more about how far we have yet to go. To even take notice of a person's race and consider it to be a factor in job performance indicates that we have not progressed as far as we might have hoped. But observing the social nature of labels like "race" and "ethnicity" is even more telling. What does it mean to be "African-American"? Obama had a black father and a white mother. He was raised by his mother's parents and only met his father once as a young boy (Meacham, 2008). Should he not at least be described as "biracial"? Is skin color the only determinant of race? Or what about Tiger Woods, the "black" golfer who is only one-eighth black and has labeled himself "Cablinasian" in order to take into account his Caucasian, black, (American) Indian, and Asian heritages (Henslin, 2007)? These two people illustrate the sociological position on the questions of race and ethnicity—they are both socially determined labels that only have meaning when society gives them meaning.

Race And Ethnicity

Race is an emotionally charged word, coming to symbolize for so many the divisiveness that has characterized our country over time. From slavery to Rodney King, much of what is made of race involves one group subjugating another.

Race does have a biological meaning, pertaining to people who share physical characteristics that are genetically transferred. However, the real meaning of race may involve a more subjective cultural definition. Biologically, race is a moot topic. There has been too much interbreeding of the world's population to speak of "pure" races. The races are more alike than they are different. But even by assigning different meanings to physical characteristics like skin color and hair texture, assuming one skin color or hair texture is superior to another, the idea of race takes on a very real meaning. It becomes a means by which people are categorized and assigned greater or lesser positions in society. As W. I. Thomas once said, "If a person defines a situation as real, it is real in its consequences" (Thomas & Swain Thomas, 1928). Defining physical characteristics as important determinants of behavior then becomes a self-fulfilling prophecy, and a way for one group to claim superiority over another. It is assumed that phenotype (appearance) relates to genotype (heredity). People who look "different" on the outside must also be "different" on the inside, and this difference is often judged in a negative way.

In the United States, Census 2000 made it possible for Americans to select more than one racial category to describe themselves for the first time. The results were that 6.8 million people—or only 2.4 percent of the U.S. population—reported more than one race. Of these, 93 percent reported two races, 6 percent reported three races, and 1 percent reported four or more races (U.S. Census Bureau, 2001). These numbers seem to indicate that Americans still view themselves as either/or, with the vast majority cleanly placing themselves in a particular racial category.

Race is a biological concept; it is an innate component of our selves (nature), rather than a personal experience (nurture) component. **Ethnicity** is a cultural definition, referring to learned behavior, and is thus due to nurture. Specifically, an **ethnic group** is a category of people with a shared cultural heritage that others regard as distinct. This cultural heritage may include language, distinctive dress and cuisine, religious beliefs, and other parts of both material and nonmaterial culture. Though the United States

is a melting pot of cultures, people are still expected to adhere to a certain set of norms and values as members of this society. Those whose beliefs and behaviors vary are labeled as "other" and suffer for that devalued status. It is not unusual for members of ethnic groups to refuse to teach their children the language of their own people in an attempt to help the child to better blend into American culture. To speak a language other than English in public would result in being labeled as "other," making assimilation more difficult, and discrimination more likely.

Minority Groups

The United States is racially and culturally diverse. Following the definition of sociologist Louis Wirth (1945), we can consider **minority groups** to be those people who are singled out for unequal treatment and who regard themselves as objects of collective discrimination. There is a strong sense of in-group solidarity, in that minority group members are aware of their devalued status and feel closer to each another than they do to people outside the minority. They enjoy fewer of the rewards and resources that society has to offer, and social stratification often follows racial and ethnic lines.

It is important to note that minority group status has nothing to do with absolute numbers—it is a matter of power. Prior to the breakdown of the apartheid system in South Africa, white Europeans in that country were the dominant group, even though they were outnumbered by the native African population by three to one. Those who control the power are referred to as the dominant group, regardless of size. Members of the dominant group occupy privileged positions in society, and possess greater power and social status.

Formation Of Minority Groups

There are two basic ways that minority groups are formed: migration and annexation. The first, migration, can be either voluntary or involuntary. Voluntary migration involves individuals leaving their home countries to resettle in another as **immigrants**. Between the years 1892 and 1924—the peak years of U.S. immigration—16 million people moved to this country. All told, between 1820 and 1990, 55 million immigrants came to the United States. Approximately one million legal immigrants come to the United States every year, and the 2000 census indicated that 30 percent of our population growth from 1990 to 2000 was due to immigration. Involuntary migration involves force, like the importation of African slaves earlier in our country's history, in which people were taken from their countries and brought to this one.

Annexation involves moving geographic boundaries. Such movements are often the result of wars or treaties. The Treaty of Guadalupe Hidalgo (1848) is an example of annexation and the formation of a minority group. In the treaty, Mexico ceded Texas, California, and much of what is now considered the Southwest to the United States. The Mexicans left behind in these areas found themselves a minority in a new country. The change in their country's boundary lines led to a change in their racial status.

Formation Of Dominant Groups

Everyone in America, or their ancestors, came from other countries, with the exception of two groups of descendants: (1) those of the original Native Americans, and (2) those of the Mexicans who lived in the American Southwest prior to 1848. How have some of these immigrating groups come to dominate the others? A look at the history of immigration to our country, and the immigration laws that came to restrict this behavior, might provide an answer.

The Spanish and Portuguese led the way in the exploration and colonization of the New World, preceding the English by more than a century. But English colonization was carried out on an unusually large scale. Jamestown was established in 1607 and Plymouth in 1620. By the middle of the 18th century, the 13 American colonies of England were well established, along with the English language, customs, and beliefs related to commerce, law, government, and religion. When the first U.S. census was taken in 1790, 78 percent of the population claimed descent from England, Scotland, or Wales. This group constituted the first "wave" of immigra-

tion to the New World, and included many people from northern and western Europe, the White Anglo-Saxon Protestants, or WASPs. And it is this group whose culture would come to dominate in the New World.

The face of the immigrant changed somewhat during the second wave of immigration, which began in the mid-to late-1800s and lasted until 1924. More newcomers arrived from southern and eastern Europe (white ethnics), and a large group of Chinese immigrants came to this country during the 1850s. These new groups of immigrants were different from the northern and western European immigrants in two major ways: religion and language. They also had different physical features, particularly those from China. It was during this time period that an anti-immigration sentiment, called *nativism*, arose. Prior to the late 1800s, immigration was encouraged. There was a lot of land in America, and a lot of people were needed to settle it. But the changing face of the immigrant, combined with the closing of the frontier in 1890, led feelings to change toward this unbridled procession of new faces. A nativist political party of the time, the American Republican Party formed in 1843, popularized the saying "I know nothing," when asked about its activities. By the 1850s, the "Know Nothing" party, as it was dubbed, was leading the way in anti-immigration activities.

The year 1882 was a watershed in American immigration history. Up to that point, the federal government had done little concerning immigration and had not even counted those entering the country until 1820. In 1882, the second-largest number of immigrants entered this country, and Congress enacted the first comprehensive immigration law, the Chinese Exclusion Act. This piece of federal immigration legislation set the tone for future laws regarding who could enter the country. The next major pieces of immigration law were the quota acts of the 1920s. The decade of 1900 to 1910 was the time of the greatest number of immigrants, with 1907 being the peak year. To stem this flow, in 1921 Congress passed the Emergency Quota Act, for the first time limiting just how many people would be admitted in a single year (300,000), and setting a quota on the countries of Europe, Africa, and the Near East, allowing only 3 percent of the number of foreign-born members of each nationality, based on the 1910 census, to immigrate to the United States. In 1924, the Johnson-Reid Act reduced the quota to 2 percent based on nation of origin and set the date of the census used back to 1890. The immediate consequence of this act was that 87 percent of the permits went to people from Great Britain, Ireland, Germany, and Scandinavia.

The national origin principle was replaced in 1965 by the Immigration and Nationality Act (Hart-Cellar Act), which established a seven-tiered preference system for entrance to the United States. The main categories of preference were family, skilled/technical worker, and refugee. This act also established hemispheric quotas for both the Eastern and Western hemispheres. This was the first time that people from countries in the Western Hemisphere had restrictions placed on their immigration to the United States, and this was the beginning of the problem of *illegal* aliens from Latino countries.

An examination of the major immigration laws indicates a tendency to favor certain nationalities over others. From the 1882 Chinese Exclusion Act, which discriminated against a whole category of people based on their nationality, to the quota acts, which favored those Anglo countries that had an early history of greater immigration numbers, to the preference system established in 1965, once the federal government began limiting entrance to our country, both the number and types of immigrants were controlled.

As a result of immigration legislation, the third wave of immigrants into the United States looked even more different from the first two. Since 1965, about 40 percent of all immigrants have come from Asian and Pacific Rim countries, and another 40 percent have come from the Western Hemisphere, particularly Mexico. The destinations of these immigrants have been different, too. California, New York, Texas, Florida, and Illinois receive the bulk of those entering the United States today (Census, 2005).

Prejudice, Discrimination, And Racism

The tendency for people to hold negative attitudes toward those different from themselves, and to treat them differently as a result, is as old as the world itself. From biblical times, and the discord between Hebrews and Gentiles, to the world today, with ethnic cleansing in China, war in Bosnia and Kosovo, and unrest in the Middle East, intolerance seems to be the norm. **Prejudice** is a feeling, favorable or unfavorable, that one has about a person or group of people that is not based on actual experience. As the root of the word suggests, prejudice involves a prejudgment about another. The prejudgment can be favorable, but, when speaking of racial and ethnic groups, prejudice typically involves a negative attitude. Prejudice relies upon **stereotypes**, rigid mental images held to be true about a group of people. These would include the belief that "Jews are greedy," or that "all Middle Easterners are terrorists."

Relying on beliefs such as these can lead to discrimination. **Discrimination** is differential treatment of people based on their membership in a specific group. Prejudice is an attitude; discrimination is an act. Both prejudice and discrimination may be based on **racism**, a set of beliefs justifying the unfair treatment of a racial minority group and its members. This set of beliefs promotes the idea of supposed inferiority of the minority group based on physical or cultural characteristics. European colonizers felt they were "civilizing the savages" when they took over the resources of the colonies, a feeling not unlike that of slave owners who felt their slaves were too "childlike" to take care of themselves. These beliefs made the subjugation of the colonials and slaves right and noble, and justified the actions of colonizers and slave owners.

Discrimination can occur at the micro or macro levels of society. At the micro level, **individual discrimination** occurs when a person treats another unfairly, and that treatment is due to the person's minority group status. These behaviors range from the less harmful, such as using racial epithets, to the more harmful, such as committing hate crimes. As a group, racial and ethnic minorities are more likely to be victims of hate crimes than any other group (Bureau of Justice Statistics, 2008).

Legal discrimination at the macro level is unequal treatment that is upheld by law. An example would be the system of Jim Crow laws that emerged at the end of the Civil War. One of these laws gave the right to vote only to citizens, or the descendants of citizens, who had voted prior to 1866. This *grandfather clause*, as it was called, denied free blacks in the South the right to vote, even though the 15th Amendment passed in 1870 gave them that right. More vividly, another example of legal discrimination would be *Plessy v. Ferguson* (1896), the U.S. Supreme Court case that made "separate but equal" the law of the land. Legal discrimination against minorities was eliminated by the 1954 *Brown v. Board of Education of Topeka* decision, and by the civil rights legislation of the 1960s.

Discrimination at the macro level, however, continues through what is now known as **institutional discrimination**. This can be defined as the way society operates that serves to ensure that some groups will be given preferential treatment over others. Social institutions are arranged such that they intentionally or unintentionally discriminate. Studies consistently indicate that minorities have more difficulty obtaining loans, renting property, and being hired for higher-status jobs. Schools in minority neighborhoods are often of poorer quality, with smaller tax bases that afford them fewer of the amenities found in wealthier areas. As a result, students in these schools receive an education of lower quality that puts them at a disadvantage when competing with members of the dominant group.

An example of institutional discrimination would be *redlining*. **Redlining** is the practice of arbitrarily denying or limiting financial services to specific neighborhoods due to the minority group status of the residents. For the most part, these were financially depressed areas and the residents posed greater credit risks. Thus, from the perspective of the lending institutions, redlining was good business practice. In the 1930s, the New Deal's Home Owners' Loan Corporation instituted a redlining policy by developing color-coded maps of American cities that used racial criteria to categorize lending and insurance risks. The Federal Housing Administration, created in 1934, adopted this method to assess locations for federally insured new housing construction (Squires, 1997). For the residents of the areas denied financial support, the results were dramatic. Neighborhoods fell into disrepair and decline. The major means of securing wealth by the middle class, accumulating equity in a home, was denied to a generation of minorities.

The Community Reinvestment Act of 1977 helped to reduce the impact of redlining by requiring banks to lend in areas from which they accepted deposits. However, some social activists have extended the definition of redlining to refer to other discriminatory practices of a financial nature that occur in minority neighborhoods. *Food redlining* means that larger supermarkets have left lower-income neighborhoods for more affluent suburbs. The low-income residents are left dependent on convenience stores that charge higher prices, so they end up spending more money, traveling farther, or purchasing lower-quality products. Predatory lending is another example of how financial redlining, though no longer officially practiced, still affects many minorities. Predatory lending, sometimes called *payday loans*, involves charging high fees for small loans, and individuals may end up owing interest rates of 300–400 percent on the money borrowed. Members of the dominant group may use payday loans; however, as a group, minorities are more likely to live below the poverty line and have more trouble securing loans, and the costs of payday loans have a greater impact in minority communities. *Rent-to-own businesses* also prey upon the financial insecurity of minorities.

Theories Of Prejudice And Discrimination

"The light within meets the light without." Plato

Our perception of others is a product of our subjective interpretation, and these subjective judgments become our objective realities. All of the messages sent to us by those around us, whether these messages are words, gestures, or personal appearances, are filtered through our own set of beliefs concerning those messages. These messages from others constitute the "light without," but the perceptions and meanings we act upon are largely added by the "light within."

Psychological Theories Of Prejudice And Discrimination

Psychologists stress that our own personalities shape our perceptions of the world. People who feel a lack of fulfillment, and experience unsatisfied expectations, may be more likely to discriminate by assigning blame for their own shortcomings to others through **scapegoating**. Scapegoating theory looks at how people may employ the defense mechanism of projection. By ascribing one's own emotions, motives, and behaviors to a less-powerful person or group, an individual can be absolved of responsibility for his or her own inadequacies. In a situation like this, frustration leads to aggression, which leads to displacement onto the less-powerful group. Minorities have historically served as scapegoats, bearing the blame for much of what is wrong with society. The case of Susan Smith serves as an example of scapegoating theory. Smith is the South Carolina mom who in 1994 let her car, with her two young sons strapped in the back, roll into a lake. The children drowned. Smith, in an effort to deflect blame from herself, blamed the crime on a black man who had allegedly carjacked her vehicle with her children in the backseat. She later admitted she was the one who committed the crime.

Other psychologists look at personality characteristics that seem to typify those people exhibiting high levels of prejudice. Theodor Adorno and his associates examined this question in the years following World War II. After surveying more than 2,000 respondents, Adorno concluded that prejudiced people exhibited an array of personality characteristics that included intolerance, insecurity, and submission to authority (Adorno, Frenkel-Brunswick, Levinson, & Sanford, 1950). Afraid to rely on their own perceptions, individuals with an *authoritarian personality* are more likely to let others define the

world and appropriate reactions to other groups. They are more likely to rigidly adhere to existing dogmas without question, fearful of threats posed by those who look or behave differently.

Sociological Theories Of Prejudice And Discrimination

Sociologists assume prejudice and discrimination are learned. How they are learned depends on one's theoretical perspective. Sociology has three major perspectives: functional, conflict, and symbolic interaction. All three perspectives attempt to determine the nature of beliefs and behaviors, and each can tell us a little about how group differences affect our reactions to others.

Functional Theory

Functional theorists believe that every part of society exists because it performs some specific function, or set of functions, for society. Prejudice is functional in that it provides strong in-group solidarity for the group exhibiting the prejudice. Think back to your high school athletic team and its fiercest rival. Negative feelings ("They've got ugly uniforms!") led to feelings of loyalty to your own school and made game night even more fun.

Prejudice can unite a group against a common enemy. After the terrorist attack on 9/11, President George Bush drew a line in the sand, telling countries of the world they were either with us in the fight against terrorism, or they were on the side of the terrorists. Bumper stickers that proclaim "America: Love it or leave it!" serve the same function of uniting us into a cohesive group, giving us a shared identity that sets us apart from "them." In fact, this "we-they" dichotomy is at the heart of the functional theory of prejudice. By assigning unfavorable traits to another group, we allow ourselves to feel superior to, and even justified in discriminating against, the devalued group.

Conflict Theory

Building on the work of Karl Marx, conflict theorists emphasize the power variable when analyzing social behavior. According to conflict theory, the *powerful* use their power to coerce the *power-*

Comparative Well-being By Race And Ethnicity

Race	Household Imcome	Poverty Rate	College Completion Rate	Unemployment Rate	Homeownership Rate	Life Expectancy	Infant Mortality Rate	No Health Insurance
White	$52,115	8.2%	29.1%	4.1%	72%	78.3	5.7	10.4%
Latino	$38,679	21.5%	12.7%	5.6%	49.7%			32.1%
African American	$33,916	24.5%	18.5%	8.3%	47.2%	73.1	13.8	19.5%
Asian American	$66,103	10.2%	52.1%	3.2%	60.0%	84.9	4.89	16.8%
Native American	$31,605	24.6%	14.2%	n/a	56.9%	74.5	8.5	32.8%

Source: U.S. Census Bureau (2007), except for white and African American life expectancy and infant mortality rates which are from U.S. National Center for Health Statistics (2007), and Native American Household Income, Poverty Rate, and College Completion Rate (2006, January), which are from the Indian Health Services, Facts on Indian Health Disparities.

less into conformity. Marx was concerned about the abuse of power on the part of the bourgeoisie, the owners of the means of production. He felt that the owners abused the workers, the proletariat, for their own advantage. This exploitation of the working class by the ruling class could only end in one way—social revolution and the formation of a classless society. Only then would the scarce resources of society, particularly wealth, be evenly distributed. In Marx's utopian society, everyone's needs would be adequately met, and there would be no stratification. No one would have more than anyone else, and all of the means of production would be communally owned.

Of course, this utopian vision has never been realized. Conflict theorists would point to the control the dominant group continues to exert over social institutions, particularly over economic institutions, as the cause. According to conflict theory, this control is maintained in one of two ways. One means of control involves the structure of the labor market. According to dual labor market theory, the work force is composed of two sectors. One sector, the primary or regular economy, contains year-round, full-time, well-paying jobs with fringe benefits like sick leave and health insurance. The second sector, the secondary or irregular economy, contains the temporary, part-time, seasonal jobs. Jobs in this sector are lower-paid, more unstable, and have few, if any, benefits. Employees in the second sector are

more likely to come from minority groups. Migrant workers would be an example of employees in this part of the economy, and most of them are minorities.

The other way in which the dominant group controls minorities and their access to scarce societal resources is by maintaining a reserve labor market. Knowing that there is always a group of unemployed workers ready to take these jobs serves to keep people in lower-status, lower-paying jobs from complaining too much. A revolution is much less likely to occur if the workers are aware of their own expendability. This situation has been exacerbated in recent years by the outsourcing of jobs to other countries like China and India. Workers are more likely to settle for less if it means job security.

Symbolic Interaction Theory

Symbolic interactionists examine the way we use symbols to create reality. In particular, when examining prejudice and discrimination, these theorists would look at the symbolic labels we use to categorize minorities. For racial and ethnic minorities, these labels are stereotypes that may be true for some members of the group, but not all. However, not having met all of the members, the labels are applied to the group as a whole and shape the way the group's members are treated. William Chambliss (1973), in his study of the Saints and the Roughnecks, found that these two groups of youth engaged in roughly the same types of delinquent behavior, but, because of their dissimilar social characteristics, were treated differently by school officials and police officers. The Saints, of higher social class and mainly from intact families, were considered "good boys who just went in for an occasional prank." The Roughnecks, on the other hand, were "not-so-well-dressed, not-so-well-mannered, not-so-rich boys heading for trouble." Chambliss reported that the Saints actually engaged in more delinquency than the Roughnecks, but their social characteristics were so labeled—stereotyped—that the Saints were seen as less of a threat than the Roughnecks. And those stereotypes had lasting results. Chambliss reported that seven of the eight members of the Saints went to college, and all seven graduated. Three of them went on for advanced degrees. As for the Roughnecks, two went to college on athletic scholarships and became coaches, two dropped out of high school and ended up in prison, one became a bookie, and the whereabouts of the other was unknown.

The symbolic interaction theory of prejudice and discrimination would also look at the meanings that the labels applied to minority groups have for the people within those minorities. Claude Steele and Joshua Aronson (1995) found that not only do negative stereotypes affect peoples' perceptions of minorities, but also affect the minorities' perceptions of themselves. In their experiment, undergraduate students were given questions from the verbal part of the Graduate Record Exam. Before taking the test, one group was asked for general demographic information: school classification, age, major. The second group was also asked to give this information, along with an answer to another question: "What is your race?" Steele said that just listing their race affected black students' performance, making them score significantly worse than blacks who were not asked to provide their race. Blacks who were not asked for race had scores equal to those of white students in the experiment.

Patterns Of Intergroup Relations

Whether it is through migration or annexation, when minority groups are formed, the patterns that will guide their relations with the dominant group must be established. It is often the dominant group that will determine how the two groups will interact because it has the power.

An historical analysis of minority/dominant relations reveals the following basic patterns: genocide, expulsion, internal colonialism, segregation, amalgamation, assimilation, and pluralism (multiculturalism).

Genocide

Genocide is the deliberate and systematic extermination of all members of a particular minority group. It may be unintentional, as the decimation of Native Americans resulting from diseases and illnesses brought by European settlers over which the Native Americans had no immunities, or it may be deliberate, such as the Holocaust. More recently, the slaughter of several hundred thousand Rwandan Tutsis by the Hutus vividly illustrates how genocide can be used as a way of dealing with a minority group. The two groups had occupied Rwanda for years, and during that time had experienced conflict and disagreements. Twenty thousand Tutsis had been killed in riots back in the 1950s. But in 1994, after the Rwandan Hutu president died when his plane was shot down, it was assumed the resistant Tutsis were somehow involved, and they were targeted by the Hutus. Of course, for the dominant group, genocide makes perfect sense—eliminate the minorities and there is no need for establishing any type of relations.

Expulsion

The forced resettlement or deportation of a group of people is referred to as **expulsion**. Forced resettlement occurs when the dominant group coerces the minority to move to a certain part of the country, as with the Native Americans in their encounters with the European settlers, or the Japanese during World War II. The expulsion of the Native Ameri-

The results of genocide.

Source: Gisela Royo

cans began early on, with the Proclamation of 1763. In that formal declaration, the word "reserve" was used to refer to the policy of the English to "reserve land west of the Appalachians" for the use of the Indians. European settlers were to be content with land to the east of the mountains. Thus began the predominant Indian policy on the part of the settlers, the reservation system. This policy was most vividly illustrated by the Trail of Tears, the forced resettlement of approximately 17,000 Cherokees from the southeastern part of the United States to what is now Oklahoma. Almost a quarter of the Cherokees died during the expulsion.

The Japanese, who had been excluded in 1924 from immigrating to the United States, faced further legal discrimination when, after the bombing of Pearl Harbor in 1941, they were rounded up and sent to *internment centers*, where most of them would live out the duration of the war. The reason given for the relocation was national security, but, although the United States was also at war with Italy and Germany, no Italians or Germans were incarcerated without due process as the Japanese were.

Deportation occurs when a group is removed entirely from a country, as happened in 1290 to Jews living in England. The Jews have a history of ostracism and expulsions, going all the way back to Moses leading his people out of bondage in Egypt to wander in the wilderness. But when the Jewish people have become so affluent that they threaten the members of the host country, or when they are no longer useful, they have often suffered expulsion. This seems to have occurred in 1290 when money lending and charging interest were banned in England, thus taking away the major livelihood for the Jews, and the way they earned money for the crown. They were then forced to leave England and find another place willing to accept them.

Internal Colonialism

Colonialism refers to the maintenance of political, social, economic, and cultural domination over a people by a foreign power for an extended period. The colonizer uses the natural resources, as well as the workforce, of the colony for its own benefit. Colonialism is largely a thing of the past, but what happens now is a situation whereby the dominant group within a society uses the minority for its own economic benefit, in what has been labeled **internal colonialism.** As is suggested by the dual labor market theory, the secondary economy tends to be dominated by members of minority groups. The better jobs of society are reserved for the dominant group, while the less-desirable jobs are taken by the minorities. Economic power stays in the hands of the dominant group.

Segregation

Segregation means physical separation. Legal segregation was supported by the *Plessy* decision. Separate railroad cars, separate schools, and separate waiting rooms for the races were all legal. Even though the *Brown* decision of 1954 overturned *Plessy*, the system of *de jure* (legal) segregation was only replaced by a system of *de facto* (institutional) segregation. Like institutional discrimination, institutional segregation occurs through the way society operates. People live in racially segregated neighborhoods, frequent stores and social venues in those neighborhoods, attend neighborhood schools, and associate primarily with those living in the same segregated neighborhoods.

Even parts of minorities can be segregated. During World War II, with the segregation of the troops by race, the Red Cross also kept the blood of black soldiers separate from the blood of white soldiers, so no black soldier's blood was given to a white soldier. And it was a black physician, Dr. Charles Drew, who developed the system for the storing of blood plasma (Wynes, 1988). He established the American Red Cross blood bank and was its first director. Drew was fired from the post when he tried to end the practice of separating black and white people's blood.

Amalgamation

The idea of the American *melting pot* is embodied by the concept of **amalgamation**, in which the cultural and physical features of various groups combine to create a new culture. The amalgamation involves both cultural borrowing and intermarriage. Indeed, the "American people" and the "American culture" are unique, existing nowhere else in the world, created by the synthesis of the various immigrant groups who arrived early on in the New World. However, the melting pot ideal changed when the face of the immigrant changed in the mid-1800s. People whose cultures or physical features were too different were not encouraged to *melt* into the culture.

Assimilation

Assimilation means that minorities are expected to be like the dominant group. The minority group members are expected to give up their distinctiveness and become part of the dominant culture. This assimilation may be forced or voluntary. An example of forced assimilation is the General Allotment Act of 1887. In that act, the tribal reservations were broken up and an allotment of land given to each family. The purpose of this act was to assimilate Native Americans into white society by making them land owners. This breaking up of the tribes was an attempt to separate the Native Americans from their tribal identity. On the other hand, voluntary assimilation allows minorities the opportunity to adapt to the dominant culture at their own rate, adopting parts of the American culture as they desire or are able.

Milton Gordon (1978) pointed out that assimilation is not a seamless blending of the foreign with the American. He said that full assimilation involves three components: cultural, structural, and marital. Cultural assimilation involves adopting the dominant group's language, foods, religious beliefs, and other components of the dominant group's ways of thinking and doing. Structural assimilation means participating in the dominant group's social system and its social structures, such as jobs, schools, and clubs. Marital assimilation involves intermarriage. Not surprisingly, these three components of assimilation occur at different rates and to different degrees, depending on the minority group. Cultural assimilation is encouraged and is the most complete. Structural assimilation involves more resistance on the part of the dominant group. And marital assimilation has faced resistance on the parts of both dominant and minority group members.

Not all groups have assimilated at the same rate or to the same degree. Several factors determine the rate of assimilation for a given minority group:

1. Similarity between the minority and the dominant group, including cultural and physical similarities.
2. Attitude of the minority and dominant groups.

The attitude of the groups might be based in part on whether or not the minority had immigrated voluntarily or involuntarily.

3. Nature of the minority group, such as size, the timing of the group's arrival, and the economic conditions prevailing at the time of their arrival.
4. Timing of immigration. More recent arrivals, and those who can easily return home, are less likely to assimilate (Schaefer, 1998). This phenomenon can be seen in the American Southwest, particularly in Texas, where Mexican-Americans hold on to their culture to a large extent, creating a Tex-Mex culture that has been labeled "Tejano". Close proximity to Mexico and frequent travels across the border have kept the Mexican culture alive and prevented a more complete assimilation of the Mexican-American population in the Southwest.

Chinatown in New York City.

Source: Herman Brinkman

Pluralism (Multiculturalism)

Pluralism allows minorities to maintain their cultural distinctiveness. Examples would be *ethnic ghettos* such as Chinatown, Little Italy, and Indian reservations. A society that truly embraces the pluralistic notion would respect a minority's cultural distinctiveness while at the same time allowing full participation in the dominant group's social institutions. Unfortunately, this is most often not the case. Native Americans may be able to continue, to some extent, their ancient tribal ways by maintaining their reservations, but it has come at the cost of isolation and abject poverty.

Most Americans may be tolerant of this pluralistic notion, but one area of contention has been language. U.S. English is a social movement formed in 1983 that seeks to make English the official language of America. If English became our official language, all government business would be carried out in English only. For example, election ballots would be printed only in English. Currently, thirty states have passed some form of English-only laws. Interestingly enough, although some may see the U.S. English movement as a racist attempt to force conformity on unwilling minorities, the movement itself was founded by an immigrant, former Senator S. I. Hayakawa. Senator Hayakawa knew that immigrants who were not English-proficient were less likely to succeed in American society, and felt that making English the official language would increase opportunities for immigrants to learn and speak English (U.S. English, 2008).

An interesting analysis of the assimilation/pluralism dialectic is Marcus Hansen's third-generation principle, or, as Hansen (1952) states, "What the son wishes to forget, the grandson wishes to remember." Hansen felt that ethnicity passed through three stages. For the immigrant generation, ethnicity is dominant as immigrants adapt to the new culture, often settling in cultural and ethnic neighborhoods with others from their homelands. In the second generation, the children of these immigrants assimilate to mainstream culture, leaving behind the ways of their fathers. The third generation, more secure in their American status, seek a return to their grandparents' roots, leading to a revival of ethnic awareness. Thus, there is a passage from pluralism to assimilation and then back to pluralism. Perhaps this third stage would be better called multiculturalism than pluralism, as the immigrant grandchildren maintain their identity with the dominant group.

Minority Groups In America

No doubt every country in the world is represented to some degree in American culture. Some, like Latinos, are here in greater numbers than others, but undoubtedly all countries have provided immigrants to America at one point or the other. So how to categorize the racial and ethnic groups that make up this great land? Any attempt to examine each separate group would lead to a list so unwieldy, and data so meaningless, that it really would be an exercise in futility! Instead, social scientists, in order to get some idea of the status of minorities in our society, group them into broad categories based on world region of origin. The resulting groups are white ethnics, Latinos, African-Americans, Asian-Americans, and Native American Indians. It is important to acknowledge the diversity of these five groups. Asian-Americans include immigrants from thirty countries in Asia and the Pacific Rim. They have different languages, different religions, different cultures, and might not even like being grouped together. But in being so, the groups are represented in sufficient numbers to provide an idea of their experiences as minorities in America.

White Ethnics

For many, identifying a minority group known as white ethnics, or European-Americans, may be difficult. Of all the minority groups, they share physical features close enough to the dominant white Anglo-Saxon Protestant group that they are able to blend. But, in terms of power and economic status, white ethnics lag behind their WASP counterparts. In large part, this is due to the timing of their arrival. The first major wave of immigrants saw the Northern and Western Europeans establish the culture that would come to dominate the New World. Coming several decades later, Southern and Eastern Europeans have not done as well as the earlier group of European immigrants, and, even though WASPs make up only about 25 percent of the American population, white ethnics still find themselves somewhat on the outside of major social institutions.

Latinos

It was not supposed to happen for another two decades, but, with the 2000 census, Latinos became the largest minority group in the United States. The reasons for their growth are high immigration rates coupled with high birth rates. In 2006, there were 44.3 million Latinos in the United States (Census, 2008a), which is about 14 percent of the U.S. population. From April 1, 2000 to July 1, 2005, the population of the United States increased 5 percent, but the Latino population increased 21 percent (Census, 2005). With continued high rates of immigration, the Census Bureau projects that the Latino population will total 106.2 million, or 24.4 percent of the U. S. population, by 2050 (Census, 2000a). The Latino population includes those from Mexico, Puerto Rico, Cuba, and Central and South America. The five states with the highest percentage of Latinos are New Mexico, California, Texas, Arizona, and Nevada. As a group, Latinos are younger than the overall population. The median age for the country as a whole is 36.2 years; for Hispanics, it is 27.2 years (Census, 2005).

One of the largest groups of new arrivals, Spanish-speaking people were in Florida in the 15th century, and in the Southwest before the Pilgrims landed at Plymouth Rock in 1620, making them also one of the earliest groups of immigrants to come to this country. Today, countries of the Western Hemisphere account for 40 percent of all legal immigrants annually.

Not only are Latinos the largest group of legal immigrants in the United States, but they also comprise the largest group of illegal immigrants. According to the Migration Policy Institute (2008), in January 2006, there were approximately 11.6 million illegal immigrants in the United States. Approximately 6.6 million of the illegal immigrants were from Mexico (57%), 510,000 from El Salvador (4%), 430,000 from Guatemala (4%), 280,000 from the Philippines (2%), and 280,000 from Honduras (2%).

Percent Distribution of Latinos by Type: 2006

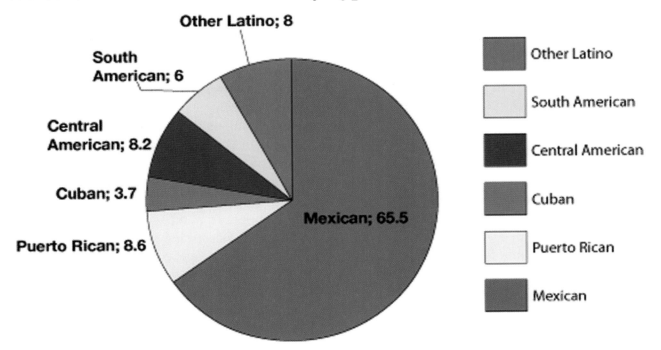

Source: U.S. Census Bureau (2006a). Current Population Survey, Annual Social and Economic Supplement.

The largest of the Latino groups is the Mexican-Americans, or Chicanos. Mexicans are descendants of Spanish colonists and Native Americans and, in 2006, numbered 28,323,000, almost two-thirds of the Latino population in the United States. The ancestors of many of these were not immigrants; they were colonized by the United States. The Indians of Mexico were first subdued by the Spaniards. This period of colonization lasted from the 16th century until 1821, when Mexico achieved political independence. After gaining independence from Spain, Mexico encouraged the colonization of Texas through immigration from other nations, mostly America, but also Czechoslovakia, Germany, Norway, and other European countries. Mexico was afraid it would not be able to secure its long, sparsely populated northern frontier from the encroachment of Americans, ever-hungry for land. To try to satisfy American settlers and maintain the status of its frontier, the Mexican government agreed to let Americans settle in Texas, but these new settlers would have to become Mexican citizens. The Mexican government hoped this buffer of Anglo-Mexican citizens would secure Texas for Mexico.

By 1834, Anglos outnumbered Mexicans in Texas by six to one. In 1836, Texas broke away from Mexico to establish an independent republic. After some ten years of independence, Texas agreed to become part of the United States.

The annexation of Texas by the United States provoked the Mexican-American War (1846-1848). The war was settled in 1848 by the Treaty of Guadalupe Hidalgo, which gave the U.S. not only Texas, but also California and most of Arizona and New Mexico. The Spanish-Mexican-Indian group that was left behind as Mexico's northern frontier receded was now a conquered group. As individuals, they had the right either to retain the title and rights of Mexican citizens or to acquire those of citizens of the United States.

Thus, the entry of large numbers of Mexicans into American society differed from that of European and Asian immigrants. The Mexican-Americans had not decided to leave their native land and go to the United States. They simply discovered one day that by a mutual agreement of Mexico and the United States, the places where they lived were no longer in Mexico. In fact, to continue being Mexicans, they either had to leave their homes and move south to the new border established by the treaty or declare officially their intention to remain Mexican nationals in the United States.

For nearly 50 years after the signing of the Treaty of Guadalupe Hidalgo, relatively few Mexican nationals moved to the U.S. with the intention of becoming permanent residents. Mexicans could cross the border with relative ease. Border patrol was not begun until 1904, and even then its efforts were directed mainly at Chinese people who attempted to emigrate from Mexico. Not until 1965 did the United States restrict immigration from Mexico.

The beginning of the 20th century marked the advent of mass migration from Mexico. Poverty and political instability, including the Mexican Revolution (1909-1922), enhanced the lure of jobs in the north. Also, World War I helped stem the flow of European immigrants, leaving more jobs for immigrants from Mexico. Those Mexicans who immigrated were generally poor and unskilled, and took jobs primarily in the secondary labor market.

The second largest group of Latinos is the Puerto Ricans, with 2006 census data indicating there are 3,704,000 Puerto Ricans in the United States. The U.S. occupied Puerto Rico from 1898, when the island was seized during the Spanish-American War, until 1952. In 1952, the Puerto Rican Constitution was drafted, establishing Puerto Rico as a self-governing commonwealth in association with the United States. Recent years have seen the residents of the island voting on the question of maintaining or changing their commonwealth status, and, so far at least, the vote has been in favor of the status quo.

Residents of Puerto Rico were made citizens of the United States in 1917. In that status, they are able to move freely from the island to the mainland, and should be considered internal migrants rather than immigrants. In the early part of the 20th century, few Puerto Ricans migrated to the mainland, but, following World War II, migration rates picked up dramatically. By 1955, nearly 700,000 Puerto Ricans had arrived, and by the mid-1960s, more than a million had migrated. Reasons for the increased migration rates included an economic depression on the island and recruiting by U.S. factory owners in Puerto Rico. Another significant reason was the availability of affordable air travel. After centuries of immigration by boat, Puerto Rican migrants became the first great airborne migration in U.S. history.

New York City had long been the destination of migrating Puerto Ricans, where they settled in Northeast Manhattan in a neighborhood that became known as Spanish Harlem. Today, there are almost as many Puerto Ricans on the mainland as on the island. New York City remains a destination for many of these migrants, although Orlando, Florida, has the fastest-growing Puerto Rican population in the United States today.

Cuban settlement in Florida began as early as 1831. Throughout the 19th century, workers moved freely between Florida and the island of Cuba, which is only about 90 miles away, trading in sugar, coffee, and tobacco. At the beginning of the 20th century, an estimated 50,000 to 100,000 Cubans moved between Florida and Cuba each year. However, the total number of Cuban Americans remained small. The 1960 the U.S. census indicated only 79,000 Cuban-born residents. The number of Cuban immigrants increased dramatically—more than one million would make their way to the United States—due to the Cuban Revolution which followed Fidel Castro's takeover of power in 1959. Many thousands more would try and fail. The first large group fleeing Castro's dictatorship tended to be wealthy and well-educated. Numbering about 200,000, many of these immigrants settled in Dade County (Miami), Florida, and most have been successful in their new country. In 1966, Congress passed the Cuban Adjustment Act, which allows undocumented Cuban immigrants to stay and, within a year, gain permanent status. This is a privilege that has never been offered to any other group of immigrants.

Several other large groups of Cubans immigrated in the next few decades; in particular, one that came in 1980. The Mariel boatlift involved the immigration of 124,000 refugees. This *freedom flotilla* began when a few boats with people seeking asylum in the United States arrived in Key West, Florida. Those migrating in the boatlift tended to have less education and fewer skills than those Cubans who had come two decades before, and they have had more difficulty assimilating to American culture. However, as a group, Cuban Americans are better educated and have higher family incomes than other Latino groups; they also have lower poverty rates.

The smallest group of Latinos in the United States includes people from the countries of Central and South America. A very diverse group, less is known about it than the other Latino groups. Many have come to the United States seeking economic opportunities, while others have come fleeing oppression and political unrest. Many have applied for refugee status but have not received it, and thus are in the country illegally. Between 1981 and 1990, nearly one million Guatemalans and Salvadorans fled political oppression and entered the United States clandestinely, seeking political asylum. Few were granted that status. As a result, religious organizations came together to help these Central American *emigrants*, starting the Sanctuary Movement to offer legal and humanitarian assistance to these refugees. **Emigrants** are people who leave their home countries to make their way to another. Upon arrival, they are referred to as immigrants by those in their new country.

One thing almost all Latino immigrants have in common is their language, Spanish. Census Bureau data indicate that approximately 28 million people speak Spanish at home. Most of these are bilingual, but almost 9 million speak English "not well" or "not at all" (Census, 2000b). This can be a hindrance to assimilation and limits opportunities for economic advancement. Attempts to implement bilingual education programs in our public schools have met with resistance. The most popular of these programs that persist are English as a second language (ESL) programs. These programs emphasize bilingual, but not bicultural, education. Ideally, ESL programs teach foreign-speaking students in their own language, while also teaching them English until they can learn in that language. Unfortunately, these programs often do not work that way and become instead English immersion programs, where students are taught primarily in English, using their own languages only when they cannot understand what is being taught (Schaefer, 1998).

African-Americans

Sociologist Nathan Glazer (1971) suggests that blacks suffer from being in, but not of, American society. There are no traditions of the "old country," no common language or common memory from overseas. They are America's *internal aliens.* Many argue that, given time, blacks will rise in society, like the Irish, the Italians, the Germans, and others. But this notion misses two points: first, the skin color of the African-American, which is not a factor for other groups in America, and, second, the African-American is an internal migrant and, as such, will face racism wherever he goes, unable to leave his oppression behind.

African-Americans have a history in America that is unique and that has had long-lasting effects. The first record of black settlers was at Jamestown in 1619. They came to the New World as indentured servants, just as many Europeans did. Indentured servants "sold" themselves into bondage for a certain number of years. However, during their period of bondage, they enjoyed certain rights and legal protection. But as the need for laborers increased, employers became reluctant to release workers from bondage. By the early 1660s, Maryland and Virginia had taken legal steps to make it more difficult for black indentured servants to gain freedom. The laws singled out black, not white, indentured servants, probably because there were fewer of them—presenting less chance for trouble—and because their skin color made them more visible and less able to escape. A constant source of cheap labor was needed to help maximize profits in developing the plantation economy in the South.

Many more blacks were brought to America as slaves. Approximately 500,000 slaves entered the country during the years of slave trading, a practice that was halted in 1807. Slaves were considered the property of their owners, and most were not allowed to learn to read or write, to marry, or to travel without their owner's permission. The Emancipation Proclamation, issued by President Abraham Lincoln on January 1, 1863, freed the slaves, but, following the defeat of the Confederacy in 1865, it took the 13th Amendment to the Constitution to completely abolish the practice. This amendment was followed by the 14th Amendment (1868), which gave blacks citizenship, and the 15th Amendment (1870), which gave black men the right to vote. This meant that a group that had, for the most part, been forced to migrate as slaves, a group that numbered almost four million, was free. Of course, the transition would not be that easy.

Lincoln felt the Southern states had never left the Union and that they continued to exist as states. Unfortunately, he was assassinated; although President Andrew Johnson attempted to continue Lincoln's policies, he was soon outnumbered by a group of Republican leaders in Congress, the Radical Republicans. They were able to pass Reconstruction bills, which declared the governments of the Southern states illegal, and divided the states themselves into five military districts. This move engendered much of the antagonism of Southerners toward Northerners. Many Northern whites, who became known as carpetbaggers, and Union loyalists from the South, known as scalawags, were elected to public office, as were many blacks. In retaliation, Southern whites planned subtle, and not so subtle, attacks against blacks. An example of this phenomenon was the Ku Klux Klan, formed in 1865. Its purpose initially was to provide amusement to white gentlemen, but it was soon discovered that their costumes and symbols could be used to frighten blacks. Accordingly, the Klan's purposes soon became the destruction of the Reconstruction government and the return of blacks to their subordinate positions. Their tactics, such as cross burnings, floggings, house burnings, and murders, proved so effective that Southern blacks found it better to show no interest in political matters, leaving that area to whites.

By 1877, the Southern states had met the requirements for readmission to the Union, those being approval of the 14th Amendment and acceptable constitutions. Federal troops were withdrawn, and Reconstruction ended. Now a new form of suppression for Southern blacks began—**Jim Crow laws**.

These laws involved proscribed behaviors that were intended to keep blacks "in their place." Many of these revolved around keeping blacks from voting. Literacy tests, poll taxes, hiding poll locations, economic pressures, threats of violence, and other strategies were used to keep newly freed blacks from voting. In the U.S. Supreme Court case *Williams v. Mississippi* (1898), the court ruled that literacy tests and poll taxes were legal, as they applied to all potential voters. Of course, it was the freed slaves who could not read or afford the poll tax. *Plessy v. Ferguson* (1896) further sealed the fate of the blacks in South, with the U.S. Supreme Court ruling that separate facilities for the races were constitutional. In other words, legal slavery was over, but oppression of the former slaves continued.

By 1900, 90 percent of blacks lived in the South, but many decided to take advantage of their new freedom and move North. World War I brought about a decrease in European immigration, and thus cheap labor for Northern factories, so blacks found employment opportunities there. But in the North, they still experienced inequity, with segregated housing and discrimination from unions. World War II also spurred black migration to the North. However, in many ways, the blacks migrating to the North fared less well than the new white immigrants from Southern, Central, and Eastern Europe. Dominant whites preferred the European immigrants over the blacks due to the disadvantage of their skin color. Of course, other non-white groups, like Japanese and Chinese, were also discriminated against because of their skin color. But, due to changes in immigration policies in the late 19th and early 20th centuries, the Chinese and Japanese population did not reach large numbers and, thus, did not pose as great a threat as blacks.

In 1954, the U.S. Supreme Court overturned the Plessy decision in the case *Brown v. Board of Education of Topeka*. From a legal perspective, discrimination had been outlawed, and freedom of the races was now the rule. The 1960s saw further progress in granting equality to a group whose ancestors had, for the most part, arrived in this country as slaves. In 1964, President Lyndon Johnson signed the Civil Rights Act, the most sweeping piece of civil rights legislation since Reconstruction. The Civil Rights Act of 1964 prohibited discrimination of all kinds based on race, color, religion, or national origin. The law also gave government the power to enforce desegregation. The Voting Rights Act of 1965 made literacy tests, poll taxes, and other measures used to restrict black voting illegal. In 1967, in the case *Loving v. Virginia*, the U.S. Supreme Court ruled that all state laws banning interracial marriages were unconstitutional. At that time, 16 states still had such laws. Another Civil Rights Act, which dealt with discrimination in housing, was passed in 1968. It would seem that all legal impediments to progress had been removed, and black Americans could stand on equal footing with their white counterparts.

In some ways, African-Americans have made remarkable gains over the last few decades. In the 110th Congress, there are 42 African-Americans in the House and one in the Senate (although he left the Senate to assume the position of president of the United States). Of course, based on their numbers, 12.7 percent of the U.S. population, those figures should be higher. Other measures of *life chances* indicate that African-Americans lag behind other groups. Economically, African-Americans have lower median family incomes ($33,916) than whites ($52,115), Latinos ($38,679), or Asian-Americans ($66,103). Only a third of black households make over $50,000 a year, compared with over half of white families. The unemployment rate is higher for blacks (8.3%) than whites (4.1%). Not surprisingly, the poverty rate for African-Americans, 24.6 percent, exceeds that of the general population, 12.5 percent (Census, 2008b). These economic variables affect the ability of African-American families to possess the most American of assets—their own home. The home ownership rate in the United States is 68.1 percent, but for African-Americans it is 47.2 percent (Census, 2007a). High school and college graduation rates are also lower for blacks than for other groups. Only 18.5 percent of African-Americans over the age of 25 have a four-year college degree, compared with 29.1 percent of white Americans (Census, 2007b).

These economic variables have an impact on health and life expectancy. In the first place, African-Americans are less likely to have health insurance than others in society. In the United States, 15.3 percent of Americans have no health insurance. For African-Americans, that number is 19.5 percent (Census, 2008b). Life expectancy for all Americans is 77.8 years, but only 73.1 years for blacks. Black males fare especially poorly, with a life expectancy of only 69.5 (Census, 2007c). The infant mortality rate for African-American babies is more than twice the national rate: 6.8 per thousand births for all races, but 13.8 per thousand births for black babies (U.S. National Center for Health Statistics, 2007). As the saying goes, when America gets a cold, black America gets pneumonia.

These inequalities extend into the criminal justice system. **Racial profiling** is a concept that has entered our language in recent years, referring to criminal justice practices that target the most suspected population. For functional theorists, it is good police practice. For conflict theorists, it is an-

other example of how the powerful use their power to control the powerless. African-Americans are certainly overrepresented in our prisons. In 2004, there were almost 1.3 million prisoners incarcerated in state prisons in the United States. Almost half a million of them (492,300) were black. According to the Bureau of Justice Statistics (2008), the lifetime chance of a person going to prison for blacks is 18.6 percent, for Latinos, 10 percent, and for whites, 3.4 percent. Perhaps, as Jeffrey Reiman suggests, the rich do indeed get richer and the poor get prison (Reiman, 2001).

For the most violent of crimes—murder—the difference is even greater. In 2005, the offender rates for murder were seven times higher for blacks than whites. Not only are blacks more likely to commit murder, they are more likely to be murder victims. In 2005, for every 100,000 blacks, 20.6 were the victims of homicide, compared with a rate of 3.3 for whites. And blacks are much more likely to be the

Asian Population by Detailed Group: 2000

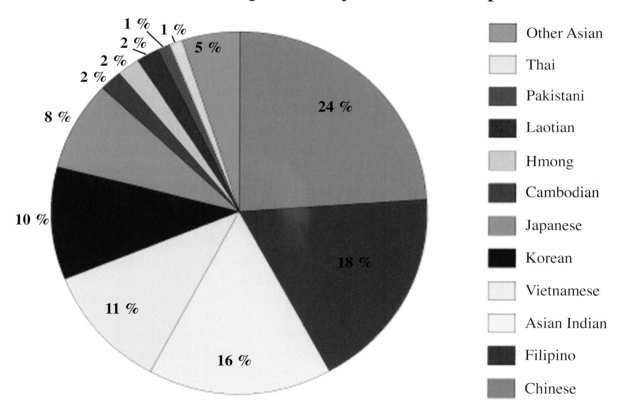

Source: U.S. Census Bureau (2002b). We the People: Asians in the United States.

victims of all types of violent crime. The rate of violent crime victimization for blacks is 32 per 1,000, compared with 23 per 1,000 for whites. Black households even had higher property crime victimization rates: 186 per 1,000 compared with 157 per 1,000 households for whites (Justice, 2008). Legal discrimination has ended; institutional discrimination has taken its place.

Asian-Americans

For the U.S. Census Bureau, the term Asian refers to people having origins in the Far East, Southeast Asia, or the Indian subcontinent (for example, Cambodia, China, India, Japan, Korea, Malaysia, Pakistan, the Philippine Islands, Thailand, and Vietnam). Data have been collected on the Chinese population since the 1860 census, and on the Japanese population since the 1870 census (Census, 2002a). These two groups have been represented in the U.S. population for generations; others, such as the Hmong, Vietnamese, Laotians, and Cambodians are more recent arrivals. Asian-Americans are the fastest growing minority in the United States. At 9 million, Asian-Americans were 3 percent of the U.S. population in 1990. In 2006, the Asian-American population numbered 14.9 million, almost 5 percent of the total U.S. population. Since 1965, 40 percent of all immigrants to the United States have been from Asia.

The Asian population in America has been labeled a *model minority* because of their success relative to other racial groups, including whites. The median family income of Asian-American families is higher—$66,103 compared with $52,115 for whites in 2007 (Census, 2008b). This is probably due to the fact that many Asian immigrants have entered the country under the "skilled and technical worker" designation, as established in the 1965 Immigration Act. Of course, not all Asian groups are so well-off. Those of Chinese and Japanese descent, with a longer history in America and more complete assimilation, are more likely to fit the model-minority stereotype, while more recent arrivals, like the Vietnamese, Koreans, and Laotians, still find themselves lagging behind others in terms of their success rates.

But even for Chinese and Japanese immigrants, success has not been a sure thing. The Chinese, the largest Asian group at 24 percent of the total Asian population, first immigrated in significant numbers in the 1860s, primarily to serve as laborers building the Transcontinental Railroad—work considered to be *coolie* labor. However, with the completion of the railroad in 1869, the labor of the Chinese was no longer needed. Fearing that the Chinese would take jobs from whites on the West Coast, the U.S. Congress was pressed to pass the 1882 Chinese Exclusion Act, ending immigration from China until 1943. This act also prevented resident alien Chinese from becoming naturalized citizens.

Japanese immigrants faced similar discrimination. Significant immigration of the Japanese to America began in the 1890s. Prior to that time, scarcely more than 4,000 Japanese had traveled to the United States, and more than half of those had returned home. The peak years of Japanese immigration occurred during the second wave of immigration, when nativism was at its peak. Most of these immigrants settled in Hawaii and along the Pacific Coast, mainly in California. They came for the same reasons as most other immigrants did: better jobs, better lives, and an escape from harsh conditions in their home country. Unfortunately for the Japanese, one other factor would serve to make them unique—they came from a country that would eventually attack the United States.

The first wave of Japanese immigrants, referred to as the *Issei*, meaning "first generation", was very successful in the United States. Their success engendered feelings of animosity and prejudice, and, in 1913, the first Alien Land Law was passed in California. This law prohibited those who were denied U.S. citizenship, including both the Chinese and Japanese, from owning land. The *Issei* attempted to transfer their land to their children (the *Nisei*), recognizing that they were citizens because they were born in the United States. The Alien Land Act of 1920 was passed, prohibiting these types of transfers, and the U.S. Supreme Court case Ozawa v. U.S. (1922) decreed that the Japanese could not obtain U.S. citizenship, a decision that was not overturned until 1952. The exclusionists were successful in their attempts to stop the flow of Japanese immigration through the Immigration Act of 1924, which prohibited further Japanese immigration to the United States. But the most dramatic example of legal discrimination against the Japanese was yet to occur.

On December 7, 1941, the Japanese attacked Pearl Harbor. Within ten weeks of the bombing, Executive Order 9066, issued by Franklin D. Roosevelt on February 19, 1942, required all people of Japanese ancestry (that is, one-eighth Japanese ancestry), whether alien or citizen, to leave their homes and report to *assembly centers* prior to being assigned to one of ten permanent *relocation centers*. The evacuation was based on fears of sabotage and espionage on the part of the Japanese on the West Coast. The relocation was started in March of 1942 and completed in November of that same year, involving 120,000 Japanese, two-thirds of whom were U.S. citizens. There were no charges brought and no trials. This large group of people, mostly American citizens, were arrested and imprisoned because of their race. It took a U.S. Supreme Court decision, *Endo v. U.S.*, in December 1944, to end the internment. Yet, at the beginning of 1945, nearly 80,000 people remained in the internment centers. For the most part, life at the internment centers had been peaceful. American flags were flown, the Pledge of Allegiance recited, and Boy Scout and Girl Scout troops formed. The *Nisei* even fought for the right to serve in the U.S. military to prove their loyalty. Restrictions barring Japanese-Americans from military service were lifted in 1943, and about 30,000 Nisei served during World War II. In fact, one all-Nisei unit, the 442nd Regimental Combat Team, went on to become the most highly decorated unit of its size in U.S. history, receiving more than 18,000 individual decorations, including 52 Distinguished Service Crosses and one Medal of Honor.

Despite discrimination, Chinese-and Japanese-Americans have gone on to enjoy success in their adopted land. And, in many ways, the model-minority label is appropriate for this group, even though not all groups so labeled have achieved success to the same extent. Fully 52 percent of Asian-Americans have four-year college degrees, compared

with 27 percent of the overall population; another 20 percent have a graduate or professional degree, compared with 10 percent for the rest of Americans (Census, 2007b). But labeling Asian-Americans as a model minority ignores the problems still facing many others with the same label. It also seems to credit one minority group with achieving the American Dream, which means that those who have not been as successful have no one but themselves to blame. In other words, if the Asians can do it, why can't the rest of you?

Native Americans

Archeological evidence indicates there were people in Alaska by 25,000 BC and South America by 15,000 BC. These tribes of people were very diverse, speaking at least 200 languages with many different dialects. They also differed in social structure and economy. Some were hunters and gatherers and other horticulturalists. Others had more advanced agricultural societies. When Columbus first came to the New World, an estimated 12 million to 15 million Native Indians were living in this part of the world—about 2 million of them in what is now the United States. Four hundred years later, in 1890, that number was 250,000. It is estimated that 90 percent of the Indian tribes died from diseases such as measles, smallpox, and influenza brought by the Europeans. Some were killed by the settlers, although the federal government never had an overt plan to eliminate the Native Americans by warfare. It is interesting to note, however, that when the Bureau of Indian Affairs was formed in 1824, it was initially a branch of the War Department; it is now located in the Department of the Interior. The 2006 U.S. Census indicated that 2.9 million Americans placed themselves in the American Indian or Alaska Native (Inuit or Aleut) category. That comes to just less than 1 percent (0.9%) of the total U.S. population.

At first, relations between the new settlers and the indigenous population were friendly. However, as more Europeans came to the New World, their demand for land began to cause problems. Being more powerful, with more firepower and a better-equipped army, the European settlers forced the

Indians to move westward to less fertile and less desirable land, yielding the land by which they had survived to the white settlers. One particularly telling example of the European hunger for land was the Trail of Tears, a result of the Indian Removal Act of 1830. This act, passed when Andrew Jackson was president, forced the "Five Civilized Tribes" living in the southeastern part of the United States to move west to Indian Territory in what is now Oklahoma. The five tribes—the Seminole, Chickasaw, Choctaw, Cherokee, and Creek—were called civilized tribes because they were, for the most part, living peacefully with the European settlers. But the desire for more land led to the forced relocation of the tribes. The Cherokee particularly suffered from this forced removal. Almost 17,000 Cherokee were forced to make the trek from Georgia to the Indian Territory in winter, during which 4,000 died. The belief at the time was that white settlers would

never go beyond the Mississippi, so moving the tribes westward would allow them to resettle and start over. Jackson promised the leaders of the tribes "an ample district West of the Mississippi…to be guaranteed to the Indian tribes as long as they shall occupy it." The leaders of the Choctaw were said to reply, "The red people are of the opinion that, in a few years, the Americans will also wish to possess the land west of the Mississippi."

Relations between Indians and white men continued to be a history of broken treaties. The U.S. Constitution (Art. 1, Sec. 8, clause 3) gave tribes the right to form treaties with the federal government. Initially, the federal government attempted to negotiate for land for the settlers, considering the tribes as separate entities. In return for giving up their land, the federal government would provide the tribes with things like schools, roads, and medical care. The treaties were to last in perpetuity, that is,

Native American ceremonies.

Source: Linda Romines

forever. However, promises were broken, American Indian land was taken, and the tribes were treated as hostile invaders in a land they had inhabited for centuries.

In an attempt to help the tribes assimilate to the dominant Anglo culture, the 1887 General Allotment (Dawes) Act broke up the tribes. Tribal land was divided and given to each American Indian family. The idea was to make self-sufficient farmers out of the Indians and to break up their tribal loyalties. American Indians who held on to their land for 25 years would gain U.S. citizenship. The Indians were forbidden by the act to sell their land for 25 years. By all measures, the Dawes Act was a failure. Almost two-thirds of the land was lost to unscrupulous land speculators, and what was left to the American Indians was mainly arid and barren acreage.

As late as 1924, one-third of American Indi-

ans were still not U.S. citizens. In 1924, Congress passed the Indian Citizenship Act, making them citizens and giving them the right to vote. In 1936, the Indian Reorganization Act acknowledged the failure of the Allotment Act, returning to the tribes their sovereignty and allowing them to reorganize. However, this was still not a satisfactory solution for either the federal government or the tribes. Both wanted the government out of tribal business, and, in 1953, the Termination Act attempted to accomplish just that. Declaring that the Indians should be free from federal supervision and control, all laws and treaties then binding the United States to the Indians were nullified. Federal assistance to the tribes was withdrawn. To the Indians, it merely looked like another way for the U.S. government to avoid fulfilling treaty obligations.

The push for termination lasted less than a decade. In the wake of demands by other groups for

A day without immigrants rally in Nebraska.

Source: Steve White

civil rights in the 1960s, President Johnson affirmed the rights of Indians to "remain Indians while exercising their rights as Indians." In 1970, President Nixon attacked the idea that the federal government had the right to unilaterally terminate its special relationship with the American Indians, believing that the American Indians were entitled by treaties and other agreements to the provision of numerous community services. This led to the passage of the Indian Self-Determination and Educational Assistance Act in 1975, giving tribes back more control over their reservation land and programs, without decreasing federal assistance. Today there are 561 federally recognized Indian tribes in America. These tribes possess the right to form their own governments, enforce laws, levy taxes, establish requirements for tribal membership, license and regulate activities, zone their lands, and exclude persons from tribal territories.

The Native Americans are the poorest of American minority groups and have suffered both legal and institutional discrimination almost since the first Europeans began to arrive. The median household income for Native Americans is $31,605, compared with $44,684 for all American households. Native Americans have a poverty rate of 24.6 percent, compared with the national rate of 13.1 percent. Native Americans also have less education than other groups in society, with just 76.6 percent of Native Americans over 25 having graduated from high school, and 14.2 percent from college. The national average for high school graduates is 83.9 percent, and, for college, 27.0 percent (Indian Health Services, 2006). It was inevitable that explorers from other countries would find this continent and begin settlement, forever changing the way of life for its indigenous tribes. One has to wonder, though, whether the price paid by those tribes was too high, and whether everyone's needs could have been met while compromising none of the groups involved.

The Future Of Racial Relations

This chapter began with the election of Barack Obama, the country's first non-white president. Leading up to the election, pundits had noted that all whites should vote for Obama. Once a man of color was elected president, the minorities could no longer complain about their subordinate status. One of them would have achieved the pinnacle, and whites could be let off the hook. This was said in jest, but it has a ring of truth. Obama's victory is an example of upward mobility and shows it is possible for anyone to make it to the top in the United States. Minorities can achieve same level as whites. But, as has been indicated throughout the chapter, for most minority groups the struggle is not over. Gains have been made, but gaps still exist. Simply having a president with dark skin is not enough to make the problems go away. And of all the issues the different groups have confronted over the past few centuries, two concerning dominant/non-dominant (minority) relations continue to cause problems: immigration and affirmative action.

Immigration

Except for those who are 100 percent Native American, or those Latinos whose families were here prior to the signing of the Treaty of Guadalupe Hidalgo in 1848, Americans all originally came from somewhere else. We are a nation of immigrants, perhaps the first self-created people ever. The idea of an immigrant, though, conjures images of strange people with different languages and religions, coming to "our" country and threatening "our" way of life. There are fears that immigrants will take jobs from hard-working Americans, or, conversely, that they will end up on welfare and be a drain on our economy. It is true that those coming to America are, for the most part, coming for employment opportunities. But many take jobs American workers do not want, in less-pleasant and lower-paid occupations.

Immigrant participation in government aid programs has fallen significantly since the passage of the Personal Responsibility and Work Opportunity Reconciliation Act (1996). The act bars those immigrants who were here prior to its enactment from receiving food stamps and Supplemental Security Income (SSI). Those arriving after the act's passage are also ineligible for food stamps and SSI, but, after entering the country, can apply for Medicaid and

Ten Source Countries with the Largest Populations in the United States as Percentages of the Total Foreign-Born Population: 2006

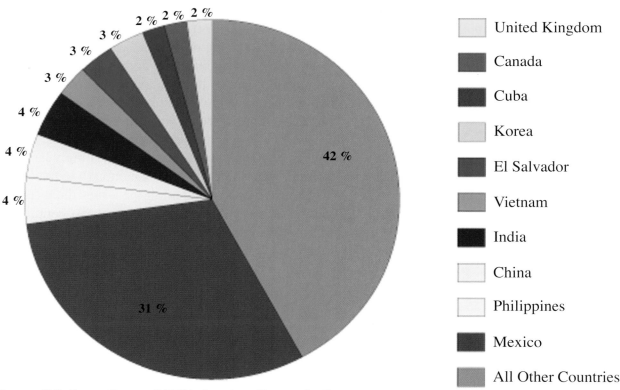

United Kingdom

Canada

Cuba

Korea

El Salvador

Vietnam

India

China

Philippines

Mexico

All Other Countries

Source: U.S. Census Bureau (2006b), American Community Survey.

Temporary Assistance for Needy Families (TANF). In 1996, immigrants represented 15 percent of all welfare recipients; in 1999, that number had dropped to 12 percent (Fix & Passel, 2002).

Other immigration concerns center on overpopulation and growth in the number of minorities. According to a report by the Pew Hispanic Center (2008), it is estimated that, if the current rate of immigration and births continues, the population of the United States will rise to 438 million in 2050, up from 296 million in 2005. Further, 82 percent of the increase will be due to immigrants arriving from 2005 to 2050 and their U.S.-born children. The report further indicated that, in 2050, nearly one in five Americans will be an immigrant, compared with one in eight in 2005. The Latino population, already the nation's largest minority group, will triple in size and comprise 29 percent of the U.S. population in 2050, up from 14 percent in 2005. The non-Latino white population will increase more slowly; by 2050, whites will become a minority (47%).

Affirmative Action

Affirmative action refers to positive actions used to recruit minority group members or women for jobs, promotions, and educational opportunities. The term was first used in 1961 when President John F. Kennedy issued an executive order stating that the government would encourage "equal opportunity for all qualified persons" through "positive measures," and that contractors would take "affirmative action that applicants are employed… without regard to their race, creed, color, or national origin" (Schaefer, 1998). This order marked a change from the passive assumption that racial discrimination could be removed by an absence of discrimination to the assumption that some positive assistance or preferential treatment was required to overcome the cumulative effects of past discrimination. Although most could agree on the goal of affirmative action, some disagreed with the policy itself. Some called it reverse discrimination, in that qualified whites would be passed over in favor of less-qualified minorities. Others said it would create an atmosphere of *tokenism*. If a minority member became successful, his or her success would not be due to personal abilities, but to a system that needed to show it was trying to be fair, and, as a token to that ideology, this particular person had been promoted.

Whatever one's sentiments about affirmative action, the results of the policy are questionable, and court rulings on cases inconsistent. Perhaps the best-known affirmative action case was *Regents of the University of California v. Bakke* (1978), a case involving the medical school at the University of California. The medical school had a quota for minority applicants, and Allen Bakke, a white applicant, argued he had been passed over for admission while less-qualified minorities were admitted to the medical school. The U.S. Supreme Court ruled in Bakke's favor, saying, however, that although quotas were unconstitutional, the school could use race as one factor in determining admissions.

More recently, in a case involving the University of Michigan, the court upheld a policy of the university's law school favoring minorities but struck down an affirmative action policy for undergraduate admissions that awarded points for minority candidates on an admissions rating scale. The decision to uphold the law school's policy was based on the desire to seek a more "diverse educational climate." The point system used by the undergraduate school, however, violated the equal protection clause of the Constitution, according to the court. The undergraduate school at the university used a 150-point system, with 100 points required for admissions, and 20 points automatically granted for minority status. Interestingly, the 20 points were granted to African-Americans, Latinos, and Native Americans, but not to Asian-Americans.

The improved statuses of minorities, with so many more moving into the middle class, sending their children to college, and achieving the American Dream, affirmative action seems to have been put on the back burner. Of course, it is also important to remember that policies like affirmative action grew out of a more activist time in our country's history—the 1960s—and that fervor has waned somewhat. Perhaps it will be as Sandra Day O'Connor wrote in her opinion in the Michigan case: "We expect that 25 years from now, the use of racial preferences will no longer be necessary to further the interest approved today." If we can look ahead just 25 years to a society that no longer pays attention to minority status, that would probably be acceptable to most. Then, no one will even notice the color of the president's skin.

Summary

This chapter looked at the different racial and ethnic groups that comprise American society, exploring the history of immigration and the immigration laws that helped create and define the dominant and non-dominant minority groups. Patterns of intergroup relations, issues of prejudice and discrimination, and theories to explain these behaviors are examined. The current status of minority groups in the U.S. is discussed, and two areas of concern in the study of race and ethnicity, immigration issues and affirmative action, are also explored.

Review/Discussion Questions

1. Give an example of legal discrimination.
2. What is redlining?
3. How have dominant groups used their position to control minority groups?
4. What is affirmative action?
5. Which of the three sociological theories concerning prejudice and discrimination do you most agree with and why?
6. Do you think the United States government should make it easier or harder to legally immigrate to the U.S., and why?

Key Terms

Affirmative action is composed of positive actions used to recruit minority group members or women for jobs, promotions, and educational opportunities.

Amalgamation occurs when the cultural and physical features of various groups are combined to create a new culture.

Assimilation means that minorities are expected to be like the dominant group.

Deportation occurs when a group is removed entirely from a country.

Discrimination is differential treatment of people based on their group membership.

Emigrants are individuals leaving their home countries to live in another country.

Ethnic groups are categories of people with shared cultural heritages that others regard as distinct.

Ethnicity is a cultural definition, referring to learned behavior, and is thus due to nurture.

Expulsion is the forced resettlement of a group of people.

Genocide is the deliberate and systematic extermination of all members of a particular minority group.

Individual discrimination occurs when a person treats another unfairly, and the unfair treatment is due to the person's minority group status.

Institutional discrimination occurs when society and its social institutions operate in a manner that ensures some groups will be given preferential treatment over others.

Internal colonialism occurs when the dominant group within a society uses minorities for their own economic benefit.

Immigrants are people who have just arrived in their new country.

Jim Crow laws covered proscribed behaviors that were intended to keep blacks "in their place."

Legal discrimination is unequal treatment that is upheld by law.

Minority groups are people who are singled out for unequal treatment and who regard themselves as objects of collective discrimination.

Pluralism allows minorities to maintain their cultural distinctiveness by respecting it and, at the same time, allowing their members to participate fully in the dominant group's social institutions.

Prejudice is a feeling, favorable or unfavorable, that one has about a person or group of people and is not based on actual experience.

Race refers to people who share physical characteristics that are genetically transferred.

Racial profiling is a law enforcement practice that targets racial minorities.

Racism is a set of beliefs justifying the unfair treatment of a minority group and its members based on race.

Redlining is the practice of denying or limiting financial services to specific neighborhoods due to the minority group status of the residents.

Scapegoating is discriminating against others through assigning them blame for their shortcomings.

Segregation is the physical separation of groups of people from each other.

Stereotypes are rigid mental images held to be true about a group of people.

Bibliography

Adorno, T. W., Frenkel-Brunswick, E., Levinson, D. J. & Sanford, R. N. (1950). The Authoritarian Personality. New York: Harper & Row.

Bureau of Justice Statistics (2008). Victim Characteristics. Washington, DC: Department of Justice.

Chambliss, W. J. (1973). The Saints and the Roughnecks. Society, 11, 24 - 31.

Fix, M., & Passel, J. (2002). The Scope and Impact of Welfare Reform's Immigrant Provisions. Washington, DC: The Urban Institute.

Glazer, N. (1971). Blacks and Ethnic Groups: The Difference and the Political Difference. Social Problems, 18 (4), 444 - 461.

Gordon, M. (1978). Human Nature, Class, and Ethnicity. New York: Oxford Press.

Hansen, M. L. (1952). The Third Generation in America. Commentary, 14, 493 - 500.

Henslin, J. M. (2007). Sociology: A Down-to-Earth Approach (2nd ed.). Boston: Pearson.

Indian Health Services (2006). Facts on Indian Health Disparities. Washington, DC: Indian Health Services.

Meacham, J. (2008, September 1). On His Own. Newsweek, 26 - 36.

Migration Policy Institute (2008). Frequently Requested Statistics on Immigrants in the United States. <http://www.migrationinformation.org> (2008).

Pew Hispanic Center (2008). Pew Hispanic Center Reports: U. S. Population Projections: 2005 – 2050. <http://pewhispanic.org> (2008).

Reiman, J. (2001). The Rich Get Richer and the Poor Get Prison. Boston: Allyn & Bacon.

Schaefer, R. T. (1998). Racial and Ethnic Groups (2nd ed.). New York: Longman.

Squires, G. D. (Ed.). (1997). Insurance Redlining: Disinvestment, reinvestment, and the evolving role of financial institutions. Chicago: Urban Institute Printing.

Steele, C., & Aronson, J. (1995). Stereotype Threat and the Intellectual Test Performance of African Americans. Journal of Personality and Social Psychology, 95 (69), 797 - 811.

Thomas, W. I., & Swain Thomas, D. (1928). The Child in America. New York: Knopf.

U.S. Census Bureau (2000a). 1970, 1980, 1990, and 2000 Decennial Census. Washington, DC: Government Printing Office.

U.S. Census Bureau (2000b). Ability to Speak English by Language Spoken at Home. Washington, DC: Government Printing Office.

U.S. Census Bureau (2001). The 2 or More Races Population. Washington, DC: Government Printing Office.

U.S. Census Bureau (2002a). The Asian Population: 2000. Washington, DC: Government Printing Office.

U.S. Census Bureau (2002b). We the People: Asians in the United States. Washington, DC: Government Printing Office.

U.S. Census Bureau (2004). The American Community – American Indians and Alaska Native: 2004. Washington, DC: Government Printing Office.

U.S. Census Bureau (2005). Population profile of the United States. Washington, DC: Government Printing Office.

U.S. Census Bureau (2006a). Current Population Survey, Annual Social and Economic Supplement. Washington, DC: Government Printing Office.

U.S. Census Bureau (2006b). American Community Survey. Washington, DC: Government Printing Office.

U.S. Census Bureau (2007a). Home Ownership Rates by Race and Ethnicity of Householder. Washington, DC: Government Printing Office.

U.S. Census Bureau (2007b). Current Population Reports, Table 217. Washington, DC: Government Printing Office.

U.S. Census Bureau (2007c). Population Division Working Paper No. 38, Table 98. Washington, DC: Government Printing Office.

U.S. Census Bureau (2008a). Population Estimates July 1, 2000 to July 1, 2006. Washington, DC: Government Printing Office.

U.S. Census Bureau (2008b). Income, Poverty, and Health Insurance Coverage in the United States: 2007. Washington, DC: Government Printing Office.

U.S. English (2008). About U. S. English. <http://us-english.org> (2008).

U.S. National Center for Health Statistics (2007, August 21). Health, United States 2006: National Vital Statistics Report. Atlanta, GA: Center for Disease Control.

Wirth, L. (1945). The Problem of Minority Groups. In R. Linton (Ed.), The Science of Man in the World Crisis. New York: Columbia University Press.

Wynes, C. E. (1988). Charles Richard Drew: The Man and the Myth. Chicago: The University of Illinois Press.

CHAPTER NINE

Inequality And Stratification By Gender And Age

Saadi N. Hassan

Social stratification is the process of ranking people according to the prestige or respect accorded to their social standing, the power they have to get others to do what they want, and their wealth, composed of material goods and resources. Social inequalities, including those based on gender and age, result from stratification. This chapter will cover the ways in which gender and age determine the roles that people are expected to fulfill in a society, depending on its stage of socio-economic development. We will look at gender and stratification, along with a number of inequality issues and a summary of how gender stratification is viewed by the sociological perspectives of functionalism, conflict, feminism, and interactionism. Age stratification is then discussed, along with an overview of the functionalist, conflict, and political viewpoints. The last section of the chapter provides a description of intersection theory.

Gender

George Murdock studied more than 200 preindustrial societies and found some global agreement on which tasks are considered feminine and which are considered masculine. He observed that hunting and warfare generally fell to men, while home-centered tasks like cooking and child care tended to fall into the category of women's work. This can be explained as a result of the simple technology used in these preindustrial societies, which assigned roles to suit the physical characteristics of men and women (Murdock, 1937). Before the Industrial Revolution, most of the tasks that needed physical effort outside the family home were performed by males. Females stayed at home, taking care of their children and doing other housekeeping tasks like cooking and cleaning. During the Industrial Revolution, men began to move to the cities to work in factories while women continued to take care of the home. This trend persisted until the beginning of the 20th century, when women in the Western world started working in factories and businesses in big cities in Europe and North America.

Gender refers to tasks and behaviors that people in a society consider to be either feminine or masculine. Gender is too variable from one culture to the next to be a simple expression of biology; it also reflects cultural values and the levels of technological development that prevail in a certain society during a specific time period. Therefore, we could say that gender is a social construct. Virtually all societies have established social distinctions between females and males. **Gender roles** are the expectations of a society regarding the proper behavior, attitudes, and activities of males and females. In most of the cultures around the world, males are expected to be ambitious and competitive; this encourages them to seek out positions involving leadership and teamwork. Females are seen as emotional and deferential; they are expected to take secondary roles that are supportive and helpful. These expectations are an important factor in determining which roles should be assigned to females and which ones to males in the stratification system. **Stratification** refers to the ranking of people in a society according to their wealth, prestige, and power.

Gender Stratification And Inequality

There are many factors that can affect social stratification and result in inequality, and these factors can change over time. This section describes some of these factors, including sexism and its role in stratification.

Peer Groups

Research shows that young children tend to form single-sex groups (Martin & Fabes, 2001). These peer groups can also teach lessons about gender. After spending a year watching children at play, Janet Lever (1978) concluded that boys favor team sports with complex rules and clear objectives, like scoring runs or touchdowns. Such games almost always involve winners and losers, reinforcing masculine traits of aggression and the desire for control. Lever added that girls tend to play team sports like hopscotch, jump rope, and dance activities which usually have few rules and where victory is rarely the ultimate goal. These tendencies indicate that girls are less competitive than boys.

Education

Gender shapes our interests and beliefs about our own abilities. It may also influence us to study certain subjects and, eventually, guide our career choices (Correll, 2001). In high schools and community colleges, more girls than boys take nursing and secretarial courses, while vocational classes in woodworking and auto mechanics attract mostly young men.

In the past, schooling was considered more necessary for men to enable them to work outside the home, but things have changed. By 1980, women were earning a majority of all associate's and bachelor's degrees, and in 2005, they received 60 percent of these degrees. In all areas of study, women earned 50 percent of all master's degrees and 48 percent of all doctorates in 2004, including 60 percent of all Ph.D. degrees in sociology. Women have also entered many graduate fields that used to be almost all male. In 1970, only a few hundred women received master of business administration (MBA) degrees, compared with more than 58,000 (42%) in 2004. Despite this progress in educational attainment for women, men still receive the majority of professional degrees. In 2004, men received 51 percent of the law degrees (LLB and JD) awarded,

54 percent of medical degrees (MD), and 58 percent of dental degrees (DDS and DMD) (National Center for Education Statistics, 2006).

Occupations And Income

In 1900, only 20 percent of women in the United States were in the labor force. This figure has nearly tripled (59%), with the majority (71%) of these women working full time. The once common view that earning an income is a man's role no longer holds true. The United States, along with most other developed nations of the world, now considers women working for income the rule, rather than the exception. Despite the increase in the number of women working outside the home, in the United States and around the world, taking care of the home and children is still considered to be "women's work." Though most men support the idea of women entering the paid labor force, and often count on the money women earn to balance the family budget, many of them still resist taking on an equal share of household duties (Heath & Bourne,

1995; Harpster & Monk-Turner, 1998; Stratton, 2001).

In the past, many younger women in the labor force were childless. This situation has changed, and among married women, 59 percent with children under age 6 are in the labor force, as are 76 percent of those with children between 6 and 17 years of age. As for widowed, divorced, and separated women, the figures for those working outside their homes are 74 percent of those with younger children, and 83 percent of those with older children (U.S. Census Bureau, 2006).

Though more women are now employed outside the home, the work performed by the two sexes remains very different. The U.S. Department of Labor (2006) reports a high concentration of women in two types of jobs. Administrative support work draws 22 percent of working women, most of whom are secretaries or other office workers. These are called *pink collar jobs* because 75 percent of them are filled by women. Another 20 percent of women are employed in service industries, including food

A woman waiting tables as a waitress.

Source: Patti Gray

service, child care, and health care. Most of these jobs tend to be at the low end of the pay scale, with limited opportunities for advancement, and male supervisors. In the field of education, women represent 98 percent of kindergarten teachers, 82 percent of elementary and middle school teachers, and 57 percent of high school educators in the United States. In higher education, 34 percent of professors in colleges and universities are women, and only 18 percent of college and university presidents (Chronicle of Higher Education, 2006; U.S. Department of Labor, 2006).

Men also dominate other job categories with higher salaries, making up 86 percent of physicians and surgeons and 63 percent of corporate managers. A recent survey shows that the top earners in Fortune 500 companies include 2,105 men (94%) and 145 women (6%). Just 17 of the 1,000 largest corporations in the United States have a woman as their chief executive (Catalyst, 2006; USDOL, 2006). In American society, high-paying professions—and the drive and competitiveness needed to succeed in them—are still defined as masculine.

Women have low representation not only in highly paid professional fields and large corporations, but also in some areas of politics. Women in the United States were legally barred from voting in national elections until the passage of the 19th Amendment to the Constitution in 1920. Today, thousands of women serve as mayors of cities and towns across the United States, and tens of thousands more hold responsible administrative jobs in the federal government. At the state level in 2006, 23 percent of state legislators were women, up from just 6 percent in 1970. In that same year, only 8 of the 50 state governors were women (16%) and women held 67 (15%) of the 435 seats in the House of Representatives and 14 of the 100 seats in the Senate (Center for American Women and Politics, 2006). Though women make up more than half of the world's population, they hold only 17 percent of the seats in the world's 185 parliaments, an increase of 3 percent from 50 years ago. Only in fourteen countries of the world, among them Sweden and Norway, do women represent more than one-third of the members of parliament (Inter-Parliamentary

A mother reading to her kids.

Source: Ned Horton

Union, 2006).

Many women, especially those who have young children, may be unable or unwilling to accept fast-paced jobs that tie up their evenings and weekends. To avoid role strain, they may take jobs that offer shorter commuting distances, flexible hours, and employer-provided child-care services. Women pursuing both a career and a family are torn between their dual responsibilities in ways that men are not. At age 40 in the United States, 90 percent of men in executive positions have at least one child, compared with only 35 percent of women (Schwartz, 1987).

Though having women in combat areas is still a controversial issue, women have served in the U.S. armed forces as far back as colonial times, though they may have signed up using male names. At the outset of World War II, only 2 percent of armed forces personnel were women. By the time of the war in Iraq in 2003, women represented almost 15 percent of all deployed U.S. troops, as well as 15 percent of all people serving in the armed forces. In the United States, almost all military assignments are now open to women. Some people support the move, stating that military women are better educated and score higher on intelligence tests than their male counterparts. Others object to opening doors in this way, claiming that women lack the physical strength of men. There are also people who argue that women are nurturers, giving life and helping others, which clashes with the image of women trained to kill.

Despite changes in the workplace, women still earn only 77 cents for every one dollar a working man earns. Median earnings for women working full time in 2005 were $31,858, while men working full time had median earnings of $41,386. Among full-time workers of all ages, 33 percent of women earned less than $25,000 in 2005, compared with 22 percent of male workers. At the upper end of the income scale, 19.3 percent of males made more than $75,000 annually, compared with only 8.3 percent of female workers (Census, 2006). This income inequality means that working women earn $1 billion less each year than men.

Not only do family responsibilities and the type of work affect the income of female workers, simply being a female is a factor (Fuller & Schoenberger, 1991). This barrier is described as a "glass ceiling" that stops qualified women from being promoted above middle management positions (Benokraitis & Feagin, 1995).

Mass Media

When television captured public attention in the 1950s, white males held center stage, and continued to do so until the early 1970s. Even then, men generally played the roles of brilliant detectives, fearless explorers, and skilled surgeons, while women played the less capable characters, often unnecessary except for the sexual interest they added to the show. Television advertisements are still apt to show

A model poses on the runway during a Christian Dior fashion show in Budapest, Hungary.　　　Source: Zsolt Dreher

women at home cheerfully using cleaning products, serving food, trying out new appliances, and modeling clothes. Men predominate in advertisements for cars, travel, banking services, manufacturing companies, and alcoholic beverages. A careful study of gender in advertising shows that men appear to be more competent and dominant, while women often appear childlike, submissive, or sexual (Goffman, 1979; Cortese, 1999).

Violence Against Women

The government estimates that 387,000 aggravated assaults against women occur annually. To this number we can add 177,000 rapes or sexual assaults and about 1.4 million simple assaults (U.S. Bureau of Justice Statistics, 2006). In regard to domestic violence in particular, it is estimated that only one of every three females who are abused by their husbands or boyfriends ever report it to the police.

The Role Of Sexism In Stratification

Men and women differ biologically in certain ways, but neither one is naturally superior. Cultures can define the two sexes differently, as demonstrated by Margaret Mead's research in Guinea (1935). Mead, an anthropologist, researched gender roles in New Guinea and Africa and found that in the mountainous home of the Arapesh, men and women had remarkably similar attitudes and behaviors. She found that both sexes were cooperative and sensitive to each other; there was no tendency for one sex to control the other. This is what can be described in our culture as a "pro-feminine" attitude. In the South of Guinea, Mead studied the Mundugumor, where she found a striking contrast to the gentle ways of the Arapesh. She found that both sexes were typically selfish and aggressive, traits defined by anthropologists and sociologists as masculine. Mead found that the Tchambuli, a third group, reversed many of the prevailing ideas of gender. Females were dominant and rational and males were submissive, emotional, and nurturing toward children.

Sexism refers to the belief that one sex is innately superior to the other. Such a belief is not just a matter of individual attitudes; it is built into the institutions of most societies, especially in developing countries where traditional values still play a vital role in the daily lives of the people. Such societies are often patriarchies, which are a form of social organization in which males dominate females. According to the United Nations gender development index, Norway, Australia, and Iceland give women the highest social standing; in contrast, women in the African nations of Niger, Burkina Faso, Mali, Sierra Leone, and Chad have the lowest social standing compared with men in those countries.

Males are dominant in the United States and just about everywhere else. In most Arab countries there is a clear distinction between what males are supposed to do in society and what females are supposed to do. Until the 1950s, the elementary (grade) schools were divided. Girls went to schools that had all female teachers and boys attended schools where the teachers were all males. Nowadays, most elementary schools in the Arab world have mixed pupils—boys and girls—and the majority of elementary teachers are female. Middle (intermediate) and high (secondary) schools, however, are divided for boys or girls only, and the majority of teachers in the girl's schools are females. As for higher education, colleges are open to both males and females, and the faculty members are also mixed.

Institutional sexism is found throughout the economies of most nations, with women highly concentrated in lower-paid, less prestigious jobs. Sexism limits the use of the talents and ambitions of women who make up half of the human population.

Perspectives On Gender Stratification

This section provides a brief explanation of how four major sociological perspectives—structural functionalism, symbolic interactionism, conflict, and feminist—explain gender stratification in modern and traditional societies.

Structural Functionalism

The structural functionalist approach, as presented by Talcott Parsons, deals with the issue of gender stratification from a macro-level perspective. Parsons (1955) described gender in terms of complementary patterns of behavior, masculine and feminine. This division of tasks gave men and women distinctive roles and responsibilities which help society operate smoothly. Gender builds social unity as men and women come together to form families and take care to help their children grow up according to the social norms of society. Parsons maintained, therefore, that gender differentiation contributes to overall social stability.

Parsons and Robert Bales, both sociologists, argued that to function effectively, families need adults who specialize in particular roles. They contended that women should take the expressive, emotionally supportive roles, and men the instrumental, practical roles, with the two complementing each other (Schaefer, 2008). According to Parsons, instrumentality emphasizes tasks, a focus on more distant goals, and a concern for the external relationship between one's family and other social institutions. Expressiveness refers to a concern for maintaining harmony and the internal emotional affairs of a family. According to this theory, women's interest in expressive goals frees men for the instrumental tasks outside the home and vice versa. Women stay at home to take care of the family as wives, mothers, and household managers; men go to the occupational world outside the home. This theory was developed in the 1950s, when many more women were full-time homemakers. It did not explicitly endorse traditional gender roles but implied that dividing tasks between spouses was functional for the family as a unit (Schaefer, 2008).

Symbolic Interactionism

The symbolic interactionist perspective takes the position that interactions between males and females perpetuate and support gender inequality. This occurs because when men and women interact, men are often the most dominant; they talk louder than women, they tend to interrupt women, they brag about themselves, and they take credit for the work of others. When women interact with men, on the other hand, they tend to speak softer and be more polite, which reinforces gender inequality. Because men are often more aggressive and forceful than women, they are more likely, as a group,

to be viewed as competent and knowledgeable, thus receiving promotions and increased earnings. Women are not as loud and tend to let men dominate conversations, so they are viewed as weak and less informed. As a result, they end up not being promoted, even though they may be more competent and valuable than the males being advanced (Thio, 2004).

Conflict

The social conflict approach also deals with the issue of gender from a macro-level perspective. This viewpoint is based on the work of Frederick Engels, who described gender in terms of the power of one sex (male) over the other (female). The conflict perspective sees gender stratification as harmful to society as a whole because it is divisive and it limits a person's development. They further this argument by saying that gender stratification gives men the power to control the lives of women, and that the capitalist system makes patriarchy stronger. This argument has lost credibility in modern developed societies where many women are holding key positions.

Feminist

The feminist perspective agrees with the argument presented by the conflict sociologists, but adds that society should adopt policies that will provide females with equal opportunities to develop their potential and obtain the positions for which they are qualified. While this approach appears to be fair and beneficial, we need to remember that some traditional societies where religious beliefs play an important role, such as Saudi Arabia, the United Arab Emirates, Kuwait, and Iran, are not yet ready to see females holding key positions, especially in judicial and other government systems. However, many women are found working in educational and health care organizations.

Those people who support a socialist-feminist perspective want to put an end to social classes and to family gender roles that encourage males to treat women as domestic slaves. This can be achieved through a socialist revolution. Radical sociologists call for an end to the family system, which means that they want to eliminate gender itself.

Age

Ageism is prejudice and discrimination against people based on their age and is most often used in reference to older individuals. It involves not just negative stereotypes, but also discrimination in employment opportunities. Elderly people do not have the same opportunities for employment because employers look for members of younger generations, whom they consider to be healthier and more acquainted with new technological developments.

The combination of age and gender stratification can be disadvantageous in the workplace, resulting in discrimination. The double jeopardy hypothesis argues that the combined negative effects of occupying two stigmatized statuses, in this case being elderly and female, are greater than occupying either status alone.

Perspectives On Age Stratification

This section offers a brief explanation of how the structural functionalist, symbolic interactionist, and conflict perspectives explain age stratification, followed by political viewpoints on the topic.

Structural Functionalist

Advocates of the functionalist perspective claim that social positions should be filled by qualified persons. However, they argue that once a person's qualifications become obsolete, new and better-qualified people should fill their jobs. Critics argue that this approach is harmful to the interests of thousands of the older employees whose jobs might be at risk. It might also encourage employers to seek to maximize their profits by replacing higher paid employees who have been with them longer with new recruits who are younger and do not expect the same wages.

A woman cooks a meal for her family.   Source: Stefanie L.

Symbolic Interactionist

The interactionist perspective follows an approach based on the participation of people, each according to his or her qualifications irrespective of age, to meet the social services needed by society. As children, we learn negative images of older people, such as they move too slowly, they forget things, and they are grouchy. Those images are then carried into adulthood. When faced with hiring or promotion decisions, those negative images can cause a person to choose a younger employee over one who is older.

Conflict

Sociologists that support the conflict perspective believe that employers always seek to maximize their profits at the expense of others. Therefore, they tend to replace older personnel with younger people who are paid less. Employers also tend to use new technology to replace human workers, reducing the number of human workers to cut the cost of production over the long term.

Political Viewpoints On Age

In the United States, conservatives may assert that although some seniors are poor, overall, elders are more prosperous and live longer than they did in the past. Conservatives believe that a culture of self-reliance encourages people to provide for their own needs throughout their lives. Additionally, when help is needed to support elder members, it should be provided by families, friends, and charitable organizations. Government programs should be a last resort.

Liberals contend that elders face a higher risk of poverty as a result of prejudice and discrimination based on their age. This prejudice would become worse in combination with other disadvantages such as those based on race, ethnicity, and gender. They argue that age discrimination is only one dimension of the social inequality caused by the capitalist economy of the United States.

Radical leftists argue that age stratification is one aspect of the striking social inequality caused by the

An elderly woman on a walk.

Source: Morgue File

capitalist economy in the United States, which seeks to maximize the profits of capitalist owners. Leftists call for replacing the capitalist economy with a socialist system to end the exploitation of the workers and to stop the practice of devaluing less productive people as they grow older in society. According to this group, the government must provide for the needs of its people at all ages.

Intersection Theory

The **intersection theory** refers to the interplay of potentially stigmatized statuses—such as gender, age, class status, race, and ethnicity—that can result in multiple disadvantages for a person. Research has shown that disadvantages linked to gender, age, and race often combine to produce low social standing for females.

Income comparisons illustrate the truth of the intersection theory. In 2005, the median income for African-American women working full time was $30,363, which was 15 percent less than the $35,797 earned by non-Hispanic white women. Hispanic women earned $25,022, or only 70 percent as much as their white counterparts. Looking at the impact of gender, African-American women earned 89 percent as much as African American men, and Hispanic women earned 93 percent as much as Hispanic men. Combining these disadvantages, African American women earned 63 percent as much as non-Hispanic white men earned, and Hispanic women earned 52 percent as much as white men (Census, 2006). These figures reflect minority women's lower positions in the occupational and educational hierarchies, confirming that although gender has a powerful effect on our lives, it does not operate alone. In a multi-layered system, class position, race, ethnicity, gender, and sexual orientation provide disadvantages for some and privileges for others (St. Jean & Fagin, 1998).

Summary

If we examine the stratification processes in most societies, we see that no single approach explains the resulting inequalities. It is a combination of both traditional and modern approaches that lead to inequalities in various societies. However, the major sociological perspectives agree that stratification leads to inequality among people based on gender and age, as well as other factors like class status, race, and ethnicity.

Gender stratification in the United States is easy to see in everyday life. Female nurses assist male physicians, female assistants serve male executives, and female flight attendants are under the command of male airline pilots. In any field, the greater a job's income and prestige, the more likely it is held by a man (Macionis, 2007).

Sexism is the belief that one sex is better than the other, and is a major factor in gender stratification. A man can be sexist if he believes that men are better than women not only in the workplace, but also in other aspects or activities of life. A woman can be sexist if she believes that women in general are better than men in many aspects of life. Unfortunately, sexism still prevails in most nations because many people believe that men are better workers and more responsible than women. This belief is widespread in third world—developing—countries, where men control most of the important positions in society; not only are they the masters at home, they are also the bosses and presidents of most workplaces, including government institutions, in the United States, Europe, and, of course, less-developed countries in Africa, the Middle East, and Asia.

The aging process is another problem facing modern societies looking for younger generations to provide newly learned skills. While it may be true that many younger people have more up-to-date skills in modern technology, elder workers have the skills and experience that enable them to deal with problems at work that younger workers may find difficult to resolve.

Finally, statuses like gender and age, race, and ethnicity, can play a negative role in the process of employing and promoting an individual in the workplace. Both the double jeopardy and intersection theories state that stigmatized statuses can combine to create even greater disadvantages for females and minorities in the workplace.

Review/Discussion Questions

1. What are gender roles?
2. What are pink-collar jobs?
3. What is ageism?
4. What is the intersection theory?
5. Have you ever broken gender roles? How did it make you feel? How did others view you?
6. Have you ever witnessed an example of ageism? What happened? How did it make you feel?
7. When it comes to political viewpoints on age, which ideology do you most agree with and why?

Key Terms

Ageism is prejudice or discrimination against people based on their age.

Gender refers to what people in a society consider to be either feminine or masculine.

Gender roles are expectations regarding proper behavior, attitudes, and activities for males and females.

Intersection theory refers to the interplay of race, class, and gender, often resulting in multiple dimensions of disadvantages for the female who is of a different race.

Sexism refers to the belief that one sex is innately superior to the other.

Stratification is the ranking of people in a society according to the amount of wealth they own, the prestige the society gives to their social positions, and the power they have to control other members of the society.

Bibliography

Arrighi, B. A. (Ed.). (2001). Understanding Inequality: The Intersection of Race/Ethnicity, Class and Gender. Lanham, MD: Rowman & Littlefield Publishers.

Ballantine, J. H., & Roberts, K. A. (2009). Our Social World: An Introduction to Sociology (2nd ed.). Thousand Oaks, CA: Pine Forge Press.

Benokraitis, N. V., & Feagin, J. R. (1995). Modern Sexism: blatant, subtle, and covert discrimination. Englewood Cliffs, NJ: Prentice Hall.

Catalyst, Inc. (2006). Catalyst Census of the Fortune 500. <http://www.catalyst.org> (2008).

Center for American Women and Politics. (2006). Women in Elective Office. <http://www.cawp.rutgers.edu> (2008).

Chronicle of Higher Education. (2006). <http://www.chronicle.com> (2008).

Correll, S. J. (2001). Gender and the career choice process: the role of biased self-assessments. American Journal of Sociology, 106 (6), 1691-1730.

Cortese, A. (1999). Provocateur: Images of Women and Minorities in Advertising. Lanham, MD: Rowman & Littlefield Publishers.

Fuller, M. (1999). Woman in the Nineteenth Century. Mineola, NY: Dover Publications.

Fuller, R., & Schoenberger, R. (1991). The Gender Salary Gap: Do Academic Achievement, Internship Experience, and College Major Make a Difference? Social Science Quarterly, 72 (4), 715-726.

Goffman, E. (1979). Gender Advertisements. New York: Harper & Row.

Harpster P., & Monk-Turner, E. (1998). Why Men Do Housework? A Test of Gender Production and the Relative Resource Model. Sociological Focus, 31 (1), 45-59.

Heath, J., & Bourne, D. (1995). Husbands and Housework; Parity or Parody? Social Science Quarterly, 76 (1), 195-202.

Inter-Parliamentary Union. (2006). <www.ipu.org> (2008).

Lever, J. (1978). Sex Differences in the Complexity of Children's Play and Games. American Sociological Review, 43 (4), 471-483.

Macionis, J. J. (2005). Sociology (10th ed.). Upper Saddle River, NJ: Prentice Hall.

Macionis, J. J. (2007) Social Problems (3rd ed.). Upper Saddle River, NJ: Prentice Hall.

Martin, C. L., & Fabes, R. A. (2001). The Stability and Consequences of Same-sex Peer Interactions. Developmental Psychology, 37 (3), 431-446.

Mead, M. (1935). Sex and Temperament: In Three Primitive Societies. New York: W. Morrow & Co.

Murdock, G. (1937). Comparative Data on the Division of Labor by Sex. Social Forces, 15, 551-553.

National Center for Education Statistics. (2006). <www.nces.ed.gov> (2008).

Parsons, T., & Bales, R. F. (1955). Family Socialization and Interaction Process. Glencoe, IL: Free Press.

Schaefer, R. T. (2008). Sociology: A Brief Introduction. Boston: McGraw-Hill.

Schwartz, M. D. (1987). Gender and Injury in Spousal Assault. Sociological Focus, 20 (1), 61-75.

Spears, G., & Seydegart, K. (1993). Gender Violence in the Mass Media (Report Prepared for the Family Violence Prevention Unit, Health Canada). Erin, Ontario: Health Canada.

Stapinski, H. (1998, November 1). Let's Talk Dirty. American Demographics, 50-56.

St. Jean, Y., & Feagin, J. R. (1998). Double Burden: Black Women and Everyday Racism. Armonk, NY: M.E. Sharpe.

Stratton, L. S. (2001). Why Does More Housework Lower Women's Wages; Testing Hypothesis Involving Job Effort and Hour Flexibility. Social Science Quarterly, 82 (1), 67-76.

Thio, A. (2005). Sociology: A Brief Introduction (6th ed.). Boston, MA: Pearson/Allyn and Bacon.

U.S. Bureau of Justice Statistics. (2006). <www.usdoj.gov> (2008).

U.S. Census Bureau. (2006). <www.census.gov> (2008).

U.S. Department of Labor. (2006). <www.dol.gov> (2008).

CHAPTER TEN

Families

Cheryl Boudreaux

I t is highly unusual to meet someone who does not have a family. That is because society considers family a birthright. The group of people we are born into is our family. Our first and most intimate social contact is with the family. In the 2000 census count, there were 33.7 million households (31% of the 105.5 million households in the United States) living in "**nonfamily households**," a census designation for people living together who are not related to the householder by birth, marriage, or adoption. If you live with roommates or an unmarried partner, for example, you count as a nonfamily household (Suchan et al., 2007).

Sociologists understand the family as a basic social institution or building block of society. The family is a *universal social institution*, meaning that it is a patterned way of solving problems and needs that exists in all societies. The family is our most important social institution. We begin life as part of a family. We are socialized in, and come to understand who we are and our place in society, as part of a family. When we are sick and dying, it is the responsibility of the family to take care of us. When we are dead, it is the family's responsibility to dispose of the body.

Which Of The Examples Listed Below Are Families?

- A mother and her child, living with the mother's partner whom the child calls "mommy."
- An unmarried man and woman.
- A grandfather and his two grandchildren.
- A married couple with no children.
- Two men who were married in Canada.
- A single woman and her child.
- A group of young adults that bought a house together and share the bills.
- A woman with her mother and her children.

Defining the family is not a simple task. The U.S. Census Bureau must have a legal definition of family to use when conducting its counts of the population in the United States. These counts are completed on a decennial basis, meaning that they occur once a decade, and the information is used to distribute scarce resources to families, as well as to inform the public about the state of the American family. The U.S. Census definition of **family** is "a group of two or more people who reside together and who are related by birth, marriage, or adoption" (Suchan et al., 2007).

While individuals may live with others in a household not related by birth, marriage, or adoption, for legal purposes, they are not considered a family even if they treat each other as family and think of each other as family. The Census Bureau distinguishes between a family and a household. According to the Census Bureau, a **household** "includes all the people who occupy a housing unit as their usual place of residence" (U.S. Census Bureau, 2003). You can therefore live together in a household, but not be considered a family. By using this distinction, the federal government defines *kinship*, or relatives, not just in the present, but for past and future generations. Definitions of family and kinship present obvious problems for the sociologist or anthropologist studying the family not only in America, where individuals may experience and define their families in ways different from the official census definition, but in other parts of the world as well.

The distinction between families and households raises a number of issues for groups that feel discriminated against when they are left out of programs and services targeted at helping families in need. These groups include gay and lesbian couples living in states that do not recognize their right to marry, heterosexual and homosexual cohabitating couples, and children living with adults not related by blood, marriage, or adoption. In Census 2000, cohabiting heterosexual households represented 4.3 percent of all households. Families come in many forms, and different societies recognize different forms as legitimate family.

Family Forms

Although the family is nearly universal, existing in all societies throughout history, it exists in many different forms. It can exist as a **matrilineal descent** system, tracing descent through the mother's line, a **patrilineal descent** system, tracing the descent through the father's line, or a **bilateral descent** system, tracing the line of descent through both the mother's and the father's families. In the United States, the family line of descent is patrilineal, illustrated by the fact that in most cases the child is given the father's last name at birth.

Families can be **consanguine families**, meaning they are formed and recognized through blood ties, or they can be **conjugal families**, meaning they are formed and recognized through the mating of a couple. When the family is formed through consanguine ties, it is usually an **extended family** including aunts, uncles, grandparents, and other blood ties. This is an important distinction from the conjugal family, which is usually a **nuclear family**, composed of two adults and their children, if they have any. While the extended family is inherited, the nuclear family is usually formed through marriage. According to Census 2000, 3.5 percent of all households were **multigenerational family** households, consisting of more than two generations living together as a family.

Patriarchy means "rule of the father" and is usually associated with **patrilocal residence**, which is the man's family residence. In a patriarchal family, the father is head of the household. **Matriarchy** means "rule of the mother" and is usually associated with **matrilocal** residence. In a matriarchal family, the mother is the head of the household. In a **matrilocal residence**, married couples live with the woman's family. There are families that have matrilineal descent systems and matrilocal residence patterns that are patriarchal. In these cases, the person considered the father might not be the biological father, but rather the mother's brother or some other man in her family of origin. In America, which is primarily patriarchal and patrilineal, young couples are more **neolocal**, meaning that they leave their parent residence and find one of their own. Young married couples living on their own in a sense have two families. The one they grew up in, their **family of orientation** made up of their parents and siblings, and their **family of procreation** made up of the spouse and the couple's children.

An Inclusive Definition Of The Family

Variations found in different parts of the world can make it difficult to study the family. In order to do a systematic study of the family, we need to have a definition that allows us to recognize family in whatever form we find it. In the United States, the family is legally defined as a household related by blood, marriage, or adoption, a definition that has been challenged because it is not inclusive of all households that consider themselves family. Researchers need a more inclusive definition of family that does not rely on blood ties, marriage, or adoption alone. Anthropologist George Murdock (1949), studying families in more than 250 different societies, developed a functional definition of the family as a social group characterized by a common residence, reproduction, and economic cooperation. Using his definition, we can observe who performs certain functions, and there we would find the family, no matter which society we are studying.

Theory And Research: Strategies For Understanding The Family

There are many theories or perspectives for understanding the family. The different views and perspectives are used somewhat like the lens of a camera. When we change the lens, we have a different focus that allows us to perceive different parts of the picture. Each theory provides a different view of what family life means at the micro or macro level. Three of those lenses or perspectives are structural functionalist, conflict, and symbolic interactionist.

Structural Functionalist Perspective

Structural functionalists look for persistent patterns in society and view them as serving a positive role or function in the maintenance of the society as a whole. The family is one such pattern that serves

certain functions in nearly all societies throughout history. From the functionalist perspective, if a function is being met in other ways, a particular pattern is no longer needed to serve its function, and that pattern will cease to exist. This leads some to conclude that the family is in danger of ceasing to exist, since professionals are paid to perform many of its most basic functions like child care, housekeeping, and education. The functionalist perspective defines the family in terms of the vital functions it serves to the individual and the society. The family functions as an institution to reproduce and maintain the society through: the reproduction and socialization of children, the passing on of rules and social status, and the provision of economic and emotional support (Eshleman, 2003; Ogburn, 1938; Murdock, 1949).

Major functions of the family include: reproduction of children, nurturing and socialization of children, emotional and economic support of its members, and sexual rules and regulations.

Reproduction and the *nurturing* and *socialization of children* are universal functions necessary for the reproduction of the family and the whole society. It is the family's responsibility to help children become good citizens in the society to which they are born.

The family is responsible for the passing on of *ascribed* or *inherited status*, including race, ethnicity, social class, and religion.

As an *economic unit,* the family must cooperate to provide for food, clothing, and shelter for its members. The family also functions to prescribe the division of labor within the family, making sure that all of the necessary tasks, such as making money, housecleaning, cooking, and laundry, get accomplished. Labor, as well as authority, in the family is divided by age and sex.

Sexual rules and regulations, taboos, are present in every society, although not every society has the same incest taboos. The family makes the distinction between kin and non-kin teaching us which individuals are off-limits for marriage and sexual relationships. In some societies it might be permissible, and even encouraged, to marry cousins, while in others it is completely taboo. A society's definition of family specifies who will be considered close relatives, and therefore off-limits.

Conflict Perspective

Conflict perspective as it relates to families suggests that our family forms develop because of the particular mode of production, or economic system, of a society. The United States has a capitalist society in which investors, workers, and consumers are important. A family in a capitalist society produces good workers trained to consume, and investors with capital ready to invest in order to produce more. Nuclear families produce more consumption and, ideally, more savings for investment. Power struggles in a capitalist society involve inequality and the division of resources perceived to be scarce.

From a conflict perspective, it is the power relationships between different groups in society, including families, that are important. Power in the society is divided by class, race, gender, and age.

Building on the conflict perspective, the feminist perspective turns our attention to gender and the inequality between men and women. An important institution in society, the family maintains and perpetuates the inequalities between men and women. The United States, along with most cultures in the world, is a **patriarchal society** where men are dominant and social institutions are set up to sustain a system of male rule. The feminist and conflict perspectives look at the division of labor both within the family and within the larger society. Within the household, women do a full extra month of work a year more than men; in society, women are still paid less than men for the same work. Arlie Hochschild (1989) calls this extra unpaid labor of women the *second shift*, representing a "leisure gap" between men and women, and illustrating the gendered unequal division of unpaid labor in the family.

An expecting couple plays with their daughter.

Source: Simona Balint

Symbolic Interactionist Perspective

Symbolic interactionism focuses on the signs and symbols that are used to construct reality. The structural functionalist perspective and conflict feminist perspectives are both macro-level perspectives that sociologists use to get a broader view. In these perspectives, the focus is on the family as an institution in the larger society. The lens is wider and we take into account the harmony or disharmony of the institutions in society.

The symbolic interactionist perspective is a micro-level perspective that focuses more closely, paying attention to symbols and their meaning created in social interaction with others. These symbols include language, gestures, body language, role making, and role taking in everyday interactions between the individual, the family, and the society. In this perspective, the formation of individual identity is important, as well as the role of the individual in the social construction of reality. The dramaturgical perspective described by Max Weber (1864-1920), George Herbert Mead (1863-1931), and Erving Goffman (1922-1982), reflects aspects of symbolic interactionism. The dramaturgical perspective examines the context of human behavior, rather than the cause, because a person's actions are dependent on time, place, and audience.

Introducing A Family Life Cycle Or Development Perspective

A family life cycle looks at the roles, problems and issues of families over the course of a lifetime. It relies on an expectation that there are major life events or stages that all families go through. Major life events include: dating, marrying, becoming parents, having children leave home (empty nest), taking care of elderly parents, and losing a partner. By looking at a family in a particular stage of this life cycle, we can spot common problems and issues. This perspective is criticized because not all families or individuals go through the same life events in the same order. For example, a single mother would not yet have faced the issues of marriage or empty nest.

Dating And Mate Selection

Almost everyone expects to, and does, marry at some point in their life. Marriage is such a strong social expectation that those who do not marry are more likely to have their motivations questioned than those who do. In many societies, and in most of human history, parents or matchmakers **arrange marriage**. In the United States, and increasingly the rest of the modern world, individuals are expected to make a *love match*, which puts the pressure on the individual to find his or her soul mate. That choice, however, feels more individual than it really is.

Turning our attention to the patterns of mate selection, we can see that we are guided by social rules to fall in love with, and marry, the appropriate person. In the United States, most people fall in love with, and marry, someone similar to themselves. Through socialization and nurturing, we have, in a sense, been programmed to fall in love with those within our group. This practice is known as **homogamy**. We tend to fall in love with and marry someone like us in race, class, education, religion, age, and *propinquity* or geographic region. Marrying someone within one's social and economic group is known as **endogamy**. Homogamy the opposite of **heterogamy**, which is the practice of choosing someone different than one's self. Those who select mates that come from different regions, or from other social and economic categories, can be said to practice **exogamy**.

Marriage: The Social Institution

Marriage is seen as an essential right all over the world. According to the Universal Declaration of Human Rights adopted by the United Nations (1948):

> Men and women of full age, without any limitation due to race, nationality or religion, have the right to marry and to form a family. They are entitled to equal rights as to marriage, during marriage and at its dissolution. Marriage shall be entered into only with the free and full consent of the intending spouses. The family is the natural and fundamental group unit of society and is entitled to protection by society and the State (Article 16).

Dating couple.

Source: John De Boer

Marriage is an important part of the formation and maintenance of the family as a basic social institution. The form of marriage tends to fit with the particular society where you find it. Forms of marriage include: **polygyny**—when a husband is allowed to have more than one wife and historically the most common form of marriage, **polyandry**—allowing a woman to have more than one husband at a time, **polygamy**—having more than one mate, **monogamy**—allowing for only one mate at a time, or **serial monogamy**—cycles of divorce and remarriage in which the person becomes less capable each time of making a permanent commitment. Many sociologists claim that the modern marriage arrangement has become one of serial monogamy as evidenced by the high divorce rate and the individual pursuit of satisfaction and personal growth over self-sacrifice for the good of the family (Cherlin, 1978; Furstenberg, 1980; Giddens, 1992).

The *marriage premise* is one of *sexual exclusivity*, which is to have only one sexual partner who is primary in a person's life, and *permanence*, the expectation that the relationship will last a lifetime. The premise supports long-lasting happy relationships, allowing for trust and the growth of intimacy. In modern society, more and more people are marrying and hoping for the ideals of sexual exclusivity and permanence, while being less able to believe in them. The divorce rate and the rate of affairs began to increase in the 1970s, and has remained high since then, leading some theorists to suggest that marriage may be in decline and, thus, less important as a social institution than it once was. Although we continue to marry, and married individuals report being happy more often than single individuals, we are less and less likely to stay together or to remain sexually faithful to our partners.

Just married.

Parenting

Fertility rates are not consistent over time but fluctuate within the social economic and historical context. They are lower than they were in the 1950s, but higher than they were in the 1970s, and currently hover around two children per woman in the United States. Perhaps this low fertility rate is due to the fact that more women are delaying having children in order to start their education and careers. Children are expensive and time-consuming, and can strain a couple's relationship. For working women, children also represent an *opportunity cost*, the value of the next-best alternative that will be forgone as a result of choosing to have a child. Even so, the average person in the United States still wants to have two children.

Children are no longer the assets that they were in preindustrial society when they could work and contribute to the family. Children are, however, seen as an important part of creating a family and living the American Dream. Having children means sharing a special kind of love and creating an environment similar to our *family of orientation*, the one we grew up in, passing on those customs that we inherited from our families. Children today are an emotional asset, rather than an economic one. Increasingly, men and women are making the decision to remain child-free.

Social programs and public policy have an effect on the fertility rate, depending on whether the society is *pro-natal*, encouraging and supporting the reproduction, nurturing and socialization of children, or *anti-natal*, putting up road blocks which make it more difficult for people who choose to parent. The pervasive assumption that everyone will have children and the need to explain a decision not to have children is pro-natal. Social programs, tax breaks, and child care that aid working parents in

A mother and daughter.

Source: Anissa Thompson

doing the work of parenting are all pro-natal. Isolating women who have children, denying parental leave from work, and cutting programs and services to families with children are anti-natal. A society can have features of both.

Three Parenting Styles

Theory and research suggest that parenting styles can have a dramatic effect on a child's grades, behavior, tendency toward substance abuse, and chances of success in life. Children have a greater chance of success if their parents are consistent, and monitor their children's activity, and discipline to train, rather than to punish. Three basic parenting styles discussed are authoritarian, permissive, and authoritative (Baumrind, 1991; Clark, 1983; Dornbusch, et al., 1987; Steinberg, et al., 1989).

Authoritarian Parenting Style

For the authoritarian parent, the child is like a lump of clay to be molded and shaped into a good citizen; a child's success or failure is seen as a reflection of the parent's ability to control that child's behavior. The parent controls the child's behavior with little emotion or explanation. The child is told to "do it because I say so" or face punishment. This parenting style is described as "demanding and directive, but not responsive" (Baumrind, 1991, p. 62).

Permissive Parenting Style

The permissive, or non-directional, parent's goal is to manipulate the child into thinking that he should behave a certain way because he wants to, because it is good for him. This parent does a lot of talking, answering the "why" questions with "because it is the right thing to do" and explaining for as long as it takes. This parent leans heavily on the child's ability to make decisions for him/herself. This parent is more "responsive than they are demanding" (Baumrind, 1991, p. 63).

Authoritative Parenting Style

Most experts agree that the authoritative parenting style facilitates success in children. It involves fewer rules, with strict adherence to those rules. This style is thought to give the child more autonomy. Parents using this style are "both demanding and responsive," wanting their children to follow the rules and be able to assert themselves and their own ideas as well. "Children from authoritative homes have consistently been found to be more instrumentally competent – agentic, communal, and cognitively competent – than other children" (Baumrind, 1991, p. 63).

Empty nest is a term used to describe the reorientation that takes place after eighteen years of parenting. This reorientation happens when parents have spent eighteen or more years raising their children, who then go off to college and start their lives as adults. As parents of adults, they then have to find a new focus and find out who they are without their children. If married, they need to reintroduce themselves to each other as individuals and as part of a couple. This can be a difficult but necessary transition.

With new technology and improvements in medicine, people are living longer, giving rise to the *Sandwich Generation* where young couples spend their time raising children and taking care of aging parents. Often, these couples do not get the luxury of the empty nest because they are sandwiched between the younger and older generations.

There is also emerging evidence that more and more adult children return home after college, so that we now have more *intergenerational households*. This number is expected to grow in the future as people wait later and later to marry (Messineo, 2005).

The Single Life

According to the U.S. Census, since 1950 there has been a continual decline in married-couple households. In 1950, one-person households represented 9.5 percent of the households counted, while in 2000, one-person households represented 26 percent of the population (Census, 2003).

In the age of "Sex and the City," a popular cable television show and movie about four single girls and their exploits in New York, being single no longer bears the stigma that it once did. Today's non-married couples are seeking satisfaction from other life experiences. They are "reworking those norms and inventing alternatives. Some strategies included having 'emotional monogamy' but not sexual monogamy; refusing to cohabit; maintaining long-distance-partner relationships; and focusing on strong ties with friends" (Budgeon, 2008, p. 319). They don't need to be married to be happy and respected by their peers (Giddens, 1992).

Some people choose to be single. Other people remain single because they never find a partner with whom they can trust their future selves. Others are single because their partner left or died. Those people who choose a single lifestyle are happier than those who look back and realize that they have lived a single lifestyle, but not by choice. Most happy singles have satisfying careers and good social networks.

Cohabitation

Cohabitation, or "living together," might be more of an emerging lifestyle than a substitute for marriage. According to Brown (2008), cohabiters are most likely to have the lowest socioeconomic status, which suggests that they may not feel their economic status is sufficient to justify marriage. Cohabiters do raise children and do not feel the need to marry because of pregnancy as in previous generations. We may see a developing trend of intergenerational cohabitation, since 40 percent of children are expected to spend some time in a cohabitating household. Just as living single has become an acceptable life choice, cohabitation is a lifestyle that has steadily increased since the 1970s. Cohabitation does not necessarily lead to marriage, especially among blacks and Hispanics (Brown, 2008; Bumpass, 2000).

Same sex or gay and lesbian couples form households and live together in most counties within the United States. Almost one-quarter of the gay male households, and one-third of the lesbian households, are raising children. These are committed relationships that are more similar to married heterosexual relationships than they are to cohabiting heterosexuals. The children of gay and lesbian parents do not have different outcomes than children raised by heterosexual parents, and they are not more likely to be homosexual themselves. Overall, "children raised in same-sex environments show no differences in cognitive abilities, behavior, general emotional development, or such specific areas of emotional development as self-esteem, depression, or anxiety" (Meezan, 2005, p. 103). Further, one study showed that preschool children raised by lesbians were less aggressive, bossy, and domineering than children with heterosexual mothers (Meezan, 2005).

The Socially Diverse American Family

America is a pluralistic, culturally diverse nation. All American families share in the larger American culture. Americans of all ethnicities are more like each other than they are like individuals from other cultures. The continually negotiated, changing American dream includes the romance of a white wedding, two kids, a house, a middle-class job, and two or more cars.

American culture includes the more static features of patriarchy, heterosexism, white privilege, and individualism. America is also a culture made up of subcultures. While we share the larger culture, which includes much of our lifestyles, eating habits, education, and national identity, we also each inhabit sub cultural identities that are important and meaningful to us.

Many people think of race as the source of our diversity; however, there is no objective biological fact of race, and cultural diversity is not based on a biological fact of race. The socially agreed upon perception of race is just as important, though. Racial discrimination and prejudice do exist. Early

studies of the black family, for example, contrasted black and white families and expected to, and did, find differences, which were seen as pathological compared with the white middle class family (Glazer, 1963). Black children were seen as coming from a culturally disadvantaged background. This influenced social policy and programs aimed at helping black children transcend their culturally impoverished backgrounds. In reality, both black and white children in poverty experience similar kinds of problems, issues, and coping mechanisms.

Belief in race and racial differences influences our families and our social policies. Although there is as yet no scientific evidence for the existence of race as a biological fact, race is a very important concept for social scientists looking to explain family experience and social status in the United States. Social scientists tend to focus on class and ethnicity, which is based on cultural tradition, experience, and identity, when looking at diversity. Families are more alike based on class than on race.

The majority of families in America are non-Hispanic white or European-American. In the 2000 census, the non-Hispanic white population represented 69.1 percent of the population, and if you include white Hispanics, the white population represented 75.1 percent of the population. The black, or African-American, population represented 12.3 percent of the population. In 2000, other large and growing racial groups in America included: Asian, 3.6 percent; American-Indian and Alaska native, 0.9 percent; and native Hawaiian and other Pacific Islander, 0.1 percent. The Hispanic population in America was seen as a language ethnicity rather than a race, and so could self-classify as any race. The perception of race in America affects a family's experiences and opportunities and its sub cultural participation. America is still segregated in terms of neighborhoods, religions, churches, and schools, not because of laws, but because of choices, economic opportunities or lack thereof, preferences, privileges, and prejudices.

Most of us associate class with income, and there is a relationship between the two; however, sociologists attribute much broader meaning to class. *Social class* represents opportunity, income, education, values, beliefs, preferences, and even family size. Whether a child is born into a working-class family or a middle-class family will greatly influence every aspect of that child's life. Parenting styles may also be related to class. The schools, churches and social programs available to any child will be different according to his or her social class.

Divorce

The divorce rate in the United States reached an all-time high in 1979 and then began to level off, so that now about 40 to 50 percent of new marriages are likely to end in divorce. Arlene Skolnick (1997) discusses the contradictory views of "Middletown" Americans on the question of divorce. We believe in marriage as a forever proposition, so we oppose divorce. We believe that no one should have to stay in a loveless or abusive marriage, so our pragmatic side recognizes the necessity of divorce. Louisiana, Arizona, and Arkansas have enacted *covenant marriage*, which is a marriage contract that is much more difficult to dissolve than the regular marriage contract. This kind of contract is very similar to marriage before the advent of no-fault divorce; at that time, couples had to have concrete evidence to prove adultery or physical abuse before a divorce would be granted. Since most people today agree that there are situations where divorce is the preferred outcome of a marriage gone wrong, covenant marriages do not seem to be the solution to the high divorce rate. Rather, we might do better to direct our energy at some of the problems that cause people to have troubled marriages. Some of these problems are related to poverty, inequality, poor conflict resolution skills, and unrealistic expectations. Many of these problems can be helped with education. As the Middletown families in Skolnick's study suggest, divorce is a remedy. If we find other remedies to these problems, divorce will cease to be functional and rates will decrease.

Remarriage

Many Americans remarry or cohabit after a divorce, forming stepfamilies. Individuals with children are less likely to remarry, and remarriages are more likely to end in divorce. Goldscheider and Sassler (2006) found that "being a co-resident father dramatically increases forming a union with a woman with children. Women's co-residential children reduce women's odds of forming unions with men who do not have children and increase them for unions with men who do" (p. 275). Overall, women have a more difficult time and are less likely than men to remarry when they have children.

Social Problems, Change, And Justice

The baby boom generation has begun to retire, and it is the largest cohort to retire since the Social Security Administration was established in 1935. This group is expected to live longer because of technology, improved health care, and a better standard of living than any other group to grow old in American history. We worry that this group will put an unprecedented strain on family resources. Social policy regarding retirement has already begun to change, expecting people to work longer and longer before retirement. Indeed, many worry that retirement will no longer be an option for many Americans.

With all of the support, joy, and love associated with the family, it is important to remember that it can also be a source of great pain for its members. The Bureau of Justice Statistics reports that although the rate of intimate-partner violence has fallen, it is still too high: "1,247 women and 440 men were killed by an intimate partner in 2000. In recent years an intimate killed about 33% of female murder victims and 4% of male murder victims" (Rennison, 2003).

In addition to intimate-partner violence, the family is host to many other social problems including child abuse, neglect, divorce, extramarital affairs, single parenthood, poverty, and the feminization of poverty, making the family a good place to direct our attention for social change.

The family can be a force for change through nurturing and socialization. With the support of positive social policy, families can lower the incidence of violence, rape, incest, alcoholism, homophobia, racism, and sexism in society.

Problems faced by today's families lead many experts to believe that the family is becoming an institution in decline. Other experts argue that the family is not in decline; rather, the modern family is described as changing to meet the demands of modern society. The concept of the family is changing. The family has existed throughout human history, and it is an essential part of the human journey. The family as a social institution has ensured that young adults find appropriate mates, children are nurtured and properly socialized, the elderly are cared for, and the dead are buried, while important customs and traditions are passed from one generation to the other. The family is not a static institution; it can be made better. The institution of family has continually changed as other elements of social reality have changed. The family in an advanced capitalist society is very different than the family in hunter/gathering, agricultural, or preindustrial societies. In the future, we may not recognize its form, but it will continue to exist as an important institution that serves basic functions in support of society.

A member of the baby boom generation looking to retire one day.

Source: Ivan Freaner

Summary

This chapter has provided a brief overview of the study of the family, along with some of the problems and concerns involved in this research. It is meant to whet your appetite so that you will want to learn more. The family is a universal social institution legally defined for purposes of the U.S. Census as a "group of two or more people who reside together and who are related by birth, marriage, or adoption" (Suchan et al., 2007). Families come in many forms, though, and this definition makes it difficult to study families that are not included. Social scientists use a theoretical understanding of the family, allowing us to recognize and include families that do not fit our expectations, and to study families in many societies and subcultures. The structural functionalist definition, for example, allows us to define family in terms of the functions that it serves to perpetuate and maintain the society. Family functions include economic and emotional support, and the reproduction and socialization of children. Additionally, conflict and feminist perspectives introduce power relations and gender into the analysis; the symbolic interactionist perspective allows us to focus more closely and look at the production of symbols and meanings for our actions. Symbolic interactionism allows sociologists to explore how socialization takes place and how identities are formed.

The family has undergone tremendous change in the last 40 years and is expected to continue to change. The society as a whole has also changed, growing through several large and important movements including civil rights, women's liberation, and gay rights. As a result of these historical changes, birth control is better and more readily available, jobs are more accessible to women and more women have careers, privacy has become a protected right, and, in some states, marriage and domestic partnerships are an option for gay and lesbian couples. Advances in technology have helped more people to have children and a new generation to live longer.

The family is also the source of many social problems, illustrating that in many ways the family is not functioning well in modern society. Examining social problems such as the high number of divorces, affairs, and single-parent families, the intergenerational transmission of divorce, the extra burden of taking care of the growing elderly population, and the rate of violence and abuse in the family, it is easy to see why some experts argue that the family is in decline.

Families are increasingly more diverse. Two categories used to deliver social programs and services based on the census count are race, a social reality rather than a biological one, and ethnicity. In recent years, the census has had to add categories for unmarried partners and for people who define themselves as more than one race. There are more people cohabitating than ever before, and more people are choosing to remain single or to not have children.

Another change in family is represented by the substantial percentage of gay and lesbian families that include children by birth and or adoption. Families are being blended through divorce and remarriage. With all of this change, we can still look to the family to serve the basic functions for the individual and society. Most people continue to describe getting married and having at least two children as a major part of their American Dream. In this chapter, we have taken a view that the family will continue to undergo tremendous change and growth, and it will continue to exist as an important institution that serves basic functions in support of society.

Review/Discussion Questions

1. What does patriarchy mean?
2. Which of the three parenting styles do you think works best? Explain.
3. Why do you think more people are choosing to cohabit rather than get married?
4. Should the government allow individuals to marry more than one person? Why or why not?
5. If one of your friends started dating someone thirty years older than him or her what would you think? What kind of advice would you try to offer your friend, if any?

Key Terms

Arranged marriage means that parents or match-makers decide who is going to marry whom.

Bilateral descent traces the line of descent through both the mother's and the father's family.

Conjugal families are formed and recognized through the mating of a couple.

Consanguine families are formed and recognized through blood ties (birth).

Endogamy involves marrying someone from within one's social and economic group.

Exogamy involves marrying someone from a different region, or other social and economic categories.

Extended family includes two parents and their children, as well as other blood relatives such as aunts, uncles, and grandparents.

Family is a group of two or more people who reside together and who are related by birth, marriage, or adoption for purposes of the U.S. Census.

Family of procreation is a family made up of a person's spouse and children.

Family of orientation is the family a person grows up in, including parents and siblings.

Heterogamy means choosing to marry someone who is different from one's self.

Homogamy involves people falling in love with, and marrying, someone similar to themselves.

Household includes all the people who occupy a housing unit as their usual place of residence.

Neolocal means that young couples leave their mother and father's residence and go out and find one of their own.

Nonfamily household is a census term used to describe people living together who are not related to the householder by birth, marriage, or adoption.

Nuclear families are composed of two adults and their children, if they have any.

Matriarchy means that the mothers rule and are in charge of the family.

Matrilineal descent traces the descent through the mother's line.

Matrilocal residence means that when couples marry, they live with the wife's family.

Monogamy allows a person only one mate.

Multigenerational family households consist of more than two generations living together as a family.

Patriarchal society is one in which men are dominant and social institutions are set up to sustain a system of male rule.

Patriarchy means rule by the father, and he is in charge of the household.

Patrilineal descent traces the descent through the father's line.

Patrilocal residence means that a married couple lives with the father's family.

Polyandry allows a woman to have more than one husband at a time.

Polygamy allows marriage of one person to two or more others of the opposite sex.

Polygyny allows a man to have more than one wife at a time.

Serial monogamy involves cycles of divorce and remarriage allowing people to marry multiple partners, but only one at a time.

Bibliography

Baumrind, D. (1991). The influence of parenting style on adolescent competence and substance use. Journal of Early Adolescence, 11, 56-95.

Budgeon, S. (2008). Couple Culture and the Production of Singleness. Sexualities, 11, 301-326.

Brown, S. L. (2008). Generational Differences in Cohabitation and Marriage in the US. Population research and policy review (0167-5923), 27 (5), 531.

Bumpass, L. L., & Lu, H. (2000). Trends in cohabitation and implications for children's family contexts in the United States. Population Studies, 54, 29–41.

Caetano, R. (2008). Intimate Partner Violence Victim and Perpetrator Characteristics Among Couples in the United States. Journal of Family Violence (0885-7482), 23 (6), 507.

Cherlin, A. (1978). Remarriage as an Incomplete Institution. American Journal of Sociology, 84 (3), 634-650.

Clark, R. (1983). Family life and school achievement: Why poor black children succeed or fail. Chicago: University of Chicago Press.

Dornbusch, S. M., Ritter, P. L., Leiderman, P. H., Roberts, D. F., & Fraleigh, M. J. (1987). The relation of parenting style to adolescent performance. Child Development, 58, 1244-1257.

Eshleman, J. R. (2003). The Family (10th ed.). Boston: Allyn & Bacon.

Furstenberg Jr., F. (1980). Reflections on Remarriage: Introduction to Journal of Family Issues Special Issue on Remarriage. Journal of Family Issues, 1 (4), 443-453.

Giddens, A. (1992). The Transformation of Intimacy: Sexuality, Love & Eroticism in Modern Societies. Stanford, CA: Stanford University Press.

Glazer, N., & Moynahan, D. P. (1963). Beyond the Melting Pot. Cambridge, MA: M.I.T. Press and Harvard University Press.

Goldscheider, F., & Sassler, S. (2006). Creating Step-families: Integrating Children into the Study of Union Formation. Journal of Marriage and Family (0022-2445), 68 (2), 275.

Hochschild, A. R. (1989). The Second Shift: Working Parents and the Revolution at Home. New York: Viking.

Kurdek, L. (2008). Change in relationship quality for partners from lesbian, gay male, and heterosexual couples. Journal of Family Psychology, 22 (5), 701-11.

Kurdek, L. (2007). The Allocation of Household Labor by Partners in Gay and Lesbian Couples. Journal of Family Issues, 28 (1), 132-148.

Meezan, W. & Rauch, J. (2005). Gay Marriage, Same-Sex Parenting, and America's Children. The Future of Children (1054-8289), 15 (2), 97.

Messineo, M. (2005). Influence of Expectations for Parental Support on Intergenerational Coresidence Behavior. Journal of Intergenerational Relationships, 3 (3), 47-64.

Murdock, G. P. (1949). Social Structures. New York: MacMillan.

Ogburn, W. F. (1938). The Changing Family. Family, 19, 139-143.

Rennison, C. M. (2003, February). Intimate Partner Violence, 1993-2001. Bureau of Justice Statistics Crime Data Brief. <http://www.ojp.usdoj.gov/bjs/pub/pdf/ipv01.pdf> (2008).

Skolnick, A. (1997). Family values: the sequel. The American Prospect, 32, 86-94.

Smock, P. J. (2000). Cohabitation in the United States: An appraisal of research themes, findings, and implications. Annual Review of Sociology, 26, 1–20.

Smock, P. J., Manning, W. D., & Porter, M. (2005). Everything's there except money: How money shapes decisions to marry among cohabitors. Journal of Marriage and Family, 67, 680–696.

Steinberg, L., Elmen, J. D. & Mounts, N. S. (1989). Authoritative parenting, psychosocial maturity, and academic success among adolescents. Child Development, 60, 1424-1436.

Suchan, T. A., Perry, M. J., Fitzsimmons, J. D., Juhn, A. E., Tait, A. M., & Brewer, C. A. (2007). Census Atlas of the United States, Series CENSR-29. Washington, DC: GPO/U.S. Census Bureau.

United Nations (1948). The Universal Declaration of Human Rights. <http://www.un.org/Overview/rights.html> (2008).

U. S. Census Bureau (2003). 2000 Census of Population and Housing, Summary Social, Economic, and Housing Characteristics, Selected Appendixes, PHC-2-A. Washington, DC: GPO.

CHAPTER ELEVEN

Education And Religion

Mita Dhariwal

E ducation and religion are social institutions that have played major roles in the development of culture and society. This chapter briefly describes the impact made by each of these institutions.

Education

Education is defined as an organized system that provides knowledge, values and skills to the next generation. The importance of education is evident in many societies. For instance, the Hindu people of India see education as the most important tool for personal development, and their scriptures describe education as providing students with a "third eye" through which they can perceive the environment and the world.

Education was initiated by religious leaders who shared their knowledge through churches, temples, and mosques. The teaching of symbols and reading and writing of a language was provided through these institutions to the youth of elite classes such as royal families, wealthy landholders, and those training to become religious leaders. The skills necessary for farming, hunting, and performing domestic duties were taught more informally by families. Education was used as **acculturation**, which is the transmission of culture from one generation to the next.

Education as a separate social institution was developed in Arabia, China, North Africa, and Classical Greece. The movement toward industrialization later transformed education to include formal preparation for jobs that required the ability to read, write, and work accurately with numbers. Thus the classic "three Rs" of the 19th century were established.

The primary role of education today is to provide credentials that are used to function in society. Many employers in the United States, for instance, rely greatly on the practice of **credentialism**, using high school diplomas and college degrees to determine who is eligible for a specific type of job.

The Functionalist Perspective Of Education

The functionalist perspective focuses on the structure and functions of education, which include its size, rules, regulations, status, and roles.

In the past, the size of the education system was small because it was only available to the upper class. Teachers were seen as the experts in passing along knowledge. They were considered gurus and given respect and admiration; their status was very high. Students were disciplined and taught to show respect for teaching and learning. Rules were part of discipline, but government regulations were not.

With the Industrial Revolution, the education system increased in size. This growth brought many changes to the rules, regulations, status, and roles of education. In the United States, schools became larger when education was made mandatory through high school. The increased size of the system caused the status and role of teachers to be viewed differently, as well as the role of students. Governmental rules and regulations became part of education, especially in regard to gaining financial support, and administrators were brought into the structure as a result.

The size of educational structures affected the quality of education. As class sizes grew, teachers started to feel overwhelmed with the demands of the

parents and students, as well as those of the bureaucracy. Overcrowded classrooms affected the ability of teachers to concentrate on meeting the needs of students, creating opportunities for them to drift away from learning.

Community also played an important role in the success of education. As societies changed, students from many different backgrounds were brought together, giving teachers the additional duty of dealing with students who had special needs to be met in order to learn. Teaching the "three Rs" was no longer the only goal, with areas such as the arts, vocational skills, and a new emphasis on social activities being added to the curriculum, changing the functions education was expected to fulfill.

Manifest Functions

1. Transmission of cultural values
2. Socialization
3. Social integration
4. Screening
5. Gatekeeping
6. Social mobility
7. Promotion of personal and social change

1. Transmission of cultural values

Education transmits the core values of a culture to the youth of a society. For example, when individualism is valued in a culture, teachers may focus on activities that promote creativity, achievement, and competition. Schools pass along the value of competition by dividing classes into competing groups for educational games and projects, and encouraging students to play competitive sports such as football, baseball, soccer, and wrestling. The custom of recognizing outstanding players and students for their achievements also emphasizes the importance of competition and reinforces individual success.

2. Socialization

Cultural norms and values are internalized in the socialization process. At first, families socialize young children regarding how to meet their basic needs, including food, hygiene, and love. Later, schools encourage students to accept cultural values as their own by internalizing the discipline, self-control, rules, and regulations of the classroom and society. Students are also socialized by being induced to social groups and formal organizations in education that they can join. By teaching occupational and social skills, schools help individuals function adequately in society.

3. Social integration

Schools aid in social integration by molding students into a relatively cohesive unit. When immigrants blend with and adopt the dominant group's culture through social integration, it is called **assimilation**. Schools allow students with different backgrounds to integrate with the mainstream culture. Saluting the flag and singing the national anthem make students more aware of their government and the society as a whole. Through this and other exercises, their sense of national unity grows and gives them a sense of pride in knowing that they are part of the society.

4. Screening

As part of the screening function, teachers establish the school curriculum according to the abilities of their students. They may use a variety of tests designed to discover the strengths and weaknesses of each student as part of this process. Screening could also include tracking, which involves sorting students into different educational programs based on their past performance. Tracking begins early, as grades and test scores are recorded from the time a student begins school.

5. Gatekeeping

Gatekeeping in education provides opportunities and job placement to individuals based on the quality of their coursework. As part of this process, schools award credentials such as diplomas and degrees to give students proof of their academic accomplishments. Learning builds upon itself, and those who graduate from high school are often encouraged to continue their educational pursuits at community colleges and universities. This type of social placement is viewed as a major task for society in order to find and recruit individuals capable of filling positions requiring high intelligence and

years of school, such as physicians and engineers (Henslin, 1995).

6. Social mobility

Education provides opportunities for students who have the ability and ambition to get ahead. Through educational attainment, poor students can improve their circumstances, because jobs that require advanced degrees often provide higher income levels and social standing.

7. Promotion of personal and social change

Schools strive to teach individuals to think critically and attain a higher level of personal achievement. Students become aware of their needs and learn to evaluate differing viewpoints and available options. They discover opportunities available to them, and they gain more freedom to express their ideas. Education provides students with increased flexibility and a greater awareness of their surroundings.

Schools provide opportunities not only for individuals to change, but for societies to change as well. New discoveries and advancements are often initiated when the knowledge accumulated by experts, scientists, professors, and teachers is passed along to their students. As education advances, so does the society.

Latent Functions

Though unintended, latent functions can be very influential and their effects may occur immediately or years later. The latent functions of education include prolonged adolescence, day care, and teenage pregnancies.

By the time students graduate from high schools in the United States, they are often eighteen—the age of adulthood—or very close to it. Children have been considered adults at much younger ages throughout history. During the Middle Ages in England, an individual was considered an adult at fourteen (Walsh & Hemmens, 2000). In the early 1800s, middle-class children in the United States went to work in their early teens, either inside or outside the family, and the concept of adolescence didn't exist (Wilson, 1983). The advent of compulsory public education extended the childhoods of students, meaning that students became adults later in life.

In some ways, schools act as day care facilities, freeing time for parents to work or engage in other activities without their children. With less time spent by parents providing for children, the educational system is left to provide for their emotional needs, which places a greater burden upon the schools.

Teenage pregnancies stem from prolonged adolescence and a lack of both societal training and parental guidance. Students with more free time and a lack of supervision may become involved in sexual activities, not realizing how their actions could affect their education. The end result could be that they drop out of school.

School counselors, administrators, and teachers have to develop programs to fulfill these unplanned functions, as well as to provide the necessary facilities. As a result of coping with teen pregnancies and prolonged adolescence, along with providing day care for parents, an extra financial burden is placed upon schools.

The Conflict Theory Perspective Of Social Inequities In Education

Uneven Distribution

Conflict theory stresses the inequalities between the "haves and have-nots," including the uneven distribution of funds and services. School budgets are based largely on property taxes. In areas with higher-priced homes, schools receive more money because property taxes increase in relation to home values. This means that wealthier communities have more funding for each student compared with poorer communities where property values are low. In well-to-do areas, teachers and staff members work in better facilities and are paid higher salaries, allowing schools there to hire more motivated teachers with superior qualifications. Well-funded schools also have the latest textbooks, computers, and a host of other learning devices available. As a nation, the United States promotes equal opportunities for all its citizens, yet offers better opportunities to children living in areas with higher property

values.

Diversity And Discrimination

Students from diverse backgrounds may feel unprepared to compete with those who are already assimilated into the culture. Most minority children come from poorer areas where the schools may not have all of the facilities and tools to prepare them for a competitive education. These students may feel discriminated against in the classroom, as well as within the whole educational system.

Discrimination in schools encompasses how students are treated by teachers. Some children might consider themselves to be "teacher's pet" and treated as such. Others might feel they are not given enough attention because of their background or appearance. Another factor in discrimination might be a **hidden curriculum** that covers the unwritten rules of behavior and attitudes such as conformity to norms and obedience to authority. The teaching of a hidden curriculum varies from one social class to another. Teachers may concentrate on teaching values, beliefs and attitudes from the point of view of their own social backgrounds, which may be different than those of their students.

Students are taught how to behave based on their position in society and according to the unwritten rules of the hidden curriculum. They learn obedience, competition, and patriotism. It is understood that students must learn respect for authority so that they can become good workers who obey the orders of their supervisors. For those who drop out of school, poor employment prospects await. A large number of students, mostly from less affluent backgrounds, still prefer to leave school because of the conflict aspects of discrimination and diversity.

The Symbolic Interactionist Perspective

Labeling And Self-fulfilling Prophecies

According to the symbolic interactionist perspective, people's behaviors and interactions with others are based in part on how they believe those other people view them. In school, this perspective focuses on teacher expectations and the possible creation of self-fulfilling prophecies. It also includes educational tracking, and labeling students as high achievers and low achievers.

The expectations of teachers are often based on past performance measures, such as test scores. When a teacher believes a student is capable of high test scores, he or she expects a higher level of performance. At the same time, teachers may lower their expectations for a student with a history of poor test scores. Even when students with low scores try to perform well, teachers may fail to acknowledge their additional effort and continue to give them their historically low grades, potentially leading to confusion and frustration.

Teachers tend to interact with students based on the labels they have assigned to them, even though the descriptive label may not be entirely accurate. Labeling theory reinforces the idea of the self-fulfilling prophecy. Robert Merton created the concept, describing self-fulfilling prophecies as false assertions that may become true simply because they were predicted (1949). For instance, a poor student who feels that he has been ignored or written off by the education system may choose to live up to his reputation by continuing to do poorly. An average student, on the other hand, might feel inspired by a teacher's high expectations and be motivated to work hard and excel.

Teacher expectations are related to student test scores in the classic Rosenthal and Jacobsen experiment (1968). In the experiment, grade school students were tested and then the teachers were told which children's intelligence scores would "spurt" that year. The test was performed again at the end of the year, and the IQ scores of the "spurters" had jumped 10 to 15 percent higher than their previous scores.

Students who displayed good behaviors and were labeled as good were found to be the most successful. Labeling can also affect children negatively if they believe that their school system views them as "not good enough" and discriminates against them on that basis. The result could be a lack of motivation, decreasing the attention spans of the students and causing them to become disinterested in school. These adolescents are more likely to be absent from school and not comply with authority because they view it as discriminatory.

The **adolescent subculture** has values and attitudes which are quite different from those of the adult world. Adolescents may be labeled geeks or nerds and treated differently by the student body as well as the staff. Students with high self-esteem show more confidence and perform better in school, which can lead to being more successful in later life. Students lacking confidence may feel like outcasts and drift away, demonstrating the important influence a student's self-image may have upon learning.

The Education System Today

Private Versus Public Schools In The United States

According to the National Center for Education Statistics, there were 30,000 private schools as of 2007. The most common private schools are parochial schools operated by the Catholic Church. These schools focus on traditional academic subjects as well as religious education. Private preparatory schools are often more expensive than parochial schools and traditionally serve a wealthier student body.

Private schools are generally recognized as superior to public schools, with their student body as a whole scoring higher on IQ and SAT tests. Students from private schools are also more likely to take academic courses, regardless of their abilities or socio-economic status, as these schools tend to groom their students for college whether or not they are financially able to attend. Public school students from lower social-economic backgrounds are more likely to be put on vocational, rather than academic, curriculum paths.

Students in private schools may view themselves as having better career opportunities because they are part of an exclusive group. These students expect to attain a high socio-economic status, according to Cookson and Persell (1985). In public schools, students may feel freer to express themselves and exhibit less discipline; in private schools, students may feel more pressure to conform to group standards and follow rules.

The role of parents in private schools is seen dif-

Many private schools require students to wear similar uniforms leading to a conformity in dress.   Source: Sam LeVan

Problems In Education

1. Unequal funding
2. Lower quality of education
3. Grade inflation
4. Functional illiteracy
5. Violence
6. Teenage pregnancy
7. Dropout rate

1. Unequal funding

Funding for education is unequally distributed between rich and poor students, and even among different geographic regions. In 2005, 7 of the 10 states spending the highest amounts per student were in the Northeast, and all 10 of the states spending the lowest amounts were in the West and South (U.S. Bureau of the Census, 2007). While higher expenditures are generally associated with higher quality in education, they do not always result in higher test scores. As an example, Iowa does not rank high in school spending, but it ranked highest in SAT scores, with an average of 1,807 (College Board, 2007).

2. Lower quality of education

Scores on SAT exams have been on the decline. One reason for this is that many students find television and video games more appealing than reading. Savell (1993) discovered that over two-thirds of school children read below their grade levels, and only one-third of high school seniors completely comprehend the information in their textbooks. Sociologists Donald Hayes and William Wolfer (Henslin, 1995) are convinced that the culprits behind declining SAT scores include "dummied down" textbooks, less homework, fewer essay assignments, grade inflation, and burned-out teachers.

3. Grade inflation

Grade inflation occurs when higher grades are given for lower-quality work. In the 1960s, high school teachers gave more Cs than As for coursework meeting the same standard. Learning declined, and in the 1990s, more As were given than Cs.

ferently than in public schools. This is particularly true in religious schools where the parents view themselves as part of their church, school, and community. In the public school system, parents might be more inclined to question their own rights along with the rights of their children and their schools. A stronger connection often exists between teachers and parents at private schools because they belong to the same groups, whereas in public schools, teachers may feel less connected to the parents because they come from different communities.

Grade inflation indicates declining standards in education and an increasing focus on passing students whether or not they have mastered the basic materials. This focus can result in students graduating from high school who are not able to function in society because they even have difficulty completing job applications. Today, an A grade may simply indicate that a student has completed the work and attended class, rather than having mastered the subject matter. Grade inflation can deceive students into thinking that they are ready for their adult lives when, in fact, they are ill-prepared.

4. Functional illiteracy

Some high school graduates may be functionally illiterate as a result of grade inflation and the desire to advance students to the next grade level. People who are functionally illiterate do not have basic reading, writing, and math skills. They may be unable to read a newspaper, a map, or even a restaurant menu. As a result, they may find it more difficult to function in society. Functional illiteracy affects society as a whole, and many public libraries offer special programs to teach adults to read in an effort to deal with the problem.

5. Violence

Basic safety has become a major issue for American schools in recent times. Once considered the safest places for youths, uniformed guards are part of daily life in some schools, with students passing through metal detectors before they are allowed to enter. In a number of schools, drive-by shooting drills have been added to traditional fire drills.

Parents are also concerned about their children being bullied by others. Students group together based on the clothes they wear, the languages they speak, and the values they share. In groupings based on social class, students from wealthier families show off their expensive possessions and engage in social activities that require money. These students may be popular and favored by teachers, and use their positions to overpower and take advantage of fringe students. Students from less affluent families may feel rejected and resent other groups. Left out socially and academically, these students may be-

come frustrated and engage in violence. Bullying is more likely to occur on school grounds, rather than in classrooms, making it harder for teachers and staff to detect.

Though a calm and secure atmosphere is the best place for children to learn and grow, schools have become places where frustrations and feelings of hatred are expressed. Parents may now be more concerned about their children's safety than their education.

6. Teenage pregnancy

Teenage pregnancies can be obstacles to education. Pregnant students might have to miss numerous classes, or even drop out of school completely because of their early involvement in sexual activity. After they give birth, teenage mothers become involved in caring for their children, and these pressures and responsibilities can get in the way of completing high school. The result is that many teenage mothers drop out of school, an interruption of education that is more likely to occur in impoverished areas. One solution to this problem is to educate youth about their bodies and the possible consequences of sexual behavior.

7. Dropout rate

The rising high school dropout rate is caused, in part, by a lack of reading and writing skills. Individuals should learn these basic skills in elementary school, but this does not always occur, especially in urban schools where students come from diverse backgrounds with lower income levels. By the time these students reach high school, they may feel alienated in the classroom. If they can't complete the assignments as well as their peers, they may feel like failures.

Lower socio-economic backgrounds may also affect how well these students adjust between school and home. They may not feel as though they belong in school. This may cause them to become socially involved with individuals in similar situations, avoiding the classroom or exhibiting deviant behavior. They are also more likely to spend time on the street where they feel comfortable, and where they are not required to display their academic deficiencies. These youths may feel more accepted by their street peers and others facing similar problems and living in comparable circumstances. Financial pressure at home can also become a catalyst for dropping out, as some students may choose to get a job in order to help support their families.

Religion

Religious institutions offer knowledge about spirituality and the existence of a higher power. Religion also serves as an anchor of identity for many individuals. Religious beliefs can help explain the meaning of life and help people to better cope with daily frustrations and anxieties.

Rituals are essential for identity and social cohesion. People may proclaim their allegiance to one particular god or many, take part in rituals, or join communes. They meditate, pray, burn incense, and chant—they may even torture themselves. Through these ceremonies, people all over the world find a purpose in life and the existence of an afterlife. The social institutions of religion are organized to meet people's spiritual need to believe in a supernatural power.

Religion as a social institution can come in many forms. A **church** tends to be large and affiliated with a religious network. Churches tend to be less strict and make fewer demands on their membership, with their primary goal being to reach more people. Most people who practice religion in the United States attend a church. A **sect** is a much smaller religious group, usually an offshoot of a larger, more mainstream religion. Sects make many demands on their members. The Community of the Lady of All Nations and the Philippine Independent Church are both considered to be Catholic sects. In a **cult**, members generally adopt views that totally reject other religions and societies. Cult members usually have a strong devotion to their leader, as was the case with Heaven's Gate. That cult believed that if all the members of the group committed suicide at the same time, they would be transported from their bodies to a UFO. In 1997, three groups of Heaven's Gate cult members, totaling 21 women and 18 men, voluntarily committed suicide (Ontario Consultants

on Religious Tolerance, 2008).

In his book, *The Elementary Forms of the Religious Life*, Emile Durkheim explains the elements common to all religions. According to Durkheim, "A religion is a unified system of beliefs and practices relative to sacred things, that is to say, things set apart and forbidden—beliefs and practices which unite into one single moral community called a Church, all those who adhere to them" (1965). This definition revolves around three elements: beliefs, practices, and moral community. Durkheim believed that moral communities emphasize the sacredness of religion, the ways to show respect, such as Buddhists bowing before shrines and Hindus bathing in the Ganges River to be purified. Moral communities bring together people who share a religious system of beliefs and practices, thus promoting cultural unity.

Organization Of Religion

Religious organizations vary from one society to another. Some societies believe in many gods and goddesses, known as **polytheism**. Hindus practice polytheism, believing that each god represents certain powers like *Brahma* the creator, *Shiva* the destroyer, and *Vishnu* the preserver. The belief in one god, **monotheism**, is shared by Christianity, Judaism, and Islam.

Followers of **animism** believe that spirits inhabit virtually everything in nature, including rocks, trees, lakes, animals, and humans. These spirits affect different aspects of life and can be influenced by performing certain rituals. Practicing these beliefs is also called **shamanism**, with spiritual leaders who are known as shamans possessing special skills like being able to heal the sick and wounded and otherwise exert influence over spirits and events in their environments. American Indians may hold these beliefs, receiving this power by using *hallucegen-peyote*, or through fasting or a lack of sleep.

Another form of religion revolving around nature is **totemism**, the worship of plants, animals, and other natural objects embodying gods and ancestors. During ritual ceremonies, people wear costumes and dance to mimic a totem object. Totemism is practiced today in Alaska by some North American

Indians, as well as by Australian aborigines and other societies and tribes around the world.

Religions Of The World

Islam

The Islamic faith is practiced by over 1.5 billion people (Hunter, 2008), and its teachings are recorded in the Qur'an. The prophet Mohammed founded the Islamic faith after receiving divine revelations from God between AD 570 and AD 630. Within the Qur'an is a code of ethics, and this system of laws and guidelines covers all aspects of Islamic life.

Islam means "surrender, resignation and submission." People who believe in *Allah* as the one and only god, and surrender or submit themselves to the will of Allah, are called Muslims or Moslems. Muslims worship in mosques, their sacred places, where the major congregations gather on Fridays. Prayers begin with, "*Lala Allah Mohammed rasool Allah,*" which means, "There is no true god but Allah, and Mohammed is the messenger of God."

Islamic families are categorized as patriarchal authoritarian. Sons are perceived as more desirable than daughters and may enjoy special privileges. Muslim males are allowed to marry non-Muslim females, but Muslim women are not allowed to marry outside of their faith. Muslim families may be polygamous, with men taking up to four wives. According to Islamic teachings, if a male wants to marry a female, there must first be a proposal and an acceptance. The proposal comes in two parts. First, a dowry is offered by the family of the groom to the family of the bride, and second, a gift known as a *mahr* is offered by the groom to the bride. By accepting these gifts, the bride and her family indicate that they agree to the proposal. In the Islamic faith, if a husband tells his wife, "I divorce you" three times, the marriage is dissolved. However, divorce is strongly condemned, and many Muslims believe that a minimum of one month needs to pass between

Grand Mosque in Dubai.

Source: Morgue File

each of the three pronouncements (OCRT, 2008).

Hinduism

An estimated 85 percent of the Indian population is Hindu, with roughly 900 million people practicing Hinduism worldwide (Hunter, 2008). Hinduism has a minimal structure and no religious hierarchy. Evolving about 4,000 years ago, this religion encompasses an enormous variety of beliefs and practices.

Followers of Hinduism worship nature, animals, and other forms of life. They believe that different powers reside in different human or animal forms. The basic Hindu belief system revolves around three main gods: Brahma the creator, god of creation; Shiva the destroyer, god of death and destruction; and Vishnu the preserver, god of past, present and future. These powers appear in different forms at different times, each as a god or goddess.

Hindus believe in reincarnation, the transmigration of the soul through a series of lives. This belief involves *karma*, meaning that destiny is decided by the actions of each individual during his or her most recent past life. In Hinduism, human life is viewed as the highest and most respected form one can obtain on earth and, because they believe that destroying any life—human or animal—is wrong, most Hindus are vegetarians.

The Hindu temple in Saint Andre on Reunion Island.

Source: Iwan Beijies

There are four major stages of life in Hinduism. The first stage is childhood, the second is learning, the third is family life, and the fourth is the renunciation of worldly things. As part of their religion, Hindus practice rituals that they believe can influence the great cosmic order. These rituals often take place at home where most Hindus have a family shrine so they can offer food before the images of their deities and meditate. Hindus see life as a ritual in which righteous individuals must strive to relate to the world as it exists. The world is a great dance determined by one's karma, with the final goal being liberation from that cosmic dance.

Hinduism is considered a way of life, and to be a part of this life a person must fit into the social system. According to *Manu* laws, each person has a duty to serve in the social order to which he or she was born. Hindus believe in a caste system in which castes represent a person's occupational opportunities, social standing, and the stage of life that person was in at the time of birth. Brahmins represent the top of the caste hierarchy and serve as priests, scholars and teachers. Below the Brahmins are the Kshatriyas, who serve as warriors and rulers. Next are the Vaishyas, who are merchants and farmers. The Shudras, the peasants and laborers, represent the bottom of the caste system. The sub caste known as pariahs, or untouchables, consists of people considered so low that they are not even formally represented in the caste system; their occupations involve handling unclean objects, such as human and animal waste.

Buddhism

Buddhism was founded by Siddhartha Gautama Buddha—*Buddha* meaning "enlightened one." As the son of the king and queen of the Sakya tribe, Siddhartha lived in great palaces, enjoying a life of

Buddhist monks shopping.

Source: Nakhon Pathom

privilege and luxury. His father tried to shield him from the worries and unpleasantness of life outside the palace walls. One day, he decided to leave the palace to explore the city. While there, he discovered a new reality consisting of the old, sick, diseased, and dead. From this he realized that people really had little control over their lives.

The prince decided to meditate in an attempt to find an end for the suffering. At the age of 29, he denounced his life of luxury and became an ascetic—one who abstains from worldly pleasures. He began studying Hinduism and was a pupil of several then-famous Brahman teachers. Later, he turned away from Hinduism as he became disillusioned with the caste system and the ascetic lifestyle. Through meditation at the age of 35 he discovered the "four noble truths": (1) the existence of suffering, (2) the origin of suffering is desire, (3) suffering ceases when desire ceases, and (4) the way to end desire is to enter the "eight-fold path." Buddhists believe that if the eight components of this path are utilized together, they can lead to a higher level of

Hanukkah Minora.

Source: Aron Kremer

consciousness and a reduction of desire. The eight parts of the path are:

1. Right view – understanding things as they really are and accepting the four noble truths.
2. Right intention – renouncing external pleasures and refraining from hurting other living creatures, be they man or animal.
3. Right speech – speaking only when necessary and choosing words carefully, focusing on truthfulness, because wrong words can damage relationships.
4. Right conduct – causing no harm to others, not stealing or acting in dishonest ways.
5. Right occupation or living – treating others fairly, only gaining wealth through honest and righteous ways.
6. Right effort – endeavoring purely, not tainted by unwholesome mental states such as envy or aggression.
7. Right mindfulness – seeing things as they really are without distortion, being clear-headed.
8. Right concentration – concentrating in a wholesome manner, focused on good and pure thoughts and actions.

Buddhism spread rapidly from India to other parts of the world, and today there are about 367 million Buddhists (Hunter, 2008). The majority of Buddhists live in India, Sri Lanka, Burma, Tibet, Laos, Cambodia, Thailand, China, Korea, and Japan.

Christianity And Judaism

There are more than 2 billion Christians, making up one-third of the world's population, and approximately 17 million Jews. Christians base their faith on the teachings of Jesus Christ as found in the New Testament of the Bible, whereas Jews base their beliefs on the Old Testament. In Judaism, the *Torah* contains the first five books of the Old Testament and is traditionally regarded as the primary revelation of God. Christians and Jews believe in one God. However, most Christians believe that their God takes the form of the Holy Trinity composed of the Father, Son, and Holy Spirit. Christians believe God is the Father, Jesus Christ is the son of God, and the Holy Spirit is the omnipresent spirit of God. Most Christians worship on Sundays, while Jews worship on Saturdays, which is referred to as the Sabbath.

Christians practice baptism, during which they accept Christ and Christ's divinity. Christians also take part in a communion, recalling the last supper Jesus shared with his disciples before his crucifixion. Communion involves the breaking of bread and the drinking of wine. Prayer also plays as important part in the lives of Christians.

Judaism has a system of civil and criminal laws, family relationship guidelines, personal ethics, and social responsibilities that govern the actions of its members. Jewish dietary laws forbid the eating of certain birds and seafood, and animals that prey upon other animals. The eating of pork is also forbidden, as the pig considered as an unclean animal. The purpose of eating kosher foods, as described in Jewish dietary laws, is twofold: first, eating only clean food and second, consuming foods that were not acquired through cruelty to animals. Judaism also governs daily prayer and study of the Torah, and reasons for wearing the *kippah* (skullcap) and the *tefillin* (two small black boxes with straps worn on the forehead and left forearm during morning prayers). Male children are circumcised on the eighth day after birth as a sign of God's covenant with Abraham. At age 13, Jewish boys undergo a bar mitzvah, giving them adult status and the responsibility of performing the commandments. Jewish girls also undergo a similar ceremony called a bas mitzvah.

The Functionalist Perspective

Manifest Functions

1. Beliefs and practices
2. Knowledge
3. Emotional security
4. Solidarity
5. Social control
6. Societal change
7. Rites of passage

1. Beliefs and practices

Religion offers beliefs and practices that separate the profane from the sacred. *Profane* relates to elements common in everyday life that do not have a religious purpose. The term sacred refers to those things worthy of reverence, a deep respect that may even inspire fear. For instance, Hindus believe that the cow is sacred, and the thought of killing one might inspire fear because the act is forbidden.

2. Knowledge

Religious institutions offer answers to perplexing questions such as whether or not there is a higher power in control of the universe. Religion offers answers to questions about the meaning of life, reasons for suffering, and the existence of an afterlife. By helping to explain how we got here and why, along with what will happen to us when we die, our lives may appear more manageable and the world more comprehensible.

3. Emotional security

Religion provides solace through its ceremonies. Religious rituals centered upon critical events such as illness and death offer emotional comfort by letting members know that others care for them and will be there to provide support in difficult times. Religion offers relief by assuring individuals that there is a purpose for their suffering.

4. Solidarity

According to Durkheim, the major function of religion is to provide and preserve social solidarity (1965). This view assumes that religion is the integrating factor of the social system, holding a place in the daily activities of its members. Religion binds its members closer to each other and to society as a whole. This solidarity is built upon shared principles and beliefs, creating a sense of belonging and a collective consciousness.

5. Social control

Religion serves as a social control mechanism, supplying rules for living in a society. Most mainstream religions are designated as **civil religions**, in that they are a collection of beliefs, symbols, and rituals that reinforce the dominant values and societal norms, such as customs, traditions, morals, and laws. Civil religions also provide for sanctions against those who violate the rules, thus helping to control the people's behavior. The social norms of religious groups apply only to their members, though some may indirectly set limits on nonmembers. Many societies incorporate religious teachings, such as the prohibition against taking a life, into their judicial systems. As a result, the religious belief that human life is considered sacred and can only be taken by a higher power becomes a control on society.

6. Societal change

Religion tends to promote the social order, which is resistant to change. Although it usually serves to maintain the status quo, religion can occasionally serve as an advocate of societal change. In the 1960s, for instance, Martin Luther King, Jr., used his pulpit and congregation to help desegregate the United States and reduce discrimination.

7. Rites of passage

Many religions have rituals tied to different life stages. Children may be baptized in order to become part of a specific belief system. Teenagers are often initiated through confirmation to prepare them for full membership in their religious communities. Adults celebrate their passage into married life through ceremonies, and funerals may mark passage into an afterlife. These rites of passage help people through emotionally charged transitions from one stage of life to the next.

Latent Functions

The latent functions of religion can include the results of extreme adherence to beliefs. Religion can place a financial burden upon followers who feel they must donate money or labor in order to be treated equally by God, or to receive rewards from a higher power. People can become so caught up in ceremonial activities that they forget their own existence. Extreme beliefs can also cause followers to worship ideas that are not even a part of their religion.

Though religions provide unity, they can also create divisions between people. They teach love for humanity, yet, at the same time, some turn that love to hatred for those belonging to different religious groups, or even very similar religious groups. Sunnis and Shiites in Iraq and Iran wage war against each other even though both groups are Muslim. Hindus may fight with other Hindus, and Protestants may fight with Catholics.

The Symbolic Interactionist Perspective

All religions use symbols to provide identity and social solidarity to their members. For Muslims, the crescent moon and star is the primary symbol, for Jews it is the Star of David, and for Christians it is the cross. These religious symbols represent sacredness and feelings of love, peace, and reverence, offering a condensed means of communicating with other members. According to Durkheim, religions use symbols to specify sacredness as different from ordinary daily life (1965). Rituals are also symbols that help unite people. Examples of religious rituals include bowing, kneeling, lighting candles, burning incense, and reading scriptures.

The Conflict Theory Perspective

Conflict theorists are very critical of religion. Karl Marx viewed society as divided into separate classes in which the rich used religion as a tool to maintain and justify their wealth and power. In this sense, religion enforces and bolsters the power of the ruling classes and justifies social inequalities. As an example, the caste system supported by the Hindu religion provides some members of society with wealth and privilege, while condemning others to poverty.

Marx himself was an atheist who believed that the existence of a god was impossible. It was his belief that religion directs people's attention toward future happiness and away from present suffering, limiting the possibility of rebellion against their oppressors. Marx stated that, "Religion is the sigh of the oppressed creature, the heart of a heartless world, and the soul of soulless conditions. It is the opium of the people" (1970).

Conflict theorists also believe that the teachings and practices of many religions promote gender and other social inequalities. Certain ceremonial rituals are only performed by men. In the Islamic faith, men and women worship separately. Men are responsible for organizing members and leading prayers in the mosque, while women are assigned the more domestic duties of cooking and cleaning.

Most theorists believe there is a strong relationship between religion and social class. Some churches are highly segregated by race and socioeconomic status. In the past, there were churches in the United States where blacks and whites were not allowed to worship together. Segregation is now more likely to be informal (Evans, Forsyth, & Bernard, 2002).

The Impact Of Religion On Capitalism

According to Max Weber, any society's religion influences the social life of its people (1958). Understanding a society, therefore, requires understanding its religion. For instance, to understand the Middle East, a person must also understand the Islamic faith, and the same is true of any related culture and religion.

There are people who believe that to understand the United States, one must also understand capitalism. Weber explains the relationship between religion and the spirit of capitalism in his work *The Protestant Ethic and the Spirit of Capitalism*. Capitalism represents a different way of thinking about work and money. The idea behind capitalism is to produce more than a person needs in order to create a surplus that can be spent, saved, or invested. In the past, some people worked just enough to meet their basic needs. Protestants believed that by working hard, glory was given to God. That glory was diminished if the proceeds of their hard work were wasted on frivolous goods. People came to consider it their duty to work hard to make profits, which in turn could be reinvested to make even more money.

Summary

The institution of education has progressed from historically informal to formal. American education is known today as a credential-based system. The rules, regulations, and bureaucracy that have developed to govern these institutions have become a major focus of education. In part, this has caused a decrease in the emotional attachment between students and their schools, as students feel that they are only there to get a piece of paper. The number of students from diverse backgrounds has increased, and treatment of these students has changed. A corresponding increase in the awareness of issues facing these students, however, is not always apparent.

Religion plays an important role in society, reassuring believers that there is a higher power and helping them to define themselves through their religion. The functionalist perspective views religion positively, as it is pro-social and reinforces the norms and values of the majority. Conflict theorists believe the power of religion is used negatively to trick the public into submission, causing them to think that what benefits the wealthy and the powerful will benefit them as well. According to conflict theorists, religion also encourages people to place their attention not on their suffering in this life, but on the rewards they will receive in the next.

Review/Discussion Questions

1. What is education?
2. List the manifest functions of education.
3. How has education impacted your life?
4. What is religion?
5. Which aspects of religion do conflict theorists study?
6. What are the manifest and latent functions of religion?
7. What does the spirit of capitalism have to do with religion?
8. What impact has religion had on the people around you?

Key Terms

Acculturation is the transmission of culture from one generation to another.

Adolescent subculture contains the values and attitudes of the youth which differ from those of the adult world.

Animism is the belief that spirits inhabit everything in nature.

Assimilation occurs when immigrants merge with the dominant group and adopt its culture.

Churches tend to be large and affiliated with some larger religious network. Churches tend to be less strict and make fewer demands of their members.

Civil religions have beliefs, symbols, and rituals that reinforce the dominant values and social norms such as customs, traditions, morals, and laws.

Credentialism involves providing documents such as diplomas, degrees, and certifications to determine eligibility for jobs.

Cults are religious groups that adopt new views rejecting society and other religions.

Education is an organized system that imparts knowledge, values, and skills to the next generation.

Hidden curriculum is one that covers unwritten rules of behavior and attitudes such as conformity to norms and obedience to authority.

Monotheism is a belief in only one god.

Polytheism is a belief in more than one god.

Sects are much smaller religious groups, usually offshoots of a larger, more mainstream religion, that make a number of demands on their members.

Shamanism is the belief that certain individuals have special skills to influence spirits.

Totemism is the worship of plants and animals or other natural objects as gods and ancestors.

Tracking is the sorting of students into different educational programs based on their past performance.

Bibliography

Basirico, L. A., Cashion, B. G., & Eshleman, J. R. (2007). Understanding Sociology. (3rd ed.) Redding: Horizon.

College Board (2007). 2007 College-Bound Seniors. New York: College Board.

Cookson, P. W., & Persell, C. H. (1985). Preparing for Power: America's Elite Boarding Schools. New York: Basic Books.

Durkheim, E. (1965). The Elementary Forms of the Religious Life. (J. W. Swain, Trans.) New York: Free Press.

Evans, R. D., Forsyth, C. J., & Bernard, S. (2002). One Church or Two? A Contemporary and Historical View of Race Relations in One Catholic Diocese. Sociological Spectrum, 22, 225-244.

Henslin, J. M. (1995). Sociology: A Down-to-Earth Approach. (2nd ed.) Boston: Allyn and Bacon.

Hunter, P. (2008). Adherents.com <http://www.adherents.com>.

Marx, K. (1970). Critique of Hegel's 'Philosophy of Right,' (A. Jolin & J. O'Malley, Trans.). Cambridge: University Press.

Massey, G. (Ed.). Readings for Sociology. New York: Norton, 1996.

Merton, R. K. (1949). Social Theory and Social Structure. New York: Free Press.

Messner, S. F. (1986). Television Violence and Violent Crime: An Aggregate Analysis. Social Problems 33, 218-234.

Ontario Consultants on Religious Tolerance (2008). ReligiousTolerance.org. <http://www.religioustolerance.org>.

Ortiz, F. I. (1982). Career Patterns in Education: Women, Men, and Minorities in Public School Administration. New York: Praeger.

Rosenthal, R., & Jacobson, L. (1968). Pygmalion in the Classroom: Teacher Expectation and Pupils' Intellectual Development. New York: Holt.

Savell, T. (1993). Inside American Education: The Decline, the Deception, the Dogmas. New York: Free Press.

Scimecca, J. A. (1980). Education and Society. New York: Holt.

Sewell, W. H. (1971). Inequality of Opportunity for Higher Education. American Sociological Review 36, 793-809.

Sewell, W. H., & Hauser, R. M. (1975). Education, Occupation, and Earnings: Achievement in the Early Career. New York: Academic Press.

Singh, S. (1982). Philosophical Foundations of the Sikh Value System. Illinois: Gurmat.

Stewart, E. W., & Glynn, J. A. (1979). Introduction to Sociology. (3rd ed.) New York: McGraw-Hill.

U.S. Bureau of the Census (2007). Statistical Abstract of the United States. Washington: GPO.

Walsh, A., & Hemmens, C. (2000). From Law to Order: The Theory and Practice of Law and Justice. Lanham: ACA.

Weber, M. (1958). The Protestant Ethic and the Spirit of Capitalism (T. Parsons, Trans.). New York: Scribner.

Weber, Max (1947). The Theory of Social and Economic Organization (A. M. Henderson & T. Parsons, Trans.). Glencoe: Free Press.

Wilson, J. Q. (1983). Thinking about Crime. New York: Vintage.

CHAPTER TWELVE

States, Markets, And Politics

Martyn Kingston

We are living in a period of significant and quickening change. Nations come and go, capitalism no longer goes unquestioned, and the role of communism has lessened in today's world. Democracy has risen where it previously seemed unthinkable, while existing democracies seek ways to rejuvenate and adapt to changing realities. Fundamentalist religious nation states exist and add to the complexity of global and regional geo-politics. The borders previously separating nations, economies and peoples have broken down, and migrants, ideas, and resources flow more freely throughout the world. The order and stability of nations, regions and peoples appear less threatened by catastrophic war between nation states, but today the world feels the threat of terrorism from small organized groups whose reach and influence transcend national territories. States, markets and politics are inextricably interwoven into a fabric which is difficult to understand let alone predict or change.

This chapter describes the way leading classical and contemporary theorists of economic and political sociology think about these foundational aspects of social order and change. Political and economic sociology originated as subfields of the larger discipline through the work of several 19th century social theorists. The early classical sociologists committed their life's work to understanding the unleashed forces of modernity including new institutional and socio-cultural arrangements associated with the rise of capitalism, democracy, socialism, religious fundamentalism and the new industrial order of nation states. They developed theoretical frameworks and paradigms so that we might better understand these developments and their relationships to the past and future. Some also offered ways to guide the actions and activism of people and institutions based on differing social philosophies and competing social and political interests.

Three themes usually characterize the work of economic and political sociologists as distinct from the way politics and economics are studied in other disciplines:

First, sociologists of politics and economy take a broad, integrated view of the social world, seeking to understand the connections between political institutions and other social institutions, especially economic and social ones.

Second, while political institutions and behavior associated with the state, political parties and voting behavior can take on a life of their own, sociologists believe them to be based in some way in other institutions or social forces. Democracy and capitalism, for example, do not arise without a set of particular historical and social circumstances. Equally, most other political phenomena, such as the collapse or rise of governments and states, cannot be adequately understood without looking at other institutional and social forces at play beyond or behind the particular characteristics and actions of individual figures or events. This characteristic of sociology comes from the core belief of the discipline that an important source of causation in the world of institutions lies in social phenomena.

Third, sociologists who study politics and economics tend to be interested in the evolutionary, comparative and historical construction of institutions and social change. Time, comparisons and history are important elements of this approach.

Key Concepts Of Political And Economic Sociology

A number of key concepts need to be examined in order to understand the contributions of classical and contemporary social theorists of the political and economic order of societies:

Power And Authority

These two concepts lie behind the key questions addressed by political sociologists and are therefore foundational to a sociological understanding of states, markets and politics.

Power refers to the capacity or ability of a person, group or institution to control, manipulate, influence or shape the views and actions of people. The concept involves the loss of freedom since at some level, some type of coercion is being applied to a person or group which in turn influences their behavior or thinking. Important sociological questions related to power follow regarding the degree and form of coercion coupled with the extent to which the person or group is aware of the imposition of power over them. Equally important is the question of agreement with the basis of that power and influence. Power takes many forms, such as within families when parents get their children to behave or when governments collect taxes and exercise power over citizens in various ways.

Authority is simply institutionalized power, whereby power is examined in the context of its institutional settings and institutionalized arrangements. A basic tenet of modern sociology is that the social world would not work effectively if obedience was simply based on force or crude forms of power leveraged by people who possessed it. Political and economic institutions exist and operate to establish rules to guide our lives just as the family exists for the same purpose regarding many key, foundational aspects of our interpersonal relationships and learned patterns of socialization. These rules represent authority. They are institutional guidelines which dictate the conditions under which one person or group may fairly ask another to comply with wishes.

Power and authority then, when taken together, refer to the exercise of influence by a person, group or society over the ideas and actions of others. It is the layered and multidimensional element that keeps our world working. When large-scale institutions break down or encounter problems that are out of the ordinary, we are faced with conditions that can result in shifting forms of institutional power and authority and changes to institutional arrangements at a fundamental level. This situation contrasts with what goes on normally, when everyday problems or situations arise which can be dealt with using the familiar, sanctioned practices of existing institutions. In the case of situations that threaten the existing order or status quo, sociologists look to recognize, explain and predict changes that may involve the very fabric of social institutions and society. In such instances, significant social upheaval results in wide-ranging consequences.

Legitimacy is another important sociological concept of political and economic systems in the modern era. The social philosopher Jurgen Habermas deals with the question of legitimation and its importance for building durable social institutions in the modern world. Legitimacy involves a sense of trust and approval between those with and without authority. It provides the foundation for the durable and stable operation of political and economic institutions. Legitimacy becomes a pivotal element in modern societies if raw forms of power are to successfully evolve into authority. Where legitimacy exists or can be created, sustained authority can be exercised. Where it fails or cannot be created, then problems occur for those holding authority and for the stability and durability of modern regimes.

The student of sociology—especially political and economic sociology—must then possess a keen interest in matters of power, authority and legitimacy and their relationships.

Institutions, Social Networks And Culture

Three additional concepts—institutions, social networks and culture—are also foundational to the work of political and economic sociologists.

In general, **institutions** represent the established and organized practices of a given society. Once they exist, they can exercise a profound influence on the form and direction of history and the lives of individuals and social groups.

Social networks involve the social ties and bonds between people and the organized relationships that link individuals to one another. There is grow-

ing interest in social networks among sociologists and across a wide range of disciplines. The focus of such work is on the idea that much of everyday life can be understood by examining the social networks in which people are embedded. For example, patterns of voting behavior can be understood by studying social networks and social relationships to determine how people come to arrive at a decision. Equally, social movements can be understood by examining various social networks in a society to gain insight into how movements originate and develop over time.

A third foundational concept is that of culture. **Culture** involves several elements by which social groups or societies solidify their ranks and navigate the social world. Culture can be understood broadly as a *way of life*, consisting of patterns of values, beliefs, norms of behavior and material technologies incorporated and used by the society or group. The term **society** is used by sociologists to describe patterns of interacting people, while *culture* is used to describe the manner in which people make sense of those interactions in terms of their meaning and significance. Culture is the human quality that allows people to differentiate themselves from others. Culture is the set of values, beliefs and norms used by people to guide and make sense of their lives and interactions, including how they understand each other and make sense of the larger institutional arrangements that surround them.

Culture involves the symbolic world of human interaction, whereby people filter the world through socially constructed interpretations of meaning and significance. A symbol is something, an object, idea or expression, that means something else, and that meaning or understanding is shared by other members of the group. Cultural analysis involves the examination of patterns of symbolic interaction between individuals and groups. The dynamics of whole societies and social institutions can also be understood using cultural analysis. Looking closely at the cultural arrangements of a society—its values, beliefs and norms, including both material technologies and its dominant idea systems—is a tool for grasping the political and economic dimensions of societies. For example, **nationalism** is a form of culture experienced by people in modern territorially bounded nation states. In the United States, nationalism is guided by beliefs and principles that are essentially political in nature and which citizens recognize as the American Creed, a political ideology shaped by the values of freedom, individualism and equality of opportunity, and a participatory democratic form of government. Another example is the manner in which modern social and political movements such as feminism and environmentalism incorporate emergent cultural beliefs concerning man's relationship to nature on the one hand and the creation of new identities concerning gender and sex on the other.

As with power and authority, the three concepts of institution, network and culture provide tools for thinking about the larger issues of politics and economics. They help students of sociology frame their discoveries and assist in directing the search for answers.

Classical Social Theorists Of States, Markets And Politics: Marx, Weber, Durkheim And Tocqueville

The foundations of a rich intellectual legacy regarding how sociologists think about politics and economics can be attributed to the work of four major historical scholars—Karl Marx, Max Weber, Emile Durkheim and Alexis de Tocqueville—who wrote during the industrial period between the 1820s and 1920s.

Karl Marx was the first of the great 19th century social theorists. His work on capitalism and social class has left an indelible mark on political and economic sociology and on the world it seeks to understand and influence. While he did not have much to say about politics and the state directly, his theoretical work on the evolution, nature and form of capitalism gives us a basic image of politics and state as reflections of the dominance of capitalism.

Max Weber is widely seen as the pre-eminent political sociologist. He dealt with themes Marx did

not consider or regarded as minor themes. Weber left us with a foundational understanding of the state and with a theoretical framework for viewing the state in relation to other social institutions.

Emile Durkheim and Alexis de Tocqueville examined social phenomena as distinct from economic or political phenomena. They gave us a set of ideas to focus attention on what we now call *civil society*—that part of the social world which is neither state nor economy—but which contains important interactions with them. Tocqueville's work provides insights into the workings of American democracy and describes key relationships between democracy and the general pattern of civic associations and participation observed in America.

One cannot understand modern political and economic systems, or the work of modern sociologists who attempt to understand these systems, without examining the contributions of these classical scholars. Their efforts were considerable and inspire the work and imaginations of today's scholars of states, markets and politics.

The questions they asked remain relevant, as do the various mechanisms and perspectives they developed to address them. How are we to explain the nature of politics? What are the forces that help us understand the nature of politics and governmental institutions in the modern world? How do we understand modern societal developments, specifically the nature and consequences of new forms of institutional arrangements? What are the key relationships that exist between modern political, economic and social civic institutions? How can we understand differences in these arrangements and social impacts across nations and societies? In order to answer such questions today, sociologists still draw largely on the intellectual foundations set by the classical figures.

The following examines the nature of such contributions and how recent scholars and social theorists build on and respond to them to address contemporary issues of politics and economy.

Karl Marx On The Economy And Politics

"It is enough to mention the commercial crisis

that by their periodic return put on its trial each time more threateningly, the existence of the entire bourgeois society. In these crises a great not only of the existing products but also the previously created productive forces are periodically destroyed. In these crises there (appears) an epidemic that in earlier epochs would have seemed an absurdity – the epidemic of over-production." Marx and Engels, The Communist Manifesto.

Writing more than a century ago, Marx offered a powerful and comprehensive view of the modern world grounded in an understanding of the rise of capitalism—a new institutional arrangement for satisfying the economic requirements of society. Marx's main contribution was to locate modern political forces and energy in an economy organized through a capitalist method of production. Many scholars today continue to follow the lead of Marx either wholly or partially by tracing the ongoing dynamics of the modern world to the workings of the economy. As capitalism has spread throughout the world, and as economic inequalities between peoples and nations have intensified rather than diminished, this view has come to take on increasing significance to many observers of politics.

The Fundamental Sociology Of Karl Marx

Social Class and Stratification: Along with his lifelong friend and co-writer, Friedrich Engels, Marx helps us appreciate the significance of social class and the notion that people's ideas about politics, religion or any set of ideas that guide social life are in some manner influenced by their wealth or property. Equally, Marx clarified another proposition familiar to people, that there are marked inequalities of wealth and power in modern societies and that these inequalities may become sources of major ideological struggles. Ironically, many people whose intellectual heritage owes the most to the theories of Marx are amongst the greatest detractors of his legacy. This is no doubt in large degree due to the way his work has been implemented by political parties and governments. His body of work has been transformed into Marxism or socialism by social and political revolutionaries, and, as a result, people have become strong proponents or equally fierce op-

ponents, regardless of the wisdom or virtue of many of the intellectual ideas he covered.

Academics and Activism: For Marx, as with most scholars, there is an inherent tension between the role of a practical human being and the role of a student of society and ideas. The former calls for action and making decisions in accordance with moral commitment of some kind. The latter role calls for theoretical or dispassionate observation. Max Weber recognized the tensions of this dilemma, and by rejecting the role of action chose to divorce himself from activism and direct himself to the world of ideas and thoughts. Marx worked to resolve the tension created by this seeming contradiction by merging the roles into one. Marx believed that through the careful study of society and history one could discover the main principles that bring about historical change and societal development. He and Engels thought they had hit upon the solution through understanding a theory of change as the product of historical development, and that by studying the development of society under capitalism in the 19th century, Marx and Engels believed and claimed that they had grasped the principles of historical change and the way ahead.

Alienation: Another reoccurring and important theme of Marx is alienation. Drawing from the humanist and rationalist traditions of the 18th century Marx described social beings as *alienated*—that is, estranged from their own unique creative capacities and from their capacity to empathize with one another. The principal causes of alienation are the institutions of society, especially social classes and the division of labor. The main manifestation of alienation is the belief by people that the institutions of society are immutable—that they possess a life of their own. Marx counters this view with the idea that institutions are continuously being created by men—in the past, present and future—and that all history, including the changing nature of social institutions, is moving society toward the single goal of eliminating alienation among men and thus revealing to them that they are masters and creators of their own social world. Each major stage of historical development brings greater progress toward this goal—an increasing capacity to be freed from alienation and from the constraints of social institutions. The final stage would involve the collapse of capitalism, the rise of state-sanctioned communism followed by a stateless form of socialism, and finally a society without social classes, since it was class that gave birth to alienation among modern peoples.

The Economy, Labor and Social Stratification: Marx's body of work speaks to the importance of labor, to man's primary role as a producer and the way in which the products of his labor become transformed. To Marx, it is this economic foundation of a society that is central to the operation of society. Until Marx, the study of the economy was just that: the study of the nature of production and the mode of production. Marx introduced the idea that the arrangements of production brought about social inequalities—inequalities which had nothing to do with the nature of human beings themselves. If some people were poor while others were rich, it was the result of the system of production and the very nature of capitalism itself.

Social groups and social stratification of those groups into higher/lower and richer/poorer is the result of the arrangement of the mode of production. Such groups represent the social stratification hierarchy of society. In a mature capitalist society there are two principal classes: the capitalists, a small minority of the population who own or control the means of production; and the proletariat, the large majority whose labor produces the goods and services in an economy and the surplus value or profit which is extracted by the capitalist in the process. The two classes differ in one essential fact: The capitalist owns the means of production, that is, the technological and scientific apparatus of production, while the proletariat owns nothing but his labor power. Ownership of property enables the owners to be the sole beneficiaries of the fruits of that process, that is, the profit or, technically speaking, the surplus value.

Materialist Philosophy: For Marx, the economy and the social relations involved in operating the economy represent the key to understanding the social world, especially its inner workings, which he claims are hidden to so many. Marx argues that people's connections to the economy shape their lives even though they may not be fully aware of these connections. The economy for Marx has a deep and profound impact on virtually every feature and institution of the social world. Economic processes not only shape politics, but they also shape religion, culture, education and the family. In this view, politics merely reflect the underlying nature and form of relations involved in production under modern capitalism. Thus, as the dominant force in the economy, capitalists are also the dominant political force since economic power is used to control political processes. The opposite also holds true, that the working class is a politically subordinate, powerless group under modern capitalism.

Base and Superstructure: A helpful way to think about this view of the relationship between the economy and politics lies in a metaphor shared by scholars of Marx called the base and **superstructure** of a society. Consider the image in Figure 12.1. The *base* or *substructure* consists entirely of the economic foundation of modern capitalism. It includes both the means of production, such things as the material requirements needed for production, along with the relations of production, that is, the nature and form of social classes. The *superstructure* that is built on top of the base or substructure consists of, among other things, the political institutions under capitalism, as well as such elements as political parties. Religion and culture are also elements of the superstructure of society. Marx believed that the economic substructure exercised

Figure 12.1 Base and Superstructure

SUPERSTRUCTURE OF SOCIETY
(State and Civil Society)
Politics, State, Religion, Culture

Base of Society
(Economy)
Social Relations
Around Means and Modes of Production
(Class Struggle)
Means of Production (Factors)
(Labor, Property, Technology & Capital)
Mode(s) of Production
(Feudalism—Capitalism—Communism—Socialism)

powerful limits over what could and could not be done by political institutions and leaders.

Politics, State Power And Class Struggle

Politics to most of us appears as a continuing conflict and struggle among different people, groups and parties. In America, politics is typically understood in partisan terms between conservatives and liberals, Republicans and Democrats, etc. According to this popular view, understanding politics means coming to terms with these groups and how they differ on such issues as the federal government's role on issues or problems. To Marx, however, the differences between contesting political groups are to be seen through differences in class and forms of property.

For Marx, and for many modern neo-Marxists, the state is a very powerful social institution. It concentrates a great deal of power and resources in the hands of a relatively small number of institutions and officials. While it might appear that such institutions can exercise decisive power over the lives of people, Marx introduced the idea that the power and leadership of the state and its officials are ultimately determined and limited by the nature of capitalism itself. States and state leaders cannot make decisions that in the long run counter the interests of capitalism itself. Both the system of capitalism as a system of private property in which the benefits of ownership belong to private individuals and groups, and the actual class of capitalists as a powerful and organized social entity, limit the freedom and exercise of power by the state. As Marx and Engels wrote, "(t)he executive of the modern State is but a committee for managing the common affairs of the whole bourgeoisie."

Marx asked "what is it that sustains capitalism, especially in the face of the existence of deep inequalities of wealth and material well-being?" For Marx, capitalism is sustained by two central tendencies. One is the power of its ideology while the other is the strength of its economy, especially over the working classes. **Ideology** is an aspect of what Marx described as the superstructure of capitalism. As such, it represents the ideals of those who propagate it along with ideas that sustain it. To

Marx, capitalist ideology fosters a form of *"false consciousness"* in that the ideology of capitalism is propounded as being beneficial to the entire society, whereas in reality, truth be told, it serves the best interests of capitalists and the modern system of capitalism itself. Any culturally dissipated belief, or set of ideas, that serves to further the interests of capitalism—for example, the dream that anyone and everyone can make it in America—constitutes capitalist ideology. It is on this basis of countering pernicious ideology that Marx argued for the need to inform and shift the consciousness of labor from a state of what he coined *"class-in-itself,"* which he viewed as a mere intellectual construct, to a realized, social, political and revolutionary movement that he called *"class-for-itself."* The main difference between these two conceptions of class is that the former lies mostly in the minds of intellectuals whereas in the case of the latter, a social class identifies and acts upon the realities of the position.

Economic Exploitation And Surplus Value

Marx developed an elaborate theoretical explanation of the economic functioning of capitalism which he viewed as an exploitative system of extraction. At a deeper level than the rejection of capitalist ideas and ideology, Marx addressed the central economic question of where value comes from under capitalism. Fundamentally, he states that wealth or surplus value can be traced back to unpaid increments of labor, meaning that under capitalism and a system of wage labor, workers are paid hourly or contracted wage labor rates that fall short of the full value of workers' labor in the productive process. At the center of the social philosophy of Marx is the belief that labor is a pivotal part of the full actualization of man, especially man as a social or communal being. Under capitalism, this potential to realize social labor power is not possible. The working classes have little or no control over labor power in terms of control over the product and process of labor. For Marx, surplus value or profit ultimately comes from the inputs of labor. Labor is needed to transform all of the other inputs or factors of production—raw materials, technology, ideas and other forms of property and financial resources—into marketable products and services. Without labor, the productive system has nothing. Marx maintained that capitalists always pay workers less than their labor is worth, and in most cases by providing subsistence wages they are able to extract huge amounts of profits or surplus value from the labor process. The overall effect, so Marx claims, is to prevent workers from accumulating sufficient capital themselves to become independent of the process of production. Marx claimed that workers possessed only their labor power, and they are forced to work because they cannot accumulate capital themselves, nor do they possess the organization or power collectively to change this situation. "Free wage labor," a term developed to describe the nature of labor under modern capitalism, is in *one* sense "free" when it is compared with the sheer brute force and ugliness of alternative feudal systems of slavery and indentured labor, but in another sense, it is anything but free for the industrial laborer, according to Marx.

Revolution And Change

Recently, sociologists have become interested in movements for political change, especially those directed toward revolutionary or fundamental change. When and how do they happen and with what effects? The collapse of the Soviet Union and its Eastern European allies and the sudden end of apartheid in South Africa are but a few of the recent situations that have sparked keen interest in such questions by scholars today.

Marx developed a powerful portrait of revolutions and fundamental institutional change that drew on his general imagery of capitalist societies and their historical conditions. He argued that the critical foundations for revolution or any set of sweeping change lay in the nature of the economy and in economic relations between social classes. He believed that every society ultimately contained within itself the materials and conditions that would spell its own downfall. Societies were to him self-contradictory forces that were promoted by one social class that in the course of its development laid the seeds of its own undoing.

Marx identified and singled out three sets of factors as antecedent causes of revolutions, economic factors, social factors and the creation of class consciousness among the working class. Marx stressed the economic causes and tended to relate the other two factors to economic causes.

Economic Causes: Marx predicted that the tendency of capitalism to pursue profits would eventually lead to an economy characterized by the overabundance of commodities, that is, a surplus of goods and services exceeding the ability of global markets to absorb them. Marx considered periodic crises and declining profits as critical to conditions favoring revolution. The second feature of markets Marx described as a necessary precondition for political instability was the centralization and concentration of capital. This includes the idea that because of capitalism's tendency to concentrate wealth, fewer and fewer owners would hold greater and greater portions of society's wealth. Marx claimed that "…one capitalist always kills many" before going on to describe the likelihood of increased oppression and the visibility of that oppression as one of the effects of the greater concentration of capital. An additional effect of centralization is the proletarization of work as more and more managers and owners fall into the ranks of the working class and as members of the ruling class identify with the conditions of the lower classes. Finally, Marx predicted that as a result of continuing crises of capitalism, the financial conditions of the majority would worsen as a result of economic instability and uncertainty, unemployment and underemployment, and the introduction of technology. This would result in a large reserve army of underutilized workers further laying the conditions of revolution. Marx wrote "(a)ccumulation of wealth at one pole is, therefore, at the same time accumulation of misery, agony of toil, slavery, ignorance, brutality, mental degradation, at the opposite pole, i.e., on the side of the class that produces its own product in the form of capital."

There is much debate over what Marx meant here. Did Marx mean that the absolute wage levels of working people would diminish, or did he mean that the relative gap in wage levels and general welfare between the classes would grow? The dispute is more than academic since under capitalism, wage levels have not become progressively worse for the majority whereas overall inequality between the classes may have. Also, the growing size and stability of the middle classes and the increasing involvement of the state in managing the capitalist economy present challenges to this overall thesis and may help explain why in fact the conditions Marx described as necessary for revolution have not resulted in many societies. In addition, the presence of institutions giving different classes a political voice from within the system may also have contributed significantly to the failed prediction of revolution. For example, political parties and trade unions dedicated, at least in part, to the interests of labor are important differences between the world Marx witnessed and today's political and economic landscape.

Social Causes: Marx wondered about the impact of the rapid urbanization of the social world. The movement of peasants from the countryside to towns and industrial cities presented Marx with a set of rapidly changing social conditions which he considered a powder-keg for revolutionary fervor. In the urban areas of Northwest England and elsewhere, Marx witnessed the most degrading and dehumanizing forms of work and sheer density of workers living in squalor. Marx thought that while the conditions of work and social life were horrifying, communication among workers was easier in the urban centers and factories than it was in the less densely populated countryside. Marx described how the "… union (of workers) is helped on by the improved means of communication that are created by modern industry and that place the workers of different localities in contact with one another." The importance of communication among the downtrodden is important because Marx argued that it has the potential to counteract the control capitalists have over the means of communication in a society and the general hegemony of the capitalist system over prevailing societal values. Of course, as bad as urban conditions were in many of the societies described by Marx, revolt let alone revolution did not uniformly follow.

Political Causes: The politicization of the work-

ing class is a major theme for Marx. Arguably perhaps, the most significant aspect or precondition of change for Marx is **class consciousness**.

In order for workers to bring about change they must be aware of themselves as a class. Adapting terminology from Feuerbach, who himself took terminology from Kant, Marx described a conditional change necessary for any social movement to be successful. In the case of labor, Marx argued that it must transform itself from a *Klasse an Sich*, or a "class-in-itself" by virtue of its members simply sharing economic and social conditions, to a *Klasse fur Sich*, a "class-for-itself," or a class whose members are aware and act upon these conditions.

Marx And Traditions Of Sociological Scholarship

The work of Karl Marx has so many facets that even though certain ideas have been discredited or have otherwise fallen away, Marxism continues to play a large and powerful role not only in how sociologists think about politics and economics, but in how politics and economics are actually conducted today. Several scholars, activists and even revolutionaries are discussed below to give a sense of how his legacy moved forward into the 20th century and beyond. One thing to also keep in mind is that it can be said reliably that the world we see today would not be the same were it not for Marx. His ideas permeate not only regimes which embraced his orthodoxy, but also those who oppose many of his ideas, too.

V. I. Lenin: Lenin and his collaborators, including Leon Trotsky, contributed to the understanding of revolutionary practice and to the body of Marxist theory. Lenin's chief contributions were to (1) the practical political application of Marxism to Russia in the 20th century; (2) the theory and practice of a socialist or workers' state; and (3) understanding the rise of imperialism and the global socialist response.

In his famous pamphlet *What is to be done?* published in 1903, Lenin outlined the position that to be a success, the socialist movement must be conducted across three fronts: political, theoretical and economic. Lenin argued against a reliance on trade unions and other reformist organizations, claiming that they alone could not succeed in transforming history. For revolutionaries and for scholars, Lenin's portrayal of revolutionary parties and organizations is of particular interest. Lenin argued for the need for full-time revolutionaries who dedicated their entire lives to the effort. In addition, he argued that detailed and ongoing study of current situations was critical to developing an effective strategy for revolutionary change. It was this combination of a dedicated cadre of revolutionaries, operating outside of the political system, along with their commitment to the careful study of local situations, including an ability to spot opportunities and exploit them, that made Lenin, and this publication especially, so influential. The neo-Marxist Georg Lukacs described Lenin as part theoretician, in that he successfully adapted and elaborated on the theories of Marx and Engels, and part politician, in that he was able to develop and command effective tactics from this theory to realize change. Lenin criticized so-called Marxists who blindly applied theory or principle and who failed to study the special circumstances operating in specific places and at specific times. His insistence in acknowledging the actual state of affairs coupled with theory, rather than blind application of theory alone, became recognized as an extraordinary contribution to our understanding of what makes for political change, especially of the radical or revolutionary kind.

In *State and Revolution* published in 1917, Lenin outlined the exact nature and form of a socialist or workers' state, something that neither Marx nor Engels was able to accomplish. He called this a temporary stage or dictatorship of the proletariat, arguing that conditions could be created to eventually see the "withering away of the state" itself. This is an interesting idea because Marx had portrayed the state as a *de facto* mechanism of oppression of the ruled by the ruling class. Lenin struggled with the contradiction in Marxist writing of foreseeing a stateless society but needing to rely on the socialist state to move society and history to this point. In the end, Lenin thought that the state could become a weapon in the struggle for the working class' emancipation by concentrating power in the hands of the workers' representatives.

Lenin's work on the analysis of imperialism was perhaps his most enduring contribution. In his writings, Marx generally focused on the operations of capitalism within nation states, whereas Lenin refocused attention on the growing realities of capitalist domination over other parts of the world. Lenin saw imperialism as a concept and framework that describe the use of transnational control and movements of key resources as an extension of capitalism beyond a national system to a global or international system. Lenin described an economic system needing an ever more abundant supply of raw materials and cheap labor for manufacturing, coupled with larger markets to sell the goods. This picture allowed Lenin to begin to explore the new dynamics of states, markets and politics in the face of such emergent global realities. Of course, developments in technology and transportation were at the forefront of this global economic transformation, and new relationships between states, economics and international politics developed.

Lenin attempted to explain these developments in his pamphlet *Imperialism: The Highest Stage of Capitalism*. He described how small numbers of monopolies within capitalist countries such as England, France, Germany and the United States worked with the state and governments of these countries to control and use the flow of finance capital to enterprise in far-away, less-developed countries. Lenin's work demonstrated the growth of monopoly capitalism and the reality of an historical stage of world history characterized by global inequities, colonization and colonialization.

Antonio Gramsci: Gramsci's analysis of the nature and role of the party showed an acute grasp of the strategic issues involved in revolutionary parties such as the communist party historically. Gramsci argued that no party could come to power unless the party became the true expression of the people and to do so meant overcoming the deep entrenchment and widespread loyalty in the public for a regime. He went on to describe how this loyalty for the regime was manufactured by a variety of social and cultural institutions. Gramsci's analysis of the historic intransigence of regimes to attempted radical penetration was helpful in the elaboration of Marx's ideas regarding party organization and activism.

The Frankfurt School and Herbert Marcuse and Jurgen Habermas: Few contemporary groups of scholars can rival the importance and influence of the Frankfurt School over political sociology. After founding the school in Germany in 1934, Theodor Adorno and Max Horkheimer were transplanted to the United States during the reign of Adolf Hitler. More philosophical and less action oriented, their work tends to return to the younger Marx regarding insights on history and society rather than the later Marx dedicated to revolutionary thought and action.

One of the principal contributions of the Frankfurt School, especially the work of Herbert Marcuse and Jurgen Habermas, is the combining of ideas emphasized by Weber with the critical assessment of capitalism emphasized by Marx.

Herbert Marcuse was less concerned with the working classes or with the fundamental virtues of labor as an activity and more concerned with the radical divorce he saw between man in modern civilization and the kind of *reason* advocated by the ancient Greeks. As it was for ancient Greek philosophers, for Marcuse *reason* was associated with the search for truth and the mind itself was not divorced from nature but could be used through deep reflection to discover those principles that were essential. In *One-Dimensional Man*, Marcuse claims that modern capitalism has created a fundamental alienation of man from nature, of reason from Reason. It has done this by repressing all those qualities that are fundamentally human, including man's need to reflect deeply on the world as well as to promote his sensual nature or Eros or love. This critical approach to modern society dominated by capitalism, and especially to the type of society developed in the United States, draws inspiration from Weber's critique of rationality. Marcuse works with Weber's distinction of *technical rationality*, or that which is concerned with technical means and calculation and efficiency, and *substantive rationality*, or that which is concerned with the ends, goals and values toward action. Marcuse identifies the problem of modern civilization as being based in the way it radically separates the two forms of reason and supplants one with the other. Substantive reason, which is the

deeper, more fundamental and ultimately necessary form, is replaced by technical reasoning, which is based on calculability, measurement and means-ends orientations. In this way, he asserts that technical reason becomes *reason* and, with it, the objects created by man thus come to stand apart from and apparently above him while at the same time his ability to reflect deeply and to imagine is itself repressed. This prevents him from seeing and recognizing this situation of fundamental alienation from reason and the essence of the human spirit. Marcuse describes this process as a dehumanizing process since, in effect, man no longer represents man, but instead his own sense of self is seen through the objects and bodies of thought he has created. Man becomes a purely technical instrument divorced from a sense of self, which had previously been realized through a capacity to reason and reflect deeply.

Jurgen Habermas, the current leading member of the Frankfurt School, also uses the work of Max Weber to critically understand the nature and impacts of modern capitalism. Working in the areas of Weber's concern for the nature of legitimacy, Habermas identifies the contradictions in modern societies characterized by social welfare, mass democracy and the nature of legal decision making. Habermas identifies an important deeper level of legitimacy based on people's shared normative understandings of what it is to be valued in the social world. This level of understanding is, he argues, obscured by institutions in the modern world and by the theories about this society. Habermas argues that only a critical theory, one that sees as problematic the very foundations of modern capitalism, can penetrate an intellectual approach he characterizes as "universal pragmatics." Only through a critical theory that involves a detailed analysis of discursive language and communication will the distortions and contradictions of modern capitalism be revealed.

Nicos Poulantzas: Arguably the pre-eminent political sociologist among contemporary Marxist scholars until his death in 1979, Poulantzas focused on how the state might become an independent actor in the history and development of the class struggle. In doing so, he pursued a notion of Weber regarding the "relative autonomy of the state" and provided some major contributions toward how we might think about capitalism and modern politics in the present era.

Poulantzas thought about societies in terms of structures, or interrelating parts which functioned to maintain their integrity and order. They are akin to the abstract notion of superstructure developed by Marx and described earlier in the chapter as a way to think about the fundamental arrangements of societies. And yet, for Poulantzas, structures are more than mere concepts because they actually shape how the world works. The main structures outlined by Poulantzas are (1) ideology, or the realm of ideas; (2) politics, or the realm of the state; (3) economics, or the realm of production; and (4) judicial, or the realm of law. Poulantzas asserts that each realm can operate independently of the other, and that in each historical situation, for example the United States in the late 20th century, one structure could dominate the others in the working of society. For example, ideological consideration could trump state or political and economic considerations, and so on. This was a major departure from the strict tenets of Marxism since it spoke to a rejection of the crude economic determinism of Marx and the base/superstructure model and dynamics. Poulantzas spoke of the economic arrangements of a social system determining other elements of a society's fundamental arrangements quite loosely.

A further and related element of the scheme Poulantzas developed involves the claim that the state, as a structure, could operate independently as an agent in the growth and development of a capitalist society. On the one hand this meant that the state could intervene in class struggles, especially when there was an impasse between dominant and subordinate classes and groups. Poulantzas even acknowledges that the state may at times intervene on behalf of the interests of the working classes over the dominant classes where it means that the system of capitalism will be able to maintain itself. The other way the state becomes an independent actor is by becoming the arena in which class struggle is contested. Poulantzas describes the modern state as being made up of different factions of classes,

including members of the subordinate classes. It is in this way that Poulantzas, for example, explains the emergence of the welfare state, many of whose programs benefit the subordinate classes. Poulantzas limits this view of the state, however, by saying that the gains are more apparent than real, since the ultimate winner behind programs such as Social Security, Medicare and poverty programs is capitalism, since it escapes fundamental scrutiny and is itself supported in the long run through the working of these efforts.

In short, the image of society, and state processes especially, is far more complicated than that of Marx. Rather than simply seeing the state and politics in a reductive and simplified way, as "being nothing but the executive of the ruling class," Poulantzas argues that the state can and does represent a battleground where conflicts and the contradictions surrounding them are waged. Ralph Milliband and most recently William G. Domhoff went on to explore this idea, and they argue that in today's societies the state remains the central vehicle through which capitalism survives largely because the key policymakers in the judicial, police, military, legislative and executive branches of the state are networked and interwoven with the capitalist class. Poulantzas takes issue with this approach and calls it simple-minded since it reduces the state and capitalism to individual actors and agents. Poulantzas sees society like Marx does, as composed of impersonal forces and structures that lie behind particular historical agents.

Max Weber On The State And Societies

"Today ... we have to claim that a state is a human community that successfully claims the monopoly of the legitimate use of physical force within a given territory ... The state is considered the sole source of the 'right' to use violence. Hence, 'politics' for us means striving to share power or striving to influence the distribution of power, either among states or among groups within a state." **Max Weber**, *Politics as a Vocation*

The claim that the institutions of the state, or government, exercise control over the workings of politics seems not only a truism but is an integral part of the view of all scholars who call themselves political scientists. And yet, sociologists since Marx have taken a slightly different perspective, arguing instead that politics cannot be understood by examining the internal workings of the state itself. One must view politics more broadly, claim sociologists. For Marx, as we have heard, this means considering the nature of social classes and the economy as well as the international circumstances among nations if we are to adequately comprehend politics.

Max Weber, writing in the early 20th century, more than 20 years following the death of Marx, not only serves as a counter-point on many issues in the writings of Marx, but his body of work also turns our attention back to the nature and role of the state and its connections to other social institutions. Weber also set out to correct the materialist philosophy of Marx by suggesting an important, if not decisive, role for ideas and ideals in the study of history and society. Weber set out to counter Marx's heavy emphasis on economic causes of social phenomena through the belief that the actual administration of politics plays a large part in shaping how power is exercised over people. Weber also countered the emphasis on social classes by showing the role played by great figures in the making of history. While acknowledging the long-term significance of societal organizations and social institutions, like the state over historical outcomes, Weber believed that individuals of great personal power and influence—**charismatic personalities**, he called them—could also exercise a decisive role in social change. Weber certainly tried to have it both ways by asserting on the one hand that the strength of state institutions was due to the rise in the force and power of law and administrative bureaucracy, while on the other hand also claiming that charismatic leadership was decisive in transforming institutional arrangements.

The Fundamental Sociology Of Max Weber

Social Science Methodology: Max Weber was an expert in many fields of study—law, anthropology, economics, history, sociology, and politics—and he used this breadth of knowledge to make sense of the development of western civilization and the modern world. Unlike Marx, he did not produce a general theory of society or history. He opposed such fanciful grand theorizing by claiming that "the more comprehensive the validity—or scope—of the term, the more it leads us away from the richness of reality since in order to include the common elements of the largest possible number of phenomena, it must necessarily be as abstract as possible and hence *devoid* of content." Taken from his *Methodology of the Social Sciences*, Weber goes on to claim that in the cultural sciences, the knowledge of the universal or general is never valuable in itself. He believed that human societies were such that it would be impossible to ever formulate some basic general laws or principles of society. At best, he said, one could offer specific explanations for particular historical events or situations. As time passed and the world changed, the questions posed by social scientists would change, reflecting new issues and concerns.

Rationality and Modern Bureaucracy: According to Weber, in order to understand the social and economic development of Western civilization, and by extension important features of the modern era, one has to examine the broad and pervasive trend toward the **rationalization of life**. Weber describes modern life as being characterized and subject to the rise of professionalism and what he termed the routinization of activities. In the modern era, more and more aspects of social life were becoming subject to a common form of rational assessment and calculability—that is, the assessment of the most technically efficient means for attaining particular ends. These new routines sprang from the growing influence of science and scientific methodology over social organization. Such rationalization developed first in the professions before it became embodied in rational bureaucracy, which for Weber became the most striking and dominant feature of all modern institutions in the West. Bureaucratic principles and practice represented major technical advances over prior civilizations; tasks were accomplished more quickly, precisely, cheaply and effectively than through any other form of prior organization. Unfortunately, and as Weber noted, the subjection of social life to the forces of bureaucratic organization and personality led to many new problems and issues introduced below.

Alienation: Like Marx before him, Weber was concerned with the effects of modernity on the alienation of man. The theme of bureaucracy is described by Weber as the structural avenue through which modern life is administered. The individual, lacking the ability to control this institution, is therefore unable to control the activities of his own life. Bureaucracy and its themes of administered process, calculation and efficiency have become so persuasive that the individual's option for action, and thus his freedom, are curtailed.

Social Status: This claim regarding the "iron cage" effect of rational bureaucracy presents something of a contradiction with his contributions regarding status groups. Weber modified the work of Marx on social stratification by pointing out the importance of *status* as an important source of group identity and solidarity. He pointed out that at times it competed with or contradicted class-based identity. Weber argued against the strict reductive and simplifying reasoning of Marx regarding social class by stressing the variety of values and beliefs that men and women might choose to commit themselves to. He spoke of such values becoming expressions, objects or "**social facts**" and that the patterns of values chosen to guide life could and did provide the basis of distinctive social groups which he termed *status groups*. Such patterns of lifestyle could, he felt, become the sources of competition and conflict among groups in the political arena.

This idea, therefore, rivals and to some degree calls into question the primacy argument on class divisions which Marx stressed. Weber claimed that race, ethnicity, religion and lifestyle are sources of status groupings and stratification hierarchies which may crisscross social class boundaries, making the analysis of community and conflict messy and less subject to general class-based theorizing. As we have seen, Marx reduced status characteristics such as race and religion to aspects of the superstructure. Weber argued that instead of seeing the full nature and consequences of race and religion, Marxist theorizing about race and religion tends to a *priori fit* the "facts" to the general theory of class divi-

sions and conflict. For example, Marx and subsequent neo-Marxists understood race and racism as a mechanism or tactic of the upper class used to control or exploit the lower subjected classes. For Marx, racial conflict and oppression were rooted in class conflict. Weber revised this formulation by showing that status or patterns of honor or prestige involved in such things as ethnicity or religion cannot always be reduced to class-based interests. He described instances where status and class attributes contradicted each other, as when members of a poorer or subjected class identify and act with rather than against members of an elite class on the basis of race or religion.

Religion and Economy: One of Weber's greatest intellectual contributions regarding economics and society involves his effort to explain broad differences between the West and what he called the Orient. Here he turned his attention to the social consequences of religion. Weber's study of the rise of ascetic Protestantism in the West stressed that besides being a major distinguishing characteristic of religion in the West, ascetic Protestantism paradoxically led to the rise of capitalism as a mode of production and economic system there. He showed how the tenets of ascetic Protestantism provide many of the socio-cultural prerequisites for the rise of capitalism and capitalist culture. They include an emphasis on salvation which became associated with work on earth, the rise of individualism and individual accountability, abstinence from self-indulgence, and the single-minded devotion to one's life and work. These ideals sprang from post-reformation religious developments and provided a moral framework for the shrewd and relentless accumulation of wealth under capitalism. In this way, Weber demonstrated that ideas, in this case religious ideas and practices, had effects on secular ideas concerning the nature and form of economic behavior. In this case, Weber linked religion indirectly to the development of new forms of production and market behavior. It is on the basis of such study and theorizing that Weber countered Marx by showing that religious ideas actually affected the emergence of capitalism rather than the reverse, that ideas were the consequence of economic arrangements.

The State, Power, Politics And Society

Weber's sense of the possibilities and influence of politics and political organizations was far more astute and developed than that of Marx. At the heart of his contributions to the study of modern society is the argument that government, and more generally the modern state, exercises as much influence over society and history as the economy. Unlike Marx, who believed that the activities of societies were grounded fundamentally in the mode of production and economic institutions and social relations, Weber believed that the exercise of political authority is central to understanding modern societies. A large part of his work was devoted to understanding the exact nature of that authority, how it worked and with what consequences in modern, feudal and ancient societies.

Weber believed that people are alienated, but from the means of administration rather than from the means of material production. While Marx believed mankind could throw off the yoke of its alienation, Weber was less certain that humankind could reduce the encroachment of bureaucracy over the individual's daily life. Unlike Marx, Weber's sociology possessed no vision or end point and no process or plan to move mankind forward. For Weber, while we can understand the major themes of the movement of history and social life based on an accurate reconstruction of the past and present, he argued that we cannot easily discern the way of the future.

The State: Weber left a considerable legacy regarding how to think about states and their operations in modern society. His framework remains one of the most influential for contemporary scholars of the state. The principal aspect of the modern state, he claimed, is that it is able to monopolize the legitimate use of physical force inside a given territory. This gives the state a power that no other institution or organization possesses in modern society. Potentially, at least, it means the state and its officials can wield its power in a way no other group, including large social classes, can. The state is indeed the ultimate authority regarding force and power. Weber argued that the state in the modern world occupies the same place of prominence and centrality as the church did during medieval times.

Weber described two key characteristics or capabilities of the modern state regarding organization. First, state bureaucracy is central to the ability of the state to administer and control. Bureaucracy provides the means by which laws are articulated and implemented through policy on behalf of the wider society. While, in a democracy, the members of parliament or congress represent the elected officials, state bureaucrats, consisting of civil servants and managers, remain decisive because they actually translate law into policy and carry out law. The second organizational feature of modern state bureaucracy involves particular groups of officials who become ascendant over others. Weber noted the rise of a political and administrative class whose power and authority comes from their expertise and skill in the administration of politics. Weber, for example, went on to argue that it is for this reason that with the ascendance of rational law over daily life, those who understood the law—modern lawyers—would become central to politics and to the administration of the force of the state.

Weber claimed that the rule of law establishes the important boundaries in a democratic society. Citizens obey the law or suffer the penalties. He portrayed a view of modern democratic society in which people go about their routines in a rational, orderly way. However, Weber suggested that beneath this surface of order lies the potential for deep threats to society in general and democratic society in particular. First, the emphasis on rational norms, efficiency and calculability and their application by the state and other modern institutions operates at the expense of issues such as justice and equality. In stressing efficiency, we become detracted by rules and bureaucratic procedures, and the focus is taken away from more meaningful ends of life and questions about such ends. Second, Weber was concerned by the consequences of the bureaucratic organization of the modern state and the fact that this meant that it was becoming more complex and powerful. He feared that this would make it far more difficult for groups and individuals to challenge the state. In contrast to Marx's fear about the accumulation of capital and power in the hands of a capitalist class, Weber illuminated an alternative threat of concentrated power under the modern state. History since the time of Weber's writing has certainly born out the wisdom of this understanding and warning given the nature and scale of global conflict and warfare.

The Power of the Ruler: Several academic interpretations exist regarding Weber's thinking about the role of individual figures or leaders in the context of modern institutions. Some scholars argue that Weber, like Nietzsche, believed in the power of great figures to transform the world, making institutions and customs mere bedfellows of those with charismatic power. Others believed that while Weber acknowledged the imprint of key figures, he also believed that institutions do take on a life of their own, as did the great sociologist Emile Durkheim. This latter view attributes power to the state to remake societies and reshape their course.

Authority and Legitimacy: Weber's study of politics addressed a fundamental sociological question: How is it that large, diverse assemblages of individuals are held together and cooperate? For Marx the answer lay in ideology. For Weber, it became a matter of authority that some sociologists term domination. Weber described how the grounds for obeying authority in modern societies lay in the rational-legal foundations of law. Law becomes an instrument of universal and impersonal rule, and it offers advantages as a governing tool in large, diverse societies. Law also provides terms in which both the officials of the state and the citizens make a contract to agree to the nature of rule. Law by itself does not, of course, ensure compliance or order. An administrative apparatus is required to implement law and monitor its effectiveness. "Organized domination," Weber said, "requires the control of those material goods which in a given case are necessary for the use of physical violence … (as well as) control of the executive staff and the material implementation of administration." Weber addressed the problem of the ruler's power being usurped from within the state apparatus by saying that solidarity must be developed between the ruler and the staff to maintain the system of authority established by law.

Although Weber characterizes the modern state as having a monopoly over the means of violence in a society, he also stresses the question of legitimacy as being important in the long run to maintaining authority and influence. State rulers can, of course, rule because they hold the means of force, but unless followers believe in this right to lead, no exercise of power by itself can maintain the ruler or the regime.

Political Power and Social Groups: Given the power or potential power of the state, Weber examined the question of state power in relation to the claims of contending social groups. State power can be seen then as a prize for competing groups seeking that control and authority. Marx argued that this prize was secured by the dominant class during each historical period or stage of historical development of societies. Under the capitalist stage, this meant that the wealthy class controlled the use of state power one way or another, in spite of the possibility of there being a democratic order with voting rights widely dispersed.

Weber considered the puzzle to be far more complex. While he acknowledged the realities of social class, he argued that such categories of people would never take decisive action unless they organized around a commonly felt basis for such action. Weber claims that such common and purposive action, especially in a modern democratic society, was more likely to spring from two other kinds of social alliance, namely status groups and political alliances. Social classes could never be organized to take decisive action because they lacked a common basis for such action.

Status groups consist of social bonds Weber described as usually springing from a shared occupational or professional position, like that experienced by lawyers, artists or teachers. As a result of a common position, they come to share values and lifestyles. They may live in certain areas of a city, shop in similar ways and think in similar kinds of ways. Status groups can become the basis of political action because their members share similar lifestyles and values.

Weber also described how *political associations* and *parties* rather than social classes or status groups in effect become the main contenders for the power of the state. The **political party**, unlike either a social class or status group, is organized specifically to pursue political ends and the exercise of power. Weber claimed that "(p)arties live in a house of 'power,'" and 'their action is oriented toward the acquisition of social 'power,' that is to say, toward influencing a communal action no matter what its content may be." Political parties direct their energy and plan their strategy based on this reality concerning power. In the end, Weber said that social classes are far too large, diverse and nebulous a social grouping to be able to obtain power and solve the complex problems of modern societies. Status groups occasionally hold power at a societal level, but the primary contenders of power to rule by controlling the apparatus of the state are political parties.

Weber And Traditions Of Sociological Scholarship

Weber's work started sociologists on the path to understanding the nature and variations of modern states. The following discusses three of the most significant contributions of recent scholars to build on the Weberian tradition regarding the state. Like Weber, each scholar regards the state as the most important and influential social institution of the modern world. Each assumes that this power should be based on the state's ability to exercise legitimate control over the use of force. Each also assumes that ultimately it is through the state that the people voice their desires about the future direction of society. Scholars of the modern states also focus attention on the considerable control the state has over various types of resources needed to mobilize change. Major questions for scholars today involve how much power and authority the state can exercise and what is to be the relationship between those who hold state and economic power. It is hard to imagine two more pivotal and relevant questions considering the current state of affairs in 2009 regarding the global economic crisis.

The following section briefly highlights important theoretical and applied issues associated with these questions considered by modern sociologists Reinhard Bendix, Charles Tilly and Theda Skocpol.

Coverage includes a description of how their work builds on the earlier work of Weber. Like Weber, each scholar takes issue with the Marxian conception of the state as simply doing the bidding of those who control the economy. Collectively, they demonstrate that the state often takes actions which run contrary to the interests of capital and to the interests of other sections of the population for that matter.

Reinhard Bendix: Fleeing Nazi Germany in 1938, Bendix introduced to American sociology comparative and historical studies involving social and political change at a large, societal level. Drawing on the work of Weber and Alexis de Tocqueville (next section), he was interested in showing the role that ideas played in the makeup of societies, including social change.

Bendix addressed the central Weberian theme of political authority. As we learned previously, authority in Weber's work played the same role as the economy and ideology did for the writings of Marx. Bendix elaborated on the idea that the central new theme of modern societies was not capitalism *per se* but rather the **rational organization** underlying *new forms of authority*. Bendix blended this theme with questions and issues raised by Tocqueville concerning the growing influence and power of the middle classes under a democratic order. Bendix made it clear that authority does not simply mean the straightforward exercise of power, even the legitimate power by rulers, but rather it represents a kind of delicate balancing act between the wishes and intentions of rulers and followers. Bendix clarified the critical idea that if one wishes to understand power and how it is used, we have to also understand the social grounds and conditions that enable leaders to exercise power, or which make it possible in the first place and on a continuing basis. Power is not simply wielded by powerful figures with no sense of the nature and character of the social conditions which surround it. Weber had emphasized that the integrity of societies arose not simply out of the material resources commanded by the wealthy but also because of dominant ideas and ideals. Bendix illuminated this argument by showing that political struggles take place over both ideal and material interests, and they occur in the context of the quite distinct ideological current which shapes and influences such political debates and conflicts. Ideal interests play a major part in the nature of politics, although they have to be discovered and studied through mores subtle and nuanced historical and interpretative analysis.

Bendix's contribution concerning the study of ideal interests and their role in responding to conflict was well-illustrated in his work on the ideologies of managerialism which developed in the early part of the 20th century. He began his analysis with the collapse of royal authority and with the forces unleashed as a result of changing authority relations in the emerging modern world. Transitioning from a society in which relations between nobility and the peasants were fixed to a society in which industry arose created opportunities for social mobility and a problem concerning the nature of labor itself. A tension existed between the individualism and freedom unleashed by the collapse of the old world and the need for workers in the new, and the need for workers to form new social institutions to deal with the changing conditions. Now that people were free, what would convince them to work for new masters? Bendix believed that ideas or ideologies were necessary to create the grounds for new forms of compliance. This was the question and issue addressed by Bendix in relation to his early work on new industrial workers and in his later writings on kings and rulers.

Charles Tilly: Tilly is a leading contemporary sociologist who treats the same questions raised by Karl Marx and Max Weber concerning the analysis of social change, economic circumstances and class differences in an historical context. Tilly uses detailed historical analysis rather than grand models to explore state-building and the struggles over the authority of government. Tilly pinpoints social change as a major theme in the nature of societies, and rather than apply broad theoretical models to its understanding, his detailed historical analysis focuses on how forces of protest and change occur among ordinary people. In addition, Tilly and his colleagues devoted considerable attention to state-making and state-building, building on the work of

Weber. Their synthesis provides us with an often-cited clear definition of the *modern state*. Tilly states that the structure of the state that became dominant in Europe after 1500 had four elements. First, it controlled a well-defined, continuous territory; second, it was relatively centralized; third, it was differentiated from other organizations; and fourth, it reinforced its claims through a tendency to acquire a monopoly over the concentrated means of physical coercion within its territory. Tilly went on to connect state-building with war-making and argued that given there were so many variations in states and state-making, that deeper analysis was necessary to account for attributes not easily explained by a general model of state-building. Tilly argued that the different characteristics of states could be attributed to various combinations of capital (resources) and coercion. Whereas the Dutch state developed because of its ability to harness capital resources, the German state grew out of its ability to harness military and administrative resources. In addition to these two predominate forces, Tilly also studied the relationship between the social class structure and the kinds of state apparatus which developed. Tilly observed that the kind and power of the social classes in a country did affect the type and form of state which developed.

Tilly is most famous for his work on social movements and revolutions. He argued that sociology needs to move away from the grand theorizing of Marx and Weber and shift to the study of the processes of political contestation itself. Tilly introduced what he called a "**resource mobilization**" model of politics characterized by the following elements: (1) interests; (2) organization; (3) mobilization; and (4) opportunity. Interests referred to the distinctive advantages and disadvantages groups held. Organization describes the common identity and social structure of the group. Mobilization relates to the resources at the disposal of the group, and opportunity describes the chances or situations the group has to move forward, harness and direct resources to compete effectively. Social movements need all such elements to be successful. Tilly describes each element in terms of particular historical situations to bring this framework alive as an explanatory tool. For example, he shows how a group's social structure can and does influence the chance of challenging existing power and authority. Strong social links and connections between members of a group can have a positive impact on the likelihood of success. Equally, Tilly shows how opportunities can exist in the wider socio-economic conditions that can allow a group or a social movement to succeed. If the established power base is threatened, distracted or extended in some way, this can provide the opportunity to challenge an otherwise repressive force. Tilly then extends the model of collective action described by Marx and Weber by identifying the types of situations and conditions needed in conjunction with the steps of a mobilization processes necessary for social resistance to be successful.

Theda Skocpol: The main contribution of Skocpol's ongoing work centers on bringing back the state as a major, independent social actor and source of explanation for different historical situations and events, such as the growth and variations of the welfare state and social revolutions in the modern era.

Skocpol takes much from the work of Max Weber as well as from Karl Marx. Like Max Weber she argues that the state is far more than a simple reflection of the interests of the dominant social class. The modern state for Skocpol operates as an autonomous and powerful institution separate from the economy and economic interests of a society. The state is made up of a variety of specific organizations, actors and interests including different branches of government, different types of administrations and forms of authority. Skocpol demonstrates that the state, like other social institutions, can take on a life of its own and in doing so impacts the whole or parts of a society independently of other institutions. The following briefly summarizes two of her most important and influential applications of this idea, one on states and social revolutions and the other on the development of the American welfare state.

Skocpol uses this conception and framework of the state as a means of explaining why in the modern era some countries, like Japan, produced

dictatorships while others, like England, produced a democracy. Skocpol argues that previous work on states and social revolutions omitted the role played by the state, or protostate, in the development of each of the countries. Skocpol summarizes her general findings and unique perspective on states and social revolutions through three central propositions. First, the causes of revolutions are to be found in the objectively observable social conditions of a society and not in the expressed intentions of revolutionaries. Second, International conditions and circumstances play a major part in promoting revolutions, influencing the ability of the incumbent authorities to control a society. And third, contrary to the assertions of Marx, the agents and institutions of the state may act independently of social classes or other economic forces to block or facilitate social movements and revolutions.

Skocpol distinguishes the social conditions that make the society and state vulnerable to a revolution and those that encourage the transformation. She examines the sets of conditions in France, China and Russia prior to the revolutionary periods, finding similar circumstances in each case. State control over the population was effective in all three cases, but in each instance the state was vulnerable to external attack by the countries' enemies. Skocpol compares this situation with others in which revolutions did not occur and notes in these cases that the external threat or pressures on the state were far less. Equally, Skocpol documents significant differences in the social and economic conditions and organization of the revolutionary forces between those countries who experienced social revolution and those which did not. In countries that avoided revolution, such as Prussia and Japan, peasant classes were unable to organize and command resources effectively, whereas in France, China and Russia they could and did. Skocpol's work in stressing the presence of social conditions has been criticized for the lack of attention given to ideological factors or beliefs and to the importance of figures such as charismatic leaders in explaining why social revolutions occur when and how they do and why in other situations they do not.

The difference in the nature and development of

welfare state policies across countries is a subject which has received a great deal of sociological attention. Along with other scholars, Skocpol is interested in explaining why it is that the welfare state in the United States was relatively late in its development and different in the provision of health care, pensions and unemployment as compared with other Western industrialized societies such as Germany, Scandinavian countries, France and Great Britain. Some trace these differences to the absence of a socialist tradition in the case of the United States, while others trace it to the presence of values such as individualism and opposition to state involvement in such functions and services which many argue typified the development of American state thinking. Skocpol argues against such explanations by comparing the nature and development of the state in different countries, emphasizing that in the case of the United States the state building processes over the nineteenth and well into the twentieth-centuries were less conducive to the evolution of a thorough going welfare state. She points out that even though Civil War pensions and benefits were evidence of early welfare traditions in the United States, they never lead to the development of a larger social program for the needy and poor because the state lacked a centralized and autonomous apparatus that could organize such a large scale program. Courts and other entities, such as political parties and economic interests, exercised greater power over the issues than the state administration. In addition, Skocpol argues that the strong paternalistic orientation of the American state, one run by men, also shaped policy initially in favor of the male breadwinner. Ironically, the exclusion of women from suffrage until the 1920s and by extension from a strong voice in government until well after this date encouraged women to pursue alternative avenues of expression. Skocpol describes in detail a history of women's voluntary associations and groups that gave them a voice and eventually suffrage in 1919, as well as an impact on the later welfare policies that would benefit mothers and children and other social groups in need. Skocpol shows that American politics was organized less on the lines of class and unions and more on the lines

of gender. This explains in part why welfare policies in the 20th century benefited housewives, women and children more than they did workers.

Regardless of differing views on Skocpol's historically based questions, her approach to understanding the nature and role of the state in modern societies provides a rich and interesting link with the earlier sociology of Max Weber and in doing so has inspired further work on the state and political institutions on the part of sociologists and political scientists alike.

Emile Durkheim And Civil Society And Politics

In earlier sections of this chapter and book we learned that the distinction between the "conflict" and "consensus" schools of sociology highlights crucial differences between leading theorists of society and politics. The conflict school dates back to the writings of Karl Marx and emphasizes the divisions and battles in societies. The consensus school presents a view of the world which is very different. It describes an underlying set of beliefs and agreements and the idea that social institutions such as education, family and religion function to give society stability and continuity. In this view, politics are approached less as a mechanism of conflict and division and more as a mechanism to create and maintain the important institutions of society.

The Fundamental Sociology Of Emile Durkheim

Along with Marx and Weber, Emile Durkheim is regarded as among the greatest foundational figures of sociology. Durkheim's main concern was to explain the basis of social solidarity or why and how societies hold together and maintain order and agreement. In doing so, he also laid the foundations for sociology as a distinctive and separate academic discipline by demonstrating the use of scientific method and approaches to the study of society. Born in 1858 in France, Durkheim followed in the tradition of the French philosopher Jean Jacques Rousseau in being absorbed by questions of "the general will" and the conditions that bind societies together.

Whereas Marx stressed the economy and Weber the state, Durkheim, like Tocqueville, emphasized civil society for understanding politics, a view which is becoming ascendant in today's political sociology through such scholars as Robert Bellah, James Coleman and Robert Putnam.

Society: The central focus of Durkheim's writings is the nature of society. Durkheim became the leading figure to implement the agenda and vocation of August Comte, who had begun to outline the broad contours of sociology as the social scientific study of human society. Society for Durkheim came to consist of several different key elements. Solidarity referred to its wholeness or integrity as opposed to its divisions and conflicts. In addition, Durkheim studied the nature and function of norms and laws, institutions, symbols and rituals, and the division of labor. Each element Durkheim studied in the context of understanding the moral order of society as well as the reasons for the failure of principal institutions in certain circumstances.

"Social Facts": Sociology, he wrote, is the study of **social facts**, which are the collective or shared ways of thinking, feeling and acting. He worked tirelessly to show that social facts existed beyond the psychology of the individual and the biological principles of humans as a species. Durkheim claimed that social facts have a force and power over humans as much as or greater than the psychological and biological facts, and that these facts are to be found in the scientific study of societies. They are external to human beings, and they influence human behavior and thinking in the same manner as psychological and biological facts and conditions.

Much of the writing and research of Durkheim set out to prove and substantiate this claim and to lay out an agenda for future sociological research. His study, *Suicide*, showed that suicide was not solely due to biological or psychological causes. He demonstrated that different societies experienced suicide at different rates and that these rates also differed across time and between different social groups and regions within those societies. Durkheim attempted to shift the focus of philosophy away from the nature of the external world and direct it to the nature of human beings, as a subject. It was society in general, and social institutions in particular, that created the ways of thinking through which the natural and moral human world was portrayed.

Social Norms and Laws: Such elements are the rules that guide behavior and thinking within societies. Durkheim viewed them as the most basic or fundamental of social facts. He went on to argue that for any society or human group to work properly, the norms and laws must carefully govern the behavior of individual members of the society or group. The nature and type of norms and laws vary with the degree of simplicity and complexity of social organization. But, Durkheim recognized, certain general patterns concerning norms and laws such as the idea of punishment; in primitive societies, laws and norms seek retribution on behalf of the entire society, whereas in larger, more complex societies, the laws seek to compensate the individual party. Penal law, characteristic of smaller, more inclusive societies, exacts harsh punishments from the offender, whereas civil law and corporate law characteristic of much of the modern system of law, simply seeks restitution on behalf of the victim, restoring things, as Durkheim describes it, "to their original state."

Social Institutions: Guiding norms and laws of a society are provided by its central social institutions. Education, religion and the economy provide examples of the central institutions of society, with each specializing in different areas of tasks or functions provided within a social system. In complex societies, education outside the home provides a central set of norms and expectations for moral order and social stability and cohesion. Education provides the earliest basis for the socialization of children into the ways and norms of a particular society. Durkheim went on to study deviance and to assert that social deviance was a sign that the social institutions of a society had failed, especially if the incidence of deviance became prolific enough. Religious institutions are also central to Durkheim's view of the social world. Religious institutions provide the values or solvent to social and moral order. Durkheim introduces the ideas of *sacred* and *profane* to separate qualities, objects and practices that are holy in nature from those which are entirely of this world. This is done to illustrate the importance of the sacred forms and their hold on profane or worldly objects such as secular moral sentiments. Durkheim shows that even though the profane or secular world may be divorced from the sacred in many societies, nonetheless it is usually affected and shaped by this other world of the sacred through the power and influence of religious institutions and ideas. Durkheim's study of religion, for example in his *The Elementary Forms of Religious Life*, is done not simply to chart the importance of religion as an institution, but to demonstrate the centrality of relationships between different social institutions, in this case religion, and the social and political systems that are shaped by it.

Culture as Symbols and Rituals: Durkheim shows that in addition to norms and laws there are commonly held **symbols** that operate to unite people into groups and societies and which in turn are important to sustaining societies and groups over long periods of time. Humans interact and interpret meaning and significance using symbols. Symbols range from the simple, such a flag or national anthem, to the complex, such as the respect given to certain historical figures or situations and events in history. In short, symbols and the rituals that surround them matter because they invoke and remind people of the meaning and significance that lie behind them. A symbol is literally a form of "social short-hand." Symbols are something, an artifact, thing or idea, whose meaning is significant and is shared or held in common by a group of people. Frequently, we speak of "symbolism" as a sense of something's full impact or deeper meaning; a meaning which is held in common by members of the in-group and which may not be viewed in the same way by other people and groups who lie outside the social ranks of those who use or revere it. Durkheim describes rituals as the "means by which the social group reaffirms itself periodically." **Rituals** are the regular and periodic occasions or situations in which people gather to celebrate themselves as a common collective. During ritual occasions, members of a shared community typically interact with each other by using symbols (ceremonial language, song, artifacts, etc.) as a form of social reinforcement or rebirth. Voting can be seen in this way, as a ritual to remind people in a democracy of the values

Political rallies, like this one for then presidential candidate Barrack Obama, excite people about the democratic process.

Source: Sally Stablein

of freedom and the importance of participatory citizenship.

The Division of Labor: Marx and Weber spoke of social class as the description of the common position of people with regard to work or occupation within an economy. Durkheim wrote of **the division of labor** as the different tasks or functions within a society to maintain the material survival of its members. Rather than seeing the division of labor as setting people apart, Durkheim regarded it as an integrating function, like norms and laws by which society is glued and solidified. People occupy particular positions or roles to ensure social order and that all important tasks are fulfilled. The job of institutions is to sort through the tasks and allocate the roles to individuals. A profound but controversial suggestion of Durkheim's is the idea that as societies grow in number and become more complex, there is a growing pressure on the division of labor.

States, Politics and Societies: Durkheim's approach to states and politics flows from his view of the nature of society and the critical role played by institutions and social facts. States and governments are simply another form or type of social institution. Durkheim's read on states is an optimistic view in that they represent the entire society and seek agreement and consensus, as opposed to the the view of conflict theorists, who see the state as operating on behalf of a dominant group or class. In this idealized Durkheimian conception, society is the basis of authority and the state must come to represent its basic workings and operations if it is to realize its idealized form. Of course, what this view fails to highlight is that the state could follow its own mandate or direction, which in turn, and as the world continues to witness, may contradict the needs and interests of the majority of the society over which it stands.

Alexis De Tocqueville On Civil Society And Politics

Alexis de Tocqueville, a great political and intellectual figure of 19th century France, wrote *Democracy in America*, which remains widely acknowledged as one of the most penetrating analyses of American politics. Born in 1805, he died in 1859 but not before he completed memorable works of comparative historical analysis. Like Durkheim, de Tocqueville emphasized the civil basis of the political order. Unlike Durkheim, he did so using a combination of historical and sociological imagination and techniques.

Tocqueville became fascinated by the question of why and how American society developed in the manner it did, especially when compared with other modern Western societies. How was America able to develop a set of political and social institutions noted for their foundations of equality and democracy, when all older societies were unable to do so? Tocqueville set about answering these questions using an extended and detailed comparative historical analysis which gave rise to comparative methods involving whole societies and nations that remain powerful and useful today.

Equality and Democracy in America: Looking around himself in the 19th century, Tocqueville could find no other society that included the notable political institutions of America. His first-hand study of equality and citizenship and the general framework of political institutions included suffrage and the capacity to influence the outcome of the political process; the abolition of a system of primogeniture which guaranteed the inheritance of wealth and privilege from one generation to the next in European societies; the idea that all people be treated the same before the legal system; and the distinctive elements of a system of government grounded in a written constitution and based on a system of checks and balances within the federal state and between its member states and the centralized state.

Notwithstanding the problem of the political exclusion of many groups of people from citizenship and other rights, Tocqueville concentrated on addressing the key analytical problem of discovering the conditions that promoted such equality. Why and how did the United States serve as the first nation to embrace seriously the principles of equality and participatory democracy largely absent from other nations?

Tocqueville stressed the presence of freedom as the principal condition of democratic equality. Even though freedom was not granted or exercised equally by all men, the foundational values of freedom and individualism were ingrained into the basic political, social and economic institutions of America. It is this foundation that would set the course of American history toward the progressive unfolding of equality and democracy, so he thought. Tocqueville went on to argue powerfully that in America, as compared with European society, men were not only free, but they were free to take actions to continually secure and show their freedom to one another. Tocqueville argued that being able to develop, engage and promote voluntary association is the most prominent and important freedom in explaining America's success. "In their political associations the Americans, of all conditions, minds and ages, daily acquire a general taste for association and grow accustomed to the use of it," Tocqueville observed that in America a strong social infrastructure of voluntary associations of all kinds grew, ensuring that democracy would continue because this became the vehicle for expressing opinions and concerns to authorities, and people grew to savor this freedom to act, to organize and to express their opinions.

Another critical institutional element observed by Tocqueville in the civil society or order of American social life is what he called a "free press" and "freedom of speech." Freedom of speech is the first principle on which the American government was established. For Tocqueville, the number and diversity of publications on display underscored the importance of this principle and its impact on the social conditions of a democratic order. He remarked that the possession of a strong social infrastructure was an absolute necessity for democracy to take root.

Tocqueville did, however, recognize several threats to equality and democracy in his study of America. Although he wrote of widespread and impressive forms of equality, Tocqueville recognized and could see the presence of deep inequalities in the social conditions of race. He described the institutions of slavery and servitude and their terrible impacts on native Indians and blacks, including the strongest forms of prejudice in states that had abolished slavery. Tocqueville was also insightful in suggesting that if and when the Industrial Revo-

lution reached America with full force that this would introduce conditions which might very well threaten rising equality, given the propensity of urban, industrial capitalism to play one group against another. These two threats notwithstanding, Tocqueville identified a third threat to democracy which he termed "equality itself." Tocqueville worried about the tyranny of majority rule and the impact this could have on minority rights and protections. He argued that since all were equal, only the greatest number could gain advantage, meaning that America would have to guard against the *tyranny of the majority* both in terms of the development of its political institutions and its social practices.

Tocqueville then provided both a vision and a map for the future of America. This was a vision not of a society divided by classes nor was it one in which the state would dominate. These were views held by Marx and Weber, respectively. Instead, Tocqueville imagined the progressive unfolding of a society directed by strong and vibrant civic institutions in which associations and organizations can give voice and meaning to the voice or will of people characterized by well-respected diversity and difference. Although this vision could be threatened by divisions between races and by excessive power forming in either the business class or the state, Tocqueville offered a clear picture of a journey well beyond the period in which it was written.

Durkheim And Traditions Of Sociological Scholarship

Over the past decade or so, civil society and social networking have merged within sociology to become the focus of attention regarding a wide range of issues and topics concerning politics and political processes. The explosion of interest in many academic disciplines and in for-profit and nonprofit organizations has much to do with the work of the following sociologists and political scientist writing toward the end of the 20th century and in the present. The interest in the work of these scholars signals a return to the kinds of arguments and positions offered more than a century go by Emile Durkheim and Alexis de Tocqueville. People are searching for ways to better understand democratic processes and to create new, workable and effective associations and organizations in civil society to aid in the process of advancing society and supplementing the institutions of the state and business. The following scholars committed themselves and their work to understanding how the institutions of civil society work and can work more effectively.

Talcott Parsons: This is arguably one of the greatest yet least understood social theorists of the 20th century. Hampered by a convoluted writing style, the complexity and importance of his ideas became somewhat overshadowed. Parsons attempted to meld the systems of Durkheim and Weber as the true foundations of modern sociology. From Weber he stressed the role and power of ideas and culture in the creation of societies and institutions, and from Durkheim he stressed the integrity of societies and the factors that sustain them. For Parsons, societies represent social systems that are able to reproduce and re-create themselves from one generation to the next. The manner in which societies continue or change is among the fundamental theoretical issues he addressed.

Parsons contributes to debates within political sociology because of the significance he placed on the values that underscore the workings of any nation or country. While Durkheim spoke of social solidarity and Tocqueville focused on the value of equality in America, Parsons described the social world as a social system and in doing so did much to articulate an approach to understanding society known as the structural-functional paradigm. Like Durkheim before him, Parsons described the civil society as a *societal community* made up of the institutions of religion, education and family; institutions which play a vital role in conveying norms and values of a society to its members. Parsons stresses an optimistic and positive sum view of politics and political process in his view of society as a social system. Rather than describe power, politics and the state as the realm and institution of division and conflict between contending views and interests and the groups that support them, Parsons describes power as "the capacity of a social system to mobilize resources to attain collective goals," and politics as "how best to proceed in the mobilization of such resources." In this view, it is the system that contains the answers through its ability to organize goals, purposes and strategies along with the specific actors who fulfill roles in the system. Parsons encouraged a positive win-win view of politics and the state rather than a zero-sum, win-lose approach in arguing that a well-run system is capable of creating more than simply the control over scarce or limited resources.

Seymour Martin Lipset: In his famous work *Political Man*, Lipset identifies Marx, Weber and Tocqueville as the main intellectual founders of political sociology. Today, Lipset himself is widely regarded as one of the principal founders of political sociology. A prolific and creative scholar, like Tocqueville, he was interested in the study of American democracy and society and by comparison the nature of other societies and their political systems. His work revealed that the main conditions making for democracy are a strong and stable middle class, a high respect for education, a prosperous and advanced economy, and the free competition among elites for the right to govern. He also drew attention to the importance of strong, sustainable and free civil institutions as an anchor to sustainable democratic government. Lipset presents a view of democratic governments as an end in and of themselves, meaning that he does not see them as simply seeking power or ruling on behalf of a small and illegitimate class. Rather, to be effective and legitimate, he argues that democracies can and should work to process the different and varied opinions and interests of people in a society.

Robert Bellah: Bellah's perspective on the study of religion has had an enormous effect on the way sociologists talk about civil society, civil order and its imprint on politics. More famous for the sociological study of religion than politics, his work in the traditions of Durkheim and Tocqueville do, however, say much about the application of a broad sociological imagination to the study of politics.

A significant contribution of Bellah's work is his work on what he calls civil religion, namely the idea that in America especially, politics has become just that—a civil religion. Bellah argues that we can now think of politics in the same sense we think of a religion, as a way of life for American citizens.

Durkheim's work contains the basis of this idea in the following quote: "There can be no society that does not feel the need of upholding and reaffirming at regular intervals the collective sentiments and the collective ideas which make its unity and its personality. … What essential difference is there between an assembly of Christians celebrating the principal dates of the life of Christ, or of Jews remembering the exodus from Egypt … and a reunion of citizens commemorating the promulgation of a new moral or legal system or some great event in the national life?"

Civil Religion: Bellah describes the historical foundations of the American civil religion as being based in ideas concerning the separation of church and state and the fact that the core political values and ideals of the American Creed stand as elements citizens hold in common. Such values include liberty, equality of opportunity, individualism, participatory democracy, and limited government. Such values and ideas are essentially political in nature and are derived from the workings and philosophy of the Enlightenment period of history. However, the way in which these values are organized and applied throughout American history leads Bellah to describe their function as far more, hence the term civil religion. For Bellah, they represent the whole fabric of American life, the symbols by which rituals are developed to celebrate the nature and elements they hold in common, and the means by which in times of national crisis a nation can restore opportunity and a sense of common fellowship among Americans.

Culture and Politics: In a widely proclaimed and best-selling book titled *Habits of the Heart*, Bellah and his co-authors explore the nature and significance of American culture using Durkheim's ideas on civil order and moral authority. Bellah points out that culture is not simply a set of habits and patterns but also involves a set of moral expectations for how people are to lead their lives. To understand the moralistic tone of American society, Bellah digs deeply into the sources of American moralism. Bellah and his colleagues argue that individualism lies at the root of American moral culture and takes three forms. First, there is the idea of self-interested

behavior and individual initiative and responsibility, the variety most often encountered in Americans of all backgrounds. They call this form of moralism utilitarianism or expressive individualism. The authors also uncover what they call the biblical and civic republican traditions of individualism, which are responsible for the energy and activity of many in the business world and which also impact other spheres of American life. A key consequence of this view is the idea that while Americans contain a strong belief in individualism, this tends to limit the civic and community orientations they experience in other societies. While noting these limits on contemporary civic and community mindedness, the authors argue that conditions of greater trust and community can be developed.

Civil Society Scholars: Recently there has been an explosion in the study of civil society and its impact on politics and political processes and institutions. Interest in civil society, especially the idea of social networking, has spread across academic disciplines and to the applied world of practice. The work of the sociologist James S. Coleman and the political scientist Robert Putnam has done much to revive the interest of both academics and practitioners.

James S. Coleman proposed a general social theory of action in *The Foundations of Social Theory*. Coleman argued that people possessed something he called **social capital**, that is, social resources individuals could use to make critical decisions and take critical actions. Coleman used this concept to describe an important aspect of the network of social relations which helped explain the quality and outcomes of social relations based largely on the trust and confidence that people had in one another. Coleman describes many examples of social capital and how important it is as an aspect of political process. One illustration covered by Coleman is the idea of "rotating credit associations" made famous in an article by Clifford Geertz. The rotating credit association is a form of cooperative economic venture in which people pool their resources and then take turns drawing on the general fund created by the larger pool. This investment strategy has been successfully used by various ethnic minority communities in American history and today in situations where no single individual has enough funds or resources to cover an economic investment, but together a system can be developed which enables and encourages economic activity and enterprise. Such a system relies on trust and social capital, and today variations of this concept are being used by many communities. In the case of strict, orthodox Muslim communities, the idea of a "community chest" is being used to pool capital and other resources for rotating investment to get around the problem of interest payments. According to the practices of many Muslim peoples, a system of borrowing based on interest payment on a loan is strictly forbidden. While the reasons behind these practices vary, the concept of social capital involving community-based trust and confidence lies at the core of the practice.

Coleman argues that there are many such examples of social trust and cooperation evident in the social world, although the prevalence, strength and use of social networks vary between cultures and locations. Coleman died before he was able to explore the range of applications of this important concept.

This task has been taken up by **Robert Putnam**, a Harvard political scientist, who acknowledges a debt to both James S. Coleman and another sociologist, Mark Granovetter, for their theoretical and empirical work on social networks. Putnam and his colleagues, Robert Leonardi and Raffaella Nanetti, studied the formation and effectiveness of regional government in Italy over a quarter century. They showed that the presence of civic traditions or "habits of the heart" are present among people, and that they can account for the effectiveness of participatory democracy and for the link between the effectiveness of government and the satisfaction of citizens. He tested various hypotheses concerning government effectiveness. First they showed that variations in levels of regional government effectiveness could not be explained by differences of wealth or other tangible resources. Then Putnam showed that measures of civic trust and traditions in a region were linked with institutional effectiveness. Patterns of voter turnout and other measures of associational involvement by local citizens confirmed his argument that the local civic community, if strong, enabled

governmental institutions to be far more effective than in situations where civic networks were weaker or not present.

In a groundbreaking book, *Bowling Alone*, Putnam reports vast new data and goes on to show how we have become increasingly disconnected from family, friends, neighbors and our democratic structures—and how we may reconnect. Putnam warns that our stock of social capital—the very fabric of our connections with each other, has plummeted, impoverishing our lives and communities. The central premise of social capital is that social networks have value. Social capital refers to the collective value of all "social networks" (who people know) and the inclinations that arise from these networks to do things for each other ("norms of reciprocity").

In this influential work, Putnam provides a masterful critical assessment of American civil society, showing periods of strong and weak commitment to civic community and social networks. The title *Bowling Alone* serves as a graphic illustration of the argument that the America of the recent past suffers from excessive individualism or what the sociologist called *The Lonely Crowd*. Putnam draws on evidence including nearly 500,000 interviews over the last quarter century to show that we sign fewer petitions, belong to fewer organizations that meet, know fewer neighbors, meet with friends less frequently, and even socialize with our families less often. We're even bowling alone! More Americans are bowling than ever before, but they are not bowling in leagues. Putnam shows how changes in work, family structure, age, suburban life, television, computers, women's roles and other factors have contributed to this decline.

Putnam painstakingly charts the presence and absence of social networks and strong civic mindedness in American society across history. He goes on to argue for the need to reestablish strong civic institutions outside of government and business so that the strengths of civic mindedness and social networking can once again enrich and benefit the general political process of democracy, including our political institutions.

Putnam describes how America has civically reinvented itself before—approximately 100 years ago at the turn of the century. And America can civically reinvent itself again. he says. To this end Putnam has helped establish various research and activist movements. The following website describes these efforts at rebuilding civic mindedness and social networking. Together.org is an initiative of the Saguaro Seminar on Civic Engagement at Harvard University's Kennedy School of Government. See http://www.ksg.harvard.edu/saguaro/primer.htm.

Types Of Modern Political Systems: Democratic, Authoritarian And Totalitarian

Politics continues to provoke the questions raised by the ancient Greeks concerning the rights of people to become involved in politics and the form governance should take. In the modern era, the world has witnessed two almost opposite forms of political rule. First, *modern democracy* retains many features of the Greek polis such as the emphasis on widespread and voluntary participation in public life. Second, totalitarianism has elements of the ancient tyranny described by Aristotle as well as a number of newer features. Totalitarianism in its purest form is represented in the modern era by the former Soviet Union, and in Germany under Adolf Hitler and the Nazis, and today its closest counterpart is the People's Republic of China, although there are signs that China is becoming a hybrid regime. A third form of political regime that lies in between democracy and totalitarianism is that of authoritarianism.

Nation States In The Modern World

With the collapse of many nations in recent decades, among them the Soviet Union, South Africa and several Eastern European nations, attention has been directed toward how to reconstruct new nation states out of old situations. Several questions have emerged regarding the models that might be used to rebuild nation states. How can the integrity of historical cultural traditions be blended with the need to establish viable new states and productive new markets? The urgency of finding answers has created a moment of some practical significance for political sociology.

The Elements of Modern Nation States: While the nation state is a relatively new construction and finding common elements is difficult, there are nonetheless several identifiable fundamental conditions associated with the emergence of nation states. For example, Charles Tilly connects the building of nation states with the activity of war-making. Going to war forces nations or peoples to consolidate and centralize operations, and gradually to construct bureaucratic organizations that will not only take on various aspects of the business of war but in turn will develop the means to collect taxes and other functions associated with the modern nation state. The historian C.E. Black takes this idea a step further in arguing that the most common feature of modern nation states is the consolidation of policy-making, that is, the centralization of political authority. This centralization of authority has been made possible by improvements in communication and transportation, which in turn has allowed for both government and private enterprise to achieve greater control and efficiencies. Another aspect of modern nation states lies in the ability to command resources to expand the tasks and purposes of the state. The provision of services to the needy or to entire populations in general was previously thought impossible and is now a characteristic of state organization. The maintenance of national defense has gradually been taken over by the modern nation state as Tilly argues, and as a result this process has given the military wing of the state power previously unimagined. States now commonly are able to collect revenues of between one-quarter and one-half of the gross national product for covering administrative costs and to fund public programs and security measures.

Max Weber claimed about a century ago that the modern nation state is also characterized by the proliferation of legal standards which in turn has led to the growth of large state bureaucracies. These developments alone have generated a large number of research questions concerning the consequences and efficiencies of such a system of distribution and regulation. Almost everywhere in the world politicians and administrators attempt to expand bureaucracy and the state apparatus, raising additional questions about competing organizational ways to meet today's problems and opportunities.

Finally, there is the question of the citizen's and the non-citizen's role in public affairs. In this area there is a great deal of difference in the way various nations approach public participation in political processes. Differences notwithstanding, whether democratic or authoritarian, all regimes appear to find it necessary to consider their authority in terms of questions of legitimacy and widespread popular support. The form this takes may vary, but it does appear to be another important feature of all modern nation state regimes.

Beyond these considerations of elementary features of modern nation states, political sociologists today are interested in the timing and sequence of events characteristic of the development of nation states, known as the process of nation-building. One reason this concern exists is because of the differences in the ways older and newer nation states develop. While countries like England took several centuries to emerge in their current form, countries like many in Africa, emerging from colonial rule, were expected to accomplish nationhood in a matter of years. Iraq is an example of how difficult it is to re-create or rebuild nationhood once the stability of an older order has been put aside. Several general questions capture frequent attention as they impact particular countries and regions. What are the effects of a country undergoing rapid transformation in nation building versus the effects of moving more slowly or gradually? Are there differences in outcomes to building large and complex political institutions before or after building economic growth and institutions? What are the relationships in the timing of the building of economic, political and social institutions? Scholars are producing some interesting work on such questions. For example, Hans Daalder claims that leaders in counties like England who were able to gradually accept the demands of full participation in politics from the new social classes were better able to develop a more

viable and widespread democracy than countries like France, whose rulers continued to discourage and to resist such involvement. Equally, the earlier and more gradual development of industrialization and capitalism in England may also account for the greater political stability of the centuries. In America, the formation of the political institutions of nationhood preceded the industrial, capitalist and urban transformations and thus, the fledgling nation was able to better guide the revolutionary economic and social changes. In the case of many nations experiencing colonialization and colonization, a less stable pattern or development is typically seen, since political reform and revolution typically followed at least the first stages of economic transformation.

Nation-Building In The Contemporary Era

It is difficult to distinguish and separate the political from the social and economic aspects of nation-building and state-building. Societal transformations such as urban migration and economic development tend to accompany political change. The following four dimensions of modern nation-building can be identified and their interrelationships studied:

1. Nationalism

Earlier in this chapter we described the Weberian notion of ideas and ideology having a powerful effect over social institutions, including those involving social change. Nowhere is this more relevant and on display than in the political arena of nationalism. Nation-building and state-building usually depend on the ability of leaders and their followers to discover and use a set of symbols and rituals concerning citizenship or other forms of common history and identity to support the construction or reconstruction of the nation state. In South Africa following the fall of apartheid, the symbolic power of the "rainbow coalition" and "rainbow nation," for example, helped facilitate an inclusive approach to post-apartheid state- and nation-building, even among previously antagonistic and warring groups. Describing the role of nationalistic ideology in nation-building, the cultural anthropologist Clifford Geertz stressed that "nationalism is not a mere by-product but the very stuff of social change in so many states; not its reflection, its cause, its expression, or its engine, but the thing itself." All modern nation states appear to use a process of developing a set of common beliefs to serve as the centerpiece of common shared identity and national sentiment. The source of such sentiments and beliefs varies and may include political, religious, socio-cultural and historical values, but whatever the source and combination of such values, the importance to galvanizing nationalism and nation-building is the same.

An example from recent writings in political sociology will illustrate. The sociologist Liah Greenfeld traced the development of nationalism in five countries—England, France, Russia, Germany and the United States. Greenfeld stresses the importance of ideas and nationalism over alternative explanations of nation-state development such as the spread of an administrative apparatus. Greenfeld argues that the sequence in which modern nation states appeared—first, England, followed by France, Russia, Germany and the United States—is also of central importance to understanding how ideas and nationalism operate to define and build nations. She states that the first modern nation, England, had the advantage of creating itself anew and thus subsequently became the model for all nation states. She argues that, in part, the nation states that followed were established and shaped out of their real and imagined struggles and differences with England and the English way. Each tried to use ideas and nationalism to distinguish its own symbolic destiny and identity from the other.

2. Legitimacy And Stability

The issue of creating a viable and sustainable nation state to which all citizens will agree and feel bound is the central issue to which Max Weber first drew attention. Earlier in this chapter we suggested that for Weber the creation and maintenance of the nation state needed to address the question of the legitimacy of the ruler and the ruled. The nature of legitimacy pointed to the fact that both those with power and authority and those without it or with less of it needed to accept the bonds and ties for law to work effectively. Habermas suggests that such

common bonds need to be grounded in widespread common consensus that depends on the ability of both governed and governors to engage in sustained dialogue and communication about that consensus. Great challenges are involved in forging and maintaining this condition. Becoming a nation state is by no means a smooth and easy task. For every success there are failures or challenges. Nation-building provides countless examples of the truth of this statement. In England, major conflicts arose in the 17th century which ultimately produced a fundamental change in the distribution of power whereby the parliament replaced the monarchy as the sovereign law-making institution. In France, the struggles were far more severe and widespread and involved revolutionary and violent change in the late 18th and early 19th centuries. Germany, too, experienced successive periods of political instability and tension across the 19th and 20th centuries. Indeed, many of these internal conflicts ended up having drastic consequences for global stability and peace. The process of nation-building in the United States began with a successful but revolutionary challenge to a colonial power and experienced successive major periods of conflict including a Civil War and severe conflicts over the issue of race. In the newly merging nation states of today, we continue to witness intense and equally violent struggles among peoples in Asia, Africa, Latin America and Eastern Europe.

How can we explain the pattern of nation-building interrupted by political and violent conflict? In other words, how can we account for the failure to obtain and maintain legitimacy in the modern world of nation states? Samuel P. Huntington, a political scientist and major scholar of nation-building, presents this widely cited explanation. Political instability exists when an insufficient number of channels and sponsors are available to embrace and channel a newly enlarged and aroused citizenry. By channels and sponsors Huntington has in mind political parties, trade unions and voluntary organizations. Others challenge this idea with examples of violent conflict coming from situations containing high levels of political institutionalization. Certainly, in the United States and England Huntington's arguments appear to ring true, whereas in other states, such as India, the opposite held. Huntington's stress on durable political and civic institutions lies in the same tradition as Robert Putnam's assertions about trust and confidence and the need for legitimate and representative civic institutions with strong links to the main sources of societal power in the polity and economy.

3. Citizenship And Shared Political Identity

Most recently, the theme of constructing national identity and a sense of citizenship has become a significant topic of academic and worldly scrutiny. Given the realities of today's world characterized by massive migrations, growing population diversity within nations and regions, and the nature of transnational and even global organizations, the nature of citizenship and national identity have resurrected themselves as among the most pressing and volatile issues of our times. Citizenship is a status bestowed on those who are full members of a community, giving them, and just them, the full complement of rights and duties associated with this status. As we know, such rights can and do involve economic rights and protections, social rights, including access to education, unemployment and medical benefits, the rights of a membership association which may include such things as the rights of movement, organization and association.

Given the potential and actual scale of conflicts both within and between nations concerning issues of citizenship, there is now little question that citizenship, and by implication national boundaries, will grow in importance. Major events such as the scale of immigration, the increased social and cultural diversity that it brings and the growth in the global or transnational economy, including international labor systems, will usher in new organizational and administrative developments in the organization of states, markets and politics. The pressure to identify exactly what it means to be a citizen and the changes in the nature and practice of institutions, including capitalism, the state and civil institutions to deal with such questions, are among the major issues of the future.

4. Economic Development And The Role Of The State

Recent events concerning the global economic crisis and the response highlight what scholars have argued for some time, that the workings of the economic system dominated by capitalism is inextricably linked to the operations of the governance and administrative system of nation states.

W.W. Rostow shows that extensive and sustained economic development and overcoming periods of deep and fundamental economic instability and crisis are achieved through a multi-staged and multi-faceted process involving the coordination of many elements of a social system of nation states. Rostow describes the economic factors within emerging or transforming nations as including: changes in the form of agricultural techniques and market organization; the emergence of an economic elite which shifts its attention from traditional practices to new forms of production; and a marked increase in the investment of a country in the technical means of production. Other scholars emphasize the need for state administration structures to undergo similar changes, especially concerning the development of the role they play in the development of the economy.

Recently, much of the most useful and interesting research on states, markets and politics has involved such questions regarding the relationship between the state and the forces at work in the economy at the local, sub-national, national, and international or global level.

The state now plays a crucial, if not the pivotal, role in the development of new markets and in the reconstruction of existing economic systems. Much research is now under way regarding the nature and form of such relationships between states and markets and the political processes that characterize their workings across and between nations. The experience of the recent global economic crisis provides an important laboratory to investigate such workings and relationships. Such analysis will undoubtedly reaffirm much of the theory and ideas of past scholars of states, markets and politics. However, no doubt, new insights and discoveries will emerge from the experience, some of which will certainly alter the dominant thinking and practice concerning the workings of economic, political and civil institutions and social life.

Summary

The concepts of power and authority are foundational to the understanding of states, markets and politics. While power refers to the ability to control or influence the views and actions of others, authority is simply institutional power and contains the rules by which society works. Legitimacy involves a sense of trust and approval between those with authority and those without. Karl Marx traced the dynamics of the modern world to the workings of a capitalist economy. He asserted that there are marked inequalities of wealth and power in modern societies and that these inequalities may lead to major ideological struggles. Marx described social beings as alienated from their own abilities as well as from each other as a result of society's institutions. The politicization of the working class is a major theme for Marx. In order for workers to bring about change they must have class consciousness. Max Weber served as a counter-point on many issues that Marx addressed, such as Marx's heavy emphasis on economic causes of social phenomena. Weber believed that the actual administration of politics plays a large part in shaping how power is exercised over people. In response to Marx's emphasis on social classes, Weber also showed the role that great figures played in the making of history. One of Weber's greatest intellectual contributions had to do with the social consequences of religion. Weber showed how the tenets of ascetic Protestantism in the West provide many of the socio-cultural prerequisites for the rise of capitalism. The principal aspect of the modern state, Weber claimed, is that it is able to monopolize the legitimate use of physical force inside a given territory, giving itself a power that no other institution or organization possesses in modern society. Weber's work started sociologists on the path to understanding the nature and variations of modern states. Emile Durkheim attempted to explain the basis of social solidarity. He was absorbed by the questions of "the general will" and the conditions that bind a society together. He emphasized civil society, not the economy nor the state, for understanding politics, a view which is increasingly seen in today's political sociology. Much of Durkheim's writing and research set out to prove the claim that "social facts," or the collective or shared ways of thinking, feeling and acting, have a power over humans as much or greater than psychological and biological facts. Rather than seeing the division of labor as setting people apart, Durkheim saw the division of labor as the different tasks or functions within a society to maintain the material survival of its members. Like Durkheim, Alexis de Tocqueville emphasized the civil basis of the political order. Tocqueville became fascinated by the question of why and how American society developed in the manner it did. He stressed the presence of freedom as the principal condition of democratic equality. He thought it was this foundation that would set the course of American history toward the progressive unfolding of equality and democracy. In recent years, civil society and social networking have become the focus of attention regarding a wide range of issues and topics concerning politics and political processes. People are searching for ways to better understand democratic processes and to create new, workable and effective associations and organizations in civil society to aid in the process of advancing society and supplementing the institutions of the state and business. In addition, politics continues to provoke questions concerning the rights of people to become involved in politics and the form governance should take.

Review/Discussion Questions

1. How do power and authority differ?
2. What does Marx mean by alienation?
3. What is social capital?
4. Think about the job you have now, or have had in the past, how much surplus value, if any, existed between the money you earned per hour and the money the business made off of your labor? Do you think it is fair or unfair? Why?
5. Do you think capitalism will ever cease to exist?

Key Terms

Alienation describes processes and a state of being characterized by estrangement and distancing from the important elements of the human spirit. It is commonly a word used to describe the dehumanizing effects of social, economic and political systems and processes. Sociologists argue that particular forms of institutional arrangements are the primary cause of alienation.

Authority is simply institutionalized power, whereby power is examined in the context of its institutional settings and institutionalized arrangements.

Base and superstructure is a Marxist concept for representing the economic foundation of modern capitalism and its dominance over the political institutions and all other institutions of social life, including culture and religion.

Charismatic personalities is a term used by Weber to describe leading figures and the influence their personalities had over people and institutions, and in social change.

Class consciousness is the idea propagated by Marx that in order for workers to bring about change, the working class must be aware of itself as a class and work together as a class-for-themselves rather than being seen as simply a class-in-itself which can be

regarded as merely an intellectual concept.

Culture is used by sociologists to describe the manner in which people make sense of the social world in terms of their meaning and significance. Culture consists of a way of life, patterns of symbolic interaction and systems of values, beliefs and meanings shared in common by a group of people.

Idealist philosophy contrasts and opposes materialist philosophy in that ideas and systems of ideas are said to be the basis of the social world rather than what goes on in and around the operation of the economy.

Ideology is a concept used to describe systems of ideas, norms and core beliefs which together represent the ideals of those who propagate the ideology along with ideas that sustain it.

Institutions represent the established and organized practices of a given society. Once they exist they can exercise a profound influence on the form and direction of history and the lives of individuals and social groups.

Legitimacy involves a sense of trust and approval between those with and without authority. It provides the foundation for the durable and stable operation of political and economic institutions.

Materialist philosophy describes the claim made by Marxists that the economy and the social relations involved in operating the economy represent the key to understanding the social world, especially its inner workings, which it is claimed are largely hidden to so many.

Nationalism is a form of normative culture experienced by people in modern territorially bounded nation states. Nationalism, or a deep-seated belief in one's nation, involves shared beliefs, values and sentiments along with social processes for creating, maintaining and transforming itself.

Political party is a modern social grouping unlike either a social class or status group in that it is organized specifically to pursue political ends and the exercise of power.

Power refers to the capacity or ability of a person, group or institution to control, manipulate, influence or shape the views and actions of others.

Rationalization of life is a phrase developed by Weber to describe modern life as being characterized and subject to professionalism and common forms of rational assessment and means-ends calculability.

Rational organization describes the underlying new forms of authority based on calculability, measurement and mean-ends orientation characteristic of modern bureaucratic organization.

Resource mobilization refers to a model of politics and political process characterized by the following elements: (1) interests; (2) organization; (3) mobilization; and (4) opportunity.

Rituals are the regular and periodic occasions or situations in which people gather to celebrate themselves as a common collective.

Social capital refers to the collective value of all "social networks" (who people know) and the inclinations that arise from these networks to do things for each other ("norms of reciprocity").

Social facts are the collective or shared ways of thinking, feeling and acting and which sociologists claim operate beyond the psychology of the individual and the biological principles of humans as a species.

Social networks involve the social ties and bonds between people and the organized relationships that link individuals to one another.

Society is used by sociologists to describe patterns of interacting people.

Symbols are something, an artifact, thing or idea, whose meaning is significant and is shared or held in common by a group of people.

The division of labor is the phrase coined by Durkheim to describe the separation and allocation of different tasks or functions within a society to maintain the material survival of its members.

Bibliography

Aristotle (1975). The Politics of Aristotle, translated by Ernest Barker, London: Oxford University Press.

Bellah, R. N. (1970). Essays on Religion in a Post-Traditional World, New York: Harper and Row.

Bendix, R. (1956). Work and Authority in Industry, Berkeley, California: University of California Press.

Bendix, R. (1968). State and Society: A Reader in Comparative Political Sociology, Boston, Massachusetts: Little Brown Publishers.

Bendix, R. (1977). Nation-Building and Citizenship, Berkeley, California: University of California Press.

Bendix, R. (1978). Kings or People: Power and the Mandate to Rule, Berkeley,   California: University of California Press.

Black, C.E. (1966). The Dynamics of Modernization, New York: Harper & Row Publishers.

Bottomore, T. (1973). ed., Karl Marx, Englewood Cliffs, New Jersey: Prentice Hall Inc.

Dahrendorf, R. (1959).Class and Class Conflict in Industrial Society, Stanford, California: Stanford University Press.

Coleman, J.S. (1996). Foundations of Social Theory, Cambridge, Massachusetts: The Belknap Press of Harvard University Press.

Domhoff, W.G. (2002). Who Rules America? Power and Politics, 4th edition, Boston, Massachusetts: McGraw Hill Press.

Durkheim, E. (1950). The Rules of Sociological Method, 8th edition, translated by Sarah A. Solovay John H. Mueller and edited by George E.G. Catlin, New York: The Free Press of Glencoe.

Durkheim, E. (1951). Suicide: A Study of Sociology, translated by John Spaulding and George Simpson; edited with an introduction by George Simpson, Glencoe, Illinois: The Free Press.

Durkheim, E. (1961). The Elementary Forms of the Religious Life, translated by Joseph Ward Swain (New York: Collins Books.

Durkheim, E. (1961). Moral Education: A Study of the Theory and Application of the Sociology of Education, translated by Everett K. Wilson and Herman Schnurer, New York: The Free Press of Glencoe.

Durkheim, E. (1964). The Division of Labor in Society, translated by George Simpson, New York: Free Press.

Feurer, L. (1959). ed., Marx and Engels: Basic Writings on Politics and Philosophy, Garden City, New York: Doubleday and Co.

Geertz, C. (1973). The Interpretations of Cultures, New York: Basic Books Inc. Publishers.

Gold, D.A.; Lo, C.Y.H.; Wright, F.O. (1975). "Recent Developments in Marxist Theories of the Capitalist State," Monthly Review Press, 27, pp. 25-43.

Gramsci, A. (1971). "The Modern Prince," in Selections from the Prison Notebooks, Antonio Gramsci, edited and translated by Quintin Hoare and Geoffrey Nowell Smith, New York, International Publishers.

Greenfeld, L. (1992). Nationalism: Five Roads to Modernity, Cambridge, Massachusetts: Harvard University Press.

Habermas, J. (1971). Theory and Practice, Boston, Massachusetts: Beacon Press.

Habermas, J. (1971). Knowledge and Human Interests, Boston, Massachusetts: Beacon Press.

Habermas, J. (1975). Legitimation Crisis, Boston, Massachusetts: Beacon Press.

Habermas, J. (1977). Communication and the Evolution of Society, translated by Thomas McCarthy, Boston, Massachusetts: Beacon Press.

Huntington, S.P. (1968.) Political Order in Changing Societies, (New Haven, Connecticut: Yale University Press.

Huntington, S.P. (1981). "The Disharmonic Polity" in Samuel P. Huntington, American Politics: The Promise of Disharmony, Cambridge, Massachusetts: Harvard University Press pp.1-12.

Huntington, S.P. (1981). The American Creed and National Identity," in Samuel P. Huntington American Politics: The Promise of Disharmony, Cambridge, Massachusetts: Harvard University Press, pp. 13-30.

Kant, I. (1929). The Critique of Pure Reason, translated by Norman Kemp Smith, New York: St. Martin's Press.

Lipset, S.M. (1959). "Social Requisites of Democracy," American Political Science Review vol. 53, pp. 69-103.

Lipset, S.M. (1959). Political Man: The Social Bases of Politics, Garden City, New York: Doubleday and Company.

Lipset, S.M. (1968). Agrarian Socialism, updated edition, Garden City, New York: Doubleday.

Lipset, S.M. (1968). "Some Social Requisites of Democracy," American Political Science Review, vol. 53, pp. 69-105.

Lipset, S.M. (1991). Continental Divide: The Values and Institutions of the United States and Canada, New York: Routledge Press.

Lukacs, G. (1971). History and Class Consciousness, translated by R. Livingstone, London: The Merlin Press, Ltd.

Marcuse, H. (1964). One-Dimensional Man, Boston, Massachusetts: Beacon Press.

Marcuse, H. (1968). "Industrialization and Capitalism in the Work of Max Weber," in Negotiations: Essays in Critical Theory, Herbert Marcuse, Boston, Massachusetts: Beacon Press, pp. 201-26.

Mitzman, A. (1970). The Iron Cage: An Historical Interpretation of Max Weber, New York: Alfred A. Kopf.

Mommsen, W.J. (1989). The Political and Social Theory of Max Weber: Collected Essays, Chicago: University of Chicago Press.

Orum, A.M. (2001). Introduction to Political Sociology, Fourth Edition, Upper Saddle River, New Jersey, Pearson Education, Prentice Hall.

Parsons, T. (1951) The Social System, Glencoe, Illinois: The Free Press.

Parsons, T. (1969). Politics and Social Structure, New York: The Free Press.

Parsons, T. (1971). The System of Modern Societies, Englewood Cliffs, New Jersey: Prentice-Hall.

Poulantzas, N. (1973). Political Power and Social Classes, Part IV.

Putnam, R.D. (2001). Bowling Alone: The Collapse and Revival of American Community, New York: Simon & Schuster Press.

Rostow, W.W. (1956). "The Take-Off into Self-Sustained Growth," in Political Development and Social Change, Ed. Finkle and Gable, pp.142-61.

Skocpol, T. (1979). States and Social Revolutions: A Comparative Analysis of France, Russia and China, Cambridge, Massachusetts: Cambridge University Press.

Skocpol, T. (1992). Protecting Soldiers and Mothers: The Political Origins of Social Policy in the United States, Cambridge, Massachusetts: The Belknap Press of Harvard University.

Tilly, C. (1975). The Formation of National States in Western Europe, Princeton, New Jersey, Princeton University Press.

Tilly, C. (1978). From Mobilization to Revolution, Reading, Massachusetts: Addison- Wesley Publishing Company.

Tocqueville, A.de. (1863) Democracy in America, the Henry Reeve text with notes and bibliographies by Phillips Bradley, New York: Vintage Books, Volumes 1, 2 and 4.

Tocqueville, A.de. (1998). The Old Regime and the Revolution, edited and with an introduction and critical appraisal by Francois Furet and Francoise Melonio; translated by   Alan S. Kahan, Chicago: University of Chicago Press.

Tucker, R.C. (1972). ed., The Marx-Engels Reader, New York: W.W. Norton Co., Inc.

Wallerstein, I. (1989). The Modern World System, Orlando, Florida: Academic Press.

Weber, M. (1949). The Methodology of the Social Sciences, translated and edited by Edward A. Shils and Henry A. Finch with a forward by Edward A. Shils, New York: The Free Press.

Weber, M. (1958). The Protestant Ethic and the Spirit of Capitalism, translated by Talcott Parsons, New York: Charles Scribner's Sons.

Weber, M. (1958). "Politics as a Vocation," in Hans H. Gerth and C. Wright Mills, eds., From Max Weber: Essays in Sociology, New York: Oxford University Press.

CHAPTER THIRTEEN

Health And Population

Bruce D. LeBlanc

O ur own health is something we might not think much about until we aren't feeling well. Health care, on the other hand, is a topic we may think about often because it has been in the news regularly for over a decade. The discussion is centered on one question: Who is responsible for a person's health care needs? Some people believe that health care is solely the responsibility of the individual; others believe that it is solely the responsibility of government. Then there is an entire spectrum of beliefs between those two endpoints.

In the United States, the health care system was originally based on personal responsibility, and each individual paid for his or her own care in what is known as a *direct pay* model. The system has since been modified to include payments from the government to health care providers on behalf of the elderly, disabled, and impoverished—a form of *socialized medicine*—and payments from private insurance companies which have created a *third-party payer* model. In the case of government payments to care providers, the taxpayers take on the responsibility of paying for the health care of certain groups of people. Third-party payments are covered by the premiums paid by individuals and their employers.

With payment comes control. When individuals pay for their own health care, they can choose who they want to see without limitations. They may choose to see a medical doctor who has met standards set by the government or professional associations, or they may choose people who offer complementary or alternative care to include herbal remedies, homeopathy, massage therapy, yoga, and meditation. Individuals are not only expected to shoulder the responsibility for paying their health care providers, but also for taking care of themselves. If they have habits that may contribute to poor health, any resulting costs of that behavior are theirs.

When the taxpayers pay for the health care of others, control over how that money spent is given to government agencies that determine who is covered by various programs and which health care providers are authorized to receive payments for treatment. Government can also determine whether a person has taken sufficient care of himself to receive treatment, and there is discussion regarding whether those who abuse substances ranging from tobacco and alcohol to food should be eligible for coverage under government-paid programs.

Under the third-party payment model, insurance companies have control over reimbursement payments and are able to set their own standards about which types of treatment are covered, different levels of reimbursement for different providers based on their participation in the company's networks. Individuals may choose where to seek treatment, or to pursue an unhealthy lifestyle, with the understanding that they may be responsible for paying for all or part of their care as a result.

The next section of this chapter provides a brief overview of four perspectives that can be used to view health care. As you read these descriptions, consider who has the responsibility for health and health care, and how their views are represented in public debates on these topics. These descriptions are followed by an overview of the foundations of sociological thought and how they relate to health, and the models of health care will be further compared. Health care as seen from the three main theoretical perspectives of sociology—structural functionalism, conflict theory, and symbolic interactionism—will be discussed and then applied to the issues of population and carbon footprinting.

Perspectives On Health

There are many perspectives from which to view health and the systems and institutions of health care. This chapter begins with a brief exploration of four such perspectives: existentialist, medical, sociological, and sociocultural.

The **existentialist perspective** focuses on indi-

vidual responsibility for health care issues. Such a perspective was advanced by LeBlanc (2000) in his health responsibility model. This model advocates individuals taking personal responsibility for not only knowing about their health status, but also taking steps to correct both individual choices and social influences that have an impact on their health. Another existentialist example is the soul life karmic perspective for an individual. Individuals, through their soul life progressions, experience certain life events, including health-related issues, as means of enlightening their souls.

The **medical perspective** views issues of health within a medical framework that attempts to examine pathogens that result in disease and illness. The medical perspective is clearly seen in the genome project through which researchers are identifying genetic factors and predispositions for diseases. Another example of the medical model is the identification of specific pathogens, such as HIV, and how those pathogens affect the health of individuals. Certainly the medical perspective is aware of, and incorporates, dimensions of the sociological perspective, but the core focus of the perspective remains the identification and treatment of pathogens and diseases.

The **sociological perspective** uses research and concepts at both a macro and a micro level to identify health care issues in a society. From a macro-sociological perspective, sociologists examine the functions of the health care system within a particular society, determining if they are functional or dysfunctional. At this level, they might also examine the tensions between groups like professional and ideological organizations (e.g., pro-life or pro-choice). Conflicts over scarce resources in the health care system, like access to primary care physicians and medical facilities, are also studied. The micro-sociological level looks at various types of credentialism illustrated, by the use of letters to designate one's professional status within the field of health care, such as CNP (certified nurse practitioner), RN (registered nurse), LPN/LVN (licensed professional or licensed vocational nurse), and CNA (certified nurse assistant).

The **sociocultural perspective** views health care

issues as not merely the responsibility of an individual, but also of his or her family members and sometimes even the community. The sociocultural perspective is different from the pure sociological perspective because of the micro level responsibility for health-related problems. Two examples of the sociocultural perspective include the Navajo tribe and Chinese families. Within both of these cultures, illness is seen as a "disease," or imbalance, in the human system, which includes not only the biological system, but also the social system—family and community. Consequently, restoring a person to health involves restoring the balance within both of the systems.

Social And Sociological Foundations And Dynamics Of Health Care

Sociologists examine health-related issues through the use of categories associated with socioeconomic status, including gender, race, and class. According to Quimby and Friedman (Blankenship, 1989), it must be recognized that power and influence are unequally distributed across the social continuum, especially for women, racial minorities, and the poor. These inequalities are seen in the lack of social institutions and activist groups that effectively address the public health issues of each of these sociocultural minorities. As a result, individuals who belong to these groups can face special challenges in maintaining their health.

One example of the unequal distribution of resources occurred when HIV infections were first being documented. Initial educational endeavors conducted by the government and nonprofit organizations were mostly directed at the male homosexual community. The lack of similar proactive HIV education programs in the African-American community led to the current wave of infections in that population.

The unequal educational systems that can exist in affluent suburban communities and inner-city minority communities are another example. The inequalities between these systems have often resulted in minority students achieving a lower educational status than their suburban counterparts. Given the positive correlation between a higher level of education and good physical and mental health, the consequences to less educated inner-city students become evident—potentially poorer health. Essentially, higher education can provide access to work with greater economic rewards, thus improving a person's well-being (Reynolds & Ross, 1998).

Demographic Factors

Sociologists are interested in demographic factors such as gender, age, race, and geographical location as they attempt to understand the nature of health and health care institutions. We will briefly explore gender and how it relates to health. When sociologists consider chromosomal and physiological data, it is quite apparent that females are the stronger sex. Females can exist with only a single X chromosome, a condition referred to as Turner's syndrome; no male of the human species has been found to exist with only one Y chromosome. Additionally females are protected by the *double X-factor*, where a dominant X chromosome blocks the expression of any recessive trait found on the second X chromosome. In comparison, the male Y chromosome is incapable of blocking the expression of a recessive trait found on the inherited X chromosome. Furthermore, from a physiological perspective, female brains have greater connectivity between the two hemispheres of the brain, which promotes quicker physiological recoveries from strokes and similar conditions. On the other hand, research on specific health conditions shows that males may be the stronger of the sexes. Women experience migraine headaches far more frequently than men, as a result of sex hormones experienced post-puberty. Additionally, women experience arthritis at higher rates than men; men are potentially protected by genetics, testosterone, and exercise. Eating disorders are also 10 times more prevalent in women, even though the risks for eating disorders are believed to be similar for both males and females. Women are more likely to experience anxiety disorders, while bipolar disorders are experienced equally for both sexes (Maloof, 2008).

The Social Nature Of The Sick Role

When we are sick, we tend to see our illness as an individual experience. Most of us, though, live and function within the social worlds of family and work. As a result of these involvements, our illness generally assumes a broader social impact. Not only do we assume the sociological status of being ill, we also take on roles associated with that status. These dynamics are referred to as the **sick role**, which involves a variety of social norms that specify the responsibilities, expectations, and rights of someone who is ill. Henderson (1935) and Parsons (1951) generally categorize the sick role as involving four characteristics. An individual who is ill first acquires the freedom to not perform certain personal, familial, and work responsibilities. Secondly, because the individual has manifested the illness, s/he is not blamed for being ill. Although not blamed for being ill, there is a third expectation that requires that the person visit an appropriate medical professional. Finally, after having sought medical treatment, the individual is expected to comply with the treatment plan in an attempt to restore his/her health (Abercrombie, Hill, & Turner, 1984).

Health Care Systems - Comparative Models

As we explore the social frameworks for providing health care to a nation's citizens, we will draw upon three prominent models: socialized medicine, socialist medicine, and decentralized national health care.

Socialized Medicine

In the **socialized medicine** model, the government exercises some, but not total, control of the health care system. Cockerham (1995) identified five characteristics associated with socialized medicine. The first characteristic allows for the financing and organizing of health care services based on capitalistic economic factors that allow for supply and demand, as well as free-market competition. There is payment by government agencies to health care providers. Ownership of health care facilities can be either private or public, providing for limited, though often expensive, private caretakers for individuals. Finally, there is guaranteed access to medical care regardless of one's financial ability to pay.

Countries that have socialized systems include Canada, Great Britain, and Sweden. In Great Britain, a primary care physician also acts as a gatekeeper, determining who should be referred to specialists. Canada ensures primary care physician coverage, as well as hospital care but limits coverage for prescription drugs for those under 65. Dental care is not provided because it is seen as the responsibility of each individual. The Swedish system provides the greatest range of benefits, including payment for travel expenses and economic losses related to health care treatments.

Socialist Medicine

Socialist medicine is a system of health care that is under the complete control of the government, or state. Hospitals and other medical facilities are owned by the government, and all health care workers are employed by the government. Medical treatment is seen as a benefit provided by a government to its citizens. Cockerham (1995) identified five key characteristics of a socialist health care system: (1) provisions for providing private health care are banned, (2) equal access to medical care is guaranteed for all citizens, (3) all health care facilities are government owned and operated, (4) health care providers are employees of the government, and (5) the health care system is financed through an economy based on socialist, and often communist, principles, wherein direct control and organization of the system falls under the auspices of the state.

Socialist forms of health care have traditionally been found in communist states like Russia and Cuba. The Russian system is outdated, and bribes are common to obtain better care, but the government is spending $6.4 billion on new facilities, equipment, and raises for doctors (Los Angeles Times, 2008). In Cuba, not only is routine health care provided by the government, but also treatment for some of the most challenging diseases, including AIDS. Although HIV-infected individuals and those who have developed AIDS often receive their care in isolated facilities, they are provided comprehensive treatment for their disease.

Decentralized National Health Care

The third organizational model is **decentralized national health care**, in which government functions primarily as a regulator of the system. Regulation typically involves the government acting as a mediator between the providers of care and those organizations that pay for health care services within the system. Cockerham (1995) also identified five characteristics associated with this model: (1) the government may own some health care facilities, (2) equal access to care is guaranteed by the government, (3) payments made to providers are regulated, (4) individuals have access to some private care at their own expense, and (5) in capitalist economies, the government often indirectly controls the organization and financing of health care services.

Countries with decentralized national health care systems include Germany, the Netherlands, and Japan. Health care plans in Germany are managed by governmental bodies and each citizen is required to belong to a plan. In the Netherlands, the fees that pay for health care are obtained through compulsory contributions from employees and employers, as well as from state subsidies. A second system exists where individuals earning higher wages can purchase private insurance with employer subsidies that equal the amount of the public contribution, supplemented by the individual's own money. Finally, in Japan the government establishes fee schedules for physicians and hospitals, but within a system that allows citizens to choose their own physicians.

United States Model Of Health Care

As with many other aspects of the social structure in the United States, the health care system offers diverse functional models that draw upon the experiences of other countries, including the three models discussed previously. For most of us, especially during our primary working years, our health care falls under an independent **direct pay model**. Under the direct pay model, each individual is legally responsible for paying all of his or her own health care costs. Most people who work are covered by employer-subsidized insurance plans, thus creating a third-party payer model.

At times in our lives, we may receive health care that incorporates features from other models. For example, both Los Angeles and Ventura counties in California have general hospitals where citizens are entitled to receive care. Although this health care is not provided free of charge, the counties will absorb the costs if the individual is indigent. Essentially, these costs are covered by the taxes paid by local residents, as they are in socialist medical systems. Medicare and Medicaid are also examples of socialized medicine. The government makes direct payments to health care providers on behalf of those people who qualify for coverage under Medicare and Medicaid. The United States health care model is a combination of several models. Fundamentally, though, it remains a direct pay system.

Health Care Controversies In The United States

In the United States, there are a number of controversies surrounding health care. Because the economy is based on a capitalist system, profit motives are enmeshed within the direct pay model of health care. Even nonprofit entities have to pay competitive salaries to their employees, raising their operating costs. It is the for-profit sector of health care that receives the most attention from legislative bodies at both the state and national level. This sector is also responsible for conducting the research to formulate new medications and developing most new technologies for the diagnosis and treatment of disease.

Unlike more socialist and socialized models of health care systems, which negotiate prices to be paid for various health care advances, individuals in the United States pay fair market value (allowing for a profit) for medications and technology. It is often argued that the direct pay system in the United States is more of a socialized or socialist health care system because it subsidizes other people's care through insurance premiums, co-payments, and other health care costs. The capitalistic for-profit nature of the United States health care system allows for the development of advanced technologies and new medications. Thus, it appears to be a double-edged sword. By paying significant health care costs, U.S. citizens have access to the most advanced health care in the world, but this access is not guaranteed because of the lack of universal health care.

The role to be played by public health departments is another controversial topic in health care. In 1920, Charles Edward Amory Winslow, a public health professor at Yale, defined public health as:

"the science and art of preventing disease, prolonging life, and promoting physical health and efficiency to organize community efforts for the sanitation of the environment, the control of community infections, the education of the individual and principles of personal hygiene, the organization of medical and nursing service for the early diagnosis, prevention and treatment of disease, and the development of the social machinery which will insure to every individual of health" (Starr, 1982).

Religious organizations raised objections, often along moral grounds, regarding any state endeavor that concerned public health. Medical professionals, particular doctors, also raised objections, particularly when public health departments tried to involve themselves in the "organization of nursing and medical service." This aspect of health care related directly to the practice of medicine, and they wanted to keep it under their purview. The antipathy toward public health services is reflected in a comment by Dr. George Shardy, who noted that "poor people do not suffer from want of skilled medical attendants…on the contrary, they obtain vastly more than they have the right to expect…vast sums of money are wasted yearly on worthless and undeserving persons" (Starr, 1982).

Dr. Shardy's comment was related to public health dispensaries, and appeared to be motivated by the fact that the dispensaries were often used as training facilities for medical interns. Physicians decreased the number of medical schools in United States, thus eliminating the need for internships at public health dispensaries, which also reduced the interns' contact with the public health system. Because it is physicians who control the training of medical students, through the legislative authority given to the American Medical Association, we can see an organized effort on the part of doctors to limit access to free or reduced-cost health care services provided by public health organizations. Such endeavors raise serious questions about the motives of both physicians and the American Medical Association, particularly regarding their economic and profit motives. We continue to see the marginalization of public health care programs to services that they are "allowed' to provide within the health care system in the United States. The services typically provided by such departments include family planning, infant and child nutrition, and environmental and community health issues, including the diagnosis and treatment of sexually transmitted infections or diseases. These services generally do not generate high revenues, demonstrating the marginalization of public health services.

Health Care Providers

There are a variety of individuals who provide health care services in the United States; yet, it is physicians who reign supreme among health care providers, regulating the practice of medicine through their legislative and legal establishments. There are three broad classifications of providers: primary care providers, secondary care providers, and alternative health care providers.

Primary care providers are physicians who can practice medicine in "all of its branches." Historically, this category has been composed of doctors of medicine (MDs). Doctors of osteopathic medicine (DOs) are another group of professionals that can function as primary care providers in the United States. These primary care providers are trained in much the same way as medical doctors, with the addition of learning holistic techniques that include physical adjustments to the body (similar to those made by chiropractors). A doctor of chiropractic (DC) can practice as a primary care provider if he or she takes additional training and refers patients as medically necessary to other primary care providers. While most states allow both MDs and DOs to practice in all medical branches, few states allow DCs to do the same. Illinois does allow chiropractic physicians this authority, provided that they complete additional courses as prescribed by the state's Department of Professional Occupations. An emergent primary health care provider, allowed in a limited number of states, is a doctor of naturopathic medicine (ND). Naturopathic doctors often use natural medicinal substances, herbs in particular, as part of their treatment protocols. Like DCs, NDs must also make appropriate referrals when a medical condition is beyond the scope of their training and practice. Depending upon where they live, individuals may have any one of these four types of doctors as their primary health care provider.

Secondary care providers include professionals who "extend" the services of doctors and nurses. Doctors have the greatest degree of authority for providing health care within the United States. Those professionals who also provide health care services, but are not physicians, are referred to as secondary care providers. This categorization is by no means a reflection of their professional training but is rather a reflection of their secondary functionality in the delivery of health care.

When the health care system experienced a decline in the number of physicians, two classifications of professionals were added to help meet demand—physician assistants and nurse practitioners. These **physician extenders** can provide basic physical diagnoses and care. In most states, physician assistants are licensed to practice under the supervision of a physician, while nurse practitioners function fairly independently. This varies from state to state, however, depending on their licensing laws.

While the impetus for the development of physician extenders was to meet the needs of the underserved, primarily those in rural areas of the United States, this health care model failed to make working in such areas a requisite for licensure. As a result, many physician assistants and nurse practitioners relocated to urban areas where they could receive higher wages.

Because of a shortage of nurses, there was a need to develop **clinical nurse extenders** (LeBlanc, 2006). These individuals provide limited nursing care to a level provided by their training and licensing. Historically, nurses were trained in three-year diploma programs, often affiliated with particular hospitals. As the nursing shortage emerged, two-year degree programs were introduced to the community college system. When the demand for nurses was still not being met, one-year training programs for licensed vocational nurses (LVNs) and licensed practical nurses (LPNs) were developed. When there was a demand for still more nurses, combined with a need to reduce costs, a third category emerged—nursing assistants. This category evolved into a certified nursing assistant (CNA) health care professional. As pressure has mounted to provide nursing care, particularly in rural areas, the scope of practice for nurse extenders has been expanded. For instance, LPNs are generally not allowed to dispense medications, administer IV treatments, or act as charge nurses, but they can, with additional training, now assume these responsibilities in some states. Not only has the scope of practice expanded for LVNs and LPNS, it has also expanded for CNAs. In some states, CNAs can now dispense medications if they complete additional training.

Within the health care field there are also a variety of professionals with specialized occupational training who provide limited health care services. These professionals include physical therapists, respiratory therapists, speech pathologists, dietitians, health care educators, medical social workers, and even chaplains. These professionals supplement primary and secondary care providers, allowing them to focus on the diagnosis and treatment of illness and disease.

Alternative health care providers do not practice health care within mainstream, Western modalities of health care. Such people have existed in non-Western societies for centuries. Many early healers, including shamans in tribal cultures, used natural plants and herbs to treat human diseases. The Chinese have used not only herbs, but also needles (acupuncture) and the manipulation of the body's soft tissues.

A more contemporary alternative practitioner is a doctor of Oriental medicine (OMDs). Doctors of Oriental medicine generally have to complete 3,000 hours of formal training, guided by Eastern philosophical principles regarding "disease" and medical treatments that promote physiological integration through a holistic approach. Herbs are often a part of their clinical practice, as are nutritional counseling and massage. Acupuncturists are a related group of alternative practitioners, specifically trained in the Chinese practice of using needles to release energy—or chi—blockages. Many states require that an acupuncturist obtain a master's degree before seeking licensure. Though they may be licensed, some states do not allow them to practice independently of primary health care providers. For instance, to see an acupuncturist in Illinois, a patient must have a referral from a primary health care provider.

Massage therapists are another type of alternative health care provider. Most massage therapists complete a 500-hour training program including more anatomy and physiology information than students in licensed vocational and practical nursing programs. Generally, the scope of practice for a massage therapist is the reduction of muscular tension in the human body. Finally, there is a range of alternative health care providers who may not be required to have much training to practice their professions. Examples include aromatherapists who use natural scented oils to work with human imbalances, and hypnotherapists who may have as few as 100 hours of training.

Theoretical Perspectives On Health Care

Structural Functionalism

As a macro-sociological perspective, structural functionalism is more concerned with the larger social and societal dimensions of health care, focusing on the functions served by the system and its institutions. Structural functionalism asserts that there is a great deal of social stability and harmony within societies, which promotes a state of homeostasis. It is hoped that the manifest (intended) functions will help promote social stability—homeostasis—but it is recognized that sometimes manifest functions can be dysfunctional because they promote social instability. There are also latent, or unintended, functions that can be either functional or dysfunctional for society.

For a society to function, it needs a healthy work force. Maintaining the health of the individual serves to stabilize the general health and well-being of the population, and it is the health of the population, particularly the work force, that allows a society to maintain itself economically. Thus, a manifest function of the health care system is to keep the citizenry healthy so they can be a productive work force serving to stabilize society.

A second manifest function of the health care system is to avoid increasing the burden placed upon the broader society to care for the health of the population. It has been proposed that one way to accomplish this is to provide, or mandate, health care coverage for all citizens. While providing health care has been discussed in the United States since the first Clinton administration, legislative efforts have failed at the national level. Massachusetts provides us with an example of how mandated universal health care coverage can be effective at dispersing the social and economic burdens that the uninsured and underinsured place upon society. Citizens of Massachusetts must have health insurance coverage or they face economic penalties. If they do not have access to insurance through their employment, they must purchase insurance within a state-sponsored plan. Thus, Massachusetts is attempting to meet this second manifest function (Massachusetts Trial Court Libraries, 2008).

The health care system in the United States is dysfunctional for the estimated 45 million uninsured and 25 million to 60 million underinsured citizens (ConsumerAffairs.com, 2007; Democratic Policy

Committee, 2005). The United States remains the only industrialized society that fails to provide comprehensive health care coverage for all of its citizens. It is interesting to note that most of these uninsured and underinsured individuals are working-age citizens, the people who contribute most to the financial stability of this country. If a significant portion of the working population became ill, it would place economic demands on the health care system that can only be described as socially destabilizing and, consequently, dysfunctional to society.

Social Conflict

Like structural functionalism, social conflict is a macro-level theoretical perspective. It deals with the larger dimensions of society and, in particular, the tensions that exist between groups within that society. Although the classic social conflict perspective articulated by Marx involved tensions between the social classes, groups can also be in conflict over scarce resources other than money, such as a significant value within society. Remember, also, that groups struggle to obtain and/or control scarce resources. Consequently, struggles for power often enter the social institutions of a society.

The health care system has many groups in conflict with one another. In the United States, we have to look no further than the power struggle over who can practice medicine, to what degree, and in what settings, to see that social conflict exists in the health care system. Historically, medical doctors (MDs) have been able to practice in all branches of medicine in the United States. When more holistic practitioners, like doctors of osteopathic medicine (DOs), entered the practice of medicine, MDs fought their acceptance, both legislatively and professionally. While legislative efforts eventually failed, the MDs succeeded professionally by limiting where DOs can practice medicine. For instance, osteopathic physicians are not permitted to practice medicine in hospitals, thus limiting their work with patients in such settings. Further, when doctors of chiropractic medicine sought professional recognition, medical doctors attempted to prevent that change. One wonders if the quality of patient care was the central concern of the medical doctors, or if

their concern was more economic, specifically the potential loss of patient revenue provided through patient care. If so, it is believed that the economic motivation, with money being the scarce resource, is central to the conflict paradigm. The exercise of power by the MDs, demonstrated by their attempts to limit the acceptance of other doctors, is the mechanism by which they maintain that scarce resource for themselves.

Two examples further illustrate the conflict dynamics within the health care system. The first example occurred in Illinois, where doctors were successful at establishing a legislative requirement that individuals must have been referred by a medical doctor, doctor of osteopathic medicine, or chiropractor before seeing an acupuncturist (Illinois Compiled Statutes, 2008). It should be noted that a number of states allow acupuncturists and doctors of Oriental medicine to practice completely independent of mandated referrals. Such states recognize a specific scope of practice within the field of medicine for these practitioners. The second example involves an attempt by physicians to limit access to natural remedies, specifically herbs. Physicians attempted to define herbs as drugs, because of their "medicinal" qualities. If classified as drugs, herbs would have fallen within the scope of practicing medicine, as only licensed physicians can prescribe drugs or medications. Individuals would then have had to acquire a prescription before purchasing herbs. Fortunately for these individuals, the efforts failed (Theil, 2003). Once again, one has to question the motives behind the actions of physicians, particularly since they have very little, if any, medical training in herbology, unlike naturopathic physicians and master herbologists, both recognized medical practitioners in other countries. Again, it appears that there is an economic, rather than a patient safety, motivation on the part of physicians to limit and control access to a variety of health care professionals and medical interventions.

Symbolic Interactionism

As a microsociological perspective, symbolic interactionism focuses on how symbols are defined and used, both contextually and socially. Equally important for symbolic interactionists are how social interactions are created and maintained and how they change society. When applying symbolic interactionism to the health care system, one needs look no further than the variety of requisite initials associated with the professional status of health care providers to see the use of symbols. The symbolic representation of something is central to this

Table 1 A

Physicians	
DC	Doctor of Chiropractic Medicine
DO	Doctor of Osteopathic Medicine
MD	Doctor of Medicine
ND	Doctor of Naturopathic Medicine
OMD	Doctor of Oriental Medicine
Nurses	
CNA	Certified Nursing Assistant
CNP	Certified Nurse Practitioner
LPN	Licensed Practical Nurse
LVN	Licensed Vocational Nurse
RN	Registered Nurse
Alternative Health Care Providers	
CMT	Certified Massage Therapist
DPM	Doctor of Podiatric Medicine
LMT	Licensed Massage Therapist
NCMT	Nationally Certified Massage Therapist
NP	Naprapathic Practitioner

perspective; therefore, it is important to recall what each of these symbols means (see Table 1 A).

Each set of letters represents the symbolic nature of a profession, which is often a socially recognized credential that defines the legal parameters for practicing that profession.

From the symbolic interactionist perspective, how individuals create, maintain, and change the social world at a microlevel is significant. We can see this within the practice of massage therapy. Historically, massage was taught through a mentoring process, and a person would be referred to as a massage therapist upon completion of the program. As society evolved, it demanded a more formal educational process for individuals studying massage; consequently, schools developed where, upon successful completion of a training program, individuals would receive a certificate recognizing their status as a certified massage therapist (CMT). Though professionally trained, these individuals often practiced without local or state licensure. The field then evolved to require licensing at a local or state level, resulting in the use of the initials LMT to represent a licensed massage therapist. A final evolution within the field of massage therapy resulted in a number of states not only requiring licensure, but also national certification. To become a nationally certified massage therapist (NCMT), individuals are required to pass an examination. The changes in this one field illustrate the importance of symbols in society and how they can change over time.

Population Issues And Dynamics

Having covered health care issues from a sociological perspective, including some issues related to population dynamics, it is time to more directly examine population from a sociological perspective. This examination of population issues and dynamics begins by reviewing some foundational terms and concepts used by sociologists. After that review, sociological population theories will be briefly highlighted. These will be followed by factors that influence population growth, as well as a discussion of limited population trends seen both globally and in the United States. The final section of this chapter will examine how each of the three dominant sociological theories views population issues and dynamics.

Within the discipline of sociology, **demography** is generally defined as the study of growth and decline in the human population caused by migration, fertility, and mortality, as well as sex ratios and age cohorts (Scott & Marshall, 2005). Like many other areas in the field of sociology, there is complexity and interrelatedness in the population characteristics and concepts related to demography. Sociologists who investigate population characteristics are referred to as **demographers**, and they focus on population projections and the social consequences of those projections.

As noted in the definition, key concepts that would interest a demographer are birth and fertility rates, death (mortality) rates, life expectancies, human migration, sex ratios, and marriage rates. We will briefly discuss these terms, as defined by Scott and Marshall (2005), and provide tables comparing these statistics for countries in several regions.

Birthrates are used to compare the fertility rates of different populations. There are two common ways to calculate birthrates, the *crude birthrate* and the *general fertility rate*. The **crude birthrate** is defined as the number of live births in a year per 1,000 people (using midyear estimates). The **general fertility rate** is defined as the birthrate per 1,000 women of childbearing age. The fertility rate is calculated as the number of live births in a year, divided by the female population aged 15 to 44 years, times 1000, and may also be referred to as the *total fertility rate*. As shown in Table 1 B [North and Central America Table], the crude birthrate in Mexico (20.04) is almost twice that of Canada (10.29), with the rate in the United States (14.18) falling about halfway between the two. Mexico (2.37) also has the highest fertility rate compared with the United States (2.10), and Canada (1.57) (Central Intelligence Agency, 2008). The terms *birthrate* and *fertility rate* are often used interchangeably, so it is important to note when the crude birthrate is being used to avoid confusion.

Death (mortality) rates are another demographic variable that interest sociological demographers. Just as with birthrates, death or mortality rates are generally defined in two ways. The **crude death rate** is the number of deaths in a year per 1,000 population in the defined geographical area. Another way of measuring death rates is the computation of a standard mortality ratio (SMR) for each sex, the sexes combined, or specific social groupings. The **standard mortality ratio** is defined as the actual or observed number of deaths of a group, divided by the expected number of deaths, and then multiplied by 100. Another key death rate examined by demographers is the **infant mortality rate**, which is defined as the number of deaths within the first year of life, divided by the number of live births in the same year, times 1000. Mexico has the lowest crude death rate (4.78), but the highest infant mortality rate (19.01). The United States has the highest crude death rate (8.27), and Canada has the lowest infant mortality rate (5.08).

Life expectancy is often used by demographers as an indicator of the standard of living within a society, in particular as it relates to the health, social,

Table 1 B North And Central America

2008 Demographic Statistics	Canada	Mexico	United States
Crude Birthrate (per 1,000 population)	10.29	20.04	14.18
Total Fertility Rate (per woman)	1.57	2.37	2.10
Crude Death Rate (per 1,000 population)	7.61	4.78	8.27
Infant Mortality Rate (per 1,000 live births)	5.08	19.01	6.30
Life Expectancy - All (at birth)	81.16	75.84	78.14
Life Expectancy - Male (at birth)	78.65	73.05	75.29
Life Expectancy - Female (at birth)	83.81	78.78	81.13
Sex Raio (at birth, males/females)	1.06	1.05	1.05
Sex Raio (under 15 years, males/females)	1.05	1.04	1.05
Sex Raio (15 - 64 years, males/females)	1.02	.94	1.00
Sex Raio (65 and over, males/females)	.77	.82	.72
Sex Raio (total population, males/females)	.98	.96	.97
NET Migration Rate (per 1,000 population)	5.62	-3.84	2.92

Source: The 2008 World Factbook, CIA.

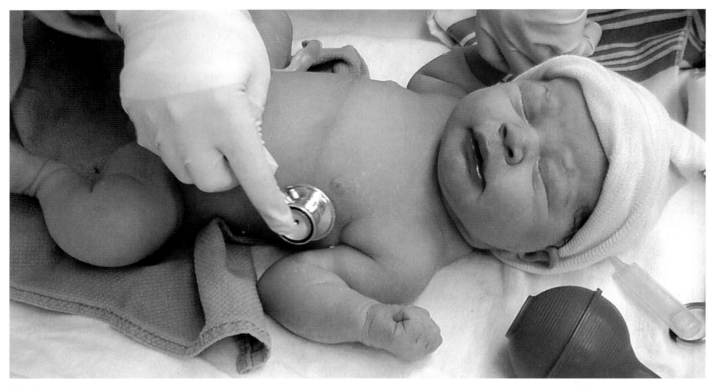

Newborn baby.

and economic standards of living. **Life expectancy** is defined as the number of years that a person can expect to live within a given society. It can also be calculated as "the number of further years of life a person can expect at a given age." Demographers often delve beyond general life expectancy to examine differences between the genders within the same societies. Among the countries shown in Table 1 B [North/Central America], Canada has the highest life expectancy rate (81.16) and Mexico has the lowest (75.84). In all three of these countries, women can expect to live longer than men, on average. The largest gap between the average life expectancy for women and that for men is in the United States, where the difference is 5.84 years.

In addition to looking at general life expectancies, demographers also examine **sex ratios**, which are calculated as the number of males per 1,000 females in the population. The sex ratios for Canada, Mexico, and the United States are fairly even up to 15 years of age, then the ratio for ages 15 through 64 in Mexico drops (0.94) compared with the United States (1.00) and Canada (1.02). That trend reverses in the 65 and older age range, with Mexico hav-

ing the highest ratio (0.82), compared with Canada (0.77) and the United States (0.72).

The sex ratio of a country is an important social indicator because it affects the **marriage rate**, which is the number of marriages per 1,000 people in a given year. The participation of women in the labor force, and the expected or actual roles for males and females, may also be affected by sex ratios (Thio, 2004). On the other hand, social policies, such as female infanticide, can have a large impact on sex ratios, affecting future trends like the availability of partners and fertility rates in a society. Too few women can relegate a significant portion of men to a single lifestyle.

Human migration is another factor that affects the population demographics of countries. Human migration is the (more or less) permanent movement of individuals or groups across symbolic or political boundaries into new areas and communities (Scott & Marshall, 2005). The definition of human migration recognizes that there may be movement between areas within a society or a country, like the migration from rural areas to more urban areas, which has been happening within the United States over the past century. The definition also recognizes migration patterns from one nation to another, such as the movement of people from Mexico and countries in Central and South America to the United States, through both legal and illegal migration patterns. In 2008, Mexico had a negative net migration rate (-3.84) which indicates net emigration, while the rates for Canada (5.62) and the United States (2.92) were both positive, indicating net immigration.

Human migration patterns can be used to stabilize population demographics, or they can challenge sociocultural and economic stability. An example of migration stabilization, including illegal migration, is seen in the agricultural sector of the United States. Many farmers could not economically produce and harvest their crops without the use of a migrant labor force that may include people who have entered the country illegally. One social consequence is the availability of affordable agricultural commodities, especially produce, for U.S. consumers. Yet, the use of this labor force can have destabilizing effects on other sectors of the economy, such as the demands placed on the health care and education systems by the illegal immigrant work force. It is estimated that five to six percent of California's K-12 student population is in the United States illegally (Miller, 1997). The presence of these students also stresses the economic resources of school districts due to the need to provide bilingual education.

Population Trends

In this section, we will examine three population trends—overpopulation, underpopulation, and resource utilization, including carbon footprinting. Each of these population issues can affect not only a particular country, but also the international community, in very different but significant ways. These issues will be examined from both a regional and a global perspective.

Overpopulation

Overpopulation is defined as the population of an environment by a particular species that exceeds that environment's carrying capacity. The effects of overpopulation can include depletion of resources, environmental deterioration, and a prevalence of famine and disease. With its over-dependence on internal resource production, Rwanda is experiencing overpopulation. It does not draw on the carrying capacity of other nations by importing significant resources. Consequently, Rwanda exceeds the carrying capacity of its own geographical and economic resources. Additionally, the rate at which the population is growing exceeds the country's ability to provide for its people, particularly when it comes to agricultural goods. This has resulted in an internal migration and a higher concentration of young men in urban areas. In turn, the level of violence committed by this group of dislocated men has increased as they struggle to survive. Finally, deaths caused by HIV/AIDS have affected the employment sector and the development of human capital through teacher deaths, and the production of agricultural resources through farmer deaths (Butler, 2004). In 2003, it was estimated that 5.1 percent of adults in Rwanda were living with HIV/AIDS, compared with 21.5 percent in South Africa and 0.6 percent in the United States (CIA, 2008).

India is also experiencing overpopulation. Though India has some of the richest agricultural land, producing the second-highest harvests of both rice and wheat in 1999, the sustenance needs of a significant portion of its population are not being met. During the same time period in which India had this significant agricultural production, only 53 percent of the population under age 5 was well-nourished and 37 percent lacked access to safe water. Furthermore, one quarter of the population lived below the poverty line, and 15 million people slept on sidewalks (Grinnell College, 2008). There is also a lack of protein to meet the demands of the population in India. In 2003, protein consumption in India was 11grams per day per person, which is much less than the standard recommended daily intake level (Gilland, 2008).

Underpopulation

In contrast to overpopulation, **underpopulation** is defined as "lacking the normal or required population density". One way of determining if a country

Table 1 C Europe

2008 Demographic Statistics	France	Germany	United Kingdom
Crude Birthrate (per 1,000 population)	12.73	8.18	10.65
Total Fertility Rate (per woman)	1.98	1.41	1.66
Crude Death Rate (per 1,000 population)	8.48	10.80	10.05
Infant Mortality Rate (per 1,000 live births)	3.36	4.03	4.93
Life Expectancy - All (at birth)	80.87	79.10	78.85
Life Expectancy - Male (at birth)	77.68	76.11	76.37
Life Expectancy - Female (at birth)	84.23	82.26	81.46
Sex Raio (at birth, males/females)	1.05	1.06	1.05
Sex Raio (under 15 years, males/females)	1.05	1.06	1.05
Sex Raio (15 - 64 years, males/females)	1.00	1.04	1.02
Sex Raio (65 and over, males/females)	0.71	0.72	0.75
Sex Raio (total population, males/females)	0.96	0.97	0.98
NET Migration Rate (per 1,000 population)	1.48	2.19	2.17

Source: The 2008 World Factbook, CIA.

is underpopulated is to learn whether it produces births equal to the necessary *replacement rate*, a figure presently established as about 2.1 children for each woman in a developed country. The replacement rate is the number of children each woman needs to have to maintain current population levels. If a country's fertility rate—the total number of children the average woman is likely to have—is below the replacement rate, underpopulation is a possibility. In 2008, the fertility rate was 1.98 in France, 1.66 in the United Kingdom, and 1.41 in Germany, as shown in Table 1 C [Europe Table]. As a result of these low fertility rates, it is estimated that by the year 2030, Europe will have about 20 million fewer workers than it needs in order to have a strong economy. It is also estimated that within two generations in France and Germany, there is a potential for a Muslim majority, due to the high fertility rate of Muslim immigrants (6.0). Additionally it is estimated that Russia will lose one third of its population, primarily through the use of abortion as a method of birth control, by the year 2050 (Smith, 2008). Furthermore, it is estimated that 15 countries have fertililty rates below 1.3, and six countries have rates between 1.3 and 1.4 (Abortion TV, 2006). As of 2001, it was estimated that 83 countries and territories had fertility rates below the replacement

level, representing approximately 2.7 billion people, or roughly 44 percent of the world's population (Eberstadt, 2001).

A decrease in life expectancy is an additional area where population declines are of concern. The U.S. Census Bureau estimates that approximately 40 countries and territories will have lower life expectancy rates in 2010 than they had in 1990. This includes the sub-Saharan region, where most of the deaths are due to HIV/AIDS, and a number of post-communist countries, including Russia, which has an average lifespan shorter than it was 40 years ago (Eberstadt, 2001). As shown in Table 1 D [Asia table], Russia's life expectancy was 65.94 in 2008, with the life expectancy for women (73.10) almost 14 years longer than that for men (59.19) (CIA, 2008).

There are several means of countering underpopulation. One means is through the regulation of abortion. In countries where abortion is illegal, such as Ireland (1.85) and Portugal (1.49), there exist some of the highest fertility rates within any European nation. Being a pro-life nation, such as Malta (1.51), also results in higher fertility rates (CIA, 2008). Another way of addressing underpopulation is through immigration. As a result of declining fertility rates, it is estimated that Europe would need

Table 1 D Asia

2008 Demographic Statistics	China	India	Japan	Russia
Crude Birthrate (per 1,000 population)	13.71	22.22	7.87	11.03
Total Fertility Rate (per woman)	1.77	2.76	1.22	1.40
Crude Death Rate (per 1,000 population)	7.03	6.40	9.26	16.06
Infant Mortality Rate (per 1,000 live births)	21.16	32.31	2.80	10.81
Life Expectancy - All (at birth)	73.18	69.25	82.07	65.94
Life Expectancy - Male (at birth)	71.37	66.87	78.73	59.19
Life Expectancy - Female (at birth)	75.18	71.90	85.59	73.10
Sex Raio (at birth, males/females)	1.11	1.12	1.06	1.06
Sex Raio (under 15 years, males/females)	1.13	1.10	1.06	1.05
Sex Raio (15 - 64 years, males/females)	1.06	1.06	1.01	0.93
Sex Raio (65 and over, males/females)	0.91	0.90	0.74	0.45
Sex Raio (total population, males/females)	1.06	1.06	0.95	0.86
NET Migration Rate (per 1,000 population)	-0.39	-0.05	N/A	0.28

Source: The 2008 World Factbook, CIA.

to quadruple its number of immigrants to prevent a decline in the working-age population. To achieve this, the net migration rates for the countries included in Table 1 C [Europe table] would have to increase substantially from their 2008 levels of 1.48 for France, 2.19 for Germany, and 2.17 for the United Kingdom. For Japan, it is estimated that nearly 600,000 immigrants are necessary to keep the working population from shrinking and having a negative impact on their economy (Eberstadt, 2001). Immigration is also a factor in the stabilization of total fertility rates within the United States. In the United States, the fertility rates for Hispanics (2.9) and blacks (2.1) were at or above the replacement level needed to maintain the current population (2.1) in 2007. The rates for Asians (1.9) and whites (1.86) were below the replacement rate (Eberstadt, 2001). Thus, it can be said that the population of United States is being stabilized mostly by the fertility rates of the Hispanic community (Currie, 2007).

Finally, China presents us with a population paradox. Some researchers believe that because China has the highest population in the world, with approximately 1.2 billion people, it is overpopulated, particularly in certain regions such as urban centers. Other researchers believe that China faces a population shortage, particularly as it deals with an aging

population. In 1979, China introduced a one-child-per-family policy to help it control its exponential population growth. As shown in Table 1 D [Asia table], China's fertility rate (1.77) was significantly below the 2.1 replacement rate, but higher than the rates for Russia (1.40) and Japan (1.22) in 2008 (CIA, 2008).

The one-child policy benefited China economically by raising the standards of living for its citizens, including the introduction of birth insurance and workman's compensation benefits (Cook, 1999). However, China still faces two emergent population concerns. By the year 2010, China's capital, Beijing, will face a water shortage because its population is expected to exceed 17 million, which is at least 3 million more than the carrying capacity of the city's water system (China.org.cn, 2009). Additionally, by 2050, China will face a shrinking working-age population that will be expected take care of the elderly, both physically and economically. Matters are further complicated by the entry of females into the labor force, as well as the decreasing number of young Chinese females, who are traditionally expected to take care of the elderly, especially in the home (Kaneda, 2006).

Next we will focus on resource utilization and carbon footprinting, as means of examining a person's impact on not only the social, but also the physical world. Using statistics for 2007, the United States consumed approximately 69 barrels of oil per person, ranking 7th in the world on this measure, behind the Virgin Islands (845 barrels per person), Luxembourg (126), Saudi Arabia (84), Guam (74), Canada (71), and Iceland (70). When looking at total consumption by country, the United States ranks first with a rate of 20,680,000 barrels per day. This difference in rank occurs because the population of the United States is much higher than that of other countries with high per capita consumption rates. China ranks second as far as total oil consumption (7,578,000) and Japan ranks third (5,007,000) (NationMaster, 2009). Other statistics for the United States may be even more revealing. It has approximately 5 percent of the world's population, yet its energy use is approximately 26 percent of that for the world as a whole. Additionally, the United States has approximately 35 percent of the automobiles in the world and represents 25 percent of the world's fossil fuel consumption (Thompson, 2000).

In this section, we will look at the geographic regions of North America, Latin America, Europe, Africa, and Asia as defined by the United Nations. In North America, we consumed 60 barrels of oil per capita. This compares with 9 barrels of oil for

Latin America, 29 barrels of oil for Europe, 3 barrels of oil for Africa, and 7 barrels of oil for Asia (Population Connection, 2007). Access and utilization of land is also significant for North America. Regarding access to arable—crop-producing—land, each individual in North America has an equivalent of 1.7 acres, compared with 0.8 acres in Latin America, 1.0 acres in Europe, 0.6 acres in Africa, and 0.4 acres in Asia.

The populations of different regions have different effects on the natural resources of the world. Concerns have been raised about the impact of unequal utilization of natural resources on environment. Out of this concern, an interest in measuring the carbon footprint of societies and individuals developed. A **carbon footprint** is defined as "the impact our activities have on the environment, and, in particular, climate change. This relates to the amount of greenhouse gases produced in our day-to-day lives through burning fossil fuels for electricity, heating, and transportation" (Carbon Footprint Ltd., 2008).

The chart below illustrates the unequal carbon footprints of different regions of the world, as measured by population versus the amount of carbon emissions.

From these statistics we see that North Amer-

Table 2 A Unequal Carbon Footprints

	Population	Carbon Emissions
Canada	0.5%	2.2%
Central and Eastern Europe	6.4%	11.0%
East Asia and the Pacific	30.2%	23.0%
Latin America and the Carribean	8.5%	4.9%
South Africa	0.7%	1.5%
South Asia	24.0%	7.0%
United States	4.0%	21.1%
Other Areas	25.70%	29.30%

Source: United Nations Development Programme

ica—the United States in particular—consumes a disproportionate amount of the world's natural resources. One final comparison will be noted; developing countries in the world hold approximately 79 percent of the world's population and emit approximately 41.4 percent of the world's carbon dioxide. This compares with the approximately 12 percent of the world's population that reside in developed countries and produce a similar amount of carbon dioxide emissions. It is this disproportionate production of carbon dioxide that has raised international concerns about the impact on the environment, specifically global warming, by the world community (United Nations Development Programme, 2008).

Our final trend affecting population is related to HIV/AIDS infection rates. It is estimated that 5.4 percent of the adult population in Uganda is infected with HIV, and in urban centers the rate is much higher (10.1%). Although rates of infection appear to have stabilized, the impact on the population of Uganda has been the death of approximately one million people, and a significantly reduced life expectancy. The labor force has been depleted, which affects agricultural productivity, and the health care and educational sectors of the economy have been weakened. Furthermore, the epidemic has resulted in more than one million orphans, and a disproportionate number of women are affected, representing 59 percent of all those infected (Avert, 2008). South Africa has a very high prevalence of HIV/AIDS (21.5%) (CIA, 2008). It is estimated that of those people under age 24, 23 percent are HIV positive. This high rate of infection, combined with a younger age of infection, is projected to result in two million orphans by 2010 (Malebo, 2002). Consequently, we again see how a health-related issued HIV/AIDS, can be a population issue that is reflected in death rates and life expectancy.

Theories Related To Population Dynamics

As we begin to examine theories related to population dynamics, it is important to recall the distinction between a theory and the theoretical perspectives used within the discipline of sociology. A theory attempts to explain a particular social behavior, and the next section will be an exploration of the theories that explain population dynamics. These explanations will draw on two classic theoretical perspectives, drawing on the works of Malthus and Marx, that attempt to explain population dynamics, as well as a more contemporary perspective based on the works of Nam. In contrast, the theoretical perspectives presented near the end of this chapter provide the overarching framework for sociological study.

Classic Approaches

Most sociologists give credit to Thomas R. Malthus for presenting the first significant theory about population and population changes. The foundations of Malthus' position were that "(1) the rapid growth of population would outstrip the resources needed to provide for it; and (2) this growth was due to the excess of births over deaths" (Nam, 1994, p. 33). Malthus recognized the necessity of resources, most notably food, as well as the reality of the birthing process, thus including the sexual drives found and expressed within the human condition. As a result of these two population dynamics, Malthus believed that population numbers would increase geometrically, while food and sustenance production would only increase arithmetically. Additionally, he believed that humans would be limited by sustenance issues. Furthermore, he believed that a set of preventative checks would address these issues. For example, preventative checks might include unsafe occupations, difficult labor circumstances, extreme poverty and diseases, military conflict, and famine—all of which result in deaths. Malthus believed that excesses were also part of population balance, particularly moral excesses. He proposed a number of checks and balances to address some of these issues, beginning with restraining excesses through acts of the will or by avoiding behaviors that may predispose a person to the miseries noted, such as avoiding the moral strain of marriage. Thus, moral restraint becomes a positive preventative check in dealing with these issues (Nam, 1994).

In response to the writings of Malthus, Karl

Marx and Friedrich Engels became his antagonists. Rather than directly challenging Malthus' dynamics of population growth and population sustenance, Marx and Engels, being true to their fundamental class position, believed that population pressures really resided within the social dimensions of one's "means of employment." Consequently, population growth dynamics are continually relevant because each stage of development will have a "law" related to population dynamics. In capitalist societies, there is often a surplus population of laborers that exceeds the needs of production demands. Regarding the surplus population, Marx and Engels maintained that Malthus failed to recognize potential progress within the sciences that could address related sustenance issues and, thus, meet the needs of a population. Additionally, the ideas of Marx, although modified, are seen within democratic socialism, which makes provisions for the less fortunate within a society based on their social class standing. The Chinese sociologist Zheng recognized the positions of Marx and Engels in a book on Chinese population issues with a quote from Engels: "If communist society should one day be compelled to regulate the production of human beings, as it regulates the production of goods, and that it and it alone will be able to do this without difficulty" (Nam, 1994, p. 72).

Zheng went on to note that a society can exercise plans to control overpopulation dynamics, in particular population reduction, "in line with the needs of the developing social productive forces" (Nam, 1994, p. 72). We can clearly see the influences of Marx and Engels within these positions articulated for Chinese society.

A Contemporary Approach

While the writings of Malthus, Marx, and Engels provide the classic theoretical foundations, it was Charles B. Nam (1994) who articulated theoretical positions of population dynamics at the macro, micro, and medial sociological levels, thus reflecting the three dominant perspectives of analysis within the discipline of sociology. Nam provided four macro perspectives that allow us to understand population dynamics at the aggregate or societal level. These perspectives include an ecological, a sociocultural, and a modernization approach, and a final approach that is institutional in nature.

The ecological perspective is based on the position that organisms adapt biologically to their environments, in this case referring to human beings adapting to their geographical areas. This approach uses a framework of technology, natural environment, and social organization. In contrast, the

Table 2 B Africa

2008 Demographic Statistics	Rwanda	South Africa	Sudan	Uganda
Crude Birthrate (per 1,000 population)	39.97	20.23	34.31	48.15
Total Fertility Rate (per woman)	5.31	2.43	4.58	6.81
Crude Death Rate (per 1,000 population)	14.46	16.94	13.64	12.32
Infant Mortality Rate (per 1,000 live births)	83.42	45.11	86.98	65.99
Life Expectancy - All (at birth)	49.76	48.89	50.28	52.34
Life Expectancy - Male (at birth)	48.56	49.63	49.38	51.31
Life Expectancy - Female (at birth)	51	48.15	51.23	53.40
Sex Raio (at birth, males/females)	1.03	1.02	1.05	1.03
Sex Raio (under 15 years, males/females)	1.01	1.00	1.04	1.01
Sex Raio (15 - 64 years, males/females)	1.00	1.01	1.01	1.01
Sex Raio (65 and over, males/females)	0.67	0.69	1.10	0.72
Sex Raio (total population, males/females)	0.99	0.99	1.03	1.00
NET Migration Rate (per 1,000 population)	2.29	4.98	0.67	0.21

Source: The 2008 World Factbook, CIA.

sociocultural position recognizes both the social and cultural dimensions of the human system as shaping demographic processes. The nature of values within a society and how these values influence where people live is of particular interest, as is how reproductive patterns are influenced by these residential choices. The third macro approach, modernization, recognizes divisions of labor within social institutions and how traditions are modernized and transformed. Thus, it is through the process of modernization that adaptations to living conditions are incorporated in societies and communities. The final macro approach, which is institutional in nature, stresses the connection between population changes and the institutional forms and mechanisms that are created within this environment. One example would be the substantive changes within the economic system that allow for improvements within health care institutions, resulting in extending life expectancy.

In contrast to these macro positions, Nam (1994) articulated a micro-level position focusing on the decision-making processes within any small group situation that includes individuals and couples. At the micro level, it is the questions regarding population dynamics that must be answered by an individual or a couple that are most relevant. Such questions might involve the number of children desired and the types of family planning to be utilized. The sociological, psychological, economical, and cultural factors that may influence these decision-making processes might also be included.

Nam concluded his examination by noting two medial approaches for understanding population changes and dynamics. His first medial approach, the normative perspective, recognizes that there are changes in societal norms at either the micro or macro level that might emerge in response to these dynamics. Changes in the norms then have an impact on the social world at the micro or macro level. Nam's second medial approach involves socialization processes, which relates to the normative perspective. As norms emerge, individuals and societies must be socialized into the emergent normative framework. Consequently, socialization is a mechanism for disseminating the new normative processes within a society.

Classic and modern theories used to understand population changes demonstrate that there are a variety of ways from which to frame these issues. Just as with the sociological theoretical perspectives and paradigms that dominate the discipline, we're cautioned not to rely on one theoretical explanation to offer a conclusive explanation for population changes and dynamics. Thus, we must conclude that these theories and theoretical frameworks should be utilized as a way of deepening our understanding of the relevant issues.

Theoretical Perspectives – Differing Views Of Population Issues

As we examine each sociological topic, it is important to recall our foundational discussions of the three dominant sociological perspectives or paradigms within the discipline of sociology. Remembering that each perspective is a way of viewing the social world and not the "correct" way of viewing the social world, we now examine how each of these three theoretical perspectives views population dynamics, beginning with structural functionalism.

Structural Functionalism

Structural functionalism asserts that there is a great deal of social stability and harmony within societies, which promotes a state of homeostasis. As the name implies, functions are part of the foundation of structural functionalism. It is hoped that the manifest—intended—functions help promote homeostasis. However, it is recognized that manifest functions can sometimes be dysfunctional if they promote social instability or disharmony. In addition, there are latent, or unintended, functions that can also be either functional or dysfunctional for a society.

China's one-child-per-family policy will be used to analyze structural functionalism. China formalized its one-child policy as a means of controlling the country's population growth. Therefore, this policy had manifest functions of controlling the population, limiting the effects of population dynamics, preventing a population explosion, and protecting the sociocultural and economic resources of the country. From this perspective, it can be argued that the one-child policy was functional for China because it resulted in direct control of population growth. While functional in this capacity, it can also be argued that the one-child policy is, at the least, potentially dysfunctional because it can create an imbalance of male to female birth ratios, with substantially more males born than what is normally seen in societies. Scholars believe that this imbalance may have resulted from sex-selective abortions, female infanticide, or the nonregistration of female births (Rosenberg, 2008). In response, China outlawed the practice of sex-selecting abortions. Another direct response from the Chinese government has been to allow families to have two children if the first child is a girl, modifying its one-child-only policy, while not officially abandoning it (Research Directorate, 2007). A latent function of China's policy, which may prove dysfunctional, is its effect on divorced individuals. Technically, divorced and remarried individuals are not allowed to have a child if their spouse has a child. This policy has been modified in Shanghai, and divorced individuals will no longer be required to wait for years before having a child (Watts, 2004). These examples illustrate the nature of manifest and latent functions and dysfunctions of the one-child-per-family policy in China.

Social Conflict

The social conflict theoretical perspective is macrosociological, dealing with the larger dimension of the social world and, in particular, the tensions that exist between groups in a society. Although

A Chinese boy, with his mother, waives to the camera.

Source: Mark Forman

the classic social conflict perspective articulated by Marx involved tensions between the social classes, modern conflict theory seeks to identify relevant social tensions between various groups in society. Within the social conflict paradigm, groups remain in conflict over scarce resources, often money, but also significant values within a society. Groups struggle to obtain, and eventually maintain, power once they control the scarce resource. Struggles for power, therefore, often enter the political and social institutions of a society. As it relates to population dynamics, there is no more salient example of social conflict than in the tensions expressed by the pro-life and pro-choice communities. The groups associated with each of these positions determine their meaning within the social conflict paradigm. Although there are many pro-life and pro-choice groups, two will be highlighted—the National Right to Life organization, which represents the pro-life perspective, and Planned Parenthood, which represents the pro-choice perspective.

In its mission statement, the National Right to Life organization (www.nrlc.org) defines its ultimate goal as "to restore legal protection to innocent human life." Although concerned with this central issue, it includes within its mission statement the "related matters of medical ethics which relate to the right to life issues of euthanasia and infanticide." The social organization, founded in 1973 as a nonsectarian and nonpartisan organization, believes that it has been influential within the legislative reforms, particularly at the national level. At that level, it has contributed to getting non-therapeutic experimentation on unborn and newborn babies banned, as well as establishing a federal conscience clause that allows medical personnel the right to refuse to participate in abortion procedures. The organization also reported being successful at advancing various amendments to appropriation bills limiting the use of federal funds for abortions and related research, both in the United States and overseas. In the 35 years since the *Roe v. Wade* decision, which it labels "35 years of death and destruction," its members believe decreases in the number of abortions are, in part, a direct result of their educational efforts. These efforts include noting the biological

developments in unborn fetuses, which they identify as children, and their "legislative measures designed to help women at time when they are most in need." The National Right to Life organization has also helped to pass laws in eleven states that require a woman seeking an abortion to view an ultrasound of her unborn fetus.

In contrast to this position, Planned Parenthood (www.plannedparenthood.org) "is committed to protecting and defending women's access to the full range of reproductive health care – including access to abortion. Decisions about childbearing are to be made by women, their families, and their doctors—not politicians." Planned Parenthood says choice is central to maintaining reproductive rights and maintains that it will work within the states, at the federal level, and around the world to "protect every woman's right to make her own decisions about childbearing." Regarding "anti-choice" activities, Planned Parenthood states that those who are "extremists" push for restrictions on basic health care and "harass women seeking preventative family planning services." Such individuals and organizations are also accused of supporting abstinence-only programs that deny medically accurate information about preventing unintended pregnancies or sexually transmitted infections. Planned Parenthood also maintains that pro-life groups distort information regarding birth control safety, condom effectiveness, and the side effects of abortion. The organization is also concerned that such individuals and organizations set up "so-called 'crisis pregnancy centers' to intimidate and confuse women seeking abortions." Planned Parenthood goes on to mention that it fights "anti-choice extremism", by advocating common-sense policies at all levels. Finally, it highlights that the legislative lobbyists at Planned Parenthood attempt to protect everyone from what it calls intrusive laws through use of the court system.

While *Roe v. Wade* established the constitutionality of abortion within the United States, it is clear from the foregoing presentations of both the National Right to Life organization and Planned Parenthood that conflict and tensions still exist over the use of abortion and other population control procedures. The scarce resource involved in this ongoing struggle is often identified as "When does life begin?" However, the positions of both organizations, as well as their organizational interventions within the sociopolitical arena, reveal that the scarce resource is really about who will have the power to choose what happens once fertilization occurs—government or the individual. Thus, even though the Supreme Court ruled in *Roe v. Wade* and 20 or more additional court rulings that abortion is legal, each of these organizations remains in a public policy, legislative, and court "battle" regarding their attempts to either change, as with the actions of the National Right to Life organization, or maintain, as with Planned Parenthood, who can ultimately decide the parameters for when abortion is utilized.

Symbolic Interactionism

The symbols that are used when discussing various sociological and societal concepts are a foundation of the symbolic interactionism perspective. Just as important is how interactions at a micro social perspective create, maintain, and also change the social world.

We only need to return to the first part of this chapter to begin to understand the various symbols associated with population dynamics. Recall that we operationally defined a number of key concepts and terms related to the study of the population, beginning with the use of the term demography or demographics as the area of study regarding population. The use of each definitional term is merely a symbolic representation of a meaning that can be used by demographers (and you as a student of sociology) to understand the issues and dynamics of population studies. Yet, the nature of symbols goes beyond their operational definitions and can often reflect sociocultural and political tensions with a society.

Though abortion is legal in the United States, considerable symbolic tensions remain regarding its utilization. The symbolic camps in the United States are commonly referred to as either pro-life or pro-choice. It is clear that each of these terms communicates a great deal symbolically, using meanings that are significant for individuals and social movements. Not only are these words symbolic socially, they are value-laden within the political arena, particularly in the United States. The symbolic value of these words is clearly seen when political candidates are asked to state their positions as either pro-life or pro-choice.

Returning to the earlier discussion of China's one-child-per-family policy, we can see a clear illustration of the creation, maintenance, and change of a social policy dealing with the attempt to control a population. While the policy in China was developed at a macro sociological level, it was the dynamics at the micro sociological level that appear to have motivated changes in their official childbearing policy. For example, the creation of the policy was the apparent result of individuals in China choosing to give birth to children at a rate that was exponentially increasing China's population. Because of these individual choices, China had to address the situation, resulting in its one-child policy. After establishing its policy, China also needed to maintain it and did so through the imposition of fines for violators. Social circumstances like divorces, remarriages, and the deaths of children resulting from the 2008 earthquake led China to change its policy in response to the child-rearing challenges faced by individuals and families who lost children through death or divorce.

Summary

This chapter presents two distinct, yet related, sociological concepts—the health care system and population dynamics. Students of sociology must remember that the foundation of any society is its inhabitants and the population issues that exist, or emerge, within that social context. There is an inherent drive for every society to perpetuate itself, not only for intrinsic psychological reasons, but as a means of perpetuating a cultural way of life. The perpetuation of life is affected by birth and death rates, immigration and emigration patterns, and social policies. The existence of overpopulation or underpopulation can place stresses on not only the economy, but the social institutions of a society. These population tensions are often addressed by a variety of social institutions.

One institution tasked with addressing population issues is the health care system. The central task, or function, of the health care institution is to maintain a healthy population for the well-being of society. A healthy population allows for the development of a strong economic sector within a society, and a strong economy promotes the maintenance of the social contract for inter-generational support and care. This well-being and care is one of the motivating factors for some form of comprehensive or universal health care as seen in socialized, and often democratic, societies. In the United States, the health care system can become a significant factor within the economic sector because of the increasing costs associated with providing technologically advanced health care to all of its citizens.

We can see a complexity regarding the health care institution and population dynamics and the various theories that attempt to explain these issues. Just as with the rest of the discipline of sociology, these issues have multiple orientations and dimensions. Within the health care institution, this is seen in the diversity of systems utilized to meet the needs of various societies. A further demarcation of sociological diversity is presented through the exposition of the three classic theoretical perspectives of the discipline and how each views either population dynamics or the health care institution.

Students should leave this chapter with a solid foundational knowledge of the sociological dynamics in societies regarding population issues and health care institutions. Within this disciplinary foundation, they should be able to articulate the diverse ways in which both of these social dimensions of life can be viewed within the discipline of sociology. Grasping this complexity will ground you well as an emergent sociologist.

Review/Discussion Questions

1. What is the sick role?
2. How does the U.S. model of health care differ from the socialized-medicine model?
3. Which health care model do you prefer and Why?
4. What is demography?
5. What factors contribute to underpopulation?
6. A hundred years from now, do you think the life expectancy in the United States will be higher or lower than it is today?

Key Terms

Alternative health care professionals are individuals providing care outside the mainstream or western modalities of health care.

Carbon footprint is the impact a person's activities have on the environment in general, and climate change in particular.

Clinical nurse extenders are individuals who are trained and licensed to provide a limited level of nursing care

Crude birth rate is the number of live births in a year per 1,000 people during a given time period in a defined geographical area.

Crude death rate is the total number of deaths per 1,000 people during a given time period in a defined geographical area.

Decentralized national health care is a system in which the government functions primarily as a regulator.

Demographers are sociologists who investigate population characteristics.

Demography is the study of the characteristics of human populations including the increases and decreases caused by migration, fertility, and mortality.

Direct pay model is a system wherein individuals are legally responsible for paying all of their own health care costs.

Existentialist perspective asserts that individuals are responsible for their own health care issues.

General fertility rates measure the number of live births divided by the female population aged 15 to 44 years (childbearing years), times 1,000.

Human migration is the more or less permanent movement of individuals or groups across symbolic or political boundaries into new residential areas and communities.

Infant mortality rate is the number of deaths within the first year of life, divided by the number of live births in the same year, times 1000.

Life expectancy is the number of years that a person can expect to live within a given society, or as the number of further years of life a person can expect at a given age.

Marriage rate is the number of marriages per 1,000 people in a given time period.

Medical perspective focuses on the medical framework that attempts to examine pathogens that result in disease and illness.

Overpopulation is the population by a particular species in excess of the environment's carrying capacity.

Physician extenders are secondary health care providers who can provide basic physical diagnosis and care.

Primary care providers are physicians who can practice medicine in "all of its branches."

Sex ratios are the number of males per 1000 females in the population of the society.

Sick roles are those that involve a variety of social norms specifying the responsibilities, expectations, and rights of someone who is ill.

Socialized medicine is composed of health care systems over which the government exercises some, but not total, control.

Socialist medicine involves a system of health care that is under the complete control of the government.

Sociocultural perspective views health issues as not merely the responsibility of each individual, but also of their family members and sometimes even their community.

Sociological perspective focuses on societal frame-works at a macro- and micro-sociological level, utilizing sociological research and concepts to identify health care issues.

Standard mortality ratio is a measure indicating the actual or observed number of deaths in the group of interest, divided by the expected number of deaths, then multiplied by 100.

Underpopulation is the lack of normal or desirable population density for economic viability.

Bibliography

Abortion TV (2006, September 7). European Countries Have Underpopulation Problem Because of Abortion. <http://www.abortiontv.com/Lies%20&%20Myths/underpopulation.htm> (2008).

Abercrombie, N., Hill, S., & Turner, B. S. (1994). The Penguin Dictionary of Sociology (3rd ed.). New York: Penguin Books.

Avert (2008). HIV and AIDS in Uganda. <www.avert.org/aidsuganda.htm> (2008).

Blankenship, K. (1998, Summer). A race, class, and gender analysis of thriving. Journal of Social Issues, 54 (2), 393-403.

Butler, C. D. (2004). Human Carrying Capacity and Human Health. Public Library of Science, 1 (3), e55. (doi:10.1371/Journal. pmed.0010055)

Carbon Footprint, Ltd. (2008). What is a Carbon Footprint? <www.carbonfootprint.com/carbonfootprint.html> (2008).

Central Intelligence Agency (2008). The 2008 World Factbook. <https://www.cia.gov/library/publications/the-world-factbook/index.html> (2008).

China.org.cn (2009). Beijing may get Yangtze water in 2014. <http://www.china.org.cn/china/news/2009-01/14/content_17104224.htm> (2009, February 23).

Cockerham, W. (1995). Medical Sociology (6th ed.). Englewood Cliffs, NJ: Prentice Hall.

ConsumerAffairs.com (2007, August 6). Study Finds 24% of Americans Underinsured. <http://www.consumeraffairs.com/news04/2007/08/cu_insurance.html> (2008).

Cook, J. (1999, December 5). Population Control and Consequences in China. <http://maps.unomaha.edu/peterson/funda/sidebar/chinapop.html> (2008).

Currie, D. (2007, September 28). Population Wars, Why Europe's demography is more complicated than you think. The Weekly Standard.

Democratic Policy Committee (2005). <http://democrats.senate.gov/dpc/dpc-printable.cfm?doc_name=fs-109-1-85-9k> (2008).

Eberstadt, N. (2001, May 18). Underpopulation, Not Overpopulation, the Real Global Problem. Washington Post.

Gilland, B. (2008). What is Overpopulation? <http://www.globalpolitician.com/print.asp?id=4818> (2008).

Grinnell College (2008). <www.grinnell.edu> (2008).

Henderson, L. J. (1935). Physician and patient as a social system. New England Journal of Medicine, 212, 819-823.

Illinois Compiled Statutes (2008). <http://www.ilga.gov/legislation/ilcs/ilcs.asp> (2008).

Kaneda, T. (2006). China's Concern Over Population Aging and Health. <http://www.prb.org/articles/2006/chinasconcernover-populationagingandhealth.aspx?.=1> (2008).

LeBlanc, B. (2000). Health Responsibility Model: Promoting Responsible Health from the Human Factor Perspective. Review of Human Factor Studies, 5, (1-2), 43-58.

LeBlanc, B. (2006). Health. Everyday Sociology (5th ed.). Elmhurst, IL: Starpoint Press.

Los Angeles Times (2008, March 16). Russia's outdated healthcare mired in corruption. <http://articles.latimes.com/2008/mar/16/world/fg-russia16plr> (2008).

Malebo, W. (2002). Country Statement on Population Matters, Policies, and Interventions, Reproductive Rights and Health, with Special Reference to HIV/AIDS. Conference on Population and Development Programme of Action, Yaounde, Cameroon.

Maloof, R. (2008). Men: The Stronger Sex? <http://health.msn.com/print.aspx?cp-documentid=100204784&page=0> (2008).

Massachusetts Trial Court Libraries (2008, October 15). Mass Law About Health Insurance. <http://www.lawlib.state.ma.us/healthinsurance.html> (2008).

Miller, B. (1997, October). Educating the "other" children-education of illegal immigrants may be necessary. American Demographics, pp. 49–54.

Nam, C. (1994). Understanding Population Change. Itasca, IL: FE Peacock Publishers.

National Right to Life (2008). <http://www.nrlc.org> (2008).

Overpopulation. (n.d.). The American Heritage® Science Dictionary. <http://dictionary.reference.com/browse/overpopulation> (2009, February 18).

Parsons, T. (1951). The Social System. New York: Free Press.

Planned Parenthood Federation of America (2008). <www.plannedparenthood.org> (2008).

Population Connection (2007). Teaching Population: Hands-on Activities [CD-ROM]. <http://www.populationeducation.org/index.php?option=com_content&task=view&id=174&Itemid=10> (2008).

Research Directorate, Immigration and Refugee Board of Canada, Ottawa (2007, June 26). Responses to Information Requests: China: Treatment of "illegal," or "black," children born outside the one-child family planning policy; whether unregistered children are denied access to education, health care and other social services (2003-2007). <http://www.irb-cisr.gc.ca/en/research/rir/?action=record.viewrec&gotorec=451354> (2008).

Reynolds, J., & Ross, C. (1998, May). Social stratification and health: education's benefit beyond economic status and social origins. Social Problems, 45 (2), 221-247.

Rosenberg, M. (2008, June 18). China's One Child Policy. About.com: Geography. <http://geography.about.com/od/population-geography/a/onechild.htm?p=1> (2008).

Scott, J., & Marshall, G. (Ed.). (2005). Oxford Dictionary of Sociology. New York, NY: Oxford University Press.

Smith, D.E. (2008, March 1). The World's Underpopulation. <http://illinoisreview.typepad.com/illinoisreview/2008/03/under-population.html> (2008).

Starr, P. (1982). The Social Transformation of American Medicine. New York: Basic Books.

Theil, R. (2003, August 9). Compromises and Betrayals: How the So-Called California Naturopathic Physicians are Digging a Hole to Bury the Natural Health Movement. <http://naturalsolutionsradio.com/articles/article.html?id=6639&filter=topic> (2009).

Thio, A. (2004). Sociology: A brief Introduction. Boston, MA: Allyn & Bacon.

Thompson, B. (2000). Ecotracs, Salt Lake City, Utah. <www.ssc.wisc.edu/~jraymo/links/soc674/674_3.pdf> (2009).

Underpopulation. (n.d.). The American Heritage® Science Dictionary. <http://dictionary.reference.com/browse/underpopulation> (2009, February 18).

United Nations Development Programme (2008). Human Development Reports. <http://hdr.undp.org/external/flash/shares> (2008).

Watts, J. (2004, April 14). Shanghai eases China's one-child rule. The Guardian.

Xinhua News Agency (2006, December 12). Overpopulated Beijing Facing Water Crisis. <http://www.china.org.cn/english/environment/192116.htm> (2008).

CHAPTER FOURTEEN

Urban And Environmental Sociology

Mark Shelley and Chris Biga

Imagine yourself, say, ten thousand years ago, as part of a group of about 30 people living in a primitive jungle, a savanna, or a plain. The other members of the group are mostly close relatives—spouses who are brothers or sisters, their children, and perhaps an aunt and uncle or two. You survive by gathering locally available edible plants and hunting animals. This group, or *band*, is the optimal size and composition, with enough female adults to take care of children, and enough grown men to carry out the hunts.

But as your group grows through births, you begin to over-gather the natural fruits, berries, roots, and plants you rely on for food. Game begins to get scarce because of over-hunting near your camp—within a one or two day's walk. You have moved camp several times, but the situation isn't improving. The threat of want and possible starvation looms large over your band. You are one of the clan leaders. What do you do?

One option would be to split the band in half: One of the divisions could migrate in one direction and the other could move in the opposite direction. Provided that you didn't encounter other bands competing for the same territory, there would be a good chance things might return to normal—that is, if enough food were available.

In this situation, growing larger doesn't make sense. In fact, it poses some formidable problems for survival. Because of this, early groups of nomadic humans rarely exceeded 100 persons.

Fast forward a few thousand years. Humans have figured out how to grow crops, as opposed to gathering those growing in the wild. They have begun to domesticate animals, so the hunt is no longer necessary. You are now a part of the *agricultural revolution*. No longer does your group need to be limited in size; in fact, it is an advantage to have a sizeable pool of people around to help plant and harvest. Now you can trade the crops you grow for other kinds of crops, and for simple farm implements, pots, and other "luxuries." An early form of specialization and division of labor has occurred. Cities come into being. You are now an urban dweller—albeit on a relatively small scale by today's standards.

During this long era of agrarian societies, cities were relatively small compared to those in existence today. Compare medieval Europe's largest city—Venice, Italy, with a population of just over 77,000 in 1363—to today's largest city—Bombay (Mumbai), India, with over 13,000,000 inhabitants.

Agricultural and trade cities dominate for many thousands of years. Then technology advances again. Steam is harnessed and engines are invented. No longer are you dependent upon your own two feet, the wind, or an animal to travel; now you can travel much longer distances in less time by railroad or steamship. Soon, oil is refined and automobiles—even airplanes—are powered by gasoline, conquering even more ground in even less time. At the center of all this is the factory, producing metal products, electrical appliances, and, eventually, plastics and composite materials. Welcome to the *industrial revolution*. Because these factories require even more labor than agricultural production, and because there is a need to coordinate finances and communications, it now makes sense for people to live in close proximity to each other in large numbers. Enter the modern (industrial) city!

As the shift from an agricultural to an industrial economy occurred, along with the rapid pace of change, rearrangement of people, and transformation of governments, a group of astute thinkers was trying to make sense of the accompanying changes in social structure and interpersonal relationships, along with the rearrangement of people and transformation of governments' rapid pace of change. This was the beginning of what we now know as *sociology*, and the movement of people to cities was a major catalyst for the discipline. Since the *classical sociologists*—including Karl Marx (1818-1883) in England, Max Weber (1864-1820) in Germany, and Emile Durkheim (1858-1917) in France—penned their seminal writings at the turn of the 20th century, sociologists have been intrigued with this ever-changing form of human organization—the city.

The Importance Of Urban Sociology

The purpose of this section is to introduce you to some of the interests and perspectives of *urban sociologists*, who focus on the study of cities and their surroundings. Why is this an important sub-field of sociology? Consider that, according to the 2000 census, 80 percent of the U.S. population lived in

Table X.1 Largest U.S. Cities (with population) in Historical Perspective

Rank	1790	1870	2007
1	New York City, NY (33,131)	New York City, NY (942,292)	New York City, NY (8,274,527)
2	Philadelphia, PA (26,522)	Philadelphia, PA (565,529)	Los Angeles, CA (3,834,340)
3	Boston, MA (18,320)	Brooklyn, NY (419,921)	Chicago, IL (2,836,658)
4	Charleston, SC (16,359)	St. Louis, MO (351,189)	Houston, TX (2,208,180)
5	Baltimore, MD (13,503)	Chicago, IL (298,977)	Philadelphia, PA (1,449,634)
6	Salem, MA (7,921)	Baltimore, MD (267,354)	Phoenix, AZ (1,552,259)
7	Newport, RI (6,716)	Boston, MA (250,526)	San Antonio, TX (1,328,984)

Source: U.S. Bureau of the Census

urban areas. Globally, more than half of the population lives in or around large cities. By contrast, in 1790, when the first U.S. census was taken, only 10 percent of Americans lived in cities. In just over 200 years, the tables have dramatically turned. Table X.1 illustrates population shifts in the United States; it also demonstrates the movement of people away from the *Rust Belt* (the Northeast and Upper Midwest regions also known as the *Manufacturing Belt*) and the *Snow Belt* (downwind of the Great Lakes) to the *Sunbelt* (particularly the Southwest).

Urban Concepts

As you may have already discovered, sociologists often have specific and technical meanings for words that are broadly used and loosely defined in casual conversation.

Population Density

One characteristic that makes an area "urban" is *population density*—how closely people are living together. In the United States, population density is calculated by the number of people living within a square mile of land. In countries using the metric system, it represents the number of people per square kilometer.

Louis Wirth (1897-1952), of the famous "Chicago School" of urban sociology (University of Chicago, beginning in the 1920s), theorized that the *size, density,* and *diversity* of urban populations (*heterogeneity*) led to a unique form of life and culture he called **urbanism**. Although subsequent research has not always supported all of the implications of his theory, there is little doubt that population density has an impact on how humans interact with each other.

So, what is considered *densely populated*? The U.S. Census Bureau considers **urbanized areas** to be spaces where more than 50,000 persons reside, with an average of 1,000 people per square mile. This may seem like a lot of people in a small space, but consider Table X.2, where we compare three U.S. cities with their global counterparts. Notice how densely populated Tokyo, Hyderabad, and Manila are compared with U.S. cities of approximately the same size!

The Central City

A city, in contrast, is not defined so much by its population as it is by its political form. A **city** is an incorporated space with boundaries that have been determined primarily by elected officials. These boundaries, or city limits, determine who lives in a particular city. As viewed by the Census Bureau, there is no size qualification for a city—it can be of any size.

A **central city** is defined as a city, or adjacent cities, with a population of 50,000, or an urbanized area with a population of more than 100,000. Until around World War II, cities were the primary focus of study among urban sociologists. At that time, however, a number of factors led many residents to flee central cities for the suburbs. These factors included home loan benefits for veterans returning from the war, federally insured and subsidized housing loans, the mushrooming of federally funded highways and automobile travel, and equal housing laws that allowed minorities to rent and purchase housing in formerly all-white neighborhoods. These

Table X. 2 Comparative Population Densities of U.S. and World Cities, 2000

U.S. City	Population	Density	World City	Population	Density
(**No U.S. cities having similar** populations or densities.)			Calcutta, India	5,021,458	70,725
			Mumbai (Bombay), India	13,662,685	58,639
New York City	8,250,567	27,051	Tokyo, Japan	8,535,792	33,342
Los Angeles	3,849,378	7,730	Hyderabad, India	3,980,938	60,317
Phoenix	1,552,259	3,002	Manila, Philippines	1,660,714	26,774

Sources: U.S. Census Bureau; United Nations.

changes created new dynamics both within the cities and between the cities and their surrounding areas.

Metropolitan Areas

A century ago, it was only necessary to refer to the name of a particular city in order to pinpoint its location on a map. Today, however, terms like "Los Angeles" and "Dallas" may refer not just to the city, but to the entire urbanized area around the city. The Census Bureau calls these places Metropolitan Statistical Areas (MSAs). These areas include at least one central city, along with those counties that are economically and socially integrated with the city. Integration with the central city is determined by people's commuting patterns. There are several subcategories of metropolitan areas, including:

1) *Micropolitan* areas: urbanized areas of 10,000 to 50,000 persons.
2) *Metropolitan* areas: central cities with 50,000 or more persons, including one or more counties.
3) *Combined Statistical Areas* (CSAs): large urbanized areas with multiple central cities, covering multiple counties, sometimes in multiple

states. Examples include the Los Angeles-Long Beach-Riverside, CA CSA, the New York-Newark-Bridgeport, NY-NJ-CT-PA CSA (including counties in four states); and the Chicago-Naperville-Michigan City, IL-IN-WI CSA, also known as Chicagoland. As of November 2007, there were 126 CSAs in the United States.

Table X.3 is a list of Metropolitan Statistical Areas with populations greater than three million based on estimates for 2007

There are two areas in the United States that have developed into contiguous (adjacent) urban areas, creating huge **metroplexes** where entire regions are virtually urbanized. On the East Coast, the metroplex often referred to as the Northeast Megalopolis or, BoWash (Boston – Washington) Corridor, stretches from south of Washington, D.C., to north of Boston. On the West Coast, the metroplex referred to as SoCal (Southern California) includes the strip of land starting at the U.S.-Mexico border just south of San Diego and extending 100 miles north of Los Angeles to Santa Barbara. Each of these regions is connected socially and economi-

Table X.3 Metropolitan Statistical Areas, 2007

CMSA	Population
New York-Newark-Bridgeport, NY-NJ-CT-PA CSA	21,961,994
Los Angeles-Long Beach-Riverside, CA CSA	17,755,322
Chicago-Naperville-Michigan City, IL-IN-WI CSA	9,745,165
Washington-Baltimore-Northern Virginia, DC-MD-VA-WV CSA	8,241,912
Boston-Worcester-Manchester, MA-RI-NH CSA	7,476,689
San Jose-San Francisco-Oakland, CA CSA	7,264,887
Dallas-Fort Worth, TX CSA	6,498,410
Philadelphia-Camden-Vineland, PA-NJ-DE-MD CSA	6,385,461
Houston-Baytown-Huntsville, TX CSA	5,729,027
Atlanta-Sandy Springs-Gainesville, GA-AL CSA	5,626,400
Miami-Ft. Lauderdale-Miami Beach, FL MSA	5,463,857
Detroit–Warren–Flint, MI MSA	5,410,014
Phoenix-Mesa-Scottsdale, AZ MSA	4,039,182
Seattle-Tacoma-Olympia, WA CMSA	4,038,741
Minneapolis-St. Paul-St. Cloud, MN-WI CMSA	3,538,781

Source: U.S. Census Bureau

cally in such a way as to form a single socio-geographic unit, or metroplex. In other places, the early development of similarly connected urban regions is evident, like the area from south of Tucson, through Phoenix, to Prescott, Arizona, which is becoming an almost 300-mile stretch of connected cities.

Urban sociologists generally agree that studying a specific city without connecting it to its metropolitan area will most likely yield unreliable and misleading conclusions, especially for larger cities. For example, one might assume that the largest metropolitan areas would include the largest cities, but this may not be true. Comparisons of the data in Table X.1 and Table X.3, demonstrate that there is not a one-to-one correspondence between city rank and metropolitan area rank. In fact, Mark Gottdiener and Leslie Budd (2005) argue that the most productive conception of modern cities is the *multi-centered metropolitan region*. In this model, the central city is seen as only one of the elements that influence life in urban environments.

Suburbs

Where a metropolitan area has at least one central city, it generally has many *suburbs*, which comprise another part of the metropolitan context. The Census Bureau defines *urban* to include all places in urbanized areas, or places of 2,500 people or more whether they are in metropolitan or non-metropolitan areas, and *rural* to include territory not designated as urban. The Census Bureau does not define the term *suburb* and rarely uses it. **Urbanologists**—sociologists and other researchers who study cities—normally define suburbs as those areas which lay between the large central cities and the rural hinterlands. Because 50 percent of Americans lived in suburbs in 2000, compared with 30.3 percent living in central cities and 19.7 percent in non-metropolitan areas, an extended discussion of *suburbia* is warranted.

Suburbs are primarily a result of advancing technology. Although some wealthier residents lived outside U.S. cities before powered transportation, for the most part, people could live only as far away from their place of work as they could walk, or as far as they could ride on a horse or in a carriage.

With the advent of steam power, trains allowed people to live farther from the center of the city. With electricity, trolleys made "streetcar suburbs" possible. These inventions, as well as the automobile, allowed more affluent families to move away from crowded and polluted central cities. Many of these early suburbs were eventually annexed into the central city itself, but the turn of the 20th century saw the beginning of a growing exodus.

The Chicago area provides a fairly straightforward illustration of suburban development that is now linked to a city. Evanston, Illinois, is home to Northwestern University and was named after the university's founder, John Evans. It lies 13 miles north of downtown Chicago. When the university was established in 1863, Evanston was already its own community, a half day's journey from Chicago. Over the years, the two cities have grown together, and there is now no visible separation between the two. In fact, Evanston is inextricably linked to downtown Chicago and much of Chicagoland, by virtue of it being the northern terminus of the "L"—the elevated train/subway system that connects Chicago and its immediate suburbs.

In 1900, only 16 percent of the total U.S. population lived in what we have defined as suburbs (outside of central cities but not in rural areas), compared with the 26 percent who lived in central cities and the 58 percent who lived in rural areas. By 1950, just less than 25 percent of the population lived in suburbs, with 60 percent of the population living in metropolitan areas. The doubling of the suburbs during this fifty-year period can be attributed to three major factors. First, framing techniques that allowed fast, relatively cheap *cookie-cutter housing* (also known as *tract housing*) to be built quickly after World War II. Second, the federal government offered guarantees for Veterans Administration (VA) and Federal Housing Authority (FHA) loans. Third, tax laws were passed allowing interest on housing loans to be deducted from income taxes. This resulted in indirect subsidies for homeowners, allowing millions to move into tract homes located on the edges of large cities.

Prospective homeowners were able to commute faster and farther due to the burgeoning Interstate

Highway System, which included bypasses and loops around major cities. These highways were heavily funded by the federal government as well.

Interstate Highways And The Growth Of Suburbia

The story of the Interstate Highway System, in itself, is an interesting one. Officially named the *Dwight D. Eisenhower National System of Interstate and Defense Highways*, it was first conceived by Eisenhower as a young officer during the Army's first coast-to-coast automobile maneuvers in 1919, which took 62 days. Following his experience as the commanding general of the Allied Forces in Europe during World War II, he realized that a large expanse of the continental United States would be difficult to defend if the country were to be attacked. He saw a strong network of high-speed automobile routes as both a military and economic necessity. Started in 1956, the system now contains more than 42,000 miles of limited-access roadways. The Interstate System includes major north-to-south arteries (Interstates 5 to 95, numbered by tens: 5, 15, 25, etc.) and east-to-west laterals (Interstates 10 though 90, numbered by tens), along with many connector routes.

Looking at a map of this highway system, one sees that, in actuality, it is an inter-city rather than an inter-state system, connecting major metropolitan areas across the country. In fact, it could be argued that suburbs have been the greatest beneficiaries of this system, allowing metropolitan housing to be spread far from the central city core. This movement has not been altogether positive for the central cities. An increasing number of people move to, live in, and pay local taxes to suburban communities while working in the central city and utilizing, but not necessarily paying for, the services of the central city during the workday. Urban sociologists often talk about **deconcentration** and **concentration effects**. In this scenario, the middle class and affluent move out of the city (deconcentration), leaving the poor and minorities in the older central cities where 100-year-old urban infrastructure like roads and bridges, sewers and utilities, are constantly in need of repair. As a result, impoverished areas are increasing (concentration of poverty), while their populations and tax bases are dwindling.

Effects Of Suburbanization

Sociologist William Julius Wilson documented these dynamics in his book *The Truly Disadvantaged: The Inner City, the Underclass, and Public Policy* (1987). Using Chicago as a case study, he identified areas where 40 percent of the population was below the poverty level. He noted that these areas offered virtually no economically viable employment, a situation which he called *spatial mismatch*. One reason for this might have been that it was often cheaper to build new factories in the suburbs than it was to repair old ones in the inner city. Wilson also analyzed the effects of unemployment and **economic restructuring**—the movement of the economy away from one based on manufacturing (which pays good wages for skilled laborers) to one based on services (which includes everything from banking and information technology to restaurants and tourism). Some of these same trends were explored by Barry Bluestone and Bennett Harrison in *The De-Industrialization of America* (1984) and *The Great U-Turn* (1990). All of these processes—highway building, deconcentration, and deindustrialization—have had negative impacts on central cities, especially those that are older.

Edge Cities

One of the most innovative and provocative approaches to the growth of modern suburbs was proposed by Joel Garreau in his book, Edge City: *Life on the New Frontier* (1991). Garreau defines an *edge city* as a location:

1) That didn't look anything like a city 30 years ago;
2) Perceived to be one place by the population;
3) With more jobs than bedrooms (differentiating it from a *bedroom community*, or suburb);
4) Providing office space for between 20,000 and 50,000 workers; and
5) Having at least one medium-to-large shopping mall.

Edge cities often compete with, as well as complement, traditional central cities. Garreau's edge cities included places like Oak Brook outside Chicago, Overland Park near Kansas City, the Galleria area near Dallas, and Scottsdale near the Phoenix area. He identified 33 central cities with two or more edge cities associated with them.

Many researchers have followed up on the edge city idea as a particular manifestation of suburban life. As we've already mentioned, most sociologists now find that viewing the metropolitan region *as a whole* is more revealing than studying any isolated feature of the urban landscape, such as the central city, the suburb, or the edge city.

Circles, Slices, Cities And Sprawl

As noted earlier, the Chicago School of sociologists pioneered American urban sociology. Robert Park (1864-1944) and Ernest Burgess (1886-1966) believed that changes in the urban environment were due to population pressures. This approach became characterized as *human ecology*. Just as weeds take over grass in a yard, some areas are "taken over" by people other than the original inhabitants through the arrival of new immigrants, the assimilation (blending in) of groups to the larger society, and the economic mobility of residents that can "move up"—and often out of their old neighborhoods. Based on their work in Chicago neighborhoods, a *concentric zone model* was developed. This model looked like a target, with the central business district, or downtown, in the middle and the suburbs at the edges, where fairly predictable movements of residents toward the outer zones would occur.

A few years later, Homer Hoyt (1916-1966) proposed a major modification to this model. He said that although the circular zones were roughly evident in the urban landscape, the circles were sliced up, so to speak, by special-use areas, which were driven by economics. For instance, activities along a railway or highway cut through the zones.

Chauncy Harris and Edward Ullman (1945) agreed with Hoyt's version of land use in the city, with one major exception. Instead of just *one* central place—the bull's eye in the previous two mod-

els—they postulated that cities had several centers, or *nuclei*. This idea foreshadowed Garreau's description of edge cities, which we discussed above, as well as the *multi-centered metropolitan region*, which Gottdiener and Budd (2005) claimed "is as qualitatively different from the traditional city as was the city itself from its predecessors 10,000 years before that." This claim seems supported by what we see today in large metropolitan areas with multiple urban cores. This has since been labeled the socio-spatial approach.

Many observers, however, bemoan the *urban sprawl* that characterizes many areas. For example, when you fly into Los Angeles from the east, you are over city lights for almost an hour before landing. This sprawl is a result of several different factors, including the in-migration of residents from other parts of the country and the world, the growth of individual cities that were once far apart but are now expanding toward one another, and the growth of housing developments that are often unplanned and uncontrolled. The process by which places turn into these highly populated areas is termed *urbanization*.

Logan and Molotch, in *Urban Fortunes: The Political Economy of Place* (1987), characterized cities as "growth machines," driven by development and encouraged by the government and private entities that stand to profit from urbanization. Six different "actors" in this "production of property" have been identified (Gottdiener & Budd, 2005). They are:

1) Speculators who buy land with the hope it will increase in value so that they will make a profit off the resale. This takes *capital* (money—over and above what one needs to live) to buy the land and patience to ride out the ups and downs of the market.
2) Developers who buy land from speculators and build offices, malls, and homes.
3) Homeowners who primarily buy homes in which they will live. A home is the largest investment that the vast majority of people ever make.
4) Local politicians who are interested in the tax revenues that the land and buildings will generate to support the city and help it grow.

5) <u>Large corporations</u> including retail, manufacturing, and other business entities that may or may not be connected to the community, whose interests are tied to the profits that they accrue from being in a given place at a certain time.

6) <u>Banks and financial institutions</u> on whom speculators, developers, homeowners, corporations—even local governments—depend for loans to accomplish their various purposes. (The financial meltdown of these institutions in 2008 and the ensuing federal "rescue packages" attest to the importance of these actors.)

With all of these different actors and all of the possible "acts" that could develop in this drama, this *political economy perspective* on urban growth is both complex and fascinating.

Cities—Old, New, And Renewed

Urbanization, the process by which a city develops, is neither a linear nor a predictable process. That is one of things that is so fascinating about

urban sociology. Different cities develop in very different ways and in different times with different results. The time during which a city comes into being—its history—is a key variable in its current shape, size and vitality. Its location is also a key factor. Look carefully at a map of the United States. Where are the cities located? Do you see any patterns?

Many large cities in the United States—especially east of the Missouri and Mississippi rivers—are located along coastlines and major waterways. More specifically, cities are located where there are significant *breaks in transportation*—where one form of transportation is exchanged for another, such as from ships to railroads, barges to trucks. These breaks were ideal places for people to settle, factories to be built, and trade to be conducted. Some cities are located where the breaks are not as obvious. Denver, for example, sits at the feet of the Rocky Mountains, the last major rest stop for travelers heading west, and the transportation origin of many products from the west going east. Some cities, like Phoenix, grew up to support military outposts,

Source: faa.gov

and stayed fairly small until technology made their geographic positions viable. For Phoenix, it was the advent of air conditioning and airplanes that helped put it on the map. The major cities in California—San Diego, Los Angeles, and San Francisco—began as Spanish missions in the 1700s. Again, the intersection of geography and technology are key factors in the development of urban areas.

Earlier in this chapter, it was noted that the infrastructure of many U.S. cities is well over 100 years old. Even when a city is younger, its original streets, buildings, and services are often outstripped by rapid growth. During the decades following World War II and the onset of rapid suburbanization, many cities felt the need to update and revitalize their downtown areas, which were physically deteriorating and rapidly losing both population and business. Downtown revitalization projects sprang up over the next 40 years, some of which demolished and almost totally rebuilt sections of traditional downtowns. Many of these ventures destroyed large public housing projects, often displacing poor residents.

Some of these revitalization efforts completely changed the skylines of cities. St. Louis, Missouri, rebuilt its riverfront to include the Gateway Arch and Jefferson National Expansion Memorial, which is now the city's trademark. Many cities added light rail systems to connect hotels, tourist spots, stadiums, and airports. Portland, Oregon, undertook a remake of its downtown area, originally designed in small blocks for easy walking, without massive demolition. Between 1976 and 1990, the city rebuilt the downtown pedestrian setting, which has become a tourist attraction in itself.

Social Relationships And Culture In The City

Up to this point, the discussion has primarily focused on issues involving social forces in a broad context. Sociologists sometimes refer to this as a *macro-social* perspective. Urbanologists are intrigued by how urban residents experience life in the city—how they form relationships and the type of relationships they form, how they create and re-create their lives in an urban space, and how they navigate their way in, around, and through the larger social forces in the city. This is referred to as a *micro-social* perspective because it exists at the level of the individual and the small group.

It is almost stating the obvious that "urban folk" are different than "rural folk." People in cities partake of a culture and array of social relations that operate differently from those outside urban areas. These differences were noted fairly early in the history of the discipline by German sociologist Ferdinand Tonnies (1855-1936). He noted that people in rural areas were bound by feelings of loyalty in their *primary relationships*, those person-to-person, face-to-face interactions that normally include family, extended family, close friends, and those with whom one has daily contact. He called this form *gemeinschaft,* which is sometimes translated as "community." Urban dwellers, on the other hand, were characterized by more individual goals, and relationships formed more as contracts, rather than being based on sentiment. This form of social relationship he called *gesellschaft*, or "society." Regardless of the terms, he realized that the social relations between urbanites were much different than those of their counterparts in the countryside.

Investigating such relationships has long been an interest of those who study life in the city. Borrowing field methods from anthropology, some of the most fascinating reading in urban sociology are *ethnographies*, or detailed accounts of the lives of urban persons and groups.

Urban anthropologist Elliot Liebow (1924-1995) made friends with a group of black "streetcorner" men in the 1960s, becoming close to them and learning how they managed their lives in Washington, D.C. His very readable account, *Tally's Corner: A Study of Negro Streetcorner Men* (1967), is a classic work of urban sociology.

At the end of his career, Liebow developed cancer. He quit his job as a professor and spent time volunteering in homeless women's shelters in the Washington, D.C. area. When the women found out who he was, they asked him to tell others of their plights. His last book, *Tell Them Who I Am: The Lives of Homeless Women* (1993), chronicles and analyzes the journeys of many of these women, exposing many preconceptions about who the homeless are and what they are, or are not, doing about their situations. In one interview, a woman tells him that she is not "homeless," but rather she is "family-less," opening up an entirely different way of understanding this population.

In this ethnographic tradition, sociologist Elijah Anderson spent years exploring where he lived, a place straddling two communities—a black ghetto (Northton) and a mixed-race neighborhood he called "The Village." *In Streetwise: Race, Class and Change in an Urban Community* (1990), Anderson tells of the uneasy tension between the two communities, and how the residents treated one another, including their stereotypes, prejudices, and misconceptions. Anderson is an African-American and was able to "switch" between the two cultures. Some of the more interesting insights from his work relate to his findings on the youth of Northton, including the impact of drugs, "sex codes" among male and female youths, and black males in public and their interactions with the police. The continuation of Streetwise can be found in *Code of the Street: De-cency, Violence and the Moral Life of the Inner City* (1999), an equally compelling read.

By undertaking these intensely personal, time-consuming studies, urban sociologists provide depth to our understanding of urban culture.

Race, Ethnicity, Immigration, And Urban Growth

Every decade of the 20th century saw a major race riot in a major city in the United States. Racial unrest and ethnic tension have been a constant focus of urban sociologists. Though much progress has been made in U.S. race relations, as evidenced in 2008 by the election of Barack Obama, the first black president, race and ethnic differences—particularly in urban areas—are alive and well.

One way to look at race and ethnicity in the city is through the use of a statistical "dissimilarity index" (Massey & Denton, 1988). The index is a number that indicates what proportion of a given group would need to move in to or out of a given

TABLE X.4 Cities with the Largest Percentage of Minority Populations by Rank, 2000 (Top 8 Ranked Cities for each race is bold-faced; **Cities in Top 8 in all 3 Races)

CITY	BLACK (Rank)		HISPANIC (Rank)		ASIAN (Rank)	
New York City, NY**	**2,129,762**	**(1)**	**2,160,554**	**(1)**	**787,047**	**(1)**
Chicago, IL**	**1,065,009**	**(2)**	**753,644**	**(3)**	**125,974**	**(7)**
Detroit, MI	**775,772**	**(3)**	47,167	(71)	9,268	(91)
Philadelphia, PA	**655,824**	**(4)**	128,928	(24)	67,654	(11)
Houston, TX**	**494,496**	**(5)**	**730,865**	**(4)**	103,694	(8)
Baltimore, MD	**418,951**	**(6)**	11,061	(168)	9,985	(84)
Los Angeles, CA**	**415,195**	**(7)**	**1,719,073**	**(2)**	**369,254**	**(2)**
Memphis, TN	**399,208**	**(8)**	19,317	(137)	9,482	(87)
San Antonio, TX	78,120	(48)	**671,394**	**(5)**	17,934	(48)
Phoenix, AZ	67,416	(60)	**449,972**	**(6)**	26,449	(34)
El Paso, TX	17,586	(131)	**431,875**	**(7)**	6,321	(124)
San Jose, CA	31,349	(102)	269,989	(10)	**240,375**	**(3)**
San Francisco, CA	60,515	(68)	109,504	(28)	**239,565**	**(4)**
Honolulu, HI	6,038	(178)	16,229	(151)	**207,588**	**(5)**
San Diego, CA	96,216	(36)	310,752	(9)	**166,968**	**(6)**

Source: U.S. Census Bureau

TABLE X.5 Cities with a Large Percentage of Minority Populations by Rank, 2000

City	Black	Hispanic	Asian
Gary, IN (Chicago area)	84.0%		
Detroit, MI	81.6%		
Birmingham, AL	73.5%		
Jackson, MS	70.6%		
New Orleans, LA	67.3%		
Baltimore, MD	64.3%		
Laredo, TX (South Texas)		94.1%	
Brownsville, TX (South Texas)		91.3%	
Hialeah, FL (Miami)		90.3%	
McAllen, TX (South Texas)		80.3%	
El Paso, TX (South Texas)		76.6%	
Santa Ana, CA (Los Angeles area)		76.1%	
El Monte, CA (Los Angeles area)		72.4%	
Honolulu, HI			55.9%
Daly City, CA (San Francisco area)			50.7%
Fremont, CA (Oakland area)			37.0%
Sunnyvale, CA (Oakland area)			32.3%
Garden Grove, CA (Los Angeles area)			30.9%
San Francisco, CA			30.8%

Source: U.S. Census Bureau

area (normally a census tract), in order for residents to be equally represented. Researchers have found that, especially in urban areas, racial and ethnic groups congregate in a rather predictable fashion, evidenced especially by the existence of black neighborhoods (*ghettos*) and Hispanic neighborhoods (*barrios*). Race, to a large degree, parallels social class—the financial and occupational well-being of the residents. Massey and Denton called the condition of cities in the United States *American Apartheid* (1993).

Certain cities have very high proportions of certain groups. Table X.4 and Table X.5 show U.S. cities with the largest numbers and percentages of blacks, Hispanics, and Asians, respectively. Do you see any geographical patterns by race?

The mix of racial and ethnic groups in a city tends to give it a unique identity, culture, and politi-cal landscape. Urban sociologists study the interactions between race and ethnicity and other variables of urban life.

During the latter part of the 19th century and into the early 20th century, there was an explosion in immigration that changed the face of American cities. However, primarily because of *xenophobia*—fear of outsiders/foreigners—immigration in the United States was severely restricted from the 1920s to the mid-1960s. With the passage of the Immigration Act of 1965, quotas based on national origin were eliminated and the doors opened to a much broader spectrum of people. Immigrants are those who voluntarily leave their country to live in another. The Refugee Act of 1980 allowed refugees, many of whom were fleeing the war in Southeast Asia and Communist Bloc countries at that time, to enter the United States and not be counted as part of the immigrant quotas. More than 90 percent of these immigrants and refugees have chosen to live in American cities. This has not only increased the diversity of city populations, but has also resulted in some conflicts between old and new immigrants of the same ethnic groups.

For instance, new Chinese immigrants (called OBCs, or Overseas-Born Chinese) did not always fit in well in the Chinatown neighborhoods where older immigrants (ABCs, or American-Born Chinese) had forged a way of life in relative isolation for almost a century. The "New Asian" immigrants (OBCs and many people from the different nations of Southeast Asia) often formed new communities that competed on some level with those that were older and more established.

In the Southwest, many cities are becoming as much Hispanic (mostly Mexican) as they are "mainstream" American. As of 2000, the Census Bureau reported that 18 cities with a population of 100,000 or more had populations with Hispanic majorities. All but one of those cities was in either California, Texas, or Florida. Immigration and immigration reform remain heated issues in urban politics throughout the United States.

Urbanism: City Culture

As we've noted, the term urbanization refers to the process of areas changing and becoming cities and metropolitan areas. Sociologists use the term urbanism to refer to the culture, or way of life, in a city. While there are many ways that cities and urban areas differ in how they "feel" from suburbs and rural towns, we will focus on three areas—nightlife, cultural institutions, and professional sports.

When living in a small town, we always joked that we "rolled up the sidewalks at sundown," which seemed more true than false. On the other hand, "the city never sleeps." The lights never completely go out in the metropolis. People move, work, and play around the clock in major cities. The presence of a *nightlife* is one of the elements that distinguish cities from their rural cousins.

Many sociologists have noted that in any large city, there is not one city, but rather many cities operating at the same time. The lives of the industrial

city, the financial city, the government city, and the college city intertwine with each other. Likewise, the work-by-day city and the nocturnal city create an ebb and flow of work, sleep, and entertainment that give a city its 24/7 character.

A variety of museums, live theaters, comedy clubs, amusement parks, hybrid shopping/entertainment centers, and concert venues are key facets of urban culture. It is not unusual for people to travel from hours away to take part in special events. One of the signs that an area is becoming urbanized is the development of these kinds of activity centers.

The rise of professional sports is a uniquely urban phenomenon. Although many of the newer teams market themselves as regional or state teams, like the Arizona Diamondbacks, Florida Marlins, and Colorado Rockies Major League Baseball teams, they are, in reality, teams related to cities (Phoenix, Miami and Denver, respectively). In fact, many residents of urban areas closely identify with their teams and become avid fans. The mass marketing of professional sports, including sponsorships by businesses of every type, has created a multi-billion-dollar industry that draws millions of tourists to major sporting events each year. Cities now stake a great deal of their reputations (self-marketing) on the success of their athletic teams.

Not surprisingly, the largest U.S. metropolitan areas almost always boast at least one team from each of the Big Four professional sports organizations—the National Football League (NFL), Major League Baseball (MLB), the National Basketball Association (NBA), and the National Hockey League (NHL). Table X.6 lists U.S. metropolitan areas with at least four professional sports franchises. Los Angeles is the only area that does not have all four sports represented; the NFL is not in Los Angeles, though at one time the city had two NFL teams. The Rams moved to St. Louis and the Raiders moved to Oakland as a result of buyouts. Many people who move still pledge allegiance to their former teams. Yankee jerseys are ubiquitous all over the United States, and it is not unusual to see more Chicago fans than Diamondback supporters at Chase Field in Phoenix when the Cubs come to town. Sports exert a powerful influence—economic, cultural, and in

TABLE X. 6 Urban Sports

Metro Area	Population	Professional Sports Teams	Combined Payroll	Average Payroll Per Team	Combined Attendance	City (population, 2006)
New York City-New Jersey- Long Island, NY:	21,961,954	Giants, Jets (NFL) Yankees, Mets (MLB) Nicks, Nets (NBA) Rangers, Islanders (NHL)	$772,374, 311	$96,546,789	8,041,089	New York City: 8,274,527 Newark, NJ: 266,736 East Rutherford, NJ: 8,716
Los Angeles- Anaheim, CA:	17,755,322	Dodgers, Angels (MLB) Lakers, Clippers (NBA) Kings, Ducks (NHL)	$449,529,970	$74,291,662	9,901,846	Los Angeles: 3,834,340 Anaheim: 377,392
Chicago, IL:	9,743,371	Bears (NFL) Cubs, White Sox (MLB) Bulls (NBA) Blackhawks (NHL)	$433,186,950	$86,637,300	7,721,881	Chicago: 2,836,658
Washington, D.C.:	8,244,965	Redskins (NFL) Nationals (MLB) Wizards (NBA) Capitals (NHL)	$284,532,041	$71,133,010	4,332,642	Washington, D.C.: 581,530
Boston, MA:	7,476,689	Patriots (NFL) Red Sox (MLB) Celtics (NBA) Bruins (NHL)	$354,475,307	$88,618,827	4,967,234	Boston: 599,351
San Francisco- Oakland-San Jose, CA:	7,264,793	49ers, Raiders (NFL) Giants, Athletics (MLB) Golden State Warriors (NBA) San Jose Sharks (NHL)	$425,784,058	$70,964,010	7,065,379	San Francisco 764,976 Oakland 401,489 San Jose 916,220
Dallas-Ft .Worth TX:	6,494,107	Cowboys (NFL) Rangers (MLB) Mavericks (NBA) Stars (NHL)	$289,329,492	$72,332,373	4,020,201	Dallas: 1,192,538
Philadelphia, PA:	6,385,461	Eagles (NFL) Phillies (MLB) 76ers (NBA) Flyers (NHL)	$316,577,946	$79,144,487	5,467,877	Philadelphia: 1,448,394
Atlanta, GA:	5,621,488	Falcons (NFL) Braves (MLB) Hawks (NBA) Thrashers (NHL)	$270,603,090	$67,650,773	4,413,381	Atlanta: 442,887
Miami, FL:	5,413,212	Dolphins (NFL) Marlins (MBL) Heat (NBA) Panthers (NHL)	$232,337,613	$58,084,403	3,340,388	Miami: 358,091
Detroit, MI:	5,405,918	Lions (NFL) Tigers (MLB) Pistons (NBA) Redwings (NHL)	$364,567,728	$91,141,932	5,420,911	Detroit: 916,952
Minneapolis, MN:	3,538,781	Vikings (NFL) Twins (MLB) Timberwolves (NBA) Wild (NHL)	$277,119,909 $69,279,997	$69,279,997	4,162,294	Minneapolis: 377,392 St. Paul: 272,217
Denver, CO:	3,000,603	Broncos (NFL) Rockies (MLB) Nuggets (NBA) Avalanche (NHL)	$297,098,824	$74,274,706	4,697,200	Denver: 566,974

Boats tossed ashore by Hurricane Katrina.

Source: Palmer W. Cook

terms of identity—in American metropolitan areas.

Access to a greater array of nighttime activities, cultural institutions, and sporting events is a key benefit of living in an urban area. One of the major downsides to living in these massive population centers is the negative impact they have had on the natural environment.

The Environment

The majority of Americans view the natural environment as separate and distinctly different from the human experience. This dichotomy can foster a belief that the relationship between human civilization and the physical environment is contentious, with humans objectifying and dominating the nonhuman world. *Anthropocentrism* is an interpretation of reality exclusively in terms of human values and experience, where humans are dominant over the nonhu-

man. Anthropocentrism "depicts nature as atomistic, passive, lifeless, and wholly devoid of purpose" (Brown, 1992). Humans assigned the purpose of serving their needs and wants to the unrefined and raw environment. While this worldview has led to great economic wealth, technological advancements, and material comforts, it has also contributed to toxic waste, air pollution, loss of biodiversity, the extinction of countless species of flora and fauna, and global warming.

Hurricane Katrina came ashore just east of New Orleans, Louisiana, on August 29, 2005, as a Category 3 hurricane. In its wake, nearly 2,000 people lost their lives across the Gulf Coast and 80 percent of New Orleans was submerged, flooded by a breached and battered levee system. Hurricane Katrina was the most costly hurricane in U.S. history, causing over 80 billion dollars in damages. Events such as Hurricane Katrina remind us that humans are not exempt from the ecological laws that govern our planet, though our western, anthropocentric worldview suggests that they are.

In this chapter we will broadly discuss how humans are one member of our global ecosystem, how the physical environment serves three functions for human civilization, how human activities lead to environmental degradation, and how this degradation affects human civilization. We will also discuss briefly several environmental problems, including air, water, and soil pollution, and provide an in-depth discussion of global climate change.

Three Functions Of The Environment

Earth serves three major functions for all living creatures that inhabit it, including humans. It is a *supply depot, waste repository,* and *living space* (Dunlap, 1994; Dunlap & Catton, 2002). When these functions break down due to overuse or competition, environmental problems emerge. On the other hand, when the earth can ensure these functions for humans and the functions complement each other, sustainability is maintained. **Sustainability** is the "ability of earth's various systems, including human cultural systems and economies, to survive and adapt to changing environmental conditions indefinitely" (Miller, 2007).

Supply Depot

As a supply depot, Earth serves as the largest shopping mall, providing all living creatures with everything necessary for survival. The air we breathe, the water we drink, and the food we eat, the raw materials like petroleum and metals needed to assemble an iPod, and even the erythorbic acid, gum arabic, and calcium disodium EDTA in a 20-ounce bottle of Mountain Dew, are materials that come directly from the earth, or are derived from earth's resources. There are two kinds of resources in this shopping mall: renewable and non-renewable. **Renewable resources**, like food grains, trees for paper and wood, and cotton for clothes, can be regenerated. The key factor in determining whether a resource is renewable is its rate of regeneration. If the need/want for a resource outpaces Earth's

ability to regenerate it, the resource is no longer considered renewable. **Non-renewable resources**, like fossil fuels (gasoline, coal, and natural gas) and rare minerals (gold, platinum, and uranium) cannot be regenerated in a timely manner, or at all, and are permanently depleted (Holechek, Cole, Fisher, & Valdez, 2000). While there can be shortages of renewable resources, such as when a freeze in Florida reduces the supply of oranges to American consumers, non-renewable resources experience *scarcities*. Diminished oil reserves in the continental United States cannot be restored, and, therefore, are considered scarce (Dunlap & Catton, 2002).

Waste Repository

As a waste repository, Earth serves as the largest treatment plant, absorbing or storing all of the waste materials from all living creatures. The earth absorbs or recycles the bodily waste of every human being, animal, and plant, the carbon dioxide and nitrogen dioxide waste from the combustion engines in our vehicles, the sulfur dioxide released from coal plants, the toxic metals like lead and cadmium released into rivers and streams from factories, and the plastic, paper, and organic matter that we place in our garbage cans that find their way to city landfills and incinerators. When waste is created faster than the earth can recycle or absorb it, pollution results. In an environment unaltered by industrialized human activity, the waste created by flora, fauna, and humans can serve as a supply depot for other organisms. Alternatively, the waste created by modern civilizations is not always a resource for other organisms (Miller, 2007).

There were approximately 4,200 passenger cars in the U.S. in 1900, whereas there are more than 600 million motor vehicles in use in the world today (Stasenko, 2001). Air pollution, a high concentration of particulate matter from automobiles and other sources, has spurred many cities to adopt a system of air quality advisories and warnings similar to severe weather warnings. In 1900, Earth's atmosphere and biotic life could absorb and recycle the waste products of these early vehicles (CO2 is absorbed by plant life and soils). While the earth will absorb today's carbon emissions, doing so will change the structure of our atmosphere. We will discuss this more later when we discuss global climate change and global warming.

Living Space

As a living space, Earth provides shelter and refuge for all of the living creatures that dwell there. The dorm room you live in, the classroom where your sociology class meets, the Grand Canyon you may visit while on vacation, and the run-down house you may visit this Friday night for a college party all take up space. As populations increase in a confined area, overcrowding can occur. Just as our resources can be overused, so can our living spaces.

Conflict Between Functions

Environmental problems occur when one of these functions is stretched beyond its capabilities, or when functions collide, keeping each of the functions from operating properly. Often, the use of the environment for one function will interfere when it is later used for another function. For example, the human health and ecological disaster at Love Canal illustrates what happens when functions of the environment conflict.

The community of Love Canal, a neighborhood of Niagara Falls, New York, is the site of one of the more notorious environmental tragedies in U.S. history (Blum, 2008; Fowlkes & Miller, 1983). Love Canal, named for William T. Love, is a half-mile trench in Niagara Falls, New York. At the turn of the century, Love had the trench excavated as part of a project to connect the upper and lower Niagara River, but the project failed. The empty, partially dug canal was turned into a dumpsite for 22,000 tons of municipal and industrial waste by Hooker Chemical and Plastic Corporation. In 1953, the Canal was capped and sold to the city of Niagara Falls for a single dollar to be the future home of an elementary school and 100 homes (Beck, 1979; Blum, 2008). Love Canal turned into a human health and ecological disaster as 421 toxic chemicals from the landfill site leeched into people's basements and yards, contaminating the water, land, and air (University of Buffalo University Archives, 2008). The overlapping functions of waste repository and living space led to high rates of miscarriages, birth defects, respiratory ailments, and cancers (Environmental Protection Agency, 2007). This site could not safely function as both a waste repository and a living space for the community of Love Canal. In the end, the elementary school closed and more than 900 families were relocated from the site at a cost of $100 million.

Causes Of Environmental Degradation

How does a society get to the point of overusing available resources, outpacing waste repository processes, and damaging its own living spaces? First, this section will discuss the three main functions served by the earth when considering environmental degradation utilizing the IPAT model. Second, the metaphor of the Tragedy of the Commons will be outlined. And, finally, we will cover the sociological theory known as the Treadmill of Production.

IPAT Model

Scientists have outlined the most important driving forces of human civilization that impact (I) the functions of the environment: population (P), social affluence (A), and technology (T) (Commoner, 1972; Dietz & Rosa, 1994; Duncan, 1961; Ehrlich & Holdren, 1971). The IPAT model has been described as "the ecological complex" to describe basic human processes that explain the relationship between human civilization and the physical environment (Duncan, 1961).

Impact

Environmental degradation can be observed on many levels, from the environmental impact of individual behaviors (electricity/natural gas usage, gasoline consumption, air travel hours, recycling habits, etc.) to the global impact of nation-states (greenhouse gas emissions, deforestation, loss of biodiversity, etc.). Later in this chapter, we will discuss several environmental problems, but first we will introduce the concept of an ecological footprint.

Environmental degradation can be broadly measured by the ecological footprint concept first proposed by Mathis Wackernagel and William Rees (1996). A city, region, or nation's ecological footprint is a measure of the land necessary to support the utilization of the three functions of the environment—resource depot, waste repository, and living space—for a specified geographic region (Wackernagel & Rees, 1996; York, Rosa, & Dietz, 2003). In our globalized economy, a region's **ecological footprint** is an important measure of environmental degradation because resources are imported and wastes are often exported. For example, a Barbie doll is not just a plastic doll. Oil that is extracted and refined into ethylene in Saudi Arabia is turned into polyvinyl chloride (PVC) plastic pellets in Taiwan. The pellets are then shipped to factories in China, Indonesia, and Malaysia where they are formed into 11.5-inch dolls by machines that were made in the United States. Barbie's hair is made in Japan; her clothes are made from Chinese cotton (Cha, 2008). One cannot measure one's complete environmental impact by looking only within one's own yard.

As an example, how much landmass does the United States need to sustain the American population at the current standard of living? An ecological footprint of "one" represents a sustainable region; an ecological footprint greater than one denotes an unsustainable region. In 2001, human civilization needed 1.2 "planet Earths" to sustain current resource consumption, waste production, and living space, and it is projected to need 1.6 planet Earths in 2015 (Dietz, Rosa, & York, 2007). In comparison, the United States alone was using 1.5 times the landmass needed to sustain our land-rich country in 1999 (Wackernagel et al., 1999). This research suggests that human civilization is coming to an age of increased ecological degradation as we outpace Earth's ability to sustain our standard of living.

You may be wondering about the size of your own ecological footprint. On average, a U.S. citizen's ecological footprint is 30 times greater than that of an average citizen in India (Miller, 2007). You can calculate your own ecological footprint on the Internet at http://www.footprintnetwork.org/gfn_sub.php?content=calculator.

Population

The U.S. Census Bureau estimates that there were 6,713,766,306 people on Earth as of August 2008. (Check out the current world population clock at http://www.census.gov/ipc/www/popclockworld.html.) Consider that it took from the dawn of human existence, approximately 195,000 years ago, until the Common Era (1 C.E.) to amass 200 million people on the planet, but it took only another 1,800 years to reach 1 billion people (Census, 2008a). Since the arrival of the Industrial Revolution, the pace of human population growth has exploded, reaching 2 billion in the 1930s, 3 billion in 1960, 4 billion by the mid-1970s, 5 billion in the late 1980s, and 6 billion in 1999 (Harper, 2008; Kemp, 2004), and it is projected to increase to 9 billion by 2040 (Census, 2008b).

Humans use resources. The more people there are, the more resources used. Two hundred years ago, Thomas Malthus, a demographer, was one of the first scientists to shed light on the issue of population growth in relation to resource consumption, specifically of the food supply. Malthus was concerned that geometric population growth would outpace the arithmetic growth of food production through technological advancements (Kemp, 2004). Population growth can also strain other resources, such as energy, water, and housing. Population concerns are especially severe in urban areas where the local ecosystems cannot absorb the waste of human activity, causing pollution of the air, water, and soil (Harper, 2008). Looking at our global measure of environmental impact, population size is directly related to ecological footprint (York, Rosa, & Dietz, 2003). The human population explosion did not happen in a vacuum; it occurred after the introduction of industrialization, a period of colossal increases in affluence and technology, including utilization of energy stores like wood, coal, and oil.

Affluence

In sociological literature, affluence refers to an individual's or group's level of social and economic abundance. Affluence is related to a person's access to resources, whether physical or social. More affluent individuals and countries utilize more

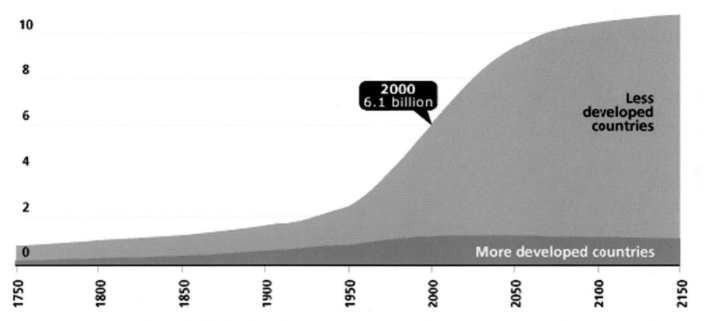

Population (in billions)

Source: United Nations

10

8

6

4

2

0

**2000
6.1 billion**

Less developed countries

More developed countries

1750 1800 1850 1900 1950 2000 2050 2100 2150

resources than less affluent individuals and countries. In research utilizing the IPAT model, affluence is often measured by a country's gross domestic product (GDP) per capita (Chertow, 2001). Although GDP per capita is a good measure of affluence, it is difficult to visualize. Photojournalist Peter Menzel (1995) provides a stunning visualization of affluence through photos of statistically average families from across the world with all their worldly possessions. Utilizing data from the United Nations and the World Bank, Menzel determined what was average based on family size, annual income, occupation, religion, and type of location (such as rural, urban, or suburban).

Thorstein Veblen (1899) described how affluence leads to greater consumption of resources, but, more importantly, to *conspicuous consumption*. Conspicuous consumption is the demonstration of affluence through lavish consumption. Think of the suburban motto of "keeping up with the Joneses." People who have more control over resources show their power and status by out-consuming their neighbors, purchasing larger homes, expensive vehicles, stylish clothing, and extravagant toys. View Menzel's photos of Material Worlds and try to identify those possessions that make up the families' conspicuous consumption patterns.

Conspicuous consumption leads to conspicuous waste. *Conspicuous waste* comes with affluence, allowing individuals to be more careless of their resources. Replacing possessions that are broken or worn, instead of reusing or repairing them, simply because one has the ability to do so, is conspicuous waste. Look at how fashion in American culture changes with the seasons. American teenagers participate in conspicuous waste by replacing perfectly usable clothing with the latest fashions to demonstrate their social status (Bell, 1998).

Technology

Technology is the useful application of knowledge to a situation. Through the use of technology, societies can accomplish tasks that might otherwise be impossible, inefficient, or difficult to accomplish. The invention of the wheel, plow, automobile, and airplane, the domestication of animals and the planting of crops, the development of medicines, Velcro, personal computers, cell phones, and the Internet, are all applications of knowledge to accomplish tasks that would otherwise be exceedingly difficult or impossible. Technology often makes life easier. The Internet, for example, has made writing college papers remarkably easier. Imagine how long it would take you to write a sociology paper if

Is a million dollars for a car too much?   Source: Luca Biagiotti

you had to actually go to the library and use a card catalog to find a book or journal article, rather than doing a search online. Or imagine how boring life would be if you could only surf through four television channels, and you had to walk to the television to change the station.

While technology can make life easier for individuals and society, it can also generate unintended consequences that damage the environment and human societies. Technologies allow society to consume more, leading to diminished resources. Technologies can also create waste matter that has detrimental environmental effects. Even though fertilizers have allowed farmers to produce vast quantities of food, the nitrogen-rich chemicals they contain find their way into streams, rivers, and oceans. Despite the fact that nitrogen is good for crop growth, it is not good for aquatic life. Nitrogen encourages the growth of plant life such as algae in water. This increase in plant life can also reduce the levels of oxygen in the water, making it difficult or impossible for animal life to exist. The nitrogen run-off from crop farming in the Midwest has led to the Gulf of Mexico dead zone, a 6,000-to 7,000-square-mile area where fish cannot live (Bruckner, 2008).

This does not mean that all technologies create environmental problems. Remember that technology is the application of knowledge, so it is also true that technology can be used to ease or eliminate environmental degradation. Front-loading washing machines and non-phosphorous laundry detergents are technological innovations that reduce the consumption of water as a resource as well as reduce the stress on environmental sinks (areas used to absorb wastes) to recycle phosphorous. Solar energy and wind turbines are sustainable energy technologies that we will be discussing later in this chapter. Because technology is the use of knowledge, it is up to the developers and users of this knowledge to understand the pros and cons involved, and to at least be cognizant of the negative consequences such technologies could have on society and the environment.

Population, affluence, and technology are those components of human civilization that have the most significant impact on the physical environment. While these components are cited by scientists as the most pressing variables that shape human-environment interaction, they do not explain how societies become unmanageably populated,

Highlighted parts of the gulf map show the areas in which oxygen levels have been depleted.   Source: nasa.gov

unsustainable societies of wealth, or technologically savvy yet ecologically destructive. The following two sections will discuss how social processes lead to environmental degradation from the perspective of "the Tragedy of the Commons" and the "Treadmill of Production."

Tragedy Of The Commons

Garrett Hardin's (1968) influential *Tragedy of the Commons* thesis suggests that, in a finite world, the short-term interests of individuals and groups can come into conflict with long-term group and global interests. Using a community of herdsman as a metaphor, Hardin illustrates how a community can unconsciously degrade its local environment. Imagine a group of herdsman sharing a community pasture (commons). Initially, each herdsman has an equal number of cattle in the pasture; the ratio of cattle to land is sustainable. This means that the cattle do not deplete the resources of the pasture or permanently damage the living space with waste.

In a competitive economy, each herdsman attempts to reap the most profit. In our example, if a single herder wants to maximize her profits, she will add more cattle to her flock. As a consequence, the added cattle will use more of the pasture's resources (food), sinks (waste storage/absorption), and living space (land). If the other herdsmen are anything like the first herdsman, they will also want to maximize profit and add cattle to the community pasture. The addition of one herder's cattle sets off a competitive battle over the shared finite resource. The new additions will apply more strain on the pasture's environmental functions, resulting in the loss of grazing foliage, increased waste matter, and a more crowded living space. The competitive behaviors of the herdsmen become unsustainable given the finite resources of the community pasture, creating a *tragedy of the commons.*

Treadmill Of Production

Extrapolating the *Tragedy of the Commons* to our global village, with the earth as one large community pasture, one can begin to see how uncontrolled growth of society can outpace the environment's ability to maintain a healthy planet. Placing Hardin's *Tragedy of the Commons* thesis in the context of our global economy, and adding a healthy dose of *neo-Marxist Theory*, one can begin to outline the theory of the Treadmill of Production. According to Allan Schnaiberg and Kenneth Gould (1994), the Treadmill of Production is the motivating force of ecological degradation driven by modern economics, especially following World War II. The modern economic market, spurred by industrialization and an abundance of wealth, requires economic expansion. In other words, corporations seek profits, and without profits, corporations fail. To maintain profits, corporations increase production. Increased production leads to competition between corporations (remember the competing herdsmen in the tragedy of the commons), which leads to more production. The competition for wealth through the production and sale of goods places the community on a treadmill.

In an attempt to increase profits, two means of minimizing costs are addressed: reducing operating costs and externalizing production costs. One way to reduce operating costs is to invest in technologies that will replace expensive labor. While investing in technological infrastructure, such as factory equipment and computer technology, is initially expensive, these costs are offset by increases in production. Companies can reduce operating costs by substituting machines for part of their human work force, because the costs related to labor—salaries and benefits—typically increase over time. The transition from labor-intensive production to technology-intensive production degrades the environment on two fronts (Gould, Pellow, & Schnaiberg, 2004). First, technologies increase production due to the increased time efficiency. Increases in production require more resource inputs, thus leading to the overutilization of environmental resources.

Second, these technologies, while efficient in time of production, are often inefficient in energy and/or chemical use. The use of these technologies leads to overutilization of environmental resources; in addition, these technologies pollute more, leading to the congestion of waste sinks. The Treadmill of Production recognizes that investment in capital leads to increased demands for natural resources.

The second method used to decrease operating costs is to externalize them, predominantly those costs related to waste disposal. Disposing of the waste resulting from the production of goods can be a costly endeavor, thereby reducing profits. Corporations may, therefore, attempt to externalize the costs of waste removal. Externalizing costs occurs when a company transfers some of its moral responsibilities to the community, either directly or as degradation to the environment. Before environmental laws, such as the Clean Air Act of 1970 and the Clean Water Act of 1972, corporations could dispose of waste in several ways that were harmful to both the environment and human health, keeping the costs of disposal to a minimum. Laws that govern the level of pollutants that can be released into the environment serve to internalize some of the costs of production, placing them upon the company rather than the community. The Treadmill of Production perspective provides an excellent blueprint to understand how a society could get to a point of overusing available resources, outpacing waste repository processes, and damaging its own living space.

Environmental Problems

In the following section, we will discuss some of the larger environmental problems that human civilization is facing. Specifically, we will discuss pollution and global climate change. When you read about these environmental effects, think of how population, affluence, and technology are leading to overutilization of, or competition for, resources, waste sinks, and living space.

Pollution

As the 2008 Summer Olympic Games began in

Beijing, China, athletes, spectators, and government officials worried about the effects that China's notoriously dismal air quality would have on the event. The Chinese government restricted car traffic, banning the use of 2 million cars, and shut down heavily polluting factories, turning Beijing into the world's largest air quality experiment in an attempt to "clean the air" for the Olympic Games (Tran, 2008). Pollution is defined as the "destruction or damage of the natural environment by by-products of human activities" (McGraw-Hill, 2003). Sources of pollution include vibration, heat, and noise that contaminate the air, water, and land.

Air pollution is the presence of particulates and chemicals in the atmosphere that have negative effects on ecological and/or social systems. More than a billion people live in communities, predominately in developing countries, where the air is unhealthy to breathe (Miller, 2007). Air pollution is so pervasive in Southeast Asia that an enormous brown cloud over the area can be seen from space, and it is intensifying the melting of the Himalayan glaciers which serve as drinking water for the people of both China and India (Environment News Service, 2007).

Most air pollution is the product of industrialization and the burning of fossil fuels. Although the atmosphere operates as an environmental sink, diluting contaminants by diffusion and wind or settling particulates to the earth by gravity or precipitation, present human activity is outpacing the ability of ecosystems to dilute pollution in many areas, leading to contaminated resources. Air quality issues are more prevalent in industrialized urban areas where population and factory density are higher, especially in communities that rely on the burning of coal as an energy source. Not only is air pollution unsightly, but approximately 150 to 300,000 Americans die prematurely each year from air pollution, while another 125,000 get cancer from breathing air pollution from automobiles (Miller, 2007).

Pastor and his colleagues (Pastor, Sadd, & Morello-Frosch, 2004) found that Latino and other communities of color in California are more likely to live in proximity to manufacturing facilities that emit toxic air pollution. Not only are there trade-offs between the functions of the environment but, also,

there are social structures that may lead to inequitable distributions of environmental problems. **Environmental injustice** occurs when a social group based on race, ethnicity, gender, age, or some other characteristic is burdened with an environmental hazard (Pellow, 2000).

Until now, we have focused on outdoor air pollution, but indoor air pollution is another major concern. In fact, indoor pollution is a greater risk than outdoor pollution. Not only does indoor air pollution have higher concentrations of harmful chemicals like carbon oxide, nitrogen oxides, and sulfur dioxide, Americans spend 70 to 98 percent of their time indoors, leading to approximately 6,000 premature cancer deaths each year (Miller, 2007).

Water pollution is the presence of particulates, chemicals, or temperature changes that have negative effects on the ecology of watersheds or the use of water sources by societies. Water is abundant—comprising 71 percent of the Earth's surface. It is also renewable because the global water system continually recycles itself. However, access to, and pollution of, water are two of the most contested environmental problems facing human societies today. Only 3 percent of the world's water supply is freshwater (drinkable), and close to 70 percent of that is locked in the icecaps and glaciers, leaving only 1 percent available for human consumption, of which the vast majority is groundwater (Geological Survey, 2008).

The most pressing global water concern is contaminated drinking water. Infectious bacteria, viruses, and parasites from human and animal waste contaminate much of the drinking water in developing countries. Approximately 17 percent of the world's population lacks access to a safe drinking water source. Contaminated drinking water causes the premature deaths of more than 2 million people, most of whom are children. There are many types of water systems that can become polluted. We will discuss the pollution of two of these systems: freshwater streams and lakes, and groundwater.

Most surface water pollution is the result of agricultural, industrial, and mining activities. Agricultural practices pollute freshwater streams and lakes with eroded sediment, fertilizer and pesticide

Polluting the air.   Source: Carlos Paes

run-off and waste and bacteria from livestock. Industrial factories use streams and lakes as a waste sink for dumping inorganic and organic chemicals, and mining is responsible for polluting water systems with toxic chemicals and eroded sediments (Miller, 2007).

Because water is constantly moving, especially in rivers and streams, the natural processes of dilution and biodegradation recycle any environmental wastes placed in water systems. Remembering the lessons that we learned from the *Tragedy of the Commons*, this recovery system becomes ineffective if overloaded. In the United States, 9 out of 10 aquifers are contaminated with volatile organic chemicals generated by people, and 50 percent of Americans get their drinking water from these aquifers (Miller, 2007). For example, in an attempt to reduce air pollution, the chemical MTBE was added to gasoline so that it would burn cleaner in automobile engines. Unfortunately, this carcinogenic chemical

is very soluble in water and has been found to leak from more than a quarter-million underground storage tanks at gas stations, contaminating groundwater that serves as drinking water.

Access to fresh water is not just a problem for developing countries. While almost every American has access to healthy drinking water, our affluent society has strained the availability of water in many communities. Because the population of Atlanta doubled between 1980 and 2007, for instance, water demands have skyrocketed. This higher demand, coupled with a recent drought, led Georgia legislators to haggle with government officials in Alabama and Florida over access to the Chattahoochee watershed, which provides water for millions of people in the three states (CNN, 2007).

Soil pollution is the alteration of the natural soil environment. In 2003, every woman, man, and child in the United States generated 1.3 tons (2,600 pounds) of garbage. This was an almost

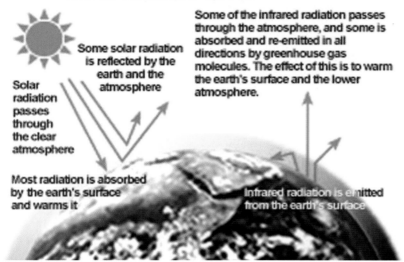

The Greenhouse Effect

Some solar radiation is reflected by the earth and the atmosphere

Solar radiation passes through the clear atmosphere

Some of the infrared radiation passes through the atmosphere, and some is absorbed and re-emitted in all directions by greenhouse gas molecules. The effect of this is to warm the earth's surface and the lower atmosphere.

Most radiation is absorbed by the earth's surface and warms it

Infrared radiation is emitted from the earth's surface

Source: EPA

three-fold increase in average waste production since 1960 (Royte, 2005). This waste included 25 billion Styrofoam cups, 22 billion plastic bottles, 186 billion pieces of junk mail, 25 million metric tons of edible food, plus countless other discarded materials (Miller, 2007). Two types of pollution that contaminate soil are solid waste and hazardous waste. Solid waste includes all discarded material that is neither liquid nor gas. These materials are often stored in landfills (66%), incinerated (8%), or recycled (27%). Some solid waste comes from individual consumer habits (municipal waste), but most of it (98.5%) comes from factories, mining operations, agriculture, and businesses that produce these consumer products and services (industrial waste). In a landmark study on environmental inequality, Robert Bullard (1983) found that African-American communities were disproportionately located in the vicinity of solid waste facilities in comparison to Caucasian communities in Houston, Texas.

The second type of soil pollution comes from hazardous waste, which includes all toxic, biological, infectious, and radioactive waste that not only is discarded, but threatens both human health and the ecosystems in which it is disposed. Household chemicals, batteries, pesticides, toxic chemicals, and ash wastes from incinerators are all examples of hazardous waste (Miller, 2007). The largest producer of hazardous waste is the U.S. military, followed

by the chemical industry. The Environmental Protection Agency (EPA) identified approximately 450,000 hazardous waste sites. Twenty-five percent of Americans live near one of these hazardous waste sites.

Global Warming

Daily temperatures can swing dramatically. The greatest temperature change recorded in a 24-hour period happened in Loma, Montana, on January 15, 1972, when the temperature rose from -54 degrees Fahrenheit to 49 degrees Fahrenheit, an increase of 103 degrees. For sustainable life to exist on Earth, though, the average global temperature cannot fluctuate dramatically. The average temperature of the earth's surface is 60 degrees Fahrenheit.

The sun's radiant heat warms our planet. While most of the sun's solar radiation (sunlight) is absorbed by the earth's surface (land and water), much of it is reflected back into space by the earth's surface and atmosphere. Earth's atmosphere—the layer of gasses that surrounds the planet—acts as a blanket, keeping much of the sun's radiation from escaping, thereby warming the planet's surface and atmosphere and making it welcoming for life. This is called the *greenhouse effect*. Water vapor, carbon dioxide, methane, nitrous oxide, and ozone are some of these heat-trapping gasses. Water vapor and carbon dioxide make up approximately 90 percent of the insulating capacity of our atmospheric blanket and are the most important of the *greenhouse gasses*.

Global warming, also called *global climate change*, is a gradual increase in the earth's average temperature (both ground and atmospheric). Earth's climate has naturally and continually fluctuated over the course of its planetary history (4.5 billion years), leading to cycles of ice ages and warm periods. For much of this time, the earth's climate was not conducive to human inhabitance outside our ancestral home of Africa (Fagan, 2004). Presently, the earth is going through a 20,000-year natural warming period (Dobson, 2002), which fostered human migration from Africa throughout six of the seven continents (all except Antarctica). The natural warming and cooling processes of our planetary climate should not be confused with anthropogenic global climate change.

Anthropogenic climate change is the relatively quick change in the earth's average temperature due to human activities. The rate of global warming has increased drastically in the last 200 years. In the last 100 years, the earth's average surface temperature has increased by 1.4 degrees Fahrenheit. The change in temperature from 1950 to 2000 was the largest increase in average surface temperature in 1,300 years, and the polar regions have not seen average temperatures this high in 125,000 years (Intergovernmental Panel on Climate Change, 2007b).

To a large extent, the type and concentration of gasses in the earth's atmosphere determine the average temperature of the planet. Greenhouse gasses are the specific gasses that have the most warming effect on the earth's atmosphere. Just as having too many blankets on your bed can cause you to be too warm, an overabundance of greenhouse gasses can over-insulate the earth's surface, influencing global warming and affecting human civilization. Water vapor, carbon dioxide, tropospheric ozone, methane, CFCs, and nitrogen oxide are the most important insulating greenhouse gasses (Harper, 2008).

Despite the fact that humans have had very little effect on the amount of water vapor in the earth's atmosphere, humans have had a major influence on the amount of carbon dioxide (CO_2) in the atmosphere (Harper, 2008). The relatively rapid warming of the last 200 years has been traced to anthropogenic sources, primarily the burning of fossil fuels (EPA, 2008; IPCC, 2007b). The burning of fossil fuels accounts for 75 percent of humankind's emissions of CO_2.

Earth's capacity to serve as a waste repository, absorbing and recycling *greenhouse gasses* produced since the Industrial Revolution, is having an impact on the planet's ability to function as a resource depot and a living space. Specifically, global warming will have negative effects on, but not limited to, food supplies and coastal living spaces (Harper, 2008). It is projected that global climate change will have a significant effect on the production of food grains. Even though many countries and regions, such as temperate regions in the mid to high latitudes, will be able to adapt to the changing climate with different crop rotations, many other countries and regions will not, such as those in tropical or dry regions in the low latitudes. Research indicates that maize production in southern Africa will decrease by 30 percent, and maize, rice, and millet production in South Asia will decrease by 10 percent by 2030 (Lobell et al., 2008).

Global warming will have an effect on sea levels due to the melting of Arctic and Antarctic ice sheets and glaciers. Because cities were often settled on trade routes, 50 percent of the world population lives on coastal lands. The Intergovernmental Panel on Climate Change (2007a) predicts significant flooding in coastal areas, especially in delta regions, like New Orleans and the Netherlands, and island regions. Inland communities are not immune to global warming; communities near river systems will also be affected. Early spring thaws will increase the probability of river system flooding worldwide. Global warming will also have an effect on human health. As the average global temperature increases, death and disease due to malnutrition, heat exhaustion, ozone exposure, and vector-borne infectious diseases like Lyme disease, plague, encephalitis, and yellow fever, will also increase in severity.

Summary

It should be clear, even from this brief introduction, that cities and their surrounding regions are complex social creations, sometimes full of surprises and contradictions. It is possible to argue that sociology in the 21st century is, by definition, *urban* sociology, in that the majority of the world's population resides in cities and their surrounding regions, and this is especially true for developed nations.

This chapter outlined how the environment provides everything for human existence, from the air we breathe to the shelters that keep us warm in the winter and cool in the summer, as highlighted in the three functions of the environment. These functions—supply depot, waste repository, and living space—have come into competition with one another throughout human history, leading to shortages in resources and polluted neighborhoods. This derogated environment can be traced to three main attributes: population, affluence, and technology, as discussed using the IPAT model. In this chapter, we proposed that the major causes of environmental degradation could be explained by the *Tragedy of the Commons* and the theory of the Treadmill of Production. This degradation can be better understood as a result of our discussion of air, water, and soil pollution, as well as in our discussion of global climate change.

Review/Discussion Questions

1. How did interstate highways help grow suburbia?
2. Who are the six different actors in the production of property?
3. Where would you rather live, in an urban or rural setting, and why?
4. If gas prices went to $10 a gallon, what do you think the impact would be on the suburbs?
5. Name some renewable resources.
6. List some causes of environmental degradation.
7. What are you doing, if anything, to reduce your carbon footprint?

Key Terms

Central city is defined as a city, or adjacent cities, with a population of at least 50,000, or an urbanized area of more than 100,000 people.

City is an incorporated space with boundaries that have been determined by elected officials and/or resident voters.

Concentration effects occur after the middle class and wealthy leave the poor and minorities in the older central cities where older infrastructures are in need of repair, areas of poverty are increasing, and the population and tax base are dwindling.

Deconcentration effects occur when the middle class and affluent move out of the city.

Ecological footprint is a measure of how much land is necessary to support the utilization of the three functions of the environment (resource depot, waste repository, and living space) for a specified geographic region.

Economic restructuring is the movement of the economy away from a manufacturing base to a service base that includes banking and financial services, shopping centers, restaurants, and tourism.

Environmental injustice occurs when a social group (race, ethnicity, gender, age, etc.) is burdened with an environmental hazard.

Global warming is a gradual increase in the earth's average temperature.

Metroplexes are areas where entire regions are virtually urbanized.

Nonrenewable resources are those resources that cannot be regenerated in a timely manner or that are permanently depleted.

Renewable resources are those resources that can be regenerated, like food and trees.

Sustainability is the ability of the earth's various systems, including human cultural systems and economies, to survive and adapt to changing environmental conditions indefinitely.

Urbanologists are sociologists and other researchers who study cities.

Urbanism is the unique form of urban life and culture.

Urbanization is the process by which a city develops.

Urbanized areas, according to the U.S. Census Bureau, are spaces where more than 50,000 persons reside with an average of 1,000 people per square mile.

Bibliography

Anderson, E. (1990). Streetwise: Race, Class and Change in an Urban Community. Chicago, IL: University of Chicago Press.

Anderson, E. (1999). Code of the Street: Decency, Violence and the Moral Life of the Inner City. New York: W.W. Norton.

Beck, E. C. (1979, January). The Love Canal Tragedy. EPA Journal.

Bell, Michael. (1998). An invitation to environmental sociology. Thousand Oaks, CA: Pine Forge Press.

Bluestone, B. & Harrison, B. (1984). The Deindustrialization of America: Plant Closings, Community Abandonment and the Dismantling of Basic Industry. New York: Basic Books.

Blum, E. D. (2008). Love Canal Revisited: Race, Class, and Gender in Environmental Activism. Lawrence, KS: University Press of Kansas.

Brown, C. S. (1995). Anthropocentrism and Ecocentrism: The Quest for a New World View. Midwest Quarterly, 36 (2), 191-202.

Bruckner, M. (2008). The Gulf of Mexico Dead Zone. Microbial Life Educational Resources. <http://serc.carleton.edu/microbelife/topics/deadzone/> (2008, August 29).

Bullard, R. D. (1983). Solid Waste Sites and the Houston Black Community. Sociological Inquiry, 53, 273-288.

Cha, M. (2008). The Creation of Barbie. <http://www.lclark.edu/~soan221/97/Barbie5.html> (2008, October 3).

Chertow, M. R. (2001). The IPAT Equation and Its Variants: Changing Views of Technology and Environmental Impact. Journal of Industrial Ecology, 4, 13-29.

CNN (2007). Feds OK drought deal letting Georgia keep more water. <http://www.cnn.com/2007/US/11/16/southern.drought/index.html> (2008).

Commoner, B. (1972). The Environmental Cost of Economic Growth. In R. G. Ridker (Ed.), Population Resources and the Environment (pp. 339-363). Washington, DC: Government Printing Office.

Dietz, T. & Rosa, E. A. (1994). Rethinking the Environmental Impacts of Pollution, Affluence, and Technology. Human Ecology Review, 1, 277-300.

Dietz, T., Rosa, E. A., & York, R. (2007). Driving the Human Ecological Footprint. Frontiers in Ecology and the Environment, 5, 13-18.

Dobson, D. M. (2002). From Ice Cores to Tree Rings. In S. L. Spray, & K. L. McGlothlin (Eds.), Global Climate Change, Exploring Environmental Challenges: A Multidisciplinary Approach (pp. 3-30). New York: Rowman & Littlefield Publishers, Inc.

Duncan, O. D. (1961). From Social System to Ecosystem. Sociological Inquiry, 31, 140-149.

Dunlap, R. E. (1994). The Nature and Causes of Environmental Problems: A Socio-Ecological Perspective. In K. S. Association (Ed.), Environment and Development (pp. 45-84). Seoul, Korea: Seoul Press.

Dunlap, R. E. & Catton, W. R. Jr. (2002). Which Function(s) of the Environment Do We Study? A comparison of environmental and natural resource sociology. Society and Natural Resources, 15, 239-249.

Ehrlich, P. R., & Holdren, J. P. (1971). Impact of Population Growth. Science, 171, 1212-1217.

Environment News Service (2007). Asian Brown Clouds Intensify Global Warming. <http://www.ens-newswire.com/ens/aug2007/2007-08-01-02.asp> (2008, August 28).

Environmental Protection Agency (2008). Climate Change: Basic Information. <http://www.epa.gov/climatechange/basicinfo.html> (2008, July 14).

Environmental Protection Agency (2007). Continuing the Promise of Earth Day. <http://www.epa.gov/superfund/20years/ch1pg2.htm> (2008, July 14).

Fagan, B. (2004). The Long Summer: How climate changed civilization. New York: Basic Books.

Fowlkes, M. R., & Miller, P. Y. (1983). Love Canal: The social construction of disaster. Washington, DC: Federal Emergency Management Agency.

Garreau, J. (1991). Edge Cities: Life on the New Frontier. New York: Doubleday.

Gottdiener, M., & Budd, L. (2005). Key Concepts in Urban Studies. Thousand Oaks, CA: Sage Publishing.

Gould, K. A., Pellow, D. N., & Schnaiberg, A. (2004). Interrogating the Treadmill of Production: Everything You Wanted to Know about the Treadmill but Were Afraid to Ask. Organization Environment, 17, 296-316.

Hardin, G. (1968). The Tragedy of the Commons. Science, 162, 1243-1248.

Harper, C. L. (2008). Environment and Society: Human Perspectives on Environmental Change. Upper Saddle River, NJ: Pearson Education, Inc.

Harris, C., & Ullman, E. (1945). The Nature of Cities. The Annals of the American Academy of Political and Social Science, 242 (1), 7-17.

Harrison, B., & Bluestone, B. (1990). The Great U-Turn: Corporate Restructuring and the Polarizing of America. New York: Basic Books.

Holechek, J. L., Cole, R. A., Fisher, J. T., & Valdez, R. (2000). Natural Resources: ecology, economics, and policy. Upper Saddle River, NJ: Prentice-Hall.

Intergovernmental Panel on Climate Change (2007a). Climate Change 2007: Impacts, Adaptation and Vulnerability. Contribution of Working Group II to the Fourth Assessment Report of the Intergovernmental Panel on Climate Change, Cambridge, UK: Cambridge University Press.

Intergovernmental Panel on Climate Change (2007b). Climate Change 2007: The Physical Science Basis. Contribution of Working Group I to the Fourth Assessment Report of the Intergovernmental Panel on Climate Change, Cambridge, UK: Cambridge University Press.

Kemp, D. D. (2004). Exploring Environmental Issues: An Integrated Approach. London, UK: Routledge.

Liebow, E. (1967). Tally's Corner: A Study of Negro Streetcorner Men. Boston, MA: Little, Brown and Co.

Liebow, E. (1993). Tell Them Who I Am: The Lives of Homeless Women. New York: The Free Press.

Lobell, D. B., Burke, M. B., Tebaldi, C., Mastrandrea, M. D., Falcon, W. P., & Naylor, R. L. (2008). Prioritizing Climate Change Adaptation Needs for Food Security in 2030. Science, 319, 607-610.

Logan, J., & Molotch, H. (1987). Urban Fortunes: The Political Economy of Place. Berkeley, CA: University of California Press.

Massey, D. S., & Denton, N. A. (1988). The dimensions of residential segregation. Social Forces, 67, 281-315.

Massey, D.S., & Denton, N. A. (1993). American apartheid: Segregation and the making of the underclass. Cambridge, MA: Harvard University Press.

McGraw-Hill (2003). McGraw-Hill Dictionary of Environmental Science. New York: McGraw-Hill.

Menzel, P. & Mann, C.C. (1995). Material World: A Global Family Portrait. San Francisco, CA: Sierra Club Books.

Miller, G.T. (2007). Living in the Environment: Principles, Connections, and Solutions. Belmont, CA: Thomson Higher Learning.

Pastor, M., Sadd, J. L., & Morello-Frosch, R. (2004). Waiting to Inhale: The Demographics of Toxic Air Release Facilities in 21st-Century California. Social Science Quarterly, 85, 420-440.

Pellow, D. N. (2000). Environmental Inequality Formation: Toward a Theory of Environmental Injustice. The American Behavioral Scientist, 43, 581-601.

Royte, E. (2005). Garbage Land: On the secret trail of trash. New York: Little, Brown and Company.

Schnaiberg, A., & Gould, K. A. (1994). Environment and Society: The Enduring Conflict. New York: St. Martin's.

Stasenko, M. (2001). Number of Cars. The Physics Factbook. <http://hypertextbook.com/facts/2001/MarinaStasenko.shtml> (2008, July 10).

Tran, T. (2008). Pollution curbs turn Beijing into urban laboratory. <http://hosted.ap.org/dynamic/stories/O/OLY_OLYMPICS_LABORATORY?SITE=NYMID&SECTION=HOME&TEMPLATE=DEFAULT> (2008, August 7).

U. S. Census Bureau (2008a). Historical Estimates of World Population. <http://www.census.gov/ipc/www/worldhis.html> (2008, August 15).

U. S. Census Bureau (2008b). World Population Information. International Data Base. <http://www.census.gov/ipc/www/idb/worldpopinfo.html> (2008, August 20).

U. S. Geological Survey (2008). Where is the Earth's Water's Located? Water Science. <http://ga.water.usgs.gov/edu/earthwherewater.html> (2008, September 8).

University of Buffalo University Archives (2008). Love Canal Collections. University Archives. <http://ublib.buffalo.edu/libraries/specialcollections/lovecanal/about.html#info> (2008, July 14).

Veblen, T. (1899, 1994). The Theory of the Leisure Class. London, UK: Constable.

Wackernagel, M., & Rees, W. (1996). Our Ecological Footprint: Reducing Human Impact on the Earth. Gabriola Island, BC: New Society Publishers.

Wackernagel, M., Onisto, L., Bello, P., Linares, A. C., López Falfán, I. S., Méndez García, J., Suárez Guerrero, A. I., & Suárez Guerrero, M. G. (1999). National natural capital accounting with the ecological footprint concept. Ecological Economics, 29, 375-390.

Wilson, W. J. (1987). The Truly Disadvantaged: The Inner City, the Underclass, and Public Policy. Chicago, IL: University of Chicago Press.

York, R., Rosa, E., & Dietz, T. (2003). Footprints on the Earth: The Environmental Consequences of Modernity. American Sociological Review, 68, 279-300.

CHAPTER FIFTEEN

Collective Behavior, Social Movements, And Social Change

Brenton Roncace

Societies change over time. This change can occur rapidly, or it can occur gradually. A coup would represent an example of accelerated social change accomplished through a form of collective behavior. In December 2008, it happened in Guinea when that African country's leader died after ruling for 24 years without a succession plan. In the absence of a leader, some mid-ranking military officers decided to take over the country and name one of their own people, Captain Moussa Dadis Camara, as the new president. At first there was resistance to the coup, but the country's politicians and prime minister surrendered their power to the military leaders in a process that took less than three days (Gettleman, 2008).

Social behavior can occur collectively or institutionally. **Collective behavior** tends to be unorganized, unpredictable, and spontaneous, with very little structure or stability. By contrast, **institutional behavior** is highly predictable and well-organized. An example of institutional behavior would be the movement of inmates in a prison yard at a medium-security prison. Depending on the time of day, inmates move in groups across the prison yard to go to work or classes, the library or the cafeteria. The inmates' schedule is predictable, with little or no deviation occurring from one day to the next. Other examples of institutional behavior would include the weekday morning commute to work, and college students walking across campus between classes.

Social Factors

Collective behavior usually does not happen on its own. Triggers of collective behavior include life-threatening danger, potential economic loss, and some forms of social injustice. The behavior chosen depends on how the people involved view the problem. If they believe it is a relatively straightforward issue, they may engage in the least organized forms of collective behavior: a panic or riot. If, on the other hand, the problem is viewed as more multifaceted with difficult-to-achieve solutions, the people involved may choose to engage in a social movement. According to Neil Smelser (1971), six factors are required to produce collective behavior. These factors, known as his *value-added approach*, must each be present and take place in order for collective behavior to occur:

1. *Structural conduciveness.* The people involved must be able to communicate their problems with each other. Face-to-face communication would be possible for people living next to each other in a neighborhood, or could occur internationally using a phone or the Internet. Once the problems have been voiced, the people involved need to be able to take action.
2. *Social strain.* An injustice or conflict needs to be present in combination with an unwillingness or inability of the side holding the power to correct the situation or make amends.
3. *Generalized belief.* The people involved must have a shared understanding about the cause or causes of the conflict.
4. *Precipitating factors.* An event or spark intensifies the conflict, which pushes people into action.
5. *Mobilization for action.* The people organize, and leaders rise up and direct the people.
6. *Failure of formal social controls.* In most situations, agents of social control like the police or the National Guard are able to prevent any collective action from occurring. This is why instances of collective behavior, such as riots,

occur so infrequently. For collective action to occur, the police and other social control agents must fail in their attempts to stop the people (Thio, 2004).

Forms Of Collective Behavior

Panic

A **panic** is a flight to safety in response to the fear of immediate danger. In most instances of panic, the fear is real—the building really is on fire, and failing to flee could result in serious injury or death. When groups of people are in panic mode together, they often act irrationally and selfishly, trying to save themselves from the perceived danger first.

An example of a panic occurred at the Hillsborough soccer stadium in Sheffield, England, on April 15, 1989. A group of 5,000 fans was waiting outside the stadium to be let in for a soccer match. When the police tried to eject someone from the stadium, twenty people rushed in. The police worried that the crowd outside might get crushed from the rush of people, and they opened a small gate. This resulted in the waiting crowd rushing to the open gate at the same time. The fans filled the gate and began getting crushed by others who were also trying to enter the stadium, pushing from behind. The trapped fans panicked and began shoving each other trying to escape, while some tried to climb over the fencing. As a result, 94 people died and 766 were injured, with 300 of those requiring medical attention (Wikipedia Foundation, 2008).

Mass Hysteria

Mass hysteria is similar to a panic except that in a panic the danger is real, while in mass hysteria the danger is absent and the participants engage in frenzied behavior without checking to see if the alleged source of the fear is real or not. In November 1994, this took place in the female dormitory at the United Arab Emirates University. The local hospital received a call that a fire had broken out in the female dorm and a number of victims were on their way to the hospital. Once at the hospital, the female students displayed a number of symptoms such as heavy breathing, shaking, dizziness, wailing, screaming, fainting, and heaviness in their chests. Physical examinations were conducted only to discover that the females were fine, with none suffering any abnormalities. So what had happened? A female student had been burning incense in her dorm room when the other women smelled the fumes and concluded the dorms were on fire, triggering mass hysteria (Amin, Hamdi, & Eapen, 1997). Mass hysteria includes situations in which one person exhibits very real symptoms and, upon seeing the symptoms, others in the group believe that they, too, are ill and begin displaying similar symptoms even though they are not sick.

Crowds

Crowds are groups of people doing something together for a short period of time (Thio, 2004). There are five types of crowds:

1. The *casual crowd* is the most loosely structured of all crowds. The term casual crowd, as coined by Herbert Bloomer (1939), is used to describe groups of people who share only a minimum level of emotional or physical interaction (Popenoe, 2000). People are able to enter and leave the crowd easily, often without even talking to one another. This type of crowd would include a group of people watching and listening to a street musician. People enter the crowd for a quick glance at what is going on, stay if they like the music, and casually move on when they are finished listening.

2. The *conventional crowd* involves a little more structure, and the behavior of the crowd is largely predictable. Examples of conventional crowds include the audience at a play, or people riding a city bus together. In these types of crowds, people rarely interact with each other and, if

Street performer in Hollywood, California.

Source: Kait Curran Palmer

they do, the interaction is often minimal, with people tending to follow conventional norms (Popenoe, 2000).

3. The *expressive crowd* forms with the intent of allowing its members an opportunity for personal expression. Examples include fans attending a sporting event who may cheer and yell in support of their team, or people attending Mardi Gras in New Orleans who shout and throw beads at one another. These crowds may appear on the surface to be out of control, but in reality there are roles and norms guiding the behavior of the individuals that make up the crowds. People in these crowds know the limits between acceptable and unacceptable behavior, and most stay within those guidelines; those that do not are often quickly removed (Popenoe, 2000).

4. *Solidaristic crowds* form with the intent of giving their members a sense of unity and belonging (Popenoe, 2000). One example of a solidaristic crowd was the Million Man March organized by Nation of Islam leader Louis Farrakhan, which took place on October 16, 1995, in Washington, D.C., the march was designed to bring black men together and strengthen their sense of solidarity. The men that attended the march reported feeling reenergized. Many new organizations emerged in response to the march, including M.A.L.E., which stands for Maturing Africans Learning from Each other. M.A.L.E. encourages men to work together to solve issues, and to use their experience and knowledge to mentor young boys (Cooper, Groce, & Thomas, 2003). Solidaristic crowds may appear spontaneous in nature, but that is largely an illusion, as these types of events are well planned and the activities are choreographed in advance.

5. *Reactionary crowds* form in response to some event or situation (Drury, 2002). Reactionary crowds are usually angry and hostile and can easily become violent. The two most common forms of reactionary crowds are mobs and riots (Popenoe, 2000). **Mobs** are angry groups of people who channel their anger onto a single target. Mobs often have leaders and some degree of structure. After the goals of the mob are met,

the crowd usually disperses. Examples of mob behavior include the Ku Klux Klan lynchings and fire bombings in the South, and the members of Islamic Jihad who target Jews (Popenoe, 2000; Borgeson & Valeri, 2007).

A **riot** is a violent crowd that moves from target to target over the course of several hours or days (Popenoe, 2000). Rioters often focus their anger on groups of people they dislike and engage in activities like violence, looting, and destruction of property. A riot occurred on the Cronulla beach in Sydney, Australia, in December 2005. During the week before the riot, three beach lifeguards had been taunting four men of Lebanese descent with comments like "Lebs can't swim" (Poynting, 2006). The Lebanese men retaliated by brutally beating two of the lifeguards. The media covered the story extensively, and a local radio show host called for a rally to take place the following weekend as a show of force. Youth in the area text-messaged each other, and when the weekend arrived, there were 5,000 participants ready to take back the beach. The crowd, many wearing T-shirts with the slogans "100 Percent Aussie Pride" and "The Ethnic Cleansing Unit" then moved across the beach shouting racist slogans and attacking anyone they thought was of Middle-Eastern descent (Poynting, 2006).

Common Traits Of Crowds

No matter the type of crowd, most share similar traits. The first is *uncertainty*–no one in the crowd is exactly sure of the outcome, nor do they all share the same expectations regarding behavior. The second is a sense of *urgency*–there is often the sense that something must be done right away, and that by simply standing around, time is being wasted. The third is *communication*–which covers how members of a crowd share ideas, as well as the mood and attitude of the group, which help force conformity among the members. The fourth is *suggestibility*–individuals in a crowd tend to be more open to suggestion and less likely to be critical of ideas suggested by others. The fifth is *permissiveness*–members of crowds often feel freed from conventional norms and, thus, act and say things differently then they would on their own (Thio, 2004).

Theories Of Crowd Behavior

Social Contagion Theory

According to Gustave Le Bon's (1841-1931) **social contagion theory**, crowds are in agreement in both thought and action, and in this sense they all share the same collective mind (Thio, 2004). According to Le Bon, it is the collective mind that represents the mind of a barbarian because it is emotional and irrational. Le Bon argues that each one of us deep down is a barbarian, but that we hide our true thoughts and feelings in order to fit into the social norms and values of society. All of that hiding is revealed among individuals who are part of a crowd because they become emboldened by their numbers, and because acting as a group takes away their own personal responsibility, releasing them to become more like their real selves (Thio, 2004).

Le Bon argued that people give up their individuality, and willfully become part of the collective mind, due to social contagion. **Social contagion** is the spreading of certain emotions or actions from one member of the crowd to another (Thio, 2004). Evidence has been offered in an attempt to prove that social contagion works on some levels, such as laughter in a movie theatre spreading from one audience member to many, and one group member's cough leading others to cough themselves (Thio, 2004).

Recently, however, evidence has been provided by sociologists that discredits Le Bon's idea of the collective mind. First, the idea of the collective mind ignores and downplays the differences among the individuals making up the crowd (Popenoe, 2000). Second, it applies individual attributes, such a mind or conscience, to a group when groups cannot possess these attributes (Popenoe, 2000).

Convergence Theory

According to **convergence theory**, people in crowds share the same attitudes, views, and beliefs, and it was because of their similarities that they came together in the first place (Popenoe, 2000). A gay rights rally is an example of convergence theory. Those people that support rights for gays are likely to be motivated, based on their views and

beliefs, to attend the rally to show their support for the cause. Others may be attracted to the rally to protest gay rights, but they, too, would be motivated to attend based on their views and beliefs.

Emergent Norm Theory

From the viewpoint of the **emergent norm theory**, crowds tend to approach unanimity because one set of behavioral norms is accepted by the entire crowd (Popenoe, 2000). Members of the crowd that refuse to adopt the emergent norms would receive social pressure from other crowd member to do so. A crowd protesting police brutality might begin throwing rocks at officers. Those in the crowd that refuse to throw rocks and remain silent still support the group and the emergent norm through their passive presence. Those members of the group that begin urging others to stop throwing rocks would likely be heckled or pushed aside (Popenoe, 2000). If a person was to view the above scene, he or she might jump to the conclusion that everyone was in agreement. That might not be the case, since those in attendance may only remain because they are too afraid to leave.

Fashions, Fads And Crazes

Fashions involve a large number of people adhering to a particular innovation. Fashions usually occur with clothes and style of dress, such as when it was popular to "peg," or excessively take in, jeans in the late 1980s through the early 1990s. Intense and short-lived, fashions tend to burn out and become unfashionable over a relatively short period of time. Fashions are also likely to be subject to traditional norms. Fashion subcultures are outside the realm of popular fashion. In a fashion subculture, the trend in question is extremely popular only among a small percentage of the population. Goth fashion is one example of a fashion subculture. Goth fashion is based in part on the dichotomy of light and dark, with the understanding that neither would exist without the other. Goths use white and black makeup on their faces to depict death and typically wear black clothing (Langman, 2008).

Fads are a temporary infatuation with a particular practice or innovation. Examples of fads include

Pet Rocks and mood rings in the 1970s, Garbage Pail Kids and jelly shoes in the 1980s, and Beanie Babies and slap bracelets in the 1990s. Current fads include Apple iPods and Texas hold 'em poker (Crazy Fads, 2008).

Crazes are fads that can bring with them serious consequences for those involved. Many crazes are financial in nature. One example of a craze, the dot-com stocks of the late 1990s, rapidly soared in value as everyone rushed in to buy, and then quickly deflated as everyone tried to sell their stock before the dot-com companies went out business. Many dot-com stocks, such as Metro One Telecom and Digital Island, went from being worth over a hundred dollars a share to only a few dollars within the span of a few years (Lewis, 2008).

Rumors And Gossip

A **rumor** is an unverified story, spreading from person to person through a variety of sources like the Internet and word of mouth (Thio, 2000). As the story is retold, bits are left out or embellished so that even if it was originally based on some facts, the resulting rumor may be entirely inaccurate. People often turn to rumors when trying to discover what is happening in situations where not a lot is known. **Gossip** involves talk about the personal and private lives of others (Popenoe, 2000). The tabloid industry is almost entirely devoted to making money off of the gossip surrounding celebrities.

Public Opinion

The **public** refers to a group that shares the same common interest, positions, or thoughts (Popenoe, 2000). Examples of public groups include the Republican and Democratic political parties, the National Rifle Association (NRA), and the American Association of Retired Persons (AARP). The attitudes and beliefs held by the public are known as **public opinion** (Popenoe, 2000).

Propaganda

Public opinion is not concrete and can change overtime. **Propaganda** refers to those methods designed to influence people's opinions (Thio, 2004). Politicians and advertisers know public opinion can change, and they use various propaganda methods aimed at influencing it to be more favorable to them. Five of the more popular methods are listed below:

1. *Ad nauseam*—repeating a message over and over again. Examples of this include television ads for the same product that are run repeatedly. In the political arena, this includes the placement of one candidate's signs in many places so that the average person encounters them wherever he or she goes.
2. *Bandwagon*—the idea that everyone is doing it, so you should, too. This method appeals to people's desire to be on the winning side and not get left behind. An example of this would be a concert coming to town with advertisements telling the public that everyone is going to be there having a great time, and you do not want to miss out on the fun.
3. *Glittering generalities*—applying emotionally appealing words to a product or cause, without presenting any factual proof to support the claim. Examples of this would include an advertisement saying that a particular restaurant has the "Best Burgers in America," without offering proof that they actually do.
4. *Transfer*—associating one thing with something else that is already widely revered or desirable. An example of this would be using the American flag in a television ad, as it is respected and admired across this country. Adding an American flag to a television commercial for an automobile might suggest that it is solid and strong like America, or that we would be performing some sort of patriotic duty if we bought the car.
5. *Testimonial*—using the reputation of the person pitching the product as an endorsement. This method uses well-known celebrities to claim a particular product or service is so good that they use it themselves (Thio, 2004).

Media Influence

When the media try to influence public opinion, they run up against several roadblocks. A roadblock occurs when diverse media sources and multiple views are transmitted, resulting in messages that sometimes conflict with one another—effectively cancelling each other out. Another roadblock involves the media shaping their opinions and viewpoints based on what "we," the public, want to hear in an attempt to garner a large audience and the advertising money that comes with it. Even if we do receive the information the media is using to influence us, we may choose to reject it, especially if it clashes with the information from one of our opinion leaders, and thus create another roadblock. **Opinion leaders** are individuals whose opinions and viewpoints are accepted by others in a community (Thio, 2004).

The media do have the power to influence public opinion because, ultimately, they choose which issues and stories they are going to cover, meaning the media serve as topic gatekeepers. The following are fours ways in which the media influence public opinion. First, they *authenticate* the information by showing images and discussing it on the air, which make it seem more real. A person would have a difficult time trying to convince others that an earthquake had not hit China if everyone was watching aftermath videos of it on their televisions. Second, they *validate* private opinions and viewpoints. People may feel stronger about their views if a commentator they respect offers similar views. Third, they serve to *legitimatize* ideas, even unconventional ones. Ideas that at first glance may appear crazy might appear more reasonable over time if a person is constantly bombarded by them in the media. Fourth, the media *concretize* unrestrained and poorly defined ideas into concrete form. The media do this by providing labels such as "global warming" or "the housing bust" that they apply to stories, making them appear to be connected (Thio, 2004).

Social Movements

Social movements are collective efforts designed to bring about some social change. Social movements are usually conducted using non-institutionalized methods (Popenoe, 2000). An example of a social movement that developed over time is the women's suffrage movement in the United States,

which had its first meeting in Seneca Falls, New York, in 1848. There the women involved signed the "Declaration of Sentiments and Resolutions," which laid out the rights they wanted to be afforded to women, including the right to vote. It was not until 1920, when the 19th Amendment to the United States Constitution was ratified, that women were granted the right to vote (Barber, 2008). Social movements have a purpose and an agenda of items they want to accomplish, so they generally involve more structure than other forms of collective behavior. Social movements also tend to have more staying power, as illustrated by the women's suffrage movement above. A riot or mob might be in action for a couple of hours; a social movement could last for decades (Thio, 2004).

Four Main Types Of Social Movements

1. *Revolutionary movements* seek to overthrow the current government and start a new one. In order to accomplish their goals, movements of this kind usually get involved in violent and illegal action (Thio, 2004). In the United States, it is considered an act of treason for a citizen to declare war on the U.S. government. One prominent example of a successful revolutionary movement was Fidel Castro's Cuban Revolution, in which he overthrew the President of Cuba Fulgencio Batista and appointed himself the leader that nation, a position he held for 49 years (Wikipedia, 2008).

2. *Reform movements* desire only limited change to the current status quo. They believe the overall social structure is good enough, so it does not need to be completely torn down, but they want minor changes and tweaking to occur in order to make the system better in their eyes (Thio, 2004). As an example, the push by workers in the United States to get government to enact a national minimum wage was a reform movement. Business owners and other capital interests fiercely fought the idea of a minimum wage, arguing that workers should be able to contract their labor at any price they saw fit, and that

it is not the business of government to determine what workers could charge for their labor (Smith, 2008). It is interesting to note that some of the arguments made by business interests against the enactment of minimum wage laws were similar to those made against the implementation of child labor laws (Fischer, 1995).

3. *Resistance movements* seek to maintain the status quo and work to prevent any social change from occurring (Thio, 2004). An example of a resistance movement involved the American Party known as the *Know Nothings*, since when asked about their movement, members would reply "I know nothing." The Know Nothings, along with the Ku Klux Klan and the Knights of Luther, were against the advancement of Catholics in society. These groups saw Catholics as a threat to democracy, believing that they were mindless followers of the Pope who had deviated from the Bible since they worshipped statues of the Blessed Virgin Mary. In an effort to stop Catholics from gaining power in society, these groups discriminated against them in employment by putting up signs such as "No Irish Need Apply." They also burned parishes, attacked convents, killed Catholics, and vehemently opposed the first Catholic to run for U.S. president, Al Smith. Catholics eventually moved into the middle class and assimilated into American culture, helping to reduce anti-Catholic sentiments. The Know Nothings eventually disbanded (Davidson & Williams, 1997).

4. *Expressive movements* want to change individuals, not society. Many religious organizations that actively try to recruit new members to their faith, such as Jehovah's Witnesses and Hare Krishna, are examples of expressive movements (Thio, 2004).

Three Possible Causes Of Social Movements

Frustration theory, developed by Eric Hoeffer (1966), claims that those who get involved in social movements are themselves frustrated or disturbed. These people join social movements as a way to di-vert their attention away from themselves and their personal problems, putting their thoughts and energies instead into their "cause." By being part of a cause, they are able to view themselves positively as people trying not only to help themselves, but others as well, by bettering society. One problem with this theory is that it focuses blame on participants in the movement instead of on society and its deficiencies. People are often drawn to social movements because racial and or sexual discrimination, societal problems that affected them, generally prompted them to get involved, not their own personal problems (Thio, 2004).

Breakdown-frustration theory contends that social breakdowns lead to social movements when frustration mounts among the masses (Thio, 2004). An example of a social breakdown that could result in social movements would be a lack of food, as deprivation and hunger can lead to rebellion (Oberschall, 1995). Imagine the social unrest that would develop if all of the supermarkets had no food, and people were going hungry and could not feed their children.

Resource mobilization theory argues that social movements are initiated only when the necessary resources and mobilization tools are available. According to this theory, movements do not come into being because of frustration. Instead, they exist because core organizers garner the support, money, and media access that is needed. This theory is often criticized for ignoring the role frustration plays in social movements. If the cause being advocated by a social movement had lots of money and resources, then it would likely rely heavily on the methods laid out by the resource mobilization theory. If the movement, however, is made up of poor people with few resources, it is more likely to be formed through frustration (Thio, 2004).

A Global Approach To Social Change

Societies change around the globe. They change, in part, due to **modernization** and the development of new technologies. When a society moves from being agricultural to industrial, sociologists would say that the move represents modernization. Modernization can serve to weaken the traditions within a culture, but this is not always the case, and, oftentimes, both may coexist (Thio, 2004). Researchers studied 496 television commercials aired on three networks in China during the summer of 2000. The researchers examined the dominant values spotlighted by each commercial's theme and discovered that both traditional and modern values were present in the majority of commercials, suggesting that tradition still plays a strong role among the modern Chinese (Zhang & Harwood, 2001).

The trend of modernization is having the greatest effect on those societies that were the least modern. In parts of Africa and South America, there were no phone lines, and people in many parts of those countries had no access to phones. With the advent of cell phone technology, people living in these areas are now able to have both phone and Internet access (Racanelli, 2008). **Convergence theory** argues that modernizations will bring Western and non-Western countries together as they become more and more technologically equal. It is believed that when this happens, countries not previously exposed to Western technology and ideas will abandon their old ways of life and traditions for more Western lifestyles (Thio, 2004).

The opposite view is offered by **divergence theory**, which argues that with modernization comes a greater and growing divide between Western and non-Western societies as the people in the non-Western societies reject Western values. Examples of this can be seen throughout Muslim societies in the Middle East. Middle Easterners may adopt Western technologies, but they still maintain their Islamic traditions. Countries practicing Islamic law, like Saudi Arabia, still chop off the hands of thieves and stone adulterers, practices that would be considered unacceptable and barbaric to many in Western cultures (Thio, 2004).

Functionalist Perspective On Social Change

Those adhering to the functionalist perspective believe that social change is a gradual process that occurs slowly. Three theories that attempt to explain how this happens are listed below:

Evolutionary Theory

Evolutionary theory purports that societies evolve gradually over time from simple to more complex forms. One of the earliest supporters of this theory was Herbert Spencer (1820-1903). Spencer believed that societies evolved on the basis of natural selection; good aspects of a society would flourish and survive, while bad aspects would cease to exist and die off. Over time, this process would allow societies to build on their strengths and discard their weaknesses. One criticism of this theory is that societal evolution does not necessarily equal an improvement. Pastoral societies had their strengths and weaknesses, as do industrial societies (Thio, 2004).

Cyclical Theory

Unlike evolutionary theory, which views change as only going in one direction, **cyclical theory** argues that societies move back and forth in a continuous series of cycles. The following three theories all stem from the cyclical theory (Thio, 2004).

Spengler's Theory Of Majestic Cycles

The majestic cycles theory was developed by German historian Oswald Spengler (1880-1936). His idea was that cultures are like living organisms: they are born, grow up, mature, grow old, and then they die. When cultures die, they are simply replaced by new ones, as once great societies like the Greeks and Egyptians have been replaced. When he wrote this theory in, he was convinced that Western civilization was in the stage of old age and close to dying off (Thio, 2004).

Toynbee's Theory Of Challenge And Response

Arnold Toynbee (1889-1975), agreed that civilizations rise and fall, but Toynbee argued that they did so not based on some life cycle as suggested by Spengler, but based on the humans within the civilization and their environment. He saw change within a civilization as prompted mainly by two sources: that of the *challenge* and that of the *response* to the challenge. The challenges could come from nature, such as a hurricane, tornado, or flood, or they could come from other humans, such as in a war. How the civilizations changed depended on their responses and whether or not those responses were successful in overcoming their challenges (Thio, 2004).

Sorokin's Principle Of Immanent Change

Pitirim Sorokin (1889-1968) believed that societies bounced back and forth between two cultural extremes, which he referred to as ideational and sensate. **Ideational culture** focuses on religion and spiritualism, and believes they are essential ingredients to understanding knowledge. This view encourages people to be spiritually active. **Sensate culture** sees science and empirical evidence as the source of knowledge. This view encourages people to engage in lifestyles which focus on being practical, materialistic, and hedonistic. Sorokin believed that

external forces, such as war, may speed up social change, but according to the **principle of immanent change**, all social change is the result of forces operating within the society. When change does occur, society simply rejects the side it currently supports and switches to the other side. Thus, societies go from being ideational to sensate, and eventually back to ideational again (Thio, 2004).

Equilibrium Theory

Equilibrium theory was developed by Talcott Parsons (1902-1979), who viewed society as made up of many interdependent parts, each contributing to society as a whole. Parsons believed that the natural condition of a social system is the state of equilibrium in which all parts of society are in balance. Parsons pointed out that a social system can change in one of two ways: Change can be generated by an outside social system, or it can come as

Man talks on his cell phone.

Source: Silvia Cosimini

a result of strain and pressure from within the same social system. Since each of the parts is dependent on the others, even a minor change to one of the parts can cause the system to become unbalanced, creating a state of disequilibrium (Popenoe, 2000). If social change does occur, then the social system needs to adjust to accommodate those changes and keep the system running as smoothly as possible. For Parsons, social change did not involve a complete revamp in which the old system would be tossed out and replaced with an entirely new one. Instead, social change would result from a slow process involving gradual change, in which new elements are added to old elements in a moving equilibrium with the goal of becoming balanced again (Thio, 2004).

Conflict Perspective On Social Change

According to Karl Marx (1818-1883), all societies are in constant conflict and it is that conflict which leads to revolutionary change. Marx viewed conflict as an even greater force in capitalistic societies, which are divided into two groups: those with money, who own the factories and businesses and decide who has access to capital, and those who sell their labor to those organizations. It is this division which creates the conflict because the two groups have different goals in mind. Business owners want to pay the workers as little as necessary in order to keep their profit high. Workers, on the other hand, want to maximize their pay and earn as much for their labor as possible. Marx believed this exploitation of labor would eventually lead to a worker revolt in which the workers would take control of the factories and businesses in which they worked. Marx's predictions have not yet come to pass for a number of reasons, including: the existence of a large middle class made up of many white-collar workers, the protection of laws requiring better and safer working conditions passed by governments in capitalist societies, and the affluence of workers, who have more today than the workers of the past, which makes them feel as though they have a stake in the system (Thio, 2004). In 1965, only 10 percent of Americans owned shares of stock, in 1980 it was 20 percent, and, as of 2000, that number was at 50 percent (Norquist, 2000).

Symbolic Interactionist Perspective On Social Change

Symbolic interactionists focus on how social interactions change within a society. People interpret the world around them in order to determine how to interact with others. Part of this interpretation of the world involves the person's own interpretation of themselves and how they want others to view them. This, in turn, influences how they interact with others. As social change occurs, people must redefine their world and their self-perceptions. People living in traditional societies often have a more concrete sense of who they are, since they were born with their social status already determined. If their parents were farmers, then they, too, are farmers; from before they could remember, to the day they die, their status as a farmers remained the same. In modern societies, this is not the case, as people assume many statuses over time. For instance, a person might go to school and become a dentist at age 32, after spending three years working as a high school science teacher. This status change, from teacher to dentist, might cause the person to feel some anxiety and nervousness as he or she tries to fit into this new status without fully knowing what is expected. People in traditional societies tend to place a high value on relationships, a sense of belonging, and their role within their group. People in modern societies, on the other hand, tend to place a high value on individualism and privacy, and may be less trusting of others.

Summary

This chapter began by discussing collective behavior and the six factors that need to be present for collective behavior to occur. The various forms of collective behavior were covered, including panics, mass hysteria, crowds, fashions, fads, crazes, rumors, public opinion, and social movements. The four main types of social movements were discussed, along with three possible causes that bring about their existence. Globally, change is occurring due in part to modernization, which different theories suggest will either push Western and non-Western societies together or pull them apart. The functional perspective on social change views change as occurring slowly and in a gradual process. The conflict perspective on social change argues that societies are in constant conflict between those who control the resources and those who do not. Symbolic interactionists focus on how people interpret and view the world around them and how that affects their interactions with others.

Review/Discussion Questions

1. List the five types of crowds.
2. Name some of the propaganda methods used to influence people's opinions.
3. What are three possible causes of social movements?
4. Which forms of collective behavior have you personally been involved in?
5. Think of some events that might trigger you to join a riot.
6. Name some things in your life that were once considered fashionable but no longer are.

Key Terms

Breakdown-frustration theory contends that social breakdowns lead to social movements when frustrations mount among the masses.

Collective behavior is behavior that tends to be unorganized, unpredictable, and spontaneous, with little structure or stability.

Convergence theory, as it relates to crowds, means that people in crowds share the same attitudes, views and beliefs, and it was because of their similarities that they came together in the first place. As the theory relates to social change, it means that modernization will bring Western and non-Western countries together as they become more technologically equal.

Crazes are fads that can bring with them serious consequences for those involved.

Crowds are groups of people doing something together for a short period of time.

Cyclical theory argues that societies move back and forth in a continuous series of cycles.

Divergence theory contends that with modernization comes a greater and growing divide between Western and non-Western societies.

Emergent norm theory asserts that crowds tend to approach unanimity because one set of behavioral norms is accepted by the entire crowd.

Equilibrium theory views society as made up of many interdependent parts, which all serve a function and are in balance with one another. Change in one part leads to change in other parts.

Evolutionary theory claims that societies evolve gradually over time from simple to more complex forms.

Fads are temporary infatuations with a particular practice or innovation.

Fashions are brief followings for a particular innovation by a large number of people.

Frustration theory claims that those people who get involved in social movements are themselves frustrated or disturbed.

Gossip involves talk about the personal and private lives of others.

Ideational culture focuses on religions and spiritualism, believing that these are essential ingredients to understanding knowledge. This view encourages people to be spiritually active.

Institutional behavior is highly predictable and well-organized.

Mass hysteria is similar to panic, except that in panic the danger is real, while in mass hysteria the danger is absent and participants engage in the frenzied behavior without checking to see if the alleged source of their fear is real or not.

Mobs are groups of people who are angry and channel their anger onto a single target.

Modernization is the transformation of a society from being agricultural to industrial.

Opinion leaders are those individuals whose opinions and viewpoints are accepted by others in a community.

Panic is a flight to safety in response to the fear of immediate danger.

Principle of immanent change states that all social change is a result of social forces operating within the society.

Propaganda refers to the methods used to influence public opinion.

Public refers to a group that shares the same common interest, positions, or thoughts.

Public opinion is composed of the attitudes and beliefs held by the public.

Resource mobilization theory contends that social movements are initiated only when the organizers have the necessary resources. Without these tools, the movement will not exist.

Riots are violent crowds that move from target to target over the course of several hours or days.

Rumors are unverified stories that spread from one person to another through a variety of sources such as word of mouth and the Internet.

Sensate culture sees science and empirical evidence as the source of knowledge. This view encourages people to engage in lifestyles that focus on being practical, materialistic, and hedonistic.

Social contagion is the spreading of certain emotions or actions from one member of a crowd to others.

Social contagion theory claims that crowds are in agreement in both thought and action; in this sense, they all share the same collective mind.

Social movements are collective efforts designed to bring about some social change.

Bibliography

Amin, Y., Hamdi, E., & Eapen, V. (1997). Mass hysteria in an Arab culture. International Journal of Social Psychiatry, 43, 303-306.

Barber, E. (1998). One hundred years toward suffrage: An overview. Votes for Women: Selections from the National American Woman Suffrage Association Collection, 1848-1921. <http://memory.loc.gov/ammem/naw/nawstime.html> (2008).

Borgeson, K., & Valeri, R. (2007). The enemy of my enemy is my friend. American Behavioral Scientist, 51, 182-195.

Cooper, R., Groce, J., & Thomas, N. (2003). Changing direction: Rites of passage programs for African American older men. Journal of African American Studies, 7 (3), 3-14.

Crazy Fads. <http://www.crazyfads.com> (2008).

Davidson, J., & Williams, A. (1997). Megatrends in 20th-century American Catholicism. Social Compass, 44, 507-527.

Drury, J. (2002). 'When the mobs are looking for witches to burn, nobody's safe': Talking about the reactionary crowd. Discourse & Society, 13, 41-73.

Fischer, L. (1995). American constitutional law (Vol. 1). New York: McGraw-Hill.

Gettleman, J. (2008, December 25). Coup in Guinea largely welcomed. International Herald Tribune.

Harwood, J., & Zhang, Y. (2006). Modernization and tradition in an age of globalization: Current values in Chinese television commercials. Journal of Communication, 54, 156-172.

Langman, L. (2008). Punk, porn, and resistance: carnivalization and the body in popular culture. Current Sociology, 56, 657-677.

Lewis, M. (Ed.). (2008). Panic: The story of modern financial insanity. New York: Norton.

Norquist, G. (2000). Elections 2000: The leave us alone vs. the takings coalition. <http://www.haciendapub.com/norquist.html> (2008).

Oberschall, A. (1995). Social movements: Ideologies, interests, and identities. New Brunswick: Transaction.

Popenoe, D. (2000). Sociology. Upper Saddle River: Prentice Hall.

Poynting, S. (2006). What caused the Cronulla riot? Race & Class, 48 (1), 85-92.

Racanelli, V. (2008, December 29). Ringing up gains around the globe. Barron's.

Smelser, N. J. (1963). Theory of Collective Behavior. New York: Free Press of Glencoe.

Smith, C. (2008). U.S. Minimum Wage History. Court's World. <http://oregonstate.edu/instruct/anth484/minwage.html> (2008).

Thio, A. (2004). Sociology: A brief introduction (6th ed.). Boston: Allyn & Bacon.

Wikipedia Foundation. http://en.wikipedia.org/wiki/Hillsborough_Disaster> (2008).

Zhang, Y. B., & Harwood, J. (2004). Modernization and Tradition in an Age of Globalization: Cultural Values in Chinese Television Commercials. Journal of Communication, 54 (1), 156.

Glossary

Absolute poverty is complete poverty, used to describe people who are desperately poor and may not know from whence their next meal will come.

Acculturation is the transmission of culture from one generation to another.

Achieved status refers to a social position that a person earns through personal effort and choice.

Adolescent subculture contains the values and attitudes of the youth which differ from those of the adult world.

Adult socialization is the process by which adults learn new statuses and roles.

Affirmative action is composed of positive actions used to recruit minority group members or women for jobs, promotions, and educational opportunities.

Ageism is prejudice or discrimination against people based on their age.

Agrarian societies are based on the technology of animal-drawn plows that support large-scale cultivation to acquire food supplies.

Alienation describes processes and a state of being characterized by estrangement and distancing from the important elements of the human spirit. It is commonly a word used to describe the dehumanizing effects of social, economic and political systems and processes. Sociologists argue that particular forms of institutional arrangements are the primary cause of alienation.

Alternative health care professionals are individuals providing care outside the mainstream or western modalities of health care.

Amalgamation occurs when the cultural and physical features of various groups are combined to create a new culture.

Animism is the belief that spirits inhabit everything in nature.

Anomie is a social condition in which norms and values are conflicting, weak, or absent.

Anticipatory socialization involves learning the skills and values needed for future roles.

Aptitude is the capacity to develop physical or social skills.

Arranged marriage means that parents or matchmakers decide who is going to marry whom.

Ascribed status refers to a social position that a person receives at birth or assumes involuntarily later in life.

Assimilation occurs when immigrants merge with the dominant group and adopt its culture.

Authoritarian leadership styles are characterized by a leader giving commands to subordinates.

Authority is simply institutionalized power, whereby power is examined in the context of its institutional settings and institutionalized arrangements.

Autonomy is when individuals have considerable control over their own work.

Back stage is the place where there is no audience and the person does not play a specific role.

Base and superstructure is a Marxist concept for representing the economic foundation of modern capitalism and its dominance over the political institutions and all other institutions of social life, including culture and religion.

Beliefs are specific ideas that people think to be true.

Bilateral descent traces the line of descent through both the mother's and the father's family.

Breakdown-frustration theory contends that social breakdowns lead to social movements when frustrations mount among the masses.

Bureaucracies are organizations with statuses and roles arranged in a fixed hierarchy. Activity is governed by strict rules and tracked through the keeping of formal records. Each status and role is specialized so that each person is only responsible for one small aspect of the organization, making each worker an expert in his or her own area. Relationships are impersonal, with everyone's main concern being their own bureaucratic role.

Bureaucratic inertia is an organizational resistance to beneficial change.

Bystander effect is a term used to describe the tendency of individuals not to get involved in emergency situations if they are part of a crowd.

Capitalist class includes the people who own the means of production.

Carbon footprint is the impact a person's activities have on the environment in general, and climate change in particular.

Caste systems are based on stratification, classifying people at birth into social levels in which they remain.

Central city is defined as a city, or adjacent cities, with a population of at least 50,000, or an urbanized area of more than 100,000 people.

Charismatic personalities is a term used by Weber to describe leading figures and the influence their personalities had over people and institutions, and in social change.

Churches tend to be large and affiliated with some larger religious network. Churches tend to be less strict and make fewer demands of their members.

City is an incorporated space with boundaries that have been determined by elected officials and/or resident voters.

Civil religions have beliefs, symbols, and rituals that reinforce the dominant values and social norms such as customs, traditions, morals, and laws.

Class conflict occurs between the owner class and the worker class as they struggle for control over scarce resources.

Class consciousness is the shared awareness of class members of their status and rank within a society, as well as their interests.

Class systems are stratification systems in which an individual's position is not fixed but instead is relatively open, allowing the individual opportunities to move between levels.

Clinical nurse extenders are individuals who are trained and licensed to provide a limited level of nursing care

Collective behavior is behavior that tends to be unorganized, unpredictable, and spontaneous, with little structure or stability.

Concentration effects occur after the middle class and wealthy leave the poor and minorities in the older central cities where older infrastructures are in need of repair, areas of poverty are increasing, and the population and tax base are dwindling.

Conformity may involve going along with peers and/or following societal norms.

Conjugal families are formed and recognized through the mating of a couple.

Consanguine families are formed and recognized through blood ties (birth).

Conspicuous consumption involves the public display and consumption of expensive items.

Control groups are those in which participants are not exposed to the variables.

Control theory is the idea that there are two control systems—inner and outer—that work against our tendencies to deviate.

Conventional morality is Kohlberg's term for people incorporating society's rules and laws into their own value systems and behaving accordingly.

Convergence theory, as it relates to crowds, means that people in crowds share the same attitudes, views and beliefs, and it was because of their similarities that they came together in the first place. As the theory relates to social change, it means that modernization will bring Western and non-Western countries together as they become more technologically equal.

Corporate crimes are the illegal actions of people acting on behalf of the corporation.

Correlation exists when two (or more) variables change together.

Counterculture describes a cultural group whose values and norms are opposed to those of the mainstream and dominant culture.

Crazes are fads that can bring with them serious consequences for those involved.

Credentialism involves providing documents such as diplomas, degrees, and certifications to determine eligibility for jobs.

Criminal justice systems include police, courts, and prisons making up the system that deals with criminal laws and their enforcement.

Crowds are groups of people doing something together for a short period of time.

Crude birth rate is the number of live births in a year per 1,000 people during a given time period in a defined geographical area.

Crude death rate is the total number of deaths per 1,000 people during a given time period in a defined geographical area.

Cults are religious groups that adopt new views rejecting society and other religions.

Cultural goals are the legitimate objectives of members of society.

Cultural imperialism refers to the widespread infusion of a society's culture into the cultures of other societies.

Cultural lag is a discrepancy between material culture and nonmaterial culture that disrupts an individual's way of life.

Cultural relativism refers to people judging another culture by its own standards.

Cultural transmission refers to a process through which one generation passes culture to the next.

Cultural universals refer to the culture traits that people share across cultures.

Culture is used by sociologists to describe the manner in which people make sense of the social world in terms of their meaning and significance. Culture consists of a way of life, patterns of symbolic interaction and systems of values, beliefs and meanings shared in common by a group of people.

Culture diversity refers to a variety of cultural differences within a society and across societies.

Culture shock refers to the disorientation that people feel when they experience an unfamiliar culture.

Cyclical theory argues that societies

move back and forth in a continuous series of cycles.

Decentralized national health care is a system in which the government functions primarily as a regulator.

Deconcentration effects occur when the middle class and affluent move out of the city.

Dehumanization involves depriving others of their humanity.

Deindividuation occurs when a person loses his or her individual identity and effectively "disappears" into a group.

Democratic leadership style is a term for involving workers in the decision-making process.

Demographers are sociologists who investigate population characteristics.

Demography is the study of the characteristics of human populations including the increases and decreases caused by migration, fertility, and mortality.

Dependency theory advocates argue that some countries are poorer and less developed because they are dependent on more developed countries.

Deportation occurs when a group is removed entirely from a country.

Detached observation involves a researcher observing behavior from a distance without actually getting involved with the participants.

Developmental socialization is the process by which people learn to be more competent in their currently assumed roles.

Deviance is a violation of rules or norms.

Differential association is a theory of deviance that believes people will deviate or conform depending on their associations.

Diffusion is the spread of cultural traits from one group or society to another.

Direct pay model is a system wherein individuals are legally responsible for paying all of their own health care costs.

Discovery is the process of knowing and recognizing something previously in existence.

Discrimination is differential treatment of people based on their group membership.

Divergence theory contends that with modernization comes a greater and growing divide between Western and non-Western societies.

Diversity is the existence of differences.

Dramaturgical analysis is the perspective of social interaction that compares everyday life to a theatrical performance.

Ecological footprint is a measure of how much land is necessary to support the utilization of the three functions of the environment (resource depot, waste repository, and living space) for a specified geographic region.

Economic restructuring is the movement of the economy away from a manufacturing base to a service base that includes banking and financial services, shopping centers, restaurants, and tourism.

Education is an organized system that imparts knowledge, values, and skills to the next generation.

Ego is Freud's term for the part of the personality that deals with the real world on the basis of reason and helps to integrate the demands of both the *id* and the *superego*.

Emergent norm theory asserts that crowds tend to approach unanimity because one set of behavioral norms is accepted by the entire crowd.

Emigrants are individuals leaving their home countries to live in another country.

Emotional labor requires workers to manipulate their feelings in order to serve bureaucratic goals.

Enclosure is the process by which the powerful and rich people fence (enclose) their land in order to exclude others.

Endogamy involves marrying someone from within one's social and economic group.

Environmental injustice occurs when a social group (race, ethnicity, gender, age, etc.) is burdened with an environmental hazard.

Equilibrium theory views society as made up of many interdependent parts, which all serve a function and are in balance with one another. Change in one part leads to change in other parts.

Ethnic groups are categories of people with shared cultural heritages that others regard as distinct.

Ethnicity is a cultural definition, referring to learned behavior, and is thus due to nurture.

Ethnocentrism refers to a tendency to judge another culture based on the standards of one's own culture.

Evolutionary theory claims that societies evolve gradually over time from simple to more complex forms.

Existentialist perspective asserts that individuals are responsible for their own health care issues.

Exogamy involves marrying someone from a different region, or other social and economic categories.

Experimental groups are those exposed to the independent variables, such as participation in a program or receiving a medication.

Experiments are controlled environments in which variables can be closely managed.

Expulsion is the forced resettlement of a group of people.

Extended family includes two parents and their children, as well as other blood relatives such as aunts, uncles, and grandparents.

Face work describes when we make an effort to give our best possible performance to avoid "losing face."

Face-saving behavior refers to techniques that people use to salvage their performance when they encounter a potential or actual loss of face.

Fads are temporary infatuations with a particular practice or innovation.

False consciousness is used to mean an attitude held by some employees that does not reflect their objective position.

Family is a group of two or more people who reside together and who are related by birth, marriage, or adoption for purposes of the U.S. Census.

Family of orientation is the family a person grows up in, including parents and siblings.

Family of procreation is a family made up of a person's spouse and children.

Fashions are brief followings for a particular innovation by a large number of people.

Folkways refer to everyday customs that may be violated without formal sanctions within a society.

Front stage is the place where a person plays a specific role in front of an audience.

Frustration theory claims that those people who get involved in social movements are themselves frustrated or disturbed.

Gender refers to what people in a society consider to be either feminine or masculine.

Gender roles are expectations regarding proper behavior, attitudes, and activities for males and females.

Gender typing refers to acquiring behavior that is considered appropriate for one's particular gender.

Genderlects are the linguistic styles that reflect the different worlds of women and men.

General fertility rates measure the number of live births divided by the female population aged 15 to 44 years (childbearing years), times 1,000.

Generalized others are people that are not necessarily close to a child but still help influence the child's internalization of societal values.

Genocide is the deliberate and systematic extermination of all members of a particular minority group.

Global perspective studies the impact our society has on other nations, and also the impact of other nations upon our society.

Global warming is a gradual increase in the earth's average temperature.

Globalization is the international spread of cultural items, practices, and ideas that were once local.

Glocalization describes when globalized items, practices, and ideas are tailored to meet local needs.

Gossip involves talk about the personal and private lives of others.

Grobalization is the desire of corporations to accommodate local needs in order to fuel their own expansion.

Groups are collections of people characterized by more than two people, frequent interaction, a sense of belong-ingness, and interdependence.

Groupthink occurs when individuals value a group enough to accept group decisions against their own better judgment.

Hate crimes are criminal acts against a person or a person's property by an offender who is motivated by racial or other biases.

Hawthorne effect describes a phenomenon in which people modify their behavior because they know they are being monitored.

Heterogamy means choosing to marry someone who is different from one's self.

Hidden curriculum is one that covers unwritten rules of behavior and attitudes such as conformity to norms and obedience to authority.

High culture refers to cultural patterns that appeal to the upper class or elite of a society.

Homogamy involves people falling in love with, and marrying, someone similar to themselves.

Homogeneity is the existence of sameness.

Horizontal mobility is the movement from one social position to another of the same rank and/or prestige.

Horticultural societies use hand tools to raise crops in order to acquire food.

Household includes all the people who occupy a housing unit as their usual place of residence.

Human migration is the more or less permanent movement of individuals or groups across symbolic or political boundaries into new residential areas and communities.

Hunting and gathering societies use simple subsistence technology to hunt animals and gather vegetation.

Hypotheses are tentative statements about how different variables are expected to relate to each other.

Id is Freud's term for the part of the personality that is totally unconscious and consists of biological drives.

Ideal culture refers to the rules of expected behavior that people should follow.

Idealist philosophy contrasts and opposes materialist philosophy in that ideas and systems of ideas are said to be the basis of the social world rather than what goes on in and around the operation of the economy.

Ideational culture focuses on religions and spiritualism, believing that these are essential ingredients to understanding knowledge. This view encourages people to be spiritually active.

Ideology is a concept used to describe systems of ideas, norms and core beliefs which together represent the ideals of those who propagate the ideology along with ideas that sustain it.

Idiosyncrasy credits are permissions granted by a group that allow high-standing members to act in a nonconforming manner, thus allowing them to break group norms.

Illegitimate opportunity structures are relative opportunity structures outside laws and social norms that frame a person's life.

Immigrants are people who have just arrived in their new country.

Impression management refers to our efforts to present favorable images to the people around us.

Inclusive communication refers to an exchange where all parties are entitled to respect and the opportunity to express themselves.

Individual discrimination occurs when a person treats another unfairly, and the unfair treatment is due to the person's minority group status.

Individual mobility is the result of hard work and perseverance by an individual.

Industrial societies are based on technology that mechanizes production to provide goods and services.

Infant mortality rate is the number of deaths within the first year of life, divided by the number of live births in the same year, times 1000.

Informal organizational structure includes any group—not formally planned—that forms within an organization and develops through personal relationships and interactions among its members.

In-groups are those in which an individual is a valued member.

Institutional behavior is highly predictable and well-organized.

Institutional discrimination occurs when society and its social institutions operate in a manner that ensures some groups will be given preferential treatment over others.

Institutional means include approved ways of reaching cultural goals.

Institutions represent the established and organized practices of a given society. Once they exist they can exercise a profound influence on the form and direction of history and the lives of individuals and social groups.

Intelligence is the capacity for mental or intellectual achievement.

Intergenerational mobility describes changes in the social positions of children in comparison to their parents.

Internal colonialism occurs when the dominant group within a society uses minorities for their own economic benefit.

Intersection theory refers to the interplay of race, class, and gender, often resulting in multiple dimensions of disadvantages for the female who is of a different race.

Intragenerational mobility relates to changes in social position over the course of person's lifetime.

Invention is the process of reshaping existing cultural traits into new forms.

Jim Crow laws covered proscribed behaviors that were intended to keep blacks "in their place."

Labeling theory is the idea that the labels people are given affect their own and others' perceptions of them, and, therefore, channel behavior either into or away from conformity.

Laissez-faire leadership style involves leaving workers to function on their own.

Language refers to an organized system of symbols that people use to think and to communicate with each other.

Latent functions are consequences of a social situation that are neither intended nor expected, and are often unrecognized.

Laws refer to formal norms that are enacted by governments and enforced by formal sanctions.

Legal discrimination is unequal treatment that is upheld by law.

Legitimacy involves a sense of trust and approval between those with and without authority. It provides the foundation for the durable and stable operation of political and economic institutions.

Life expectancy is the number of years that a person can expect to live within a given society, or as the number of further years of life a person can expect at a given age.

Looking-glass self is Cooley's theory that we are influenced by our perception of what others think of us and develop our self-image on that basis.

Manifest functions are the intended and expected consequences of a social situation.

Marginal working class includes the most desperate members of the working class who have few skills and little job security. They are often unemployed.

Marriage rate is the number of marriages per 1,000 people in a given time period.

Mass hysteria is similar to panic, except that in panic the danger is real, while in mass hysteria the danger is absent and participants engage in the frenzied behavior without checking to see if the alleged source of their fear is real or not.

Master status is a status that determines a person's overall social position and identity.

Material culture refers to physical or tangible creations that members of a society make and use.

Materialism occurs when people are able to satisfy their basic needs and have money left over to spend on ostentatious goods and services.

Materialist philosophy describes the claim made by Marxists that the economy and the social relations involved in operating the economy represent the key to understanding the social world, especially its inner workings, which it is claimed are largely hidden to so many.

Matriarchy means that the mothers rule and are in charge of the family.

Matrilineal descent traces the descent through the mother's line.

Matrilocal residence means that when

couples marry, they live with the wife's family.

Measurement is the systematic process of assigning values or labels to concepts for research purposes.

Mechanical solidarity is a form of social cohesion in which people do similar work and share the same values and beliefs.

Medical perspective focuses on the medical framework that attempts to examine pathogens that result in disease and illness.

Medicalization of deviance means to relate deviance to an underlying illness that needs to be treated by physicians.

Metroplexes are areas where entire regions are virtually urbanized.

Micromanagement is the unrelenting managerial control of even the smallest tasks.

Minority groups are people who are singled out for unequal treatment and who regard themselves as objects of collective discrimination.

Mobs are groups of people who are angry and channel their anger onto a single target.

Modernization is the transformation of a society from being agricultural to industrial.

Modernization theory advocates argue that societies started as simple and traditional, then moved, or are moving toward, being modern (developed) societies.

Monogamy allows a person only one mate.

Monotheism is a belief in only one god.

Mores refer to strongly held, formally enforced norms with moral overtones.

Multiculturalism refers to the coex-

istence and equal standing of diverse cultures within a society.

Multigenerational family households consist of more than two generations living together as a family.

Nationalism is a form of normative culture experienced by people in modern territorially bounded nation states. Nationalism, or a deep-seated belief in one's nation, involves shared beliefs, values and sentiments along with social processes for creating, maintaining and transforming itself.

Neo-colonialism is the indirect continuation of colonialism through economic means.

Neolocal means that young couples leave their mother and father's residence and go out and find one of their own.

Nonfamily household is a census term used to describe people living together who are not related to the householder by birth, marriage, or adoption.

Nonmaterial culture refers to abstract or intangible things that influence our behavior.

Nonrenewable resources are those resources that cannot be regenerated in a timely manner or that are permanently depleted.

Nonverbal interaction is the exchange of information among people without the use of speech.

Norms refer to established rules of expected behavior that develop out of society or group values.

Nuclear families are composed of two adults and their children, if they have any.

Opinion leaders are those individuals whose opinions and viewpoints are accepted by others in a community.

Organic solidarity is a form of social cohesion in which people work in a wide variety of specialized occupations, and thus gain their social consensus from their need to rely on one another for goods and services.

Out-groups are those in which an individual is not a member, but is, instead, an outsider.

Overpopulation is the population by a particular species in excess of the environment's carrying capacity.

Panic is a flight to safety in response to the fear of immediate danger.

Participant observation allows a researcher to observe a group's behavior from within the group itself.

Pastoral societies use technology that supports the domestication of animals in order to acquire food.

Patriarchal society is one in which men are dominant and social institutions are set up to sustain a system of male rule.

Patriarchy means rule by the father, and he is in charge of the household.

Patrilineal descent traces the descent through the father's line.

Patrilocal residence means that a married couple lives with the father's family.

Peer group includes a person's same-aged friends with similar interests and social positions.

Personal space is the private area surrounding a person.

Personality refers to a person's patterns of thoughts, feelings, and self-concepts that make him or her distinctive from others.

Physician extenders are secondary health care providers who can provide basic physical diagnosis and care.

Pluralism allows minorities to maintain

their cultural distinctiveness by respecting it and, at the same time, allowing their members to participate fully in the dominant group's social institutions.

Politeness theory is the idea that communicators change and adapt their messages to protect and save the "face" of their listeners.

Political party is a modern social grouping unlike either a social class or status group in that it is organized specifically to pursue political ends and the exercise of power.

Polyandry allows a woman to have more than one husband at a time.

Polygamy allows marriage of one person to two or more others of the opposite sex.

Polygyny allows a man to have more than one wife at a time.

Polytheism is a belief in more than one god.

Popular culture refers to widespread cultural patterns that appeal primarily to the middle and working classes.

Populations are entire groups of people to be studied.

Post-conventional morality is the highest level of morality available, according to Kohlberg. At this level, people use broad ethical principles to guide their behavior, such as showing respect for human dignity, equality, and, of late, respect for one's environment—even for the rights of animals and other living creatures.

Post-industrial (postmodern) societies are based on computer technology that produces information and supports service industries.

Power determines who gets the best of a society's resources, who gives orders, and who obeys orders. It can also refer to the capacity or ability of a person, group or institution to control, manipu-

late, influence or shape the views and actions of others.

Power elite is a term used to describe a small group of high-ranking leaders from government, corporations, and the military.

Pre-conventional morality is Kohlberg's term for abiding by the law chiefly to avoid punishment or to gain some benefit.

Prejudice is a feeling, favorable or unfavorable, that one has about a person or group of people and is not based on actual experience.

Primary care providers are physicians who can practice medicine in "all of its branches."

Primary deviance is the first occurrence of a violation of a norm which the committing actor does not view as deviant. Thus, it would have little to no effect on a person's self-concept.

Primary groups are organized around togetherness and are assumed to be long-lasting.

Primary socialization is the period during which children learn language and basic behavioral patterns that form the foundation for later learning.

Principle of immanent change states that all social change is a result of social forces operating within the society.

Propaganda refers to the methods used to influence public opinion.

Public refers to a group that shares the same common interest, positions, or thoughts.

Public opinion is composed of the attitudes and beliefs held by the public.

Qualitative data measures intangibles like people's feelings and can include focus group results, interviews, and observations.

Quantitative data is data that can be measured in numbers.

Race refers to people who share physical characteristics that are genetically transferred.

Racial profiling is a law enforcement practice that targets racial minorities.

Racism is a set of beliefs justifying the unfair treatment of a minority group and its members based on race.

Random samples are those in which each person who is part of the population has an equal opportunity to be selected for participation in a study.

Rational organization describes the underlying new forms of authority based on calculability, measurement and mean-ends orientation characteristic of modern bureaucratic organization.

Rationalization of life is a phrase developed by Weber to describe modern life as being characterized and subject to professionalism and common forms of rational assessment and means-ends calculability.

Real culture refers to the values that people actually have.

Recidivism rates represent the number of people rearrested for committing the same types of crimes.

Redlining is the practice of denying or limiting financial services to specific neighborhoods due to the minority group status of the residents.

Reference groups include any group that an individual admires enough to use as a standard for his or her identity.

Relative poverty is the feeling or belief that you are poor when you compare yourself with other people.

Reliability refers to consistency, or receiving the same results every time the same study is conducted.

Renewable resources are those resources that can be regenerated, like food and trees.

Resocialization is the process by which people must leave behind their old selves and develop new ones.

Resource mobilization refers to a model of politics and political process characterized by the following elements: (1) interests; (2) organization; (3) mobilization; and (4) opportunity.

Resource mobilization theory contends that social movements are initiated only when the organizers have the necessary resources. Without these tools, the movement will not exist.

Riots are violent crowds that move from target to target over the course of several hours or days.

Rituals are the regular and periodic occasions or situations in which people gather to celebrate themselves as a common collective.

Role conflict refers to conflicting demands connected to two or more statuses.

Role exit is the process by which people disengage from a role.

Roles are socially defined expectations associated with a given status.

Role set refers to a number of roles attached to a single status.

Role strain refers to conflicting demands connected to a single status.

Routinization is the reduction of innovation into bureaucratic routine.

Rumors are unverified stories that spread from one person to another through a variety of sources such as word of mouth and the Internet.

Samples are smaller groups of individuals selected from larger populations.

Sanctions refer to rewards for normal behaviors and penalties for abnormal behaviors.

Scapegoating is discriminating against others through assigning them blame for their shortcomings.

Secondary deviance is a response to primary deviance by which a person repeatedly violates a norm and begins to take on a deviant identity.

Secondary groups are organized around a task and assumed to be short-term.

Secondary socialization takes place later in childhood and into maturity. In this phase, other agents of socialization take over some of the responsibility from family.

Sects are much smaller religious groups, usually offshoots of a larger, more mainstream religion, that make a number of demands on their members.

Segregation is the physical separation of groups of people from each other.

Self-efficacy is a person's confidence that he or she can accomplish what is desired and manage what is necessary.

Sensate culture sees science and empirical evidence as the source of knowledge. This view encourages people to engage in lifestyles that focus on being practical, materialistic, and hedonistic.

Serial monogamy involves cycles of divorce and remarriage allowing people to marry multiple partners, but only one at a time.

Sex refers to the biological feature of sexual identity that each of us plays, such as in reproduction.

Sexism refers to the belief that one sex is innately superior to the other.

Sex ratios are the number of males per 1000 females in the population of the society.

Shamanism is the belief that certain individuals have special skills to influence spirits.

Sick roles are those that involve a variety of social norms specifying the responsibilities, expectations, and rights of someone who is ill.

Significant others are those people who are the closest to, and have the strongest influence on, a child, and whose approval and affection they desire most.

Social aggregates include people who share a space and purpose but do not interact.

Social capital refers to the collective value of all "social networks" (who people know) and the inclinations that arise from these networks to do things for each other ("norms of reciprocity").

Social categories have members that share similar traits, but do not interact or know one another.

Social class is made up of people in relatively similar situations with roughly the same power, income, and prestige.

Social conflict perspective views society as a compound filled with inequalities in regard to the allocation of resources.

Social consensus occurs when nearly all members of a society want to achieve the same goals and work cooperatively to achieve them.

Social contagion is the spreading of certain emotions or actions from one member of a crowd to others.

Social contagion theory claims that crowds are in agreement in both thought and action; in this sense, they all share the same collective mind.

Social control involves techniques and strategies for maintaining order and preventing deviant behavior in a society.

Social facts are the collective or shared ways of thinking, feeling and acting and which sociologists claim operate beyond the psychology of the individual and the biological principles of humans as a species.

Social groups involve two or more people who have a shared a sense of identity and shared interaction.

Social institutions are established ways that society organizes to meet basic needs.

Social interaction involves reciprocal communication between two or more people through symbols, words, and body language.

Social mobility is the movement from one social position to another.

Social movements are collective efforts designed to bring about some social change.

Social networks involve the social ties and bonds between people and the organized relationships that link individuals to one another.

Social order includes social arrangements upon which members depend.

Social rituals are sets of behaviors that symbolize a relationship.

Social stratification is the ranking of people within a society.

Social structure refers to the social relationships that exist within society.

Socialist medicine involves a system of health care that is under the complete control of the government.

Socialization is the process whereby we internalize our culture's values, beliefs, and norms. Through this experience, we become functioning members of our society.

Socialized medicine is composed of health care systems over which the government exercises some, but not total, control.

Societies are diverse groups of people who share distinctive cultures in defined geographic locations.

Society is used by sociologists to describe patterns of interacting people.

Sociocultural perspective views health issues as not merely the responsibility of each individual, but also of their family members and sometimes even their community.

Sociological imagination is the process of achieving a better understanding of our own experiences. We do this by discovering our place within society, including our experiences with social institutions and the historical period in which we live.

Sociological paradigms provide frameworks that allow us to study society and analyze data and research using sociological tools, methods, and theories.

Sociological perspective focuses on societal frameworks at a macro- and micro-sociological level, utilizing sociological research and concepts to identify health care issues.

Sociological perspective involves being able to see the general in the particular.

Sociology is the scientific study of human society and social interaction.

Spurious correlation occurs when two variables change together, not because of a causal relationship between the two, but because of a third variable. This result reminds us that "correlation does not imply causation."

Standard mortality ratio is a measure indicating the actual or observed number of deaths in the group of interest, divided by the expected number of deaths, then multiplied by 100.

Status is recognition given to a person or group.

Status inconsistency occurs when a person is given conflicting statuses.

Status set refers to all the statuses that a person occupies at a given time.

Status systems rank people based on their social prestige.

Stereotypes are rigid mental images held to be true about a group of people.

Stigmas discredit a person's claim to a normal identity.

Strain theory is an idea developed by Robert Merton to describe the great strain felt by some members of society when they do not have access to the institutional means to achieve cultural goals.

Stratification is the ranking of people in a society according to the amount of wealth they own, the prestige the society gives to their social positions, and the power they have to control other members of the society.

Stratified sampling makes sure that the people randomly selected to be in the sample match the proportions of the population being studied.

Street crimes include mugging, rape, and burglary.

Structural-functionalism views society as an intricate structure, with many different levels or parts all working together in collaboration for stability.

Structured mobility involves societal events that allow entire groups of people to move up or down the social structure together.

Subculture refers to distinctive lifestyles and values shared by a category of people within a larger society.

Subordinates are individuals or groups with less or little power in a coercive interaction.

Superego is Freud's term for the part of the personality that acts as the "executive branch" because it uses reason and it deals with whether something is right or wrong.

Superordinate goals involve people or groups working together to achieve a goal that is deemed important to everyone involved. The people tend to become friends and their attitudes, values, and goals will become similar, even if those involved originally disliked one another.

Superordinates are individuals or groups with more social power in a coercive interaction.

Sustainability is the ability of the earth's various systems, including human cultural systems and economies, to survive and adapt to changing environmental conditions indefinitely.

Symbol refers to anything that carries a meaning and represents something else.

Symbolic interactionism contends that society exists due to the everyday interactions of people.

Taboos refer to strongly held mores, the violation of which is considered to be extremely offensive.

Techniques of neutralization are ways of thinking or rationalizing that help people deflect society's norms.

Theories are integrated sets of propositions that are intended to explain specific phenomena and to show relationships between variables in order to gain understanding.

Total institutions are places where people are cut off from the larger society and forced to follow a strict set of rules.

Totemism is the worship of plants and animals or other natural objects as gods and ancestors.

Tracking is the sorting of students into different educational programs based on their past performance.

Underpopulation is the lack of normal or desirable population density for economic viability.

Urbanism is the unique form of urban life and culture.

Urbanization is the process by which a city develops.

Urbanized areas, according to the U.S. Census Bureau, are spaces where more than 50,000 persons reside with an average of 1,000 people per square mile.

Urbanologists are sociologists and other researchers who study cities.

Validity means that indicators used in research, like rating scales, accurately measure the concepts they are intended to measure.

Value contradictions refer to values that conflict with each other, either within a culture or across cultures.

Values refer to collective ideas about what is right or wrong, good or bad, desirable or undesirable in a particular culture.

Variables are attributes that may change their values under observation. Variables can be assigned numerical scores or category labels.

Vertical mobility is the movement from one social position to another of a different rank and/or prestige. This change can be in an upward or downward direction.

White-collar crimes include illegal acts committed by affluent and/or respectable individuals in the course of business activities.

Work spillover refers to the effect that work has on individuals and families, absorbing their time and energy and impinging on their psychological states.

Photo Credits

Chapter 1 p. 10 " Beach crowd" Source Andre Monteiro

Chapter 2 p. 32 "Statue" Source Lukas Patkan

Chapter 3 p. 68 "Kids playing" Source Anissa Thompson

Chapter 4 p. 94 "Stage" Source Morgue File

Chapter 5 p. 124 "Marching band" Source T.A.

Chapter 6 p. 158 "Graffiti" Source Elena Gorgievska

Chapter 7 p. 182 "Street" Source Simon Pintar

Chapter 8 p. 212 "Race" Source Dominic Morel

Chapter 9 p. 242 "Gender and age" Source Photo Rack

Chapter 10 p. 256 "Family" Source Benjamin Earwicker

Chapter 11 p. 274 "School bus and church" Source Sam LeVan and Yarik Mission

Chapter 12 p. 294 "Money" Source Jorge Vicente

Chapter 13 p. 332 "Health care" Source Andrew Richards

Chapter 14 p. 360 "Urban environment" Source Photo Rack

Chapter 15 p. 390 "Baseball" Source Aaron Schwab

Name Index

Subject Index

Canada 34, 59, 189, 200, 257, 336, 343, 344, 345, 348
cancer 79, 87, 98, 126, 369, 376, 382
capital class 166
capitalism 20, 60, 102, 113, 289, 295, 296, 298, 300-306, 308, 311, 318, 323, 325
capital punishment 174
carbon dioxide 349, 375, 384, 385
carbon footprint 334, 345, 347, 348
Caribbean 58, 111
castes 185, 187, 188, 285
Catholic Church 279
Catholicism 18
Caucasian 19, 24, 165, 213, 384
cellphone 25, 26, 42, 61, 84, 89, 378, 399
Central America 186, 227, 343
central city 363-367
Chad 248
charismatic personalities 307
Cherokee 221, 233
Chicago 15, 21, 364-367, 372
Chicago School 21, 102, 363, 367
Chickasaw 233
children 17, 18, 21, 25-27, 35, 39-41, 43, 44, 46, 52-54, 60, 70-72, 74-85, 87, 98, 99, 112, 118, 129-131, 138, 167, 185, 186, 191, 193, 194, 198, 200, 214, 218, 224, 231, 236, 237, 244, 245, 247-249, 251, 257-259, 261, 263-268, 276-281, 287, 288, 296, 314, 315, 346, 351-354, 361, 382, 398
China 38, 45, 48, 51, 58, 101, 140, 201, 215, 216, 219, 231, 276, 287, 313, 322, 347, 351, 352, 354, 377, 382, 397, 399
Chinatown 43, 54, 224, 372
Chinese Exclusion Act 215, 216, 231
Choctaw 233
Christianity 38, 46, 129, 282, 287
Chrysler 196
church 40, 78, 86, 87, 99, 266, 267, 275, 279, 280, 282, 289, 309, 320
citizenship 228, 231, 234, 317, 323, 325
city 14, 17, 34, 49, 142, 166, 195, 286, 310, 347, 362-372, 375-377, 393
civil law 50, 315
civil religions 288, 319, 320
Civil Rights Act of 1964. 97, 229
civil rights movement 60, 173
civil society 298, 314, 315, 317-321

class conflict 20, 166, 308
class consciousness 204, 302, 303
class system 185, 188, 204, 205
class-for-itself 301, 303
Clean Air Act of 1970. 381
Clean Water Act of 1972. 381
clinical nurse extenders 339
clothing 14, 44, 45, 58, 117, 259, 378, 395
Coca-Cola 43, 58, 144
Code of the Street: Decency, Violence and the Moral Life of the Inner City 370
coercion 102, 112, 114, 296, 312
cohabitation 265
collective behavior 391, 392, 397
college 12
Colorado Rockies 372
Columbine High School 167
communication 12, 40, 51, 54, 58, 59, 84, 97, 100, 101, 103, 106, 108, 109, 111, 114-118, 303, 305, 322, 324, 392, 394
communist party 173, 304
community education centers 83
Community of the Lady of All Nations 282
community outreach 16
Community Reinvestment Act 1977. 217
competition 54, 55, 97, 102, 112-114, 130, 144, 196, 276, 278, 308, 319, 336, 375, 381
concentration effects 366
concentric zone model 367
concrete operational stage 67, 77
conflict theorists 19, 20, 22, 60, 166, 173, 203-205, 218, 219, 230, 289, 317
conflict theory 60, 100, 102, 166, 218, 219, 278, 289, 334, 353
conformity 49, 50, 55, 81, 83, 127, 128, 131, 132, 134-136, 139, 161, 164, 165, 167, 173, 219, 224, 278, 394
conjugal families 258
Connecticut 54, 133
consanguine families 258
conservatives 251, 301
conspicuous consumption 184, 378
conspicuous waste 378
consumer 42, 140, 143, 144, 146, 260, 345, 375, 384
contact comfort 72
containment theory 165
content analysis 27

continuity theory 86
control group 26
control theory 165, 166
conventional morality 79
convergence theory 395, 399
cookie-cutter housing 365
cooperation 51, 96, 101, 112, 113, 126, 189, 259, 321
corporate crimes 171
correlation 25, 115, 335
Council on Foreign Relations 189
counterculture 55
covenant marriage 267
crazes 395, 396
credentialism 276, 334
credit card 172
Creek 233
crime 14, 15, 17, 50, 83, 125, 126, 128, 131, 159, 162, 163, 165, 166, 170-174, 186, 191, 204, 218, 230, 231
criminal justice system 166, 173, 230
criminal law 50, 204, 287
critical sociological research 22
crowds 132, 393-395
crude birthrate 343
crude death rate 343
Cuba 225, 227, 336, 337, 397
Cuban Adjustment Act 227
Cuban Revolution 227, 397
cult 282
cultural change 58, 59
cultural goals 164, 165
cultural imperialism 58
cultural lag 58
cultural relativism 55, 56
cultural transmission 52
cultural universals 60
culture 12, 20, 21 33, 34, 43-61, 70, 78, 80-82, 85, 87, 89, 96, 97, 102, 104, 106, 109-112, 115, 118, 144, 146, 160, 161, 163, 173, 214, 215, 222-224, 227, 234, 244, 248, 251, 266, 275-289, 297, 298, 300, 308, 316, 319, 320, 369-372, 378, 399, 400
culture shock 43, 58
customs 38, 43, 44, 46, 47, 49, 54, 56, 107, 113, 215, 263, 268, 288, 310
cyclical theory 399

D

Dalit 188
Dallas 364, 367
day care 82, 139, 277, 278

death certificates 27
death penalty 49, 174
decentralized national health care 336, 337
deconcentration effects 366
Defense of Marriage Act 170
dehumanization 132-134
deindividuation 132, 134
delinquency 83, 220
delinquent behavior 15, 220
democracy 41, 48, 60, 295, 296, 298, 305, 309, 313, 316-323, 398
democratic leadership style 145
democrats 159, 301
demographers 342-344, 354
demography 342, 354
Denver 368, 372
dependency theory 202
deportation 220, 221
detached observation 27
Detroit 196
developmental socialization 85
deviance 159-170, 173, 174, 315
deviant behavior 159, 160, 162, 163, 165-169, 174, 281
dialect 115-117
differential association 167
diffusion 39, 56-59, 382
Digital Island 396
direct pay model 336, 337
disability 86, 97, 98, 115, 175
discovery 59, 71, 160
discrimination 47, 80, 97, 138, 188, 214, 216-222, 229, 231, 232, 235, 236, 250, 251, 266, 278, 288, 398
disengagement theory 86
Disney 43
divergence theory 399
diverse people 16, 53, 54
diversity 33, 47, 52-54, 56-58, 60, 105, 110, 112, 116, 135, 136, 138, 144, 170, 224, 266, 278, 318, 325, 363, 372
divorce 27, 35, 98, 99, 136, 262, 267, 283, 299, 305, 354
DNA 162, 174
doctor of Oriental medicine 340
domestic violence 240
domestication revolution 36
dominat groups 19, 215, 223
do-not-resuscitate order (DNR) 89
dramaturgical analysis 106
dramaturgy 106
drives 44, 73-75, 77, 349
dropout rate 280, 281

drug abuse 131, 168
drug use 163
dysfunction 17, 55, 56, 334, 340, 341, 351, 352

E

Eastern Europe 201, 215, 229, 302, 322, 324
eating disorders 335
ecological footprint 376, 377
economic determinism 184, 306
economic exploitation 202, 301
economic restructuring 366
economic sociology 295-298
economic unit 35, 259
economics 15, 16, 19, 82, 100, 296, 298, 303, 304, 306-308, 367, 381
economy 35, 37-40, 42, 85, 164, 189-191, 200-202, 219, 222, 228, 232, 235, 252, 296, 298-303, 307-309, 311, 313, 315, 317, 319, 325, 336, 337, 345-347, 349, 362, 366-368, 377, 380, 381
edge cities 366, 367
Edge City: Life on the New Frontier 366
education 12, 14, 17, 19, 23-25, 35, 37-42, 46, 48, 50, 56-58, 71, 77, 79, 82, 83, 85, 88, 96-100, 115, 116, 118, 137-139, 141, 164, 171, 189, 191, 192, 195-200, 202, 217, 227, 235-237, 244, 246, 248, 249, 252, 259, 261, 263, 266, 267, 275-281, 300, 314, 315, 319, 325, 335, 338, 342, 345, 349, 353
egalitarianism 185
ego 74, 78, 106
Egypt 38, 221, 320
eight-fold path 286
Emancipation Proclamation 228
Emergency Quota Act 215
emergent norm theory 395
emigrants 227
emotion 108, 109, 140, 142, 264
emotional labor 147
empirical data 15, 22
employment 14, 40, 50, 88, 97, 129, 138, 146, 199, 200, 202, 229, 235, 250, 278, 340, 345, 350, 366, 398
empty nest 261, 265
enclosure 186
Endo v. U.S. 232
endogamy 261

England 14, 40, 53, 71, 186, 189, 215, 221, 277, 303, 304, 313, 323-325, 362, 392
English 51, 52, 54, 55, 58, 108, 115, 189, 214, 215, 220, 224, 227, 324
English as a second language programs (ESL) 227
Enron Corporation 171, 172
environmental injustice 382
Environmental Protection Agency (EPA) 384
Equal Employment Opportunity Commission 97
equality 47, 48, 57, 79, 110, 140, 205, 229, 298, 309, 317-320
equilibrium theory 400
estate system 186
ethics 28, 128, 283, 287, 353
ethnic ghettos 224
ethnic group 29, 55, 214
ethnicity 15, 34, 53, 56, 96, 97, 105, 115, 160, 175, 198, 200, 213, 214, 224, 251, 252, 259, 266, 308, 370, 371, 382
ethnocentrism 47, 55-58, 102
ethnographies 369
European 48, 53, 118, 199, 202, 215, 216, 220, 224, 226, 229, 232, 266, 302, 317, 318, 322, 346
European Union 189
euthanasia 353
Evanston 365
evolution 34, 71, 298, 314, 342, 399
evolutionary theory 399
exchange 39, 101, 112, 114, 141
existentialist perspective 334
exogamy 261
experiment 26
experimental group 26
expulsion 220, 221
extended family 127, 258, 369
eye contact 108-111, 117, 133

F

face work 106
Facebook 59
face-saving behavior 106
facial expressions 108-110, 117
factories 14, 19, 40, 229, 244, 303, 362, 366, 368, 375, 377, 382-384, 401
fads 395, 396
false consciousness 204, 301
family 82, 83
family of orientation 259, 263

family of procreation 259
farmers 14, 38, 39, 116, 143, 195, 201,
    204, 234, 345, 379, 401
fashions 378, 395
Federal Housing Authority (FHA) 365
feminist theory 166, 172
fertility rates 263, 343, 344, 346, 347
feudalism 185, 186
first world countries 13, 200, 201
FISH! 147
five stages of dying 87
Florida Marlins 372
folkways 49, 50
food redlining 217
Ford 196
formal norms 49, 50
formal operational stage 77
formation of cities 14
four noble truths 286, 287
France 14, 17, 304, 313, 314, 317, 323,
    324, 346, 347, 362
Frankfurt School 305
freedom of speech 47, 318
friends 83, 86, 100, 113, 128, 136, 167,
    251, 369
front stage 107, 108
frustration theory 398
functional illiteracy 281

G

game stage 74
Garbage Pail Kids 396
gatekeeping 277
gays 169, 395
gemeinschaft 369
gender 52, 80, 81, 118, 172, 200, 243,
    244, 248, 249
gender conflict 19
gender inequality 38, 39, 118, 249
genderlect 117
gender role 80, 83, 244
gender stereotypes 81
gender typing 80
General Allotment Act of 1887. 222
general fertility rate 343
General Motors 196
generalized others 74
generation X 54, 105
generation Y 53, 54
genital stage 75
genocide 41, 50, 220
genotype 214
Germany 13, 14, 112, 131, 145, 200,
    216, 221, 226, 304, 305, 311,
    314, 322, 324, 337, 346, 347,

362
gerontology 87
gesellschaft 369
gestures 111
Ghana 111, 183, 184, 186, 197, 198,
    202, 203
global climate change 375, 376, 381,
    384, 385
globalization 144, 145
global perspective 12, 14, 345
global stratification 200, 202
global village 42, 381
global warming 349, 374, 376, 384,
    385, 397
glocalization 144, 145
god 38, 49, 87, 188, 282-284, 287-289
Google 43
gossip 49, 50, 396
goth 395
grade inflation 280, 281
greenhouse effect 384
greenhouse gases 348, 384, 385
grobalization 149
groups 12, 14, 26, 34, 36, 53, 56, 57,
    83, 89, 96, 100, 112, 126-130,
    134, 135, 224-235
groupthink 134
Guam 348
Guinea 248, 391

H

Hare Krishna 398
Harlem 165, 227
Harry Potter 60
Harvard University's Kennedy School
    of Government 322
hate crime 175
Hawthorne effect 27
hazardous waste 384
health care 335-337, 340
health responsibility model 334
Heaven's Gate 282
heterogamy 261
heterogeneity 363
heterosexuals 19, 266
hidden curriculum 83, 278
hierarchy of needs theory 77
high culture 57
Hillsborough soccer stadium 392
Hindu 187, 188, 275, 284, 289
Hip Hop 58, 84
hippies 55
Hispanic 24, 96, 104, 106, 195, 236,
    252, 266, 347, 371, 372
HIV 334, 335, 337, 345, 346, 349

Hmong 231
Holocaust 131, 132, 220
homeostasis 340, 351
homogamy 261
homogeneity 135, 136, 138, 139
homosexuals 19, 71, 159
horizontal mobility 398
hormones 71, 80, 335
horticultural societies 35-39
household 258
Huaxia Chinese School 54
human behavior 11, 15, 16, 95, 104,
    162, 261, 315
human development 70, 74, 75
human ecology 367
human migration 334, 344, 345, 384
human resources 16
hunting and gathering societies 34, 35
Hurricane Katrina 374
Hutus 220
Hyderabad 363
hypothesis 22

I

I.Q. 136
Iceland 248, 348
id 74
ideal culture 48
ideational culture 400
identical twins 71
identity crisis 75
ideology 301
Idiosyncrasy credit 135
illegal aliens 216
illegitimate opportunity structure 165,
    171
immigrants 214
Immigration and Nationality Act 216
Imperialism: The Highest Stage of
    Capitalism 304
impression management 106, 107
incest 50, 259, 268
inclusive communication 114
income 184, 191-193, 245-247
India 51, 145, 187, 188, 201, 219, 231,
    275, 287, 325, 345, 347, 362,
    377, 382
Indian Removal Act of 1830. 233
Indian reservations 224
Indian Self-Determination and
    Educational Assistance Act 235
individual discrimination 216
individual mobility 196
Individualism 47
Indonesia 377

Industrial Revolution 14, 39, 40, 140, 244, 276, 318, 362, 377, 385
industrial societies 39-41
infant mortality rate 200-202, 230, 343
Infanticide 35, 37, 344, 352, 353
informal norms 49, 50
informal organizational structure 142
information technology 41, 59, 366
in-groups 129, 130, 131
innovation 164
instinct 44, 46
Institute for Research on Poverty 197
institutional behavior 391
institutional discrimination 217, 222, 231, 235
institutional means 164
institutional sexism 248
institutions 35, 37, 39, 40, 100, 297-301, 315, 316, 368
intelligence 70, 76, 80, 87, 102, 116
intergenerational households 265
intergenerational mobility 198
Intergovernmental Panel on Climate Change 385
internal aliens 228
internal colonialism 220, 222
internalized norm 126, 129
International Red Cross 101
Internet 12, 26, 42, 43, 58, 59, 144, 378, 392, 396, 399
internment centers 221, 232
interpretive sociological research 22
intersection theory 243, 252
interstate highway system 366
intragenerational mobility 198
invention 59
Iowa 280
IPAT model 376, 378
iPods 42, 59, 84, 396
Iran 131, 249, 289
Iraq 41, 111, 130-132, 247, 289, 323
Ireland 216, 346
Italy 116, 131, 221, 321, 362
Ivy League 164

J

Japan 13, 41, 45, 46, 55, 58, 104, 111, 112, 129, 131, 142, 160, 189, 200, 202, 231, 287, 313, 337, 347, 348, 377
Japanese business model 142
Jehovah's Witnesses 398
Jim Crow laws 217, 228
Johnson-Reid Act 216
Judaism 38, 282, 287

K

Kansas City 367
karma 284, 285
kinship 35, 37, 113, 258
Kippah 287
Koreans 111, 201, 231
Kosovo 216
Kshatriya 187, 188
Ku Klux Klan 55, 56, 129, 165, 228, 394, 398
Kuwait 249

L

labeling theory 167, 279
labor 36, 39, 40, 41, 113, 139, 200, 202, 235, 246, 260, 300, 317
laissez-faire leadership style 145
language 51, 52
Laos 48, 287
Laotians 231
latchkey kids 83
latency stage 75
latent functions 17, 277, 288, 352
Latin America 14, 111, 202, 324, 348
Latinos 53, 224-227, 229, 230, 235, 237
laws 50
leftists 252
legal discrimination 217, 221, 231, 232
legal equality 47, 48, 97
legitimacy 297, 305, 310, 323, 324
lesbians 169, 266
liberals 25, 30
libido 75
life expectancy 196, 197, 200-202, 343, 344, 346, 347, 350
Little Italy 224
looking-glass self 72
Lou Gehrig's disease 98
Louisiana 116, 267, 374
Love Canal 376
love match 261
Loving v. Virginia 229
Luxembourg 348

M

macrosociology 33
Maine 116
Major League Baseball 372
Malaysia 34, 201, 231, 377
Mali 248
Malta 346
Mandarin Chinese 51, 54
manifest functions 17, 276, 287, 340, 351
Manila 363
Manu laws 285
Manufacturing Belt 363
Mardi Gras 394
marginal working class 166
Mariel boatlift 227
marijuana 83, 163, 174
market research 16
marriage 261-263, 267
marriage premise 262
marriage rate 344
mass hysteria 392, 393
Massachusetts 116, 340
master status 97, 98, 169
material comfort 47, 55, 60
material culture 44, 45, 47, 51
materialism 184
materialist philosophy 300, 307
matriarchy 258
matrilineal descent 258
matrilocal residence 258
Maturing Africans Learning from Each other 394
McDonald's 13, 50, 58, 141, 145
McDonaldization 141
measurement 24, 25
mechanical solidarity 17
media 84, 85, 247, 396, 397
Medicaid 235, 337
medical perspective 334
medicalization of deviance 174
Medicare 89, 171, 306, 337
melting pot 55, 214, 222
metaphysical stage 15
methodology of the social sciences 307
Metro One Telecom 396
metroplexes 364
metropolitan statistical areas 364
Mexican Revolution 226
Mexican-American War 226
Mexico 41, 58, 144, 186, 215, 216, 223, 225, 226, 343-345, 364, 379
micromanagement 145
microsociology 33
Middle Ages 14, 186, 277
Middle East 36, 38, 39, 46, 111, 112, 130, 131, 201, 216, 289, 399
migration 58, 214, 215, 220, 225, 226, 343-347
Migration Policy Institute 225
Million Man March 394
minorities 195, 200, 217, 218, 222-224
minority groups 224-235
Mississippi 195, 233, 368
Missouri 368, 369

mobility 36, 37, 197, 198
mobs 394
model minority 231, 232
modern democracy 322
modernization 202, 351, 398, 399
modernization theory 202
monogamy 48, 262, 265
monotheism 39, 282
mores 50
mortality 200-202, 230, 242, 343, 346, 347, 350
mosques 275, 283
motherhood penalty 138
Mountain Dew 375
MTV 53, 58
multi-centered metropolitan region 365, 367
multiculturalism 55-57, 223, 224
multigenerational family 258
Mumbai 362
Muslim 111, 130, 283, 289, 321, 346, 399
MySpace 84

N

NAFTA 144
National Basketball Association 372
National Center for Education Statistics 245, 279
National Football League 372
National Geographic News 188
National Hockey League 372
National Rifle Association 396
National Right to Life 353, 354
nationalism 55, 297, 298, 323, 324
nation-building 323, 324
Native Americans 232-235
nativism 215, 231
Navajo tribe 335
Nazi 75, 131, 132, 311
Neo-colonialism 202, 203
neolocal 258
Netherlands 337, 385
New Deal's Home Owners' Loan Corporation 217
New Guinea 109, 248
New Jersey 54, 116
New Orleans 374, 385, 394
New York 43, 53, 54, 105, 116, 160, 165, 174, 216, 227, 362-364, 370, 376
New Zealand 200
Niagara Falls 376
Niger 248
nightlife 372

nonfamily households 257
non-material components of culture 20
nonmaterial culture 45
nonprofit organization 318, 335
non-renewable resources 375
nonverbal 50, 51, 106-110, 117, 118
norms 49, 50
North America 160, 244, 348
Norway 200, 226, 247, 248
nuclear family 258

O

object permanence 77
observation 27
occupational socialization 85
occupations 245-247
Odwalla 144
Oklahoma City bombing 126
Olympic Games 60, 144, 381, 382
one-child-per-family policy 351, 352, 354
One-Dimensional Man 305
opinion leaders 397
opportunity cost 263
oral stage 74
Oregon 89, 369
organic solidarity 17
out-groups 129, 131
overpopulation 236, 345, 350
Oxford University 198
Ozawa v. U.S. 231

P

Pakistan 231
panic 392
Parkinson's disease 86, 87
participant observation 27
pastoral societies 35, 37, 38
patriarchal society 167, 260
patriarchy 249, 258, 266
patrilineal descent 258
patrilocal residence 258
payday loans 217
Pearl Harbor 221, 232
peer groups 83, 167, 174, 244
peers 17, 22, 43, 72, 82, 83, 112, 128, 163, 265, 281, 282
penis envy 75
permissive parenting style 264
Personal Responsibility and Work Opportunity Reconciliation Act 235
personal space 112
personality 72, 736
Pew Hispanic Center 236
phallic stage 75

phenotype 214
Philippine Independent Church 282
Philippines 48, 225
Phoenix 365, 367-369, 372
physician extenders 339
physician-assisted suicide 89
physicians 175, 189, 234, 246, 337-339, 341, 342
Planned Parenthood 353, 354
play stage 74
Plessy v. Ferguson 217, 229
pluralism 47, 220, 223, 224
police 82, 174, 230, 248, 392, 395
politeness theory 101
political changes 14
political economy perspective 368
political party 215, 311
political power 310
political science 16
political sociology 295, 305, 315, 319, 322, 324
politics 295, 298, 301, 309, 314, 317
pollution 381
polyandry 262
polygamy 262
polygyny 262
polytheism 282
popular culture 57, 58, 96
population density 363
Portland 369
Portugal 346
positivism 15
post-conventional morality 79
post-industrial society 41
poverty rates 14, 195, 227
power 127, 129, 185, 296, 301
power elite 185
pre-conventional morality 79
prejudice 216-218
preoperational stage 77
preparatory stage 74
Prescott 365
prescriptive norms 49
presentation of self 106, 107
prestige 185
primary care providers 338, 339
primary deviance 168
primary groups 128, 129
primary relationships 369
primary socialization 82
primogeniture 186
principle of immanent change 400
prison 49, 85, 132, 133, 166, 173-175
pro-choice 353, 354
proletariat 19, 219, 300, 354
pro-life 346, 353, 354

social work 16
socialist medicine 336
socialization 69, 70, 80-82, 85, 86
socialized medicine 333, 336
societal community 319
society 34, 41, 42, 257, 309, 314, 317
sociobiology 71, 162
sociocultural evolution 34
sociocultural perspective 334, 335
sociological imagination 12
sociological paradigm 12
sociological perspective 12, 334, 335
sociological research 21, 22
sociologists 160
sociology 11, 14, 15, 162, 163
Somalian 118
South Africa 14, 302, 322, 323, 345, 349
South America 37, 112, 225, 227, 232, 345, 399
South Korea 41, 201
Soviet Union 302, 322
Spanish 51, 215, 225-227, 369
spatial mismatch 366
spurious correlation 26
Sri Lanka 287
St. Louis 369, 372
standard mortality ratio 343
Starbucks 59
State and Revolution 304
status 96, 97, 135
status groups 308, 310, 311
status inconsistency 98, 185
status set 97, 98
status system 185
stay local movements 141, 143
stereotypes 56, 81, 83, 216, 219, 220, 250, 370
stigma 160, 169, 265
strain theory 164
stratified sampling 23
street crime 170, 172
streetcar suburbs 365
Streetwise: Race, Class and Change in an Urban Community 370
structural functionalism 17, 203, 261, 334, 340, 341, 351
structured mobility 197
subconscious 75
subculture 53, 54
subordinate 114
subsistence technology 34
substantive rationality 305
suburbs 365-367, 372
Sudan 46
suicide 17, 18, 26, 127, 282, 315

Sunbelt 363
Sunnis 289
superego 74, 75, 163
superordinate 114, 131
supply depot 375
supportive interactions 100, 101, 103, 112, 113
surplus value 301, 302
survey research 26
sustainability 375
Sweden 247, 336
symbol 21, 50, 51
symbolic interactionism 20, 102, 249, 261, 334, 341, 342, 354

T

taboos 50
Taiwan 41, 58, 377
Tally's Corner: A Study of Negro Streetcorner Men 369
tattoos 160
technical rationality 305
techniques of neutralization 167, 169, 172
technological advancements 14
technology 34, 36, 38, 40, 41, 378
teenage pregnancy 280, 281
teenagers 59, 80, 84, 86, 100, 102, 126, 288, 378
tefillin 287
Tell Them Who I am: The Lives of Homeless Women 369
temples 188, 275
terrorist attack 114, 126, 218
Texas hold'em poker 396
Thailand 41, 111, 231, 287
The American Dream 164, 171, 232, 237, 263
The Communist Manifesto 19, 299
The de-industrialization of America 366
the division of labor 39, 259, 260, 299, 315, 317
The Federal Housing Administration 217
The Great U-Turn 366
The Heritage Foundation 193
The Lonely Crowd 321
The Mam 144
The Real World 52
The Red Cross 50, 101, 222
The Treaty of Guadalupe Hidalgo 215, 226, 235
The Truly Disadvantaged: The Inner City, the Underclass, and Public

Policy 366
theological stage 15
theory 17, 19, 20, 60, 80, 163-167, 202, 218, 219, 252, 259, 278
theory of challenged and response 399
theory of majestic cycles 399
theory of moral development 78
third world countries 141, 188, 200-202
third-generation principle 224
third-party payer model 333, 337
Tibet 287
tokenism 236
Tokyo 363
Torah 287
torture 125, 132-134
total fertility rate 343, 347
total institution 85
totalitarianism 322
Totemism 282
tract housing 365
traditionalists 54
traditions 43, 303, 311, 318
Tragedy of the Commons 376, 380, 383, 386
Trail of Tears 221, 233
Transcontinental Railroad 231
treadmill of production 381
Trilateral Commission 189
trokosi 186
Tucson 365
Turkey 111
type A personalities 112
type B personalities 112

U

U.S. Census Bureau 80, 174, 192, 193, 230, 258, 346, 363, 377
U.S. Department of Labor 245, 246
U.S. Supreme Court 217, 229, 231, 232, 237
unconscious 74, 75
underpopulation 345, 346
unilever 144
United Arab Emirates 249
United Arab Emirates University 392
United Nations 50, 248, 261, 348, 391
United States 183, 189, 279, 337
universal social institution 357
University of California 237
University of Chicago 15, 71, 102, 363
University of Ghana 197
University of Michigan 237
University of Wisconsin 162
untouchables 188, 285
urban 361-363, 370

Urban Fortunes: The Political Economy of Place 367
urban sociologists 362, 363, 365, 366, 370, 371
urbanism 363, 372
urbanization 367, 368
urbanized areas 363-365
urbanologists 365, 369
utero 71

V

Vaishnava 188
validity 25
value contradictions 48
value-added approach 392
values 43-47
variable 24, 25
Venice 362
verbal 50, 51, 71, 81, 106, 115, 116
vertical mobility 197, 198
Veterans Administration (VA) 365
Victorian Era 75
Vietnam 48, 231
Vietnamese 231
Virgin Islands 348

W

wage labor 301, 302
Wal-Mart 43, 59
Washington, D.C. 369
waste repository 375-377, 381, 385
wealth 184, 191
welfare state 306, 313, 314
westernized culture 12
white ethnics 53, 215, 224, 225
white-collar crime 171
widowed 18, 245
Williams v. Mississippi 229
Wisconsin 116
women's suffrage movement 397
work spillover 99
work world 81, 82, 85
World Bank 378
World War I 72, 226, 229
World War II 88, 218, 220, 222, 226, 229, 232, 247, 363, 365, 366, 369, 381
world-systems analysis 202

X

Xboxes 84
xenocentrism 55
xenophobia 56, 371

Y

Yahoo 43
YMCAs 83
Yugoslavia 54

Z

Zamboanga 48

Notes

Notes

Notes

Notes

Notes